The Light and Fire of the Baal Shem Tov

Other Books by Yitzhak Buxbaum:

Jewish Spiritual Practices
Jewish Tales of Mystic Joy
Jewish Tales of Holy Women
Storytelling and Spirituality in Judaism
The Life and Teachings of Hillel
An Open Heart: The Mystic Path of Loving People
Real Davvening: Jewish Prayer as a Spiritual Practice
  and a Form of Meditation for Beginning and Experienced Davveners
A Person Is Like a Tree: A Sourcebook for Tu BeShvat
A Tu BeShvat Seder: The Feast of Fruits from the Tree of Life

The *Light* and *Fire*
of the
Baal Shem Tov

Yitzhak Buxbaum

continuum

NEW YORK • LONDON

2008
The Continuum International Publishing Group Inc
80 Maiden Lane, New York, NY 10038

The Continuum International Publishing Group Ltd
The Tower Building, 11 York Road, London SE1 7NX

Printed in the United States of America

Library of Congress Cataloging-in-Publication Data

Buxbaum, Yitzhak.
    The light and fire of the Baal Shem Tov / Yitzhak Buxbaum.
      p. cm.
    Includes bibliographical references.
    ISBN 0-8264-1772-8 (hardcover : alk. paper)
    ISBN 0-8264-1888-0 (paperback : alk. paper)
    1. Ba'al Shem Tov, ca. 1700-1760. 2. Hasidim—Ukraine—Biography.
  3. Rabbis—Ukraine—Biography. 4. Hasidism. I. Title.
BM755.I8B89 2005
296.8'332'092—dc22

                           2005019630

Dedication:

*I often had the great privilege of sitting at the feet of a tzaddik and hasid
who resembled the Baal Shem Tov in the qualities of his soul,
my rebbe and master, Rabbi Shlomo Carlebach,
the memory of a tzaddik for a blessing.*

*Knowing Shlomo and seeing his loving ways, gave me many insights
into the personality of the Besht. I am sure that Shlomo is now
sitting beside his dear friend, the holy Baal Shem Tov,
playing for the Besht on his guitar,
melodies from the Garden of Eden.*

Acknowledgments.

I would like to thank Rabbis Jacob Immanuel Schochet of Toronto and Dovber Pinson of Brooklyn for reading the manuscript of this large book, checking it for errors, and helping me correct some mistakes. Since I did not always follow their suggestions, any remaining mistakes are my responsibility. I would like to express my appreciation to Rabbis Schochet, Pinson, and Meir Fund of The Flatbush Minyan, and Aaron Raskin of Congregation B'nai Avraham, both of Brooklyn, New York, for making themselves available to answer questions of all sorts concerning the subject of this book. I would like to thank my dear wife, Carole Forman, who spent many hours helping me with this book, particularly in creating the map. I would also like to thank my friend Christopher Blosser for printing up a number of drafts of the book, in addition to his excellent work as webmaster of my website, "The Jewish Spirit Online," www.jewishspirit.com. May God, blessed be He, repay with good and with blessing all those who have helped in preparing this book.

Contents

List of Stories and Sections

HIS LIFE

A Mission as a Teacher and Baal Shem

A Movement Forms and Opposition Grows

A Mature Teacher Full of Wisdom and Love

Toward Redemption
with the Sting of Persecution and Heresy

To Death and Beyond

Appendix

Preface

FOR YEARS I HAVE BEEN ATTACHED HEART AND SOUL TO THE HOLY Baal Shem Tov and finally was inspired to produce a book about his life and teachings. The famous book of stories about him, *Shivhei HaBaal Shem Tov* (*Praises of the Baal Shem Tov*), published in 1814, fifty-four years after his death in 1760, is not worthy of the holy Baal Shem. It is teeming with miracles and depicts the Besht (an acronym for **B**aal **Sh**em **T**ov) superficially, not as an elevated teacher but as a mere miracle-worker. When I asked my master and teacher, Rabbi Shlomo Carlebach, about *Shivhei HaBaal Shem Tov*, he said, "The Rebbes* considered it a joke." There is also a problem regarding the corpus of Baal Shem Tov tales as a whole. Over time, many stories came into being about the Baal Shem Tov, yet some of them contain hardly any spiritual or moral teaching. Books of Baal Shem Tov tales have been published from time to time. But as is often the case with hasidic stories, they are collected without any discrimination between what is edifying and what is of little value. Typically, when one reads stories about the Besht from the various sources, the huge mass of relatively commonplace tales overwhelms the really important ones. The situation is different with regard to the Besht's teachings, which are uniformly exalted. Rabbi Shlomo Carlebach once explained to me the reason for the difference between collections of tales and of teachings: Whereas tales were often first told and then passed down by ordinary hasidim¶, who may or may not have been spiritual people, teachings were typically transmitted by learned rabbis. This does not mean that the stories are inferior to the teachings; the Baal Shem Tov himself highly valued stories. But the task in producing a worthy book of stories about the Baal Shem Tov is to pick out the wheat and remove the chaff, selecting the stories that truly portray such a great and holy figure, to create not a biography but a "life-in-stories." That has been my goal and purpose in writing this book.

My father, Mac (Meyer) Buxbaum, of blessed memory, came from Kolomaya (then part of Poland in Austria-Hungary; now in Ukraine). How thrilled I was when I discovered that the Baal Shem Tov lived in Kolomaya for two years. I had returned to Judaism and was strongly drawn to hasidic tales and teachings. It seemed that my profound attraction for Hasidism came from deep roots. A story (which I did not use in

---

* Title for hasidic sect leaders.
¶ A hasid (sing.) is a follower of the Baal Shem Tov; a member of the hasidic movement; literally, "a pious person."

xxiii

this book) tells that the Besht once knew by the holy spirit that violent bandits were about to raid his town. He told the townspeople to flee, and they all escaped by crossing the Dniester River. The editor of *Shivhei HaBaal Shem Tov*, who records this tale, says at the end that he does not know if the Besht was living then in Tlust or Kolomaya. I like to imagine that it was Kolomaya and that, since the whole town fled with the Besht, my ancestors were with him too. According to the hasidic tradition, the first person to "reveal" the Baal Shem Tov's light was Rabbi David of Kolomaya. My hope is that this book, written by a descendant of a Jew from Kolomaya, reveals the Besht's light and his fire, which will burn until the coming of the Messiah.[1]

A Note to the Reader

THE STORIES, TEACHINGS, AND OTHER MATERIAL IN THIS BOOK ARE TAKEN from traditional hasidic sources and translated from the Hebrew. It is usually their words you are reading, not mine (except for necessary adaptation and editing). This book is written for those who are Jewishly knowledgeable as well as for those who are unfamiliar with Jewish religious customs and terminology. Items in the text that may be unclear to some readers are explained in many footnotes, endnotes, and in the Glossary. Please see the Appendix for "*Baal Shem* and Faith Healer," "About Towns and Places," and "How This Book Was Constructed."

Light and Fire

ON THE BAAL SHEM TOV'S BIRTHDAY IN 1941, REBBE YOSEF YITZCHOK Schneersohn of Lubavitch said:

Today, the eighteenth of [the Hebrew month of] *Elul*, is the . . . anniversary of a day which is holy and luminous for all of Jewry—the day on which the Almighty brought gratification both to Himself and to the House of Israel by bestowing upon them a great pillar of light and a great pillar of fire, namely, the soul of our godly master and eminent teacher, Rabbi Israel the son of Rabbi Eliezer (whose soul reposes in Eden), the Baal Shem Tov.

The Rebbe continued, saying:

[The Baal Shem Tov's] path was lit up by a pillar of light, namely, the teaching that "I have set God before me always," and there burned within it a pillar of fire, namely, the love of his fellow Jew.

On another occasion, the Rebbe said:

Light illuminates and fire burns. [The teaching of the Baal Shem Tov] comprises both the *avodah* [divine service] of the brain and the *avodah* of the heart. The *avodah* of the brain is called . . . light and the *avodah* of the heart is called . . . fire.[1]

Introduction: Praise, Promise, and Prayer

Praise of the Baal Shem Tov

Let the pious rejoice, and the lovers of God be glad,
when they see the crown of the Baal Shem Tov
restored to its former glory.

For who is like our master, teacher, and rabbi,
the holy of holies, the light of Israel and its holy one,
with the halo of God on his head,
the light of the seven days of creation, that godly man,
Rabbi Israel Baal Shem Tov, who was like a son of God,
an angel who came down from heaven,
a great and holy light, whose glory illumined the earth.

Sparks from that precious and holy torch
penetrated the hearts of many,
even to the innermost chambers.

Who can describe his awesome holiness and purity,
his total separation from all worldliness,
his love of God and of the people of Israel?

In the same way that he was ready to sacrifice his life for God, blessed be He, so was he ready at every moment to give up his life for the least of the least in Israel.

With his special love for the simple working people and for the poor and downtrodden among the Jewish folk, he showed them they were not forgotten by God and he drew them back to the waiting embrace of their Father in Heaven.

The prophet said, "Behold, days are coming, says the Lord God, when I will send a hunger in the land, not a hunger for bread, nor a thirst for water, but to hear the Word of the Lord." In reading this book, precious Jews, your hunger will be satisfied and your thirst will be quenched, for these stories and teachings of the holy Baal Shem Tov are bread of the Divine Presence and a fountain of waters from the living God. The prophet cried out, "Everyone that thirsts, come to the water! And he who has no money, come, buy and eat!"[1]

Praise of the Tzaddikim

Praise to God and praise to His *tzaddikim**,
who believe in the Holy One, blessed be He, with perfect faith
and serve Him with devotion and fervor, whose hearts are directed
to their Father in Heaven, every hour and every minute.

The foundation of faith and the pillar of divine service is to believe that the Creator, blessed be He, is one, single, and unique, that He watches over and directs all the worlds and all the nations of men, as it says in the holy *Zohar*¶: "He is the master and ruler, and before Him everything is accounted as if non-existent. He fills all worlds and surrounds all worlds, and there is no place where He is not present."

Precious Jews! The time has come for us to return to our heavenly root and cleave to the Holy One, blessed be He, and to His servants, the tzaddikim. The holy Torah says about our ancestors: "And they believed in God and in Moses, His servant." If not for our teacher Moses, peace be upon him, and all the holy prophets and tzaddikim, where would we be? Is it not by their teachings and the scriptures and writings that tell of their direct experience of God that we know of Him, blessed be He? Praise, praise to the holy Baal Shem Tov, the Moses of Hasidism, who has led us out of the spiritual Egypt and whose teachings will light our way until we exit the physical "Egypt," ending our long and bitter exile, with the coming of our righteous Messiah, soon and in our days.[2]

Praise of the Stories of the Tzaddikim

The glory of the Baal Shem Tov shines most brightly in the stories of his life.
How great are the tales of the tzaddikim!
They are the brilliant jewels in the Torah's crown,
and fragrant flowers on the Tree of Life.

The holy Baal Shem Tov, may his merit protect us, said that a person who tells or listens to stories praising the tzaddikim is as if engaged in studying and meditating on the Torah's deepest mystic secrets—*Maaseh Merkavah*, the Account of the Divine Chariot—for the tzaddikim are the chariot of God.

The Maggid§ of Mezritch, the Baal Shem Tov's disciple and successor, quoted the psalm verse: "Give praise, O servants of the Lord, give praise to the name of the Lord!" and read the Hebrew as: "Giving praise to the servants of the Lord is like giving praise to the Lord."

---

* A *tzaddik* (sing.) is a pious or holy man, or a hasidic rebbe. Plural *tzaddikim* (includes women).
¶ The "Book of Splendor," the main text of the Kabbalah.
§ Preacher.

Praising the tzaddikim with stories is like praising God.

Precious Jews! Children of holy ancestors! I beg you to read the stories in this book praising the holy Baal Shem Tov with reverence. Remove the shoes from your feet and tread softly, for you are approaching holiness.

The Torah scroll is not a mere book, just ink on leather parchment. The Western Wall of our holy Temple is not just a wall, a pile of old stones; nor Jerusalem a city like other cities. Neither are the stories of the holy tzaddikim mere stories.

The Torah is the Word of Him who Spoke and the World Came into Being, and the letters of the Torah scroll are black fire written on white fire. The Divine Presence has never left the Western Wall, and Jerusalem is the Holy City, the navel of the earth. The stories of the tzaddikim are the stories of God's doings in this world; they tell of the meetings of heaven and earth. Whoever thinks that they are "just stories" desecrates his own soul.

Tales of the tzaddikim awaken the heart and kindle the inner fires of love for God, blessed be He, with great longing and yearning. When reading the stories of the pure servants of God, those mighty in power, who perform His word, your heart will awaken from its slumber and say to you, "Why should not I also seek intimacy with my Father in Heaven?" The story of the deed is even greater than the deed itself—because the story inspires many others to imitate the deed. Many tzaddikim said that their own arousal to love for God came from hearing stories of the deeds of tzaddikim. Rebbe Nachman of Bratzlav, the Besht's great-grandson, spoke about the importance of storytelling and said, "I myself was greatly motivated to serve God through stories of tzaddikim. Many famous tzaddikim used to visit the home of my holy parents. We lived in Medzibuz, in the same house that had been the home of the Baal Shem Tov. Many pious Jews would come and visit the Baal Shem Tov's grave, and they would usually stay at my father's house. It was from them that I heard many stories of tzaddikim, and this moved me toward God." It was through this that Rebbe Nachman attained the great things that he did.

Pious people are delighted when they hear stories of the tzaddikim, which are sweeter than honey. But those with a closed heart have no taste for them and say, "What's in them? It's all exaggeration and foolishness, entertainment for children." It is a good sign for a person, if, on hearing stories of the virtuous deeds of the tzaddikim and their sincere and holy service of God, blessed be He, his heart yearns for God as the deer longs for the waters of the desert stream, that his heart ignites with flaming coals of fiery devotion and earnestly offers a silent prayer that he too will merit to serve God in truth.

So, precious Jews, if you have opened this book, open your heart as well. Do not read these stories about the life of the holy Baal Shem Tov as worldly people read secular tales for amusement, a diversion for a spare hour. Read these tales with devotion, for they are dear to God Himself.

When one Jew tells his earnest friend stories about the tzaddikim who love and fear God, blessed be He, God Himself turns to listen, as it says: "Then those who feared the Lord conversed with one another: and the Lord hearkened and heard it, and a book of remembrance was written before Him for those who feared the Lord and that thought upon His name."

This book of stories about the holy Baal Shem Tov and his teachings is a book of remembrance written before the Holy One, blessed be He. It is written for all those who seek to love and fear God and desire His nearness. It is written for you.[3]

Praise of the Stories about the Baal Shem Tov

Stories of the Besht Save

STORIES OF THE HOLY BAAL SHEM TOV HAVE THE POWER TO DRAW GOD'S salvation into the world. When told with faith, a story about a tzaddik is like a prayer and, like a prayer, it saves. Rebbe Nachman of Bratzlav said that telling the story of the deed of a tzaddik arouses the holy impression of that deed. Rebbe Yisrael of Rizhin told:

"Once, to save the life of a sick boy, the Baal Shem Tov went into the forest, attached a candle to a tree, and performed other mystical actions and meditations, and he saved the boy, with the help of God. After the Besht's passing, there was a similar matter with his disciple, the Maggid of Mezritch, who said, 'I don't know the mystical meditations my master the Baal Shem Tov used, but I'll simply act, and God will help.' So he lit the candle in the forest and performed the other mystical actions, and his deeds were acceptable on high and had the desired effect. In the next generation, there was a similar urgent matter with Rebbe Moshe Leib of Sassov, a disciple of the Maggid of Mezritch. He said, 'I don't even know how to do what is necessary, but I'll just tell the story of what the Baal Shem Tov did, and God will help.' And so it was, with God's help.

The Rebbe of Helish was once asked to tell a tale. He said, "A person should tell a tale in a way that the telling itself saves. My grandfather, who was a disciple of the Baal Shem Tov, was lame. When he was asked to tell a story of his master, he began to tell them how the holy Baal Shem Tov leaped and danced when he prayed, and as he recounted what he had seen, he stood up. The story so aroused his fervor, that he began to show them by his own leaping and dancing how his master did it. That moment, he was cured of his lameness and became a healthy man."

Once, the Besht's disciples saw him weeping greatly and then he began to rejoice greatly. A close disciple asked him why he had cried so much and then became so happy. The Besht replied, "At first, I sat down and pondered over how the prophet Elijah and I both learned from the same master, Ahiyah ha-Shiloni. But whereas Elijah merited that every time people mention him, they say, as is customary, 'May he be remembered for good' [good for the person recalling Elijah], I only merited that they would tell stories about me. So I wept, begging God, that when a Jew tells a story about me, he also benefit 'for good,' and if the story is about spirituality, he be saved spiritually; and if it is about worldly matters, he be saved in worldly matters. After my prayer, I heard a heavenly proclamation: 'Everyone who believes that all the divine service and all the striving and efforts of Israel the son of Sarah were not for himself but only for the benefit of the people of Israel, collectively and individually, and tells stories about him, will have salvation and success and will receive an abundance of goodness and blessing.' So," the Besht concluded, "When I saw that even when I'll be in the upper world, the Jewish people will be saved because of me, I became happy and joyful." May the merit of his holiness sustain us, that we be saved with all good. Amen.[4]

What to Believe

MANY MIRACLE TALES ARE TOLD ABOUT THE BAAL SHEM TOV, AND A person may wonder, "What should I believe?" The Rebbes were not so simpleminded as to naively believe any story they heard.

Rebbe Mordechai of Neshkiz said, "I don't give much credence to the miracle stories told about the tzaddikim, because many of the stories are fabricated, and others are riddled with errors—except for the stories told about the Baal Shem Tov, may the memory of a tzaddik be a blessing for the life of the World-to-Come. For even if a story about him never actually occurred, and there was no such miracle, it was in the power of the Baal Shem Tov, may his memory be a blessing for the life of the World-to-Come, to perform everything."

Rebbe Yaakov Yitzhak, the Seer of Lublin, said, "If someone would come and tell me that he saw the Baal Shem Tov go up on a ladder into heaven while alive, bodily, with his clothes on, I would believe him. Because it's fitting to believe everything told about the Baal Shem Tov."

Rebbe Shlomo of Radomsk said, "Whoever believes all the miracle stories about the Baal Shem Tov in *Shivhei HaBaal Shem Tov* is a fool, but whoever denies them is an *apikoros* [a nonbeliever]."

Rebbe Naftali of Ropshitz said, "All the miracles people tell about the Baal Shem Tov were certainly in his power to do, and even many more, but in actuality, most of them never happened." Yet something profound may be learned even from a miracle story that never happened, for the tale can send a ray of holy light into our soul to elevate and enliven us.[5]

Tell of the Baal Shem Tov's Piety

REBBE MENAHEM MENDEL OF RIMANOV ONCE VISITED THE BAAL SHEM Tov's grave in Medzibuz and said afterward that the Besht appeared to him and told him that he was upset that people were telling stories of his miracles and not about his love and fear of God.

Rebbe Yehuda Tzvi of Strettin once remarked about the many miracles recorded in *Shivhei HaBaal Shem Tov*, "Are *these* the praises of the Baal Shem Tov? *I* can do those miracles! It was the Baal Shem Tov's love and fear of God that made him great!"[6]

The Power and Preciousness of Baal Shem Tov Tales

REBBE TZVI HIRSH OF ZIDITCHOV, REBBE YITZHAK EIZIK OF KOMARNA, and Rebbe Avraham Mordechai of Fintshov—who knew a thousand stories about the Besht—all cherished stories about the Baal Shem Tov and appreciated their great power. Each of them told a story of the Besht every day.

Rebbe Menahem Mendel, the Tzemach Tzedek, of Lubavitch could not talk about the Baal Shem Tov or tell stories about him for more than a few minutes, because he became so aroused that it was a danger to his life.[7]

The Promise and the Hope

PRECIOUS JEWS! YOU HAVE THE PROMISE OF THE BAAL SHEM TOV HIMSELF that reading stories about him is mystically potent to bring salvation and help, whether your need is material or spiritual—if you read with faith that all the Besht's deeds were only for the benefit of the Jewish people and for you too. If you read these stories with devoted attention, the darkness of your daily troubles will lift and the light of joy will enter your mind; strong waves of love for God will arise in your heart. Know that with each story that you read, your sins are forgiven and you are coming ever closer to God, blessed be He and blessed be His name.

Precious Jews! Brothers and sisters! There are those who say that the fire of Jacob has been extinguished, that Israel will no more seek its God. They claim that you have finally lost the pious instincts of your holy ancestors. They say that skepticism will keep you from appreciating a book that speaks openly of devotion and fans the coals of divine love; that it will only embarrass you. I, Yitzhak son of Meyer and Charna, deny it. The spark of holiness in each Jew will never disappear (God-forbid)! The Jewish people will soon arise once again in all their glory, to glorify the living God. May it be His will.

Aim High

WHEN REBBE MENAHEM MENDEL OF KOTZK WAS A YOUNG DISCIPLE of Rebbe Simha Bunim of Pshis'cha, he would walk around in the *beit midrash**, immersed in his thoughts, in an intense mood of *d'vekut*[¶]. Some of the other hasidim were annoyed by his behavior, feeling that he was arrogantly acting as if he were different from everyone else sitting and studying Torah. One of them rebuked him, "Why are you pacing about like this? Who do you think you are, the holy Baal Shem

---

* Torah study hall.
¶ Devotional God-consciousness.

Tov?" "Did the Baal Shem Tov make everyone swear," replied the Kotzker with fire, "that no one would be as great as him?"

Rebbe Mordechai of Neshkiz would tell his son, Noah, stories about the holy Baal Shem Tov's great spiritual attainments and after each story said, "Look, my son, what a Jew can achieve if he doesn't sleep."

Dear friends, fellow Jews, let us read about the life and teachings of the Baal Shem Tov not only for enjoyment but to learn to imitate his holy ways. The Jewish people needs heroes, both men and women, to aim for the highest.[8]

The Author's Prayer

PRECIOUS JEWS! CHILDREN OF THE LIVING GOD! I HAVE READ MANY books whose pious authors recounted religious tales with holy charm and grace. I know that I possess no such literary ability. Therefore, I beg you to judge my efforts with a good eye. Only your kindness will make my words pleasant and my storytelling sweet. As I begin this book, I prostrate before the Holy One, blessed be He, and beg all the tzaddikim, foremost among them the holy Baal Shem Tov, to intercede for me and make my work acceptable to Him, blessed be He. How can I write a book about the holy Baal Shem Tov and tell his stories when I can only understand him and write according to my own lowly spiritual level? Yet, although I know that my deficiencies mar my writing, I also believe with firm faith that this book is being written not by my hand but by the hand of the Holy One Himself, blessed be He and blessed be His name. The One who makes lamp-oil to burn can make even vinegar burn and shed light. This book has been written by inspiration of the holy spirit. Whoever reads it will be impelled to love God, the Torah, the Jewish people and all people, God-willing. Blessed is the one who ignores the faults of my writing and seeks the deep meanings of these stories and teachings. Although the author is unworthy, I pray that this book reveal the Baal Shem Tov's light and fire. May it become a devotional scripture for all those who cherish the Besht and his teaching. The author promises whoever buys this book that he will receive blessings and whoever keeps it in his home that he will be protected from harm.

Finally, I offer my obeisance to my fellow Jews and also to non-Jews who read this book. You are all in the image of God and are beloved of God. That is the firm conviction of my mind and heart. The Rabbis teach us, when mentioning a tzaddik, to add to his name, *zecher tzaddik livracha*, "may the remembrance of a tzaddik's name be for a blessing." May this book, which mentions the holy Baal Shem Tov's name with reverence, transmit a powerful blessing to carry you to the goal of a human being on this earth, the purpose for which we were all created, to unite in love with the One and Only One and with all humanity. Amen.

His Life

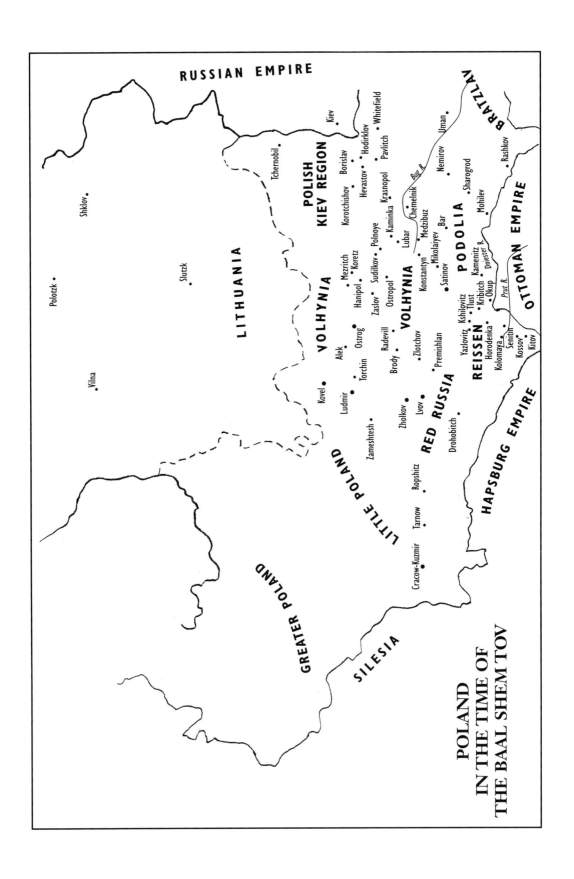

POLAND
IN THE TIME OF
THE BAAL SHEM TOV

The Setting

Decline and Turmoil in Poland

THE BAAL SHEM TOV WAS BORN DURING AN ERA OF DECLINE AND turmoil in Poland, which was then a very large backward country composed of many lands and peoples, including Lithuania and much of the Ukraine. Most of the Besht's activity was in the Ukrainian areas of Poland, such as Podolia, Volhynia, and Reissen. The Polish nobility, which was at that time more powerful than the king, harshly oppressed the Ukrainian peasantry. In 1648, the notorious Bogdan Chemielnicki led a rebellion of Cossacks and Ukrainian peasants against Polish rule and in the process slaughtered large numbers of Jews. The Chemielnicki rebellion led to ten years of internal and external wars for Poland. Her neighbors exploited her weakness and attacked her, ripping away chunks of territory. All sides in these various conflicts attacked the Jews, who were between the hammer and the anvil, always the victims. Nearly a thousand Jewish communities and villages were destroyed. Hundreds of thousands of Jews were massacred. Others fled and became impoverished refugees.[1]

Antisemitism and Its Depredations

WHAT WAS THE SOURCE OF THIS VIOLENCE AGAINST JEWS? THE fiercely antisemitic Catholic Church fomented many of the attacks against the Jewish people. During the lifetime of the Baal Shem Tov, there were twenty blood libels, in which Jews were accused of using Christian blood for their Passover matzahs; most of these blood libels were incited by priests. There were social and economic aspects to this antisemitism as well. Being legally denied entrance to many professions and occupations, Jews often became agents of the Polish nobles and therefore dealt directly with the Ukrainian peasants. Although many Jews were poor farmers, peddlars, craftsmen, and simple laborers, others collected taxes for Polish nobles or leased taverns and other properties from them, inspiring the envy and hatred of the ignorant peasantry. The oppressed peasants gathered in the tavern after work to drink away their troubles and paid their last coins to the Jewish tavern keeper. But the Jews were as powerless and oppressed as the peasants and, in addition, were exposed to savage religious persecution. The constant wars and rebellions that ruined the Polish economy also severely affected the Jews. And from time to time in Polish Ukraine, the Haidamaks—robber bands of discontented peasants and other renegades—attacked and ransacked Jewish communities, further disheartening the Jews.

Divisions and Decline in the Jewish Community

AS A RESULT OF ALL THESE FACTORS, POLISH JEWRY WAS GRAVELY weakened. Corruption among community leaders became rife and rabbinic positions were frequently bought and sold. But despite the disruptions and the terrible poverty, there was a high level of Torah knowledge among the elite—the rabbis and Torah scholars—who intensively studied not only Talmud and *halacha* (religious law), but Kabbalah too. Too often, however, their study was not from spiritual motives but for prestige and gain. Unlike in earlier and better times, religious education was lacking among the common folk, because of reduced prosperity. Yet, although the troubled Jewish masses were usually ignorant of Torah, they were still devout and wanted to serve God! Despite that, many of the rabbis and scholars viewed the downtrodden and uneducated Jewish working people with contempt and provided them with little comfort in their suffering.

The False Messiah, Shabtai Tzvi

EVENTUALLY, THE PERVASIVE FEAR CAUSED BY UNSTABLE AND DANGEROUS conditions infiltrated Judaism itself, and the most pious people, whether educated or not, inclined toward an unhealthy fear of sin and followed a severe ascetic path. This wretched situation produced a yearning for release among the people that broke out in the welcome with which many—even great rabbis and scholars—received the false messianic claims of Shabtai Tzvi, who had announced himself as the redeemer in 1648—in the very midst of the disastrous Chemielnicki rebellion. Shabtai Tzvi was originally from Turkey, which then had a border with Poland. His messianic movement grew and increased in strength until, in 1666, the Turkish sultan had him arrested and offered him the choice of death or conversion to Islam. When Shabtai Tzvi converted, his confused followers explained away his betrayal of Judaism, and his movement continued underground. There were secret groups of Shabteans in Podolia, the Polish-Ukrainian province where the Besht was born. The rabbis, of course, fervently opposed the insidious Shabtean influence that threatened the very integrity of Judaism. Clearly, Shabteanism reflected a dangerous sickness in the Jewish religious community.

The Pre-Beshtian Hasidim and the Hidden Tzaddikim

❧ THE TWO MOST HEALTHY AND VIBRANT SEGMENTS OF THE JEWISH religious community in Poland at this time were the pre-Beshtian hasidim (pious) and the hidden tzaddikim (righteous).* Both these groups were ascetically inclined kabbalists; the former were part of the establishment, and the latter had separated from it. Most of the hasidim were great Torah scholars, an elite group that concentrated on the spiritual elevation of members of their own mystic circles. They were held in high regard by the rabbis and masses alike. The hidden tzaddikim were also often scholars and kabbalists, but they were populists, motivated by their love for the oppressed Jewish people and their desire to comfort them and uplift them spiritually. They were a movement of mystics who rejected the aloof attitude of a religious establishment that focused on the external aspect of Torah scholarship and religion and looked down on the uneducated and imperfectly observant simple people. The hidden tzaddikim taught simple working Jews the basics of Judaism with an emphasis on *musar* (character development and ethics); qualified members of their group also studied Kabbalah. Because of the terrible repercussions from the heresy of Shabtai Tzvi, who had used erroneous kabbalistic interpretations to support his messianic claim, the rabbinic establishment discouraged the study of Kabbalah, except for the elite few, the scholarly hasidim. The rabbis were wary of anyone who attempted to spread kabbalistically oriented ideas to the populace. The hidden tzaddikim, who taught Kabbalah even to some laborers, fell under suspicion and, as a result, were forced to go underground. Thus, there were two secretive societies working within the Jewish community at that time—the Shabteans and the hidden tzaddikim. Some of the rabbis confused the two groups. But while the Shabteans were a negative influence, the hidden tzaddikim were a positive force in many ways. Unhappy with the elitism of the rabbis and the scholars, the hidden tzaddikim threw in their lot with the common people. Some of the hidden tzaddikim worked at manual occupations; others were wanderers. Some worked or wandered at different times. Either way, they quietly influenced the working people through their close association with them. They were all "hidden," meaning that they hid their identities as pious mystics who were totally devoted to God and the Jewish people. They also kept themselves hidden owing to an acute sense of modesty and humility, believing that the truest service of God is that

---

* Both terms are potentially confusing. In Hebrew, *hasid* means "a pious person." Before and during the Besht's time, the term was especially used for members of exclusive circles of devout and scholarly kabbalists. A second meaning of *hasid* later developed—as a designation of a follower of the Baal Shem Tov or of his movement. To avoid confusion in the use of the term *hasid*, I will refer in the body of this book (after the Setting) to the pre-Beshtian hasidim as "the Pious." *Tzaddik* in Hebrew literally means "a righteous person," but it typically means a holy man. A "hidden tzaddik" is someone whose exterior conceals his inner holiness, perhaps by his being a manual laborer or by his modest demeanor. In the Besht's time, there was a movement of people called "hidden tzaddikim," who should not be confused with the legendary thirty-six hidden tzaddikim in whose merit the world exists. The term in this book usually refers to someone connected to the movement of hidden tzaddikim, but occasionally it is used in its general sense, without any relation to the movement; the meaning must be determined from the context.

which is unknown to others. Yet they made great efforts to raise the spiritual and material level of the Jewish masses. And in small numbers they recruited other Jews into their fold. The Baal Shem Tov's parents were members of this movement.

Baal Shems

ANOTHER DYNAMIC ELEMENT IN JEWISH SOCIETY AT THAT TIME WAS THE faith healers and miracle workers. Although few in number, they loom large in our story. Knowledge of Kabbalah was very prestigious, and practical kabbalists who used divine Names to do healing, oppose demonic forces, and perform miracles were usually held in great esteem; yet some Torah scholars and medical doctors scorned them. They were called *baal shems*, masters of the divine Names (however, some impostors claimed the title without the reality). The movement of hidden tzaddikim was always led by a tzaddik who was a *baal shem*, such as Rabbi Eliyahu Baal Shem of Wurms in Germany; then, all from Poland, his successor, Rabbi Yoel Baal Shem of Zameshtesh; his successor, Rabbi Adam Baal Shem of Ropshitz; and finally, his successor, Rabbi Israel Baal Shem Tov of Medzibuz.[2]

Beginnings to Revelation

Awakening the Jewish People from a Faint

AFTER HALF A CENTURY OF SUFFERING AND DESTRUCTION THAT BEGAN in 1648–1649, and despite the best efforts of the hidden tzaddikim, the people of Israel were in a faint. It was then that the soul of the Baal Shem Tov, who bears the name of the whole people, "Israel," was revealed to revive them. It is similar to when a person has fainted and someone calls his name into his ear to revive and awaken him. Rabbi Israel Baal Shem Tov awakened the people of Israel from their faint and brought them renewed joy in the nearness of God.[1]

The Baal Shem Tov's Soul and the Sin of the Tree of Knowledge

ACCORDING TO THE MYSTIC TEACHINGS, ADAM'S SOUL IN THE GARDEN of Eden contained the souls of all the people who would ever be born. When Adam sinned and ate from the fruit of the Tree of the Knowledge of Good and Evil, all were affected. But some few souls fled before that fateful moment and remained pure and untainted. The soul of the Baal Shem Tov was one of those pure souls that never tasted from the Tree of Knowledge.[2]

The Satan's Accusation

ALL UNBORN SOULS ARE STORED IN A TREASURY BELOW THE THRONE OF glory. When their moment arrives and parents are chosen for them, they are sent down to this world to be clothed in a body. The Baal Shem Tov's soul was so pure, so holy, so radiant—its light shining from one end of heaven to the other—that the Satan, fearing the trouble this would cause him and the threat to his power, vehemently objected whenever parents were selected, claiming they were unworthy. Although the angels always interceded for the couple, the Satan's arguments time and again succeeded. Thus, the Baal Shem Tov's soul was unable to descend and remained in heaven for many years. But for all that time, tzaddikim had been praying that the Besht's soul would descend to this world. Finally, their prayers bore fruit.[3]

The Besht's Parents Tested

DEAR READER, THE NEXT STORY CALLS FOR YOUR DEVOTED ATTENTION. It tells why the Baal Shem Tov's parents merited such a holy son. So open your heart to receive its deep teaching, which explains a key aspect of Rabbi Israel Baal Shem Tov's mission to the Jewish people.

Rabbi Eliezer and Sarah (the future parents of the Baal Shem Tov) lived in Okup, a village in the Polish province of Podolia, near the border with Turkey. They had reached old age but had no children, because Sarah was barren. Both husband and wife were very devout and especially dedicated to the *mitzvah** of hospitality. But they lived in an area with a sparse Jewish population and guests were hard to find! So they hired a servant to sit at the outskirts of their village, to watch for any passing Jewish traveler and direct him to their home. The servant was instructed to promise the traveler he would be well treated and to do everything possible to persuade him to accept their hospitality. When a precious guest arrived at their home, both Rabbi Eliezer and Sarah quickly attended to him and cared for him diligently, offering him food and drink and preparing for him a comfortable bed. If he was a poor man, traveling to collect charity to support his family, they first gave him a generous donation, even before he ate, so his mind would be at ease during the meal, knowing he had accomplished his purpose. They treated every guest, no matter who he was, with respect and reverence, for they faithfully fulfilled the teaching of the Rabbis, who say that receiving a guest is like receiving the *Shechinah*[¶]. When the guest was ready to depart, Sarah prepared provisions for his journey, while Rabbi Eliezer gave him another liberal donation. Such was their loving way with guests. Their kindness to their fellow human beings was constant, because their minds and hearts were always on God.

The exceptional hospitality of this devout couple made a great impression in heaven, and the angels began to praise them, saying it was fitting to repay them for their many good deeds. A decision was made that they would be rewarded by having a very holy soul born to them as their son. Since Rabbi Eliezer and Sarah were not only pious but elderly and had long ago passed beyond lust, their conjugal relations were entirely pure, just for the sake of heaven. So they were worthy and able to bring down that most radiant soul that shone throughout heaven.

But while the angels were praising them, the Satan stepped forth to cast aspersions and accuse them. When he saw that his accusations against this pure couple were ineffective, he argued that before they were excessively rewarded they must be tested.

---

* Divine commandment.
¶ The Divine Presence.

When this was agreed upon in heaven and it was asked, "Who will go to test them?" the Satan himself eagerly replied, "I'll go." But the one who announces good tidings, the prophet Elijah, may he be remembered for good, came forward and said firmly, "If you test them, as is your way, you will cleverly try them with a test beyond their power, which they will surely fail. If they must be tested, it's not good that you be the one to do it. I'll go!"

Since the couple's greatest virtue was hospitality, their hospitality was tested, to see if they had reached its deepest truth. So one Sabbath afternoon, Elijah went to them in the guise of a poor Jewish wayfarer. He appeared at their home with a staff in his hand and a knapsack over his shoulder. He greeted them with "Good *Shabbos!*" showing that he knew it was the Sabbath, but he had desecrated its sanctity, for it was clear from the dust on his feet that he had traveled on the holy day.

Yet the pious couple uttered not a word to rebuke him. They warmly welcomed him into their home, sat him down to their *seudah shlishit** and later their *melave malka*¶ and gave him food and drink to satisfy his appetite and thirst. All the while they never even mentioned to him his desecration of the Sabbath, nor did they reproach him about it.

When three stars appeared in the night sky, signaling the Sabbath's end, their guest announced his intention to depart. At first, they tried to dissuade him, telling him to wait until morning, because of the danger from highwaymen who lurked in the dark of night to waylay travelers. But when he insisted on leaving, Sarah quickly set herself to preparing provisions for his journey. Then, after Rabbi Eliezer had given him a generous donation of charity, the husband and wife accompanied the traveler on his way for a good distance, fulfilling the *mitzvah* to escort a guest and do everything possible to ensure his safety. During all this time, Rabbi Eliezer and Sarah had never once mentioned his Sabbath desecration.

When they reached the outskirts of the village and were about to part from him, Elijah revealed himself to them and told them that he had come to test them to see if they were hospitable even to someone who violated the Torah and *mitzvot*. It is one thing to warmly welcome those who adhere to one's religious values; but it is another thing, and far more difficult, to warmly receive those who openly flout the Torah and its commandments. Having seen Rabbi Eliezer and Sarah's fine behavior, which showed that they grasped the inner essence of piety and hospitality, Elijah promised them that as their reward a son would be born to them who would lighten the eyes of all Israel, and they should call his name, "Israel."

The Rabbis say that the deeds of the ancestors of the Jewish people—the Patriarchs and Matriarchs—foretell the future deeds of their descendants. So too with parents and children. This tale, which tells why the Baal Shem Tov's parents merited having a son like him, also explains him and his mission. His parents, who belonged to the movement of hidden tzaddikim, were pious and kind even to those who transgressed

---

* The third Sabbath meal.
¶ The feast of "Escorting the Departing Sabbath Queen."

the Torah and its commandments. The holy Baal Shem Tov followed in their footsteps and loved all Jews, even those who did not keep the tenets of Judaism fully. He learned from his parents that judging others prevents a person from fulfilling the commandment to love your neighbor. And only love can bring the straying children back to their Father in Heaven.[4]

Sixty Heroes

RABBI ELIEZER AND SARAH WERE DEEMED WORTHY OF BRINGING DOWN that radiant soul from heaven. But the Baal Shem Tov's pure soul feared the Satan's power on earth and did not want to descend to this world. Perhaps he would be overcome by the snakes and scorpions that exist in each generation, namely, the satanic opponents of those who are holy and faithful. Through the grief caused by their venomous enmity, he might be weakened and destroyed and separated from his spiritual root. So he refused to descend to this world, until he was given an escort of sixty heroes, like the sixty heroes who surrounded King Solomon's bed to guard him against the demons of the night. These were the holy tzaddikim, the disciples of the Baal Shem Tov, who came down to earth with him and surrounded and guarded his soul. With their help, he would be able to accomplish his task and uproot evil from the midst of the earth.[5]

Holy from the Womb

SO SARAH CONCEIVED A SON, A CHILD WITH A PURE AND HOLY SOUL. When the Baal Shem Tov was still a baby inside his mother's womb, he thought, "What *mitzvah* can I do now?" He decided that the only *mitzvah* an unborn child can perform is to not struggle or kick in his mother's womb, in order to fulfill the commandment to honor your mother. So he was very quiet and did not thrash around or kick.[6]

His Birth and Infancy

ON *HAI** *ELUL*, THE 18TH DAY OF THE HEBREW MONTH OF *ELUL*, IN THE year 1700, Israel Baal Shem Tov was born to his father, Rabbi Eliezer, and to his mother, Sarah, in the small village of Okup. After he entered the world, he held on to

---

* In *gematria* (Jewish numerology), the number 18, in Hebrew *hai*, *het-yud*, means "life" and is auspicious.

the *mitzvah* of honoring one's parents and as an infant was careful not to trouble his mother by crying or screaming. He rested quietly in his cradle so as not to bother her. But when she briefly left the house, he could not restrain himself and he would wail and cry.

While still an infant, little Israel already showed signs of his future greatness. When he heard anyone studying Torah, he fell silent and listened intently, his child's face beaming with delight. He was always attracted to good people and his little heart vibrated in sympathy with whomever he met. Any unhappy event that caused another person pain provoked his tears. But each time his mother helped a poor man—as she often did—with food or money, he smiled with pleasure.

The Song of Songs, the love song between God and the Jewish people, says: "Honey and milk are under your tongue." Like the infant Isaac with his mother Sarah, little Israel had imbibed piety with his mother Sarah's milk. At three years of age, the day came for him to begin learning the Hebrew alphabet. When his father took him on his lap and wrote down the letters *aleph* and *bet* on a slate, Israel's eyes shone with joy. According to the hallowed custom, Rabbi Eliezer was about to put honey over the letters, to touch it with his finger and then to his son's lips—to teach him, from the earliest age, the Torah's sweetness. But before he could dip his finger in the honey, little Israel, who saw the divine light nestling within the holy letters, bent down and kissed them. Astonished at his son's action, Rabbi Eliezer recalled the psalm verse: "How sweet are Your words to my lips! Sweeter than honey to my taste!"

It is natural for a child and its parents to be bound in love, but this is even more true when the child is born to them in their old age. Such was the case with Israel and his parents. Being so devoted to them, little Israel quickly absorbed their holy traits, for both of them were pious and loving people. From the child's earliest days, his father and mother raised him and taught him according to the principles of the movement of hidden tzaddikim, to which they belonged, especially regarding love for fellow Jews.[7]

His Father's Last Words

WHEN ISRAEL WAS FIVE, THE TIME CAME FOR HIS ELDERLY FATHER TO leave this world. While on his death-bed, in his last moments on this earth, Rabbi Eliezer, the hidden tzaddik, called his son to him, took him in his arms, and said, "My dearest son, I see that you'll soon light my *yahrzeit* candle*, and I won't have the pleasure of raising you. Israel, always remember what I'm telling you now: Never fear anyone or anything except the Holy One, blessed be He!"

Then Rabbi Eliezer spoke to his son again, saying, "Remember that God is always with you. Think about this constantly. Ponder this thought more deeply every hour and every minute, wherever you are. But keep your ways hidden. Study the holy Torah

---

* A memorial candle to commemorate the anniversary of a parent's death.

but let it appear to others as if you're an ignorant person. And remember this also: With all your heart and with every fiber of your being, love each and every one of our Jewish people, regardless of who or what he or she is."

In these last few words, the father gave his only son provision for his journey through life. This short testament was to Israel like the two tablets of the covenant for all his days on this earth. During all the events of his life, his path was lit up by a pillar of light—"I have placed the Lord before me always," and within that pillar there burned another, a pillar of fire—love of Israel.* [8]

Kaddish

AFTER RABBI ELIEZER'S DEATH, ISRAEL'S MOTHER SARAH MADE SURE THAT her precious only son said the *Kaddish*¶ for his father during the *shiva*, the seven days of intense mourning. After the *shiva*, she took him to the synagogue every day, to say *Kaddish*. She taught him the prayer's meaning, and Israel recited it with devotion— earnestly praying for God's kingdom to be revealed on earth.

Anyone who heard Israel recite the *Kaddish* would have his eyes well up with tears and he would begin to sob. People said that whoever had not heard little Israel say the *Kaddish* had never experienced the sweetness of a child's prayer in his life. In heaven too there was a great commotion over the *Kaddish* of little Israel, the son of Rabbi Eliezer.

Every morning, Sarah rose early and woke her small son, calling out to him, "Wake up, my darling 'Kaddish.' It's time for the morning prayers!" The small house in which the widow and her son lived was far from the synagogue, which was on the other side of the village. Holding her son's hand in her own, Sarah walked with him down the long street to get there. As he walked along with his mother, the little boy would recite the first part of the *Shema*§, which his mother had taught him. He recited the *Shema* and *V'Ahavta*# so sweetly and softly in his child's voice, that—as they passed down the street—the people in all the houses along the way would wake up from their sleep and, overcome by a mysterious yearning for God, rush to the synagogue to pray.

When little Israel recited the *Kaddish* in the synagogue, it often seemed to him that he saw his dear father, who had come from the Garden of Eden to listen to his prayer, standing beside him. When he thought he saw his father nodding his head in approval and moving his lips to answer "Amen" as Israel recited the *Kaddish*, he always became more inspired and fervent in his praying. The memory of his pious father was very dear to him.

Now without her husband's support, Sarah worked as a midwife, and everyone

---

* That is, love for the Jewish people.
¶ The memorial prayer for the dead.
§ The "Hear O Israel" prayer.
# The prayer that follows the *Shema*, about love for God.

called her "Sarah the Midwife." But her poor earnings were not enough to provide for their daily needs, so she also sold clothing and other household items to the gentile peasants. That is how she eked out a meager living for herself and for her son. Since Sarah could not afford to pay the full tuition for a *melamed** to teach Torah to Israel, she arranged, partially in place of tuition, for him to work for the *melamed*. Little Israel swept the teacher's house, which also served as the *cheder*¶, drew water for him, and did his errands.[9]

Fulfilling His Father's Words

AFTER HIS FATHER'S DEATH, LITTLE ISRAEL TRIED TO FULFILL HIS FATHER'S last words to him. He immersed himself in the thought that the Holy One, blessed be He, is everywhere and is always with him. Israel frequently recalled what his father had told him: that Abraham had come to know his Creator when he was only three years old. Israel also knew God at an early age and wanted to know Him more and to be even closer. Orphaned from his earthly father, he felt a great yearning for his Heavenly Father. He thought about God constantly and felt that he never had to be afraid of anything or anyone. He firmly believed that since God protected him, no one could harm him. Because of such thoughts, this pious boy was always a happy child. Whenever he was with people, he was openhearted and friendly, and he tried to follow his father's instructions to treat everyone in a kindly way, no matter who he or she was.[10]

His First Test

ISRAEL OFTEN WENT INTO THE FIELDS OR THE WOODS OUTSIDE THE town because he felt a need to be alone. He once went to walk in the woods and was there as it became dark. Trusting, with a child's innocent faith, what his father had told him—that God protected him—he was fearless. When he saw a distant glow, he went to see what it was and, reaching it, found a large house, with a mysterious illumination emanating from within. As he entered, the light became brighter. But although the house was full of light, he felt surrounded by darkness.

When he came to the innermost room, he saw many demons, Satan's henchmen, seated around a large table laughing raucously. They turned to him fiercely and snarled, "Why are you not afraid to enter here?" "My father told me to fear nothing except the Holy One, blessed be He, alone!" he replied. They laughed scornfully at the

---

* Teacher.
¶ Primary religious school.

orphan and said, "Little boy, don't you know that God has abandoned the earth?" "'Let all the workers of iniquity be scattered!'" he shouted. The demons immediately vanished, as if they had never existed. The house too and everything in it instantly disappeared. Little Israel saw that he was standing alone in the woods at night, in pitch darkness, but he felt the light of the living presence of God surrounding and protecting him. The Torah says: "With Him light dwells," and: "Even darkness is not dark for Thee, but the night shines like the day. The darkness and the light are both alike to Thee."[11]

No Longer an Orphan

ISRAEL'S PIOUS MOTHER SARAH ALWAYS HAD A BOOK OF PSALMS IN HER hand. And she taught him to recite psalms at every opportunity and to use them as the basis for his personal prayers. One day, when he was reciting psalms and had reached the verse "You are My son; today, I have begotten you"—he felt that God was speaking to him through this verse, and his eyes filled with tears. He thought, "God said to David, 'You are My son,' and from that day David was God's son. That must be especially true for me too, because I don't have a father. But God is a Father of orphans. And He has now said to me too, 'You are My son; today I have begotten you'!"[12]

A Wayward Youth

A YEAR AFTER HIS FATHER'S DEATH, ISRAEL'S MOTHER ALSO PASSED AWAY. The townspeople, who revered the memory of his saintly parents, arranged for his upkeep and education. They put him in the charge of two guardians, who paid part tuition to the *melamed* to teach him Torah, together with other children. Israel went to live in the *melamed*'s home and, to help with his own support, continued to perform various menial services for the teacher and his wife.

Israel succeeded in his studies, for his love of Torah was deep and strong. After finishing his daily studies in the *cheder*, he would go off into the fields or woods away from people and other children, to repeat from memory, undisturbed, what he had learned. His progress in *Tanach** and Talmud was outstanding. Although the circumstances of his life were difficult, he tried to behave in the way that his parents had taught him, and to be kind to everyone he met. He even made an effort to like the *melamed*, who rudely ordered him about on his different errands, and the other children, who looked down on him as an orphan. But he did not always succeed in his

---

* Bible; acronym for *Torah, Nevi'im, K'tuvim*, that is, Torah (Five Books of Moses), Prophets, and Writings.

attempt to be good. And he often felt cramped in the *cheder*, which was in the *melamed*'s home. Not only was the one-room house small and unclean but the *melamed* treated the children harshly and his wife added to the disorder by her own yelling at the students, who were less than studious and sometimes even impudent. Being indoors all the time also depressed Israel. And the *melamed*'s rote teaching was so different from the sparks of fire that he had seen emanate from his father's holy mouth when his father had taught him Torah! Israel felt freer when he was outside in the open air, as he walked through the woods pondering the teachings and stories of the Torah and Talmud. While among the trees and grasses, he also meditated on the presence of God, as his father had taught him. He considered how each created thing, whether a blade of grass, a leaf, a flower, or a stone, is kept in existence every moment by God's will, and, were His will removed, it would immediately disappear. "There is nothing but God!" he repeated aloud countless times, and he frequently uttered a mystic verse that his father had taught him: "He fills all worlds and surrounds all worlds and there is no place where He is not present!"

The pious boy constantly reminded himself that God created everything only for the good of His creatures, and especially for His people, Israel. Often, in the intensity of his meditation, young Israel felt, when he was looking at the world around him, that he was looking at God, and God was also looking at Him. He felt the comforting presence of his Heavenly Father very close to him then. He believed with complete faith that God was watching over and caring for him, and would protect him from any harm. When he encountered anything frightening, he uttered the psalm verse his father had taught him for such situations: "Let all the workers of iniquity be scattered!" Whereas other children were afraid of the forests that surrounded the town, in which bears, wolves (and even demons!) roamed, young Israel was fearless. Sometimes, he even slept in the fields or in the woods. And, trusting in God, no harm ever came to him.

Little Israel prayed often, with intense fervor. Even as a boy, the spirit of God rested on him, and he yearned to pour out his soul before his Creator. He spoke to God as if he were speaking to his own father, for he fully believed that God, blessed be He, was actually present—with him, by him, near him. But following his father's instructions, he hid his piety from people. Because of that, to others, he appeared wayward. Usually, he would study for a few days with his teacher, but afterward he would run away from school and go out to the forest.[13]

A Blessing of Eyes to See

ONCE, HE RAN AWAY TO THE WOODS BECAUSE HE COULD NOT BEAR the *cheder* anymore. The *melamed* was always screaming, his wife acted like a crazy woman, the schoolchildren were fighting, and the house was filthy. To make matters worse, he was also unhappy when he remembered his father's last words to him to love every Jew. How was it possible? When he came to the forest, he stood there for a while, crying and praying for some sort of salvation, because what kind of life did he have? He was a little boy, all by himself in the world and surrounded by troubles! Although Israel believed that God was always with him, a little boy also needs to have adults to love him and guide him. Israel could not help but feel alone.

Suddenly an old man appeared and called him by name. "Israel," he said, "I want to give you a blessing that you should have eyes to see." "What do you mean by that?" Israel asked. "Who are you?" The man just said, "May you have eyes to see." And he left.

Israel never learned who the man was. Later, he wandered back to *cheder*. But now, when he walked in, things looked different: The teacher was still screaming, but Israel realized that sometimes, when a person experiences poverty and other difficulties, he is no longer in control of his temper. And when Israel saw that the teacher's wife, it was true, was still agitated and upset, nevertheless, he understood what she had been through; and he saw the unruly students and the unkempt house too in a different way.

Israel understood that he had received a precious blessing from the elderly stranger, who, he now realized, was a holy man. That blessing helped him to understand that if there are Jews who are acting in ways they should not act, he should seek to comprehend why that person is behaving that way, what that person is going through. After this mysterious encounter with the unknown man, who was a hidden tzaddik, Israel had "eyes to see."

At that time, there were more than a few hidden tzaddikim who wandered about the countryside with their knapsack on their back. On a number of occasions, little Israel came across these holy men in the forest or in town and talked to them about the Torah and asked them questions about God and His world and about divine service.[14]

Different from Other Children

WHEN ISRAEL RAN AWAY FROM THE SCHOOL TO THE WOODS, AND HIS guardians searched for him, they often found him sitting somewhere under a tree or lying on the grass gazing at the sky and communing with himself. They attributed his peculiar behavior to his being an orphan and unsupervised, and each time they returned him to the teacher. But young Israel's strange habits were due not to his being wayward but to a streak of holy brazenness. His actions were the result of a fiery youthful piety. His soul yearned without cease for God's closeness and, for that, he needed solitude and space. The cramped *cheder* and the *melamed*'s rote teaching did not allow his soul to soar into heaven. So, though his guardians kept returning him to the *melamed*, he kept running away to be alone. Thus matters went on for two years. But after this happened numerous times, his guardians finally gave up hope and stopped searching for him and returning him to the teacher. They withdrew him from the *cheder*, and Israel, who was then seven years old, grew up differently from other children. He was very independent. Although he no longer attended the *cheder*, he continued to work for the *melamed* and to do odd jobs for other people. Some of his parents' friends took him in to live with them and he paid for his keep. He occasionally studied Torah alone, or with a study partner, young or old, in the *beit midrash*. He also spent much time praying and meditating as his father had taught him, whether in the synagogue or while wandering outdoors.[15]

Israel Goes Away with a Hidden Tzaddik

ONE MORNING, AFTER PRAYING WITH THE EARLY *MINYAN** OF DEVOUT Jews who worshiped at dawn, Israel went into the forest, as he often did. Suddenly, he heard a voice at a distance and, following the sound, saw a distinguished white-bearded elderly Jew wrapped in a tallis[¶] and *tefillin*[§], praying with a fervor that Israel had never before encountered. His voice wafting heavenward was a symphony of longing . . . of joy . . . now expressing entreaty amidst tears . . . then changing to rapture. Israel was spellbound. He was attracted to this amazing Jew in a way beyond anything he had ever felt. He hid behind some trees and watched, unseen, the man's every movement. It gave him great pleasure just to listen to the enchanting sound of this Jew's prayer. Israel was so impressed and in wonder that he was certain this must be one of the thirty-six hidden tzaddikim, on whom the existence of the world depends. He could not take his eyes off this holy Jew. He did not let his eyes blink, lest he lose this precious sight for even a moment.

The tzaddik finished his prayer, removed his tallis and *tefillin*, and took out a small Book of Psalms and chanted a number of psalms in the sweetest and most melodious voice. Then he sat down and studied Torah with rapt concentration and delight for a long time. Israel had observed many people *davvening*[#] and studying Torah in the synagogue and *beit midrash*, but *davvening* and studying like this were unique in his experience. After the man finished his studying, he took some dry bread and a water bag from his knapsack, washed his hands and ate, then said the Grace After Meals, again with great devotion and fervor. Finally, he gathered his books, tallis, and *tefillin*, kissed them lovingly, and returned them to his knapsack. Then he slung the knapsack over his shoulder, took his staff in his hand, and set off on his way.

At that moment, Israel came out of his hiding place and approached the man, saying, "*Shalom aleichem*, Rebbe**." Seeing him, the man replied, "*Aleichem shalom*[¶¶]," and asked, "What is a young boy like you doing in the woods alone?" Israel answered that he loved the fields and forests, adding, "I'm an orphan, but I'm not afraid, because my father, of blessed memory, before his death told me not to be afraid of anything, except

---

* Prayer-quorum of ten men.
¶ Prayer shawl.
§ Ritual leather boxes, containing Torah verses written on parchment, strapped to the head and arm while praying.
# The ordained form of Jewish prayer.
** Peace be upon you, Teacher (or: Master).
¶¶ Upon you be peace.

God, blessed be He!" The man asked him, "Are you perhaps the son of Rabbi Eliezer?" When Israel answered in the affirmative, the man asked him his name and then said, "My name is Shlomo Zalman. I knew your holy father." Then he took from his knap-sack a volume of the Talmud tractate *Pesahim*, asked Israel to sit down with him in a grassy spot, and together they studied for two hours. Israel's knowledge, eagerness to learn, and quick grasp gratified the tzaddik greatly. He said, "Your father, of blessed memory, would be very proud of you."

Reb* Shlomo Zalman realized that Rabbi Eliezer's son was a precious vessel that might be damaged without proper care, and he asked the boy if he would like to accompany him on his travels. Israel, who was all alone in the world, was irresistibly attracted to this holy Jew. He attached himself to Reb Shlomo Zalman and went with him without any idea of where they were going.

Reb Shlomo Zalman, who took Israel under his wing, was a hidden tzaddik. Unex-pectedly meeting his friend's orphan son, he felt certain that heaven had appointed him to the task of caring for the boy and teaching him about the Torah and about life.[16]

Wandering with Reb Shlomo Zalman

HIDDEN TZADDIKIM WERE ESPECIALLY CONCERNED TO EDUCATE orphans and occasionally "recruited" them into their movement. (There were many orphans at that time, because of the poor living conditions and medical treat-ment, and the frequent pogroms.) Reb Shlomo Zalman recruited the young orphan, Israel, who was then eight years old, to accompany him on his travels. In their wander-ings, they stopped in various towns and villages. For much of the day, Reb Shlomo Zalman taught Israel Torah. And the boy never once saw him receiving donations, as itinerant beggars did, yet he supported Israel all the time. Israel did not know that his father and mother had been hidden tzaddikim, nor did he know that his mentor was a hidden tzaddik and was supported by the movement. Reb Shlomo Zalman occasion-ally performed various missions for the movement of hidden tzaddikim, but he kept these activities secret from Israel. Israel accompanied Reb Shlomo Zalman in his wan-derings for three years.[17]

In the Home of Rabbi Meir

ONCE, WHEN THEY WERE IN A SMALL SETTLEMENT, REB SHLOMO ZALMAN told Israel that, in the forest nearby, there lived a pious and learned Jew named Rabbi Meir. He said that he would leave Israel with him. He then took the boy to

---

* An honorific equivalent to "Mr."

Rabbi Meir, left Israel in his care, and, after a tearful parting, during which he bestowed many blessings for spiritual success on the boy, went off on his own.

Israel stayed in that isolated house in the forest with Rabbi Meir. And he diligently studied Torah with his new teacher and master. Every day, Rabbi Meir took him to the nearby settlement to pray with the congregation. To the local people, Rabbi Meir was just a simple laborer, a tar-maker. None of them knew that he was a *gaon** and the leader of a group of hidden mystics.[18]

He Joins the Society of Hidden Tzaddikim

BEFORE THE BAAL SHEM TOV TURNED THIRTEEN ON *HAI ELUL*, 1713, RABBI Meir taught him the secrets of the *tefillin* and other *mitzvot*—how to bind himself to God in *d'vekut*. After he became bar mitzvah, Rabbi Meir introduced him to the study of the Kabbalah. And he began to tell Israel about the hidden tzaddikim and revealed to the boy that his parents had been members of the movement. He also told him about their leader, the great *gaon* and tzaddik Rabbi Adam Baal Shem, originally of Ropshitz in Poland, who lived far away, near Vienna, in the German-speaking lands. At the age of fourteen, Israel joined the "Camp of Israel" (*Machane Yisrael*), the society of hidden tzaddikim. Some of them were wanderers, like Reb Shlomo Zalman; others were manual laborers, like Rabbi Meir. The young Israel had, at first, been "adopted" into this movement that he later joined. But his lineage was in the movement, for both his parents had been members, and they had raised him, while they had the chance, according to its highest standards. Israel now left Rabbi Meir and became a wanderer. He began, this time alone, to travel from city to city, and from settlement to settlement, fulfilling various missions that the leadership of the hidden tzaddikim placed on him.[19]

Elijah's Teaching about Simple Devotion

BEFORE HE WAS SIXTEEN YEARS OLD, ISRAEL ALREADY HAD A FAIRLY extensive knowledge of Kabbalah. He prayed using the *yehudim* (kabbalistic divine-Name-unifications) of the Ari[¶], which had been taught to him by a hidden tzaddik named Rabbi Hayim.

On his sixteenth birthday, on the 18th of *Elul* in 1716, Israel was in a small settlement, where he was staying at an inn. The innkeeper was the simplest sort of Jew, who was able to pray only with great difficulty, without knowing the meaning of the Hebrew words. He was very devout, however, and had a pious custom of continually uttering in every situation and circumstance: "Blessed is He forever and ever!" His wife, who helped him run the inn, also had a habit of continually saying: "Blessed be

---

* Great Torah scholar.
¶ The great kabbalist, Rabbi Yitzhak Luria, also called the Ari, the "Lion."

His holy name!" Although they were occupied with their daily tasks, they kept their minds and hearts always focused on God by repeating these holy sentences.

That day, Israel went out to the fields, according to the age-old custom to seclude oneself with one's Creator for a period of time on one's birthday. Standing in a field near some trees, he began to recite psalms while meditating on unifications of the divine Names. While he was immersed in this recitation, he entered a trance and ceased to be aware of his surroundings.

Suddenly, he saw the prophet Elijah standing in front of him, gazing at him with an enigmatic smile on his lips. Israel was greatly surprised that he had merited to see Elijah. When he had been with Rabbi Meir or with a group of hidden tzaddikim, he had, on a number of occasions, seen the prophet Elijah. But this was the first time that he had ever seen him when he was alone.

As he was puzzling over Elijah's mysterious smile, the angelic prophet spoke to him, saying, "You are struggling with such effort to perform complex kabbalistic meditations on the words of the psalms. But Aharon Shlomo the innkeeper and Zlateh Rivkah his wife know nothing about the cosmic effects caused by the 'Blessed is He forever and ever' that he says, and the 'Blessed be His holy name' that she says. Yet, their simple utterances make all the worlds tremble, even more so than the meditations of great kabbalists!"

Elijah told Israel of the great pleasure in heaven when men, women, and children praise God; especially when the praise is uttered by simple people; and most especially when it is continual; for then they are always cleaving to God, blessed be He, with pure faith and pious innocence. Israel took Elijah's words to heart and later pondered them deeply.[20]

A Turning Point in the Besht's Views

THIS ENCOUNTER WITH ELIJAH GREATLY INFLUENCED THE YOUNG Baal Shem Tov's views. The Besht knew that some hidden tzaddikim who worked as manual laborers engaged in the practice of repeating holy phrases or sentences. They also taught that pious custom to working people who were unable to study Torah or even recite psalms. Israel's seniors and teachers in the movement had told him that this simple but powerful practice was used by none other than the biblical Enoch, who had been a humble shoemaker. Enoch, they said, constantly repeated a holy sentence at all times, even during work. While sewing together the uppers and lowers of the shoes, he recited with each and every stitch, "Blessed is His glorious kingdom forever and ever!" By this, he was able to bind together the upper and lower worlds, heaven and earth.

The hidden tzaddikim had a special connection to Elijah the Prophet. Because he ascended to heaven alive in a fiery chariot and never died, Elijah can return to earth to help Jews in need. He also appears in visions to mystic adepts to teach them the Torah's secrets. Elijah, who often makes visits disguised as a poor wayfarer, was, so to speak, the angelic guide and teacher of the hidden tzaddikim. Elijah and Enoch, one a wanderer, the other a laborer, were the only individuals that the Torah says entered heaven alive, and both were spiritual models for the hidden tzaddikim, who were themselves wanderers or laborers. The hidden tzaddikim also sought to "enter heaven while alive"—to experience godly reality during their lifetime—by means of a fiery devotion to the mystic path.

After this meeting with Elijah, the Baal Shem Tov began frequently to repeat a holy sentence. At different times he used the verses uttered by the innkeeper, his wife, and Enoch. He also used the psalm verse "I have placed God before me always," the common pious phrase *Baruch HaShem* ("Praise God"), and "The power of the Doer is in the deed"—meaning that the divine life-force pervades every aspect of reality.

Elijah's appearance to the young Baal Shem Tov to teach him about the spiritual value of repeating a holy phrase praising God, was a turning point in the Baal Shem's religious life. The hidden tzaddikim already sided with the common people against condescending rabbis. The hidden tzaddikim encouraged the devotion of the working people. But now the young Baal Shem Tov went a step further. Elijah had revealed to him that the simple devotions of pious working people can produce a spiritual effect even more profound than the meditations of accomplished kabbalists. Torah study, especially of the Kabbalah, can lead to spiritual levels to which no simple person has access. But in matters of faith, trust in God, and self-sacrifice, Torah scholars and even great kabbalists can learn from pious simple people. The young Baal Shem Tov realized that certainly he too could learn from them! As a result, his opinion of simple faith and of devout simple people was greatly elevated.

This pivotal encounter with Elijah also transformed the young Baal Shem Tov's attitude to prayer. From then on, even after having learned all the complex kabbalistic meditations for prayer, he tried to pray with the innocence and simplicity of a child. He came to believe that simple, childlike devotion is the key to entering the presence of one's Father in Heaven.

The Besht passed on these profound teachings to his comrades among the hidden tzaddikim and to the working people whom he met. He told them with great enthusiasm that even an uneducated laborer can become very close to God! Even someone who is not a Torah scholar or a kabbalist can immerse himself in holiness. The Besht often told laborers, "While your hands are working below, keep your heart turned to God above by fervently repeating pious phrases." Hidden tzaddikim who worked as manual laborers inspired many fellow laborers with this teaching that the young Besht had transmitted from the mouth of Elijah the Prophet.[21]

Baruch HaShem

 IN TEACHING THE WORKING PEOPLE, THE HIDDEN TZADDIKIM TOLD tales about how Elijah the Prophet instructed Jews to remember God and show their faith in Him by using traditional pious phrases, such as "God-willing" and (when bad things happened) "This also is for good." The Baal Shem Tov, like other hidden tzaddikim, encouraged simple people to express their devotion by constantly using these phrases. When asked "How are you?" pious Jews respond, "*Baruch HaShem*," (Praise God), meaning: "Whether my situation is good or bad, I thank God." Realizing that this response arouses mercy on high for the Jewish people, the Besht always asked every Jew he met about his health, welfare, and livelihood, knowing that he would piously answer, "*Baruch HaShem*, all is well!" By this practice, the Baal Shem Tov expressed his love for the Jewish people, because he enabled them to find favor in God's eyes. At a gathering of the hidden tzaddikim, he proposed that they adopt this custom of his, and they accepted it as a group, for they agreed with the Besht, who said that it was an entrance into the divine service of the love of Israel.[22]

Elijah Becomes His Master and Teacher

FOR THREE YEARS THE BAAL SHEM TOV HAD LEARNED TORAH FROM REB Shlomo Zalman, the hidden tzaddik who took him from Okup. For four years he had learned Torah and Kabbalah from Rabbi Meir, and occasionally from Rabbi Hayim—who taught him kabbalistic praying. But after the revelation of Elijah on his sixteenth birthday, the angelic prophet appeared to him regularly and became his foremost teacher. Elijah had announced Israel's birth to his father and mother, and now on his birthday he became his master and teacher.

A New Program for the Hidden Tzaddikim

IN 1718, WHEN HE WAS EIGHTEEN YEARS OLD, THE BAAL SHEM TOV suggested a program for a new direction in the work of the hidden tzaddikim. At that time, many Jews were still suffering economically and socially from the dislocations caused by the events of 1648–1649, and, especially in outlying areas, parents could not afford to educate their children in Torah. Many children were growing up without even knowing the Hebrew alphabet. The Baal Shem Tov wanted to rebuild the community of Israel from the foundation up, for if the foundation is strong so is the whole building. And the foundation of the people of Israel, he realized, is the education of the children. The Besht wanted the hidden tzaddikim to accept on themselves the task of educating children, and to arrange that there be teachers in every town and settlement, no matter how small. He also wanted the hidden tzaddikim to occupy themselves in a more regular way with teaching uneducated adults who knew nothing about Judaism. He discussed his ideas first with a hidden tzaddik named Rabbi Mordechai, who was his close friend and who accepted the Besht as his teacher. The Besht's program was then passed on to the leadership and accepted by the movement. The Besht, Rabbi Mordechai, and a third comrade, Rabbi Kehot, were appointed to work together to develop a plan for its fulfillment. Large amounts of money would be required to support this program, and two hidden tzaddikim, Rabbi Aharon David, a carpenter in Brody, and Rabbi Shlomo Hayim, a tailor in Lvov, were appointed by the movement's leaders to coordinate the efforts to raise funds. The society of hidden tzaddikim also resolved that in any place where there was a lack of teachers for the children, they themselves would perform that service. Then, following the adage of the Sages that "he who reads the letter should himself fulfill its instructions," the Baal Shem Tov decided to become a teacher's helper.[23]

An Assistant Teacher

ISRAEL HAD LEFT OKUP AT THE AGE OF EIGHT, AND NOW TEN YEARS later at eighteen he returned to live in his hometown; but he wanted to remain hidden. As he was not held to be knowledgeable in Torah, he would be regarded as unfit for a job as a teacher. Yet he had previously lived in the home of a *melamed*, had done his errands, and occasionally assisted him at the *cheder*. That *melamed* had left Okup for different parts. So Israel now obtained a job as an assistant to the new *melamed* in a *cheder* for little boys in his hometown of Okup. Each day, he took the children from their homes to the *cheder* and brought them back at the end of the school day. When he went into their homes in the morning to pick them up, he would say the "*Modeh Ani*" prayer with them, help them to put on their *tzitzit** and to say that blessing and the other blessings. Then he would recite with them the morning *Shema* and the traditional verse for children: "Moses commanded us the Torah, the inheritance of the Congregation of Israel." He always responded "Amen" to their blessings, with great devotion and fervor. During the school day, he also performed other tasks, such as reviewing the teacher's lessons with the students. When he took the children home at the end of the day, he recited the evening *Shema* with them and the verse: "Into Thy hand I commend my spirit," for they would soon be put to sleep.

Many of the parents had trouble making a living and could not spend enough time with their children. The young Besht took every opportunity to teach and train the children to respect their parents and to appreciate them. Every day, when he picked them up, he asked, "Shlomele" or "Moshele, how are you this morning?" And the child would answer, "*Baruch HaShem*, Reb Israel, I'm well, and I thank God that I have such good parents and such good brothers and sisters!"

While most other assistant teachers elsewhere would wake up the children in the morning, roughly by yelling, the young Baal Shem Tov would sit on a child's bed and softly sing a *niggun*¶ to wake him. When the boy opened his eyes, the Besht asked him if he knew it was time to get up. The Baal Shem Tov took so long to go from house to

---

* Ritual fringes on a square-shaped shirt or *tallis* (prayer shawl).
¶ Melody.

house and bring all the children to the *cheder* that the *melamed* became angry at him and the Besht almost lost his job as a result! But the children cried so much when they heard that the *melamed* was firing him that they protected him! The Besht's attitude to the children was totally loving. If one of them was difficult and refused to go to the *cheder*, the Besht pleaded with him and urged him, and would even persuade him by giving him a penny to buy some candy. The children loved him with all their hearts because they knew that he loved them. He often hugged and kissed them. His most special tender care was reserved for those children whose parents had neglected their religious training. To them, he told the beautiful stories of the *Chumash**—about the Patriarchs and Matriarchs, about Moses—the tales of the Prophets, and of the Sages of the Talmud.

The hidden tzaddikim had pioneered a new way of drawing the common people to religion: by telling them tales of the Torah and of the Talmud. The Baal Shem Tov was an excellent storyteller who fully appreciated the power of stories. And he used his abilities to great effect with the children. When the Besht told them Torah stories, his storytelling was so vivid that the children felt they were actually present at the scene. The Rabbis say that every Jewish soul was at Mount Sinai when the Torah was given, and the Torah itself says to remember "what your eyes have seen." Once, the Besht told the children about the giving of the Torah to the Jewish people at Mount Sinai, and he described the scene so graphically that the children felt that they were present at the foot of the mountain, and experienced the thunder and lightning, and heard, "I am the Lord your God!" Later, on the following *Shavuot* (the holiday commemorating the giving of the Torah), the event at Mount Sinai was clearly before their eyes. When the Besht asked them, "Do you remember being at Mount Sinai?" They all answered, "We remember!"

The Baal Shem Tov's job as an assistant teacher was part of his divine service of the love of Israel, and he reached exalted spiritual levels because of his excessive love for the children. He confided to his comrades among the hidden tzaddikim that he loved children even more than holy books. The Besht greatly enjoyed his work as an assistant teacher, which allowed him to express and deepen his piety, which was as pure as the piety of the children he taught. When one of his comrades among the hidden tzaddikim wondered why a person of exceptional spiritual talents such as he spent his time with children, the Besht replied, "The Torah study of innocent children is more precious in heaven than the studying of even great scholars. And by being with children you can learn how to be childlike." He taught the children for their sake, but also because of his own strong desire to be close to God; he wanted to be around children, to absorb their sweet qualities of innocence and trust.

In *cheder*, the young Besht repeated with the children the lessons they had learned from the *melamed*, such as the alphabet—*aleph-beis*—and the vowels—*kametz-aleph: aw . . . kametz-beis: baw*. He felt that heaven received great pleasure from the children's simple "Torah study." He was sure that even the angels envied his holy little flock!

---

* Five Books of Moses.

Each day, he brought the children to the synagogue and, as the congregation prayed, he taught the children to recite, in a loud but pleasant voice, the congregational responses, such as "*Amen*" and "*Y'hai shmai rabba mevorach!*"* To him, the "amen" of a child was not something small but something great. When the Torah scroll was taken around in procession during the synagogue service and returned to the holy Ark¶, the Besht always lifted the children up to kiss it, and when they entered and left the synagogue, he lifted them up to kiss the *mezuzah*§. All this was his holy work with the little children, the breath of whose mouths is pure and without sin.[24]

A Werewolf

WHEN THE BESHT LED THE CHILDREN BETWEEN HOME, *CHEDER*, AND synagogue, he walked with them at the head of the line and enthusiastically sang religious songs with them in his own sweet voice. Their raised voices could be heard far away, and their pure and innocent singing inspired whoever heard it. Their songs also ascended into the heavens, and there was as much pleasure from them in heaven as once there had been from the songs the Levites sang in the holy Temple in Jerusalem. It was a time of great favor on high.

Sometimes, young Israel took the children by a roundabout path through the fields and woods, for he wanted them to see the glories of God's creation in Nature. As he walked with the children and led them in song, the angels gathered to listen. But the Satan too came among them, for he perceived a serious threat to his power. He was afraid that the time had arrived when he would be removed from the face of the earth. So he possessed a certain gentile sorcerer and incited him against the Baal Shem Tov.

One day, when the Besht was walking with the children and leading their singing, the sorcerer transformed himself into a werewolf and attacked them. The children fled in panic, scattering in all directions. Later, some of them even became sick, they were so frightened. After this incident, the fearful parents refused to send their children to the *cheder*. So the "daily offering"—of the children's study and prayers—was halted. It was as if the daily sacrifices in the Temple had ceased!

Then, the Baal Shem Tov mustered his faith and trust in the Lord his God. Out of his great love for the children, he was ready to risk his life for them. So he went from house to house, pleading with the parents to have faith that in the merit of the children's study they would come to no harm. He begged the parents to trust him to protect their children and promised to return all their children to them safe and sound. If need be, he would fight with the wolf and slay it in the name of the Lord. Why should they stop the children's studies, which were so precious in heaven? He persisted until he finally persuaded them to trust him with their dear little ones.

---

* Amen, blessed be His great Name!
¶ The cabinet containing the Torah scrolls.
§ A small container, holding a parchment with Torah verses, which is attached to a doorpost.

Taking a good, strong stick in his hand, he set out with the children in tow to the *cheder*. When his little band was happily singing, the vicious beast attacked again. Israel confronted it, struck it a mighty blow on the forehead, and it died on the spot. The next day, the corpse of the sorcerer was found lying on the ground. But not a hair of the children's heads had been harmed. They were all returned safely to their parents, as Israel had promised.

The Rabbis say that God tested Moses and David as shepherds of sheep before He put them in charge of His flock. The Holy One, blessed be He, also tested the Baal Shem Tov with his little flock of children before He raised him to be a shepherd of the Children of Israel.[25]

A Gentile Youth Throws a Stone

ONE DAY, A PARENT OF ONE OF THE SCHOOLCHILDREN WAS TRAVELING to visit a certain Torah scholar. Israel asked to go with him, since he craved the chance to see this great sage. But the man did not want to take the Besht in his coach. So Israel rode concealed on the running board protruding from the back of the coach, without the man knowing it.

As they were traveling, a gentile youth, seeing a Jewish youth riding this way, threw a stone at him. It found its mark and wounded Israel, who began to bleed from his head. But the youth who threw the stone immediately became paralyzed. His feet sank into the ground, so that he became fastened where he stood. When his friends tried to move him, he sunk even farther into the earth. The youth's parents, who had seen the whole incident, ran to the coach yelling and would not let it move on. They begged and pleaded with Israel to pray that their son be saved from his calamity. Only after the culprit promised—by nodding his head since he could not speak—that he would never again throw stones at Jews did Israel yield to their pleading. He prayed for him, and the offending youth was miraculously freed from his trap, safe and healthy as before.

After this amazing event, the man whose coach it was treated Israel with respect and awe and took him inside. But later, when Israel returned to his work as a teacher's assistant, an even greater miracle occurred: The first miracle was forgotten. Although it was an astonishing wonder that happened before a number of people, it made no impression at all, either on Israel or on those who had seen it. It was God's will to keep Israel hidden until the time when he was ready to be revealed.[26]

Shammos *of the* Beit Midrash

AFTER THIS, ISRAEL FELT A NEED FOR A DIFFERENT ENVIRONMENT to further his spiritual development. He wanted to be among Torah scholars and near a library of holy books. So he became the *shammos** of the *beit midrash* in Okup. He also attended to the needs of a number of Torah scholars who studied there regularly. As was the custom then, these scholars stayed in the *beit midrash* the whole week, only returning home for the Sabbath. They were completely immersed in Torah study and prayer all their waking hours. When they felt hungry, they paused just long enough to eat a little bread or a meal that was prepared at home, and immediately resumed their divine service. At night, when they became drowsy, they rested their head on the table where they studied or stretched out on a hard bench for a short nap, just enough to regain the energy they needed to return to Torah study and prayer.

The Besht, whom they called "Israel the Shammos," brought them food and water from their homes. In the winter, he heated the stove for them. He put holy books back on the shelf and every day swept up the *beit midrash*. He was deeply gratified by his divine service of cleaning and honoring the "miniature sanctuary" of the house of Torah study. He also humbly performed the *mitzvah* of personally serving Torah scholars and fulfilled his earnest desire to be a servant of the servants of God. This work allowed the Besht to spend all his time in the *beit midrash* and secretly study the Torah when possible.

The Baal Shem Tov's father, himself a hidden tzaddik, had instructed his young son in holy modesty. So the Besht was content to appear ignorant and to serve God behind a veil of concealment. He kept his divine service well hidden. When the Torah scholars were awake—during the early part of the evening—after *Maariv*[¶] and the evening meal, he slept. When they went to sleep, he woke up. He engaged in his pure divine service almost until dawn, and just before they awoke, he went back to sleep. They thought that he slept the whole night, from beginning to end. As he was never seen studying Torah, they never suspected anything. They assumed that he was just a simple, uneducated youth. Yet, during the night hours, he usually studied Kabbalah, mainly the holy *Zohar*. Often, when the scholars were awake in the early evening and the Besht was stretched out on a bench in the *beit midrash* with his eyes closed, he was merely pretending to sleep and was actually engaged in silent mental Torah study, prayers, and meditations, in intimate communion with his Creator.[27]

He Remains Unmarried

ISRAEL WAS NOW TWENTY YEARS OLD, AN AGE AT WHICH HE WOULD have already been married, had his parents been alive to arrange it. Israel himself was consumed with spiritual matters. Previously, moving about on his missions for the hidden tzaddikim, he had little time to think about a wife. Now that he was settled and working as an assistant *melamed* or synagogue caretaker, he made so little money that

---

* Caretaker.
¶ The daily evening prayers.

he was not considered an attractive prospect by the girls' parents. Moreover, since he was thought to be unlearned, the parents of pious girls from good families did not want him for a son-in-law. But occasionally, young Israel thought about fulfilling the *mitzvah* to marry, to be fruitful and multiply.[28]

The Secret Manuscript of Rabbi Adam Baal Shem

NEAR VIENNA, VERY FAR FROM THE BESHT'S VILLAGE, THERE LIVED A holy, elderly tzaddik named Rabbi Adam Baal Shem. Rabbi Adam was a great kabbalist and *baal shem* and was the leader of the movement of hidden tzaddikim. He was in possession of a hand-written manuscript of a book that contained the deepest secrets of the Kabbalah, including the practical Kabbalah—how to use divine Names to perform miracles. The hidden tzaddikim quietly spread the study of the theoretical Kabbalah, the understanding of divine wisdom. The practical Kabbalah, however, is very dangerous, and those fit to learn it are few. Rabbi Adam used this potent knowledge and these powerful practices for good, but when he became old he realized that he had to decide what to do with the mystic manuscript in his possession. God-forbid that it fall into the hands of the wrong person! Neither his son nor any of his disciples was qualified to handle this fiery Torah without being burnt. Since he did not want to destroy the manuscript, he was tempted to hide it in a cave. However, he knew that it could be used to do great and good things. These secret teachings had been passed down from time immemorial. They had first been revealed to Abraham, and since then had been in the possession of only four others before they reached Rabbi Adam. Uncertain about what to do, he prepared a dream question before sleep: "To whom should he give the manuscript?" The answer from heaven was: "Give it to Rabbi Israel, the son of Rabbi Eliezer in the town of Okup in Poland. He will be the leader of the hidden tzaddikim after you."

Upon awakening, he called his only son, Rabbi Nachum, to him and said, "I have a manuscript containing teachings that you are not yet worthy of knowing. Take it and seek out a certain distant town named Okup in Poland. There you'll find one of our comrades named Rabbi Israel the son of Rabbi Eliezer, who is twenty years old. He's a special young man who instigated our program to educate neglected children. Deliver the manuscript to him, for it belongs to the root of his soul. If you're fortunate, he'll permit you to become his disciple. And it is in that town, my son, that you'll find your soul-mate for marriage."

After Rabbi Adam passed away, Rabbi Nachum traveled by horse-drawn carriage from city to city until he reached Okup. There he lodged with the head of the community, who asked him, "Where are you from, and where are you going? Because you don't look like someone who's seeking charity donations"—for he was an impressive-looking young man; his shining face testified to his Torah wisdom and deep piety. He answered truthfully, but concealed his essential purpose, saying, "My deceased father, of blessed memory, who was a famous tzaddik, instructed me before his death to take a wife from the town of Okup, and I'm obligated to fulfill his wishes." Immediately, the whole town was buzzing with the news, and before long a number of desirable marriage proposals were offered to him, for he was well thought of by everyone who saw him. After considering the proposals, he entered into a marriage agreement with a certain wealthy man.

After the wedding, he lived with his wife in his father-in-law's home. His father-in-law provided the young couple with everything they needed, so his son-in-law could study Torah full-time, without disturbance. Then, Rabbi Adam's son began to search for the person he was seeking. But he found no one named Israel the son of Eliezer, except for the *shammos* in the *beit midrash*. After paying close attention, however, it seemed to him that this simple young man was not what he appeared to be and that he might be the hidden tzaddik that his father had sent him to find. So he said to his father-in-law, "It's difficult for me to concentrate on my Torah study in your house because of the distractions. Would it be possible for you to have a small part of the *beit midrash* screened off for me so that I can study there undisturbed? Then, as the Rabbis recommend, I'll be able to study in the same place as where I pray."

His intention in asking this was so he would be able to be with Israel the Shammos—who was always in the *beit midrash*—at all times, so he could watch him closely to discover who he was. The wealthy man, who regarded his son-in-law very highly, fulfilled his request without delay. He also instructed the Baal Shem Tov to serve his rabbi son-in-law (as he served the other scholars), promising to pay him for his trouble.

One evening, when everyone was asleep, Rabbi Nachum pretended he also was asleep, and he saw the Baal Shem Tov, as was his custom, get up and engage in Torah study and prayer. Rabbi Nachum did the same thing the next night also, and again saw him doing this. He then decided to make a test. On the third night, the Baal Shem Tov arose and studied Torah, but in the middle of the night he dozed off sitting on the bench. Rabbi Nachum quietly got up, put a page of the secret manuscript on the table in front of the Baal Shem Tov, and then he returned to his place and again feigned sleep.

When the Besht woke up after a short nap and saw the page in front of him on the table, he visibly shuddered. He studied it and then tucked it inside his coat. Rabbi Nachum put another page in front of him the following night with the same results, until he was certain that this was the person to whom his father had sent him to deliver the manuscript.

He called Israel over and said to him, "My master and father, of blessed memory, Rabbi Adam Baal Shem, commanded me to deliver this manuscript to you. Here—this is all of it. I have only one request: I beg you, my master, to have pity on me and allow me to study with you." The Besht quickly realized that this manuscript was heaven-sent, but he realized that if he was found teaching Rabbi Nachum, his life of secret piety would be exposed. So he answered, "I agree to what you've asked, but only on condition that no one else knows of it, and that you not give the slightest hint of our changed relation. You mustn't show me the least sign of honor. Instead, you must continue to order me about to serve you, as before." That is what they did. Publicly, Israel still served Rabbi Nachum; privately, the Baal Shem Tov was his spiritual master.

But when the Jews of the community saw that Israel the Shammos was occasionally studying with Rabbi Nachum (for they could not completely hide their joint Torah study), they said that it was certainly due to the merit of his saintly parents that providence had arranged for Rabbi Nachum to come to the town to lead him back to the straight path. Since the time when he had been withdrawn from the *cheder* as a boy, they had never seen him studying Torah. They thought he was just a pious but ignorant young man. Now that they saw him studying with Rabbi Nachum, their opinion of him began to change. They felt he had returned to the ways of a decent and respectable youth, someone with a bit of Torah education. As a result, since he was an orphan and had no father to arrange a marriage for him, they found a wife for him. Israel married, but his new wife, Chava, died soon afterward. This trauma caused Israel to immerse himself even more deeply in his intense Torah study and piety.

However, as Israel and Rabbi Nachum continued to study together, it became increasingly difficult for Rabbi Adam's son to carry on the charade that he was the master and Israel the servant. It was particularly painful for him to have his spiritual master serve him menially. So he decided that the only solution was to get away from the town and its people. The greater solitude would also enable them to delve even deeper into their studying and divine service.

He went to his father-in-law and said, "I'd like to separate myself even more from worldly distractions. Perhaps you can arrange to obtain for my use a small hut of some sort, outside the town, so I can be entirely secluded and immerse myself completely in Torah study and prayer." And his father-in-law did this for him. Then he also requested that his father-in-law hire Israel the Shammos to stay with him there, to serve him and attend to all his needs, so that he could send him to town to get his food and so on. His father-in-law did that for him also.

When Israel and Rabbi Nachum began to stay in the small secluded hut, they were able to study Torah to their hearts' content—including the *Zohar* and Rabbi Adam's kabbalistic manuscript. One day, Rabbi Nachum asked the Baal Shem Tov to summon from heaven the angelic Prince of the Torah in order to teach them a certain secret of the practical Kabbalah. The Besht refused, saying "If we make an error, God-forbid, in our *kavvanot**, it might be dangerous, God-forbid, since we haven't any ashes of the red heifer to purify us if we become unclean." Regardless, Rabbi Nachum continued to urge him day after day until the Besht could no longer refuse. So they fasted from one Sabbath to the next and immersed in the *mikvah*¶ many times, as was required. On that second Sabbath, they meditated with great intensity. After the Sabbath ended, they performed certain specific *kavvanot*. Immediately, the Besht cried out, "Oh, oh! Because of what we've done, it's been decreed that both of us die this very night. The damage can only be repaired if we can concentrate on our *kavvanot* the whole night

---

* Mystical meditations or incantations.
¶ Ritual bath or natural body of water used for immersion.

without sleeping; then, 'a decree is nullified if the night passes without its being executed'! But if we doze off, God-forbid—since sleep is from the side of death—the Satan will have a finger hold and will be able to overcome us completely."

So they remained awake, meditating the entire night. Before dawn, Rabbi Nachum weakened and began to doze slightly. When the Baal Shem Tov saw this, he rushed over and yelled at him, but he could not rouse him. The Besht carried him into town and they tried to wake him, but were not able to do so. They buried him with great honor.

The Baal Shem Tov then took the manuscript he had received from Rabbi Adam Baal Shem and sealed it within a large stone in a mountain cave. When he uttered an invocation, the stone opened. After placing the manuscript inside, the stone closed up again. The Besht then appointed an angel to guard it.[29]

Remarriage

AFTER THE SUDDEN DEATH OF RABBI NACHUM, THE BAAL SHEM TOV, who was shaken by the losses of his wife and his friend, pursued a different path. The dangers of being involved in the study of practical Kabbalah made a strong impression on him. He began to lead a more normal life and was not as hidden as before.

At that time, the Baal Shem Tov left his village of Okup in Podolia and moved to the large city of Brody in Reissin. He was drawn there mainly by the renown of the city's Torah scholars, particularly those who studied in the famous Brody *Kloiz**. He settled in a small town near Brody, where he became a *melamed*.

The Baal Shem Tov quickly won the hearts of the townspeople, because he was an outstanding scholar and very wise. Since there was no rabbi in the town, all community affairs were brought to him for his decision. When there was a quarrel, he rendered a judgment so clear and wise that the one who was favored by his decision and the one who was not were both pleased with him, because he explained the Torah's verdict so convincingly.

In nearby Brody, the head of the religious court was a great Torah scholar, named Rabbi Gershon Kitover, who was a member of the Brody *Kloiz*. His father, Rabbi Ephraim, an exceptionally pious individual, once became involved in a dispute with someone from the small town where the Besht was living. So Rabbi Ephraim went there and suggested to the other man that they travel to Brody and put the matter before the religious court. The other man, not wanting to deal with a court where Rabbi Ephraim's son was so influential, said, "We have here in this town a *melamed* who's an outstanding Torah scholar. He's also a fair and just arbiter. Let's go to him.

---

* Yiddish for a Torah study hall or a house of prayer. The famous *beit midrash* of the great scholars in Brody was called the Brody *Kloiz*.

We'll both present our arguments and hear his ruling. If for any reason you're unhappy with his judgment, I'll go back with you to Brody." Rabbi Ephraim accepted the man's suggestion, and they brought their case before the Besht.

As soon as the Baal Shem Tov met Rabbi Ephraim, he saw with the holy spirit that Rabbi Ephraim's daughter was ordained by heaven to be his wife. It was the custom then for a Torah scholar to welcome a worthy visitor by interpreting some difficult passage in the Talmud or *halacha*. To indicate to Rabbi Ephraim that he would be a fitting son-in-law and that Rabbi Ephraim would not be giving his daughter to an ignoramus, the Besht offered a penetrating explanation of a passage in the Rambam*, and also told Rabbi Ephraim some of his other brilliant talmudic interpretations. Rabbi Ephraim was extremely impressed by the young man. He was greatly attracted to him and felt that their souls were connected. Rabbi Ephraim and the other party to the lawsuit presented their arguments, and they disputed heatedly about the matter in contention. After about an hour, however, the Baal Shem Tov drew light out of darkness, and gave a judgment so eminently fair and just that Rabbi Ephraim was in awe. He began to love this young man very much.

Meanwhile, he found out that the Baal Shem Tov was a widower, and Rabbi Ephraim had a divorced daughter named Chana. A divorced woman was considered a fitting match for a widower. So Rabbi Ephraim spoke to the Besht privately and said, "I've heard that you need a wife. Would you perhaps find my daughter acceptable?" "I agree to your proposal," replied the Besht, "but since so many of the wealthy men of this community want me as a son-in-law, we must conceal the matter, so that no one knows of it. I don't want to appear to be snubbing them, since they've treated me so well and have given me a great deal of prestige in the community. If you consent, we'll sign the engagement contract without witnesses. And I have one more request—that you make this engagement for your daughter with *me* and not with my Torah knowledge or wisdom, for I won't allow any exaggerated praises of myself or my scholarship to be put on the engagement agreement. Simply write my name: 'Israel the son of Eliezer,' without any titles or praises." As Rabbi Ephraim felt himself completely of one mind with the Baal Shem Tov, he readily agreed to anything he asked. They wrote an engagement contract with mutual wishes for good luck and the conditions of engagement, simply, without noting either their learned titles or their places of origin or residence. Each one had a copy. And the whole thing was kept secret. The Besht planned to soon return to his life as a hidden tzaddik, which would be difficult if his Torah expertise was written in black and white on an engagement contract for others to see, or if it was read aloud, as is traditional, at the wedding ceremony.

During Rabbi Ephraim's journey home to Brody, he suddenly fell ill and departed to his eternal world. His son, the renowned Rabbi Gershon Kitover, was informed of the disaster and came to bury and eulogize his father, as the Torah requires. When he took possession of the various papers that were on his father's person, he found among

---

* The *Mishneh Torah*, a book by Maimonides, who is referred to by the acronym for his name, Rabbi Moshe ben Maimon.

them his sister's engagement document, showing that Rabbi Ephraim had engaged his daughter Chana to someone named Israel the son of Eliezer. He was dumbfounded at this discovery. His father was a prominent man from an illustrious family. How could he have engaged his daughter to some obscure person whose family and place of residence were unknown, as they were not recorded in the engagement contract? No titles of praise about his status or accomplishments were attached to his name at all (which would have been customary had he merited them)! He reported this shocking revelation to his sister, who had a different view of the matter. "If our father found this betrothal fitting," she said, "we should certainly not question it."

Meanwhile, the Besht, who was still working as a *melamed*, waited for the school term to end and then went to the householders whose children he taught and said, "I've decided to move to Brody." They were very reluctant to let him go and did everything possible to persuade him to remain, even offering him a large increase in salary. But he would not change his mind, for he had other plans.

So he left and traveled to Brody. The Besht's brief stint as a respected teacher and leader in the small town where he had resided had allowed him to obtain a wife that befitted him. But now he wanted to return to his former concealment. So, on the way to Brody he dressed in clothes like those worn by simple villagers, including a short sheepskin coat with a broad belt. He also changed his demeanor, speaking and acting as if he were a coarse and uneducated man.

Disguised this way, he entered Brody and went to the home of Rabbi Gershon, where he found two rabbinical courts in session. Rabbi Gershon, as the head judge, was supervising both courts and was engaged in researching the Torah rulings of the cases that were coming before them. The Baal Shem Tov stood at the doorway, and Rabbi Gershon, assuming that he was a beggar, offered him a coin. But the Besht said, "I have something to discuss with you in private."

He went with the rabbi into another room, showed him his copy of the engagement contract and said to him, as would a crude person, "Give me my wife." The rabbi was shocked by his coarse appearance and speech, and became very upset and confused. What had his father done? After telling the Besht that he would take care of the matter, and asking him to return later, he summoned his sister and explained the situation to her, describing the whole scene. He urged her not to go through with the marriage. Perhaps their father was not even in his right mind when he engaged her to this man! Chana, however, who was more pious and less calculating than her scholarly brother, answered as before, saying that as this was undoubtedly their father's will, it was not their place to question it. Even if he were correct about their father's mental state, certainly it was by God's will that this had come about. Perhaps exceptional children would result from the marriage. So they agreed to go through with the marriage and set a date for the wedding.

Before the Baal Shem Tov and Chana entered under the *huppah** for the ceremony, the Besht said that he first wanted to speak to his bride-to-be (as the Sages recom-

---

* Bridal canopy.

mend). So he spoke to Chana privately and told her the truth about himself—everything there was to know. And he made her swear that she would not reveal a word of it to anyone, even if a long time passed and they lived in great poverty. At some point, she might be tempted to reveal the secret of his Torah knowledge and stature to gain prestige or to provide them with a decent living. But his mission in life required concealment, and he had to know if she agreed to that life. Israel was aware that his spiritual path would impose heavy burdens on Chana and he had to be sure she was ready to endure them. Chana asked him one question. "Israel, why must you wear peasant clothes and pretend that you are a coarse person?" "My dear Chana," replied the Besht, "Let me tell you a parable to explain myself. A king exiled his son to a distant village so that the prince would appreciate and enjoy his father's palace all the more when he returned. But the prince forgot who he was and assimilated to the peasants and their rustic ways. Realizing that his son would not return on his own, the king sent a minister to bring him back. But the minister failed, because he could not gain the confidence of the prince, who distrusted him because of his strange appearance and manner. Another of the king's ministers, however, cleverly removed his courtly garments and donned peasant clothes. He succeeded in befriending the prince and returned him to his father the king. My mission in life," said the Besht to his wife-to-be, "to help return the Children of Israel to their Heavenly Father, requires that I be hidden among the common working people, that I become one of them and dress like them." "Now I understand," said Chana, and she expressed her desire to share Israel's life and mission, come what may, including any hardships.

After the wedding, Rabbi Gershon began teaching Torah to his new brother-in-law, who he thought was an ignoramus. Perhaps Chana's husband would be able to absorb something. The Baal Shem Tov, however, continued to conceal his great Torah knowledge. He maintained the pretense that he was incapable of learning even the simplest matters.

Seeing this, the rabbi—who was a renowned scholar, the head of the religious court, and a prominent man in the community—said to Chana, "Dear sister, I'm mortally embarrassed by your simpleton of a husband. If you're willing to seek a divorce from him, good; but if not, I'll buy you a horse and wagon and you and he can go live wherever you want, but, please, not in the same town with me. I can't bear the shame any longer." His sister agreed to his offer, and she and the Besht set off for other parts.

After wandering for a while, they settled down in the Carpathian Mountains. The Baal Shem Tov arranged a place for his wife to live in a small village between the towns of Kossov and Kitov in Reissen (her family was originally from Kitov). Then he went off to seclude himself and pursue his religious practices. The Besht chose to live in a mountainous wilderness, and to do his spiritual work not in a *beit midrash* but among shepherds with their flocks, near caves inhabited by bears and near the lairs of wolves.

The young couple struggled to make a living by manual labor. The Besht dug clay, which was used to make primitive dishes, bowls, pots, and ovens; and two or three times a week Chana went out to him with the horse and wagon. Although tender and delicate, and from a wealthy family, she helped him load the clay on the wagon. Then she carted it to the town to sell for a small sum that was just enough for the two of them to live. This way of life was fairly typical for some of the hidden tzaddikim, who lived secluded in sparsely populated wilderness areas and supported themselves by the sweat of their brow.[30]

Spiritual Labor

THE BESHT WORKED HARD DIGGING CLAY, BUT MOST OF HIS TIME was spent laboring in divine service. He lived in a room-like crevice in the side of a mountain, with large stones serving as his table and chair. He kept his mind fastened on God, studying Torah, praying, and meditating. He spent countless hours reciting psalms, the preferred practice of simple unlearned Jews. He fasted continually with interruptions, eating scantily at lengthy intervals. During the summer, he dug a shallow pit, put some flour and water in it, and let the sun's heat bake the mixture into a crude bread. This was all he ate after his fast. And he remained in solitude, constantly engaged in Torah study and other divine service. His favorite books were *Ein Yaakov** and the holy *Zohar*.

The Besht studied Torah with great devotion and diligence, but to express his soul's yearning, he turned even more to prayer, in which one stands face to face with God. When he looked into a book of Torah or a *siddur*¶, he saw clearly that God had poured the fiery light of His presence into the holy letters on the page, and the Besht fervently poured out his soul, to unite with God in the letters. When praying, his determination to encounter God was so powerful that he was prepared to die for the sake of the *kavvanah*§ of the prayer. Ready to die after two or three words, he put all his energy into each word he uttered. He would call out, "Why should I continue to live if I can't see You?" Totally engrossed in his spiritual striving, the Besht was utterly indifferent to his bodily needs and desires. His only desire was to see God; as David pleaded in the psalm, "When will I come and see the face of God?" The whole day, he pined for God, hoping that that day he would reach his goal. His soul's separation from its Source cast him into a holy despair. Amidst weeping, he called out, "Father, Father, reveal Yourself to me! When will I see You?" Standing alone in the woods, far from human ears, he poured forth his burning prayers at the top of his voice, oblivious to his surroundings. Having subdued his bodily desires, his soul soared aloft on the wings of prayer into the spiritual realms.

Prayer was his main vehicle for spiritual ascent. But to purify himself and prepare for prayer and other divine service, the Besht frequently immersed himself in the nearby Prut River. He often stood in the water up to his neck for long periods of time,

---

* Book containing the *Aggada*, the non-legal matter of the Talmud, such as legends and parables.
¶ Prayer book.
§ Intention.

chanting psalms from memory. As he advanced spiritually, moving rung by rung up the ladder of holiness—due mainly to his fervent praying and his frequent *mikvah* immersions—he realized that the only other time he had made such rapid spiritual progress had been when he had taught children as an assistant teacher. His devotion to the children had also opened him up to great spiritual lights. He came to believe that fasting was no longer helping him and that his frequent *mikvah* immersions served the same purpose; so he ceased fasting.

Aside from his special zeal for prayer and his love for people, the Baal Shem Tov sought to have *d'vekut* at every moment and in everything he did, according to the verse: "Know Him in all your ways." He entered more and more deeply into the thought that God's Presence fills the earth and there is no place where He is not present. Day and night, day after day, week after week, month after month, his single thought was to remember God. His longing was intense; every fiber of his being craved nothing other than nearness to God and the experience of His presence at all times. The Baal Shem Tov's bodily lusts were burned up in the flaming desire he felt in his flesh for the living God. He often went to favorite places in the forest and on the mountains to pour out his heart in songs and praises to God, blessed be He, with love, yearning, and fervor, until the verse applied to him: "In her love you will be ravished always." He was always abstracted and absorbed in his inner thoughts due to his intense *d'vekut* and his great yearning for the holy *Shechinah*.

Sometimes his fervor was so all-consuming that he lost awareness of the world and of his own body. Once, he walked for three days and three nights in a state of powerful *d'vekut*, completely unaware of the outer world. He did not realize that he had not eaten or slept all that while. At other times his awareness was so heightened that the world around him became alive. He walked in the woods and listened to the birds in the trees singing to God, and sang along with them. He walked beside the rivers and ponds and heard the frogs croaking, and he lifted his voice to join their chorus of praise to God. It was then that he learned the languages of the animals and birds.

He frequently immersed in the river for spiritual purity. He immersed even during winter, when it took hard work to break the thick ice with an axe. When the Besht came up, blue and shivering, from the frigid water, he was exposed to brisk winds that made the air even colder. Before he had a chance to put on his clothes or shoes, the soles of his feet would stick to the ice. When he lifted his feet to move, the skin would rip off and his feet would bleed. But he felt no pain, because of his intense *d'vekut*.

Once, a gentile shepherd boy passed near the place at the river that the Besht frequented and was astonished to see this young Jew immerse through a hole in the ice. When he walked over after the Besht left, he saw spots of blood on the ice. The next day, when he passed that way again and saw the Besht go down and, after immersing again and again, stand in the freezing water up to his neck, he ran back to his village and returned with some straw to put next to the hole, so that this saintly young Jew would be able to put his feet down without suffering injury. The boy did this every day for weeks. When the Besht became aware of it and of who was helping him, he thanked and blessed him for his kindness.

This shepherd boy told the other gentile peasants about the Besht and they all came to revere him as a holy man. So as not to disturb his devotions, they did not water their animals at the place in the river where he immersed and prayed. Once, when the son of one of the peasants was sick, they brought him water to drink from the place where the Besht always immersed, and the boy immediately recovered. From then on they considered the water from that spot to be "holy water" and they drank it for healing. The Baal Shem Tov loved these peasants and other decent gentiles. Although some gentiles were hostile and antisemitic, others were not, and he appreciated their goodness. Because of their great respect for him, these peasants who knew about him tried to help the Besht, whenever possible, with his few needs. And he also helped them whenever he could.[31]

With the Shepherds

SOMETIMES THE BESHT CEASED FROM HIS CONSTANT STUDYING AND praying and befriended the shepherds who roamed about in the fields or on the hills with their flocks and herds. From time to time, he helped a shepherd who was seeking a lost sheep. Though the shepherds talked with him about ordinary, profane matters, their words entered the Besht's heart, because they were simple, trustworthy, and direct people, without any deceit or guile. The young Besht thought that perhaps their simple work of caring for their animals had a good effect on their character. After all, Moses and King David had been shepherds! He decided that being out in Nature, without worrying constantly, but simply being happy, was healthy, both physically and spiritually. Now and again he sat down with shepherds he met and learned their songs; he also taught them Jewish melodies. The Besht felt that the shepherds' songs, which he liked so much, expressed their basic trust in the world around them and their longing for something elevated. Sometimes he raised a shepherd's song into the realm of holiness by giving it Jewish words and singing it before God.[32]

The Besht Protects a Shepherd Boy

ONCE, A GENTILE SHEPHERD BOY WHO WAS GRAZING HIS SHEEP ON THE mountainside saw a wolf approaching his flock and he cried out for help. But there was no one nearby to come and help him and he was terribly afraid. The wolf killed one of the sheep and dragged it off. The next day the wolf returned and the frightened boy again did not know what to do. The wolf snatched another sheep and ran off. On the third day, the shepherd boy was terrified to see a pair of wolves approaching his flock. But this time, seeing the pious Jewish youth, Israel, sitting on a crag higher up on the mountain, he called out, "S'ruel, S'ruel!" Hearing his cry, the Besht ran to the boy's aid. The two wolves attacked him but he fought back using his walking stick and, with his strength and his trust in the God of Israel, slew them both. He then called to the shepherd boy, "Don't be afraid, the wolves are dead." The boy cautiously approached, and saw that they were indeed dead. The Besht asked him if he had a knife, and when told yes, said, "Skin the wolves. You'll have a fur coat to wear and so will I." From then on, the Besht wore this wolf-skin coat in cold weather.[33]

The Mountain Moves

 THE TOWERING CARPATHIAN MOUNTAINS WHERE THE BESHT WAS LIVING are separated by deep valleys. The mountains are flat on top with steep sloping sides that have few landings. Once, the Besht was walking along on one of these mountaintops, deeply immersed in meditation, oblivious to the world. Meanwhile, from a mountaintop across the valley, a band of robbers were eyeing him as a potential victim. When they saw that he was walking dangerously close to the edge, like someone lost in thought and unaware of where he was, they said, "He'll surely fall off the cliff and break every bone in his body." But when the Besht reached the cliff's edge and extended his foot, the adjacent mountain suddenly moved right up to the first one and the ground became level under his step! As he continued walking, the two mountains parted as before! Although a tzaddik's absorption in God seems to make him vulnerable, God guards his footsteps and he comes to no harm.

Seeing this astonishing miracle, the robbers realized that this young man was a saint and that God was with him. Instead of planning to harm him, they decided to befriend him. They went to him and told him what they had witnessed. "We saw with our own eyes that you are a saint," they said, "so we beg you to pray on our behalf that God help us, for we're always risking our lives." "Why do you rob?" said the Besht. "You should earn your living by doing honest labor with your hands." "Master," they answered, their eyes to the ground, "we only do this because our wives and children are hungry." "It doesn't matter," said the Besht, "it's forbidden for gentiles—who are Children of Noah—to steal or rob." "Master," they answered, "we can't change our ways." "I know that poverty and hunger can turn a man's mind away from his Creator," said the Besht. "But if you can't completely free yourselves from this sin, at least do so in part. If you'll swear to me that you'll spare other poor people and never rob or harm Jews, I'll pray for you." They swore. From that time on, if there was any strife or argument among the robbers, they went to the Baal Shem Tov and he mediated between them and found a compromise.[34]

Protected from a Robber

 ONCE, TWO ROBBERS ASKED THE BAAL SHEM TOV TO JUDGE A DISPUTE between them. Afterward, one of them was angry at the Besht's decision and thought, "When he's awake, it's impossible to harm him, but when he's sleeping, I'll kill him." Later that night, the man approached the sleeping Baal Shem Tov and raised his axe to chop off the Besht's head. But, suddenly, he felt himself grabbed by many hands, and he was mercilessly beaten until every inch of his body was covered with welts and bruises. The Baal Shem Tov then woke up and, seeing the man's pitiful condition, said, "Who did this to you?" But he was too weak to answer. The next day, when the robber had recovered somewhat, he repentantly told the Besht the whole story. The psalm verse says about those who trust in God: "He will give His angels charge over you to guard you in all your ways; they will carry you on their hands, lest you strike your foot against a stone."[35]

Traveling as a Hidden Tzaddik

THE BAAL SHEM TOV SOUGHT THE SOLITUDE OF THE MOUNTAINS and wilderness to be alone with his own soul and with his Maker. But he could not bear to be away from people for too long. Just as he yearned to be close to God, he also yearned to be close to his beloved fellow Jews.

The Besht sometimes traveled for weeks at a time "in exile"—as did other hidden tzaddikim—wearing the rough clothes of a villager. The mystics teach that the *Shechinah* is more readily found on the road, and the light of the *Shechinah* rested on the young Besht as he journeyed from one village or town to the next, working to help the common people in any way possible. The Besht believed that whatever he encountered or experienced was intended by divine providence for a purpose. Whenever he met a fellow Jew, he asked himself, "Why did God send this person to me? How can I help him?"—materially or spiritually. From his numerous travels as a hidden tzaddik, the Besht knew that many of his fellow Jews eked out a precarious living as humble merchants and peddlars, trudging from village to village with their wares—of pots, utensils, needles, and so on. The Besht often met them on the road. He frequently encouraged and comforted these Jews who were separated from their families and were prey to loneliness and dejection. A holy saying that he often repeated to them was: "A Jew is never alone. Wherever he is, wherever he stands, God is with him."

The Baal Shem Tov regularly went on various missions for the hidden mystics. Sometimes he collected charity money from movement sympathizers and others. This money was used to support other hidden tzaddikim or to aid poor Jews, such as Jewish innkeepers who could not pay the rent to their landowners or had to be ransomed if they were imprisoned because of their inability to pay. Everywhere he went, the Baal Shem Tov spent his time with the common people, preaching and encouraging them to have simple faith and not assimilate to gentile customs, but to be faithful to Jewish ways, and to avoid slander, talebearing, and cursing. He was also always alert, when he encountered people of spiritual potential, to make new recruits to the movement of the hidden tzaddikim.[36]

Helping Body and Soul

IN 1721, THE MOVEMENT OF HIDDEN TZADDIKIM EMBARKED ON A NEW plan to relieve the Jewish people from the difficult conditions that still persisted because of the Chemelnicki massacres of 1648–1649. Hundreds of thousands of Jews had died, countless communities ceased to exist, and much property had been pillaged and destroyed. Many Jews had taken refuge in the large cities where they had no work. The dislocation and material poverty also produced religious poverty.

The Baal Shem Tov had already instigated a program to concentrate on teaching children in isolated areas; later, it was decided to also teach uneducated adults. Now, to further repair the situation, the Besht, together with his fellow hidden tzaddikim, began to propagandize among the Jews of Podolia, Volhynia, and Galicia that they should leave the cities (where the poverty was great and opportunities to earn a living were few) and go to live in the villages and small settlements. They encouraged the men to work the land or engage in manual labor and the women to do spinning and raise small animals and chickens or grow vegetables.

In his extensive wandering, the Baal Shem Tov had passed through many small villages and settlements, some of which, before the Chemelnicki massacres, had had Jewish residents, and some of which had not. As he traveled, he had investigated the condition of the villagers and peasants in these areas. He had also learned the names of the feudal lords in different areas and paid attention to their character. He was instrumental in the decision of the hidden tzaddikim to spur the Jewish refugees to return to the villages. Now, when the hidden tzaddikim began their campaign to persuade the Jews to move, the Besht went around telling the refugees about this or that village or lord, recommending one place or another, telling them that the gentile inhabitants of this village were good people or that that lord was a good and decent person, and that there were opportunities there for a Jewish family to make a living.

The first task of the Baal Shem Tov and his comrades among the hidden tzaddikim was to heal the body of Israel, and later to heal the soul of Israel. At this time in his career, most of the Besht's efforts were in helping Jews to provide a livelihood for themselves, and his work was mostly with the simple people, who are the body of Israel. Only later did he occupy himself with Torah scholars who are the soul of Israel.[37]

The Children

THE FIRST THING THE BESHT DID WHEN HE ENTERED A TOWN WAS TO ask about the children and their education; afterward he inquired about the adults. The Besht loved to tell the children Torah stories, according to their level. He often distributed nuts and apples to the little ones, to give them a treat and bring them some happiness, but also to accustom them to recite blessings. He would ask all the others to be silent while one child made the *beracha**, telling them, "We must all answer 'Amen' after the *beracha*. Our Rabbis say that whoever answers 'Amen' after a blessing receives a greater reward than the one who makes the blessing." He made sure the child reciting the blessing said it correctly. Then he led all the children in saying "Amen" with great feeling. When the children saw the tremendous devotion and fervor with which he said the "Amen" it made a lasting impression on them. He would then put his pure hand on the heart of each child—sending a current of divine power directly into his soul—and bless him, saying, "Be a warm Jew!"[38]

A Hug, a Touch, a Glance

ONCE, WHEN THE BESHT WAS VISITING IN THE HOME OF A JEWISH FAMILY in a certain village, he saw that one of their children was an exceptionally soulful boy. The Besht became so enthused that he took the child on his lap. He then entered into an ecstatic mood and, without realizing it, began hugging the boy so tightly that the child fainted. They had to shake the Besht to wake him from his trance, so that he would release his grip. Everyone in the house became frantic and there was a big commotion, but after much effort, they revived the boy. Before he left, the Besht blessed the boy to become a tzaddik and a servant of God. The Besht was always looking for children with high souls, who were fit vessels for holiness. When he was a child, he too had been taken under the care and tutelage of hidden mystics, who had seen his great spiritual potential.

An ordinary tzaddik must offer many prayers to inspire a person to repent. A rare tzaddik like the Besht can fill a person's soul with light through a hug, a mere touch, or even a glance. Just as an evil person can cast an evil eye with his glance, a great tzaddik can by a good eye bless with his glance; in fact, as the Rabbis teach, the power of good is greater than the power of evil.[39]

Arousal by a Glance

ONCE, WHEN THE BAAL SHEM TOV WAS IN A CERTAIN TOWN ON THE Sabbath, he went along with others to the home of the rabbi, to celebrate the rabbi's son's beginning to study the *Chumash* at the age of five, as is customary. The boy stood on the table and began to give a little Torah talk before all the guests in the crowded room. In the middle of his speech, the boy's mother suddenly grabbed him and took him down from the table. Her husband asked her, "Why did you grab him like that in the middle of the talk?" "Because of the evil eye, God-forbid! Don't you see," she

---

* Blessing.

said, her voice trembling, "that strange man standing by the door, dressed in a peasant's fur coat, pushing his way into the crowd and staring at the child? I'm frightened! Tell him to leave!" She was worried that the man was casting an evil eye on her son, because the boy was brilliant. That "strange man" was the Baal Shem Tov. Later, he told one of his hidden mystic comrades, who was with him in the town, "I was standing by the door, pressed in among the crowd. But I saw from across the room the child's glowing face—the *Shechinah* was resting on him. I set my eyes on him to draw down on him a flow of even more divine light. And I accomplished something. Who knows what more I could have done for him if his mother had not insisted that I leave the house!"[40]

Visiting Towns and Villages

WANDERING THROUGH THE COUNTRYSIDE AND VISITING MANY TOWNS and villages as a hidden mystic, the young Baal Shem Tov brought many people back to God. When he entered a town he would stand on the street and strike up a conversation with some simple Jews, talking to them about everyday matters, asking them about their livelihood and health. But before long he would be telling them Torah legends and other religious tales, holding them spellbound with his storytelling.

Once, the Besht visited the town of Tarnow in Galicia and had soon gathered a crowd around him. "You should know," he said to them, "that each Jew is more precious to the Holy One, blessed be He, than an only son born to a father in his old age. A Jew is never alone. God is always with him. And the Holy One, blessed be He, derives great pleasure when a simple Jew prays, says psalms, or does a *mitzvah* with simple faith. Let me tell you a story from the time of the Temple to explain:

"A rich man was bringing a large fattened ox to the Temple to offer as a sacrifice. The ox was a massive, powerful animal, and the men were unable to budge it when it refused to be led. A poor man happened to pass by on his way home from the market, carrying a bunch of vegetables for his family's meal. Seeing the difficulty, and sympathizing with the plight of the man who was trying to bring a sacrifice to the Temple, he held the bunch of vegetables in front of the animal to let it nibble at them, and led it along peacefully, until they brought it to the place of sacrifice. That night, the owner of the fattened ox was shown a vision in his dream, and he heard a voice saying, 'The sacrifice of the poor man, who gave up his family's meal of vegetables to help you, preceded your offering.'

"God desires the heart," said the Baal Shem Tov to his audience. "The rich man brought as his burnt-offering a large fattened ox, and he was so happy he had merited to sacrifice such an animal that he also sacrificed a sheep as a peace-offering and made a celebration feast for his family and all his friends and acquaintances. He also gave the *kohanim** their shares of the sacrifices. All this because of his great joy at the *mitzvah* he had performed. The poor man, broken and crushed by his poverty, was bringing home

---

* Priests; sing. *kohen*.

some vegetables for his family's meal. What were his few vegetables—that he gave up to help his fellow Jew—compared to the massive ox and the sheep that the rich man sacrificed? But He who sits in heaven, blessed is He and blessed is His name, had more pleasure from the offering of the poor man's few vegetables than from the rich man's fattened ox. For the rich man offered much, but his family sat down that night to a hearty meal. The poor man sacrificed his family's food, everything he had, to help another Jew, and that night his family went hungry."

The Besht explained the story's lesson to his audience of simple people, saying, "Anything a Jewish man or woman does because God commanded it is judged according to the intention of the person's heart. Therefore, even the least thing in the world that a Jew does for the sake of God—such as offering something that costs just one penny—and he does it willingly and joyfully, with purity of heart, is very precious and dear to the Creator of the world, blessed is He and blessed is His name. God proudly relates it, so to speak, to the ministering angels, and says, 'Look at the good deed that this one of my sons or daughters has done!' and He blesses him or her."

When the Besht concluded and left, his listeners all went back to their work and chores, this one to his work as a water-carrier, that one to her cooking. But the Besht's story about the poor man's bunch of vegetables, and his teaching that the smallest service for the glory of God, blessed be He, if done joyfully and with purity of heart, is precious to the Creator of the world, stayed alive within them, and many of them silently prayed and pleaded to God that they might merit to do some *mitzvah* and be able to serve Him with all their hearts and with great joy. The Besht spoke to them from the heart and, as the Rabbis say: "What comes from the heart, enters the heart."[41]

May His Great Name Be Blessed!

ONCE, WHEN THE BAAL SHEM TOV WAS VISITING A CERTAIN TOWN, a crowd of simple Jews—men, women, and children—gathered around him. Knowing that the working people felt inadequate because of their lack of Torah knowledge, he sought to show them that God loved them too. He began to preach and said, "It's written: 'Happy is the one You [God] choose and bring near, to dwell in Your courts! We shall be satisfied with the goodness of Your House, Your holy Temple!' There are certainly different spiritual levels among Jews. Some are on the level of being in God's 'courts'; others are on the more inner level of being in 'Your holy Temple.' But all Jews are happy and fortunate, because they are all chosen and have all been brought near, as it says: 'Happy is the one You choose and bring near.' When is that most evident? When the whole congregation stands in the synagogue and, as one, recites: '*Amen, y'hai shmai rabba*' [May His great name be blessed!]. Then, they are all equal, because all Jews magnify and sanctify God's name." By making clear to them that their praise of God was heard in heaven and their divine service greatly valued, the Besht inspired these and other simple Jews to recite the congregational response "*Amen, y'hai shmai rabba!*" with devotion and fervor. And the Rabbis say that whoever utters this powerful phrase praising God's name with all his might has the gates of paradise thrown open before him.[42]

The Sermon in Kolomaya about Love of Israel

ONCE, THE BAAL SHEM TOV VISITED THE TOWN OF KOLOMAYA IN REISSEN, stood in the middle of the marketplace, and before long was surrounded by a large crowd of men, women, and children. He began to preach to them about love for the Jewish people, one of his favorite themes. He said:

"There are three loves every Jew must have: love of God, love of the Torah, and love of Israel. We should love God because He is God, and we should love Him above and beyond any understanding or comprehension on our part. We should love the Torah, not because we understand everything in it, but because it is God's Torah. And that is the way we should love the Jewish people and each Jew, not because of their special individual qualities, because this one is intelligent or that one is good, but simply because they are all His people.

"On the level of their souls, all Jews are alike. We should love every Jew, regardless of who or what he or she is—whether rich or poor, learned or unlearned, even whether righteous or, God-forbid, wicked. We should love a Jew just because he is a Jew. We should seek to do good to any Jew, to help him in any way we can, with self-sacrifice, just as we should have self-sacrifice for the sake of God. A Jew should be willing to sacrifice himself for any other Jew, even someone he never met before in his life. It's so important to help a fellow Jew! I tell you that sometimes a soul comes down to this world for its full life span of seventy or eighty years only to do one favor for another Jew. Let me tell you a story about something that actually happened. There was once a difficult case before the heavenly court, concerning a simple man who had passed away and whose fate in the next world was being decided. This Jew was not learned in the Torah and only knew how to pray and say psalms. But his love for the Jewish people was very strong, with total self-sacrifice. He loved other Jews with all the powers of his soul: in thought—for he continually thought about his love for Israel and pondered how he might help and do favors for his fellow Jews; in speech—for he talked continually with love for Israel, always speaking of the good qualities of the Jewish people as a whole and of individual Jews, and always discussing with others how to do favors for this person or that person; and in deed—for he tirelessly helped every Jew as much as he was able. He was sad whenever any other Jewish man or woman was sad; and he was happy at their joy. It was decided in the heavenly court that, even if this simple Jew did not know how to study Torah, his place in the Garden of Eden would be among those great tzaddikim and Torah scholars who were famous for having been lovers of Israel.

"I tell you, the sigh of a Jew at the distress of a fellow Jew shatters all the iron barriers of the heavenly accusers*, and his joy at the happiness of a fellow Jew and the blessing he wholeheartedly gives him, are accepted by God, blessed be He, as if it was the prayer of the high priest when he prayed for the people of Israel in the holy of holies in the ancient Temple.

"We can understand how great our love for fellow Jews should be from the love that the Holy One, blessed be He, has for them, even for the simplest Jew." (The Besht had been in Kolomaya for a few days and had come to know a certain Rabbi Yaakov, who was a great Torah scholar. So he said:) "Let me explain by an example: You all know that Rabbi Yaakov's mouth never ceases from studying aloud. He studies Torah day and night, without a minute's cessation. He knows the *Tanach, Mishna, Gemara, Rashi, and Tosafot*⁋ by heart, and he studies from memory. Now, when a person studies from memory, he's more engrossed in what he's studying. One day, Rabbi Yaakov was studying from memory a long and complicated comment in the *Tosafot* that takes up almost the whole page in a volume of the Talmud. Nothing could require more concentration. Yet, when his little son, who is just a child, came over to him and spoke a word of Torah that showed a spark of wisdom, Rabbi Yaakov was so delighted that he interrupted his own studies. This, in turn, made a great impression on the child, who knew what it meant for his father to interrupt his studies, and he was thrilled by his father's approval.

"God too, blessed be He, is deeply engrossed in Torah study, so to speak, as the Sages, of blessed memory, say: 'The first three hours of daytime He sits and studies Torah.' But then He interrupts His study, so to speak, and listens to the prayers and requests of His children, Israel, who pray to Him at that time! So great is His love for the Jewish people!

"When the Holy One, blessed be He, was about to create man, He told the angels of His intention, as it says: 'Let us make man.' The angels answered, 'What is man that You should think of him? What need is there for a man like this?' But the Holy One, blessed be He, created man anyway. And when a Jew gets up early in the morning and runs to the synagogue to pray with a congregation, and then, later, although he's busy and troubled all day earning his living, leaves everything he's doing and again runs back to the synagogue to pray *Minha*§; then, between *Minha* and *Maariv*, he listens to someone teaching *Ein Yaakov*; then he prays *Maariv* and on his way home he thinks about the Torah teaching that he heard—the Holy One, blessed be He, summons the angels and tells them of His pride in this man that He created, saying, 'You angels have no millstones around your necks. You have no families to support, no troubles or taxes. But a man has all these burdens to contend with: He has a wife and children, and it is I who commanded him to have a family and to accept all these responsibilities, and he did so, according to what the Torah said. And he has to support his family, and is beset

---

* Prosecuting angels in the heavenly court.
⁋ Five traditional Jewish texts that are subjects for study; see the Glossary for definitions.
§ The daily afternoon prayer service.

with troubles because of it. He must pay taxes and he suffers from the hard yoke of the exile too. Yet he still serves Me so faithfully!' So does the Holy One, blessed be He, express His pride in the divine service of even the simplest Jew—who prays, says psalms, and does *mitzvot*, all with simple faith. And, as with Rabbi Yaakov's son," concluded the Baal Shem Tov to his rapt audience, "hearing this should make a great impression on you, and you should realize how important the divine service of a Jew is to your Father in Heaven!"[43]

A New Approach in Love of Israel

THE HIDDEN TZADDIKIM WORKED TIRELESSLY TO STRENGTHEN JUDAISM among the Jewish masses, but generally they did so in the manner popular then: preaching with rebukes and warnings that God would strictly punish each sin, no matter how small. The Besht, however, paved a different path that was old but which he renewed. He taught his comrades among the hidden tzaddikim that it was necessary to encourage and console Jewish men and women by concentrating on their good points and virtues. This would also, he said, arouse heavenly compassion on them.

Slowly but surely this new approach was accepted among the movement of hidden tzaddikim. Their methods of dealing with the people changed accordingly and benefitted their efforts to elevate the Jewish people spiritually. As they traveled extensively, they then spread this approach to communities far and wide.[44]

Hershel Goat

THE BAAL SHEM TOV COULD SEE THE INNER LIGHT AND BEAUTY OF simple Jews. He was always on the lookout for diamonds in the rough—simple people with undeveloped spiritual potential—to draw into the movement of the hidden tzaddikim, where they would be taught, elevated, polished, and made to shine.

When the Besht was twenty-two, he once traveled with a group of hidden mystics to Brody. Some of them passed through, but the Besht and two of his elderly comrades remained in the city. On his third day there, he was standing in one of the markets and talking with some of the working people—as was his holy way, to encourage them in their reciting of psalms and in their love of fellow Jews—when suddenly he was startled by someone passing close by to them. The man, a porter, was walking bent over under a heavy sack of flour that was on his shoulder. His clothes were tattered and he had reed shoes on his feet. His cheeks were sunken, his eyes bulged, and his face, pale as whitewash, was dripping with perspiration. But above his head shone a light so brilliant that the Besht had never seen its like. Looking at him, the Besht realized that despite his humble exterior, this porter was a great and holy man. When the other townspeople who were standing there saw this porter lugging his heavy sack, some of them called out sarcastically, "Hey, Hershel, heave ho!" Others called him by a mocking nickname, "Hey, Hershel Goat!" Although they were making fun of him in a mean way, he replied with a warm blessing, "Be well and healthy, my friends!"

The Baal Shem Tov later told his fellow hidden mystics, Rabbi Yehezkel and Rabbi Ephraim, what he had seen and asked them if they knew this man, if perhaps he was also a hidden mystic. But they knew nothing about him being one of their comrades. Later, when they saw the porter themselves, they were as astonished as was the Besht, his light was shining so brightly.

The Besht decided to investigate the matter. He asked around and found out that Reb Hershel was a simple man, who had been widowed for ten years. He had two sons, who were studying in the town's yeshivahs and were supported by his wife's relatives. Although he made enough to live on as a porter, he spent all his earnings to support four goats, because, people said, he loved goat's milk. So his nickname was "Hershel Milk," but the town jokers called him "Hershel Goat." The Besht also found out that he lived in a dilapidated house on the outskirts of town.

The Baal Shem observed him closely for a few days, but could not discover any clue to his character. Disturbed at his inability to solve the puzzle, the Besht prayed for heaven to reveal the secret to him. Why did this man, who seemed to be a simple laborer, have such a pure and brilliant halo shining above his head, so that even the Besht's elder comrades, the hidden tzaddikim, Rabbi Yehezkel and Rabbi Ephraim, were moved to wonder when they saw it—for the dazzling lights that glowed above the head of the "hidden tzaddik" Reb Hershel—hidden from his peers—were like the rays of glory that radiated from Moses himself!

Heaven took notice of the Besht's unhappiness, and his prayer began to bear fruit. But since it had not yet been answered, he decided to press his request by means of a fast. So he waited until the Sabbath ended and, after the *melave malka* feast, began a fast of interruptions of three days and three nights.* When the Besht completed his daily fast after *Minha* on the third day and was leaving the free community hostel where he and his comrades were staying, he met Reb Hershel in the street. The Besht decided to use this providential meeting to get closer to Reb Hershel to learn his secret. After exchanging greetings, he said, "Reb Hershel, I'm very hungry and feel weak. I'd love to drink some of the goat's milk I hear you have to sell." "My dearest friend," answered Reb Hershel joyfully, "I'd be so glad to give you some goat's milk, but I refuse to take any money for it. The way I see it, I'm obligated to give my food and everything I have to a needy fellow Jew. Come home with me and I'll gladly give you some fresh milk to drink."

They walked together for a long time, until they came to a narrow, muddy alley, full of garbage, lined with tumble-down shacks without real roofs or windows. One of these sad ruins was the home of Reb Hershel. The moment he opened the door, his goats ran over to him bleating, and began licking his hands and feet and frisking about,

---

* Fasting daily until evening, then eating, for three days.

as is their way. Reb Hershel took a pot, milked the goats, and then gave the fresh milk to the Baal Shem Tov, who drank it with pleasure. The Besht then prayed *Maariv* and stayed in Reb Hershel's home overnight.

All the time he was with the Baal Shem Tov, Reb Hershel was in a cheerful mood. He told the Besht everything about himself—how he had been widowed for ten years from his dear wife, who had spent all her time doing *mitzvot*—especially visiting the sick poor and being a midwife for poor women. While he was in his period of mourning for her, his wife had appeared to him in a dream, he said, and told him of the great reward she was receiving for her good deeds. "She told me," said Reb Hershel, "that a number of times while she was alive she had heard visiting preachers say that after death, in the World of Truth, a person's judgment begins with the beating he receives while still in the grave. Then, the angel Dumah asks you your name and angels of punishment lead you to the heavenly court. After the judgment is pronounced, the soul is punished by being cast about in the Sling and then you are taken to *Gehinnom**. But when she passed away, she said, it was not like that at all! They carried her to the 'house of the living'¶ and buried her. When her sons said *Kaddish*, those standing there answered 'Amen,' and the angels also called out, 'Amen, may it be His will!' When they finished covering her with earth, an angel came and asked her her name, and she answered, 'Rachel Leah.' Then they escorted her to the heavenly court. There she saw men, women, boys, and girls, all of whom she recognized, for they were the sick poor for whom she had cared for and helped to cure, for twenty-seven years, from the time she was a girl living in the house of her father, Daniel the Peeler, until the day of her death. She continued to tell me how she was led to the Garden of Eden and she said that in heaven they greatly treasure someone who has been charitable and kind to a Jewish man or woman. 'And you, Hershel,' she said, 'you're a simple person. You don't know how to study Torah. So occupy yourself with tending the sick and women giving birth. And try as much as possible to keep your good deeds secret.'

"After that," said Hershel, "I bought goats. I feed and care for them and take their milk to the sick and to women after childbirth, to heal and strengthen them. I distribute the milk secretly, leaving full containers on their doorsteps. And God, blessed be He, gives His holy blessing and they are healed and recover. All these years since my dear wife's passing I've supported myself with great difficulty, because all the money I earn goes to take care of the goats. And everything I do, I do secretly, as my wife told me, because the best charity is in secret. But last night, my wife appeared to me in my dream and told me that if, after *Minha*, I meet a poor man who asks me for something, I should invite him to my home and give him some milk to drink. And I should tell him my secret because, with his help, I'll be saved eternally."

The Besht stayed in Brody for about another month, and during that time he closely observed the divine service of Reb Hershel. He saw that he served God with pure and simple faith, paying no attention to the disparaging nicknames people called

---

* Hell.
¶ Traditional euphemism for a cemetery.

him; that he was diligent in his service of love of Israel with self-sacrifice—and because of all this he had merited that wonderful, brilliant light.

The Baal Shem Tov then told Rabbi Ephraim Tzvi—who was the leader of the group of hidden tzaddikim with which the Besht was associated—what he had discovered about Reb Hershel. And Rabbi Ephraim Tzvi recruited Reb Hershel into their group. Reb Hershel was taught by a number of hidden tzaddikim and became increasingly elevated in Torah, holiness, and piety. Finally, he became a famous healer and helped many people with his prayers and remedies. All this happened because of his holy wife's advice and because the Baal Shem Tov had seen Reb Hershel's inner light and helped bring it into revelation.[45]

Yonah the Tinsmith

AFTER THIS, THE BAAL SHEM TOV DISCOVERED TWO OTHER DIAMONDS in the rough and helped a simple Jewish couple fulfill their potential.

In a certain town where Jews lived, there was a child who was orphaned of both his parents by the age of five. His uncle raised him and hired a *melamed* to teach him Torah. But the boy, whose name was Yonah, was a very slow learner; no matter how many times his teacher went over the lesson with him, he could not master it. When the other boys his age were already beginning to study *Gemara*, Yonah was still trying to master the Hebrew alphabet. He finally learned to make the blessings over what he ate and drank; but that was the limit of his progress. When his relatives saw that nothing was being accomplished, they decided to discontinue his studies with the *melamed* and gave him over to the community *Talmud Torah* school.

He studied in that school until the age of twelve, and there too, since nothing was being accomplished, the community leaders made arrangements to apprentice him to a tinsmith. The tinsmith, who was a pious Jew, did a good job of teaching the boy his craft and also supervised Yonah's religious conduct. By that time, Yonah knew how to say blessings over what he ate and drank, but did not always know exactly which blessings applied to which foods, so the tinsmith taught him that. Yet, although Yonah was a slow learner, he still had a deep-seated craving to study Torah. Since he wanted to study even while working, he would sit and recite blessings, thinking that he was fulfilling his obligation to study Torah. This went on until the tinsmith heard him once and explained to him that saying a blessing without eating is a blessing made in vain, which is considered a sin. Then the boy began to repeat the Hebrew alphabet during work.

Although he was painfully slow when it came to Hebrew or religious studies, Yonah easily mastered his trade of tinsmithing. Meanwhile, he reached the age of thirteen and became bar mitzvah. When the tinsmith saw how well Yonah had learned the trade, he encouraged him to set up his own business and work for himself.

Yonah opened a tinsmithy, did good work, and was successful. He gave charity generously, but was still depressed that he was religiously ignorant. When he came of age, he married the daughter of a tar-maker who lived in a village next to the forest where he worked. The son-in-law also settled in that village and made a good living as a tinsmith. He prospered and had everything he needed. But he was so unhappy about his inability to study Torah that he sometimes wept in despair.

In that village there were a number of Jewish families, among them a Torah scholar, although there was no synagogue. Once, the young tinsmith Yonah went to the Torah scholar and poured out to him his pain and heartache at not being able to study. The scholar advised him to secretly support needy Torah scholars. God desires the heart, he said, and simple Jews who financially support scholars are as important to Him as those who study Torah. From then on, Yonah devoted himself to supporting Torah scholars.

It was a custom in the village that when a visitor arrived—a rare event—everyone wanted to fulfill the *mitzvah* of welcoming guests, so they cast lots to see who would have the honor of hosting the guest. Once, when a visitor who was suffering from a severe skin ailment that covered his body came to the village, they cast lots and the young tinsmith won him as a guest. He joyfully took the man home, gave him his own room, bathed him, and applied to his skin different salves that greatly eased his discomfort. A number of days later, the visitor wanted to move on, but Yonah was so gratified at the chance to fulfill the *mitzvah* of hospitality, especially as the guest was a Torah scholar, that he pleaded with him to stay for a few more days.

Once, when they were together, he asked his guest about the cause of his malady. The guest told him that he had been knowledgeable in the Talmud but, desiring to master the early and later commentaries, a difficult task, he had harshly afflicted himself and fasted, while studying diligently and unceasingly. His severe regimen finally affected his health. He became weak and sickly and developed a skin ailment from which he was suffering. But he had accomplished his goal.

A short time later, the guest left Yonah's home and went on his way. The young tinsmith, having heard the cause of his guest's sickness, prayed and pleaded with the Holy One, blessed be He, saying that he was willing to suffer any bodily afflictions, if God only granted his wish to be a Torah scholar. When days passed, and there was no change in his ability to learn, he decided to do what his guest had done. He began to fast. He also went out to the woods, sat down on an anthill, and allowed the ants to bite him—while he recited psalms, for, over time, he had learned to pronounce the Hebrew. He did not know the meaning of the words he recited, but he uttered them amidst tears and sighs.

Once, as he was sitting in the woods reciting psalms and weeping, he saw in front of him a Jew with a staff in his hand and a knapsack on his shoulder. At first Yonah was frightened to suddenly see someone in this isolated place, but he soon calmed himself. This wayfarer was the Baal Shem Tov, who was traveling on a mission for the hidden tzaddikim. The Besht asked him why he was sitting in the woods weeping. Yonah told the Besht that he was crying from his grief at being ignorant of the Torah. He explained to him that another wayfarer, a Torah scholar who had been a guest in his home, had told him how he had increased his ability to study by afflicting himself and fasting. So he accepted this on himself, until God, blessed be He, would help him to be a Torah scholar.

The Baal Shem Tov listened sympathetically to Yonah's story. He then took a holy book out of his knapsack and said to him, "Why don't we study a little Torah now?" They sat down and studied, and the words of Torah revived the spirit of the despairing young man. Yonah saw that the Baal Shem Tov was a great scholar and sage. And the Baal Shem Tov saw the young man's true mettle and decided to recruit him as a hidden mystic. The Besht said, "You can achieve your goal of becoming learned in the Torah by fasting and self-affliction. But if you want, I can tell you an easier path to becoming a Torah scholar." Hearing this, Yonah begged the Baal Shem Tov to tell him how. The Besht told the young man that he had to transfer to him everything he owned—his house, his money, and all his possessions—and go into exile. He would accompany the Besht and be under his direction for three years. If he agreed to these conditions, the Besht promised him that he would be a Torah scholar. "The suffering of 'exile,' of traveling from place to place without possessions, will subdue your ego and make you a chariot for the *Shechinah*. Then," said the Besht, "you'll be able to receive every blessing, including the blessing of Torah wisdom."

(According to the Baal Shem Tov the "easier" way was for the young man to give up everything he owned and wander in exile for three years! God and the Torah cannot be won by half-measures. To achieve spiritual perfection, Yonah needed to abandon home and possessions and rely on God alone. The money that he gave to the Besht would be used for good causes, to support hidden tzaddikim and other needy Jewish poor.)

Yonah immediately agreed to do as the Baal Shem Tov proposed, but the Besht said to him, "Don't be hasty. First speak to your wife, and ask your father-in-law's advice too. After eight days, meet me again at this same place in the woods. Then you can tell me your decision." The Baal Shem Tov then went on his way. Yonah returned home and told his wife, whose name was Devorah Leah, everything that had happened. After hearing the story, she said to him, "My dear husband, don't I know your long-standing grief at not being able to study Torah? Now, when this door has suddenly opened up before you, you certainly must enter and agree to the conditions. I willingly give you my consent, but with a condition of my own. Before we deliver all our possessions into this holy man's hands, he must visit our home as our guest to eat a meal, so we can fulfill for one last time the *mitzvah* of welcoming guests, for after we give him everything we own, we'll no longer be able to fulfill this *mitzvah*."

After this conversation with his wife, Yonah went to his father-in-law and told him too everything that had happened. His father-in-law's reaction, however, was quite different from his wife's. "It's true," he said, "that it's written that the Torah is more precious than pearls—and it would seem that one should be willing to give up all one's possessions to acquire it. But my opinion is that the Torah forbids such a radical step. You have a wife and children you're obligated to support. How can you leave them and give this man all your possessions?"

His father-in-law's words made a strong impression on Yonah and, as a result, he became confused and full of doubts. For eight days he agonized over his situation without being able to decide what to do. During that time he fasted and wept. On the eighth day, he again spoke to his wife about his dilemma and of her father's opinion. With gentle fervor, she said, "Your having so many doubts shows that your tears and sighs all these years at not being able to study Torah were not truly sincere. If they came from the deepest place in your heart, you wouldn't hesitate now when given a chance to become a Torah scholar!"

Yonah listened to his wife's words and then went out to the place in the woods where he once again met the Besht, who was standing there waiting for him with his staff in hand. The Besht asked him what he had decided, and he answered that he agreed to everything. They sat down and began to converse, when suddenly the young tinsmith emitted a deep sigh. "Why are you sighing?" said the Besht. "Are you already having regrets? You can still change your mind!" Yonah told him the truth, that the contrary advice from his wife and his father-in-law had confused him. "Your father-in-law is right," said the Besht. "There are many simple Jews who financially support Torah scholars and fulfill the *mitzvot*, and they are even higher than Torah scholars." "Even so!" exclaimed Yonah, who finally decided that his wife's words came from a holy source. "I agree to give up my possessions and go into exile for three years! But my wife suggested I make one condition: that you visit our home and allow us to serve you a meal, so that before we become poor, we can have at least one last chance to fulfill the *mitzvah* of hospitality." The Baal Shem Tov agreed to the "condition" and together they went to Yonah's home. They arrived at his house some time after *Maariv* and found the table set with all kinds of delicious food, and candles shedding a warm, joyous glow, as if for a holiday. When the Baal Shem Tov asked Yonah what the holiday was, he answered that he did not know, and they would have to ask his wife. Devorah Leah said, "Today is a holiday, a time to celebrate, for two reasons: First, that we're able to fulfill the *mitzvah* of welcoming a guest; and second, I see that the Holy One, blessed be He, wants to take all our possessions from us. When He's shown us such kindness—by giving us Torah in exchange for our possessions!—isn't that a reason to make a holiday, that the Holy One, blessed be He, is taking back what He deposited with us, in such a fine way?" Before they sat down to eat, the couple put all their money into a pouch, signed a document stating that their house and everything they owned were a gift to the Baal Shem Tov, and brought in two of their neighbors to sign as witnesses. Then they and the Baal Shem Tov enjoyed the meal and went to sleep.

The next morning, before the Baal Shem Tov and Yonah left, the Besht said to Devorah Leah, "Although your house now belongs to me, I give you permission to live here with your children, as a tenant, until your husband returns from exile." He also gave her, as a gift, sacks of flour and potatoes that had been in their possession, and permission to sow the garden next to the house and to make use of its fruits and vegetables—but all this as a tenant, not an owner. He blessed the woman and their two boys and daughter, took the pouch with the money, and left, together with Yonah the Tinsmith.

By taking away everything the couple had, while giving the woman some meager "gifts" and permission to use the property, the Baal Shem Tov actually wanted to give her the same great gift he hoped to give her husband, who had to abandon his family and possessions and go into exile. She too would now be freed from the corrosive influence of "me and mine," of ego and ownership. As a truly pious woman, Devorah Leah already knew that God was only taking back what was His. Now, she could live that truth—for "the earth is the Lord's and all that is in it." Although their money would be used to help those more needy than they, little in her actual circumstances would change. She would live with her children in the same house and eat from the same garden, but now—after transferring ownership to a holy man—as a "tenant" of God.

Eventually, Yonah became a Torah scholar and a hidden tzaddik. He also made a good living as a tinsmith, and he and his wife were prosperous. Devorah Leah became a great *tzaddeket.** Before Yonah parted from the Baal Shem Tov at the end of three years, the Besht told him, "Everything you've attained is only because of your wife. And what's the essence of her greatness? her joyful self-sacrifice for Torah and *mitzvot.*" Yonah and Devorah Leah knew that they both owed their salvation to the Baal Shem Tov, who had seen their potential and helped them to fulfill it.[46]

Rabbi Meir's Blessing

 THE BAAL SHEM TOV HAD INSTIGATED A MOMENTOUS CHANGE IN THE propaganda methods of the hidden tzaddikim, replacing rebukes and warnings of divine punishment with encouragement and consolation. Two years after the hidden tzaddikim had accepted this new approach of the Besht and had seen the tremendous advances it produced for the work of their movement, the venerable Rabbi Meir, one of the movement's leaders and the Besht's former teacher, summoned the young Baal Shem Tov to him. The Besht traveled to Rabbi Meir and, when he arrived, Rabbi Meir placed his hands on his head, and said, "May God's blessing come upon you, because you blazed a new path in the love of Israel." Shortly thereafter, the Baal Shem Tov was chosen as one of the three members of the committee in charge of the activities of the hidden tzaddikim, who served as the movement's leadership after the death of Rabbi Adam Baal Shem.[47]

God's Livelihood

ONCE, WHEN THE BAAL SHEM TOV WAS WANDERING FROM PLACE TO place and arrived in a certain village, he followed his usual practice of asking every

---

*A pious or holy woman.

Jew he met about his welfare, enabling him to answer "*Baruch HaShem*" (Praise God). Now, in that village there lived an elderly Torah scholar, who was a *parush* (ascetic) who separated himself from the world. At that time, some of the most pious people sat isolated for years studying Torah. This *parush* had been sitting, studying the Talmud, for more than fifty years. He had fasted almost his whole life. He would sit studying in his corner of the *beit midrash*, wrapped in his tallis and *tefillin*, until the evening, when he had his only meager meal of the day with some bread dipped in water.

The Baal Shem Tov entered this *gaon's* separate little room off the *beit midrash* and asked him in a friendly way about his welfare. The *gaon*, who was immersed in his studying, paid no attention to this intrusive stranger who was dressed like a simple peasant. He was annoyed that his holy studies were being interrupted by what seemed to him an attempt at idle conversation. When the Besht persisted and repeated his question, the *gaon* angrily gestured with his hand toward the door, as if to say, "Leave me alone." The Besht responded, "Rabbi, why are you depriving God of His livelihood?" The *gaon* was confused by this peculiar remark, a villager saying that one needed to provide God with a livelihood? He replied irritably, "What are you talking about?" The Besht explained, "Rabbi, a person's livelihood comes from what God decrees for him. You can sit and study because God provides you with a livelihood. But what is God's livelihood? Don't the Rabbis say: 'Israel provides a livelihood for their Father in Heaven'? And the psalm says: 'You [God] are holy, who dwells amidst the praises of Israel! When two Jews meet and ask each other about their welfare and livelihood, and one answers, "Praise God! I make my living this way"; and the other says, "Praise God! I make my living that way"—that praise is *His* livelihood, blessed be He. He is holy and exalted, separated far from the world, but that praise brings Him down, so to speak, into the world; that is the place in which He dwells. When you refuse to talk to anyone or to praise God's goodness to you, but just study Torah, secluded in your own little corner, you deprive God of His livelihood!"

The Baal Shem Tov's words and manner of speaking touched the heart of this man, who realized that he was not listening to a simple peasant. The Besht continued, "The goal is not to imprison yourself within the four walls of Torah study. Torah study alone is not enough. The Rabbis say: 'Whoever says, "I have only the Torah," hasn't even the Torah.' You have to uproot every bad trait from your personality, including every bit of impatience and anger. Even if it takes time away from Torah study, you should mix with other people and take an interest in their welfare. And you should try to help and encourage them when they have troubles." After these words, the elderly *gaon's* demeanor changed, and he and the Besht entered into an animated Torah conversation. As a result of this encounter, the *gaon* was invigorated with new life, to become a better Jew and a better person. The Baal Shem Tov had changed his view of what was required from someone devoted to God—not isolation and separation, but engagement with the world and love for people.[48]

The Father of Orphans

A CERTAIN ELDERLY JEWISH WIDOW LIVED IN A SMALL UKRAINIAN town with her only daughter, who had already reached marriageable age. This young woman was rather ugly and her widowed mother would sit alone pondering with concern her daughter's future, thinking, "Didn't they announce in heaven forty days before she was created who will be her soul-mate?"

This widow served as the women's preacher who taught in the women's section of the synagogue; she sewed shrouds for the dead, wove long wicks for the lengthy candles put at ancestral graves on Rosh HaShanah, and she stayed awake to keep night guard over new corpses. For all this she earned a few pennies. On weekdays, the mother and daughter ate coarse black bread with salt; on Sabbaths and holidays, they ate salted fish. But the woman made do with little and did not complain against the Holy One, blessed be He, about the demands of her stomach. She had only one prayer, and it came from a broken heart: that she merit to see her daughter nursing children.

After some time the woman became ill and her time to die drew near. This happened during the winter, when the air was so fiercely cold that crows fell dead out of the sky. The frozen air became hard to breathe; the water turned to ice, even in the house. The old woman lay in bed covered with pillows and rags and moaned in pain. Inside the house it was frigid; the glass windows were overlaid with thick ice; the walls of the one-room dwelling were frozen and silvery with snow. There was no food to revive the sick woman; there was no firewood for the heating oven. The daughter sat like a stone next to the sickbed, hungry and crushed. Her heart turned to her mother, who was leaving her forever. She would be a miserable orphan, with no friend or support. She too had only one prayer: "Oh, Compassionate Father, Father of widows and orphans . . . !"

Just then the door opened and a man entered, a poor Jew wearing peasant clothes, with a leather belt around his waist, a knapsack over his shoulder, and a thick walking stick in his hand. His beard and *payot** were one solid piece of ice. This was the Baal Shem Tov. Immediately after saying, "*Shalom aleichem*," he threw his knapsack into a corner, shook the snow off of him, and vigorously clapped his hands together to warm them up, like the peasants do. Then he saw the sick woman in bed and noticed her yellowish face. As she dozed, she took in short breaths with difficulty. He looked at the young woman who was sitting like a living block of ice.

The Besht disappeared out the door and after a short while returned with a bundle of sticks for firewood on his back. He dropped them on the ground and began to light the oven. He then covered the girl with his tattered overcoat. He took some potatoes out of his knapsack, searched around the room and found a pot, sat down on the

---

* Ritual side-locks of hair commanded in the Torah for men.

ground and prepared a meal. Since there was no water in the barrel, he broke some icicles off the eave of the roof and while they were melting from the fire, he turned over the sick woman's bed, and rubbed her cold hands as he whispered the words from the daily prayers directed to the One "who heals the sick of His people Israel."

Meanwhile, the elderly sick woman awoke from her difficult sleep and asked for a little water to revive her. The Besht quickly got it for her. She cast a glance at him, her eyes wide open and filled with pain, her chapped lips twisted as she asked with difficulty, "Who are you?" "I'm a Jew, a poor wanderer," he replied, "I came in seeking to warm up a little." As he entered into a conversation with her, he began to encourage her and revive her spirit with the hope that she would recover from her illness and would merit to see grandchildren studying Torah and fulfilling *mitzvot*. Hearing these words of consolation, the sick woman's face contorted with weeping. She shook her head in disbelief and turning her deadened eyes on her dejected daughter, sighed and whispered, "A poor orphan! Who'll care for her? Who'll lead her to the *huppah*?" "God-willing, I will!" said the Baal Shem Tov. A little life flickered in the woman's dull eyes. "Promise me!" The Besht's face glowed. He did not hesitate for a minute. With complete trust in God, he said, "I promise you that I'll take care of your orphaned daughter!"

The widow passed away and the Baal Shem Tov began to look for a groom for the orphan girl. He also collected donations for her dowry and for the wedding. Some time later, the Besht happened to be in a village near Kossov at the end of the summer, where he met a Jew who invited him to stay in his home. This man was a simple villager in every respect; only the merest spark of Jewishness remained within him. During the conversation between the villager and his guest, the Baal Shem Tov learned that the man had been widowed for two years. The villager then began to reveal himself to his guest. "As far as making a living, thank God, I have everything I need. I have two milch cows out in the courtyard, I always have enough bread to eat, and there's plenty of fruits and vegetables. What I don't have is a wife to look after my home! If I lived in the city among other Jews, I'd have married a widow or a divorced woman by now. I don't need a dowry either; I have enough money, thank God. If the woman has her own clothes, good; but if not, I have a trunk full of my late wife's clothes—silk and velvet dresses, and fine pieces of fabric."

The Baal Shem sat silently. He remembered with great pity the poor and lonely orphan girl, and saw in this meeting the finger of God. When the man finished speaking, the Besht said to him, "I have someone for you." "A widow or a divorcee?" "A single woman." "Where does she live?" The Baal Shem Tov told him the name of the town. "Who's her father?" "Our Heavenly Father!" replied the Besht innocently. "She's an orphan!" That night they decided to travel the next morning to see the woman.

When dawn came, the skies were clear, the trees gave off their fragrance and the earth emitted its own pleasing odor. It seemed as if the whole creation was praying: the birds were chirping overhead, the frogs were croaking in the ponds, the rooster was crowing in the yard, the water was muttering its soft gurgle, and the forest making its gentle murmur. Heaven and earth joined in a pure prayer, the upper and lower worlds praying together one hymn, "How great are Your deeds, O Lord, You have done them all with wisdom!"

At that dawn hour, the Baal Shem Tov wrapped himself in his tallis and *tefillin* and stood focused in prayer. His face glowed with divine grace, his eyes sparkled like sapphires as a supernal radiance flickered in them. The Besht's heart filled with joy and his legs danced as if on their own; his soul was drawn upward to the Source of light and love and with his whole being he sang a song from the morning psalm, "Praise God, call out His name, tell the peoples of His deeds; sing to Him, play music for Him, speak of all His wondrous acts!"

Seeing this pious ecstasy, the astonished villager realized that his guest was a hidden tzaddik, and after the Besht had finished his prayers, the man turned to him and said, with trembling and great reverence, "Rabbi, I'd like to marry this young woman under the *huppah* today." That very day, the Besht and the villager went in a wagon hitched to a strong horse and traveled to the woman's town. In the wagon were wine, chickens, fine flour, and also clothes of velvet and fine wool, with gold jewelry, all gifts for the bride. The villager was happy and joyful, and the Baal Shem Tov was quietly singing, "Blessed is the Father of orphans!"[49]

The Light of Storytelling

🔥 THE BAAL SHEM TOV GREATLY VALUED STORYTELLING; BUT AN EXPERIENCE he had in a certain town raised his appreciation even higher. He was once passing by a *beit midrash* with another hidden tzaddik, when he saw a supernal light emanating from within. "There must be great scholars inside," he thought, "studying the Torah in holiness." But when they entered, he saw two simple Jews, not studying Torah, but sitting and conversing with each other. The Besht asked them, "What are you talking about?" They answered, "We're telling stories about the deeds of the tzaddikim." When he heard that, the Besht realized that storytelling produces the same divine illumination as does Torah study.

Afterward, he told his hidden tzaddik friend, "This makes clear to me the meaning of the verse: 'Then they that feared the Lord spoke one with the other: and the Lord hearkened and heard, and a book of remembrance was written before Him, for them that feared the Lord and that thought upon His name.' Now I understand that speaking about tzaddikim causes a revelation of the light of the *Shechinah* and elevates both the tzaddikim themselves—those 'that feared God'—and those who tell and hear the stories—'that thought upon His name,' because storytelling about tzaddikim is like meditating on God's name."

This incident convinced the Baal Shem Tov of the great power of storytelling. He himself was a master storyteller and he often praised storytelling to his fellow hidden tzaddikim, telling them it was the best way to inspire the common people. He also told them that storytelling would elevate them spiritually too. The next time he was with a group of his comrades, he spoke about storytelling and said, "Whoever tells or listens to stories about tzaddikim, or even about ordinary people who at times rise to holiness, is as if engaged in the mystic study and meditation on the Divine Chariot—because the tzaddikim are the chariot, the vehicle for Godliness* in the world."[50]

The Besht Values the Common People

THE BAAL SHEM TOV WAS PAINED TO SEE THAT MANY OF THE RABBIS and Torah scholars viewed the pious simple Jews he loved so much with undisguised condescension and contempt, treating them as if they were strangers, and not the children of Abraham, Isaac, and Jacob. There was an abyss separating the Torah scholars from the common people. The scholars held that the essence of Judaism is Torah knowledge—which the common people lacked. The Besht could not understand how the scholars did not take into account that the ignorance of most simple Jews was not because they had no desire to learn Torah, but because of their grinding poverty, which chained them to the yoke of their livelihood even while they were young. But in the hidden chambers of their hearts they wept bitterly at not being able to study Torah.

The Besht felt that the simple Jews were full of concealed treasures of good qualities, and he had a higher regard for them than for Torah scholars. Many scholars were cursed with pride and arrogance, while many simple Jews were blessed with true piety and humility. He cherished the common people who prayed with simple devotion, full of faith and trust in the Holy One, blessed be He. In those unlearned people who could barely pray and chant psalms, one could expect to find the most prized religious virtues and character traits, more so than in others. "God desires the heart," the Besht used to say, "and the simple Jew who, to his sorrow, is not able to read the words of the Hebrew prayers properly, let alone understand their translation, is precious to the Holy One, blessed be He. Simply by saying the words, he brings great pleasure to the Creator, blessed be He, and causes a flow of divine beneficence to all the worlds."[51]

The Tale of the Sigh and the Sneer

ONCE, THE BAAL SHEM TOV ARRIVED IN THE TOWN OF CHEMELNICK IN Podolia early in the morning, stood in the street in his rough peasant clothes, lit his pipe and began to smoke. Soon, as two women passed by on their way to the market, he asked them a few questions and engaged them in conversation. Then he began to tell them a story, followed by another, until a few men overheard that he was telling

---

* Divinity.

stories and walked over to hear; soon there was a large crowd gathered around him. Then he told this story:

"In a certain town there lived a poor man with a wife and many children, who made a hard living as a porter. He knew how to recite the prayers, although he didn't know the meaning of the Hebrew words. Every morning, he rose before dawn, ran to the synagogue, quickly recited the prayers, then rushed off to a day of back-breaking labor—to earn enough for a crust of dry bread for his hungry children. In the evening he always went to the synagogue to pray, but was usually late to arrive. His prayers were often disjointed and incomplete and, exhausted by his labors, he would doze off standing or sitting. Then he returned home, physically broken and crushed, only to be pained by the sight of his family's suffering.

"In the same neighborhood, there lived a young Torah scholar who studied full-time. He received a weekly stipend from the community to sit and study, and had no financial worries. When he came to the synagogue in the morning, he prayed slowly, as proper, with full concentration, then sat down for his regular morning session of in-depth Talmud study. Afterward, he went home for a meal, and then returned to study more Torah with an untroubled mind. He was always early for *Minha* and *Maariv*, which he recited carefully and slowly.

"Every day, after the evening prayer, the porter and the young Torah scholar met on the street as they walked home. The porter, who walked bent over, with sloped shoulders, let out a deep sigh when he saw his neighbor, the Torah scholar. He thought to himself how his neighbor spent his day under the yoke of study of the holy Torah, while his day was spent bent under the yoke of heavy burdens. How he wished he could pray and study Torah like his neighbor, like a Jew should!

"Meanwhile, the young Torah scholar, who walked erect with an arrogant bearing and a sense of his own dignity, cast a dismissive glance at the porter. On his lips was a contemptuous sneer, as he thought of the chasm that separated him from his ignorant neighbor—as if to say, 'What do I have in common with you?'

"Days, weeks, months, and years passed, until both the porter and the scholar left this world. When the Torah scholar appeared before the heavenly court, he came before the bench with head held high and confident steps. "Heavenly judges!" he said, "I studied much Torah, I prayed with concentration, I was careful to do all the *mitzvot*, the light as well as the heavy!" The judges were satisfied with his deeds and about to pronounce a favorable judgment, but at the last moment an angel approached and asked for their attention. Without speaking further, he put on one side of the scale of judgment all the oversized and heavy Talmud books that the Torah scholar had studied and the large *siddur* from which he prayed. On the other side of the scale he placed only the contemptuous sneer that used to pass over the scholar's face as he looked at his porter neighbor—and it outweighed the other scale.

"After him, the porter appeared before the heavenly court, with bent head and weak knees. He approached the bench and said, 'Righteous judges! I'm ashamed to come before you. I wasn't able to study Torah and didn't pray as I should have; my prayers were often shortened and incomplete. Almost all my time every day was spent carrying burdens, to support my wife and children. . . .' But even before he could finish speaking, an angel came and put on the scale the sigh the porter emitted when he saw his Torah scholar neighbor—at not being able to study and serve God like him—and that sigh weighed down the scale of judgment to the side of good."

The Baal Shem Tov broke the gate of the Garden of Eden and flung it wide open before the simple folk and working people; and he dared to expel from the Garden of Eden those Torah scholars who were sure of themselves and of the share in Paradise that was waiting for them.

The simple Jews who surrounded the Besht in the street and heard his story understood its clear message. They were deeply moved to realize that this wandering preacher and storyteller appreciated their piety and they rededicated themselves to serving their Father in Heaven.[52]

The Besht Opposes Preachers of Rebuke

MOST OF THE PREACHERS IN THE BAAL SHEM TOV'S TIME TYPICALLY emphasized stern rebuke and reproof. They used threats of punishment in the afterlife and descriptions of the terrible suffering in hell to frighten people into repenting of their sins. The outstanding preachers knew how to use every rhetorical device to extract tears from their listeners, and a sermon's quality was judged by the amount of tears shed. Since these preachers claimed that the people's suffering was because of their sins, the more troubles that afflicted them, the more the preacher chastised them and frightened them with further punishments, to bring them to repentance.

The Baal Shem Tov had worked to reform the approach of the hidden tzaddikim to preaching so that they encouraged the people rather than rebuked them. And he could not bear to see these regular preachers tormenting the simple people. He knew the poverty and tribulations of the common Jews and the persecutions they suffered at the hands of the gentiles. He also knew their pure and simple faith.

He once told a preacher he encountered at a roadside inn, "The God of Israel is not a tyrant, God-forbid, but a compassionate Father, who wants to draw His children to Him with love! It's not the remembrance of the day of death, or fear of the punishments of hell that awaken a person's heart to the service of God, blessed be He, but the yearning to cleave in devotion to the Source of all, to the Life of all that lives."

Once, the Besht arrived in a small town, most of whose inhabitants were simple Jews—peasants and craftsmen—but they were also faithful Jews who trembled at God's word. The whole week they worked hard. They prayed with the congregation three times a day, and recited the entire Book of Psalms every day before dawn. On the Sabbath, the whole congregation together said the Book of Psalms twice, once before dawn and once in the afternoon. From time to time, someone would teach them and interpret a verse in the *Chumash* or a teaching in *Pirkei Avot**.

---

* The ancient rabbinic text *Ethics of the Fathers*.

It was during the summer when the Besht arrived in this town. He stayed there a number of days and, as the hidden tzaddikim often did, he mixed with the working people and listened to their deep sighs as they spoke about the difficulties they faced in making a living. It had been unusually hot that summer and their field crops and vegetable gardens had been severely damaged. Indeed, it was a pity for the whole town.

The Baal Shem Tov had intended to leave the town after a few days but the desperate situation of its inhabitants touched his heart and aroused his compassion. He decided to summon a few of his fellow hidden tzaddikim and together they would pray to arouse heavenly mercy on the townspeople. The next day the Besht arranged for some of his comrades to visit and when they arrived they all made a *pidyon nefesh** for the whole town. They prayed, and God, blessed be He, who yearns for the prayers of the tzaddikim and fulfills their requests, answered the prayers. The skies filled with clouds and plenteous rain poured down on the parched fields and vegetable gardens. The people could not contain their joy. Their faces shone from their great happiness and reflected profound thanks to the Life of the worlds, for God's salvation comes in the blink of an eye, may His name be blessed for ever and ever. Men came in from the fields and told of the miracles of the Creator—that abundant rains had revived the crops. The town was filled with joy and gladness: men, women, elders, youths, and children—all talking about the miracles and compassion shown them by God, blessed be He, in sending to them His messengers of good tidings—blessed rain.

This was on a Thursday evening, and the head of the congregation and the leaders of the community decided that they would specially dedicate the coming Sabbath. The congregation would recite the whole Book of Psalms not twice but *three* times. In addition, they would prepare sweet pastries for the third Sabbath meal, to distribute to the children when they told them of God's kindnesses.

When the Baal Shem Tov and his companions, the other hidden tzaddikim, saw the great joy and the *kiddush ha-Shem*¶—that the whole town gave thanks to God—and when they heard the announcement about the coming Sabbath, they shared in the mood of elation. They decided to stay in the town for the Sabbath, to participate in the rejoicing and the sanctification of God's name.

Before dawn on Friday, an itinerant preacher arrived in town. He immediately went to the head of the congregation to request permission to preach the next day in the synagogue. According to his letters of recommendation he was an exceptional preacher. His sermons were so effective in causing people to repent that it took him only a few minutes to have the whole congregation drenched in tears. Although the head of the congregation was a simple Jew, he was also pious and God-fearing. He treated the preacher with the utmost respect, but explained to him that this Sabbath was dedicated as a Sabbath of thanksgiving, and the time that would normally be appropriate for his sermon was already set aside for an additional recitation of the Book of Psalms.

When the preacher heard this, he lashed out at the head of the congregation, curs-

---

* The "soul-redemption" was a sum of money from funds of the hidden tzaddikim that the Besht donated to charity on behalf of the town.

¶ Sanctification of God's name by a noble deed of self-sacrifice.

ing him for showing contempt for the holy Torah. "How dare you tell a Torah scholar like me that you have no time to hear my sermon! You have time enough for a *Shabbos* nap and eating pastries, but to hear words of Torah and rebuke you don't have time? You'll all go to hell!" And he continued to shower more curses on him and on the townspeople. The head of the congregation, who was shaken and terrified by this unexpectedly vehement reaction, fell over himself desperately trying to appease the raging man and begged the preacher's forgiveness. With great difficulty, he finally got him to agree to meet with the town's rabbi to decide on a fitting time for him to give his sermon. The preacher informed him that according to old and established custom, when a preacher visits a town he is obligated to request permission to preach from the head of the congregation. But he has no obligation to go to the town rabbi. An ordinary preacher waits until the rabbi sends a delegation of honor to invite him to the rabbi's house; but a preacher who is a Torah scholar, like himself, waits until the rabbi comes to him and accompanies him back to the rabbi's house. The head of the congregation hastened to the rabbi and fretfully told him everything that had happened. Since the rabbi was humble and lowly in his own eyes, he answered that certainly there is nothing greater than the honor of Torah scholars, and especially a scholar such as this, whose preaching brings many people to repent, and who sacrifices himself to that noble end, wandering from one place to another. He declared himself not only ready but happy to go to the preacher and bring him back to his home.

The preacher was lodging at the home of the caretaker of the synagogue. On his way to the town he had decided that since he needed to find someone in town who could direct him to the right people and run various errands for him, the best place for him to stay would be with the synagogue caretaker. Later, he would be able to see how things turned out; perhaps he would find an even better place to stay.

When the rabbi and the head of the congregation arrived at the preacher's lodgings, the preacher was finally satisfied that he was being shown the proper respect and he calmed down. The rabbi and the preacher immediately began to engage in a Torah conversation and the rabbi saw that the preacher actually was an outstanding scholar. The head of the congregation stood to the side and listened to the discussion with the utmost respect, although he was unable to follow much of it. When the rabbi and preacher finished conversing, they fixed a time for the sermon: after the third Sabbath meal, until the time for *Maariv*. Word quickly spread throughout the town that a famous preacher had arrived, a great scholar and tzaddik, who roused people to repentance, and that he would be preaching on the Sabbath after the third meal.

The women of the town meticulously attended to the arrangements for this Sabbath of thanksgiving. Instead of the single candle they would ordinarily light in the synagogue, they each lit two, for the honor of this special Sabbath. So the synagogue was full of lit candles. The overflowing joy and elation that prevailed on this Sabbath, inspired by the lighting of the extra candles, the Sabbath meals, the Sabbath hymns that were sung, the additional recitation of the psalms, the distribution of the sweet pastries to the children as they were told of God's kindnesses—all made a powerful impression. The Baal Shem Tov and his fellow hidden tzaddikim were delighted and gratified to witness this remarkable sanctification of God's name and were very happy that they had remained in the town for this Sabbath.

When the time for the preacher's sermon arrived, all the townspeople eagerly gathered in the synagogue. The preacher ascended the *bimah* (platform) and began his sermon with the teaching of *Pirkei Avot* that begins: "There are seven kinds of punishment for seven chief transgressions: When some give tithes and some do not, famine through drought comes, some go hungry and some are full." The preacher went on to expound about the continuation: "Pestilence comes to the world on account of the sins for which the penalty of death is appointed in the Torah, and which have not been brought before a court of justice." The people's crops had just been afflicted with drought. But God had sent abundant rain to answer the prayer of the Besht and the other hidden tzaddikim, who had pleaded the merits of the people's simple faith. Now, this preacher of sin and punishment threatened them with drought and worse—with pestilence!

When the congregation heard these terrible threats, they erupted in sobbing. The eyes of men, women, elders, youths, and children flowed with bitter tears. The preacher continued his harsh rebuke, warning them that the Holy One, blessed be He, would punish them also with blood: First, their children would die and then their parents; so that they would be widows and orphans, like during the horrendous pogroms of 1648 and 1649. When they heard these awful things, a loud groan came from all those gathered there. Many fainted and the clamor and tumult grew from minute to minute.

In the midst of this uproar, the Baal Shem Tov entered the synagogue. When he saw the weeping and wailing, and heard what the preacher was saying, the anguish of the townspeople touched his heart. He jumped up on a table and shouted to the preacher, "Rabbi! The *Midrash* says that God, blessed be He, told Moses to, so to speak, rebuke Him!* Why then are you rebuking the people of this town, who serve their Creator so faithfully? Rebuke the Holy One, blessed be He, for not having enough compassion on His children and His people! And pray to Him that now, after He already had compassion on them and sent them rain, His children will continue to serve Him faithfully!"

"Yes, yes!" people called out throughout the synagogue. They immediately ended the preacher's sermon by reciting *Kaddish D'Rabbanan*¶, and all together they joyfully and fervently began to recite Psalms of Ascent, praising the Holy One, blessed be He, for His mercies are forever.[53]

An Esrog *from Elijah*

AFTER THIS, THE BAAL SHEM TOV AND HIS WIFE LEFT THE VILLAGE between Kossov and Kitov that they had made their home. They wandered around for months with their horse and wagon until they finally settled down again in

---

* A preacher would be a rabbi. Do not confuse him with the town rabbi. The *Midrash* is an ancient rabbinic commentary on the Torah.

¶ The prayer said at the conclusion of a sermon.

a village near Senitin. This place too was in Reissen in the foothills of the Carpathian Mountains on the Prut River. As the Days of Awe approached, the Besht went into the city during the days of *Selichot* and planned to stay there until after *Sukkot**. When the cantor in the synagogue where he prayed became ill after the morning and additional prayers the first day of Rosh HaShanah, everyone was worried; they wondered where they would find someone to lead the prayers the second day of the holiday. The innkeeper where the Besht was lodging said, "There's a pious person staying in my inn who has a good voice. Maybe he would agree to lead the prayers the second day." The *gabbai*¶ of the synagogue said to them, "My advice is to ask him to lead the afternoon and evening prayers today, and we'll see if we like his praying." They decided to do as he suggested, and the community leaders approached the Baal Shem Tov. Being a hidden tzaddik, the Besht was very reluctant to place himself in a position where his ecstatic praying could hardly be concealed and might draw to him unwanted attention. But the circumstances forced his hand. After they pleaded with him, he agreed to do as they asked.

Later that day, he went before the Ark§ and led the prayers. They all saw that his praying was as sweet as honey. The congregation was so aroused by his devotion and fervor that there was no question that they wanted him to be the prayer-leader the next day too, and they begged him to fulfill their request. The second day of Rosh HaShanah, he prayed the morning and also the additional prayers with the sweetest voice, and with holy enthusiasm.

During the Ten Days of Repentance, between Rosh HaShanah and Yom Kippur, the regular cantor recovered from his illness. The townspeople were now in a predicament, because they longed for the Baal Shem Tov to lead the prayers on Yom Kippur too. On the other hand, they could not just push aside the regular cantor. Finally, they decided to ask the Besht for his advice. When they went and asked him, he said, "I suggest that you tell the regular cantor that you'll pay him his set fee, as every year, on the condition that he asks me to pray in his place, since he hasn't completely recovered." Seeing that this was a tactful way to handle a delicate situation, they followed the Besht's advice. The regular cantor immediately consented and went to the Besht to ask him to pray in his place. The Besht agreed.

After Yom Kippur, the Baal Shem Tov summoned the householders and asked them, "What are you paying me?" "Set your own fee," they said, "We'll give you whatever you think is fitting." The Baal Shem Tov was so indifferent to anything except divine service that he had not even discussed a fee with them earlier. "My fee," he said, "is that you arrange to get for me a beautiful and perfect *esrog*# for *Sukkot*." They read-

---

* There is an extended sequence of holidays at the beginning of the Jewish year, from the Days of Awe—Rosh HaShanah through Yom Kippur—and until after *Sukkot*. *Selichot*, early morning penitential prayers, are recited on the days leading up to Rosh HaShanah.
¶ Synagogue manager and ritual director.
§ The prayer-leader prays at a stand facing or near the Ark.
# Citron ritually waved on the holiday of *Sukkot*. There is a special merit in the citron being as beautiful and perfect as can be, and pious people make great efforts and spend much money to acquire a splendid *esrog* for the *mitzvah*.

ily agreed and promised him that they would make every effort to obtain for him a perfect *esrog*.

That year, however, *esrogs* were simply not to be found. In most towns it was impossible to obtain one. The householders sent people to search for an exceptional *esrog* and agreed to pay whatever it cost. They searched in all the towns, but could not find even an ordinary *esrog*, let alone a perfect one.

On the day before *Sukkot*, the Baal Shem Tov, who did not yet have an *esrog*, sat at home dejected and depressed the whole day. For someone like the holy Baal Shem, who lived only to serve God, not having an *esrog* to perform the *mitzvah* was an actual tragedy. He was so miserable he felt himself on the edge of darkness and did not go to pray the afternoon prayer with the congregation on the eve of the holiday. The householders waited for him to arrive, but he did not appear. For their part, they were extremely embarrassed at not being able to provide him with the *esrog* they had promised, so they did not send anyone to bring him, but continued to wait.

As evening approached, the prophet Elijah, disguised as a gentile, came racing into town on a horse, carrying in his hand an *esrog*, a *lulav**, and the other of the "Four Species," all of them as perfect as could be. He rode right up to the front of the synagogue and shouted out in Russian, "Does Israel live here?" "Yes," they said, and told him where the Besht's house was. The man turned and rode there at a gallop, pulled up his horse, jumped off, and ran into the Baal Shem Tov's house. The moment he handed the Baal Shem Tov the Four Species, the Besht revived, as if new life had been breathed into him. The horseman immediately rode away and the Baal Shem went to pray the afternoon and evening prayers, joyfully and with a happy heart. God, blessed be He, would not deprive His devoted servant of the means to serve Him. That *Sukkot* the townspeople also merited having an *esrog* because of the Baal Shem Tov[¶]. And it was clear to all of them that the prophet Elijah had brought him the Four Species. Seeing that he was no longer hidden, the Baal Shem Tov left the town immediately after the holiday. He went to live in Kshilovitz, near the town of Yazlovitz in Podolia, where he continued as a hidden tzaddik, and no one knew of him.[54]

His Movements and Encampments

DURING THIS PERIOD IN HIS LIFE, THE BESHT SOMETIMES TRAVELED around performing missions for the society of hidden tzaddikim and leading the people to repentance; at other times he dwelt in a particular place and worked for his living. But he usually did not stay in any one location for a long time. He lived in many different places and worked at many different jobs. Sometimes, as when he suddenly

---

* A date palm branch waved as one of the Four Species on *Sukkot*.
¶ Other people also used that *esrog* to perform the *mitzvah* of ritual waving.

left the area of Senitin, he did so because he was in danger of being revealed and could no longer maintain his disguise as a common person. At other times, he moved according to the instructions of the rest of the leadership of the hidden tzaddikim, who wanted to spread his influence to people in different areas. There were also occasions when he moved because of his own personal spiritual or material needs.

As a Shochet

Tears

🔥 WHEN HE HAD LIVED WITH RABBI MEIR THE HIDDEN TZADDIK, THE BAAL Shem Tov had trained in the holy work of *shechitah**, learning all of its laws, rules, and techniques. When he went to live in Kshilovitz, he served as the *shochet* for that village and also for many of the nearby villages. At that time, he innovated what came to be called the "Ukrainian" method of whetting the slaughtering knife, to make it especially sharp, so the slaughter would be as painless as possible for the animal. But the Besht's own practice as a *shochet* went beyond that. When he sharpened his knife, he did not pour water on the sharpening stone as did the other *shochtim*; he wet the stone with his tears. Before he slaughtered an animal, he wept, thinking, "How can I kill a living creature? Am I better than it?"[55]

Inspecting His Knife

🔥 AT THAT TIME, THE GREAT *GAON* RABBI YAAKOV YEHOSHUA, THE P'NAI Yehoshua¶, was the rabbi of Lvov and the district that included Kshilovitz. Once, the P'nai Yehoshua wanted to make an inspection to see if all the *shochtim* in the villages under his authority were properly expert and knew how to sharpen their knives correctly. So he ordered them all to come to him and show him their knives. When the Baal Shem Tov came, he took his knife out of its sheath, which was stuck in his boot. But the P'nai Yehoshua took one look at him and said, "I was not speaking of someone like you." He could see from the Baal Shem Tov's face that he was a person of great purity and piety.

The Besht then lifted up his knife to heaven, for the inspection of the Holy One, blessed be He. And in the glint of the sunlight on the blade, the P'nai Yehoshua was astonished to see the four-letter name of God. At that moment he realized that this *shochet* was a great hidden tzaddik. The Besht then asked the rabbi not to tell anyone about him.[56]

---

* Ritual kosher slaughter. A slaughterer is a *shochet* (pl. *shochtim*).
¶ Great rabbis are often known by the names of their most famous book or commentary.

Attraction

() FROM TIME TO TIME, THE BESHT WAS AT THE HOME OF THE *GAON* Rabbi Tzvi Margoliot, the head of the religious court of Yazlovitz, where he met the rabbi's two sons—Yitzhak Dov, age seventeen, and Meir, age eleven—both of whom were Torah prodigies. The Besht saw that they had high souls and were of refined character owing to their great *yichus* (family lineage). In telling a comrade among the hidden tzaddikim about the boys he said, "There are three famous Jewish families that are pure, generation after generation: Horowitz, Margoliot, and Shapiro."

Whenever the Besht was in Yaslovitz he visited its *beit midrash*, to use its library and listen to the Torah teaching of its scholars. On one visit he found the two Margoliot boys there and broke in upon their studies with a story about his horse. The boys did not give the simple *shochet* a second thought and, slightly annoyed at his interrupting them, they returned to their books. They never considered the deep spiritual teaching in what seemed to them idle conversation. But after he left, the two brothers were suddenly filled with a burning desire to travel to the *shochet* of Kshilovitz. They had no idea why they had such a strange attraction for him. Since no one could possibly understand what they felt, they did not tell anyone else about it. And since their father would never allow them to visit the *shochet*, they stole away without permission and secretly went to Kshilovitz, to the Besht's home.

Once they were with the Besht, they did not want to leave. Meanwhile, back at their home, there was a great commotion about the missing boys, and people went out in all directions to search for them. Finally, after two weeks, someone said that he had seen two boys of their description walking near Kshilovitz. So the searchers went from house to house in the village, until they found the brothers with the *shochet*, and they had to return home.

Greatly relieved at finding his sons safe and sound, their father, the *gaon*, did not demand an explanation of their rash escapade. And the Besht had ordered them not to reveal to anyone what they had done there. But, later on, their father asked them, "Boys, what did you see in the *shochet* of Kshilovitz that Torah scholars such as yourselves should run to him and want to spend all that time with him?" "Father," they replied, "it's impossible to explain what he's like. But believe us when we tell you that he's wiser and more pious than anyone in the whole world!"[57]

The Besht's Prayer Tested

() THE BESHT LEFT KSHILOVITZ AFTER HAVING BEEN THE TOWN'S *SHOCHET* for about two years. For a while, he was a *melamed* in a village close to Lvov. The Besht also served as the prayer-leader in the village, because no one else was qualified to lead the prayers properly. And the Besht could no longer bear being so concealed, when his soul yearned to soar aloft while praying, and to draw others with him. How could he allow someone else to lead services in the synagogue, if that meant the praying would be rote and uninspired? On the Sabbath, he led the prayers and also taught the villagers Torah. When Rosh HaShanah approached, the Besht prayed before the Ark during the days of *Selichot* and then on the holiday itself. He also blew the *shofar** for them.

When the community leaders of Lvov found out about this, they were furious that the villagers had made their own holiday *minyan* in the village. The custom was always for Jews from all the villages to go every year for *Selichot* and the Days of Awe to pray in the city. When they prayed with their own *minyan* in the village, the city of Lvov lost the income that their attendance brought to the community treasury. So the leaders of the Jewish community of Lvov decided that they would wait until the villagers came to the city for Yom Kippur. Then they would deal with them.

But when the villagers prayed in the village for Yom Kippur too, the Jewish leaders of Lvov saw that they had to act. They ordered all the cities and towns in the area not to sell the Four Species needed for *Sukkot* to the men of that village, so they would be forced to come to Lvov for the holiday. They also ordered that when the villagers arrived in the city on the eve of *Sukkot*, they should submit themselves to public disgrace by walking barefoot from the city gate to the synagogue, wearing their white *kittles*¶, as on Yom Kippur. After praying the afternoon prayer, they must then go to the rabbi's house to receive a reprimand. They also ordered that the villager who had led the prayers be tested in the synagogue by praying the afternoon service. If he recited the prayers properly, they would not fine the villagers. But if their prayer-leader made mistakes, they would all be punished further, in addition to the disgrace of their barefoot march and the rabbi's censure.

The villagers submitted to the communal decree. They were greatly humiliated as they marched through the town, for the town's children trailed behind them on their way to the synagogue, taunting them with jokes and jibes.

The Baal Shem Tov, who was considered the prime offender, went before the Ark in the synagogue to be tested by leading the prayers. He said the prayers perfectly, correctly pronouncing the words and chanting the melodies properly. But when he reached the "blessing of the Patriarchs" at the beginning of the *Shemoneh Esreh*§, he turned to the congregation and said, "Whoever hasn't completely repented of his sins should leave the synagogue." Fear and dread descended on many there and they began to flee the synagogue in panic and confusion. The community leaders also fled. They were ready to judge and test others, but they could not stand in the test.

Afterward, they brought the Baal Shem Tov, for rebuke, to the P'nai Yehoshua, who was sitting in his house wrapped in tallis and *tefillin*. The saintly rabbi, who had not

---

* Ram's horn blown in synagogue during the Days of Awe, through *Selichot*, Rosh HaShanah, and Yom Kippur.
¶ Penitential robes.
§ The most important prayer of every Jewish prayer service.

been told by the community leaders who the offending villager was, immediately recognized the hidden tzaddik he had met earlier when inspecting the *shochets'* knives. He greeted him warmly and spoke to him in the friendliest way. It was only through the intervention and prayers of the P'nai Yehoshua that those who had persecuted and humiliated the Baal Shem Tov were saved from heavenly punishment.[58]

Tlust

AFTER THIS, THE BAAL SHEM TOV MOVED TO THE PODOLIAN TOWN OF Tlust, in the foothills of the Carpathian Mountains, not far from Kshilovitz, and was a *melamed* there too. He was so poor when he lived in Tlust that all he had to wear was a rough overcoat, and his toes stuck out through the holes in his shoes. He and his wife ate so poorly that their special *Shabbat* "delicacy" was a humble *farfel tzimis**.

The Besht started to attract some followers in Tlust, as he had in Kshilovitz. At first, he was not able to arrange a separate *minyan* in his home, but he did gather some men who prayed with him. Since it was against custom and tradition to form a separate *minyan*, the community leaders in Tlust tried their best to thwart the Besht, but he persisted, because the set synagogue ways could not satisfy him. In the ordinary synagogues, rich and poor, learned and unlearned were separated. The rich and the scholars prayed in the front by the prestigious eastern wall (close to the Ark and the prayer-leader); the poor and the unlearned were relegated to the back rows. A poor person was hardly ever honored by being called up to make a blessing over the Torah. Being poor himself and having often posed as an unlearned, common man, the Besht knew how this discrimination in the house of God felt. He also loved and respected the Jewish poor and could not bear their unequal treatment. In his view, all Jews were equal before God, and if there was any superiority in virtue, it was usually in favor of the poor and unlearned. Did not the Sages say that the poor are God's special people? The Besht also began to feel that if he was to lead Jews to repentance, he must also lead them in the prayers, which he could not do without his own, separate *minyan*. Prayer was at the center of the Baal Shem Tov's religious path. If he wanted to pray without concealing his fervor, he could not be in a regular synagogue, where they would frown on his "excessive" devotion and try to restrain him. And how could he show others how to pray with self-sacrifice to the living God if he did not have freedom to pray as he wished? Praying with his own small group in Tlust, he was spared these problems. Early every morning he went to the *mikvah*, even in the middle of winter, when the air was frigid and the water iced over. Afterward, while praying, drops of perspiration the size of large beans dripped from him due to his holy exertions.[59]

* A grain dish mixed with glazed carrots.

A Tap on the Window

ONCE, THE BAAL SHEM TOV HAD NO MONEY TO GIVE TO HIS WIFE TO buy what they needed for the holy Sabbath—candles, wine for *kiddush**, challahs[¶], and food. So, early on Friday morning, *erev Shabbat[§]*, he went and tapped on a neighbor's window. When no one answered, the Besht gave a quick glance through the window, to see if anyone was inside. Not seeing anyone, he immediately started walking home. The neighbor, who was in the other room and slow getting up, opened the door and, finding no one there, went outside to see who had been knocking. Looking down the street, he saw the Baal Shem Tov walking away. He ran after him, caught up with him, and asked, "What did you want? Why were you knocking on my window?" "I don't have any money to buy what's needed for *Shabbos*," replied the Besht. "If you need money for *Shabbos*," said the man, "why did you run away so quickly? Why didn't you wait for me to come to the door or go to the other neighbors?" "When a man is born," replied the Baal Shem Tov, "his livelihood comes into the world with him and, by rights, he should receive his sustenance without working, like the animals and birds. But because of his sins he has to work to earn his living, as the verse says: 'In the sweat of your brow shall you eat your bread.' But how much a person must work varies. The more he's deteriorated spiritually, the more he has to work. Whereas one person can earn his living without stepping out of his house, another has to travel great distances. As for me, I felt this morning that I didn't have to do much. I only had to make a little effort to provide an opening for God's providence to act. So I tapped on your window. Now that I've done my part, I have complete trust that God will do the rest and provide for me. How He does that—whether through you or in any other way—is not my concern. I have other things to attend to now." Deeply impressed by the Baal Shem Tov's faith and trust in God, the man ran home and brought back a generous donation for the Besht's Sabbath needs.[60]

He Learns Holy Eating from a Village Innkeeper

THE BAAL SHEM TOV WAS ONCE TOLD BY ELIJAH THAT HE COULD learn how to sanctify his eating from a certain villager. The Besht had rejected the ascetic path of fasting, but did not yet know how to maintain his profound *d'vekut* while eating. Part of the answer came from a simple Jew. The Besht was always eager to meet pious people and absorb some of their ways in serving God. He traveled to a small village and, when he arrived, found that the man he sought ran an inn. Deter-

---

* The "Sanctification" blessing recited by the man of the house over wine before Sabbath or holiday meals.
¶ Fine, braided bread.
§ The day before *Shabbat*, particularly Friday morning and afternoon.

mined to learn holy eating from his host, he carefully observed him during meals to see the manner in which he ate. But although he watched him carefully, he saw no exceptional behavior whatsoever from the innkeeper. As far as the Besht could tell, he was an ordinary man and ate like an ordinary man. There seemed to be nothing special at all about him, and nothing to learn from him. But since the Baal Shem Tov could not doubt what heaven had revealed to him about the holiness of the man's eating, he continued to watch his doings closely, and noticed that while sitting at the table before every meal the man quickly shut his eyes, scrunched up his face, and then ate. When the Besht asked him why he did this, the villager at first refused to answer, but after much pleading he revealed his secret. He told the Besht, "I realized that because of my many sins, I'm not worthy to eat the food that the Holy One, blessed be He, prepares for those He created to do His will. But knowing that God desires that the wicked repent, I offer my life to Him. I say, 'God, I'm willing to die for Your sake. If I don't do Your will, it's only because of the leaven in the dough, my evil inclination! If You don't want me to live, take my life now!' If the Holy One, blessed be He, doesn't take my life at that moment, I know that He wants me to live and I'm permitted to eat." After meeting this man, the Baal Shem Tov always completely repented with self-sacrifice before every meal, until he was certain that God was feeding him with favor.

The Besht, of course, made the traditional ordained blessings before and after food, which put eating in a spiritual context. And he now prepared for eating by repenting before every meal. By using knowledge gleaned from holy books and by his own experiments, he also learned how to serve God and have *d'vekut* while eating too. Once he had mastered the basic techniques of holy eating on his own, he was told by Elijah that his teacher for eating in perfect holiness would be Moses himself, who had been on the mountain for forty days and forty nights without eating or drinking. The next day, Moses came to the Besht in a vision and taught him many *kavvanot* for meditative eating. After that, Moses sometimes appeared to the Baal Shem Tov while he ate and taught him this or that specific *kavvanah*.[61]

He Learns Self-sacrifice for Fellow Jews from a Woodcutter

ON ANOTHER OCCASION, THE BAAL SHEM TOV WAS TOLD BY ELIJAH that he could learn a great lesson in holiness from a certain tzaddik named "Rabbi Yitzhak son of Yaakov" in the town of Koretz in Volhynia. He traveled to Koretz, and when he arrived in town asked around as to where a Rabbi Yitzhak ben Yaakov the Tzaddik lived, but no one knew about any such person. They told him that the only Yitzhak son of Yaakov was a certain woodcutter nicknamed Itcheh, who lived in the gentile part of town near the forest. In answer to his questions, the Besht found out that this Itcheh was not a Torah scholar and not even considered to be religious. The only things special about him were that he worked chopping wood in the forest from morning to evening, with tremendous energy, like a madman, and he had an incredible appetite! He did the work of three men and ate enough for four! The Besht decided that the man he was sent to learn from must be a hidden tzaddik who concealed his Torah knowledge and holy ways from the eyes of men.

When the Besht went to Reb Itcheh's home in the late afternoon, the man's wife told him where in the forest her husband was working. The Besht went there, followed the sound of the axe and of falling trees, found him, and watched in amazement as Reb Itcheh chopped trees and wood like a wild man, without taking a moment's rest. It seemed that he had supernatural powers.

When evening was approaching, Reb Itcheh stopped working and noticed the Baal Shem Tov who was standing at a distance observing him. The Besht greeted him, asked for lodging, and Reb Itcheh cheerfully offered him hospitality. As soon as they returned to Reb Itcheh's home, his wife served their guest, and then served her husband a gigantic loaf of bread, half as big as the table, with a meal fit for four people. The Besht watched in amazement as Reb Itcheh ate, and he saw that the townsfolk had not exaggerated when they spoke in awe about his appetite, for during the meal he shoveled down his throat a mountain of food, plate after plate! No sooner had he finished this huge meal, than he jumped into bed, fell asleep, and his snoring could be heard from one end of the forest to the other, like a storm wind passing through the trees! The Besht was at a loss as to what exactly heaven intended him to learn from Reb Itcheh.

The Baal Shem Tov stayed with Reb Itcheh for a few days and watched him carefully to see why in heaven they considered the woodcutter a tzaddik; the Besht was certain he was a hidden holy man, but he saw nothing that was holy, only working, eating, and sleeping. The woodcutter did not pray or study Torah or behave in any other way that a Jew is supposed to act! Not knowing what else to do, the Besht revealed to Itcheh that he had been told that Itcheh was a tzaddik and that he wanted to learn from him. Reb Itcheh said, "I'm not religious at all and know nothing about it. I became an orphan when I was five and I never learned how to study Torah or to pray. I'm no tzaddik!" Itcheh had no idea why the Baal Shem Tov would come to learn from him, when he was just a plain and ignorant woodcutter. When the Besht said he would not leave him until he revealed his secret, Reb Itcheh insisted that there were no secrets. Knowing that if heaven said this man was a tzaddik, it was certainly true, the Besht persisted and asked, "Then at least tell me why you eat so much and work so hard that you seem insane?" "I'll explain," said Reb Itcheh. And when he explained, it became clear that his eating and chopping wood were truly for the sake of heaven.

Once, he said, he was in the forest working near an isolated road, far from any habitation, when he heard in the distance cries from a Jew who was being assaulted by robbers. Despite the danger to his own life, Itcheh ran to try to save the Jew from them, and attacked the robbers with his axe. He was a strong man, but there were five of them and they too had weapons—axes and knives. He was certainly risking his life by fighting with them, and only through the merit of the love of Israel that burned within him at that moment was he able to save himself and the other Jew. But as he battled with the robbers, wondering if he would survive the fight, Itcheh vowed that if God would save him from them, he would eat a lot and work hard, with all his might—to become even stronger to fight against anyone who threatened Jews. "What I vowed then," said Itcheh, finishing his story, "I've fulfilled!" When the Baal Shem Tov heard this tale, he realized why he had been sent to Reb Itcheh, who was truly a holy Jew. Later, when telling another hidden tzaddik about what he had learned, he said with fervor, "With each swing of Reb Itcheh's axe chopping wood and with each bite of food that he eats to increase his strength, he fulfills two commandments with self-sacrifice—love of Israel, and not standing idly by the blood of a fellow Jew—even if he doesn't have these commandments in mind!"[62]

As a Coachman

AFTER HAVING BEEN AWAY FOR FOUR YEARS, THE BAAL SHEM TOV AND HIS wife, Chana, left Tlust and returned to Brody to the Besht's brother-in-law, Rabbi Gershon. When they arrived, and Rabbi Gershon asked his sister how she was and where they had been, she told him that they had wandered from place to place and town to town and had experienced poverty and suffered a great deal. Rabbi Gershon had little sympathy for his ignorant and eccentric brother-in-law. He had been the one to suggest that the couple leave Brody to spare himself embarrassment. But now he pitied his sister and he found a place for the couple to live close to his own home. He also tried to provide them with a way to support themselves, by taking on the Baal Shem Tov as his personal servant. He considered the Besht a simpleton, unfit for any serious work. But he felt he could at least use him for errands and driving his coach.

Once, Rabbi Gershon had to travel somewhere and he took the Besht along as his coachman. The rabbi dozed off during the trip, since he usually stayed awake for most of the night in his divine service—of Torah study and prayer—and slept little. Meanwhile, the Baal Shem Tov, who could hardly keep his attention on what he was doing because of his total absorption in God, drove the horses deep into a large mud puddle. Rabbi Gershon was awakened by the jolt as they came to a sudden stop, and he saw that they were in serious trouble. The horses were so deep in the mud it would be impossible to get them out without help. Not only was he exasperated at the gross stupidity and ineptitude of his brother-in-law, but he was also vexed because he felt that if he sent him to a nearby village to bring back some villagers to pull out the horses, he might wander off somewhere and get lost! Having seen how the Besht sometimes walked around as if in a daze, Rabbi Gershon considered it one more sign of his being a simpleton—but actually the Besht was lost in his ecstatic love of God. Because of his single-minded *d'vekut*, he sometimes had "lapses" of attention, such as in not seeing the mud puddle. (Later, the Besht learned how to act with awareness of the world while retaining his elevated God-consciousness.)

Reluctant to send his unreliable brother-in-law, Rabbi Gershon decided to go himself to find help, even though it was hardly befitting his honor as an important rabbi. He had to begin by stepping down from the coach and wading through the mud!

Then, he walked to a nearby village and started back with some men and horses to pull his coach and horses out of the muck and mire. But when he was on his way back with the villagers, what did he see but the Baal Shem Tov driving toward him! "Who pulled you out of the mud?" he asked in astonishment. "I simply tapped the horses once," the Besht replied, "and they walked out easily." Not wanting to hurt animals, the Besht never whipped the horses. He simply talked to them in their own language or tapped them gently. And at his tap, the horses had hurried to do his bidding and the mud parted like the waters of the Red Sea. Rabbi Gershon, who did not recognize whom he was dealing with, did not know what to make of this strange answer. Still fuming about plodding through the mud and his long walk for help, he had lost any interest in the Besht's services. "If I can't even use him for simple tasks like this," he said to himself, "he's not fit for any kind of work!"[63]

The Besht and His Wife Chana Run an Inn

RABBI GERSHON THEN RENTED AN INN—AS CUSTOMARY, WITH A TAVERN and guest rooms in the innkeeper's house—for the Baal Shem Tov and his wife Chana in a small village near Kitov, close to the Prut River, hoping that they could earn a living there. "Let my sister take charge of running the inn!" he thought. In any case, he would no longer be bothered by having his strange brother-in-law near him. But he would occasionally see them, since he was not only a member of the Brody *Kloiz* but also a member of a circle of pious scholars in Kitov, his original hometown, and he regularly visited there. So the Besht and Chana returned to Kitov where they had formerly lived.

At this time, the Besht was deeply involved in the spiritual labor that would bring him to perfection. In the forest near the inn, he built for himself a secluded hut, where he prayed, studied Torah, and meditated day and night the whole week. He was only at the inn for the Sabbath. On Friday he returned home, where there was a bathhouse and a *mikvah*, to wash and immerse, in honor of the Sabbath. After immersing in the *mikvah*, he donned the white Sabbath garments he kept at the inn, for he always wore white on the Sabbath, according to the kabbalistic custom.

His wife Chana took care of running the inn, and God blessed the work of her hands with modest success. They received guests for lodging and meals, and served them graciously. When guests arrived during the week, she sent for the Baal Shem Tov, and he came and did the kosher slaughtering for the guests' meat meals. He also helped serve the guests. It was all one to the Besht whether he served God by Torah study and prayer in his secluded hut or by waiting on guests in the inn. Of course, the Besht and his wife had to take money for their services, for otherwise they would not have the means to perform the *mitzvah* of hospitality. When serving guests in the inn, the Baal Shem Tov zealously fulfilled the Rabbis' teaching that receiving one's fellow man is like receiving the *Shechinah*. The Besht had learned this kind of devoted hospitality and service in his parents' home. While the Besht and Chana were living in this inn, their first child was born, a daughter, whom they named Edel.[64]

His Infant Daughter Edel Grasps Her Father's Beard

THE BESHT REMAINED IN SOLITUDE IN THE FOREST THROUGHOUT the week and on Friday he came home. He often fasted from Sabbath to Sabbath, not intentionally—from an ascetic impulse—but being totally absorbed in his divine service and in a state of intense *d'vekut*, he simply forgot to eat. At the beginning of the week, Chana gave him a bag of loaves of bread when he left for his secluded hut and, at the end of the week, when he was about to return home, he looked, and realized that the bag was still full.

On Sabbath evenings, when he sat down at the table for his Sabbath meal, he was in a state of such awesome *d'vekut* that he almost did not eat. He took one bite of the challah and his mind soared into the upper worlds. His wife Chana, who was anxious that he eat after having fasted the whole week, called to him, so that he would return to the normal plane of consciousness; but she was not able to draw his mind down to this world.

Once, she put their infant daughter Edel on her father's lap, as the Besht sat at the table in a deep trance, and the child began to pull at her father's holy beard, as children do. This drew the Besht back to body consciousness and he began to eat. From then on, Chana always placed the child on her father's lap at the table, to draw his mind down, so he would eat, for although the Besht's thoughts might be roaming in the highest heavens, his mind was immediately drawn down to attend to a child, because a child is in the image of God. The Besht attained a state of intense *d'vekut* by means of his prayer, study, and meditation. But he also saw God in people, particularly children.[65]

His Wife Sells Her Shterntichel

ALTHOUGH THE INN WAS USUALLY SUCCESSFUL ENOUGH TO SATISFY their basic needs, the Baal Shem Tov and Chana occasionally suffered from great poverty. But regardless of the circumstances, the Besht had to have some expansiveness on *Shabbat*—some item of better food or some other small luxury in honor of the holy Sabbath. Like many Jewish women, Chana's most precious possession was an expensive *shterntichel*, a decorated and bejewelled head covering for *Shabbat*. Once, when she had no money to buy any special food for the day of rest, she pawned her *shterntichel* to provide her holy husband with some expansiveness on *Shabbat*.[66]

The Helper of the Helpless

ONE YEAR BEFORE PASSOVER, WHEN BUSINESS AT THE INN WAS VERY poor, the Baal Shem Tov had no money at all, and none with which to buy matzahs or meat for the *seder**. So he harnessed his horse to his wagon and set out to travel to the nearby villages to earn some money as a *shochet*. He worked until he had enough money to buy what he needed, and brought back flour and meat for Passover. When he arrived home at the inn, he said to his wife, "Chana, please call someone to take the flour and meat off the wagon and bring it into the house." Meanwhile, he went off to his secluded hut. But, before Chana could arrange for someone to unload the wagon, there was a sudden rainstorm, which made the flour *hametz*¶ and spoiled it. So Chana went and told her husband what had happened.

The Besht inspected his slaughtering knife and set out again, this time to the villages in the other direction. Again, he earned some money and was bringing back flour for the holiday. But this time also something happened. There was a steep hill not far from the Besht's house, and the horse could not pull the wagon up the hill. So the Besht climbed down and pushed the wagon from behind. But half-way up, the horse died from the strain. The Besht unharnessed the horse and left the dead animal on the road. Then he was forced to push the wagon himself. He could not go for help, because this was "guarded flour" for matzahs, which if left unattended, would become unusable; or it would be stolen.

Before long, he was completely exhausted from his efforts and sunk down by the side of the wagon, weeping, as he uttered a silent prayer before God for help in his distress. In the midst of his weeping he fell asleep and Elijah appeared in his dream and said, "Your tears have been received with favor and your prayer has been accepted. I will send a peasant to take your wagon and the flour to your house." The Baal Shem Tov asked Elijah, "Master, why was I punished this way—first, the rain spoiling the flour; then, the horse dying—since I was willing to give my very life for the *mitzvah* of guarding the flour for the matzahs?"

"You were punished," Elijah answered, "because although you guarded the flour with total self-sacrifice and your last ounce of energy, you forgot the most important protection of all—to pray first to the only true Guardian, as the verse says: 'If God does not watch over the city, the watchman stays awake in vain.' In everything you do, always say first, 'With God's help,' then you will be successful. Even when doing *mitzvot*, one cannot succeed without God's help. After you exhausted yourself pushing the wagon, when you realized you were helpless and turned to God in prayer, then your prayer was answered, for He is Helper of the helpless."

The moment the Baal Shem Tov awakened from his sleep, Elijah appeared again, as a gentile peasant, who came along with a wagon pulled by two horses and said, "Israel, hitch your wagon to mine, and I'll take you home." When they arrived at his house, the man said, "What will you give me to go back and skin the dead horse?" The Besht offered him a fair amount for the work—a silver coin. The peasant returned to the hill, skinned the horse, and brought its hide back to the Besht. After receiving his payment, he left. But another peasant immediately came and offered the Besht the extravagant

---

* The festive meal and home religious service celebrating Passover.
¶ Leavened.

sum of four gold coins for the horse hide. He then said to the Baal Shem Tov, "Use this money to buy yourself and your wife some nice clothes for the coming Passover holiday!" The Besht realized that this too was Elijah in still another disguise.

The Besht knew that the money he was given for the horse hide, which was much more than it was worth, was help directly from the hand of God. He now had enough money to buy not only matzahs and his other Passover needs, but also new holiday clothes for himself and his wife Chana.[67]

The Source of the Money

 WHEN THE JEWISH *MOCHSIN**, WHO RENTED OUT THE INN ON BEHALF of the local lord, and who supplied the Baal Shem Tov with liquor to sell, saw that the Besht had bought fine new clothes for himself and his wife, he became suspicious that his tenant was buying liquor from someone else and cheating him of his profit. So he complained about him to Rabbi Gershon (who rented the inn on behalf of his brother-in-law), and said, "Because of my respect for you, I'm coming to you first and not taking immediate action. But if your brother-in-law doesn't confess to his wrongdoing, and make up my loss, I'll have him beaten by the lord's strong-arm men in the citadel of the manor house." Rabbi Gershon, who believed the accusations against his brother-in-law, promised to be severe with the Baal Shem Tov and told the *mochsin*, "I'll take care of the matter." Soon after this, Rabbi Gershon visited the Baal Shem Tov in his village near Kitov and admonished him. But the Besht denied the accusation and said, "I never did any such thing, God-forbid." "Then where did you get the money," said Rabbi Gershon, "to buy new clothes for yourself and your wife?" "God gave it to me," said the Besht. Exasperated at what he considered to be the simple-minded piety of his brother-in-law, Rabbi Gershon said scornfully, "Why doesn't God give it to me?" "He doesn't give it to you," said the Besht, "but He does give to me." Rabbi Gershon said, "See that the *mochsin* doesn't inform on you to the manor house and have you beaten up." "I'm not afraid of him," replied the Besht.

The Baal Shem Tov knew that the money and everything he received, came to him from the hand of God, blessed be He. And if God protected him, what could the *mochsin* or any man do to him? So he feared no one except God. And no harm came to him from the *mochsin*, who never followed through on his threats, for God protects His servants who take refuge in Him.[68]

His Horse Returned

 AFTER SOME MONTHS, THE BAAL SHEM TOV EARNED ENOUGH MONEY, together with his brother-in-law's help, to buy another horse. But not long after-

---

* Agent of the feudal lord; tax collector.

ward, the new horse was stolen. Rabbi Gershon was angry at him for not properly guarding the animal. "The other horse dies and now this one is stolen!" He considered his brother-in-law a hopeless fool. The Besht was so totally absorbed in his *d'vekut* then that he could not deal with practical matters carefully, like a normal person. But God watches over His holy tzaddikim, who are distracted by their excessive love for Him and cannot always care for themselves, let alone their animals or possessions.

When Rabbi Gershon chided the Baal Shem Tov about the theft of the horse and the Besht felt himself cornered and wanted to escape from his brother-in-law, he blurted out, "They'll return my horse!" Hearing this, Rabbi Gershon thought him a greater fool than before. Every time the Besht visited Brody or Rabbi Gershon was in Kitov, Rabbi Gershon asked him sarcastically, "Israel, have the thieves returned your horse yet?"

The Baal Shem Tov had spoken without thinking, but by saying "they" would return his horse, he meant heaven, not the thieves. He believed with perfect faith that everything that happens is from God, blessed be He, as Job said: "The Lord gave and the Lord has taken away; blessed be the name of the Lord." Since God had decreed that the horse be taken away, He could also decree that it be returned. About two months later, a gentile on a horse rode up to the Besht's house, tapped on the window, and asked him to please bring out a light for his pipe. The Besht came out, recognized his horse, and said, "Isn't that my horse?" Immediately and without saying a word, the man got down from the horse and returned it to him. This was, again, Elijah the Prophet.

The Baal Shem Tov had said, under duress, that the horse would be returned, yet God fulfills the words of a tzaddik, even if they are spoken carelessly, as it says, "The tzaddik decrees and God, blessed be He, fulfills."[69]

S'micha *from Heaven*

THE BAAL SHEM TOV OFTEN EXPERIENCED REVELATIONS OF ELIJAH, who taught him the Torah's secrets and saved him in times of need. One day, when the Besht was alone in the forest, Elijah the Prophet and many angels appeared to him. Elijah asked the Baal Shem Tov to bow his head; then he laid his hands on the Besht's head, the angels lent their strength and support, and they together gave him *s'micha*, heavenly ordination, as a rabbi and teacher in Israel. Before Elijah left, he said to the Besht, "Much is expected from you." Later, the Besht wondered what Elijah was hinting at.[70]

Soul Revelation

THE BAAL SHEM TOV HAD ACHIEVED AWESOME REVELATIONS AND LEVELS in holiness. But more than visions of Elijah or the Torah's secrets, the Besht yearned to see God's light always and everywhere. He wanted to fully reveal his own soul, because the mystics teach that only when a person lives from the center of his being, his soul, can he meet the Source of his soul. The Besht was extremely sensitive to what raised or lowered his spiritual state, which he considered the subtle teachings of his own soul. His soul taught him that he had reached exalted spiritual levels not because of his study of the Talmud and halachic codes, but because of his fervent praying and his frequent use of the *mikvah* to prepare for prayer. He became aware of the limits of fasting, a typical ascetic practice for pious people and mystic aspirants at that time. The Besht realized that fasting and self-affliction were sometimes necessary when a person needed to repair something in his soul. But he saw that fasting usually depressed his spiritual state and weakened the intensity of his praying. Contrarily, immersing in the *mikvah* added power to his praying, so he could work with his body, rather than try to break or subdue it. The Besht also discovered that fasting usually produced an angry disposition. He thought, "If fasting and self-affliction make a person angry at his fellow men, how they can they advance him spiritually?" He came to realize that breaking the body through fasting and self-mortification was a path of darkness. He chose the path of light.

The Besht's soul also taught him that certain spiritual levels simply could not be reached through solitary devotions. He realized that when he acted selflessly to help another Jew, his heart opened. And the time he spent with children—particularly playing with his little daughter, Edel—opened his heart more than any praying or meditating. When he taught children or did a favor for a fellow Jew with self-sacrifice, not just with money but with his body, he found that he gained access to new spiritual realms. By opening himself to people, he became more open to God. So he acted with complete self-sacrifice for any Jew, even for someone whom he had never met.

Determined to achieve perfection, the Besht went deeper and deeper in his devotions: Torah study, prayer, psalms, and meditation at his secluded hut; loving service of human beings created in the divine image at the inn. He rejected the excessive fasting of the kabbalists and instead served God by elevating the "divine sparks" in the food, relating to the spiritual aspect of the food and of eating. Every time he sat down to eat, he ate as a sacred meal, meditating on the presence of the *Shechinah*—in his surroundings, at the table, in the life-energy entering him through the food, in the taste of the food, and in the pleasure of the experience. The kabbalists sacrificed their body and afflicted it with fasting and mortifications. The Besht cared for his body, but everything he did, all his spiritual practices, were with complete self-sacrifice. That was his key to revealing his soul: by being totally present to God at every moment, he gained an answering revelation of God's presence. When he prayed, he was ready to die after a few words and he took it as God's mercy that he lived to the end of the prayer. When he studied Torah or helped a Jew in need, he did so with single-minded devotion and all his energy.[71]

Self-sacrifice for Hand-washing

 ONCE, THE BESHT AND A COMPANION WERE TRAVELING TO A DISTANT town on a mission for the hidden tzaddikim and were on the road when the time came for *Minha*. When the Besht realized that they had forgotten to take along water to ritually wash their hands before prayer, he became very upset, as if the worst disaster had befallen him. As his companion looked on in amazement, the Besht cried out to heaven, with tears running down his cheeks, "Master of the world, why should I live if I don't have water to wash my hands before prayer?" According to Jewish law, one may clean one's hands by wiping them with any material, such as pebbles or earth, if water is not available, but the Besht could not be satisfied with allowances and leniencies; he wanted complete and pure divine service. Everything that the Besht did was with fervor and fire: He studied Torah with fire, he prayed with fire, he helped people with fire, he ate with fire. He served God with utter self-sacrifice, and that was why he attained what he attained.[72]

Loving God without the World-to-Come

THE BAAL SHEM TOV, LIKE OTHER TZADDIKIM, JUDGED HIMSELF strictly, to a hair's breadth. Therefore, he was humble and lowly, considering himself as never having properly served God, blessed be He. Because of this, he sometimes felt that he was far from God (God-forbid)!

The Besht once became so depressed that it seemed to him that he certainly would not have a portion in the World-to-Come. He could not think of a single redeeming quality he had or a single good deed he had ever done that was utterly pure. And he could find no way to inspire and enliven himself. But then he said, "I love God, blessed be He, even without a reward in the World-to-Come!"[73]

One Flutter of an Eyelash

THE BAAL SHEM TOV'S LOVE FOR GOD WAS SO INTENSE THAT HE CHERISHED any speck of divine service that he was able to perform. He used to say to his friends among the hidden tzaddikim, "One flutter of an eyelash for God's sake, makes the creation of the whole world worth while."[74]

Ahiyah Becomes His Spiritual Master

ALTHOUGH THE BAAL SHEM TOV EXERTED HIMSELF TO THE UTMOST to serve his Creator, in his humility he felt that everything he attained was ultimately due to the merit of his saintly parents, who had pleaded and prayed before the Throne of Glory that heavenly mercy be shown him and that he be granted exalted spiritual levels. He also felt that if he had a high soul it was due to their merits, not his own. But because of his constant devotion with self-sacrifice, it was decreed in heaven that the Torah's hidden light be revealed to him and that he be shown the way the Torah is studied in the Garden of Eden. The Besht was chosen to lead the Jewish people, and a special, exalted angelic teacher was appointed to teach him the Torah's innermost secrets. The Torah's hidden light would evoke the hidden light of his own soul.

One fall day, in the early afternoon on Friday, the Baal Shem Tov lay down for a nap to prepare for the Sabbath and fell into a deep sleep. In his dream he saw a venerable old man who said, "Israel, I have been sent from heaven to teach you. After *Shabbat*, on the first day of the week—which is your birthday, the 18th of *Elul*—wait for me in the mountains outside the city. I will meet you there to teach you. But tell no one about this, not even your wife, for you are forbidden to reveal anything until I give you permission to do so." When the Besht asked him his name, he said, "In time you will know it."

The old man disappeared and the Besht awoke. He thought it was merely a dream and there was no point in giving it heed. He went to the *mikvah* to immerse for the honor of the Sabbath, but when he put his head below the water and opened his eyes (as was his custom), he saw the old man in front of him. A holy fear and trepidation descended on him. When he came up from the water, he felt that he had become a different person, and that the holy spirit was hovering over him.

The Besht traveled to Kitov for that *Shabbat*. He prayed with the Pious of Kitov, a group of exceptionally devout scholars and kabbalists who were based in the town *kloiz*. At *Kabbalat Shabbat**, he saw that they were staring at him, but he did not know why. On the night of the Sabbath, as he slept, the old man appeared in his dream and said, "Do not think, my son, that this is just a dream. Everything you have seen is true. The proof is that on Sunday, when you go out of the city, you will meet me between two mountains." (He indicated to the Besht which place he meant.) "But before you leave the city, immerse in the *mikvah* four times, with holy intentions." Then he disappeared. When the Besht awoke, he realized that this was not a mere dream, but a heavenly vision.

During the Sabbath morning prayer service, they called him up to read the *haftorah* portion from the prophets. This made him wonder, for they had never honored him this way. At the third Sabbath meal, his brother-in-law, Rabbi Gershon, who was visiting Kitov, called him over and said, "Israel, your appearance has changed; your face looks different. Are you feeling well?" But the Besht did not reveal anything, as the old man had charged him. When he returned home at the conclusion of the Sabbath, and recited the hymn "*Eliyahu HaNavi*"after *havdala*¶, Chana asked him, "Why is your face so pale?" He did not reveal anything to her either.

Sunday was *hai Elul*, the Baal Shem Tov's birthday; he was twenty-six years old. The Besht followed the instructions he had been given. An hour before noon, he immersed in the *mikvah*, and immediately left for the designated meeting place between the mountains. Then the old man appeared and told the Besht to follow him. The old man

---

* The Friday night prayer service for welcoming the Sabbath.
¶ End-of-Sabbath ceremony that separates sacred from profane time.

led him into the entrance of a cave in the side of the mountain. They walked inside and came to an underground chamber, where there was a table and two chairs. The old man then took from a fold in his garment a copy of the holy *Zohar* that glowed in splendor and lit up the darkness. He handed the book to the Baal Shem Tov and told him to read it. When he began to do so, he felt a powerful influx of divine light into his soul. He was filled with a new wisdom: The pathways of heaven were shining before his eyes and the gates of understanding were flung wide open before him. Then the old man began to teach him. After two hours, the old man said, "My son, that is enough for today. With God's help, we will continue tomorrow. But be careful not to reveal anything about this to anyone." The Besht again asked his teacher's name, but the old man replied that the time for that had not yet arrived. He took the Besht by the hand, led him out of the cave, and accompanied him to the Besht's village near Kitov. Then he put his hands on the Besht's head and blessed him.

Every day, the old man taught the Baal Shem Tov, who did not know his master and teacher's name. One day in the middle of the summer, before parting at the entrance to the village, the old man told the Baal Shem Tov his name, and from the great fear and awe that descended on the Besht, at having merited being taught Torah by such a holy and awesome master—none other than Ahiyah ha-Shiloni—he fell to the ground from weakness. But with the help of God his strength returned.[75]

Ahiyah's Spiritual Lineage

IN THE CHAIN OF THOSE WHO RECEIVED AND TRANSMITTED THE concealed Torah, Ahiyah ha-Shiloni was the seventh generation: Moses received this secret Torah at Mount Sinai and passed it on to Joshua. Joshua transmitted it to Pinhas, and Pinhas to Eli, Eli to Samuel, Samuel to David, and David to Ahiyah. Ahiyah ha-Shiloni lived through all those previous generations. He saw Amram (Moses' father). He was a disciple of Moses and among those who made the Exodus from Egypt and was present at the splitting of the Red Sea. He was at the Giving of the Torah at Sinai, and sat in the religious court of David the King of Israel. He was the master and teacher of Elijah, the heavenly teacher of the mystics, and of Rabbi Shimon bar Yohai, the great mystic and author of the *Zohar*.[76]

The Besht's Teachers

THE BAAL SHEM TOV ATTAINED AWESOME KNOWLEDGE OF THE revealed and concealed Torahs*. His first teachers were his saintly parents. He

---

* Respectively, the Bible, Mishna, Talmud, halachic codes; and the Kabbalah.

then learned much Torah and Talmud from the hidden mystics, particularly from Rabbi Meir, his foremost earthly teacher, who also taught him Kabbalah. But the prophet Elijah ha-Tishbi was his heavenly teacher, until he merited being taught by Elijah's own teacher, namely, the prophet Ahiyah ha-Shiloni, who was his preeminent teacher and master. Later, the Besht would have an even greater heavenly teacher: the Messiah.

Ahiyah was called by the Besht: the *Baal Hai* (Master of Life), meaning that he won eternal life and lives forever; the name also means that he is a master of revealing the two highest of the five soul levels described in Kabbalah—*haya* and *yehida* (that is, *Baal Het"Yud*)*. *Haya* (living) and *yehida* (single) are the two soul levels in constant contact with God¶. Ahiyah helped the Baal Shem Tov to reveal those levels of his soul and to reach a perfection that few have attained. The Besht was a soul from the world of *Atzilut* (Nearness)§. When such a high soul attains revelation, all of its soul levels are in constant *d'vekut* with God. The first three soul levels of *Naran* (*Nun"Resh"Nun*)—*nefesh*, *ruach*, and *neshamah*—relate to the Torah of the head; the two highest soul levels of *Hai* (*Het"Yud*)—*haya* and *yehida*—relate to the Torah of the heart. The soul levels of *haya* and *yehida* permit one to comprehend the mystic Torah. When someone reveals the soul level of *yehida*, he attains prophecy and the holy spirit, and God, blessed be He, actually speaks with him. That is the level eventually attained by the Baal Shem Tov, when he reached perfection and heard Torah from the mouth of God Himself.[77]

Ahiyah Teaches Him Daily

EVERY DAY, AHIYAH TAUGHT TORAH TO THE BAAL SHEM TOV. HE BEGAN on the first day with the first verse of the Book of Genesis: "In the beginning, God created the heavens and the earth." Ahiyah taught him many mysteries of the revealed and concealed Torahs, including how the holy *Zohar* is studied in heaven. Every day, many changes occur in all the worlds and the meanings of the *Zohar* correspondingly change, with different interpretations each day. In the heavenly academy of the Holy One, blessed be He, in the Garden of Eden, souls of the tzaddikim and angels learn the *Zohar* each day with a new interpretation from the Holy One, blessed be He. That is what Ahiyah ha-Shiloni revealed to the Baal Shem Tov and what the Besht himself heard in the heavenly academy. Ahiyah taught the Besht theoretical Kabbalah and also practical Kabbalah, the secrets of working miracles. But the great mystics do not use divine Names for performing miracles except in special circumstances, in situations of great need.[78]

---

* The five levels are *nefesh*, *ruach*, *neshamah*, *haya*, and *yehida*—animating force, spirit, breath-soul, eternal life-force, singleness in union with the One.

¶ *D'vekut*.

§ The highest of the four worlds. See Glossary: Four Worlds.

The Besht Crosses the River

AHIYAH HA-SHILONI TAUGHT THE BAAL SHEM TOV THE MYSTIC USE of divine Names. Being young, the Besht desired to test his knowledge and see if he had the power to perform a miracle. So, uttering a divine Name, he lay his belt on the Dniester River and crossed over the water on it.

Immediately afterward, he realized his error in using a divine Name for no purpose, and he repented and fasted. He also vowed never to use a divine Name to perform a miracle unless directed by heaven to do so. But he felt that an impression of his transgression still remained. For many years after this incident, the Besht kept his sin before him and repented.[79]

Soul-Ascent

THE BAAL SHEM TOV HAD LEARNED ABOUT *ALIYAT NESHAMAH*, THE mystic soul-ascent, from Rabbi Adam Baal Shem's secret manuscript, and was told now by Ahiyah to apply what he had learned. Soul-ascent became his pinnacle spiritual practice. When a tzaddik is consumed with fervent devotion for God, his soul can ascend into heaven. That is one meaning of the story of the prophet Elijah ascending into heaven in a fiery chariot. In making a soul-ascent, the Besht first cleaved to the *Shechinah* with total devotion and became established in a trance state of God-consciousness. Then, by uttering an invocation, his soul exited from his body and ascended to heaven, where he encountered angels, deceased prophets, and sages, and received from them Torah secrets. When in the upper worlds, the Besht also learned of accusations against the Jewish people and appeared before the heavenly court to argue in their defense. In his earlier years, the Besht had declined to use this practice of soul-ascent, which, like the use of divine Names, is dangerous and only for a few of the spiritual elite. But now, under the guidance of Ahiyah, he began to visit the upper worlds. Whereas previously, Elijah and then Ahiyah came to teach him, now he could rise into heaven and seek them out, or seek out other heavenly teachers, when he desired.

Two Thrones

THE BAAL SHEM TOV, AT THIS TIME OF HIS LIFE, WAS STILL SEEKING THE correct way to serve God and he was often anxious and worried that perhaps he was not performing God's commandments in the proper way. His fear of sin was so excessive that he made himself depressed, as he was constantly troubled that he was not serving God as He deserved. He was particularly anxious about his Sabbath obser-vance, because the rules restricting work on the Sabbath are very intricate, and it is difficult to keep them all perfectly. Indeed, there are countless restrictions in the Torah; who can adhere to all the detailed halachic requirements without some fault or deficiency?

So one *Shabbat* he asked his master, the prophet Ahiyah ha-Shiloni, to show him the place in the Garden of Eden reserved for those who most perfectly observe the Sab-bath. The prophet accompanied the Besht on a soul-ascent and led him higher and higher, from one chamber to another in the heavenly palace, until they ascended to a place so high and exalted that even the angels are not permitted to enter. He saw what no eye ever had the privilege of seeing. In this exalted chamber were two glowing, golden thrones, inlaid with sparkling diamonds and other precious jewels.

The Baal Shem asked Ahiyah ha-Shiloni, "Master, for whom are these two thrones prepared?" Ahiyah replied, "One throne is for you, if you are wise, and the other is for a companion whom you must find." What he meant was that the Baal Shem would merit that throne if he followed the example of this other person's Sabbath ways and would become his companion in the Garden of Eden. The Rabbis teach that each per-son has a companion in paradise whose spiritual level somehow matches theirs.

That night, at the conclusion of the Sabbath after *havdala*, the Baal Shem set out to find this person who kept the Sabbath best. He prepared his horse and coach and trav-eled at once. Because the journey was so long, his master, Ahiyah, revealed to him for this single occasion the divine Name for shortening a journey, by which the earth con-tracted under his horse's racing hooves. After the Baal Shem Tov left the vicinity of the village, he dropped the reins and the horse went on its own, under divine guidance, to the place the Besht needed to go. He traversed enormous distances at miraculous speed. Although the coach flew like the wind, the destination was so far away that the journey still took days. The horse raced on and on; it flew over mountains and valleys, fields and forests, rivers and lakes, until the Besht arrived in a large, foreign city where no Jews resided. Finally, the horse stopped in front of a house on the outskirts of the city, a sign that this was the place the Besht was seeking.

The Besht knocked on the door and a man who appeared to be a gentile came out and greeted him. The Besht spoke to him in a foreign language and asked if he could stay with him for a few days. The man said yes and warmly welcomed the Besht into his home. The Besht soon noted, however, to his astonishment, that there seemed to be nothing Jewish about his host! He did not dress like a Jew, he ate nonkosher meat, he did not ritually wash his hands before eating, nor did he make blessings or pray. The Besht thought, "Will this person be my companion in paradise?"

But the Besht realized that if this was where his horse stopped, this must be the man who kept the Sabbath best! He *must* be holy, his holiness was simply very hidden. The Besht therefore decided to stay and observe the man carefully. But after the most thor-ough scrutiny, he realized to his dismay that there seemed to be nothing even remotely Jewish about the man, let alone holy!

The Besht spent the Sabbath there as well. After all, he had been told that this was the man who kept the Sabbath most perfectly! Needless to say, the Besht's own Sabbath was a great disappointment. There was no kosher food in the house (certainly not the traditional fish or *cholent**). All he could eat were a few dry loaves of bread that he had taken along for the trip. He was not able to read the Torah portion on the Sabbath, since there was no Torah scroll available. Although the Besht watched everything the man did very closely, he did not see a shred of Sabbath observance. This from the man who "kept the Sabbath best"! But on Saturday afternoon, his host gave a party for all his gentile friends. Men and women mixed together freely, eating, drinking, and dancing, as is the custom among gentiles; the men also smoked cigars! The host himself was in a happy mood, rushing about and doing everything possible to cheer up his friends. But what a miserable Sabbath for the Baal Shem, who, of course, did not participate in this raucous merriment! He became depressed, thinking, "Will this coarse person who is desecrating the Sabbath in every way possible, be my partner in the Garden of Eden?"

Discouraged and confused, the Besht was about to leave on Saturday night after making *havdala*. But before departing, he asked his host out of curiosity, "Why did you make that party earlier in the day?" The man said to him, "I'll tell you the truth: I'm a Jew, but I know nothing about Judaism. I was orphaned when I was a little boy and was raised by gentiles, who took me far away from where I was born. I remember only one thing about my parents: that every Saturday afternoon they made a big party for all their neighbors; they were very happy and did everything possible to make their neighbors happy. So I try to be a good Jew in the one way I know—by rejoicing on the Sabbath and making a party for my neighbors to make them joyful. That's all I know of Judaism, but I do it with all my heart!"

The Besht then realized that this man was indeed holy and had a true Jewish heart. He actually had an exalted soul. How many people taken from their Jewish home as he had been and raised in those circumstances would do what he did with such faith? The Besht wanted to return this great soul to its Jewish root and explain to him in detail all the laws of Sabbath observance and tell him how Jews really keep the Sabbath. But when he tried to open his mouth to speak, he felt something pressing down on his tongue. All the limbs of great tzaddikim are trained to do only God's will: Their eyes do not see what they should not see, their ears do not hear what they should not hear, and their tongue does not speak what should not be said. On reflection, the Besht realized that heaven was preventing him from speaking, for if this man would know the many Sabbath laws, how would he, with his meager background, ever be able to keep them all? As he was, he was holy, but if he learned all the many rules, he would never attain even an average observance. God was more pleased with the way he kept the Sabbath now, than if he changed his ways and abided by more of its laws. Now, he kept the Sabbath with all his heart, with holy simplicity and joy. He was actually a very high soul. If he knew the correct and traditional way to keep the Sabbath, he would never reach that level. His observance would fall short and, inevitably, the happiness that he

* Sabbath stew.

felt in the Sabbath, which he kept according to his own capacity of understanding, would disappear.

After this experience, the Baal Shem returned home and asked his master, Ahiyah ha-Shiloni, to show him the place reserved for those who keep the Sabbath the worst. This time, Ahiyah led him through barren deserts and past the Mountains of Darkness into a cave. They descended farther and farther down until they reached *Gehinnom*. Then they passed through dismal chambers, until they reached the lowest pit in *Gehinnom*. There, the Besht saw two black-as-coal thrones, smouldering and smoking and emanating an acrid odor. The Besht asked Ahiyah, "Master, for whom are these terrible thrones prepared?" Ahiyah replied, "One throne will be for you, if you are unwise, and the second will be for a companion whom you must find." If the Besht kept the Sabbath like this other person, he would inherit the second throne.

That same day, which was Friday, the Baal Shem set out to find this person who kept the Sabbath most poorly. He set off in his coach and let the horse go as it pleased. This time, the trip was short and before long he was in a nearby town, traveling through a densely populated Jewish neighborhood that was bustling with activity in preparation for the Sabbath. As his coach moved through the narrow streets, he saw Jews hurrying to and from the market, making their final purchases for the holy day. He could smell the odors of the Sabbath cooking—challah, gefilte fish, *cholent*—as he passed by. Finally, the horse came to a stop in front of a house from which the chanting of Torah study could be heard. When the Besht climbed down, he asked whose house it was and was told by someone on the street that this was the home of the town rabbi, a man who strictly adhered to the minutest details of Jewish law. The Besht knocked on the door and was let in by a servant, but could not speak to the rabbi, who was too engrossed in Torah study at his desk to look up and greet a guest. The Besht waited patiently for half an hour, until the rabbi finished his study session and looking up and noticing him, offered him a weak greeting. The Besht asked, "May I stay with you for the Sabbath?" The rabbi consented, ordered his servant to take care of the Besht's accommodations, and went back to his study—a cool greeting. Now, it is holy to study Torah uninterrupted, but did not Abraham interrupt his conversation with God Himself to greet three visitors?

That Sabbath was a miserable one for the Besht. Gloom and darkness reigned in the rabbi's house. The rabbi was so afraid of violating the prohibition of *muktzeh* (not to touch any forbidden object on the Sabbath) that he would not stretch out his hand, lest he accidentally touch a work implement, such as a pen. Now, this is certainly holy, but he went to extremes! He was so afraid of stepping on an ant (for one is forbidden to kill anything, even a noxious insect, on the holy Sabbath), that he would not stretch out his foot. This too is holy, but again he took it to extremes! As a result, he could not stretch out his hands or his feet, and he sat like a prisoner in his chair, with his arms crossed and legs tucked in, the whole Sabbath day.

The Besht understood why this rabbi's Sabbath observance caused displeasure in heaven and he wanted to explain to him how to truly keep the Sabbath—with joy! But when he opened his mouth to speak, no words came out and he felt something pressing down on his tongue. On reflection, he realized that heaven was preventing him from speaking. The Torah says that it is a *mitzvah* to instruct another person and to correct his behavior; but the Sages add that if you know that the person will not listen to you, it is a *mitzvah* to refrain from correcting him, for you will only cause strife. The rabbi was so proud of his Torah scholarship and certain of his own way that he would never have listened to correction.

From these two journeys, the Baal Shem Tov learned how important it is to observe the Sabbath and to do all the *mitzvot* with joy; and also that an excessive fear of sin, which produces worry and anxiety and deprives one of joy, gives no pleasure to God. From then on, the Besht always taught that God wants us to serve Him joyfully. One should never allow the fear of sin to stifle the great happiness one gets from Judaism.[80]

A Simple Man's Trust

AS A HIDDEN TZADDIK, THE BAAL SHEM TOV OFTEN WENT ON MISSIONS to help hard-pressed Jews in the villages—whether they were innkeepers, millers, or *mochsins*. At that time, the lord was an absolute ruler over his villages and lands. If one of his Jews failed to pay the rent, the lord had him severely beaten and often imprisoned him and his family; they would be thrown into a deep pit and left there to languish until someone redeemed them by paying their debt. The Besht, along with other hidden tzaddikim, collected donations and distributed the money to those in need—to pay the rent for their inn or mill, and also used the money for the great *mitzvah* of redeeming captives. The Baal Shem Tov knew the plight of debt-ridden innkeepers, since he and his wife also ran an inn.

Once, it was revealed to the Baal Shem Tov from heaven that in a certain place there was a man who never worried, because he had total trust in God. So the Baal Shem Tov traveled to meet him, to learn this pious quality. When the Besht arrived, the man, who was an innkeeper, gave him a warm welcome and a fine meal. During the meal, the Besht asked him, "What is your yearly rent?" "3000 *rheinish*," the man said. The Besht asked further, "Do you pay the whole sum in advance or at the end of the year?" "I pay at the end of the year," the man answered." In fact, the whole amount is due in eight days." "Do you have the money?" the Besht asked. "I don't have a penny," the man answered matter of factly. "Do you have any way to get the money? There's not much time left!" "I don't have any prospects at all." "What will you do, then?" the Besht asked. "Won't the lord throw you and your family in prison?" The Baal Shem Tov's host replied simply and calmly, "I trust in God, who has helped me to pay every year. He'll help me this year too, for 'His is the silver and His is the gold'—and He gives it to whomever He pleases." Wanting to test the man, the Besht said, "What will you do if you can't get the money? The lord will punish you, God-forbid. Wouldn't it be wise to borrow the amount you need before the deadline?" "Isn't it better to trust in God," replied the innkeeper, "than to depend on a man of flesh and blood?"

The Baal Shem Tov decided to remain with this pious innkeeper, to see how things would turn out. He stayed in the man's house for the week and was treated with the same graciousness as on the day he arrived. He also noticed that his host's brow showed not the least trace of worry. He was as untroubled as a wealthy man with large sums of money in the bank.

Two days before the deadline, a servant came from the lord's house, shouting at the innkeeper that he better have the money ready. When the innkeeper heard the servant yelling, he answered back, "Why is the lord harassing me now! Aren't there two days left? I'll pay him the full amount before the deadline!" When the Baal Shem Tov heard this, he was surprised and asked him if he had found some source of money. "I just trust in God," said the man. "I'm certain I'll have the money when I need it."

On the day payment was due, the lord's servant returned at the break of dawn, yelling, "Today's the day! Where's the 3000 *rheinish*?" "I have until sunset to pay," the man replied. "Why are you harassing me now?" "Do you have the money?" asked the Besht. "No," he said. "Where can you get 3000 *rheinish* today?" asked the Besht. "Watch," he replied, "and you'll see that God will help me." There was not the slightest sign of anxiety or worry on his face. He then went to pray, and acted as if it were any ordinary day. After the prayers, they were sitting in his house when they heard knocking at the door. The Baal Shem Tov reacted, but the innkeeper was utterly calm. Three merchants were at the door and said to him, "We want to buy a large quantity of grain from the lord"—and they specified the number of measures of wheat, barley, and spelt they needed. "Since we know that he's a hard man and difficult to deal with, we thought that you might act as a middleman for us. We've heard that he holds you in high regard." "How much are you willing to pay per measure?" he asked. They specified a price for each kind of grain. "Good," he said. "You'll be able to buy everything you need from the lord, maybe even at better prices than what you're willing to pay. But I want to earn a profit of 3000 *rheinish* for myself." "What?" said the merchants. "Isn't it enough if you make 500 *rheinish* from the deal?" But he would not give in. "I won't accept a penny less than 3000!" So the merchants went elsewhere. Meanwhile, the Besht was astonished to see that the man showed not the least regret that they left. "Listen, my friend," said the Besht. "Wouldn't it be better for you to take the 500 *rheinish*? What will you lose by that?" "That won't get me the 3000 I need," he answered. "If God, blessed be He, sends me 3000—well and good; but if not, what do I need the 500 *rheinish* for?"

As the evening deadline approached, two servants came from the lord, yelling, "Give us the money!" "I'll deliver it myself!" he answered, and taking his walking stick in his hand, he set off for the manor house. The Baal Shem Tov, who was astonished at this, followed, to see the end of the matter. As they were on the way he asked him, "Did you somehow get the money to pay him?" "God will help me," the man said, "but the truth is, I don't have a penny." As they were walking down the road, the merchants, who were coming back in the other direction, met them. They had gone to other villages and were not able to buy what they needed. When they saw the innkeeper, they told him that they were willing to give him a 1000 *rheinish* commission. Saying that he would not take less than 3000 *rheinish*, he walked right past them and continued on his way to the lord's house. Since the merchants knew that even if they gave him the 3000, the grain would still be cheaper than what they would have to pay elsewhere, they ran after him. Meanwhile, he was walking, staff in hand, to pay the lord, when he did not have a penny to his name—but he had a lion's heart, serene and untroubled! When they caught up with him, they tried to bargain with him, saying, "Will you take 1500? . . . 2000?" He told them, "I won't take a penny less than 3000!" So they finally agreed to give it to him, on condition that they would be able to buy all the grain at the price he had quoted. He told them that whatever price the lord asked, they should offer less than what they had agreed upon, and he would compromise between them, and the final price would be what he had told them. And so it was. The innkeeper went with the merchants to the lord, who welcomed him graciously. They soon began to talk about the purchase, and the lord asked for a higher price than the innkeeper had set for them, and they offered less. Then, acting as a middleman, he suggested the price he had set, as a compromise. "If my innkeeper says that's fair," said the lord, "I won't demand more." The merchants counted out the money to the lord, gave the 3000 *rheinish* to the innkeeper, and they all went home satisfied. The Baal Shem Tov also went home, thinking, "How great is trust in God, when you trust Him completely!" From this memorable incident, the Besht learned never to worry about money or other material conditions, but to be calm and to completely rely on God.[81]

The Besht Summons the Satan

THE BAAL SHEM TOV ONCE SUMMONED THE SATAN, BY MYSTICAL MEANS, to this world. The Adversary appeared to him in the form of a large black dog that stood up on its hind legs outside his window and growled to him furiously, "You putrid drop, why were you not afraid to call me to this world? I've only rarely been here: when Adam ate from the forbidden fruit; at the sin of the Golden Calf; at the destruction of the two Temples. Otherwise, my work is done through agents." "I'm not afraid of anyone, except the Holy One, blessed be He!" replied the Baal Shem Tov. "What do you want?" barked the Satan. "I want you to give me the key to piety!" demanded the Besht.

Why would the Baal Shem Tov seek the key to piety from the Satan? The Rabbis teach that to achieve spiritual perfection a person must serve God not only with his good inclination, but with his bad side as well, turning all his evil tendencies to good uses, turning lust into divine love, anger at others into anger at his lower nature, pride of self into pride at being a servant of God. The Besht sought this secret of transformation from the Satan, who is the outer manifestation of the inner evil inclination. Why would the Satan accommodate him? According to the Rabbis, the Satan himself does all his work in God's commission, for the sake of heaven, and wants to be defeated. But he is not easily conquered!

When the Besht boldly asked for the key to piety, the Satan was still seething with anger at having been summoned by a mere human. He refused to reveal his secret and was about to return from whence he had come. Seeing this, the Besht sought to pacify the Satan's rage and gazed at him compassionately. The Satan stared back and, seeing the Besht's shining forehead and saintly appearance, was soothed. He gave the Besht the secret he sought, whispering to him how to totally transform his lower nature. Then, instead of leaving, he said gently, "Son of the living God, permit me to stay a while longer, to gaze at the divine light on your face."

When a person's ways please God, the whole creation will be pleased with him. When he fulfills the purpose for which he was created, even his enemies will make peace with him. The Baal Shem Tov could treat his lower nature harshly for the sake of God. But he was also able to gaze compassionately on his chief enemies—the Satan and his own evil inclination—and that won him the great prize of true piety.[82]

A Village Tailor's Psalms Save a Settlement

WHEN THE BAAL SHEM TOV ONCE BECAME AWARE OF A HEAVENLY decree that a certain Jewish settlement would be destroyed, he summoned two of his fellow hidden tzaddikim, Rabbi Mordechai and Rabbi Kehot, to form a *beit din** and consider how they might nullify it. But when he made a soul-ascent in their presence, he saw that the decree was final and could not be changed. On his return descent through the different heavenly palaces, he saw a brilliant light emanating from one of them. He investigated within and found that this was the palace prepared as a heavenly reward for a certain Jewish tailor, who had memorized the whole Book of Psalms and recited it five times each day as he worked. It was the letters of his psalms that were sparkling with such a dazzling light in that palace.

After completing his soul-ascent, the Baal Shem Tov immediately traveled to visit that tailor and said to him, "If you knew that by using your merit in the World-to-Come you could save a Jewish settlement, would you do so?" "If I have a portion in the World-to-Come," the tailor replied, "I willingly give it as a gift to save that settlement." That moment, the decree was nullified.

The Baal Shem Tov knew that the simple piety of ordinary people was highly valued in heaven, and that sometimes the merit of a simple person could elicit divine mercy when even the Besht and his hidden mystic comrades could not annul a heavenly decree.[83]

Ahiyah Teaches the Besht How to Talk

EVERY DAY, AHIYAH TAUGHT THE BAAL SHEM TOV TORAH AND ALSO spiritual practices, including practices for speech. It is a very high spiritual level to maintain one's *d'vekut*—to be in the immediate presence of God—while conversing

* Religious court.

with people. Ahiyah taught the Besht how, when talking with someone, he should consider himself as if talking to God. If he asked a favor from someone, he should actually ask it—as a prayer—of God. Or, when he conversed, he could think that it was God's power and vitality, the *Shechinah*, that was giving him the ability to talk, and the same was true for the other person; the *Shechinah* was speaking through him too. Thus, the Besht achieved equanimity by considering his speech and the other person's speech as coming from one mind (for according to the mystic teachings, all souls are one, and parts of the *Shechinah*), and he could hear what the other person said as a heavenly message spoken to him by God (regardless of the other person's intention).

Ahiyah also taught the Baal Shem Tov to train himself to elevate other people's conversation to its heavenly root. When someone else was speaking about a worldly matter, such as a desire, a love, for food, the Besht would remind himself of his love for God; when the other person was speaking about his fear of sickness, the Besht reminded himself of his fear and awe of God, and so on.

The Besht found it particularly difficult to have *d'vekut* when he had to converse about or deal with worldly matters. So Ahiyah directed him to practice this, for example, by buying something even when he had no need, in order to work on maintaining his *d'vekut* while doing it. Another technique the Besht used when speaking to someone about a worldly matter, was to consider himself like a person who had left his home and, all the while he is away, is constantly thinking about when he will return. "God is our true 'home,'" said Ahiyah, "and when you have to deal with worldly matters, you should be thinking of your desire to turn your full attention back to Him as soon as possible." Ahiyah ha-Shiloni taught the Besht these and many other spiritual practices for how to have a constant, devotional awareness of God's presence in all his activities—to fulfill the verse: "Know Him in all your ways."

As the Baal Shem Tov progressed spiritually and his God-consciousness became more and more profound, for a period of time he even became unable to talk with people about mundane matters, because of his great *d'vekut* with God, blessed be He. When he tried to speak, he talked incoherently. This was especially the case before *Shabbat* when his mood elevated and his mind soared into the upper worlds. Whereas formerly it had been difficult for him to maintain his high level of God-awareness when speaking to people, he now had the opposite problem: He could not turn his attention to converse with people because of his intense *d'vekut*. But his master Ahiyah directed him to recite, every day, Psalm 119, which begins: "Happy are those whose way is pure," and a number of other special psalms. He also taught the Besht several other practices so that he would be able to converse even while in an elevated spiritual state. As a result, the Besht could once again converse with people normally, without his *d'vekut* being disturbed.

Most tzaddikim must work to keep their minds above in *d'vekut*; but the Baal Shem Tov eventually reached the exalted level that he had to force his mind down to focus on something worldly. Ahiyah taught him how to lower his mind to this world. After much prayer and fasting to achieve this, the Besht attained a still more exalted spiritual level where his mind was so expanded that a worldly affair took up very little space; he could deal with it and yet not be disturbed, no more than a pebble makes waves in the ocean.[84]

He Sees Godliness Within and Without

ONE DAY, AHIYAH ASKED THE BAAL SHEM TOV TO IMMERSE IN THE nearby Prut River, eighteen times. Then he kept the Besht in the cave, as they studied, for three days and nights without any food. At the end of three days, at dawn, Ahiyah led the Besht outside by the hand. He put his hands on the Besht's head and blessed him, saying, "May your eyes be opened to see the Truth!" Then, Ahiyah disappeared. Standing outside the cave, the Besht felt the most intense yearning for God he had ever known; his soul and body were shattering for God, his whole being ached for God. Then, suddenly, his eyes revealed a new light, more powerful than a thousand suns. Everywhere he looked, he saw God's light shining out through everything. The sky, the trees, the stones, the earth beneath his feet, the very air—were all Godliness, shimmering with divine vitality. Waves of joy thrilled his body. He saw God with his physical eyes. He saw Godliness first and everything else afterward, by the way. It was clear to him: God is everything and everything is God. Even as a boy, the Besht had believed in the kabbalistic teaching that "God fills all worlds and surrounds all worlds; His glory fills the earth and there is no place where He is not present." Indeed, the Besht had for a long time seen the divine reality. But now he saw it with greater intensity and without cease. He knew and saw that God is more real than the world, for He is the essence of all that exists. Every tree, every stone is Godliness; there is nothing but Him. "Everything above and below is One!" he whispered to himself. From that day on, the Baal Shem Tov was established in God-awareness. He realized that he was surrounded by Godliness and that God was within and without. He knew clearly that everything that exists is constantly being created by God and everything that happens is from God. Even every movement of his, every feeling, every thought, was also from God. He saw God in all things and heard God in all sounds. He heard the divine voice in the rustling of tree leaves, in the flowing sounds of the river, in the singing and chirping of birds. When he listened to the inner sound that his ears heard, he heard the voice of God, which enlivened and brought into being the sound he was hearing. He felt at every moment that God was with him. His bliss was boundless.[85]

He Reveals the Levels of His Soul

ACCORDING TO THE KABBALAH, THERE ARE FIVE WORLDS AND FIVE corresponding soul levels: the worlds (from lower to higher) of *Asiyah, Yetzirah, Briyah, Atzilut, Adam Kadmon* (Action, Formation, Creation, Nearness, Cosmic Man); and the soul levels of *nefesh, ruach, neshamah, haya, yehida* (animating, spirit, breath-soul, life-force, singular). The holy *Zohar* says: "When a person merits it, he is given a *nefesh*, then a *ruach*, then a *neshamah*, then a *neshamah l'neshamah* [soul of the soul, which is another name for *haya*]." The Baal Shem Tov revealed each of these soul levels in turn. When he had revealed the soul of his soul from the world of *Atzilut*, he attained a complete awareness of Godliness within and without.[86]

The Besht Finds God in Nature

THE BAAL SHEM TOV EXPERIENCED GOD'S PRESENCE VERY POWERFULLY in Nature. He often traveled by foot through fields and woods, gazing in awe as he went, at the world's many wonders, reveling in the beauty of God's creation, the work of His hands. The Besht rejoiced with all his being in the majesty of the sky, the sun by day and the moon and stars at night. He listened with open ears to birds singing praises to their Creator and to the lowing and bleating of herds of cows and flocks of sheep exulting in the fields. He bent his ear to hear the "speech of palm trees" and songs from the mystic Book of Songs, *Perek Shira*. At these moments, his soul was filled with love for God and for all His creatures on the face of the earth. He rejoiced with God between the blue sky overhead and the green grass beneath his feet. Sometimes he was so entranced by his surroundings that he began to sing, and it seemed to him as if the heavens and earth and all they contained—the trees, grass, birds, and animals, even the stones—sang with him. His ear caught the chirping of the birds and the buzz of the bees; it seemed as if the spirit of God was moving in waves through all animals, all plants, even all inanimate creation. At times of ecstasy like this, he felt nullified before the infinite light of God. Feeling the divine wind pass through him, he sang to the living God "who has all this in His world." Often, unable to bear the intensity of his longing, he prostrated on the ground, amidst the grass that also humbly bends and prostrates when a strong wind passes over it.*

Once, after traveling in the countryside under the open sky for a number of days, on a mission for the hidden tzaddikim, the Besht stopped in a town and went to the *beit midrash* to study Torah. Inside, he suddenly felt depressed and realized why. The rabbi of the town came over, introduced himself, and started a conversation with the visitor. The Besht innocently revealed to the rabbi that he experienced a feeling of great expansiveness outdoors, that he found God in Nature and felt that seeing natural beauty purified his soul in a mysterious way. The rabbi was critical and said, "Who gave you permission to create a new path in Judaism? Didn't our ancestors purify their souls by studying Torah and doing *mitzvot*? Why do you need to view the creation to purify your soul?" "This is not a new path to God at all," replied the Besht. "Didn't our Sages say in the Talmud, 'When someone goes outside in the month of *Nissan* and sees trees in new bloom, he should say: "Blessed is God who lacks nothing in His world and created beautiful creatures and trees to benefit and delight human beings"?' When I'm out in the wide fields, I realize how poor language is to express even the least bit of the holy feelings that pass through my heart then. Only singing can convey a little of the ecstasy and joy I experience. When I turn my ear to hear the speech of all creation, I learn to know the One who spoke and created the world, and to love Him and every part of His creation, without exception or distinction. That's the meaning, I think, of

---

* The Hebrew *ruach* means both "wind" and "spirit."

Perek Shira, which our early Sages composed; that is the secret of the 'language of birds and animals,' which King Solomon knew; that is the 'language of the palm trees,' which Rabbi Yohanan ben Zakkai understood. The Midrash says on the verse: 'no shrub* of the field was yet in the earth . . . because there was yet no man to till the soil'—All the trees are as if speaking to each other; all the trees are as if speaking to human beings.' How happy is our lot if we understand the speech of the trees, the palms, the shrubs, and grasses, because they all tell one thing: the glory of the one and only God, blessed be He and blessed be His name, the Creator of heaven and earth!"

Despite the Baal Shem Tov's enthusiastic explanation, the rabbi was unconvinced by his views, and the Besht left, considering their encounter as he went. He realized how difficult it is for a scholar whose whole life is lived within the four walls of the *beit midrash*, whose religious ideal is to just sit and study for as many hours as possible, to understand his love for Nature and appreciate his path up the mountain of God.[87]

Elevating the Creation

ONCE, DURING THE SUMMER, THE BESHT WAS TRAVELING ON ANOTHER mission for the hidden tzaddikim and had to spend *Shabbat* alone in an isolated area. During the late afternoon of a warm day, when he welcomed the holy Sabbath outside in a field, the sheep grazing there gathered around him. They all stood on their hind legs, like people, lifting their forelegs to heaven and bleating all the while he prayed. By his prayer, the Baal Shem Tov elevated all the lower levels of creation, until even the animals had the understanding to recognize their Creator—so they all cried out to God with him.[88]

The Besht Is Chosen as Leader and Perceives the Limitations of the Camp of Israel

ON HIS DEATHBED, BEFORE HE DIED, RABBI ADAM BAAL SHEM HAD conveyed to the leading figures of the movement of hidden tzaddikim that Rabbi Israel ben Eliezer should one day—at the time of their choosing—succeed him as head of their society, the Camp of Israel. For years, this information was kept from the Baal Shem Tov, while he served on a committee of three that acted in place of a single leader. Finally, the other senior figures in the movement decided that the time was right and the Besht was made the sole leader of the hidden tzaddikim; he was then thirty years old.

The leaders of the movement hoped that Rabbi Israel would add new vigor to their

* *Siah*. The word for "shrub" also means "speech."

attempt to spread the teaching of Torah, *musar*, and Kabbalah even to isolated areas of Poland and beyond. He had many tools with which to work. By this time, the Camp of Israel was highly organized and there were strong links between its members. They had established centers from which to conduct their propaganda, in many different places. Each hidden tzaddik worked in his center and from time to time sent detailed reports to the Baal Shem Tov.

For the next six years, the Baal Shem Tov worked diligently to improve the movement's efforts to reach and benefit the masses of Jews. He was both energetic and effective. During this time he continued to refine his religious thinking and his message, but he also pondered the very nature of the Camp of Israel as a secret society. Having taken over the leadership and responsibility for the movement as a whole, the Baal Shem Tov began to be acutely aware of its limitations. The Besht had spent years traveling on missions for the hidden tzaddikim and living among the common people while working at various kinds of jobs. He had met and intimately knew the Jewish people, from their water-carriers and woodcutters to their rabbis and scholars. The Baal Shem Tov's heart ached because of the terrible suffering and degradation, both material and spiritual, of the Jewish people and because of the suffering of the *Shechinah* in exile—for the *Shechinah* was cast down in the dust. He was zealously engaged, heart and soul, in the noble work of the hidden tzaddikim, but he finally realized that, although they had accomplished great things, so much was beyond their grasp! The strict secrecy of the hidden tzaddikim placed burdensome restrictions on their freedom of activity, and hindered their ability to propagandize and to organize the simple people. The movement's kabbalistic focus also reduced its effectiveness in spreading their message of devotion and piety, for the Kabbalah is so intellectually demanding that only an elite can master it. The Besht decided that what was required was a presentation of the Kabbalah's wisdom in a way that everyone could understand. After all, he thought, if a child cannot understand something, how can it be the Torah's essence? Had not he himself received the essential mystic teachings from his father when he was still only a child? What were they? They were simple: to love God, to do His will, and to be aware of Him at every moment! With this compact but potent teaching, he could initiate the simple people into the threshold of mysticism. Had not Elijah told him that the pious utterances of the simple innkeeper and innkeeperess were in certain ways more spiritually powerful even than the meditations of the great kabbalists? Love, he realized, is the key. Love of God, the Torah, and the Jewish people is everything; the rest is commentary.

The Besht also realized that the asceticism prevalent in kabbalistic and *musar* teaching was not the prescription needed for the ills of his generation. The Jewish people were suffering from antisemitic persecution and a desperate economic situation. They had absorbed blow after blow and were already terribly afflicted. By telling them to afflict themselves to repent, they were only being pushed into despair and hopelessness. Instead, they needed to be encouraged and inspired, given new hope and new joy.

The Besht yearned to help lead his beloved Jewish people back to the joy of closeness to their Father in Heaven. He had himself tasted the divine fruit of the Tree of Life. How could he keep that happiness for himself? He wanted to cry out to his brothers and sisters, "Taste and see that the Lord is good!" He felt that he must reveal himself and set up the Eternal's banner on the highest hill. But concealment and modesty were so deeply ingrained in him from the holy training he had received from his parents and the hidden tzaddikim! What is purer than divine service in secrecy? Is not piety soiled by being exposed? Is not pride the greatest threat to sincere devotion? So he doubted his own motives in wanting to lead openly and could not break with the path established by the hidden tzaddikim. But his inner struggle continued.[89]

Ahiyah Tells Him He Must Reveal Himself

AHIYAH HA-SHILONI, THE *BAAL HAI*, BEGAN TEACHING THE BAAL SHEM TOV on his twenty-sixth birthday, and continued for ten years. He had started with the first verse of Genesis in the Five Books of Moses: "In the beginning, God created the heavens and the earth," and now finished with the last words of its final verse: "in the sight of all Israel." Then Ahiyah laid his hands on the Baal Shem Tov's head and gave him a heavenly *s'micha* as a leader for the ages. And he told the Baal Shem Tov, on his thirty-sixth birthday, that the time had come for his light to be revealed in the sight of all Israel.[90]

The Besht Refuses to Be Revealed

THE BAAL SHEM TOV RESISTED HIS MASTER'S REQUEST AND REFUSED to be revealed, saying he had chosen for himself the way of a hidden tzaddik. Moreover, he was troubled by what Ahiyah said, and asked him how he had fallen lower than his comrades who were allowed to remain hidden. Was he being punished by being asked to reveal himself? If it was necessary that someone act as a leader of the whole Jewish people, certainly many others, better than he, could be found. Although the Besht had been chosen as leader of the hidden tzadikim, humility pervaded his personality. He was so modest, he was hidden even among the hidden tzaddikim, who did not know his true greatness. And he did not consider himself worthy to be the singular leader of his own generation, let alone beyond that!

As the Baal Shem Tov wrestled with Ahiyah's demand and his own inner doubts, he was also disturbed by the realization that if he were revealed, there would inevitably be scandals and disputes; he would arouse opposition and have opponents who would try to swallow him alive, without any provocation. Although his heart trusted in God's mercies (which had never forsaken him and never would), why did he need all this trouble? Was he not happy as he was—separated from worldly vanities, living in a spiritual paradise of his own and studying secretly with his holy master and teacher every day? His leadership of the Camp of Israel was a great task, but he still had a private existence. If he were revealed, he could expect only trouble and suffering. His master told him, however, that the heavenly decree was signed and sealed: At thirty-six years of age, he must be revealed. When the Besht continued to refuse, Ahiyah told him, "The light you have attained through a life of concealment and solitude does not compare to the light you will attain by revealing yourself and working with the larger community, because the Holy One, blessed be He, desires a dwelling place in the lower world. Moreover, the decision of the heavenly court is final. If you do not agree to what is asked of you, you have nothing more to do in this life, God-forbid, for the whole purpose of your soul's descent to this world was to be revealed, so that the fountains of your teaching would flow outward. If you refuse to fulfill your divine mission, you will end up as a robber waylaying travelers in the forest! And if you think yourself happy, studying with me secretly," said Ahiyah, "I tell you that you will not see my face again until you agree to the divine decree."

It was not easy for the Besht to oppose his heavenly master, but he felt that Ahiyah's command was a test—for him to refuse the personal honor and glory that would come with being revealed and to steadfastly cling to the modesty and secrecy that were the rule among the hidden tzaddikim. Yet his heart also yearned to save his beloved Jewish people from their religious decline and degradation! What if his being revealed was necessary for that task? What if the test was whether he could give up his desire for modesty in the service of God?

The great struggle of the Baal Shem Tov against becoming the unique leader of Israel, was similar to the struggle of Moses—who did not want to accept the holy mission of being Israel's redeemer from the Egyptian exile—for the Baal Shem Tov was the Moses of Hasidism.[91]

God's Desire That He Be a Leader

FINALLY, THE BAAL SHEM TOV COULD NO LONGER RESIST, EITHER HIS own inner promptings or the demands of his master, Ahiyah. His burning desire to save the Jewish people overcame his doubts about his motives and his concern about his own fate. He confided to his wife Chana, "It has been decreed in heaven that I become the leader of Israel." "What will you do?" she asked. "We must fast," he replied, "and plead for God's help." The two of them fasted night and day for three days, and lay prostrate on the floor in supplication, until they were weak and exhausted. On the evening, when the third day was coming to a close, the Baal Shem Tov heard a heavenly proclamation, "My son, go and lead the people. Do not delay your revelation, for the world needs you." The Besht rose to his feet and said to his wife, "If it is God's will that I lead the people of Israel, I must accept it."[92]

Ahiyah Tells Him of the Previous Incarnation of His Soul

AFTER THIS, AHIYAH APPEARED TO THE BAAL SHEM TOV AND REVEALED to him the previous incarnation of his soul. He said, "In the year 1573 there lived in the holy city of Tzfat* in Israel a simple Jew who knew only how to pray, not to study Torah; but he was pure in his deeds and modest and hidden in his ways.

"One night, after completing *Tikkun Hatzot*¶, he heard a knock on the door. To his question, 'Who's there?' he heard a heavenly voice answer, 'Elijah the Prophet, may he be remembered for good.' He opened the door and Elijah the Prophet entered his room, which became filled with light and joy. 'I have come to reveal to you the year of the coming of the Messiah,' said Elijah. 'But there is a condition: that you tell me what you did on the day of your becoming bar mitzvah that led the heavenly court to rule that you merited that I appear to you to reveal divine secrets.' 'What I did then I did only for God's glory. How can I reveal it to others? If for this reason you can't tell me what you were sent to reveal, so be it; it's not necessary. Because I have a tradition that what a Jew does for God should be hidden from the eyes of humans. It should be just for the Holy One, blessed be He, alone.'

"Elijah, of blessed memory, disappeared and ascended to heaven, where there was a great commotion. They were impressed by this man's sincere piety, that he rebuffed Elijah the Prophet and his offer to reveal the End and the time of the Messiah's coming, because he wanted to act for the sake of heaven alone. The heavenly court considered the matter and ruled that Elijah the Prophet should appear to this tzaddik again in Tzfat; he should teach him Torah and reveal to him secrets. This simple Jew became unique in his generation, a pure tzaddik, hidden in his pious modesty, so that no one knew of his greatness and holiness.

"The day came when he was elderly and passed away to the next world. After discussion and argument, the heavenly court decided that his reward would be to descend again to this world, and heaven would this time force him to reveal himself. And through him a new path would be revealed—to establish and revive the world with a spirit of purity and a spirit of holiness, and a new light would shine in each and every heart, and through him God's name would be sanctified and the earth filled with divine knowledge that would hasten the End. You," said Ahiyah to the Baal Shem Tov, "are that soul."[93]

Serving the Great Torah Scholars

AT THIS TIME, THE BAAL SHEM TOV WAS TOLD FROM HEAVEN THAT before his revelation he still needed to fulfill the *mitzvah* of personally serving the eminent Torah scholars of the generation. The Rabbis say that personally serving

---

* Safed.
¶ Midnight lamentation prayer service and vigil. See Glossary.

Torah scholars is more spiritually potent than studying with them. So the Besht traveled to the town of Zholkov in Reissen (near Lvov), to the greatest Torah scholar of the generation, the *gaon*, Rabbi Ephraim Zalman Shor, the author of *Tevu'ot Shor*. But when he arrived, the *gaon*—who was exceedingly humble and would not accept personal service from anyone—did not allow the Baal Shem Tov to serve him. After the Besht was there for a few days, Rabbi Ephraim Zalman dozed off for a moment, and his pipe became extinguished. The Besht went over and relit it, saying, "At least I merited to serve the *gaon* of the generation while he slept."

From there, the Besht traveled south in Reissen to visit Rabbi Yitzhak of Drohobitch, the tzaddik of the generation, who was greatest in righteousness and holiness. Rabbi Yitzhak received him, and said, "When a Jew gets enjoyment from doing a favor for another Jew, why should I deprive him of his pleasure?" Once, the Baal Shem Tov served Rabbi Yitzhak a cup of tea. When Rabbi Yitzhak finished the tea, the Besht returned the cup to the kitchen. The *rebbetzin** asked him, "I can understand why you wanted to serve my holy husband, but why did you have to trouble yourself to remove the empty cup?" He replied, "On Yom Kippur, after the high priest used the spoon and incense bowl in his holy service in the Temple, he returned them to their place; so did I do."

Finally, the Baal Shem Tov went to visit the Maggid of Brody, Rabbi Ephraim, the son of the Hacham Tzvi, who was the sage of the generation, excelling in wisdom. Rabbi Ephraim was sickly and weak. It was a harsh winter, and the rabbi, who was desperately poor and could not afford to keep his house heated all the time, suffered greatly from the cold. The Baal Shem Tov arrived wearing a heavy fur coat like the peasants wore, yet even he was cold. "It's freezing in here," he said to the rabbi, "We have to light the stove." "I have a little wood," answered Rabbi Ephraim, "but it's not ready to be used. I don't have anyone to chop it up." "I chop wood for a living," said the Besht, who was concealing himself and posing as a simple laborer. So he got up, chopped some of the wood, and lit the stove.

The *rebbetzin*, who was not in the house then, returned a few minutes later and was surprised to find the house heated. Seeing that some of the little wood that they had left was missing, and had been used for heating, when she needed it for cooking, she began to scream, "Who wasted the wood?" When she saw the Baal Shem Tov and realized that he had lit the stove, she took a broom and wanted to chase him out of the house. Suddenly, Rabbi Ephraim saw a pillar of fire above the Besht's head, and trembled. He cried out to his wife, "Stop! Stop! If you touch even a hair of his head, the world will return to *tohu v'vohu*¶, for his name is great in heaven!"

When she left the room, Rabbi Ephraim said to the Besht, "I realize now that you are destined to be the leader of this generation and that your words are heeded in heaven. Therefore, I beg you not to be angry with my wife. Our terrible poverty has made her bitter and irritable. I beg you to excuse her; she's not a bad person." The holy

---

* A rabbi's wife.
¶ The emptiness and void before Creation; that is, the world would be destroyed.

Baal Shem Tov, who was compassionate and forgiving, reassured him and, after engaging in an animated Torah conversation with the rabbi, left and went to his village near Kitov.[94]

The Besht's Light Is Revealed by Rabbi David of Kolomaya

AT HOME, THE BESHT'S WIFE CHANA CONTINUED TO RUN THE INN, while he secluded himself throughout the week, studying Torah with his master, Ahiyah ha-Shiloni. On Friday he returned home for the Sabbath. From time to time, when there were guests staying at their inn, the Besht's wife called for him and he came and served them.

One day, as was the custom of many rabbis, Rabbi David, the Maggid of Kolomaya, was traveling through the local villages before Hanukkah to collect *tzedaka** money for the poor. He took a wrong turn, however, and ended up at the Baal Shem Tov's house when night was coming on. The Besht was not at home then, being engaged in divine service at his secluded hut, and his wife received the guest warmly and graciously. The rabbi asked the Besht's wife where her husband was, and she, to protect his secret, answered that he had gone to help the *mochsin* water the animals and would be back soon. The *maggid*, who was hungry, asked her what there was to eat. She told him that her husband had slaughtered a chicken that day. If he inspected the knife and approved it, she would make him some chicken soup. She showed him the knife and, when he approved, began to make the soup. Then she went off quietly to inform her husband that they had a guest.

The Baal Shem Tov returned home, pretending that he had just come from the *mochsin*. He served the *maggid* in the humble manner of a lowly person serving a great man. He prepared the bed for him and then he went to sleep in the same bed with his wife, like villagers do, so the *maggid* would think him a simple man.

At midnight, the Besht arose, for he never slept more than two hours, and sat behind the oven, quietly chanting psalms with great fervor. Rabbi David also woke up and, seeing an intensely bright light behind the oven went over to see what it was. When he approached the oven, he saw an incredible sight. The Baal Shem Tov was sitting there, with brilliant rays of light streaming over him, arched in the shape of a rainbow. This awesome vision was beyond what the *maggid* could bear and he fainted. At the sound of his fall, the Besht's wife woke up, and seeing the *maggid* lying unconscious at her husband's side, she shook the Baal Shem Tov to bring him out of his trance—for he had no awareness of his surroundings—to help her revive their guest.

The next morning, Rabbi David told the Baal Shem Tov what he had seen, and asked for an explanation. The Besht, who continued to pretend he was a simple man,

* Charity.

answered, "I don't know. I was just reciting psalms. Perhaps somehow I became attached to God and you saw what you did." Rabbi David realized that his host was concealing his identity, and, as the rabbi of the district, ordered him to tell the truth. The Besht then removed his "mask" and revealed himself to the rabbi. From that day on, Rabbi David of Kolomaya frequently traveled to be with the Baal Shem Tov and hear Torah teaching from him. The teachings were so profound and soul-stirring that he often repeated them to his friends and colleagues. Seeing how wonderful these teachings were—for they were like the Torah taught in the Garden of Eden—and knowing that they were beyond his own spiritual level, they asked him from whom he had heard them. He would always reply, "I heard them from a certain poor man." And whenever Rabbi David heard Rabbi Gershon abusively scolding his brother-in-law, the Baal Shem Tov, he said to him, "Leave him alone. He's wiser than you are." He did not tell him that the Besht was a hidden tzaddik, for the Baal Shem Tov had ordered Rabbi David not to expose him.

After this, the Baal Shem Tov occasionally revealed himself to exceptional individuals whom he encountered. When the time came for him to be revealed to the world, they were among the first to become his disciples and followers.[95]

Rabbi Gershon Complains about the Besht

IT WAS THE PIOUS CUSTOM OF THE BAAL SHEM TOV, WHEN HE TRAVELED to the nearby town of Kitov for Rosh HaShanah to remain there for the entire month—until the end of *Sukkot*. When praying in the city, he insisted on standing by the prestigious eastern wall that was reserved for Torah scholars and the wealthy. Since people held him to be a poor *am-ha'aretz**, no one important, they considered this peculiar and eccentric, and thought he was "not all there." But it was not prestige that the Besht was seeking. He simply wanted to be close to the holy Ark when he prayed. And since he opposed the custom that allowed only scholars and the wealthy to be near the Ark, his standing there also expressed a silent protest.

Once, during the intermediate days of *Sukkot*, Rabbi Gershon, who was visiting in Kitov and also prayed by the eastern wall, noticed that his brother-in-law was praying without *tefillin*. "Why don't you have *tefillin* on today?" he asked. "Because," replied the Besht, "I saw in the Yiddish books that anyone who wears *tefillin* during the intermediate days of a holiday is committing a grave sin that deserves the penalty of death." The rabbi became very angry to hear that his ignorant brother-in-law was making religious decisions for himself, based on the Yiddish books no less! (Torah scholars read Hebrew books. Yiddish books in the vernacular were only for the unlearned.) If he continued this way, who knows where it might lead! The Sages say: "An ignorant person cannot be God-fearing," because, despite his good intentions, he will err, and act improperly—

---

* Someone unlearned in the Torah.

especially if he tries to set his own course, rather than relying, as he should, on the teaching of those who are learned in the Torah. Actually, in not putting on *tefillin* during the intermediate days of the holiday, the Besht was following a kabbalistic custom different from the one that prevailed in Poland. But to conceal the source of his practice and his knowledge of Kabbalah, he claimed that he had seen it in one of the Yiddish books written for unlearned men and women who could not read Hebrew.

Knowing from past experience that the Besht was stubborn and would not obey him, Rabbi Gershon took him to Rabbi Moshe, the rabbi of the religious court of Kitov. Both Rabbi Moshe and Rabbi Gershon were members of the circle of the Pious of Kitov; other great rabbis, such as Rabbi Nachman Kossover, Rabbi Arye Leib of Polnoye, and Rabbi David of Kolomaya were also members. Since the Baal Shem Tov was pious, perhaps, Rabbi Gershon thought, he would accept the authority of Rabbi Moshe, who was a great tzaddik. When they arrived at the rabbi's house, Rabbi Gershon touched the *mezuzah* at the door and kissed his fingers, following the pious custom. The Baal Shem Tov touched the *mezuzah* but did not kiss his fingers. Rabbi Gershon became angry with him over this as well.

When they entered Rabbi Moshe's house, the Besht removed his "mask" and the rabbi saw a great light and stood up before him. Then, the Besht put the mask back over his face and the rabbi sat down. This happened a number of times, and the rabbi became confused, because he did not know who the person standing in front of him was: One moment, he appeared to be a holy man, but at the next moment, he appeared to be someone coarse and uncouth. When Rabbi Gershon complained about him, concerning the *tefillin* and *mezuzah*, Rabbi Moshe took the Baal Shem Tov privately into an adjacent room and said, "I order you to tell me the truth! Who are you?" Since the rabbi was a great tzaddik, the Besht feared to disobey him, and he revealed to him that he was a hidden mystic. But then the Besht ordered him, in turn, not to reveal to anyone else what he had told him. When they emerged from the other room, Rabbi Moshe said to Rabbi Gershon, "I've reprimanded him sternly. I don't think he'll do anything improper again. He was just acting innocently." After they left, the rabbi took the *mezuzah* off the wall to have it inspected, since he had noticed that the Baal Shem Tov had not kissed it upon entering. It was found to be defective.[96]

Rabbi Gershon Harasses the Besht

THE BAAL SHEM TOV DID NOT ALWAYS OWN A COPY OF THE *ZOHAR*, his favorite book. At times of financial hardship he had occasionally sold or pawned a copy of a volume he did own to buy food for his family or to give urgent charity. The Besht once borrowed a volume of the *Zohar* from Rabbi Moshe of Kitov. When he was walking home with it concealed under his coat, he met his brother-in-law, Rabbi Gershon, who was passing by in a coach. Rabbi Gershon asked him, "What are you hiding inside your coat?" When the Baal Shem Tov did not want to tell him, Rabbi Gershon got down from his coach, took the book from him, and said in amazement, "*You* need a copy of the *Zohar*?" After finding out from whom he had borrowed it, Rabbi Gershon brought it back to the rabbi.

The next day, the Baal Shem Tov left his village to go into the city to pray in the synagogue and, during the *Shemoneh Esreh*, he sighed deeply. After the prayers, Rabbi Moshe asked him, "Why were you sighing like that during the prayers?" The Baal Shem Tov was evasive and tried to avoid telling him, saying that it was nothing important, and so on. But the rabbi insisted, and said, "Tell me the truth. I know that something is bothering you deeply, because that sigh came from the heart." The Besht then told him that he was still upset by what had happened the previous day with Rabbi Gershon taking the *Zohar* away from him. The rabbi, with an understanding smile on his face, gave the volume of the *Zohar* to him again, and blessed him that this time he would not meet Rabbi Gershon on his way home.[97]

The Besht Exorcises a Madwoman

THERE WAS A MADWOMAN IN KITOV, WHO WAS POSSESSED BY A *DYBBUK**
that revealed the vices and virtues of everyone who appeared before her. Once, when the Baal Shem Tov came into the city, Rabbi Gershon urged Rabbi Moshe to take the Baal Shem to her, hoping that she would rebuke him for his misbehavior, and he would return to the proper path. Although by this time Rabbi Moshe knew that the Besht was a hidden tzaddik, he took the Besht to the woman, as asked, to keep his secret from Rabbi Gershon. They were accompanied by many people, including many of the Pious of Kitov.

The rabbi entered first, and the madwoman addressed him, saying, "Welcome to you who are holy and pure!" She called out greetings to everyone who entered, each according to what he deserved. The Baal Shem Tov entered last. When she saw him, she rose to her feet, and said, "Welcome, Rabbi Israel!" Then, changing her tone from respectful to defiant, she continued, "Do you think I'm afraid of you? Not at all! I know that you've vowed not to make use of the divine Names and can't expel me!"

The Baal Shem Tov had hidden himself behind some other people when he came in, so they did not see whom she was talking to and could make no sense of her words. They asked her, "What are you saying?" She repeated to them what she had said, until the Baal Shem Tov scolded her, saying, "Be silent, or I'll appoint a *beit din* to release me from my vow not to use the divine Names and I'll cast you out of this woman!" Then she began to plead with him, saying, "I'll be silent!"

Those among the Pious of Kitov who had come with him urged him to allow them to release him from his vow and to exorcise the *dybbuk* from the woman. The Baal Shem Tov was reluctant, saying that the spirit can be very dangerous when it is cast out. But they would not relent. Finally, he agreed, and after being released from his vow,

---

* The spirit of a dead person.

said to the *dybbuk*, "See what you've caused by your own doing! My advice is that you now leave the woman peacefully. If you do, we'll all study Torah for your sake." The *dybbuk* agreed to exit. The Baal Shem Tov then asked it for its name. "I can't reveal my name before all these people," it said. "Let them leave, and I'll tell it to you." (For it would mortify the dead man's children, who still lived in the city, to have this known.) When the others had gone outside, he revealed his identity, and told the Baal Shem Tov that he had become a *dybbuk* because he had mocked the Pious of Kitov. The spirit then exited from the woman without harming anyone or doing any damage.

When a report of this event got back to Rabbi Gershon, his attitude to his brother-in-law began to change. Although he still considered him ignorant, he realized that his peculiar piety had nonetheless won him powers of a sort. But he was still unclear what to think about him.

The townspeople also began to change their opinion of the Baal Shem Tov and held him in higher regard. But they too still considered him to be basically uneducated.[98]

He Is Revealed to the World and Accepted as Master by the Pious of Kitov

THREE MONTHS AFTER HIS THIRTY-SIXTH BIRTHDAY, THE BAAL SHEM TOV was revealed publicly in a wondrous way. That day, the Pious of Kitov were gathered together, with Rabbi Moshe, the rabbi of the community, and with Rabbi Gershon among them, and the conversation turned to Rabbi Gershon's brother-in-law, Israel. A few of them mentioned that they had seen amazing things from him, but for some reason had neglected to pay much attention at the time and had afterward forgotten what they had witnessed—but today they remembered. This one told one story, that one told another. Before long it dawned on them that he was an extraordinary hidden tzaddik. They considered all the puzzling things about him that had never made sense—and now, once they realized that he had been pretending to be ignorant and concealing himself from them, everything suddenly became clear. All their previous doubts and suspicions about him disappeared. To this point, Rabbi Moshe of Kitov and Rabbi David of Kolomaya, who knew the Baal Shem Tov's secret and had been ordered by the Besht not to reveal him, had been quiet. But now they spoke up. "There is a great light nearby," they said. "It's fitting that we bring it into the city." They then all set out together to travel to the Besht's village, to accept him as their rabbi and leader, and to ask him to come live in the city.

When the Baal Shem Tov saw with his holy spirit that they were traveling to him, he set out in the direction of the city. They met just outside his village near a field with a few trees, and they all got down from their coaches. The Besht sat down on a tree stump, and they all came before him and accepted him as their master, teacher, and rabbi. Most of these men were great scholars who followed the ascetic path of the Kabbalah.[99]

The Sermon to the Pious of Kitov: The Parable of the Magic Palace

THE BESHT TAUGHT THEM, AND SAID, "'LIGHT IS SOWN FOR THE righteous, and joy for the upright in heart.' The way wherein light dwells is that of love and joy in the service of God, blessed be He. Excessive fasting and self-affliction lead to sadness and depression and are the way of darkness. The Sages say that the *Shechinah* does not rest on someone who is sad, but only on someone joyful in doing the *mitzvot*. I tell you, a person can achieve what the greatest rabbis and mystics of former times attained, but sadness will prevent it. Therefore, you should always be joyful, especially when engaged in divine service, for without joy one cannot cleave to the Holy One, blessed be He. Sadness is not a sin, but there is no sin a person will not commit because of sadness. So if you stumbled and sinned, be regretful and repent your error, but immediately return to being joyful in the service of God. Abandon fasting and self-affliction! I have come to this world to show another way, that a person should seek to attain three loves: love of God, love of Israel, and love of the Torah. Fasting and self-affliction are not necessary.

"Your body may seem to be the enemy of your soul, which yearns for Godliness; for the body is drawn to material things, while the soul is drawn to spiritual things. And the body is lazy and reluctant to fulfill the divine purpose for which it was created. You might think that in order to compel the body to fulfill its mission you will deny it food, sleep, and its other physical needs; you will torment it with fasts and afflictions, to break its materiality. But that is not the way wherein light dwells. Rather, you must illuminate the body, clarify and purify it, not break it with afflictions, for the Holy One, blessed be He, created the body so that its physical matter would be a vessel for Godliness. Therefore, I tell you that you must not treat the body like an enemy and seek its defeat. Instead, you must work with the body and help it.

"There are two kinds of doctors: Those who heal with bitter medicine and those who heal with sweet medicine. It is better to be a doctor who heals with sweet medicine, for then the patient will take the medicine prescribed. There are those who teach the way of fasting and self-affliction—but many refuse to take their bitter medicine. My way is with eating and drinking and fulfilling the body's needs, not in a lowly way, but as an exalted service of God, for that is the higher path, the path of light.

"Those who imbibe this sweet medicine—which is an elixir of life—look on their fellow men with love and compassion. But the other way, of fasting and self-affliction, is harsh. It is also dangerous, for I have seen that those who imbibe bitter medicine become embittered and cannot look at their fellow men without being angry and judgmental.

"I tell you, you must love every one of our people—regardless of who or what he or she is—with all your heart and soul. There is nothing greater than helping a fellow Jew—materially and spiritually. You must do a favor for another Jew with devotion and self-sacrifice. You must even be willing to give up your life to help him. There is nothing greater than helping another Jew. I tell you, love of Israel with self-sacrifice brings more light to the soul and produces a greater soul-revelation than the deepest solitary meditation on Godliness.

"Purify yourselves in the *mikvah* every morning to prepare for prayer and divine service. The *mikvah* is better than fasting, which weakens the body and deprives you of energy that can be devoted to the service of God.

"When you pray and study Torah, attach yourselves with love and joy in *d'vekut* with the holy letters. Pour your soul into the letters to meet God, who dwells within them. Pray with all your energy and concentration, with dedication and self-sacrifice, ready to die for the sake of the *kavvanah*—and I promise you that you will attain great things. You will subdue your body and God will be with you.

"How can a person hide from God, whose light fills all the worlds? King David said in the psalms: 'Where can I go to flee from Your presence? If I ascend into heaven, Thou art there; if I make my bed in the netherworld, behold Thou art there!' Is there no place where you can hide from the Holy One, blessed be He? I tell you, a person can hide *in* the body, because the body is concealment and forgetfulness; that is the way of worldly people. What then should a person do? Should he seek God and hide *from* his body, with fasting and afflictions, like the ascetics? I tell you, 'hide not from your own flesh'; rather, fulfill: 'From my flesh will I see God'!

"To join silver with silver you must first remove the rust. You have to purify the flesh, until you see Godliness. You have to clean and polish the flesh for many years— with perspiration from exertion in Torah study, with perspiration from exertion in prayer, with tears from *Tikkun Hatzot*, with much labor of the heart and much labor of the brain. But finally—someone one year earlier and someone one year later—when the Holy One, blessed be He, has compassion, you will remove the bodily rust and corrosion, you will succeed in cleaning and polishing the flesh, and then you will see Godliness.

"I tell you, the world is full of great lights and awesome secrets, but a person can keep himself from seeing them simply by holding his little hand in front of his eyes!

"It is a high level of spiritual attainment when a person is constantly aware of God's presence—that He surrounds him on all sides—and his *d'vekut* with God is so great that he does not need to remind himself again and again that God, blessed be He, is present with him, because he sees God with the eyes of his mind, for He is the place of the world.

"What this means is that He was before He created the world, and the world exists within the Creator, blessed be He. Therefore, a person's *d'vekut* should be so great that what he primarily sees is God, blessed be He. His vision should not be, first, of the world and then, by the way, of God. No, but his sight should be primarily of God. When a person is on this level, all the Shells*—the unholy forces that surround and block what is divine—disperse and remove themselves from him, for it is they that darken his vision and the eyes of his mind so that he cannot see God, blessed be He.

---

* *Kelipot.*

"There is another high spiritual level of a different kind, to always see God, just as you would see a person. And you should be aware that God is also looking at you, just as another person would look at you. Always be joyful, believing with complete faith that the *Shechinah* is with you and guards you. Meditate on this at all times. You should always be looking at God and seeing Him, and also realize that He is always looking at you.

"I tell you, there is nothing that exists in the world except the light of the Infinite One, blessed be He, concealed within all things. And all the verses in the Torah, such as 'There is nothing but Him,' 'The whole earth is full of His glory,' and 'I fill the heavens and the earth'—are to be understood literally, according to their plain meaning: that there is no place and no action, speech, or thought that has not the essence of Godliness concealed and contracted within it. Even a speck of dust is pervaded by divinity. Therefore, someone who gazes with his mind's eye and a piercing glance on everything that he sees—at their inside and their inner vitality, not their surface and outside alone—will not see anything other than the divine power that enlivens them and brings them into being and keeps them in existence, every moment and every second."

Then the Baal Shem Tov told them a great parable that expresses the essence of his teaching:

"A king, by magic, surrounded his palace with many walls. Then he hid himself within the palace. The formidable walls were arranged in concentric circles, one inside the other, and they grew increasingly larger—higher and thicker—as one approached the center. They had fortified battlements and were manned by fierce soldiers who guarded from above; wild animals—lions and bears—ran loose below. All this was so that those who approached would have proper awe and fear of the king and so that not all who desired to approach would be allowed to do as they pleased.

"The king then had proclamations sent throughout the kingdom saying that whoever came to see him in his palace would be richly rewarded and given a rank second to none in the king's service. Who would not desire this? But when many came and saw the outer wall's awesome size and the terrifying soldiers and animals, most were afraid and turned back. There were some, however, who succeeded in scaling that wall and fighting past the soldiers and animals, but then the second wall loomed before their eyes, even more imposing than the first, and its guards even more terrible. Seeing that, many others turned back.

"Moreover, the king had appointed servants to stand behind the walls to give money and precious stones to whoever got beyond each wall. Those who had crossed one or a few walls soon found themselves very rich and satisfied with what they had gained from their efforts; so they too turned back. For one reason or another, either from fear at the increasing obstacles or satisfaction with the accumulated rewards, none reached the king . . .

"Except for the king's son. He had only one desire: to see the face of his beloved father. When he came and saw the walls, soldiers, and wild animals, he was astonished. He could not understand how his dear father could hide himself behind all these terrifying barriers and obstacles. 'How can I ever reach him?' he thought. Then he began to weep and cried out, 'Father, Father, have compassion on me; don't keep me away from you!' His longing was so intense that he had no interest in any rewards. Indeed, he was willing to risk his life to attain his goal. By the courage of his broken heart, which burned to see his father, he ran forward with reckless abandon and self-sacrifice. He scaled one wall and then another, fought past soldiers and wild animals. After crossing the walls, he was offered money and jewels, but he threw them down in disgust. His only desire was to see his father. Again and again he called out to him.

"His father the king, hearing his son's pathetic cries and seeing his total self-sacrifice, suddenly, instantaneously, removed the walls and other obstacles. In a moment they vanished as if they had never existed. Then his son saw that there were no walls, soldiers, or animals. His father the king was right before him, sitting on his majestic throne, while multitudes of servants stood near to serve him and heavenly choirs sang his praises. Gardens and orchards surrounded the palace on all sides. And the whole earth shone from the king's glory. Everything was tranquil, and there was nothing bad or terrible at all. Then the son realized that the walls and obstacles were a magical illusion and that his father the king had never really been hidden or concealed, but was with him all the time. It was all just a test to see who truly loved the king.

"You must know," said the Besht, looking at his disciples sitting around him, "that all the worlds were created by and from Him and are garments for Him, like the snail, whose shell garment is part of its own body. Everything that exists is created and kept in existence every moment and every second by the divine power that is within it. Were it removed, that thing would instantaneously return to nothingness. You must realize with complete faith and know with absolute clarity that the whole earth is full of God's glory and there is no place where He is not present. When you know that God is in every object, movement, and thought—and that everything is from Him, for everything is a covering and garment wherein He is concealed—when you know that He is hiding there, there is no longer any concealment, and all the 'workers of iniquity' are scattered. There is no barrier separating us from God; He is always with us.

"You must not only believe this and know it, but must realize it in your own experience. To do so you must meditate more and more deeply on this thought until it becomes part of you. You should have one thought in the service of your Creator, blessed be His name. Many thoughts confuse a person. Simply think that everything in the world is filled with the Creator, blessed be His name. And think: 'I want to serve Him and give Him pleasure always.' Let your mind always be in *d'vekut* with Him, blessed be He.

"The Torah says: 'Know Him in all your ways.' You should try to have *d'vekut*, God-awareness, in every activity you engage in, whether religious or worldly. You should strive to attain continuous *d'vekut*, without a moment's cessation, throughout the whole day. Continuous practice leads to continuous *d'vekut*; you will become established in *d'vekut* and, because God-consciousness is blissful, you will experience the bliss and joy of the Garden of Eden.

"Who can attain all this? Only someone who strives with total self-sacrifice, who truly believes that he is a child of God, and is restless for God and yearns to see his

Father's face. When your only desire is to see the face of your Father in Heaven, you will not be deterred by any obstacles or barriers, whether material or spiritual, for there are no barriers; they are all illusory. Everything that happens to you, whether for good or 'to become better*,' is only a means to aid you, when you truly desire to achieve *d'vekut* with God, blessed be He. Neither will you be distracted by rewards or punishments, by attractions or aversions, whether material or spiritual, for they too are illusory. Whether the mask is frightening or smiling, you will pay it no heed, you will see right through it—for your only desire is to see the face of your compassionate Father."

The Baal Shem Tov paused and sat silently for a while. His disciples too sat silently; all were immersed in a profound spiritual mood. Then, one of them spoke up and said, "Master, when I first decided to seek God in truth I experienced great light and joy. But then that awesome feeling left me, until this moment, when I'm experiencing it now in your holy presence." The Besht replied with a parable.

"A person went into a store to buy sweets and the shopkeeper let him taste some of the candies. But when the customer wanted to continue tasting, the shopkeeper said to him, 'I let you have a taste so that you'd know how good everything is. But if you want to have more, you have to pay. I didn't treat you for nothing!' God gives a person a taste of the sweetness of the Hidden Light. But after that taste, he must 'pay'; he must exert himself to achieve and earn that joy and delight in the future, to make it a spiritual possession, to win mystic consciousness and the bliss of *d'vekut*. That is your task now."

Another disciple said, "Master, why is it that sometimes I have great *d'vekut* and feel close to God, blessed be He, but then suddenly my *d'vekut* ceases and I feel far from Him?" The Baal Shem Tov answered, "When a father teaches his infant child how to walk, he stands in front of him and, with his arms outstretched, slowly walks backward a step or two, holding his hands close to the child so that he won't fall. Then the toddler walks toward his father. The father takes a few more steps backward, and again the child moves forward. In that way, the child learns how to walk. That is also how the Holy One, blessed be He, acts with people. If when a person had fervent *d'vekut*, God did not remove Himself from him, his *d'vekut* would not increase; it would decrease. But when God removes Himself again and again, a person must continually increase his *d'vekut*, so it becomes stronger and more fervent. Each time that he sees that God, blessed be He, has separated Himself, he is inspired to increase his *d'vekut* more than before. No matter what rung you are on," continued the Besht, "there are always times of expanded consciousness and of constricted consciousness; that is the secret of the holy animals [*hayot*] that pull the Divine Chariot by running and returning, for the divine life-force [*hiyut*] that we receive from the Source of all life ceaselessly ebbs and flows."

"Master," asked the disciple, "is this true of you too? Are there times when you don't feel God's presence?"

---

* A euphemism for "bad," to avoid saying something negative.

"Everyone has times of expanded and constricted consciousness," said the Besht, "but one can also reach levels from which one does not fall. When a father wants to play with his little child, he hides his face with his hand, and then shows his face to him—doing this again and again. But the father's pleasure is even greater when the child is clever enough to push his father's hand away, so that it no longer conceals his face. God's glory fills the earth and there is no place where He is not present. When it seems that He is absent, He is merely hiding His face from you. But if you know that He is hiding, there is no more concealment. If you truly want the game to end, and to see Him always, push your Father's hand away to see His face."

As he said this, the Baal Shem Tov closed his eyes and entered a trance of intense *d'vekut*. His face shone like the sun at its zenith. Gazing at the radiance of the *Shechinah* on his face, the souls of his disciples were aflame with the words that came from his holy mouth. The Besht remained in that state for a short while as the disciples sat silently and watched in awe. Then the Besht slowly opened his eyes as if waking from a deep sleep.

Moved to the core of their souls by what they had heard and seen, they wove a leafy crown of twigs and, placing it on the Baal Shem Tov's head, they affirmed their devoted allegiance to his leadership and declared him to be the Rabbi of all the Jews in the Exile.[100]

Hai Elul

THE HOLY ONE, BLESSED BE HE, IS LIKE THE SUN, AND A TZADDIK IS LIKE the moon that reflects His light. Like all the tzaddikim, the Baal Shem Tov's growth in holiness resembled the waxing of the moon, for while the light of the sun is always the same, the moon waxes to fullness. Although the new moon's light is small, it is still the moon. In the same way, a young tzaddik is still a tzaddik; he is still radiant, but his light is small. So the light of the Baal Shem Tov grew and grew; his light waxed greater and greater, until it fully reflected the light of the sun, the Holy One, blessed be He and blessed be His name.

On *hai Elul* (*hai*, 18, signifying Life), the eighteenth day of the month of *Elul*, in 1700, Rabbi Israel Baal Shem Tov was born.

On *hai Elul*, 1703, at the age of three years, he recognized his Creator, and the light of his soul began to be revealed.

On *hai Elul*, 1713, the Baal Shem Tov became bar mitzvah. His mentor and teacher Rabbi Meir initiated him into the study of Kabbalah and taught him secrets of *d'vekut*. The light of the Besht's soul shone forth with increased strength.

On *hai Elul*, 1716, at the age of sixteen, the prophet Elijah ha-Tishbi, may he be remembered for good, appeared to the Baal Shem Tov for the first time, became his heavenly teacher, and taught him the secrets of divine wisdom.

On *hai Elul*, 1726, at the age of twenty-six, his foremost master and teacher, the prophet Ahiyah ha-Shiloni, the *Baal Hai*—the master of eternal life and of the higher soul levels—appeared to the Baal Shem Tov for the first time, to teach him the secrets of the secrets of wisdom. The Baal Shem Tov's eyes saw great light; his soul was filled with light and emitted light.

On *hai Elul*, 1736, at the age of thirty-six, when Ahiyah ha-Shiloni completed his teaching, he told the Baal Shem Tov that he must reveal his light to the world. Three months later, the Besht revealed himself and his soul came into full revelation, like the full moon reflecting the light of the sun. His soul united with the light of the holy *Shechinah*. Then, Elijah's promise to Rabbi Eliezer and Sarah, the Besht's parents, began to be fulfilled, that a son would be born to them who would illumine the eyes of all Israel.[101]

Adam Kadmon

AT THE AGE OF THIRTY-SIX, THE BAAL SHEM TOV HAD REACHED THE ultimate spiritual perfection: The essence of his divine soul, the soul of *Adam Kadmon*, the Cosmic Man, sitting on the Throne of Glory, taught him at all times—to elevate his body with all its physical needs, as well as everything in his worldly, material sphere, as decreed by divine providence in place and time, to purify and illuminate them with the light of Torah and divine service. The Baal Shem Tov, so to speak, lived on the ground floor and upper story of the house at the same time. When he wanted, he put on his body like a garment; when he wanted, he took it off like a garment and was like an inhabitant of the upper worlds. He became a living embodiment of the divine form of *Adam Kadmon*. He had achieved perfection: a fleshly human being and elevated soul together. He was above and below at the same time. Praise God for He is good, for creating a tzaddik of goodness and love to be a foundation for all the worlds until the coming of the Messiah![102]

A Mission as a Teacher
and *Baal Shem*

He Moves to Kitov

THE BAAL SHEM TOV WAS A GREAT TZADDIK, BUT HE WAS VERY POOR. And his new disciples, who were also poor, could not afford to support him and his wife and child. In any case, the Besht would not take money from them. Yet his disciples could not bear to see the difficult conditions in which their master and his family lived. And they would no longer allow him to stay in an isolated village. They brought him to the city of Kitov and arranged for him to earn a living by teaching the sons of a local *mochsin*. The disciples were embarrassed that they could not support their great master. The Baal Shem Tov, however, did not consider working as a *melamed* to be beneath him; he loved teaching children. But God had other plans for him.[1]

He Becomes a Baal Shem

AT FIRST, THE BESHT WAS NOT CONSIDERED BY THE TOWNSPEOPLE OF Kitov to be anyone special. But after hearing that he had expelled the *dybbuk* from the madwoman, and that great rabbis had accepted him as their leader, his fame quickly grew. Some sick people now began to come to him for healing, but he refused to receive them. One day, they brought him a madman, and the Besht would not see him. But that night he was told from heaven that he should use divine Names for healing to sanctify the name of God. When he awoke, he told them to bring the madman to him and he healed him. Then he gave up working as a *melamed* and became a *baal shem*. And people came to him from all over.

Having traveled for years around the countryside as a hidden tzaddik, the Baal Shem Tov had learned much about medicinal herbs from a few fellow hidden mystics and from folk healers, both Jewish and gentile. The kabbalistic manuscript the Baal Shem Tov had received from Rabbi Adam Baal Shem also contained the secrets of using divine Names for healing. But faith, not secret knowledge or techniques, explained the Besht's power as a healer.

By choosing to work as a *baal shem*, the Besht could help the sick and suffering, and earn his living in a way that expressed his love for the Jewish people. He could now be close to them and influence them. With his miracles of healing, he could show them that there is a God in Israel and make them receptive to his religious message.

Many Jews lived in fear of their gentile neighbors. They were afraid of church-inspired blood libels and pogroms. They were terrified of marauding groups of Cossacks, Tartars, Haidamaks, and bandits. They were also afraid of gentile sorcerers and hostile demons. Their world was dark around them. These fears had insinuated themselves into their religious life and produced a morbid, ascetic piety that was based on an exaggerated fear and terror of God. The Baal Shem Tov broke out of this trap. He first conquered his lower fears by fearing only God; then he burst through to attain the higher level of love of God. The Besht, who even as a child had overcome his fear of the forest, of its wild animals and demons, taught the people to trust in a God of love and compassion. His fearlessness in confronting antisemites, defeating gentile sorcerers, and casting out demons, proved to the people that God would protect them. And he taught them a piety based on love of God and of their fellow Jews. By overcoming the often irrational fears that depressed the people, he opened the gate before them to the path of joy in the service of God.

At this time in his life, Israel ben Eliezer assumed the title of "rabbi" and became known as the Baal Shem Tov. *Baal shem* means a master of divine Names and a healer; *baal shem tov* means the possessor of a good name or reputation among one's fellows. Rabbi Israel merited both titles. There was also another meaning of Baal Shem or Baal Shem Tov: It was the title for a leader of the movement of hidden tzaddikim, although this meaning was only known to members of their group. Now Rabbi Adam Baal Shem's successor was called Rabbi Israel Baal Shem Tov.[2]

Amulets

LIKE OTHER *BAAL SHEMS*, THE BAAL SHEM TOV EMPLOYED AMULETS AS a token of divine protection and for various other purposes. Shortly after becoming a *baal shem*, the Besht hired a scribe, Rabbi Alexander, to write amulets for him. The Besht's amulets became so popular and he received so many requests for them that he soon hired a second scribe to produce them—Rabbi Tzvi.

A *mochsin* from a small town once came to the Baal Shem Tov seeking his help against a gentile who had worked a magic spell on him, so that anything left overnight in his house, whether money in a wallet or something in a vessel, was reduced by half. The Besht ordered one of his scribes to write protective amulets for all the rooms of the man's house. Then, the Besht traveled back to the man's home with him.

When they arrived at his house, the Besht placed all the amulets in a pile on the table, and went to the market. The members of the household then saw that the evil spirit began to spin around like a whirlwind from one corner of a room to another, until it quit the house altogether. However, there was a large, fenced-in yard surrounding the house, and the spirit remained at the gate.

When the Baal Shem Tov returned from the market, the spirit appeared in the form of a huge Cossack standing at the gate. But the closer the Baal Shem Tov approached, the smaller it became, until it disappeared completely. Then the Besht placed the amulets throughout the house. When the occupants of the house told him how the spirit had whirled about before it left, he searched around in the straw bed, in the rooms, and among the barrels that were standing there, in order to expel the evil spirit, for that was his practice in these matters. Then he traveled home.[3]

Increasing Fame

THE BAAL SHEM TOV'S FAME GREW UNTIL HE WAS KNOWN FAR AND WIDE. His herbal medicines and amulets, his prayers and blessings worked many miracles and he healed many people who came to him from all the surrounding areas. He began to travel regularly to towns and villages throughout Poland—to Podolia, Volhynia, Galicia, Reissen, Lithuania—and beyond, to serve as a *baal shem*, his reputation as a wonder-worker preceding him.

Everyone who came to tell him of the success of his treatment or to thank him for a miracle he had wrought was asked to thank God, blessed be He, because, said the Besht, "Everything that happens is in God's hands and it's God, blessed be He, who puts miraculous powers in medicinal herbs and amulets; it's God, blessed be He, who answers prayers and fulfills a tzaddik's blessings."

His extensive traveling as a *baal shem* gave the Besht an opportunity to see firsthand the social, political, and economic conditions of his fellow Jews and to become acutely aware of their pressing needs. This intimate knowledge of his people's often difficult and sometimes desperate situation prepared him as a leader and served him well when the time came to act on their behalf.[4]

The Besht Attracts Disciples and Followers

THE BAAL SHEM TOV, WHO WAS ALREADY THE LEADER OF THE HIDDEN tzaddikim, had, over the years, won the allegiance of other isolated individuals to whom he had revealed himself. Now that he was revealed to the world, he began to attract many more disciples, particularly among Torah scholars and kabbalists. Some scholars were aroused and inspired by the Baal Shem Tov, but others rejected him and disapproved of his having abandoned the ascetic path of the Kabbalah, which they followed. Most members of the circle of the Pious of Kitov became the Besht's disciples. Most, though not all, of the members of the Brody *Kloiz* rejected and opposed him. Rabbis Meir Margoliot, Nachman of Horodenka, Menahem Mendel of Bar, and Yehiel Michal of Zlotchov were members of the Brody *Kloiz* who became the Baal

Shem Tov's disciples. The Besht also had a great appeal to young Jews, who were excited by his new teaching and radical ways.

In general, his approach as a spiritual guide and teacher was two-fold: On the one hand, he offered to the religious elite and spiritual aspirants a path to the highest mystic attainment. Such people became his disciples, were part of his inner circle, and followed his discipline and direction. On the other hand, he offered to the Jewish masses the joy of closeness to God. These people became ordinary hasidim (followers). He taught his disciples the ideal of continuous *d'vekut* throughout the day, *without a moment's cessation.* He taught his regular hasidim that they should strive to have true *d'vekut* for *at least one moment* during the day; as he often said, "He who grasps a part of the whole, grasps the whole." If a person cleaves to God for even one moment, by doing one holy deed, no matter how small, he derives tremendous spiritual benefits: He is cleaving to the One and Only God, the true Reality and receives a great influx of divine light.[5]

Reading Thoughts

The *Shivitti*

🔥 THE BAAL SHEM TOV'S ABILITY TO READ OTHERS' THOUGHTS—A SIGN of his possessing the holy spirit—not only astonished doubters, but won them over as disciples and followers.

When the Besht visited the town of Whitefield (Biala Cerkiew) in the Polish Kiev region for the first time, the religious judge was a tzaddik named Rabbi Hayim. That morning, the Besht had prayed in a field on the way there and, when he arrived in the city, they were still praying in the synagogue. So he went to hear the *Kedushah* recited. He stood listening in the synagogue courtyard, and then ordered the *gabbai* to go in and remove the *shivitti** from the wall facing the rabbi. (It serves as a visual focus to remind the prayer-leader to have God-consciousness every moment while praying.) The *gabbai* did as he was told and removed the *shivitti*. When the rabbi took three steps back after concluding the *Shemoneh Esreh*, he saw that the *shivitti* was no longer on the wall and asked about it. They told him that the Baal Shem Tov was in the courtyard and had ordered that it be taken down.

Immediately after the *Kedushah*, the rabbi went out and asked the Baal Shem Tov why he had it removed. The Besht told him, "Every day you have a certain distracting thought when you pray the *Shemoneh Esreh*, because the scribe who drew the *shivitti* was a wicked person and was not meditating on holy thoughts when he made it, but

---

* A kabbalistic picture in the form of a candelabra, at whose center is the psalm verse: *Shivitti HaShem l'negdi tamid*—"I have placed God before me always" (Psalm 16:8).

was playing with a dog." The rabbi realized, to his amazement, that the Baal Shem Tov was right—each day he lost his focus and had a foreign thought while praying the *Shemoneh Esreh*. Now he knew why. Rabbi Hayim became the Besht's disciple and traveled every month to Kitov to spend a Sabbath with him.[6]

The Imprint of the Maker in What Is Made

WHEN THE BAAL SHEM TOV SAW A CRAFTED OBJECT, LIKE THE KABBALISTIC picture of the candelabra, he knew by his holy spirit the craftsman's thoughts when he made it. After this incident in Whitefield, he explained the principle behind his ability to some disciples who were with him, "When a craftsman shapes crude matter, he leaves the imprint of his intelligence, which is his life-force, in the object he makes. The spirit of the maker is impressed and imprinted in the object made. If you have the eyes to see it, you can recognize the spirit of the maker and his behavior in the object. The same principle," said the Besht, "applies to this world, which is the work of God's hands."[7]

Continuous D'vekut

THE BAAL SHEM TOV TAUGHT HIS DISCIPLES VARIOUS SPIRITUAL PRACTICES to keep their mind always on God and to achieve mystic awareness. He told some of them to continually repeat the phrase "The power of the Maker is in what is made." When they merited to see the power of the Creator in the creation, their eyes would behold their Maker and see Godliness revealed.

Rabbi Meir Margoliot and his brother Rabbi Yitzhak Dov had become attached to the Baal Shem Tov when they were still youths and the Besht was the *shochet* in Kshilovitz. Later, when the Besht became famous and they had grown up and become accomplished Torah scholars, they traveled to be with him every year. On one such visit, the Besht gave Rabbi Meir, as a gift, a piece of parchment on which he had written in his own hand the four-letter name of God, Y-H-V-H. He told Rabbi Meir to keep it with him and to gaze and meditate on it occasionally while studying Torah and while eating. Then he said, "Meir, try each day to increase your focus on God, blessed be He, and your absorption in Him, blessed be He. Godliness is found in everything in the world, even in inanimate objects. One can learn how to serve God even from stones or trees. All the worlds yearn to worship Him. The sun's race across the sky that we see each day is because the sun too yearns, longs, and desires every day to achieve more supernal light than it achieved the day before."

Soon after this, when Rabbi Meir sat down to study Torah and placed the parchment from the Besht in front of him, he gazed at it and saw that the four-letter name of God was glowing with divine fire—black fire written on white fire.[8]

Rabbi Yaakov Koppel the Shivittinik

THE BAAL SHEM TOV HAD A GREAT DISCIPLE IN KOLOMAYA NAMED Rabbi Yaakov Koppel, who earned his living as a storekeeper. The Besht told him to keep his mind constantly on God by repeating "*Shivitti HaShem l'negdi tamid*" or just "*shivitti*." The gentiles of the town called him "the Shivittinik," because he always passed his hand over his eyes—to concentrate—and repeated "*shivitti, shivitti*," even when taking care of customers; they considered him a holy man, which he was.[9]

Rabbi Gershon Becomes a Disciple

RABBI GERSHON KITOVER, WHO HAD PREVIOUSLY HARASSED HIS BROTHER-in-law and even encouraged his own sister to leave Brody with her husband, out of his embarrassment at the Baal Shem Tov's seeming ignorance, had been the one most stunned and embarrassed when the Besht revealed himself as a great tzaddik. Rabbi Gershon, who was a member of the circle of the Pious of Kitov and the Brody *Kloiz*, now accepted the Baal Shem Tov as his master. But he could not forget his earlier treatment of the Besht. Look to whom he had condescended! It did not take Rabbi Gershon long, however, to completely change his attitude. He became a devoted follower and friend of the Baal Shem Tov, whom he loved more than anyone in the world. He yearned with great thirst to hear the sweet Torah teaching that came from the Besht's holy mouth. He considered the Baal Shem Tov to have the holy spirit and to be able to prophesy the future. And he always kept on his person a protective amulet from the Besht. The Besht, in turn, was very fond of his brother-in-law, for Rabbi Gershon was truly a great person.[10]

The Baal Shem Tov's Praying

WHEN THE BAAL SHEM TOV PRAYED, HE WAS COMPLETELY IMMERSED in the spiritual world. He lost awareness of his body and the material world, so that he could not even speak. It was only by a miracle that his lips moved to utter the words of the prayers. He often stood praying for hours at a time. His *d'vekut* then was exalted and total. Sometimes, his face burned like a torch; at other times, his eyes streamed nonstop with tears of joy. He often leaped and danced while *davvening*. In the morning, when he put on *tefillin* and recited the *Shema*, his mind and thoughts elevated, and he sometimes ran around the synagogue as if he was in another world.

Once, after services, when his disciples gathered around him, he said, "The *Shechinah* is called 'prayer,' because God's presence in the world is revealed when someone prays with utter devotion. The *Shechinah* is the inner impulse to real praying. The

Shechinah, so to speak, prays to the Holy One, blessed be He, as the verse says: 'O Lord, open my lips and my mouth shall declare Your praise!'"

It was the Baal Shem Tov's fervent praying, even more than his Torah teaching, that won him followers. He told one of his disciples, before he sent him back to his hometown to organize a *minyan* and lead prayers, "When a person prays from the depths of his heart, with true love and fear of God, then whoever hears his praying, even if he's the worst sinner, can't help having thoughts of repentance, at least for those few minutes, and he yearns to be a Jew who also knows how to stand in prayer before the One and Only One. I tell you," said the Besht, "if someone who hears your praying doesn't yearn to repent, it's a sign that you haven't really prayed."

The Baal Shem Tov elevated all those praying with him. They became fervent and enthusiastic; everyone would pray at the top of his voice. Being in the Besht's presence when he *davvened* was an unforgettable experience. Those who saw and heard him praying were changed forever. They wept and did not know why they were weeping; they knew only that they were moved to the root of their souls.

The Besht's awe of God was so great that it could hardly be contained in his body. During prayer, he often trembled and shook uncontrollably. Once, one of his disciples overheard him saying to himself, "I'm amazed at you, wretched body! How is it that you haven't crumbled to bits from awe of your Creator?" His shaking and trembling when *davvening* made a powerful impression on those who saw it. The divine vitality that filled him was so great that it reached even into his *tzitzit*, which moved and swayed as if alive. Once, when the Besht was traveling, he stopped in a village, and prayed *Minha* in a room used to store grain. The Besht prayed at the eastern wall and everyone present saw how the grain in the barrels near the western wall shook and trembled while he was praying.

It was clear to those who saw his *davvening* that a struggle and transformation were taking place within him, back and forth, between "running and returning." He seemed to be melting in emotion: On the one hand, running to God in intense longing almost until expiration, his movements and chanting being like those of a person withering from the absence of some ultimate pleasure and racing to attain it; on the other hand, a return to the divinity in this world, his body reviving and his voice expressing delight and bliss. They would see moments of longing, when his face would be as white as lime; his eyes fixed, staring straight ahead, without any sign of life, as if all his body were shattering. Then, suddenly, the reverse: swaying and movements that indicated intense vitality. His death-white face would flush with color; his eyes reddened, delight pouring out of them; and all his body became enlivened, moving and swaying, slowly and gently, according to the melody of the prayer.

Once, during prayer, the Besht threw himself onto the Ark, as one does in desperate supplication. Later, when some of his disciples asked him why he had done this, he knew nothing about it; he had no recollection. When he prayed, he was not in his normal consciousness.

Sometimes, he would stand stiff and unmoving, like a statue, or fall down to the ground seemingly lifeless. Those who saw his trances and his extreme states during prayer were awed and occasionally even terrified. Once, when the Baal Shem Tov was in Kolomaya, and praying the *Shemoneh Esreh*, his face covered with his tallis, a little boy named Nachman, the son of Rabbi David of Kolomaya, snuck under his tallis (as children do) and looked at his holy face. He saw that each moment the Baal Shem Tov's color changed: One moment his face was entirely white, without a drop of blood, like a dead man; the next moment, his face shone like the sun with a supernal light. From his fright and terror at seeing this, the boy became ill with a high fever, until they told the Baal Shem Tov, who healed him.

Even gentiles who heard the Besht's praying knew it was for real and from the heart, without any trace of falsity, and were affected by its holy power. Charna Ashkenazi, the mother of one of the Besht's disciples, Rabbi Shimon Ashkenazi, was once traveling somewhere with a gentile wagon-driver, and they stopped beside a field near the woods to graze the horses. The Baal Shem Tov happened to be in that field, praying with his *minyan*, and the gentile stood at a distance, staring at the Baal Shem Tov; he would not take his eyes off him. Afterward, he asked Charna, "Who was that Jew under the tree?" "Why do you ask?" she said. "I felt such a great fear and awe come over me," he said, "that the whole forest seemed too small to hide in."[11]

The Besht's Daughter, Edel

A Fiery Daughter

THE BAAL SHEM TOV ONCE SAID THAT HE TOOK THE SOUL OF HIS daughter Edel from the Torah verse *Esh daat lamo*, "a fiery law unto them"—because she was a fiery personality, fervently devoted to God.

By prayer and meditation, a great mystic like the Besht can "select" the kind of soul he wants for his child from the heavenly treasury of unborn souls. And he can also draw the divine energy that resides in a particular Torah verse to infuse and inspire that soul.[12]

The Sleeping Child

WHEN EDEL WAS A YOUNG GIRL, SHE SOMETIMES MISBEHAVED. BUT BEING clever and bold, she was able to defend herself against charges of wrongdoing.

One Rosh HaShanah, the Baal Shem Tov refused to begin the sounding of the *shofar*, because Edel was not present, and he wanted to be sure that she heard the *shofar* blasts correctly, according to *halacha*. Edel was a high soul, and her father was willing to delay the congregation for her sake.

After searching for Edel, they found her sleeping in her bed. Now, to sleep during the day on Rosh HaShanah, when one is being judged in heaven, is considered perilous. When her father woke her and asked, "You know that one is not supposed to sleep during the day on Rosh HaShanah, don't you?" Edel replied, "Mother always says: 'When a child sleeps, they save the best portion for him.'" (This saying encourages a child to sleep or nap by telling him that when the meal begins, the best portion of food will be kept for him until he awakens.) On hearing these words, the Baal Shem Tov immediately went, with Edel, to the synagogue and began the sounding of the *shofar*.

One purpose of the *shofar* is to awaken the "sleeping" Children of Israel and call them to repentance. Yet that they are asleep itself gives a pretext for heavenly judgment against them: Why are they asleep? Edel's clever reply gave the Baal Shem Tov an answer to the heavenly accusations against the Jewish people, and he went immediately to wake them up to receive the best portion that had been saved for them. When they will fully awaken, the final redemption will come.[13]

The Gates of Divine Help

WHEN EDEL WAS A YOUNG WOMAN, SHE ONCE PARTICIPATED IN A vigorous debate among the Besht's disciples about the recitation said at the end of the Sabbath: "May the Holy One, blessed be He, open for us the gates of light, the gates of long life, the gates of patience, the gates of blessing, the gates of understanding, the gates of joy," and so on, with a long list of many different gates. They argued over which of the gates was the most important, each offering his opinion. Edel said that the gates of divine help were the greatest of all and that all the others were included in it.

When they went and asked the Besht, he said, "She's right, because when a person attains any one of these gates—the gates of Torah, wisdom, or repentance; or in materiality, the gates of sustenance, livelihood, and so on—he should understand that it was all due to divine help, and that the gates of divine help include all the others, for without God's help it's impossible to accomplish anything, even the smallest thing, or to make the smallest movement. Even the understanding that everything depends on God and that you yourself do nothing, also comes from God, blessed be He, who has granted you this understanding." Edel always used to say, "Heavenly help is better than anything."[14]

The Or HaHayim

A Meeting of Souls

IN 1741, THE *GAON*, RABBI HAYIM BEN ATTAR OF MOROCCO, WENT UP TO live in the holy city of Jerusalem. In 1742, *Chumashim** with his commentary, *Or HaHayim* (The Light of Life), were published in Venice and quickly reached Poland.

---

* Plural of *Chumash*.

When the Baal Shem Tov saw this commentary, he was excited and enthused, for he found in the Or HaHayim a kindred spirit who shared his most precious thoughts and dreams, someone whose heart was full of holy fervor and devotion to God.

The Besht told his disciples that during the soul-ascents the Or HaHayim made every night, he heard Torah from the Holy One, blessed be He, Himself, and that his awesome holiness was beyond description. He was among those who descended into the Divine Chariot during soul-ascents, he had revelations of the souls of tzaddikim of past generations, and he had reached exalted levels of the holy spirit. "During my own soul-ascents," continued the Besht, "I've often tried to meet the Or HaHayim in the upper worlds, but I saw him only fleetingly. To whatever heavenly palace I ascended, I saw him there for only a moment, and then he had moved on to an even higher palace. Not that he's greater than me," the Besht added with a smile, "he's just quicker on his feet."

The Baal Shem Tov was constantly pained by the terrible suffering and humiliation of the Jewish people. His heart ached to save them by speeding the redemption. Now he saw his chance. The souls of Rabbi Israel Baal Shem Tov and Rabbi Hayim ben Attar were both sparks of the soul of King David, and the Besht yearned to go up to Jerusalem to meet the Or HaHayim, for he believed that if they would meet, the Messiah son of David would come. But it was not yet time for the End, and heaven prevented the meeting of these two awesome tzaddikim.[15]

Rabbi Gershon Goes Ahead

IN 1742, THE BAAL SHEM TOV SENT RABBI GERSHON KITOVER TO Jerusalem as his emissary to Rabbi Hayim ben Attar. Before Rabbi Gershon went, the Besht told him that the Or HaHayim had two yeshivahs, one whose activity was in the open, for studying the revealed Torah, and another secret one, for studying the concealed Torah, the Kabbalah. The Besht told his brother-in-law to make every effort to gain entrance to the secret yeshivah also. He further instructed Rabbi Gershon not to tell the Or HaHayim about him or praise him until the Sephardic sage said something on his own to indicate that he knew him. And he gave Rabbi Gershon a letter to deliver at that time.

When Rabbi Gershon arrived in Jerusalem, he immediately went to the Or HaHayim to request permission to attend his yeshivah. The Or HaHayim asked him who he was, and he answered simply that he was a Jew from Poland who earnestly desired to learn Torah from him. He was given permission to enter the open yeshivah and he studied there for a week. Then he went to the Or HaHayim's house again and this time asked permission to study in the secret yeshivah. The sage was taken aback that Rabbi Gershon knew about this at all. But when he gazed at Rabbi Gershon from head to toe, he saw that he was worthy of studying Kabbalah, and gave his permission.

The secret yeshivah (called Yeshivat Beit El) met in a cave. After Rabbi Gershon had studied there for three days, the Or HaHayim ordered the gatekeeper not to allow him to enter anymore. Rabbi Gershon immediately went to the Or HaHayim's house to find out why he had been denied entrance. "I'm angry at you," said the sage. "Why didn't you tell me that your master is Rabbi Israel Baal Shem Tov? I know of your holy master and have seen him in the upper worlds. If he's your teacher, you have no need for another rabbi."

Rabbi Gershon then delivered the letter the Baal Shem Tov had given him. In it, the Besht asked permission to travel to Jerusalem to meet the Or HaHayim face-to-face, for he knew that if they would meet, they could bring the redemption. The Or HaHayim sent a letter back to the Baal Shem Tov, by the hand of a Jew returning to Poland, asking him, if when he saw him in the upper worlds, he saw his face and all his limbs, or not. When the Baal Shem Tov wrote back, in another letter delivered by a disciple who was traveling to Jerusalem, that he did not see his heels, the Or HaHayim wrote to him again that he should not trouble himself to come, because it would be for nought. The Baal Shem Tov never received this final letter. And in the winter of 1743, although he was told from heaven not to go, he set out to travel, with great self-sacrifice, to the Holy Land. To bring the redemption and save the Jewish people from their suffering, he was willing to endure any hardship.[16]

To Israel

Forty-two Journeys

THE TORAH SAYS THAT ALL THE WANDERINGS OF THE JEWISH PEOPLE IN the Sinai Desert, their camping and journeying, their stopping and going, were divinely ordained; by the word of God they traveled and by the word of God they encamped. Forty-two separate journeys are recorded in the Torah. According to the mystic teachings, all the journeys of each Jew in his lifetime—everything that happens to him, from the day he is born, to the day he dies and returns to his eternal world—are symbolized by those same forty-two journeys. The day of his birth and exit from the womb is like the Exodus from Egypt; then he goes from journey to journey during his time in this world, until after death he comes to the land of eternal life, which is like the Promised Land. On the spiritual plane too, all his traveling and halting are according to divine decree. Sometimes he is in expanded consciousness, other times in constricted consciousness. The forty-two journeys are recorded in the Torah to teach every Jew how to travel through life, with all its ceaseless ups and downs, through deserts and oases, from journey to journey.

When the Baal Shem Tov traveled to the Land of Israel, his master, the prophet Ahiyah ha-Shiloni, showed him, at every stage of his journey, where it was hinted at in the forty-two journeys of the Jewish people in the Sinai Desert.[17]

Setting Out and Stranded

THE BAAL SHEM TOV PAID THE FARE FOR A SHIP, AND HE, HIS DAUGHTER, Edel, and his scribe, Rabbi Tzvi, set sail for the Land of Israel. The captain of the ship was a scoundrel, and when they were approaching their destination of Istanbul (Turkey), he told them that they would have to dock at a nearby island for two or three days to make urgent repairs. The Baal Shem Tov, Edel, and Rabbi Tzvi disembarked to get some fresh air and relax from the rigors of the voyage. As soon as they were out of sight, however, the captain ordered the sailors to put out to sea, which they did, leaving the Besht and his daughter and scribe stranded on the island. The captain had stolen their money and valuables and had cast their clothes and their other few possessions onto the beach.

When they realized their dire situation, they began to explore the island, to see if there was some way they could reach Istanbul. While they were wandering about, they came upon robbers, whose language they did not understand, who attacked them, bound them with ropes, and began to sharpen their knives to slaughter them. But when the robbers suddenly felt hungry, they left their bound captives and sat down to eat. Rabbi Tzvi said to the Baal Shem Tov, "Master, why don't you do something to save us! Now is the time to use your powers!" "I don't know a thing now," answered the Besht, "all my powers have been taken from me." (Heaven was punishing him by removing his expanded consciousness and his ability to work miracles.) This had never happened before to the Baal Shem Tov, and he began to weep. Then he recovered and said to Rabbi Tzvi, "If you remember anything that I taught you, remind me!" "I also remember nothing," said Rabbi Tzvi," except for the *aleph-bet**." "Recite it to me!" cried the Besht. Rabbi Tzvi began reciting, "*Aleph, bet, gimel, dalet . . .*" and the Baal Shem Tov recited it after him—word by word, letter by letter—loudly and with awesome fervor, as was always his holy way, until all his powers were returned to him as before.

At that moment, they heard the clanging of a bell. An old navy captain suddenly arrived with a troop of soldiers and frightened off the robbers. The soldiers quickly cut the ropes that bound the three captives and set them free. They then took the Besht, his daughter Edel, and his scribe Rabbi Tzvi to their ship, and brought them to Istanbul, where they arrived two days before Passover. The Baal Shem Tov realized that this incident was a heavenly warning that he should return home, but he refused to abandon his mission.[18]

Passover in Istanbul

ONCE AGAIN, THE BAAL SHEM TOV WAS PUNISHED FROM HEAVEN AND HIS exalted state of expanded consciousness was taken away. He went to a *beit midrash* in the city and sat down, but he was not able to study Torah; he knew nothing. He was now also destitute and without resources, all of their valuable possessions and money having been stolen. Since no one there knew of the Baal Shem Tov, he was in a difficult situation, without anyone to help. Edel kept asking, "What will we do for Passover,

---

* Hebrew alphabet.

father? What will we eat?" He answered with simple faith, "God will provide for us." But when the morning before Passover arrived, they still had no matzah or wine.

That morning, Edel went to the shore to wash the white garments her father wore in honor of Sabbaths and holidays. While she was washing them, tears rolled down her cheeks without cease, for the night of the first *seder* was approaching and they still had nothing of what they needed for the holiday! Just then, a passenger ship docked in the port. Among those who disembarked was a wealthy, pious Jew returning home after having been abroad on business. When he saw a young Jewish woman crying, he went over to her and asked what was troubling her. Edel wiped her tears and answered, "My father is a famous tzaddik, but because of events, heaven has punished him by removing his exalted state of consciousness. He's sitting now in the *beit midrash* and I don't know what to do, because we have no place to stay and nothing prepared for Passover."

After telling him the story of their journey, the wealthy man took pity on her and said, "Bring your father and his scribe to me. The three of you can stay in my house for the whole holiday, and I'll take care of all your needs." He gave her his address and she went immediately to the *beit midrash* and told the Baal Shem Tov everything that had happened. Then they went to the wealthy man's home.

Their host welcomed them warmly, although he did not see anything in the Besht's face to indicate that he was the tzaddik his daughter had said he was. The Baal Shem Tov did not want to eat, because it was already past the hour when eating *hametz* is allowed, and eating matzah is forbidden during the daytime before Passover. They gave him wine and he drank a large amount. After drinking the wine, the Besht went to the room his host had given him. Tired from the rigors of the journey and the trials that they had endured, he lay down to rest and fell asleep. The Baal Shem Tov slept until nighttime, while his host went to the synagogue to pray the evening service and returned home to find him still sleeping. Needless to say, he was very surprised that a "holy man" would sleep into the night when the holiday had begun. He asked Edel to wake the Baal Shem Tov because it was time for the *seder*, but she answered that, according to the Torah, it was forbidden for her to wake her father. Rabbi Tzvi also was afraid to wake him. So the wealthy man went into the room himself to wake the Baal Shem Tov.

When he entered, he saw that the Besht's face was burning, it was as red as fire, and both his eyes were bulging out, with streams of tears flowing from them; strange noises were also coming from his mouth. Startled by this sight, he quickly left the room. He realized that his guest was indeed a holy man of God and he gave up any thought of waking him.

After some time, the Baal Shem Tov woke up by himself, washed his hands, and stood up to pray the evening service, in amazing *d'vekut*, because while he slept, his expanded consciousness and spiritual levels were returned to him. After he prayed, they sat down for the *seder*, and the Besht recited the *Haggadah** with great fervor, as

---

* The traditional Passover *seder* text recounting the Exodus story.

was his holy way. He read the story of the Exodus from Egypt and came to the words: "It is this that has stood by our ancestors and us. For not only one has risen against us to annihilate us, but in every generation they rise against us to annihilate us, and the Holy One, blessed be He, saves us from their hand." Then—out of its proper order in the service—he immediately began to recite the verse from the *Hallel**: "To Him who alone does great wonders, for His kindness is forever!" and loudly repeated this verse many times with awesome fervor.

All during the *seder*, their host did not dare ask the Baal Shem Tov anything. But later, when they had concluded the *seder* in the early hours of the morning, he asked him to explain his strange behavior—his weeping during sleep and his loud repetition of the verse: "To Him who alone does great wonders." The Besht said, "A terrible decree was issued by the government against the Jews of Istanbul and, when I was on my bed, I made a soul-ascent to try to annul it. Only because I was ready to sacrifice myself was I able to annul the decree. I was about to expire and my soul was ready to leave my body; but in the merit of my love for Israel, they had mercy on me in heaven and returned my soul to me. Thank God, I succeeded, and my prayer was granted; the decree was annulled in heaven. During the *seder*, when I recited the *Hallel* verse: 'To Him who alone does great wonders,' the decree was annulled on earth. Tomorrow in the synagogue, God-willing, you'll hear the full story of what happened."

The next day, before the morning service, a wine merchant, who was a prominent member of the community, entered the synagogue and announced, "*Mazel tov, mazel tov*, my friends! We've all been saved! God has delivered us from an evil decree!" And he told them the whole story of what had happened.

The Baal Shem Tov's host now knew that the Besht was not only a holy man, but a miracle worker, whose prayers were listened to in heaven. When he heard of the Besht's desire to go up to the Land of Israel, and knowing that the Besht had no money, he offered to pay for all the expenses of the journey. And he said he would be honored to send the Baal Shem Tov money to support him when he would be living in the Land of Israel. The Baal Shem Tov accepted his first offer, but declined the second, saying that he could not think about his maintenance there; his only desire now was to merit being in the Holy Land.[19]

A Visit to the Rabbi of Istanbul

AFTER THIS, THE BESHT VISITED THE CHIEF SEPHARDIC SAGE OF ISTANBUL, and during their conversation in the holy tongue told him about the evil decree against the Jews of Istanbul that had been averted. He then told him that the Jews in his own country were suffering from a very harsh and terrible exile inflicted by the angel-prince¶ of Poland. Hearing this, the sage's head convulsively flew back as if he

---

* Psalms of praise that are part of the *Haggadah*.
¶ Each nation has its angel in heaven that represents it at the heavenly court.

had been struck by a blow, and he uttered a deep groan. The Baal Shem Tov saw that, with this groan, the angel of Poland was wounded and the coming of the Messiah brought closer.[20]

Disaster and Return

THE BAAL SHEM TOV PREPARED TO SET OUT FOR THE LAND OF ISRAEL. When he and his companions boarded the ship, he was told from heaven to go ashore again, to return home and continue his work in Poland. But he refused to obey and they took away all his spiritual levels, including his ability to study Torah and pray. He could not even recite the first word of a blessing, "*Baruch*" (Blessed), from the *siddur*, because he did not recognize the letters of the Hebrew alphabet. "What does it matter?" he said. "I'll travel to the holy Or HaHayim and to the Land of Israel as an ignorant and unlearned man."

The Baal Shem Tov accepted with love whatever difficulties and afflictions came to him, until something overwhelmed him, for a great storm arose and battered the ship. The Besht knew that it was because of him, and that heaven was blocking his way. Suddenly, a huge wave swept over the ship and carried his pious daughter Edel overboard. Drowning, she cried out, "Father, help me!" This was more than he could bear, and he began to weep. At that moment, because of his great distress at his daughter's suffering, and because all his spiritual levels had been taken from him, the Satan (may his name be blotted out!) came and tempted him to apostasy. When the Besht realized the disaster that was threatening him, and that he had reached the gates of death, he cried out, "Hear O Israel, the Lord our God, the Lord is one!—Master of the world, I'll return home!" Immediately, his teacher, the prophet Ahiyah ha-Shiloni came, snatched Edel from the sea, and quickly carried them all back to Istanbul, through the clouds.

The Baal Shem Tov was terribly depressed by what had happened, but Ahiyah was surprised at him and said, "Didn't I long ago teach you the divine Names to meditate on when you encounter trouble and are suffering? The Besht answered that heaven had not revealed to him beforehand how great the trouble would be that would come upon them. Then, Ahiyah showed him where he was in the 42 journeys and in which spiritual worlds he was now and which divine Names he should meditate on. The Baal Shem Tov strengthened himself to sweeten those worlds in their source by finding the sweet in what is bitter. So he accepted this reversal too with love and joy. Then he returned home.

Three months after the Besht returned to Poland and Kitov, Rabbi Hayim ben Attar passed away in Jerusalem.[21]

He Moves to Medzibuz

AFTER THE FAILURE OF HIS ATTEMPT TO BRING THE MESSIAH BY JOINING the Or HaHayim in Israel, the Baal Shem Tov had to reconsider his plans and hopes for the Jewish people. In 1745, he moved to Medzibuz in Podolia (which was part of Poland, although the population was mostly Ukrainian). To attract him to their town, the Jewish community provided him and his family with a rent-free house near the synagogue. The Besht later told one of his disciples that heaven had given him a choice whether to move to Nemirov, Medzibuz, or a third city in Polish Ukraine, and that he chose Medzibuz so that on *Shabbat* he would always have fish to eat, for the Bug River had many fish. (According to the Kabbalah, eating fish on *Shabbat* has mystic importance.)

But there was another reason why the Besht settled in Medzibuz. He had decided to make Medzibuz the center of a large, organized movement to revive Jewish life. When the Besht was first revealed, he concentrated his efforts on drawing near simple Jews. But now he wanted to reach the Torah scholars and the religious elite, and for that he had to live in a town like Medzibuz that was full of outstanding scholars in the revealed Torah and the Kabbalah. With their help, he would be able to spread his message widely. After his extensive travels as a *baal shem*, he was now famous, and many people, even gentiles, came to him for healing; the city of Medzibuz became renowned because of his presence there. The Besht continued to travel to Jewish communities in Podolia, Volhynia, Galicia, Reissin, and Lithuania. He worked as a *baal shem* as before, but his journeys now were mainly directed to gaining adherents to his new movement. He especially concentrated on winning over rabbis and scholars, men of stature, who could aid him in his holy task and mission.[22]

The Birth of His Son, Tzvi

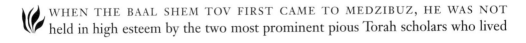 SHORTLY AFTER HIS MOVE TO MEDZIBUZ, THE BESHT'S SECOND CHILD was born to his wife Chana, a boy, whom he named Tzvi. At his son's *bris**, the Besht gave a brief talk in which he said, "The name Tzvi is an acronym for the words of the prophet: *Tzaddik b'emunato yichyeh*—'a tzaddik lives by his faith.' May my son Tzvi grow up to fulfill that verse! The Hebrew can also be read as: *yichayeh*—'a tzaddik enlivens others by his faith.' There are two kinds of tzaddikim. One enlivens himself by his faith. But a greater tzaddik has enough faith to influence and enliven others too. I bless my son Tzvi with all my heart that he also fulfill that reading. May it be God's will!"[23]

The Pious Scholars in Medzibuz

WHEN THE BAAL SHEM TOV FIRST CAME TO MEDZIBUZ, HE WAS NOT held in high esteem by the two most prominent pious Torah scholars who lived

---

* Circumcision.

there, Rabbi Zev Kitzes and Rabbi David Forkes, the *maggid* of the town. They considered his being a *baal shem* unworthy of a tzaddik, because there were charlatans who claimed that title and took advantage of people's gullibility to exploit them. The two rabbis soon discovered, however, that the Baal Shem Tov indeed possessed exceptional spiritual qualities and had miraculous powers. They became his disciples and—living in Medzibuz—became intimate with him. A group of close disciples, who were all great scholars and kabbalists, formed around the Besht in Medzibuz. Some of them stayed in his house the whole week and went back to their families only for *Shabbat*. They and others were the core group of the Besht's Holy Society, his circle of close disciples, his "sixty heroes." This Holy Society was the seed that grew into the great tree of the Baal Shem Tov's new hasidic movement.[24]

His Minyan

THE BAAL SHEM TOV'S PRAYER *MINYAN* IN MEDZIBUZ WAS COMPOSED of extraordinary men of intense spirituality. He elevated all of them and they prayed with tremendous *d'vekut*, with devotion and fervor. Once, one of them, Rabbi Yaakov, who was called Rabbi Yakil, took his son to the synagogue with him, where the Baal Shem Tov was leading his *minyan* in prayer. Rabbi Yakil said, "Look well at this, my son, because there won't be something like this again in the world until the coming of the Messiah!"[25]

Rabbi Yaakov Yosef of Polnoye

Drawing Him Close

RABBI YAAKOV YOSEF WAS THE RABBI OF SHAROGROD IN PODOLIA (HE was later the rabbi of Polnoye). As a boy he had become famous throughout Podolia and Volhynia as a Torah prodigy. As a man he was a great talmudic scholar and kabbalist who was committed to a rigorous interpretation of *halacha* and righteousness. He was also intensely spiritual and followed an ascetic regimen of frequent fasting. But his fault was that he was strict on others as well as on himself. He was prone to anger and often engaged in disputes with the people of his town.

Rabbi Yaakov Yosef did not know the Baal Shem Tov and had never seen him. Although he had heard that the Besht was a great tzaddik and miracle worker, he gave these reports no credence. The Baal Shem Tov, however, was aware of Rabbi Yaakov Yosef's outstanding qualities, and desired to make him a disciple.

One summer, the Besht visited Sharogrod. Arriving in the early hours of the morning, when people were leading their animals to pasture, he stopped in the middle of the street and climbed down from his coach. When a Jewish peasant passed by leading his cow with a rope, the Besht motioned to him to come over and began telling him a story. Before long, the man had entirely forgotten where he was going and why, and stood fastened to the spot next to his cow, listening to the Besht weave his enchanting tale.

Someone else passed by and, catching a few snatches of a story, he too drifted over to hear what the Besht was saying. Soon, another of the passersby stopped, then a few more. The crowd around the Baal Shem Tov grew larger and larger, until he had attracted almost everyone in the town. They all stood spellbound within the charmed circle of his storytelling, listening to his delightful tales that were suffused with love of God. Among them also stood the *shammos* of the synagogue.

During the summer, Rabbi Yaakov Yosef prayed at eight o'clock in the morning, and the *shammos*, who had the key, opened the door of the synagogue every day at 6:30. That day, the rabbi came to the synagogue and found it still closed. Being by nature an irritable person, this infuriated him. The *shammos*, meanwhile, was listening to the Baal Shem Tov with the others, some of whom were standing with their tallis and *tefillin* bags under their arms. They had been on their way to the synagogue and had completely forgotten where they were going. However, just then the Baal Shem Tov signaled to the *shammos*, motioning with his hand as if opening a door with a key, and the *shammos* suddenly remembered about the synagogue! He ran as fast as his legs could carry him and, when he arrived there out of breath, found the rabbi standing outside, alone and fuming. Not only was the synagogue locked, but the regulars, who came every day for the morning prayers, were not there! The *shammos* explained that a visitor to the town was standing in the street telling stories, and everybody was listening to him. The rabbi was greatly incensed by this, but it did him no good, and he had to pray alone.

After praying, the rabbi ordered the *shammos* to bring the storytelling visitor to him. He would have him given stripes for preventing the congregation from praying together! Meanwhile, the Baal Shem Tov had finished his storytelling and returned to the inn where he was staying. The *shammos* went looking for him and, when he found him, conveyed the rabbi's order that he come to him at once. The Besht went immediately. When he arrived, the rabbi, who was still furious, said to him, "Are you the one who stopped the community from praying as a congregation?" "I'm the one, master," the Baal Shem Tov replied humbly, "but I beg the rabbi not to be angry at me, and allow me to tell him a story." "Go ahead," said Rabbi Yaakov Yosef gruffly.

The Besht told him a story, and the rabbi was so moved by it that he calmed down. He began to talk to the Baal Shem Tov respectfully, addressing him as "sir." The Besht, on the other hand, stopped calling him "rabbi" and "master" and began to speak to him as an equal, addressing him also as "sir." Then the Baal Shem Tov said, "If you'd like, I'll tell you another story." "Please do," said the rabbi. When the Besht finished that story, he asked the rabbi if he would like to hear still another. When he said yes, the Besht said to him, "Listen closely. I was once driving a coach with three horses—one brown, one black, and one white—and they were not able to neigh. A gentile peasant called out to me from his coach, 'Slacken the reins!' I slackened the reins, and once again the horses were able to neigh. Do you understand what I'm saying?" asked the Besht. "I understand, master," said Rabbi Yaakov Yosef humbly.

What did the parable teach the rabbi? The body's animal powers—represented by the horses—must be reined in and directed to do the will of the soul, whose purpose is to serve God. But if they are controlled too strictly—if "the horses cannot even neigh"—the person becomes tense and angry; all joy is suppressed. And there can be no true divine service without joy.

At that point, Rabbi Yaakov Yosef began to converse with the Baal Shem Tov, and during their conversation he attached himself to him—as disciple to master—with all his heart and soul. Then the Besht said to him, "I still haven't prayed, and I want to go now and do so." While he went to the synagogue to pray alone, Rabbi Yaakov Yosef went home and showed the Besht great honor by having a fine meal prepared for him. After the meal, the two of them went for a walk and all the people of the town accompanied them, and saw that the Baal Shem Tov had attracted their rabbi to him. From then on, Rabbi Yaakov Yosef became one of the foremost disciples of the Baal Shem Tov.[26]

Crying

SOME TIME AFTER THIS, RABBI YAAKOV YOSEF HEARD THAT THE BAAL Shem Tov was in the town of Mohilev, not far from Sharogrod, and he went to see him. Arriving early Friday morning, he was surprised to find the Besht puffing on a pipe before the prayers, and thought it peculiar. The time before prayer should be used to prepare to meet one's Maker; how could the Besht engage in a pleasurable diversion? But it was the holy practice of the Baal Shem Tov—as of some others then—to prepare for the prayers by meditatively smoking his pipe. During the service, Rabbi Yaakov Yosef sobbed as never before in his life. And he understood that the crying was not from himself, but from the holy power of the Baal Shem Tov.[27]

The Reward for Personal Service

ONCE, RABBI YAAKOV YOSEF FELT SPIRITUALLY DRY AND STALE. KNOWING that offering personal service to one's master makes one receptive to his influence, he walked for three days straight from Sharogrod to Medzibuz to visit the Baal Shem Tov (it being especially meritorious to travel to one's spiritual master on foot). When he arrived in Medzibuz, the Besht was about to prepare for the morning prayers by smoking his pipe, and had taken it out. Rabbi Yaakov Yosef served the Besht by lighting his pipe with a live coal. "As your reward for serving me," said the Besht, "may you merit new fire in your service of God!" After the morning prayers, Rabbi Yaakov Yosef immediately returned home, without having heard any new teaching from the Besht. He had accomplished his purpose by lighting his master's pipe and had no need to stay further.[28]

Elevation

THE BAAL SHEM TOV USED TO SAY TO RABBI YAAKOV YOSEF, "YOSSELE, I have to elevate you spiritually." Once, after staying with the Besht for five weeks, Rabbi Yaakov Yosef humbly asked him, "Master, when will you elevate me?"[29]

His Fasting

FOR THE FIVE YEARS PRECEDING HIS MEETING THE BESHT, RABBI YAAKOV Yosef had fasted continuously with interruptions—daily until evening, when he ate a meal—and once every month he fasted for the whole week, from one Sabbath to the next. In the sixth year of this practice, he met the Baal Shem Tov.

One week, when he was fasting from Sabbath to Sabbath, the Besht, who was on the road traveling, heard a heavenly proclamation, saying, "Hurry to him, for if he continues fasting for one more day, he will go insane!" The Besht raced to his disciple so furiously that one of his horses died from the exertion. When the Besht arrived, he ordered Rabbi Yaakov Yosef to end his fast, and added, "One of my best horses died because of you. May it be your atonement." Immediately, the rabbi obeyed him and ate. Later, the Besht sent him a letter that said, "I'm very upset by your fasting. As your master, I order you, by the decree of the angels, and of the Holy One, blessed be He, and His *Shechinah*, to desist from any more fasting. Abandon this dangerous path, which leads to depression and sadness, for the *Shechinah* does not rest on someone sad and depressed, but only on someone joyful from doing *mitzvot*. Subdue your body and evil inclination not by fasting, but by attaching yourself completely in *d'vekut* to the holy letters of your Torah study and prayer. If you obey me in this, you brave man, all the judgments will be sweetened, and I promise you that God will be with you."

The next time Rabbi Yaakov Yosef visited the Baal Shem Tov, the Besht said to him, "I've effected in heaven that when a man uses the *mikvah* in the morning, before prayer, it's considered by the Holy One, blessed be He, as if he had fasted a full day."[30]

His Soul's Torah

RABBI YAAKOV YOSEF FULFILLED ALL OF HIS MASTER'S TEACHING, instruction, and advice as best he could. Before the next Rosh HaShanah, the Baal Shem Tov was serving as prayer-leader and reciting *Selichot*. When he recited the verse: "God shall circumcise your heart," Rabbi Yaakov Yosef fainted. At that moment, after all Rabbi Yaakov Yosef's mighty efforts, the Besht finally circumcised his heart and elevated him spiritually. While in a deep trance, Rabbi Yaakov Yosef received his soul's Torah with thunder and lightning and the accompaniment of all sorts of musical instruments, as it says in the *Zohar* about the Giving of the Torah at Mount Sinai. Just as the Jewish people received the Torah as a nation at Mount Sinai, the Baal Shem Tov caused Rabbi Yaakov Yosef to receive the Torah as an individual.[31]

A Yossele like This

THE BESHT RETURNED THE LOVE THAT RABBI YAAKOV YOSEF HAD FOR HIM, and he was very proud of his great disciple. He once said, "I won't seek any reward from the Master of the world for the Torah and *mitzvot* I've done, but only for having given Him a Yossele like this."[32]

Rabbi Yosef of Kaminka

RABBI YOSEF OF KAMINKA WAS ALREADY AN EXCEPTIONAL TORAH SCHOLAR and servant of God before he met the Baal Shem Tov. But he followed an ascetic path. The first time he met the Besht, the Besht was with his holy disciples in the woods. When Rabbi Yosef approached, the Besht greeted him and said, "*Shalom aleichem*, Rabbi Yosef. Tell me, why do you torture your body so much?" He asked this as if Rabbi Yosef were a close friend, but he had never met him in his life. Rabbi Yosef answered, "I afflict my body in order to subdue it." "If you want to subdue your body," said the Besht—and he pointed to Rabbi Yaakov Yosef who was praying the *Shemoneh Esreh* standing next to a tree—"pray like that person there; then you'll subdue your body."

Rabbi Yosef became very attached to the Baal Shem Tov, who drew him close. In a short time, he attained the holy spirit. The Besht once said, "If the Redeemer comes in this generation and needs a prophet and a high priest, Rabbi Yosef will be the prophet, and Rabbi Yaakov Yosef [who was a *kohen*] will be the high priest." If the Besht praised his disciples this way, testifying to their greatness, how great was he?[33]

Rabbi David Leikes and the Besht's Pet Bear Cub

THE BAAL SHEM TOV DISCOURAGED EXCESSIVE FASTING, BUT TAUGHT that if a person knew that something in his soul could be fixed only by fasting, he should fast until he had accomplished what needed to be done. One of his foremost disciples, Rabbi David Leikes, used to fast from one Sabbath to the next. One day, he entered his master's house and came into the Besht's room, where a pet bear cub was tied by a rope. The Besht had found an orphaned cub alone in the woods and was rais-ing it until he could return it to the wild. The cub began to yelp in fright when Rabbi David came in, and struggled desperately against the rope, trying to escape. The Besht said to Rabbi David, "Please leave; you're frightening him. Since you have the divine image on your face, and it's written: 'The fear and dread of you shall be upon every beast,' he's terrified of you." Rabbi David thought, "Since the master said to me that I have the divine image, that means I can stop fasting." Knowing his thoughts, the Besht said, "Your task now is to eat and care for your body, and to manifest God's love and compassion, more than His fear and awe." Then, Rabbi David's face would lose its severity and he would be similar to his master, the Baal Shem Tov, who was like Adam in the Garden of Eden, whom all the animals loved.[34]

Still Hidden

WHEN THE BAAL SHEM TOV REVEALED HIMSELF, HE DREW MANY OF his close disciples from the ranks of the elite circles of pious Torah scholars and kabbalists. At the same time, some of his comrades in the movement of hidden tzad-dikim gave up their secret identities to assist him in his new task. But even after he revealed himself and had many disciples, he was still the leader of a network of hidden tzaddikim. These were comrades and followers from the time when he was a hidden tzaddik, who remained hidden tzaddikim. They appeared to be poor laborers or trav-eled around as wandering beggars with torn clothing. The Besht also told some new disciples to be hidden tzaddikim and he sent them on various missions. Even after the Besht had long been revealed, he once confided to a close disciple that he still felt he was more among the hidden tzaddikim than the revealed ones—meaning that he was still more hidden than revealed.[35]

Reb Yaakov Shammos

ONE HASID OF THE BESHT WAS CALLED REB YAAKOV SHAMMOS (REB YAAKOV the Servant). He was a hidden tzaddik who made his living by stoking the ovens in the homes of new mothers and preparing food for the other children and feeding them. The Baal Shem Tov once said, "Reb Yaakov Shammos sees Godliness with his physical eyes."[36]

Lighting His Pipe with a Candle of Non-kosher Fat

ONCE, WHILE THE BAAL SHEM TOV WAS SMOKING HIS PIPE TO PREPARE for prayer, it occurred to him that he was acting wrongly by lighting his pipe with a candle made from non-kosher fat. (Although one is forbidden to eat such fat, one may derive other benefits from it, such as using it for candles; but it cannot be used for Sabbath candles.) The Besht felt that for someone on his spiritual level, perhaps it was impermissible to use such a candle to light his pipe. After all, he was using his pipe to prepare for *davvening*. He even recited a blessing over his pipe-smoking! He decided, however, that now was not the time to be worrying about this, since he was preparing for prayer. His only purpose should be to focus his mind for that divine service. Yet he could not get the matter out of his mind. He tried many techniques to clear his mind, but nothing worked. He kept thinking that perhaps he should not be lighting his pipe with a candle of non-kosher fat. When he realized that he was being prevented from preparing for prayer, he jumped up and swore that from then on he would *always* light his pipe with a candle of non-kosher fat! And, indeed, from then on, the Besht always lit his pipe with a candle of non-kosher fat.

Later that day, between *Minha* and *Maariv*, the Besht sat with his disciples, lit his pipe, and began to teach them. And he told them the story of what had happened earlier, and explained, "I could have sworn *never* to use a candle of forbidden fat. But that wouldn't have solved the problem. The usual impulse of people who want to be more pious is to become more ascetic, to deprive themselves of something. They think that being more holy means separating oneself from the world. As their fear of sin becomes ever stronger, they constantly worry that they are somehow transgressing. And they steadily narrow the scope of their activity in the world: They refuse to eat at this or that place, or associate with these or those people, or let their children befriend these other children. Their world grows smaller and smaller. Finally, a person becomes like a rabbi I once met, who sat in his chair almost the whole Sabbath with his arms at his sides and his legs tucked in for fear of touching something *muktzeh* or stepping on an ant!

"There are two kinds of holiness in Judaism. The root meaning of *kadosh*, 'holy,' is 'to be separate.' One kind of holiness is to separate from sins and materialism and from sinners and gentiles. That's the holiness of the fear of God, and it is good when kept within reasonable bounds. But there's another kind of holiness that comes from love of God, where the goal is to infuse holiness into the world. That's my hasidic way and the way I want you to follow. I never want to isolate myself; I want more and more contact and involvement with God's world and with people. This morning while smoking my pipe, I heard the voice of what seemed to be my good inclination whispering in my ear, telling me not to use a candle of non-kosher fat. But then I realized that this was actually my *yetzer ha-ra*, my evil inclination. And I refused to listen to it, because there's no end to that path. One restricts oneself more and more until finally, one lives in a small world of a just few pious people like oneself. I could have vowed never to use a candle of non-kosher fat. But I wanted to *kill* that impulse, that *yetzer*. And I did so, by vowing to *always* use a candle of forbidden fat." The Besht concluded, "When you have a 'pious' impulse to separate from the world, consider: There are times when it's holy to separate; but there's usually a second possibility, another kind of holiness—to engage with the world, to infuse the world with holiness and elevate it."[37]

Leib Saras Dances before the Besht

A YOUTH OF FIFTEEN, NAMED LEIB SARAS, WHO HAD BEGUN TO VISIT THE Baal Shem Tov, once burst into the Besht's room and began to dance in a wild ecstasy from one end of the room to the other. The Besht's mature disciples, infuriated by his chutzpah*, wanted to throw him out, but the Besht calmed them, and said to him, "I know you're on fire, and I know what's going on with you. But I want you to know that you're on a dangerous path; you're on the edge of a sharp sword. Leave that path and cling to me!"

The Besht saw that the impetuous youth was on a high spiritual level and had a great soul. But he needed a rebbe, a spiritual master, to guide him. The Baal Shem Tov would teach him balance, to know when to let his spirit free and when to control his passions, lest they lead him to fall into unrestrained wildness. Soon after this incident, the Baal Shem Tov appointed Rabbi Leib Saras as his liason with the hidden tzaddikim.[38]

When to Visit the Teacher?

A TORAH SCHOLAR ONCE VISITED THE BAAL SHEM TOV AND ASKED TO BE his disciple. The Besht asked the man if he would like to come to him when he was teaching his circle of disciples or when he was playing with his little son Hershele (Tzvi).

If he was an outsider, he would ask to be with the disciples, thinking that he would learn kabbalistic secrets; otherwise, he would want to see how a father should relate to his child.

Even more than the Baal Shem Tov wanted to teach Torah or Kabbalah, he wanted to teach by example how to love people, particularly children. By observing how the Besht behaved with his child, a perceptive disciple could learn many mystic secrets about how God behaves with His children. The man who was being tested understood what to do. He asked to watch the Baal Shem Tov play with his son. Later, the Besht invited this new disciple to join his circle of disciples, when he taught them the deepest secrets of the Kabbalah.[39]

His Torah Teaching

SOMETIMES, WHEN THE BESHT TAUGHT TORAH, HIS WORDS WERE SO fiery they set the hearts of his listeners aflame. At other times, his words of Torah were as sweet as honey and produced an ineffable peace and joy. Someone who heard Torah teaching from the holy mouth of the Baal Shem Tov never forgot it all his life.

The joy the Besht's disciples felt when he taught them Torah was indescribable. It

*Brazen behavior.

was not only what he said, but how he said it and who was saying it. As soon as he opened his holy mouth, they felt elevated. The very sound of his sweet voice was like a balm to troubled souls. His face shone like an angel of God and his words were the words of the *Shechinah* speaking from his throat. He was always in a state of intense *d'vekut* when he taught Torah, every word he said being spoken before God. He taught them Torah the way it is taught in the Garden of Eden, and his disciples could smell the fragrance of paradise that filled the room. Its perfume was so ravishing that their souls almost flew away with each word that he uttered. Everything he said was perfectly true, directly from heaven; nothing missed the mark by the least bit. His teaching was not measured out, because there was no end to the divine wisdom that poured from his holy mouth. An ordinary Torah teacher studies and then teaches. After having scattered what he gathered, he stops speaking. Not so the holy Baal Shem Tov, who was an ever-flowing stream, so attached to the supernal source that, when he began to speak, the fountain of divine wisdom never failed.

He once remarked to a disciple, "God tells me the Torah to speak. I don't have to work hard over it." He told another disciple, "When I teach, I first attach myself in *d'vekut* with the Creator, blessed be He. Then I let my mouth say what it will." Before one of his disciples left Medzibuz to return to his hometown where he would teach and preach, the Besht said to him, "When you speak words of Torah before people, bind your mind first to the Creator, blessed be He. The souls of your listeners are also bound to the Creator, since no one lives except from the flow of life-energy from God, blessed be He, who bestows life on all creatures. You should think that you are speaking before the Creator, blessed be He, to give Him pleasure. Say to yourself: 'I'm not speaking before people, because what do I care if they praise or criticize me?' Don't be concerned about your own honor but about the honor of heaven. Bind yourself to God and to your listeners, and speak to their souls, which are sparks of divinity, and speak before God."

When he was teaching Torah one day to his disciples, he interrupted himself and uttered with intense fervor the verse from the Song of Songs: "New as well as old, have I laid up for thee, my beloved." And he continued, "For You alone, Master of the world, for no one but You." His disciples later questioned him, "Have we not also merited to hear our master's teaching?" "As a full barrel overflows," he replied.

Once, when his disciples asked him to teach after the prayers, he did so. But while he was teaching, he began to tremble and shake as he did during prayer. Then he interrupted himself and said, "Master of the world! It's revealed and known before You that I'm not speaking for my own honor, or for the honor of my father's or my mother's families!" After pausing, he said, "Much do I know and much am I able to do, but there's no one to whom I can reveal it."[40]

The Melamed's Dream

 THERE WAS A CERTAIN RICH MAN IN MEDZIBUZ WHO WAS OPPOSED TO THE Baal Shem Tov because of the Besht's unconventional and innovative ways. The *melamed* who lived in his home and taught the man's children—a pious young Torah scholar—also kept his distance from the Besht. The Baal Shem Tov, for his part, very much wanted to draw this *melamed* to the true service of God, for he was a young man of great spiritual potential, a vessel fit to receive everything good. Nevertheless, it was not obvious to the Besht how he could accomplish this purpose, for not only did the *melamed* avoid the Besht, but the householder he worked for kept a strict watch over him in this regard.

One Sabbath night, the *melamed* dreamed that he was taking a stroll through Medzibuz, when he saw a magnificent palace of exquisite beauty. He was stunned by the sight and could not have his fill of it, for the more closely he looked at it the more wonders he saw. After gazing at it for a while, he thought to himself: If the building's basic design is this magnificent, how much more astonishing must its fine work and ornamentation be! When he inspected the building more carefully, he was even more charmed, because in every little section that he focused his eyes on, he saw wondrously expert workmanship, whose equal could not be found in all the world. He profoundly contemplated all this beauty until he fell into a rapture. Again, he thought to himself: If the palace's exterior is so amazingly beautiful, what must its interior be like?

When he approached a window to peer inside, he looked and—behold—he saw within, the Baal Shem Tov and all his holy disciples sitting around a table, and the Besht was teaching Torah. The young man's heart yearned to enter the inner sanctum, and he ran to the door. But when he tried to enter, the servant pushed him away and would not permit him to go in. Although this broke his heart, his longing to hear the words of the living God was so overpowering that he stood by the window and listened with devotion to all the holy teachings uttered by the Baal Shem Tov. Then he woke up . . . and it was a dream! He began to go over all the Torah teachings he had heard, and they were sweeter than honey. He repeated them to himself a second and a third time, but since it was still the middle of night, he had to go back to sleep.

When he woke up on the Sabbath morning and got out of bed, he remembered the dream with total clarity, but he had completely forgotten the teachings. This bothered him so much that he actually became confused and could hardly pray. At the Sabbath table after prayers, he sat as if bewildered, and the householder said to him, "What's the matter? Did you have a bad dream? If you did, you can have three friends change it to good." The *melamed* did not answer. He would have run off to the Baal Shem Tov that moment, but he remembered how the doorkeeper in the dream had rejected him, and he was afraid the same thing would happen to him while awake, and he would be completely humiliated. That whole day he was in a state of extreme agitation.

During the third Sabbath meal, the Baal Shem Tov said to one of his disciples, "Go to the house of that wealthy man and invite the *melamed* to come here." All the disciples were surprised, since they knew that the *melamed* had previously wanted nothing to do with the Baal Shem Tov. But as soon as the disciple the Besht had sent opened the door and said to him, "The Baal Shem Tov invites . . ." the *melamed* jumped up like a madman, raced outside without his coat, and ran to the Baal Shem Tov.

There he sat at the table and listened to the Torah teachings of the Baal Shem Tov and, when he realized that they were the same teachings he had heard in his dream, he immediately fainted. Some of the Besht's disciples quickly attended to him. When he came to, the Baal Shem Tov said to him jokingly, "If you'd heard something new, I might understand why you were so excited, but I know that you already heard all this last night!" At that moment, the *melamed* realized that everything that had happened to him was from God, and from then on he became a devoted disciple of the Baal Shem Tov.[41]

Rabbi David Leikes Is Appointed to Lead the Dancing

RABBI DAVID LEIKES USED TO ENJOY TREATING THE HOLY SOCIETY, the Besht's inner circle of close disciples, to drinks, which he himself brought from a local tavern. Although he was a great Torah scholar, even among the inner circle, he was not concerned about his honor, and was happy to get the liquor himself, feeling that bringing the liquor, wine, or mead, which make men happy, is a *mitzvah*; it was a cherished task he would not delegate to anyone else. The Baal Shem Tov rewarded him for this holy service of his with the honor of leading the dancing at every celebration, because Rabbi David was an outstanding dancer and his fervor in dancing was unlimited. After Rabbi David had abandoned—at the instigation of the Baal Shem Tov—his ascetic habit of fasting, he fully absorbed the Besht's teaching, that a Jew should always be joyful. One of his favorite melodies was set to the verse 'Only the living, they shall praise You!'" He used to sing this melody with all his heart and soul, when the Baal Shem Tov sat amidst his Holy Society of close disciples and all of them danced around him with fervor and flaming devotion.[42]

Rabbi David Leikes Reaches into His Pocket

ONCE, THE BESHT ATE A THIRD SABBATH MEAL WITH HIS DISCIPLES THAT continued for a number of hours into the night. Finally, they said the Grace After Meals, stood up where they were to pray *Maariv*, made *havdala*, and sat down again immediately for the *melave malka* feast. After the *melave malka*, the Baal Shem Tov said to Rabbi David Leikes, "David, let's have some money to buy some mead for us to drink." Of course, Rabbi David would not have money on his person right after the Sabbath! Regardless, Rabbi David had no doubts about a command from his holy master, who had asked him for money for something to drink. Although he knew that he had not a penny with him, he put his hand into his pocket, took out a coin, and gave it for the mead. The faith of the Baal Shem Tov's disciples in their master was total; and great faith draws down heavenly blessings.[43]

His Tear-Stained Siddur

THE BESHT WROTE THE NAMES OF MANY OF HIS CLOSE DISCIPLES IN THE
margins of his *siddur*, next to specific prayers and also on blank pages, along with
requests to make for them during his prayers—to succeed in Torah study, to attain true
piety, to merit going up to Jerusalem, and for worldly needs too. One of the Besht's
disciples once had an opportunity to look through this *siddur* and he saw that these
places and pages were spotted with tears that the Besht had wept while praying for his
disciples and those close to him.[44]

Even One Moment's Consolation

THE BAAL SHEM TOV ONCE VISITED A WOMAN WHO WAS CRITICALLY ILL
and he comforted her and blessed her, "May the Merciful One send you a complete healing!" "No, Rebbe!" the woman on her sick-bed pleaded, "Swear by your portion in the World-to-Come that I'll get well!" "I swear to you," said the Besht, "by my
portion in the World-to-Come that you'll get well! Be strong and trust in the Healer
of all flesh." Some time later, word came that the woman had died. The Besht's close
disciples, who were embarrassed by what had happened, asked him, "Master, why did
you swear by your portion in the World-to-Come that she would get well?" "I knew
that she wouldn't recover," said the Besht. "The heavenly decree was sealed and nothing I could do would change it. But she was so afraid, it was making her terribly
depressed and miserable and was ruining her last few days on this earth. What do I
care about my portion in the World-to-Come, if by losing it I can bring even one
moment's consolation to a Jewish woman?"[45]

With Joy and with Sadness

MOST OF THE RABBIS IN LITHUANIA WERE TOTALLY COMMITTED TO THE
absolute primacy of Torah study in Jewish life. Lithuanian Jews were the least
receptive to the Baal Shem Tov's message, and Lithuania became a bastion of opposition to his new hasidic way. The first time the Besht visited the town of Slutzk in
Lithuania, he arrived shortly before *Rosh Hodesh*, the New Moon celebration. In
Slutzk, they followed the custom of observing the day before *Rosh Hodesh* as a *Yom Kippur Katan*, a Lesser Day of Atonement, a day of fasting and repentance. At noon before
Yom Kippur Katan, which began that evening, they announced that all work in town
should cease, so that everyone—men, women, and children—could come to the synagogue for the afternoon prayers. Following the afternoon and evening prayers, they
announced that everyone should return to the synagogue at midnight for *Tikkun
Hatzot*, and that the following day too would be a day of fasting until the evening and
of a cessation from work.

That night, after *Tikkun Hatzot*, the town preacher delivered a sermon in the synagogue, to arouse people to repent. He took his theme from a puzzling saying of the Sages:

> The purpose of the days is the nights;
> the purpose of the nights is the Sabbaths;
> the purpose of the Sabbaths is the New Moons;
> the purpose of the New Moons is the holidays;
> the purpose of the holidays is Rosh HaShanah;
> the purpose of Rosh HaShanah is Yom Kippur;
> the purpose of Yom Kippur is repentance;
> the purpose of repentance is the World-to-Come.

The preacher chose this saying because of its connection to their holy task that night—to repent on *Yom Kippur Katan* before *Rosh Hodesh*—and he explained it this way: "'The purpose of the days is the nights' because at night we have time to study the Torah, as the Rabbis said: 'The night was created for study.' 'The purpose of the nights is the Sabbaths' because on the Sabbath we are completely free from work and can dedicate ourselves to Torah study for the whole day, not just at night. 'The purpose of the Sabbaths is the New Moons' because on *Rosh Hodesh* life for that month is decreed in heaven and life is given to us to study the Torah. 'The purpose of the New Moons is the holidays' because, as is known, a special heavenly light is revealed during a holiday that illuminates our Torah study. 'The purpose of the holidays is Rosh HaShanah' because on Rosh HaShanah light and life for the whole year descend to us from heaven. 'The purpose of Rosh HaShanah is Yom Kippur' because on Yom Kippur we are detached from all worldly concerns and are like angels. 'The purpose of Yom Kippur is repentance'—is self-evident. 'The purpose of repentance is the World-to-Come' because by repentance, we gain the World-to-Come."

The preacher expounded each part of the saying at length, explaining it according to his understanding, as best he could. And the whole congregation—of men, women, and children—were aroused by his words and they all began to sob as they wept in repentance.

After the preacher's sermon, he and everyone else went home to go to sleep, but the rabbi remained in the synagogue and sat down to study. The Baal Shem Tov sat down next to him and began singing a wordless *niggun*. The rabbi did not want to be impolite to a guest to the town, so he did not interrupt, and waited until the Besht finished his song. Then the rabbi greeted him. The Baal Shem Tov returned his greeting and sang another song. After he finished this one, the rabbi asked, "Why are you singing?" "The people truly repented and their sins were forgiven!" replied the Besht. "How could I not sing?" "You're right!" said the rabbi. "Let's dance!" said the Besht. So the two of them jumped up, joined hands, and danced in joy. Although this rabbi did not become a disciple or a follower of the Baal Shem Tov, he was very impressed by him and considered him to be a great person. He saw that the Besht was a Jew who sang and danced in joy when the sins of his fellow Jews were forgiven, and he was someone who could share that joy with him, the rabbi. While the Besht was in Slutzk, many rabbis and scholars were critical of him for what they perceived as his innovations, but this rabbi rejected their disparaging comments.

The next day, the day of *Yom Kippur Katan*, two young Torah scholars were sitting in the synagogue studying. The Baal Shem Tov had noticed them the previous night. When the preacher had been speaking to arouse the congregation to repent, they had ignored his sermon and continued studying, sitting by themselves in the back of the synagogue. Such behavior was fairly typical of the scholars of that time, whose ideal in divine service was continuous, uninterrupted Torah study. They felt free to separate from the congregation. So, while everyone else was weeping in repentance, they sat and continued studying. But this was not the Besht's attitude. He sat down next to these two young men and began to weep. When one of them asked him why he was weeping, he said, "I'm weeping for you, because you're pushing God away by your arrogance. You're studying the Torah but forgetting the One who gave it." "*Oy!* You're right!" said the young man, who was very moved by the Besht's words. How could you not be moved when seeing someone weep for you? Yet his study partner did remain distant; but this young scholar became a disciple of the Baal Shem Tov.

The Besht's spiritual path was broader and more many-sided than the exclusive Lithuanian focus on Torah study. The Besht appreciated the theme of the preacher's sermon—that the ultimate purpose of Torah study and divine service is repentance. He saw that the preacher had touched people's hearts and brought them to repent. But the preacher did not fully understand the final part of the saying, that by repentance you attain the World-to-Come. He had led the congregation to tears of repentance; but if you truly repent and your sins are forgiven, you should be singing and dancing in joy. How much more should you be dancing if a whole congregation, a whole town, repents! That was what the Besht taught the rabbi. But the Besht's own joy came from an even deeper source, for the mystics teach that the World-to-Come is here now if one is immersed in the bliss of God-consciousness.

When the Baal Shem Tov saw the two young scholars separate themselves from the congregation, ignoring *Yom Kippur Katan* and the preacher's sermon, it was clear to him that they did not understand that the true purpose of Torah study is to turn to God. How could you turn to God if you thought you did not need to repent and if you ignored the congregation when they were repenting?

The Besht was so devoted to God and to the Jewish people that, after seeing the congregation repent, he sang and danced. But when he saw that two fine young men had become lost on the path of Torah, he wept for them. That is why he could lead people back to God in repentance, for most people, when they see that someone loves them, love him in return, and listen to his words with an open heart and mind.[46]

Serving God with Joy in Song and Dance

❧ THE BAAL SHEM TOV WAS A GIFTED SINGER WITH AN EXPRESSIVE VOICE. He considered singing a service of God, for music touches the soul and produces an outpouring of the soul. He often led his disciples in song, especially at the Sabbath table. Sometimes he asked them to close their eyes and put their hands on each other's shoulders as they sang, so that they were all connected in a sacred circle. He used to say, "When you put your hand on your brother's shoulder, you physically express your resolve to fulfill the commandment to love your neighbor as yourself." The Besht also danced before God as a divine service. And he revived the circle dance among the Jewish people. In a circle all are equal; there is no first and no last.

Once, the Baal Shem Tov sang and danced with his disciples for hours on *Shabbat* evening after the meal. When he sat down to rest for a while, his disciples surrounded him and he said, "By means of music you can attain joy and *d'vekut* with the Infinite One, blessed be He. The holy *Zohar* says that there are heavenly palaces whose gates are only opened by song. But you have to sing before God, and let the *Shechinah* sing through you. When you dance, dance before God. I tell you, the dances of a Jew are prayers and the purpose of dancing is to lift up the holy sparks. In a sacred dance, the lower rung of spirituality is raised up to the higher. The Rabbis say: 'In the future, the Holy One, blessed be He, will make a circle dance for the tzaddikim in the Garden of Eden. He will sit in their midst and each will point with his finger to God in the center, as the verse says: "It will be said on that day: 'This is our God, *this* is the One for whom we waited, that He would save us. *This* is the Lord for whom we waited, and we will be glad and rejoice in His salvation!'"' I tell you, if we dance with real faith, we can taste now in our circle dancing that great day in the future. May it come soon in our time. Amen!"

One of his disciples said, "Master, some of your opponents criticize us for what they say is our excessive joy and our dancing." The Besht replied, "I'll answer them with a parable. Once, a talented fiddler stood in the street playing in an ecstasy of passion. Many people gathered to listen and were so enchanted by his music that they began to dance, lost to the world. A deaf man happened to pass by and, since he couldn't hear the ravishing music, was utterly astonished by the bizarre scene before his eyes. Not knowing why the people were dancing, he was certain that they were actually madmen! The truth is that if he heard the music and experienced the tremendous joy and ecstasy, he would have danced with them! My disciples," said the Besht, "hear and see the song that emanates from each and every thing that God, blessed be He, has created. If so, how can they keep from dancing?"

Gazing at his loyal disciples surrounding him, all fastened on his every word, he continued, "I tell you, a Jew should always be joyful. He mustn't allow any opening for the evil inclination of sadness. Pious people consider sadness a sin according to the Torah; and joy—the joy that comes from seeing that everything is good—they consider a commandment of the Torah. The Torah says about the Holy One, blessed be He: 'There is joy in His place.' How can you not be happy, if you know that you're in God's world and that He's always near? You're like a king's son—and there's always joy in your father's palace. If you understand this and truly believe it, how can you experience any suffering? I tell you, the deepest truth is that there is no bad or evil, no sorrow or sadness, and no death. There's only joy. But not everyone can hear or understand this teaching. Just remember that the Torah says: 'Serve God with joy.' Just as the 'serve God' must be always, so too must the 'with joy' be always. You must always be joyful!"[47]

His Disciples Dance on the New Moon

ONE YEAR DURING THE YOM KIPPUR PRAYERS, THE BAAL SHEM TOV saw with his holy spirit that harm would come to the Jewish people if he and his disciples did not make the traditional blessing of the new moon immediately following the holiday. Then, this great *mitzvah* would weigh down on the scale of merit and incline the heavenly balance of judgment to good. But the new moon was not visible at the end of Yom Kippur and the blessing could not be recited. The Besht, who was depressed about this, attempted by his mystic powers to cause the moon to appear. He asked his disciples several times to go outside and see if the moon was visible, but in spite of his great efforts, the skies remained overcast with dark clouds and it seemed unlikely there would be a moon that night.

The Besht's disciples knew nothing about this, however, neither about their master's depression, nor about the heavenly decree and how important it was that they bless the moon after Yom Kippur. It was their custom to celebrate at the end of Yom Kippur, since they had completed their divine service successfully, led by their holy master, the Baal Shem Tov, whose service on Yom Kippur was like that of the high priest in the Temple. They were confident that their prayers were accepted and that they were signed and sealed for a good year. So this time too they were joyously dancing with holy fervor. At first, they danced in the outer room of the Besht's house, but afterward, carried on the wave of their exuberant joy, they burst into their master's room and danced in his presence. When the joyful ecstasy of their dancing surged even more strongly, they dared to draw the Baal Shem Tov himself into their circle. They swept their holy master into their midst and he began to dance with them. While they were dancing this sacred dance, those outside suddenly called out loudly that the moon was visible, and they all went out quickly to bless the moon that night. The Baal Shem Tov then said that what he could not accomplish by his mystic powers, his disciples had accomplished by their joy.[48]

The Besht Dances with the Spiritual Torah

BEFORE ONE *SIMHAT TORAH**, THE BESHT TOLD HIS DISCIPLES, "WE MUST always be joyful, but especially on holidays, which are the special times for joy; and most especially on *Simhat Torah*, for then our joy must be unlimited."

That *Simhat Torah* night, the Baal Shem Tov danced ecstatically with his holy disci-

---

* The holiday of Celebrating the Torah.

ples, as he embraced a Torah scroll, clasping it to his breast. Then he handed it to one of his disciples and continued to dance without it. Rabbi Yitzhak, another disciple, saw this, and said, "Our holy master has now handed over the physical Torah and has taken to himself the spiritual Torah."

Afterward, when the Besht heard this comment repeated, he said, "I'm surprised that Rabbi Yitzhak is able to see such things."

The Baal Shem Tov taught that a Jew must absorb the Torah so deeply into himself that he *becomes* a Torah. And when a Jew becomes a Torah, he dances in joy.[49]

There Won't Be Enough Wine!

AT ANOTHER *SIMHAT TORAH* CELEBRATION, THE BAAL SHEM TOV'S disciples were joyously dancing in the outer room of their master's house and they were also drinking a lot of wine. The Besht's wife Chana complained to the servant who was bringing the wine up from the cellar, "There won't be any wine left for *Shabbat!*" So she went into the Besht's room and said to him, "Tell them to stop drinking and dancing, because you won't have any wine for *kiddush* and *havdala!*" The Besht replied with a laugh, "You're right! Go in and tell them to go home!" When she opened the door, the disciples were dancing in a circle, and she saw that there were flames blazing all around them like a canopy of fire. Taking the pitchers out of the hands of the servant, she herself then went down to the cellar and brought up as much wine as they wanted. A short while later, she again entered the Baal Shem Tov's room, and he asked her with a smile, "Did you tell them to leave?" This time, she laughed and said, "You should have told them yourself!"

The Besht knew when it was the time to measure and calculate and when it was the time for unlimited fervor and boundless devotion.[50]

Chana and Edel

THE BAAL SHEM TOV'S WIFE, CHANA, DID NOT KNOW HEBREW AND WAS even unable to pray from a *siddur* or recite psalms. Yet it was known that she was a great *tzaddeket* and it was with her help that her holy husband attained his awesome spiritual levels. Chana's daughter Edel, however, was a great *tzaddeket* and also a great scholar. She was an expert kabbalist who meditated on special *kavvanot* when she prepared challah for *Shabbat*, when she lit the Sabbath candles, and at other times.[51]

The Perfect Groom

WHEN EDEL REACHED MARRIAGEABLE AGE, A PROPOSAL WAS MADE TO THE Baal Shem Tov to take Rabbi Yehiel Ashkenazi as a bridegroom for her. They said that he was an excellent scholar and very pious, with all the good qualities one would seek in a young man. The Besht sent his disciple Rabbi Arye Leib of Polnoye to the town where Rabbi Yehiel lived, to test his Torah knowledge. When Rabbi Arye Leib returned, the Besht asked, "What happened? What did you hear from him?" "When I questioned him to see what he knows of the Torah," replied Rabbi Arye Leib, "he said, 'I never knew, I don't know, and I won't know.'" "That's just the kind of groom I'm looking for!" said the Besht as he laughed with pleasure. He immediately agreed to the match, then went in to his daughter, Edel, and said, "*Mazel tov, Kallah**!"

Modesty, concealment, and the humility of knowing that one does not know were at the center of the Besht's own spiritual path.[52]

Edel and the Book of Remedies

EDEL HELPED HER MOTHER CHANA IN RUNNING THE BESHT'S HOUSEHOLD and was in charge of the money, dealing with the many expenses. She was the Baal Shem Tov's daughter, but also his disciple. The Besht transmitted to her many kabbalistic secrets and she was known to have the holy spirit. Edel's heart was on fire for God; she constantly yearned for God and never ceased to think of how she might give Him pleasure.

The Besht kept a book of remedies and *segulot*¶ for his own use as a healer. Once, when he was leaving Medzibuz on a trip, he said to Edel, "My book of remedies is very precious to me. But you have my permission to use it while I'm away, if someone comes who desperately needs healing and can't wait for my return. But don't let anyone else even touch the book or look into it, and you speak to the sick person directly, not through someone else. If you need to, ask one of my scribes to write an amulet for the person." Edel used the book of remedies on a number of occasions when her holy father was away, and effected several miraculous healings.[53]

Shoes in the Garden of Eden

ONE OF THE BAAL SHEM TOV'S CUSTOMS WAS TO SPEND A GREAT DEAL of time with simple Jews on *Simhat Torah* and encourage them to rejoice on this most joyous of holidays that comes at the end of *Sukkot*. Most of these common people were unable to study Torah, and their prayers were often mangled and recited with faulty Hebrew; but their dancing could reach the highest heights! During *Sukkot*, the Besht always invited everyone into his *sukkah*§ and surrounded himself with these sim-

---

* Congratulations, Bride!
¶ Mystically potent remedies, incantations, objects, or actions.
§ A temporary booth used for eating, living, even sleeping on *Sukkot*.

ple Jews, whom he loved. Once, he said to his disciples, "Other people decorate their *sukkahs* with all kinds of pictures and ornaments, but I decorate my *sukkah* by filling it with simple Jews, because their pure faith causes great joy in heaven." Then he told them, with a smile, this story:

"On the morning of Sabbaths and holidays, the Jews usually sleep late, because the time for *Shaharit* [morning prayers] is typically later than on weekdays. Especially on *Simhat Torah* morning they sleep a little more, because of all their exertions from dancing with the Torah scrolls in the synagogue and because of all the food they ate the previous evening at the festive meal. However, since the angels' service of God doesn't include either dancing or eating, they wake up bright and early on the morning of *Simhat Torah*, like any other day, eager to begin their divine service of singing songs of praise. But since—as the Rabbis tell us—the angels aren't permitted to begin singing in heaven until Israel has first sung God's praise below in their prayers on earth, they go instead to the Garden of Eden, where they occupy themselves with cleaning up and sweeping the garden. But suddenly they find strange items that they don't recognize—shoes, soles, heels, broken shoelaces—and they're astonished. They're accustomed to finding holy things like *tzitzit* and *tefillin* in the Garden of Eden, but not shoes! Perplexed, they went to the angel Michael to discover the meaning of these mysterious objects. Michael—the angel-advocate of the Jewish people, who praises their merits before God—explained to them that this was his 'merchandise,' and that these things were left over from the Jews' dancing with the Torah. He then began to look over all the shoes strewn about—that had fallen off or become ripped during the vigorous dancing—and to point out: These are from Kaminka, those are from Mezritch, and so on [towns where the Besht's followers resided]! And that," said the Besht, "is how the angel Michael was able to boast to the angel Metatron, who weaves crowns for his Maker from the prayers of Israel, that he, Michael, made a better crown—from the torn shoes of the *Simhat Torah* dancing!" To the Besht, not even praying was higher and more exalted than the fervent, joyous dancing on *Simhat Torah*.[54]

Why All This Dancing and Joy?

THE BAAL SHEM TOV WAS ALWAYS ESPECIALLY JOYFUL DURING THE PERIOD of Counting the Omer*. Every day after the blessing of the counting, from the second day of Passover until the eve of *Shavuot*, his joy increased from day to day. On the new moon of the month of *Sivan*, his joy began to peak¶. Together with his hasidim who surrounded him, he danced in joyous ecstasy, until even Rabbi Yaakov Yosef of Polnoye, who was often morose and frequently wept over the exile of the *Shechinah*,

---

* The forty-nine days from Passover to *Shavuot* are ritually counted.
¶ *Shavuot* occurs in the early part of the month of *Sivan*.

was also overcome with joy and danced together with the Besht's other disciples. Finally, after exhausting himself dancing, Rabbi Yaakov Yosef almost collapsed into one of the chairs to rest. When the Besht too sat down to rest, Rabbi Yaakov Yosef asked him, "Master, you've greatly influenced me and I too am numbered among your hasidim and occasionally dance with them. But I have to ask in amazement, 'Why all this dancing and joy specifically during the period of the Counting of the Omer?'"

His face beaming with divine joy, the Besht answered, "There are many paths in the service of the living God and He, so to speak, cherishes them all. One path followed by many great rabbis and their students is to stand in silent fear and awe before the Lord who created the world. Everything is contained in that silent awe—whatever the mouth can utter or the body can express by its movements. When a person experiences the joy that he's actually a part of God, that he is bone of His bones and flesh of His flesh, so to speak, that there's nothing separating him from his Creator, then, words and movements are superfluous, because they're only garments—mere external coverings—for the feelings and thoughts within them. The naked thoughts and feelings are absolutely pure, on the level of *Ein Sof**, infinity. In their total silence, these great rabbis speak with their Creator, just as the trees of the forest speak with Him in their quiet vitality, just as the sea speaks in its silence and the sky in its blue wordlessness . . . and so too all of existence and the *sefirot*¶ also before they are clothed in the worlds, before the universe was formed.

"But there is another path, that of Hasidism. Great sages of our people followed this path even hundreds of years ago. When Rabbi Akiba prayed, he began standing in one corner of the room and ended up in another corner, because of all his bowing and prostrating. He couldn't pray quietly; his love for his Creator was so strong that it couldn't be contained within the four cubits of his personal space. He had to sway and move and, as it says in the Song of Songs, 'leap over the mountains and jump over the valleys'; that was how he served his Creator! That's the hasidic path. When hasidim are engaged in worship, an explosive spirit swirls within their souls that cleave to the living God. It shakes their body and limbs until the body starts to dance ecstatically, because dances are the body's prayers, on the level of 'All my bones shall say, "O Lord, who is like unto You!"' The body and all its limbs dance to the rhythm of the heart, which moves and flows with the prayer of the universe. And the heart feels that its beating is only an echo of the motion of the worlds and that with its beating it embraces those worlds that unite with their Creator and become, so to speak—like the union of male and female—'one flesh.'"

The Baal Shem Tov continued his explanation to Rabbi Yaakov Yosef, saying, "I chose the second path, or really, my soul chose that path. I was impelled to choose it by some hidden force. When I dance with the joy of doing a *mitzvah*—a joy I experience every moment—I'm rejoicing that I merited to serve my Creator, to pour my heart out before Him in prayer, to eat and drink with devotion (since that is too one of the ways

---

* The "Infinite," a kabbalistic appellation for God.
¶ The ten divine emanations as described in Kabbalah.

of serving God, on the level of 'Know Him in all your ways'). When my heart is filled with joy, I feel an ecstatic delight in jumping and dancing, in elevating above the earth beneath my feet, in separating myself from earthliness below, and getting closer to heaven above. I become even more joyful as I get closer and closer to the day on which the Torah was given. From Passover, the Day of our Freedom, to *Shavuot*, the Day of the Giving of the Torah, when I count every one of the forty-nine days—I also count every hour and every minute. And as I get closer to the festival of *Shavuot*, my joy becomes greater and greater within me, until it becomes boundless and limitless. That's why I dance ecstatically after the Counting of the Omer."[55]

Hearing the Inner Song

WHEN THE BAAL SHEM TOV LISTENED TO A MUSICIAN PLAYING, IT WAS as if the instrument was speaking in a language that he knew, and he could hear in the music everything the musician had ever done in his life. Once, the Besht listened to a fiddler and understood through his music all the sins that he had committed since the day he was born. But he listened in the way of "perceiving sin but not dwelling on it." If he could hear these things in the music of an instrument, how much more so when someone sang! Another time, when the Baal Shem Tov was walking along with his disciples, they came across a drunken gentile who was standing in the street singing. The Besht stopped and listened intently to the man's song until he had finished. Afterward, his disciples asked him what he found so interesting in the singing of a drunken peasant. "When a person sings," replied the Besht, "he confesses about his whole life. And when someone confesses, you're obliged to listen."[56]

His Charity

Everything He Took In, Went Out

THE BAAL SHEM TOV WAS SO DEVOTED TO THE *MITZVAH* OF CHARITY that he was always poor, even after he became famous. Although he received large sums of money from people who came to him for advice, blessings, and prayers, he used the money exclusively for charity and not for his household needs. This was also true of the money he collected in donations when he traveled through the towns. Everything he took in, went out in the large amounts of money he expended on charity, to ransom captives, or to provide wedding expenses for poor brides.[57]

He Gives More than a Fifth with Joy

THE BAAL SHEM TOV'S INCOME FOR HIMSELF AND HIS FAMILY CAME from his work as a *baal shem*, which included his amulets. He gave more than a fifth of this income too for *tzedaka*. People asked him, "Don't the Rabbis say that a person shouldn't give more than a fifth to charity, lest he also become poor and need charity himself?" He answered, "If someone has to fight with himself to pry the money loose for charity—that's the person who the Rabbis said shouldn't give more than a fifth. But if someone can give freely and joyfully, and actually gets pleasure from his *tzedaka*, how is that different from the large amounts of money other people spend on their various worldly needs and pleasures?" Since charity gave the Besht such great joy and pleasure, he felt entitled to give even more than a fifth.[58]

Infinite Charity

THE BESHT HAD TWO HASIDIM WHO GAVE GENEROUSLY FOR EVERY needy case he presented to them. He once said to his disciples, "I have two very charitable hasidim, but they're not on the same level. If the police unjustly arrested a Jew, threw him in prison, and demanded ransom, and I went to the first hasid and told him, 'Someone is rotting away in prison. I need money to ransom him,' he would ask, 'How much do you need?' If I said, 'A thousand gulden,' he would say, 'Wait a minute.' He would go to his office, get his money box, and count out a thousand gulden. He's truly generous! But if I went to the second hasid and said, 'Somebody's in prison,' he wouldn't ask me how much money the ransom was. He would say, 'Here's the key to my money box. Take out what you need.' I tell you, our giving to others must be on the level of being infinite, boundless." That was the way the Besht himself gave.[59]

He Gives Away Money on the Road

ONCE, WHEN THE BAAL SHEM TOV PASSED THROUGH HORODENKA ON his way to Brody (both in Reissen), he stopped at the home of his disciple, Rabbi Meir Margoliot, and asked Rabbi Meir to accompany him. Rabbi Meir was excited to see his master, and happy that the Besht was asking him along. He rushed out, taking only his overcoat and his tallis and *tefillin*, and they set out.

When they arrived in Brody, the Baal Shem Tov had to stay at an inn, like a merchant would (rather than being received in a private home like a great rabbi). No one came to welcome him except for two men, one wealthy, the other not, both of them outstanding Torah scholars. They greeted him and came to him often while he was there. Most of the scholars of the Brody *Kloiz* thought nothing of the Besht and hardly anyone in town considered him to be special or worthy of note. (Although the Torah scholars of the Brody *Kloiz* showed no respect for the Baal Shem Tov, he held them in high regard. During his stay in Brody, he told Rabbi Meir that he saw the *Shechinah* resting on the *kloiz*.) So the Besht was staying at the inn and paying for himself and Rabbi Meir, while no money was coming in from people seeking his blessings or healings to cover the expenses. When Rabbi Meir saw that the money the Besht had with him was quickly used up, and he had nothing left, he regretted not having taken with him any money for the road. Then he heard the Besht say to the coach driver, "Get ready to travel!" So he went and told the two scholars that the Besht was about to depart, and they came to take their leave of him and honor him by accompanying him on his way out of town. However, when they saw that the Besht was not quite ready to leave, they said to Rabbi Meir, "We'll go to the *beit midrash* to study. When the Baal Shem Tov is ready to leave, please send someone to tell us and we'll come back."

When the Besht was about to leave, Rabbi Meir sent someone to tell them, and they returned. The wealthy one of the two men had already given the Besht a generous donation the first time he had come to take his leave, and Rabbi Meir had been happy that there would be some money to pay for the travel expenses. But when they returned the second time, the Besht took that money, gave it back to the man, and said, "Give one half of this to the Brody *Kloiz* and distribute the other half among the poor." Then the Baal Shem Tov and Rabbi Meir left the town.

When Rabbi Meir realized that the Besht had given away all of the donation, his heart sank, for he knew that the Besht now had no money and he himself did not have a penny. When they were on the road he said, "Master, why did you have to give away all the money? Now we don't have a single penny for our travel expenses." The Baal Shem Tov answered him with words that stir the soul. He said, "Meir, you can be sure that as long as God is alive, we have nothing to worry about!"

And so it was, that when they arrived at their next destination, Radevill in Volhynia, the townspeople came to the Baal Shem Tov seeking blessings and remedies, and they gave him ample money. The same thing happened in all the other places they traveled to, and the Besht returned home with enough money to pay his debts and to give charity to many poor people.[60]

Tzvi and the Silver Objects

THE BAAL SHEM TOV ONCE WENT WITH HIS SON TZVI TO PAY A VISIT TO Rabbi Moshe of Kitov. The boy, who was used to living in straitened circumstances, was astonished at some of the things he saw in the rabbi's home. His eyes opened wide at the array of silver religious objects—such as the *kiddush* cup and the Sabbath candelabra in the breakfront. There was nothing like that in his home. On their way back to Medzibuz, the Besht said to his son, "You must be envious of the rabbi, and wondering why your father doesn't have such silver things." "Yes," the boy answered. "If your father had money to buy such silver objects," said the Besht, "he'd use it instead for *tzedaka*, and to help poor people."[61]

A Feast for the Poor

THE BAAL SHEM TOV ONCE VISITED THE TOWN OF UMAN (IN THE Polish-Ukrainian province of Bratzlav) and while there instituted a number of customs for his hasidim in the town. One of them was that anyone who was sick and recovered, should make a thanksgiving feast for a *minyan* of ten poor people and give them *tzedaka*.[62]

An Open House

THE BAAL SHEM TOV AND HIS WIFE CHANA CONDUCTED AN "OPEN HOUSE"— opening their doors to any traveler or wanderer who needed a place to lodge or to eat. There were always people of all sorts staying with them or eating at their table. The Besht and his wife never examined whether a guest was "worthy" or "of questionable character."[63]

No Money Overnight

THE BAAL SHEM WAS ALWAYS RELUCTANT TO TRAVEL TO EARN MONEY. He did so only when his wife brought him a list of debts from buying flour, meat, and other household items on credit. Only when the debts had grown to a large sum would he agree to go. When he returned from his travels with money, he paid off his debts that same day and gave what was left over for charity. He never kept money in his house overnight, as that would not be showing complete trust in God.

Once, he returned from a trip with a large amount of money. He paid his debts, gave charity, and asked some of his disciples to get him the names of poor people to give donations to. But before they were able to do that, the Besht's wife took some of the money, thinking that for a few days at least she would not have to ask the storekeepers to let her buy their household needs on credit (because she almost always had to buy on credit).

Late that night, the Besht was in the *beit midrash* and felt that something was hindering his divine service. Sensing what the cause might be, he went home, woke everyone up, gathered them together, and said, "Let whoever took some of the money confess." His wife admitted that it was she who had taken the money and she returned it. The Besht then ordered that they go immediately to the homes of poor people and distribute the money to them by slipping an envelope under their door. The Besht used to say, "When I keep even a penny in my house, I can't sleep the whole night; that penny causes my body more pain than if I had a stone for a pillow."[64]

The Jingle of Charity Coins

THE TOWNSPEOPLE OF MEDZIBUZ ONCE WANTED TO ABOLISH THE custom of passing around charity collection plates during the morning prayer service on *erev* Yom Kippur. They claimed that it was disruptive and disturbed them.

When the Besht heard about this, he refused to allow them to do away with the custom. And he told them a story. "Once, before Yom Kippur, the accusing angels gathered together to prevent the prayers of Israel from ascending into heaven. But when the Jews began casting coins for charity into the plates on *erev* Yom Kippur, the jingling sound disturbed their gathering and caused them to disperse. In the heavenly judgment on Yom Kippur," said the Besht, "there are always accusing angels who argue that the people don't deserve to be forgiven. But in the merit of their charity, called to mind by the jingling of the coins, the decree for punishment is averted."[65]

Turning the Stove to Gold

ONCE, REBBETZIN CHANA BROUGHT THE BAAL SHEM TOV A LIST OF THEIR debts, thinking that he would certainly travel to earn some money. When days passed and he still had not set out, and the debts kept increasing, she went again and gave him a new list. "Why are you pressuring me to travel?" he said. "Do you see the stove over there? If I want, it'll immediately turn into gold. Maybe you think I would do this by using divine Names, God-forbid! No, I could do it just by praying with great faith. But I'm ashamed to ask my Creator for something like this!"[66]

His Wife Builds a New House

TO ATTRACT HIM TO MEDZIBUZ AND SHOW HIM THEIR REGARD, THE Jewish community had provided the Baal Shem Tov with a house for himself and his family. After years had passed, his wife, Rebbetzin Chana, saw that they needed a new house, because the one they were living in was not only too small but in poor condition. They always had so many hasidim and guests visiting, there was hardly any place to put them. Yet, because the Besht gave everything he had to charity and kept only the barest minimum for his household needs, he could not afford to purchase anything larger or more suitable. Moreover, he would never agree to the expense. So his wife decided to build a new house without his knowledge. Where would she find the money? She economized on her household expenses and saved money little by little. She also accumulated money given to her by the Besht's closest disciples, whom she had confidentially told about her plan to build a larger house.

Finally, the house was finished and ready for occupancy. The Baal Shem Tov was taking a walk with his disciples, who directed their path past the new house, knowing that the Besht would surely ask them to whom it belonged. When he did, they told him that the house he was living in was too small and in pitiful condition, so the *rebbetzin* had built this house, and that it belonged to him. The Besht was pleased and said, "It's written in Proverbs: 'A house and wealth are from a father's inheritance, but a wise wife is from God.'" Freely translating and interpreting the verse—different from its literal meaning—as a question, he continued, "How can a man obtain a house if he's constantly occupied serving God to the exclusion of everything else? Perhaps he might inherit a house from his father. But what if he doesn't inherit a house? If it's God's will, blessed be He, that he have a house, then God gives him a wise wife, and as it says elsewhere in Proverbs: 'A woman's wisdom builds her house.'" The Besht appreciated his wife's cleverness, in slowly and secretly saving the money, and in hiding the building of the house from him. If her scheme succeeded, it was only because God, blessed be He, wanted him to have a house and so had given him a clever wife. After they moved into their new home, the Besht had a small house of seclusion built adjacent to it, where he could have privacy for his divine service.[67]

The Hose-Maker

ONCE, WHEN THE BAAL SHEM TOV VISITED THE TOWN OF HANIPOL IN Volhynia, he was standing by the window in his host's home in the early morning, smoking his pipe to prepare for the morning prayers. As he looked out, he saw a laborer with his tallis and *tefillin* bag in his hand, walking by so intently on his way to the synagogue, as if he were walking straight to the gates of heaven. Sensing his holiness, the Besht actually trembled when he saw him, and said to the householder, "Run outside and see who that was walking by with his tallis and *tefillin* bag." The householder went outside, looked, came back in, and told the Besht it was a certain hose-maker. "Call him here." said the Besht. "I know him," said the householder. "He's so stubborn, he's like a madman. When he's on his way to the synagogue, he wouldn't turn aside even if the king himself called him." When the Besht heard this derogatory comment about the hose-maker, he became silent, because he knew that the man's "madness" was his stubborn piety: He was so devoted to the synagogue that he went there with a single-minded intention to serve his Creator and would not stop for conversation, business, or any other reason.

After the morning prayers, the Baal Shem Tov asked another of his local followers about this man and was told that the hose-maker regularly prayed in the synagogue, and never failed to attend, whether it was summer or winter, and regardless of the weather. If there were fewer than ten men present for a *minyan*, he still prayed in the synagogue (for the Rabbis say it is good to pray in a sanctified place even without a *minyan*). And he always prayed in his fixed place (as the Rabbis say: "He who fixes for himself a place in the synagogue, the God of Abraham will help him").

This simple hose-maker had made such an impression on the Baal Shem Tov that he decided to meet him and find out more about him. After returning to his host's home, he sent for the hose-maker, asking him to bring four pairs of socks. The man came and brought the socks. The Besht looked them over, saw that they were of good quality, and asked him, "How much do you want for a pair?" "Each pair is one and a half gulden" the man said. "Will you give them to me for a single gulden?" asked the Besht—who was testing him. The man did not answer, because he would not change his price, but was ashamed to refuse the rabbi. When the Besht saw that the hose-maker did not answer, he thought that perhaps the man was ashamed to bargain with a rabbi, so he asked someone there to bargain with him. This other person said to him, "Perhaps you'll sell them for less than one and a half gulden apiece?" "If I had wanted to sell them for less," he said simply, "I would have asked for less." He was a straightforward, honest person who did not bargain; the price he asked was the true price. This too could be considered stubborn, but it was the stubbornness of unshakeable honesty. Without further discussion, the Besht paid him the full price for the four pairs of socks.

Then the Besht asked him, "How do you spend your time? What do you do during the day?" "I work at my trade," the man answered. "How do you do that?" continued the Besht. "I make at least forty pairs of socks a day," he said, "sometimes as many as fifty. Then I put them in a large basin and press them until they're properly done." "How do you sell them?" asked the Besht. "I never leave my house except to go to the synagogue," he replied. "If there's a *minyan*, I pray with the congregation; if there isn't a *minyan*, I pray alone in my set place in the synagogue." (He trusted God to provide him his livelihood, even without his running after customers. And because he was so honest, the buyers came to him and even supplied him with the materials he required to produce his socks. Aside from his work to support his family, his only other interest was serving his Creator, and the synagogue, to which he was devoted heart and soul.) "What do you do," asked the Besht, "if you need money to marry off your children?" (This was the problem that weighed most heavily on poor working people and led them to run after every opportunity to make money, or to travel around seeking charity from fellow Jews.) The hose-maker answered simply, "God, blessed be He, helps me. He gives me the money I need, from my work, and I marry off my children." His trust was like a strong pillar. The Besht said, "When you get up very early in the morning, how do you spend your time before you go to the synagogue?" "I make socks then too," he answered. "Do you say psalms?" asked the Besht. "What I'm able to say from memory, I recite while working." The Besht then dismissed him.

The Baal Shem Tov's host had disparaged this hose-maker, calling him a madman, but the Besht knew well the madness that comes from fervor and zeal, and he admired the holy stubbornness that produces scrupulous honesty and unwavering piety. He turned to his host and said, "This simple man and others like him will be the foundation of Judaism and the synagogue until the coming of the Redeemer, may he come soon and in our days."[68]

The Old Merchant without Sin

THE BAAL SHEM TOV ONCE WENT WITH SOME OF HIS DISCIPLES ON a journey, and on the way they met a coach full of merchants coming from Breslau in Silesia (Germany). The Besht ordered his coachman to stop and he warmly greeted a certain white-haired old man among the merchants, treating him with great respect. His disciples were very surprised at this, for they knew that man, and considered him just an honest but simple person, and not at all a Torah scholar or anyone special.

When they were traveling again, they asked the Besht why he had shown him such respect. He said to them, "In our generation, a person like this is a tzaddik. He's been going to Breslau on business for forty-three years now. He stays there almost the whole year, and he's at home for just three weeks a year. Yet he's not aware of committing any sin, either in Breslau, or on his way there or back."

It is difficult for a person to maintain his religious standards when he is far from home on an extended business trip. There are temptations in a big city; and so too while traveling. The Besht saw this simple old man's white beard and innocent face that shone with piety and was inspired with respect for the many years he had kept himself pure, although he spent so much time away from home and on the road. The Torah says: "The glory of elders is their white hair" and "White hair is a crown of glory; it is found in the way of righteousness." The Besht could see people's goodness and piety, even if they were not Torah scholars, and even if their qualities were hidden from others.[69]

Heikel the Water-Carrier

THE BAAL SHEM TOV ASKED EVERYONE HE MET "HOW ARE YOU?" TO elicit the pious response "*Baruch HaShem*" (Praise God)! And he wanted his disciples to understand the deeper meaning of that traditional reply.

One day, when the Baal Shem Tov was standing outside his house with his disciples, they saw Heikel the Water-carrier coming down the street with two heavy pails of water on his shoulders. As he approached, it was clear from his face that he was unhappy. The Besht asked him, "How are you today, Reb Heikel?" Heikel answered, "I won't sin by lying, Reb Israel. I'm feeling miserable. My strength is getting less every day, and our fellow Jews have come up with a new custom: They're building their houses on the hillsides, right up to the top! It's hard for me to climb all the way up, lugging these two heavy buckets on my back! So my livelihood is suffering; I'm not making much of a living these days. May God have mercy!" Then Heikel continued on his way.

The next day, the Baal Shem Tov was again standing with his disciples outside his house, and again they saw Heikel coming along with two full buckets of water on his shoulders. As he approached, they could see the happy and contented look on his face. Once again the Besht asked, "How are you today, Reb Heikel?" This time, Heikel smiled broadly and replied, "*Baruch HaShem*, Reb Israel! God-forbid that I should complain about the Master of the world! Everything's fine with me. There's nothing a person can't get used to. Why, when I was young, the two water buckets felt so heavy and tired me out. But now, thank God, I no longer even feel their weight; they're like two feathers on my shoulders. I'm only happy that God gives me the strength to help my fellow Jews and bring them the water they need!"

After he left, the Baal Shem Tov said to his disciples, "Do you see this? It's as if there are two Heikels! It's the same person, the same pair of water buckets, the same houses high up on the hillsides. Yet look at how different the Heikel of today is from the Heikel of yesterday! When he's dissatisfied, he grumbles and complains, and actually feels as if he has no strength left. But when he's content with his lot, he blesses and praises the Creator of the world for giving him the strength to serve people by bringing water to their homes. It's Heikel's lot in life to be a water-carrier. But it's his decision every day whether he'll labor joyfully at his work, or, God-forbid, drudge away in bitterness and misery, groaning and complaining about his difficulties. You might think: Yesterday Heikel had a bad day, today he had a good day; it's not true. *I tell you, there are no good times and bad times, there are only happy times and sad times, for every*-thing *that God does is for good. It only depends on how we receive it!*"[70]

The Sermon in the Field about Love of Israel

AS A BOY, THE BAAL SHEM TOV'S FATHER TAUGHT HIM TO LOVE EVERY JEW, regardless of who or what he or she is. The Besht learned to love simple Jews without any condescension. As an assistant *melamed*, he loved the Jewish children he had under his care so much that he often kissed them. After his marriage, when he ran an inn with his holy wife, Chana, he served the guests as if he were serving the *Shechinah*. The Besht's self-sacrificing love of his fellow Jews carried him to great attainments in holiness and God-awareness. He developed his way in love of Israel all his life, until it became a complete book of four hundred chapters. The Rabbis say that a Jew should be especially careful about one *mitzvah*, fulfilling it in all its depth and in all its details. For the Baal Shem Tov, that *mitzvah* was the love of Israel. When a Jew was in trouble, the Besht prayed for him and made a *pidyon nefesh*. Although a Jew was on the other side of the world, the Besht heard his sigh. He was ready to sacrifice himself and even give up his life for any Jew, even someone whom he had never met. The Besht used to say, "'Love your neighbor as yourself' means to love the person you are with at that moment." His disciples saw that when he met someone new, his whole body actually shivered.

One summer day, the Baal Shem Tov went with his disciples in a few wagons to the countryside. They stopped next to an open field and got down for a walk. After walking for a while, when they came to an area of soft grass, the Besht sat down and his disciples sat around him. Then he said, "Let me teach you about the love of Israel.

"You must love a fellow Jew just because he is a Jew—even if you don't know him at all.

"The Holy One, blessed be He, told our father Abraham, 'Look at the heavens and count the stars, if you can; so many shall your descendants be.' From the earth, the stars appear small, but in the heavens above they are very large. The Jewish people are likened to stars because they appear small in this world, but in the upper world, in heaven, they are very great. I tell you, each Jew is as precious to the Holy One, blessed be He, as an only child born to its parents in their old age, and even more than that.

"Love of Israel is the first gate leading to the courtyards of God. You cannot enter except by passing through that gate. You might think, 'I'll seclude myself in the world of Torah, prayer, and meditation.' There's a time for seclusion, but I tell you, love for fellow Jews and self-sacrifice for their sake will lead you to much higher mystic attainments than any solitary practice.

"'You shall love your neighbor as yourself' is the commentary and explanation of 'You shall love the Lord your God.' When you love another Jew, that is, his essence, his soul, you are loving the Holy One, blessed be He, Himself, since every Jew is actually a part of God from above. Love of Israel *is* love of God, for it's written: 'You are children to the Lord your God,' and when you love a father, you love his children. The Torah says 'love your neighbor as yourself,' because your neighbor *is* your self. You and he have the same essence: the *Shechinah*, which is the Soul of all souls.

"There are three loves you should strive to acquire: love of God, love of Israel, and love of the Torah, for as the holy *Zohar* says: 'God, the Torah, and Israel are mystically one.' Just as you love the Torah, because it's God's Torah, so must you love Israel, because they are *His* people—not because they are good, intelligent, or possess any other virtue. If you see something in the Torah that you don't understand, you don't express doubts about it, God-forbid; you try to explain it. So too with any Jew: If you see something wrong, God-forbid, about him that you don't understand, try to explain it and justify it.

"The House of Israel is basically divided into two groups—although there are many grades within each group: the simple, unlearned Jews and the Torah scholars. The commandment to love Israel is to love both these and those. You must love the simple people because they believe in God and His Torah with a pure and simple faith. And you must love the scholars because of their Torah knowledge. The Talmud says that the greater a person is, the greater is his evil inclination. Although scholars tend to be arrogant because of their knowledge, they are still good Jews—and you should love them. You must also love Jews who don't observe the Torah. There are two main reasons to love a Jew: simply because he's a Jew or because he knows and obeys the Torah. Only the first relates to a person's essence and is equal for every Jew. You must love a Jew just because he's a Jew. Love of Israel means loving each and every Jew, regardless of who or what he or she is—whether a man or a woman, a rich person or a poor one, a Torah scholar or a simple Jew, whether he is good or someone who needs to become better."

After this teaching, the Besht and his disciples returned to Medzibuz. Once they arrived home, the Besht went to his room, but his disciples went to a special house that they rented outside the town, where they often gathered after their master taught them Torah and reviewed what he had said. They continued to discuss these teachings far into the night, because they were part of the essence of the Besht's message.[71]

The Title "Jew"

THE BAAL SHEM TOV CONSIDERED BEING A JEW VERY SPECIAL. THE NEXT day, after the morning prayers, he said to the members of his *minyan*, "If I knew for certain that I was a son of Abraham, Isaac, and Jacob, I'd wear my hat at an angle!" He surely had no doubts about his lineage; he was simply trying to communicate his deep joy at being a Jew. Later that day, he said, "If I knew that when I passed away, they'd say: 'A Jew died,' I'd be so happy, I'd tell them to strike up the band!"[72]

The Pleasure in Heaven from Jewish Worship

LATER THAT SAME DAY, THE BAAL SHEM TOV SAID TO HIS DISCIPLES, "The pleasure that the Holy One, blessed be He, derives from the divine service of His children, the Jewish people, is greater than the pleasure He gets from the worship of the angels in all the worlds. It's like a little talking bird from which the king derives more pleasure, even though it speaks nonsense, than from the eloquence of all his ministers and servants. The angels themselves know this. But the angel who most appreciates and values the service of the Jews is the archangel Michael, who pleads their merits in heaven. I tell you, even Michael, that great prince among angels, would give all of his divine service for one *tzitzit* of what a Jew is able to fulfill."

The Baal Shem Tov's unstinting love for his fellow Jews led him to interpret every movement of theirs as reflecting their inner yearning for the living God. In a Jew's every gesture, the Besht saw a prayer addressed to the Creator; in every sigh, he perceived a penitent turn toward the Master of the world.

The Baal Shem Tov deeply appreciated the simple faith of the common folk, and looked at each pious deed of theirs with the eyes of Michael, the angel-intercessor for Israel; like Michael, he exploited it fully for the merit of Israel in his pleading before God's throne. What seemed small to others was to him great—and he made it great. The Baal Shem Tov once overheard a Jew comfort his friend by saying, "The Holy One, blessed be He, will surely help!" The Besht made of this tiny morsel a complete meal, telling his disciples that because of this simple man's utterance, God, blessed be He, would surely help—and that this man had saved hundreds and thousands of Jews from evil decrees![73]

The Besht's Love of Simple Jews

The Besht Teaches His Disciples to Appreciate Simple Jews

ONE DAY, AFTER THE MORNING PRAYERS, WHEN THE BAAL SHEM TOV'S disciples were sitting with him in the *beit midrash*, they asked him to teach them how to love simple people, because they found this difficult. The Besht said, "Many rabbis and Torah scholars look down at the Jewish masses, most of whom are uneducated peddlars and laborers. They call them 'the psalm-sayers' or 'those who don't know what they're reciting'—because these simple Jews don't understand Hebrew. In many towns the community leaders don't even allow common folk who are obligated to say *Kaddish* for a deceased parent to serve as prayer-leader! Sometimes, the working people are even made to pray in a separate room in the synagogue!

"But I tell you, loving and respecting simple Jews is at the center of my teaching. Simple Jews possess so many virtues! The simplicity with which a simple Jew prays, recites psalms, and does the *mitzvot*—just because the Holy One, blessed be He, commanded it—produces great pleasure in heaven. Every Jew, even the least of the least, can and must be a servant of God. Every Jew, whoever he is, can accomplish great things to fulfill God's purpose in creating the world and, specifically, in bringing his soul down to earth. All that's required is a pure heart, even if it's the heart of the simplest Jew. What is purity of heart? In essence, it's sincerity—a person's inner intention, for 'God desires the heart.' And the heart of a simple Jew—whose misfortune is that he doesn't know how to recite the Hebrew words of the prayers, let alone know their translation—is precious to the Holy One, blessed be He. By merely reciting the words as best he can, even without understanding them, he gives the greatest pleasure to the Creator of the world and causes a flow of divine goodness to all the worlds. The Holy One, blessed be He, is pleased when simple people, who are grateful for His many blessings, praise Him in their everyday conversations. When a Jew, who's asked about his health and livelihood and his family's welfare, answers with praise to the Creator of the world: '*Baruch HaShem*, I'm making a good living!'; 'Thank God, my children are well!'; 'The Healer of the sick granted me a complete recovery!' and so on—this produces such satisfaction in heaven that it cannot be comprehended. If you remember the joy in heaven over the virtues of even these simplest Jews, you'll love all the Jewish people, including those who are simple and uneducated."[74]

Hershel the Ditch-Digger

THE BAAL SHEM TOV HAD A CERTAIN HASID, WHO WAS A SIMPLE MAN, but very pious. He earned his living digging ditches, and was called "Hershel the Ditch-digger." This Hershel was totally indifferent to material concerns. His whole life was Torah. Every fiber of his being was devoted to God. Although he supported his family to the best of his ability and provided them with bread and vegetables, he himself ate only the minimum that he needed to subsist. He only drank water and, in his whole life, had never tasted meat. He had memorized the Hebrew of the *Chumash* and the Book of Psalms, word for word, and recited them while he worked digging ditches and when he was moving about. Although he knew the meaning of most of the words, whether he knew the meaning or not, he still recited them. The Rabbis say that the Holy One, blessed be He, takes into account the views of the tzaddikim in directing the affairs of the world. The Baal Shem Tov said that among the tzaddikim treated with such heavenly esteem are also some pious, simple people, whose service gives God deep pleasure. He used to say, "Hershel the Ditch-digger's views are given consideration above."[75]

Remember the *Mah*

ON TWO DIFFERENT OCCASIONS, THE BAAL SHEM TOV SAID A PRAYER based on the verse in the Book of Lamentations: "Remember, O Lord, what happened to us [*meh haya lanu*]; look and see our degradation!" Each time, he first said, "Although Jews differ in their knowledge and observance of the Torah, they are all alike in the innermost essence of their souls. They all have the potential of the *mah**— the ability to nullify themselves in their devotion to God."

Once, when he was in a gathering of prominent *gaonim*¶, who were engaged in sharp talmudic arguments, he saw that they were filled with pride and conceit. He prayed that God would have compassion on them and let them see where they had gone astray: "'Remember, O Lord, what happened to us!'—Remember, O Lord, the loss of the 'what,' the humility of our souls; 'look and see our degradation'—look, and let us see our degradation and how low we have fallen!"

On another occasion, he was in a village of simple Jews, who, out of love for their fellow Jews, were making great efforts with tremendous self-sacrifice, to ransom a captive, a Jew who had been unjustly imprisoned. Although they were all poor people, they were giving away almost everything they owned to rescue this Jew who just happened to be passing through their town and was being held for ransom—despite the fact that they knew nothing about him. The Baal Shem Tov said in the presence of his disciples, "'Remember, O Lord, what happened to us!'—Remember, O Lord, that this was done because of the 'what,' the humility of their souls; 'look and see our degradation'—look at how they devalue themselves, endangering their lives and livelihoods because of their love for a fellow Jew!"

In these two incidents, the Baal Shem Tov compared some scholars and simple peo-

---

* The Hebrew word *mah*—"what"—mystically stands for the spiritual level of humility. In Kabbalah, the letters of *chochmah* (wisdom) rearranged, form *co'ach mah*, the power of self-nullification that produces the potential for what can be.

¶ Plural of *gaon*.

ple for his disciples, showing them how he viewed each group. He wanted them to imitate the good qualities of the simple people, for the Besht taught that by loving and helping fellow Jews with self-sacrifice, one achieves a great revelation of the *mah*—the spiritual potential—of the soul.[76]

The Gloomy Tailor

IN VILNA, LITHUANIA, THERE LIVED TWO SIMPLE TAILORS, NOT PARTICULARLY skillful in their craft, who made plain clothes for common people and for peasants in the villages. One day, the two of them decided to become partners and, leaving Vilna for a period of time, travel throughout the countryside from village to village plying their trade, until they would accumulate a certain amount of money, when they would return home. They were on the road for several years, made the sum they had set for themselves, and were traveling back to Vilna.

On the way, they came to a certain village and went, as they always did, to the home of the Jew who lived in the village. This Jew was the *mochsin* for the lord who owned the village. When they greeted him, the tailors could see from his face that he was very worried and downcast. Being good people and sympathetic to the troubles of a fellow Jew, they asked him why he was so anxious and depressed.

At first, he refused to answer, being in no mood to talk. But when they urged him to relieve himself by telling them his problems, he told them, through tears, that he was in a terrible predicament. "The lord of the village is marrying off his daughter and he ordered me to find an expert tailor to make her wedding gown. I've already traveled to a number of cities and brought him a few expert tailors—but he didn't like any of them! Not only that, he threatened that if I didn't bring him a good tailor quickly he'd kick me out of the village! I'm desperate. I don't know what to do!"

Both of these tailors, who had Jewish hearts, listened to him sympathetically. Although they were simple people, they were pious and looked for God's hand in their daily affairs. They thought to themselves, "Has God perhaps brought this work to us?" "My friend," they replied gently, "we're both tailors. Go and tell the lord that you've found two expert tailors, and that he should give us a chance to make the clothes." The man looked at them as if they were crazy and laughed derisively. "Shall I make fun of him? Didn't I tell you that famous tailors couldn't please him? Forgive me for saying so, but how can I bring him tailors like you, who wander around the villages patching peasants' clothes?" The tailors, however, did not give up. "What's the harm," they said, "in telling him about us? Since it seems that he's acting crazily, rejecting even the best tailors, maybe just for that reason he'll like what we do!" In short, they persisted until he agreed and went and told the lord that he had found two new expert tailors.

The lord, who agreed to try them out, said that they should make him a sample garment, and when they did—wonder of wonders—he liked it more than anything he had seen! He could not stop praising their work, and gave them the job of making all of his daughter's wedding trousseau. The tailors stayed in the lord's manor for a few weeks, until they had finished the whole job, and he was extremely pleased with that too. He thanked them profusely, praising their skill, and paid them generously. Then the lord summoned the Jewish *mochsin*, whom he thanked for finding such excellent tailors, and told him that he could continue living peacefully in the village. Meanwhile, the lord's wife, noticing that the tailors seemed overjoyed that the *mochsin* would be able to stay in the village, said to her husband, "These Jews seem delighted that their co-religionist won't be expelled from the village. Why not tell them about the other Jewish *mochsin* we've imprisoned in the pit? Perhaps they'd consider paying his debt and ransoming him from us?" The lord said to them, "Another of my Jews didn't pay his rent, so I was forced to put him and his family in prison. They've been there for so long that they're begging to be put to death. Since I've seen how sympathetic you are to your fellow Jew here, maybe you'd want to ransom this other one?" The tailors, whose hearts went out to a Jewish family in such terrible distress, asked, "How much money does he owe?" He said, "300 gulden." One of the tailors said to his friend, "What do you say?" "What can I say?" said the other. "If it was a smaller amount, I'd agree to share the *mitzvah* to ransom captives. But how can we afford the enormous sum of 300 gulden without ruining ourselves?" The first tailor stood thinking for a few moments and then said to the other, "Listen to me, my friend. I want to end our partnership. Let's figure out what my share of the money is; then I'll take what's mine." Without further ado, they made an accounting and determined that each of them was entitled to exactly 300 gulden. The second tailor saw that his friend was preparing to give all his money—which it had taken him years to earn—to fulfill the *mitzvah*, and he tried his best to dissuade him from doing so. After years of wandering and hard work, he would reduce himself to becoming a beggar. Certainly, there is no greater *mitzvah* than ransoming captives; but how can you willingly make yourself a pauper? Nevertheless, the other one was unshakeably determined to perform this holy deed of mercy with self-sacrifice and would not be swayed by logic or arguments. The only language he was listening to was that of his heart. He would not even consider changing his mind. They divided the money, and the first tailor took his 300 gulden and gave them to the lord to pay the debt of the captive Jew and his family. The lord then released the captives, had them brought before the tailor, and told them that this Jew had paid their debt, and he, the lord, was freeing them. Overcome with emotion, the whole family fell on the tailor's neck weeping tears of joy, and the tailor also wept with them.

After that the two tailors returned to Vilna. The one who came back with all his money started a business selling ready-made clothes and became very successful, his business growing by leaps and bounds. The second one, who came back without a penny, descended to the depths. His wretchedness was so great that he became depressed and went around always bent over and in a sullen mood, earning himself the nickname: the Gloomy Tailor. His grinding poverty sometimes brought him close to starvation and, when the pangs of hunger made him desperate, he begged from people on the street. And no one knew what had befallen him.

One day, a Jewish merchant was walking down the street, when the Gloomy Tailor approached him with outstretched hand and mumbled a request for a few coins to buy some bread. The callous merchant scornfully said, "And what will I gain by my charity?" "I'll bless you with success," answered the tailor humbly. The merchant smirked cynically and murmured, "The blessing of a *shlimazal* [luckless fool]." He flipped him a few small coins, and the tailor blessed him saying, "May God, blessed be He, give you success in all your doings!" The merchant walked on and immediately forgot about this chance encounter. This merchant dealt in linen and occasionally traveled to the estates of various lords to buy their linen, which he then sold in the city. The day that he encountered the tailor, he had to visit a certain lord who was a very hard man. Every time he did business with him the deal was only concluded after much wrangling and a difficult struggle. But that day, there was a miracle of sorts: When the Jewish merchant visited him, the lord finished his business with him easily without any trouble at all and in a way that he could expect a big profit. He was amazed at his strange good luck and suddenly recalled the tailor's blessing for success. The thought flickered in his mind, "Who knows? Maybe his blessing was effective!" In any case, he made a mental note of what happened and stored it away for future reference.

A few weeks passed, and the linen merchant again had to travel somewhere on business. This time he sought out the Gloomy Tailor and, when he found him, gave him some *tzedaka* and asked for his blessing for a successful trip. The tailor blessed him and the merchant set out. Again he was successful in an almost miraculous way. Now he was certain that the tailor's blessing was effective and, from that time, he made it a rule, whenever he went on a business trip, to first give the tailor some charity and obtain his blessing. This went on for half a year, and during that time the merchant became a wealthy man from the tailor's blessings. However, no one but he knew a thing about this.

Between Rosh HaShanah and Yom Kippur, the merchant hosted a family gathering in his home for many of his relatives. When he was somewhat tipsy and in a happy mood after imbibing some wine, he carelessly revealed to them the source of his recent success: the tailor's blessings. The secret ceased to be a secret, for, as the saying goes: "Your friend has a friend; and your friend's friend also has a friend." It quickly became known throughout the city that the Gloomy Tailor had the power of blessing. People began to stream to him to ask for his blessings. And his blessings were fulfilled; when he blessed someone, that person succeeded. But although he brought blessings to others, he himself remained poor and depressed.

At that time, it happened that two disciples of the Baal Shem Tov passed through Vilna and heard many stories about the tailor who gave blessings. Later, when they visited the Baal Shem, and told him about these miraculous doings in Vilna, he told them that the next time they were there they should try to bring the tailor to him. On their next visit to Vilna, they persuaded the tailor to travel with them to the Baal Shem Tov.

When the tailor visited him, the Besht tried to discover how this seemingly simple man came to possess this great power of blessing. The tailor himself had no idea. The Besht asked the tailor to tell him the story of his life. So the tailor began recounting everything that had happened to him, until he came to the incident of the wedding clothes that he made for the lord and how he had ransomed the captives, giving up all the money it had taken him years to earn. When the Baal Shem Tov heard that story, he immediately stopped him, saying, "That's it!"

The Baal Shem Tov kept the tailor with him and began to work on him, as a master craftsman works on his raw material. This kind and humble man possessed great light, but not having the vessels to contain it, was dark and gloomy. The Besht could see the gold coin, though its luster was dimmed, underneath the encrusted grime of many layers of mud. First of all, the Baal Shem Tov cured him of his depression and melancholy. Then, he began to teach him the revealed and the concealed Torah, and opened before him the fountains of divine wisdom, until the former tailor became a great tzaddik and kabbalist and thirstily drank the holy teachings of the Besht. Finally, he became joyful in God's light and his own light shown out to all.[77]

Simple People Reveal God's Simplicity:
The Parable of the Fields

THE BAAL SHEM TOV WAS ONCE WALKING WITH SOME OF HIS DISCIPLES outside of Medzibuz, taking a stroll down a road that had planted fields on both sides, with irrigation ditches to bring water from the nearby Bug River. When they stopped to rest, he said, "The simple essence of the Infinite One, blessed be He, manifests more in the simple faith and religiosity of simple Jews than it does in Torah scholars. When an artist paints a country scene of a field and its crop, he demonstrates his skill by painting them as they truly are, showing the natural beauty that the Holy One, blessed be He, bestowed on them. The more closely his painting depicts Nature, the more beautiful it's considered to be. The situation is similar when comparing a simple person and a Torah scholar. A simple person is more natural, like a field dependent upon rain, while a Torah scholar is like a field irrigated by a farmer. An irrigated field almost always yields more than an unirrigated one. But the field that depends on rain, whose appearance is not marred by the ridges and ditches of irrigation channels, displays more of the natural beauty that the Holy One, blessed be He, placed in the field. I tell you, the simple essence of the Infinite One, blessed be He, manifests more in a pious simple Jew than in a Torah scholar."

After the Baal Shem Tov and his disciples returned to Medzibuz, they sat down in the *beit midrash*, and he continued to teach them. "One should fulfill the Torah and *mitzvot* with simplicity of heart. But scholars like yourselves, whose divine service is, to a great degree, intellectual and rational, often feel that they have to understand everything beforehand and consider themselves ready and on the right spiritual level before they act. Simple people have an advantage in their divine service. They do the *mitzvot* not based on reasoning, but because they accept the yoke of the kingdom of heaven with simple faith. You should aspire to that kind of simplicity and innocence!"[78]

Loving Even the Least of the Least

WHEN THE BAAL SHEM TOV ONCE SAW HIS DISCIPLE RABBI DAVID OF Kolomaya kissing his son Nachman, he said to him, "David, the person who in your eyes is the least of the least and the lowest of the low, is dearer to me than your only son is to you."

Rabbi David said, "Master, I want to love all the Jewish people, as you do. But I know that I love Torah scholars more than others." The Besht replied, "Although a scholar is very precious, being an intellectual, he's usually spiritually cold, and often even cools off other people's fervor. He should try to overcome that weakness. But a simple person, who has simple faith and good character traits, is so precious! God loves all Jews, whether man or woman, the greatest *gaon* or the simplest person, for He loves the essence, the inside, of the person. Whether someone is learned or unlearned is just the outside; on the inside they're all equal. Therefore, we should love and honor the simplest Jew as much as the greatest *gaon*, because 'we all have one Father,' and as it says: 'you are children to the Lord your God' and: 'I love you,' says the Lord.'"[79]

An Expert Eye

THE BAAL SHEM TOV HAD THE EXPERT EYE OF A JEWELER WHEN IT came to simple Jews: He could see virtues that others would not even notice. And he trained his disciples to recognize what their eyes saw. One day, he told his disciples, "Pay attention to Reb Pesach the Water-carrier when he enters the synagogue to pray."

The disciples knew Pesach the Water-carrier and considered him merely a simple uneducated Jew. They never paid any attention to him at all. But now they watched him before he entered the synagogue for the afternoon prayer. They saw how, with great care, he ritually washed his hands a number of times and wiped them with a towel. When he opened the synagogue door, his facial expression changed due to his awe and reverence. When he went in and looked at the holy Ark, they heard him utter the verse: "*Shivitti HaShem l'negdi tamid!*" ("I have placed the Lord before me always!") He became so aroused when he said this, that they saw that his face actually changed colors!

This was a profound lesson to the disciples about entering a synagogue and also about noticing and appreciating the piety of a simple Jew. Later, when they reported to the Besht what they had seen, he said, "Nothing a person sees or hears is accidental. It's all providential, for everything that you see or hear conveys heavenly instruction. But you must pray to be able to understand what your eyes are seeing. Every Jew is a heavenly messenger to reveal Godliness. Each one has some good quality that you can train yourself to recognize and emulate. Simple Jews, with their innocent faith and guilelessness, are true servants of God. But you must learn to see their good qualities, which are often concealed from undiscerning eyes." The Baal Shem Tov, as a master teacher, knew what to point out to his Holy Society, and his devoted disciples trained their eyes to see.[80]

Different Paths to the Same Goal

THE BAAL SHEM TOV WAS ONCE RECEIVING VISITORS AND SAID TO ONE man, "You reached your spiritual level by reciting psalms," and to another, "You reached your level because of your Talmud study." Both of them had attained something spiritually, which the Besht saw at a glance, one achieving what he did with a favorite practice of working people and the other with the typical practice of religiously educated people.[81]

Learning from Simple People

ELIJAH HA-TISHBI AND AHIYAH HA-SHILONI* HAD TAUGHT THE BAAL SHEM TOV to learn from the simple people and sometimes had even sent him to learn from them. The Rabbis say: "Who is wise? He who learns from every person." The holy Baal Shem, with the humility of a tzaddik, always learned from the simple folk with whom he came in contact the virtues in which they excelled, such as faith, trust, and love of Israel. He used to say, "The greatest of the great should learn from the least of the least, who embody the essence of holy simplicity." He also often said, "In each Jew are hidden treasures of virtues—for, as the Rabbis teach about all Jews: 'They are modest, compassionate, and doers of kindness.'" He valued the typical virtues of the common folk more than the virtues of the scholars. What characterized the virtues of the simple people was their holy simplicity and pious innocence.[82]

The Importance of Sabbath Guests

THE BAAL SHEM TOV ONCE SAID TO HIS DISCIPLES, "MY WHOLE LIFE I'VE traveled widely, and some of my trips were to learn from the good deeds and holy practices of others—sometimes from very simple people. You can learn to serve God from everyone you meet, if you want to and if your eyes are open. Wherever you travel, regardless of the apparent 'reason' that led you there, there are also hidden divine purposes at work, and you should learn how to serve God from everything that happens to you and from everyone you meet. Once, I had some reason to travel to the German-speaking eastern lands, but I discovered once I was there that the real reason I was there was to learn hospitality from a certain innkeeper. When I had lodged with him for a few days and was about to leave on a Thursday, he offered me a large sum of money to stay, so that he wouldn't have to celebrate the holy Sabbath without a guest at his table! My parents ran after Sabbath guests, but this innkeeper taught me some-

---

* Elijah the Prophet, the Tishbite (from Toshav), and Ahiyah the Prophet, the Shilonite (from Shilo).

thing new about the importance of Sabbath guests and the preciousness of a *mitzvah!*"[83]

The Besht Learns Love of God from a Shepherd

THE BAAL SHEM TOV WAS ONCE SHOWN FROM HEAVEN THAT A CERTAIN simple man called Moshe the Shepherd served God, blessed be He, better than he did. He longed to meet this shepherd, so he ordered his horses harnessed to his coach and traveled, with a few of his disciples, to the place where he was told the shepherd lived.

They stopped in a field at the foot of a hill and saw above on the hillside a shepherd who was blowing his horn to call his flock. After the sheep gathered to him, he led them to a nearby trough to water them. While they were drinking, he looked up to heaven and began to call out loudly, "Master of the world, You are so great! You created heaven and earth, and everything else! I'm a simple man; I'm ignorant and unlearned, and don't know how to serve You or praise You. I was orphaned as a child and raised among gentiles, so I never learned any Torah. But I can blow on my shepherd's horn like a *shofar*, with all my strength, and call out, 'The Lord is God!'" After blowing with all his might on the horn, he collapsed to the ground, without an ounce of energy, and lay there motionless until his strength returned.

Then he got up and said, "Master of the world, I'm just a simple shepherd, I don't know any Torah and I don't know how to pray. What can I do for You? The only thing I know is to sing shepherds' songs!" He then began to sing loudly and fervently with all his strength until, again, he fell to the earth exhausted without an ounce of energy.

After recovering, he got up again and began to call out, "Master of the world! What is it worth that I blew on my horn and sang songs for You, when You're so great? What more can I do to serve You?" He paused for a moment and said, "There's something else I know how to do and I'll do it for Your honor and glory!" He then stood on his head and began to wave his feet wildly in the air. Then he did somersaults one after the other, until he collapsed on the ground, exhausted. The Baal Shem Tov and his disciples watched all this from a distance in amazement.

The shepherd lay there silently until his strength returned. Again, he began to speak and said, "Master of the world, I've done what I can, but I know it's not enough! What more can I do to serve You?" After pausing to reflect, he said, "Yesterday, the lord who owns the flock made a feast for his servants and, when it ended, he gave each of us a silver coin. I'm giving that coin to You as a gift, O God, because You created everything and You feed all Your creatures, including me, Moshe the little shepherd!" Saying this, he threw the coin upward.

At that moment, the Baal Shem Tov saw a hand reach out from heaven to receive the coin. He said to his disciples, "This shepherd has taught me how to fulfill the verse: 'You shall love the Lord your God with all your heart, with all your soul, and with all your might.'"[84]

Reciting the *Aleph-Bet*

THE BAAL SHEM TOV ONCE TOLD A FEW OF HIS DISCIPLES, "GO TO A certain village near Medzibuz, where you'll find a simple Jewish villager who is one of the tzaddikim of the generation."

They went there and found a Jewish villager who knew almost nothing of the Torah except the Hebrew alphabet. He would sit the whole day in a field under a tree and, with great devotion, recite the letters of the *aleph-bet*: *aleph, bet, gimel, dalet.* . . . When he finished reciting all the letters, he said, "Master of the world, You created all the letters of the alphabet, which join together to become all the words—all the prayers, praises, and requests. I don't know how to pray or to praise You, so here, my Heavenly Father, are all the letters of the alphabet. Please, You put them together into prayers, songs, and praises more beautiful than any I could ever say!" Then he began to fervently recite the alphabet again.

When the disciples returned to the Baal Shem Tov, and told him what they had seen and heard, he said to them, "Sometimes the childlike innocence of a simple Jew has more holy power to shake the supernal worlds than even the Torah study and praying of the great tzaddikim of the generation."[85]

The Besht Sends Scholarly Disciples to Learn from Simple People

MANY TIMES THE BAAL SHEM TOV SENT GREAT TORAH SCHOLARS TO remote places to learn good character traits from simple Jewish villagers and peasants. Once, he sent a great scholar to a tiny village to learn trust in God from a carpenter; he sent a second scholar and tzaddik, who was the rabbi of a large congregation, to a butcher, to learn the fear of heaven; a third great scholar and tzaddik, who had spent many years in solitude undergoing ascetic disciplines, was sent to the *shammos* of a synagogue, to learn humility; a fourth scholar he sent to a tailor to learn truth-speaking; a fifth, to a water-carrier to learn what it meant to have a good heart; a sixth, to a mason to learn the love of fellow Jews. All those who were sent by their master, the Baal Shem Tov, to learn these good character traits were great scholars, while those to whom they were sent were the simplest people.[86]

A Movement Forms and Opposition Grows

The New Movement Forms

BY THE TIME THE BAAL SHEM TOV MOVED TO MEDZIBUZ, HE HAD already begun to surround himself with a circle of disciples who were men of stature and accomplished scholars; these were in addition to the many hidden tzaddikim who were still actively working under his direction. All of these exceptional individuals joined together to further the goals of their holy master, the Baal Shem Tov. Now that he was living in Medzibuz, the Besht continued to focus on drawing to himself rabbis and scholars who became part of his inner circle. Then, after being perfumed with his teachings, they were sent out to widen the circle further and spread their master's teachings to the masses. As the numbers of his followers continued to grow, the Baal Shem Tov established centers for the new movement in different towns and, in each center, appointed one of his close disciples; or he established a center in a disciple's hometown. All of his own activities and the efforts he directed were planned, orderly, and efficient. Over the course of a number of years, all of this steady labor for the sake of the new movement spread its influence far and wide. At the same time, the Baal Shem Tov began to appoint rabbis, *shochtim*, cantors, and so on in towns where his followers held sway. Only a few years after his revelation, the Besht's movement in Podolia and Volhynia alone numbered ten thousand souls. As years passed, the number grew to twenty, then thirty thousand. But as his movement expanded and grew, so too did the opposition to it.[1]

The Reasons for Opposition

AS THE BAAL SHEM TOV'S FAME SPREAD, MANY RABBIS AND TORAH scholars opposed him, for a variety of reasons: One, they mistakenly believed that he was not a Torah scholar; two, he de-emphasized Torah study in favor of praying; three, according to their opinion, he elevated the common people at their expense; four, he challenged their authority, asserting his own; five, he was an innovator, changing the liturgy, the method of *shechitah*, and other customs; six, they felt that he promoted light-headedness and wildness, with singing and dancing; and finally, seven, he based himself in the Kabbalah. In the preceding century the Jewish people had experienced a disaster from a false messiah who justified himself by the Kabbalah—Shabtai Tzvi. These rabbis and scholars thought that the Baal Shem Tov was another disaster-in-the-making. Some of the Lithuanian rabbis even suspected him of having connections with the Shabtean movement.[2]

Innovations in the Liturgy and Shechitah

THE BAAL SHEM TOV COULD NOT BEAR TO PRAY WHERE THE WORSHIP was rote and without devotion. He needed his own separate *minyan*. But there was another reason for his separate *minyan*: The Besht perceived that the root of his soul was not directed to the heavenly gate connected to the traditional Ashkenazi liturgy, and he instead used the kabbalistic *siddur* arranged by the Ari, which is based on the Sephardic rite. The Ari taught that there are separate gates in heaven for each of the twelve tribes of Israel and that the prayers of each tribe rise through its own specific gate. But he claimed that his prayer book provided entry to all the gates. So the Besht directed his disciples to form their own *minyans* and to use the Ari's version of the liturgy. The Besht was also particularly strict about *shechitah*; he refused to eat meat if he was not sure that the *shochet* was skilled and expert, according to his views. Again, he departed from customary ways by directing his followers to follow his rigorous standards and instructed the *shochtim* among them to use his own "Ukrainian" method of sharpening the slaughtering knife. These radical steps in changing ancient customs aroused the ire and opposition of many rabbis and Torah scholars who feared the rise of a new separatist sect.[3]

A Visit to Slutzk

THE BESHT ONCE VISITED A WEALTHY COUPLE IN SLUTZK, LITHUANIA, who had built a new mansion but were afraid to move in because a new house can become a dwelling place for demons. They had sent for Rabbi Israel, the famous *baal shem*, to purify their home and remove their fear. When he arrived, the woman of the house wanted to make the Besht a meal, but he asked to first see the knife that the *shochet* would use to slaughter the animal. So the *shochet* was called to come and show the Besht his knife. When some of the townspeople heard about this request, they were furious with the Besht; how dare he ask to see the knife of the local *shochet*, especially in a big community like theirs, as if to question the *kashrut** of the meat they

* Kosher fitness.

were all eating! They wanted to forbid the *shochet* from going, but since the woman hosting the Besht was so prominent, they could not oppose her order summoning the *shochet*. After the meal, she took the Baal Shem Tov to the new house where almost everyone in town watched as he made strange movements in different places in the dwelling, as if he saw something—presumably to exorcise the demons. But some of them who were already angry at him suspected he saw nothing and was merely a charlatan. Later, when the time came for *Minha*, the Besht led the prayers, and they were again startled to hear that he was praying according to the Sephardic rite of the Ari, so they became even more incensed. Finally, the situation became so hostile in Slutzk that the Baal Shem Tov was forced to leave before his opponents seriously embarrassed him. Some of the local rabbis and Torah scholars were extremely vehement and even vicious in their opposition to the Baal Shem Tov. The Besht called such opponents "Jewish demons." But there were also some in the city of Slutzk who believed in him.[4]

Protecting the Besht from Opponents

RABBI MEIR MARGOLIOT, ONE OF THE BAAL SHEM TOV'S FIRST DISCIPLES and a famous Torah scholar, occasionally had to defend his master against the insults of rabbis and scholars who opposed him. Once, after an incident of that nature, the Besht said to him, "When a great soul descends to earth to be clothed in a body, an accusation is aroused above. The Satan complains, 'Now, I won't be able to do my job, because he'll make the whole world repent! Why was I created to no purpose?' In response, they give him a demonic Torah scholar, who is also sent down to earth at that time, and this scholar will mock and insult the perfect tzaddik. Whoever wants to can cleave to this one or to that one, and free choice is preserved. Because of such snakes and scorpions, my soul refused to descend to this world if I were not accompanied by sixty disciples, like the sixty heroes who surrounded King Solomon's bed to protect him from demons of the night. Meir, you are one of my sixty heroes."[5]

A Disciple Revives the Besht's Spirit

THE BAAL SHEM TOV WAS ONCE IN A STATE OF SUCH PROFOUND DARKNESS and depression—feeling that he had never served God as He deserved—that his last trace of vitality had almost been extinguished. But then, through the wondrous doings of divine providence, a devoted disciple, one of his "sixty heroes," came in to him at just that moment. Standing before the Besht in fear, awe, and trembling, he whispered, "Holy master!" These two words, uttered with the utmost reverence, revived the Besht and caused a spark of life to enter him, until his life-force was quickened and fortified, and he returned to his spiritual rung. Without that, he would have fallen from his exalted level.[6]

Saved When Sick

THE BAAL SHEM TOV ONCE BECAME VERY SICK AND LOST THE POWER OF speech. A number of his disciples were standing around his bed when he gestured to them to put *tefillin* on him. They did so, and he lay there in bed with the *tefillin* on for a long time. Then he began to talk. When they asked him what had happened, he told them that there was a heavenly accusation against him for something he had done when he was a little boy, which brought on this illness. Suddenly, his master, Ahiyah, appeared to him in a vision and said, "Quick, put on *tefillin*!" "Then," said the Besht, "the satanic accuser appeared to me in the form of a gentile peasant, carrying a scythe in his hand, ready to cut off my head. But he couldn't come near me because of the *tefillin*. He yelled at me in Russian, 'Take off those leather straps!' I ignored him and he kept on yelling until he disappeared. It says in the holy *Zohar* that certain *mitzvot*, such as *tefillin*, protect a person, so that he's sheltered under the wings of the Divine Queen, the *Shechinah*, and no accuser can approach or harm him. I also saw in a vision that my brother-in-law, Rabbi Gershon, tried to go before the heavenly court to plead on my behalf, but the gates were shut and he couldn't get in; so he grabbed a big piece of wood and started to pound on the gates until he forced them open. Then he began to yell, 'How can you threaten his life for such a minor sin?' It was the *tefillin* and his pleading that saved me."

The Rabbis say that God judges the holiest people, those closest to Him, most strictly. That is also how they judge themselves. When the Besht asked himself why he had become sick, the only sin he could think of to explain it was a minor transgression he had committed when he was a boy. But Ahiyah and Rabbi Gershon, the *tefillin* and the *Shechinah* Herself, together protected him from punishment.[7]

The Besht Stays Aware of His Opponents' Activities

THE BAAL SHEM TOV'S OPPONENTS—*MISNAGDIM**—MADE CONSTANT efforts to impede the rapid growth of his movement. But the Besht was usually aware of their activities. At that time, travel between Medzibuz and the centers of the opposition in Shklov and Vilna in Lithuania took a number of weeks. Yet there was a constant flow of visitors to Medzibuz, arriving and departing, who supplied the Besht with necessary information, and everything was kept secret from all but his inner circle.[8]

Speaking with Women

THE BAAL SHEM TOV WAS A MAN OF THE PEOPLE WHO WAS FRIENDLY with everyone. He walked the streets of Medzibuz, smoking his pipe and talking

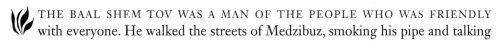

* A *misnaged* (sing.) is an opponent of the Besht and his hasidic movement.

with whoever he met, including women. This scandalized those excessively pious people who were stricter about limiting interactions with women.

It often happened that women came to the Baal Shem Tov before the men, that a wife visited him before her husband had any interest. After talking with her and relating to her need or request, the Besht would always tell the woman that when she returned she should bring her husband with her.[9]

A False Rumor

ONE *SIMHAT TORAH*, THE BAAL SHEM TOV WAS DANCING WITH SUCH enthusiasm that he fainted. While he was lying on the floor, his daughter Edel brought him a pillow so that he would feel better as he lay there resting. In the meantime, he told the hasidim, "Don't stop; keep dancing!" So Edel was standing in the middle next to the Baal Shem Tov and the hasidim were dancing around them. One of the Besht's opponents came in at this point to see what the hasidim were doing and, not realizing that the Besht was lying on the ground, reported to others that he saw the hasidim dancing around a woman. This false rumor further increased opposition to the Baal Shem Tov.[10]

Ya'ale V'Yavo

THERE WAS A CERTAIN OUTSTANDING TORAH SCHOLAR WHO SUSPECTED the Baal Shem Tov of being a fraud. He thought, "How can a person ignorant of the Torah have the holy spirit and do miracles, since the Rabbis say that an ignorant man can't be pious?" So he decided to travel to the Besht, to test him.

When he arrived, the Besht was dressed in his usual rough village clothing and certainly did not appear to be a Torah scholar. The rabbi addressed him in a condescending tone and, alluding to the Besht's fame as a miracle-worker, said, "Some people claim that you have the holy spirit, but others say that you're ignorant of the Torah. So I'd like to see if you know something about the *halacha*." As the rabbi considered what to ask the Besht, he remembered that it was *Rosh Hodesh* and that he had forgotten to recite the additional *Ya'ale V'Yavo** section in the morning prayers. He then asked the Besht a question so simple that any scholarly boy would know the answer: "If someone forgets to say *Ya'ale V'Yavo* in his prayer, what must he do?" "Rabbis like yourself," replied the Besht, "study the Torah day and night. I'm just a simple man who spends a lot of time on the road traveling. So I know a lot about horses. To answer your ques-

---

* "Let our remembrance rise and come before You"—a special prayer inserted into the prayer service on New Moon and other holidays.

tion, I first have to ask you a question from my area of expertise. Now, some horses are much more expensive than others. My question is: Why would someone pay—as happens—ten times more for one horse than for another?" The rabbi answered immediately, "Because one horse can run ten times faster than the other." "I see that you also know something about horses," said the Besht. "You're right. But there's another question: If the fast horse leaves the path, it strays ten times farther than the other! Doesn't that remove its advantage?" The rabbi had no ready answer to this question and remained silent. The Besht continued, "The answer is simple: When a fast horse turns around and goes back on the right path, it also runs ten times quicker than the slow horse does when it's returning from going the wrong way. So its advantage makes up for its disadvantage. Now here's the point: Just like a fast horse, someone who's quick and clever has an advantage. Even if he goes astray, God-forbid, he can quickly correct his path and repair the damage. It's you, Rabbi, who have gone astray, and it's up to you to use your intelligence to quickly reverse your course and repair the damage! As for your forgetting *Ya'ale V'Yavo*"—and here the rabbi was astonished that the Besht knew by the holy spirit that he had forgotten the prayer—"whether or not a person should repeat the whole prayer after forgetting *Ya'ale V'Yavo* doesn't apply either to you or me, although we're both obligated to say the whole prayer again if we forget. Because if you forget it once, even if you say the whole prayer again, you'll still forget that part a second time; and I'll never forget to say *Ya'ale V'Yavo* even the first time." After saying this, the Baal Shem Tov left the room, while the rabbi stood there stunned and speechless, for he realized at that moment that although he had prayed the whole prayer over a second time that morning, he had also forgotten to say *Ya'ale V'Yavo* the second time! He quickly absorbed the Besht's meaning and immediately began to ponder how he had gone astray and how he could repent and repair the damage. He then decided to become a disciple of the Besht.

Why did this rabbi forget *Ya'ale V'Yavo* the second time? Because he had become lost on the path of Torah, and in planning to test and challenge the Baal Shem Tov, he had separated himself from God. Why would the Besht never forget to say the proper prayer? Because there is no forgetfulness before God. Someone who truly stands before Him, during prayer and at all times, never forgets anything.[11]

He Admonishes a Preacher

THE PREACHERS IN THE BAAL SHEM TOV'S TIME WERE FOREVER rebuking their listeners and terrifying them with graphic descriptions of the divine punishments for sin. They portrayed God as jealous and vengeful, sternly meting out strict retribution for every offense. Their sermons were based on Torah verses such as: "God acts so that men will fear Him," and on similar talmudic quotations that warn of punishment. Warming eloquently to their dire theme, they often made statements that sounded like curses, such as: "For such-and-such sin, the Holy One, blessed be He, will visit upon you, God-forbid, such-and-such fearsome punishment!" Needless to say, their sermons often lowered the spirits of their listeners and left them in a depressed mood. In fact, by their harsh words of rebuke, they actually disparaged the Almighty, for the simple men and women who listened to them learned to picture the one who is "a merciful and gracious God," who "is good and does good to all," as a vengeful God, relentlessly strict and unsparing.

The Baal Shem Tov so loved the Jewish people and particularly the simple folk, that he could not bear to hear preachers berate and accuse them. For him, praising the Jewish people was as much a divine service as praising God Himself.

The Besht once spent the Sabbath in the town of Alek in Volhynia, as a guest in the home of the community leader. On Saturday afternoon, when his host went to hear the sermon of a visiting preacher in the synagogue, the Besht stayed at home, waiting for him to return for the third Sabbath meal.

Meanwhile, some people coming from the synagogue told him that the preacher was castigating the Jewish people for their sinfulness. The Baal Shem Tov became angry upon hearing this and told his attendant to go to the synagogue and tell his host to come home immediately and not listen to the rest of the sermon. While engaged on this errand, the attendant also informed some other people in the synagogue about the Besht's anger at the preacher, and word of this quickly spread throughout the congregation. In a few minutes, the preacher saw that people were leaving one by one, and he stopped his sermon in the middle.

The next day, the preacher paid a call on the Baal Shem Tov and greeted him. When the Besht (who did not know him or recognize him) asked him who he was, he identified himself as the preacher and said, "I wanted to ask you why you were so angry at me yesterday." The Baal Shem Tov jumped up, with tears in his eyes and his voice choking with emotion, and said, "Why do you speak badly of the Jews! I tell you that after a Jew spends the whole day in the marketplace running around struggling to make a living for himself and his family, and when evening arrives he sighs and anxiously reminds himself, 'I mustn't let the time for prayers pass!' and goes into a house and prays *Minha*—even without understanding the meaning of the words—yet, I tell you that the angels in heaven tremble from his holiness!"[12]

Rebuking God's Children

WHEN THE BAAL SHEM TOV ONCE CRITICIZED A PREACHER OF REBUKE FOR focusing on the sins of a congregation, the preacher justified himself by arguing that the Torah in many places rebukes the Jewish people for their sins. "It's true," replied the Besht. "The Holy One, blessed be He, often chastises us and punishes us too. Yet when Moses said, 'Listen, you rebels!' it was decreed, because of his angry condemnation of the Jews, that he not enter the Land of Israel. Everyone knows that a father rebukes his own children, but he won't allow anyone else to do so. For God it's permitted, so to speak, to rebuke the Jews, because they're His own children. But for flesh and blood, even Moses himself, it's forbidden!"[13]

Curing a Spiritual Sickness

IN A TOWN NOT FAR FROM MEDZIBUZ THERE LIVED A MAN AND HIS UNCLE, both of whom were wealthy and gifted Torah scholars. The uncle was a follower of the Baal Shem Tov; the nephew was a vociferous *misnagid*. The relations between uncle and nephew, which had once been warm, became cold and tense after the uncle, who had earlier been an opponent of the Besht, became his disciple. The nephew was angry at his uncle for following someone he considered to be a false teacher, and he frequently insulted the Baal Shem Tov in his uncle's presence. Whenever he heard the Besht's name mentioned, he became agitated and immediately launched into a tirade against him, while his elderly uncle tried in vain to silence him. The nephew derisively called his uncle and his uncle's hasidic friends "the holy dancers," for that is what some of the Besht's opponents called his hasidim. When the Baal Shem Tov occasionally visited this town, the *misnagid* nephew did not cease vilifying him to whoever would listen. There seemed to be no end to his hostility to the Besht.

When the uncle became a hasid of the Baal Shem Tov, the nephew had moved to another synagogue for prayer and study. His house was in the same courtyard as his uncle's house, and his animosity to his uncle became so intense that he separated off his section of the area with a fence so that they would not even meet in their shared courtyard.

During the days of *Selichot*, the Baal Shem Tov unexpectedly visited that town and the joy was tumultuous, for since the elderly uncle, who was well respected and influential, had become a disciple of the Baal Shem Tov, almost the whole town had also become his hasidim. Therefore, the Besht's sudden arrival created a great stir.

At that time, the *misnagid* nephew was very sick in bed. However, even ill, as soon as he heard that the Besht had arrived in the town and that everyone was jubilant, he began, as usual, to slander and insult him.

The Baal Shem Tov taught Torah while he was visiting there, and one of his teachings was on the verse: "You shall not hate your brother in your heart; you shall surely rebuke your neighbor, and not bear sin because of him." He said, "'You shall not hate your brother in your heart.' The way of the world is that people hate someone who hates them. But the Torah's way is to return love for hate. If someone responds to hate by hating a fellow Jew in his heart alone, even without doing him harm or speaking against him—that itself violates a prohibition of the Torah. The way to avoid transgressing the commandment not to hate your brother in your heart is found in the continuation of the verse: 'You shall surely reprove your neighbor.' His hatred for you certainly has a reason behind it, which is undoubtedly religious. [The Besht, in his goodness, always charitably judged the motives for others' animosity.] Evidently, he sees something in your conduct that he considers contrary to the Torah's teaching. Therefore, the way to deal with him is: 'You shall surely reprove your neighbor'*—go and *prove* to him that your conduct is correct and proper. If you ask, 'Why am I required to do all this?' It's because of the obligation you have to love your fellow Jews. That's why the verse continues: 'do not let him bear sin because of you[¶],' that is, don't let him continue to sin by hating you. Your love of Israel should be such that you don't want him to consider you sinful. When you've proven to him that your conduct is according to the Torah, you'll remove from *him* the sin of: 'Do not hate your brother in your heart.' But since you know that you're in the right and he's wrong to hate you, and that you are fulfilling the important commandment of love of Israel in trying to save him from the sin of: 'Do not hate your brother,' you might be inclined to speak to him harshly. Therefore, Rashi comments on: 'Do not bear sin because of him': 'Do not embarrass him in public. Speak to him privately and gently.'"

Before leaving town, the Baal Shem Tov told the uncle that he wanted to visit his opponent, the sick nephew. Accompanied by the uncle and some other townspeople, the Baal Shem Tov went to fulfill the commandment to visit the sick and the Torah's teaching to return love for hate, which he had taught about earlier. As he entered the *misnagid's* home, he found the family weeping and wailing. The sick man was lying in bed with closed eyes, running a high fever and mumbling incoherently, and his movements were those of someone critically ill. When the Besht entered the room, the family offered him a seat, and he sat down at the bedside of the sick man. He then placed his hand on the sick man's head and in the melody of Talmud study, chanted,

"Sickness can come from Amalek[§]. Amalek is doubt. Doubt is arrogance. Arrogance is bitter.

"Sickness of the body may be caused by sickness of the soul. Sickness of the soul is caused by doubts about faith in God. Doubts about faith are caused by Amalek.

"Amalek can cause doubts about faith in God through doubts about the Torah's holiness, by accepting only its plain meaning and being skeptical about the rest, by stubbornly refusing to study the other three of the levels of the Torah's holy orchard—hint, homily, and secret. When you're proud of your knowledge of the plain meaning, that's the arrogance of Amalek, and it's truly bitter.

'Where do these doubts about the Torah come from? How does Amalek gain entry and a foothold? Amalek begins with doubts about a fellow Jew, when you look at him hatefully, with an evil eye, because his behavior displeases you. You should instead approach him and reprimand him, and not, God-forbid, gaze at him from a distance while seething with anger against him. Because judging from afar is the arrogance of Amalek and is very bitter."

The touch of the Besht's holy hand and the sound of his pleasant voice chanting in the melody of Talmud study had great healing power. The sick man's head cleared and

---

* The Besht read the Hebrew *tochei'ach*, reprove or rebuke, as "to offer proof" to someone.

¶ Usually read (see preceding and following) as: "do not bear sin because of him."

§ The tribe of Amalekites, who attacked the stragglers and the weak among the Jews who left Egypt in the Exodus, traditionally symbolizes the force that seeks to lessen and cool down faith, that produces doubt.

he regained full consciousness; his high fever immediately subsided. His heart also opened after years of being constricted in anger and censure. He carefully followed the reasoning of the Besht's words with full comprehension, and he saw that the Besht had diagnosed his spiritual illness as an expert doctor. Not only that, but this compassionate doctor, who returned his hate with love, had actually healed him in body and soul. He gazed at the Baal Shem Tov sitting at his bedside, and then gazed at his uncle, who was looking at him with loving concern. Tears welled up in his eyes and streamed down his cheeks, as he realized that not only was he well, praise God, but he also had become the Besht's disciple.[14]

Loving Someone Who Hates or Harms You

THE BAAL SHEM TOV'S DISCIPLES FOUND IT DIFFICULT TO UNDERSTAND how their master could be so loving and mild to those who persecuted or insulted him. Once, when he was teaching them, one of them asked, "Master, how is it possible to love someone who hates or harms you?"

"When someone abuses you and causes you suffering," said the Besht, "you have to make every effort to love him even more than before, for three reasons: First, because you'll be strongly tempted to hate him, and loving your neighbor is a great principle of the Torah. So you must exert yourself to overcome your evil inclination and love him even more. Second, if you love him, he may repent. So you should love even wicked people, while hating their evil deeds. But it's forbidden to draw too close to them. It's written about Aaron that he loved and pursued peace, loved people and drew them to the Torah. *By* loving people he brought them to repent, and drew them to the Torah. Because when I love someone, he'll love me in return, for: 'As water reflects a face, so does the heart of a person reflect the heart of his fellow.' Since I hate his evil deeds, he too will begin to hate them and will repent. Third, you must love someone who harms you even more than before, because the Congregation of Israel is a vessel for holiness, and when they are united and love each other, the *Shechinah* and all holiness dwell among them. But when, God-forbid, there's any schism between them, the holiness falls among the evil Shells, which is a disaster. So when a person sees that someone is withdrawing from him, he should love that person even more and move toward him, to close the empty space."[15]

Rabbi Nachman of Kossov

RABBI NACHMAN OF KOSSOV WAS A GREAT TZADDIK AND A MEMBER OF THE Pious of Kitov. At first an opponent of the Baal Shem Tov, he later became a disciple and close friend.

An exceptional preacher of the fiery kind, who focused on people's sins and rebuked them for their failings, Rabbi Nachman had great success in bringing people to repent. Although he valued the Baal Shem Tov's ability to read minds, he knew that the Besht could not match him in speaking ability. He once suggested that they form a team and travel all over the world to bring people back to God. "You'll read people's thoughts and tell me what their sins are," he said, "and I'll convert them with my fiery sermons. Together, we'll make everyone repent!" The Besht could imagine how "delighted" people would be to hear Rabbi Nachman denounce their sins—which the Besht would reveal to him—in his fire-and-brimstone sermons. He smiled at this suggestion and said, "If we joined forces, I don't think we'd even have a *minyan* to pray with, because everyone would flee from us without looking back."

The Baal Shem Tov knew that many of the rabbis and preachers who harshly rebuked people's sins suffered for their misguided zeal by provoking disputes against themselves.

He once joked, "People say: 'With truth you can travel from one end of the world to the other.' When a rabbi can't stand sin or falsehood, and stubbornly insists on the truth, exposing the sins of the people in his town, he can go from one end of the world to the other—they'll chase him out of each town he lives in, one after the other, until he finally reaches the other end of the world!"

The Besht's way was not of rebuke but of love and encouragement. He once said to Rabbi Nachman, "You should arouse sinners to repent by your love of Israel, by drawing them so close that, even without your saying anything directly, they become aware of their sins and correct themselves."

On another occasion, the Besht told his friend a parable about preaching. "A king banished his only son from his realm. He later sent two servants to report on his son's conduct. One servant returned and slandered the son to his father by reporting all of the prince's wrongdoing and bad deeds. The other servant reported the very same things, but when he spoke he shared the king's pain and explained that the prince's bad behavior resulted from his long exile, during which he had forgotten the ways of royalty. Then the king was filled with pity for his son. He restored him to the palace, and rewarded the loyal servant. In the same fashion," said the Besht, "when a preacher admonishes the Jewish people, he should always act like the second servant. Jews don't sin because they want to, but only because they've become separated from their Heavenly Father. All that's needed is for them to return and become close to God. Then they'll abandon their sins on their own. If a preacher takes this approach, it'll surely please our Father in Heaven." Eventually, the Besht convinced Rabbi Nachman to become a preacher of the kind word, of love and uplifting. He then turned even more people back to God than he had done previously.[16]

The Penance

 RABBI YEHIEL MICHAL, THE SON OF RABBI YITZHAK OF DROHOBITCH AND one of the outstanding young scholars of the Brody *Kloiz*, lived in the small town of Borislav (later, he achieved fame as the Maggid of Zlotchov). At first skeptical about the Baal Shem Tov, he became his disciple when he saw that the Besht could elevate his praying to new spiritual heights.

One Friday during the winter, a Jewish peddlar from Borislav, who was returning home for the Sabbath after a week on the road earning his living, had problems with his wagon and could not reach the town as early as expected. If evening arrived when he was on the road in the open country, he would have to remain there for the whole Sabbath, alone in a dangerous area. So, to reach safety, he was forced to travel into town as evening fell.

Deeply troubled at having unintentionally desecrated the holy Sabbath, he went to pour out his grief to the pious young man who sat day and night studying Torah in the *beit midrash*, to ask him how to repent. Rabbi Yehiel Michal prepared a penance for the man according to the strict rules prescribed in some holy books—to fast many times, roll naked in the snow, break the ice and immerse in the freezing water of a river or lake, and so on. The man did as he was told, but before long the severe penance proved to be more than he could physically bear.

Soon afterward, the Baal Shem Tov happened to visit the nearby town of Hodirklov. When the man heard that a great tzaddik was in the area, he immediately traveled to Hodirklov to ask him also what to do to repent. How could he fix the damage to his soul when he did not have the strength for the severe penance? In his anguish, he wept profusely before the Baal Shem Tov, confessing that he had committed a terrible sin by traveling as the Sabbath arrived!

After listening intently, the Besht told him to bring a pound of candles to the synagogue on *erev Shabbat*, light them in honor of the coming Sabbath, and his sin would be atoned. Since he had desecrated the Sabbath, let him now honor its sanctity. The man was dumbfounded when he heard this, and stood there speechless. Would such a small offering, such an easy penance, rectify a serious transgression like desecrating the Sabbath?

Understanding what he was thinking, the Baal Shem Tov asked the man to tell him exactly what had happened that Friday. With tears streaming down his face, he told the Besht the whole story, and the difficult penance that Rabbi Yehiel Michal had given him. With great anguish and regret, he explained that he had not been able to stand up under the fasts and afflictions. The Baal Shem Tov then repeated his instructions, saying, "My son, do as I told you. Bring a pound of candles to the synagogue in honor of the Sabbath. Go home; your sin will be atoned. And tell Rabbi Michal that I order him to visit me in Hevastov, where I'll be for the coming Sabbath."

The man fulfilled the Baal Shem Tov's command. Rabbi Yehiel Michal did also, and on Friday he harnessed his coach and traveled from Borislav to Hevastov. At a crossroads on the way, his coach sunk deeply into the mud and he could not get it out. He hurried to the town on foot, walking as fast as he could to arrive before the Sabbath began. But the hour was already late and he did not succeed in reaching the town before the sun had set and the stars had appeared. When he entered the house where the Baal Shem Tov was staying and found him standing at the table holding the wine cup, about to make *kiddush*, Rabbi Michal's heart fell. He could not believe what had happened to him.

The Besht put down his *kiddush* cup and greeted Rabbi Michal with "Good *Shabbos!*" Then, reading the anguish on the young man's face, he gazed at him compassionately and said, "So, Michli, perhaps you'll understand now how to deal with a Jew who unintentionally desecrates the Sabbath! Someone like yourself, who's been pure and sinless all his life, can't imagine the pain and grief of a Jew who's stumbled and sinned. How could you give him a penance like that? You should know, Rabbi Michal, that his heart was broken, and because of his sincere regret his sin was already repaired and his transgression removed completely!" Humbled, Rabbi Michal listened in silence. He had learned a profound lesson. Then the Besht made *kiddush* with his usual fervor and devotion.

The Baal Shem Tov knew that Rabbi Michal lacked sympathy and had prescribed a harsh penance for the simple peddlar, because he himself was so holy and removed from sin. But the Besht, who was the holy of holies, sympathized with the man's failings and recognized his anguished regret, because the Besht's path was based on leniency and love.[17]

A Cold House, a Cold Jew!

THERE WAS A CERTAIN PROMINENT TORAH SCHOLAR IN MEDZIBUZ WHO was not respected by the townspeople, which was surprising. Finally, this scholar himself asked the Baal Shem Tov what the reason was. The Besht did not immediately answer him. But later—and this was during the winter—he told some of his disciples to visit the man's home and see if his house was cold inside. When they visited him, they found that his house was indeed very cold and that he did not heat it properly, although he could have afforded to do so. When they reported this to the Besht, he said, "A cold house, a cold Jew!" Asked to explain his remark, he said, "He's cold to himself and cold to others. So people are cold to him, measure for measure." This scholar did not want to spend money on himself, even when there was a real need, and he did not want to spend on others. Because of his stingy nature, people treated him accordingly. When the scholar later spoke again to the Baal Shem Tov, the Besht told him, "Be a warm Jew, and others will be warm to you!"[18]

His Disciples Praise the Jewish People Halfheartedly

ONE EVENING AFTER MIDNIGHT, SOME OF THE BAAL SHEM TOV'S DISCIPLES were sitting in his *beit midrash* praising the virtues of the Jewish people. The Besht, who was in the adjoining room, saw with his holy spirit that they were not sincere and were not speaking from the heart. They were saying these things only to please the Creator. So instead of arousing love and pleasure in heaven, they were stirring up accusations and judgments. Indignant and incensed, the Besht went to them and complained, "You are praising the Jewish people the way a woman praises the children of her husband's first wife in his presence. She does it just to please him, but in her heart she despises them. But I, Israel, say that Israel, the holy people, are holy! They are good, good, good; full of kindness and Torah and countless virtues!" He went on praising the Jewish people for a long time, until he truly caused great pleasure and delight in heaven, and drew down kindness and blessings on all of Israel.[19]

Witness for the Defense

ONCE, WHEN THE BAAL SHEM TOV WAS LEADING THE PRAYERS BEFORE THE Ark, he interrupted himself, turned around, and walked right out of the synagogue. Seeing a peasant selling firewood from a wagon on the street, the Besht bought the full load from him—for use in heating the synagogue—and the gentile followed him back in, carrying some of the wood into the building. The man made a number of additional trips to bring in the whole wagon load.

Needless to say, everyone was astonished by the Besht's strange behavior. One is not supposed to interrupt the prayers; for the prayer-leader to walk out and buy firewood on the street—what could be more bizarre? But at that moment, they were too surprised to question the Baal Shem Tov and, in the middle of the service, it was inappropriate anyway.

When the peasant finished carrying in the wood, the Besht told one of the synagogue officers to pay him for it and to add something extra for his trouble in bringing it into the synagogue. He also asked them to give the man a glass of liquor. Feeling honored by the rabbi's consideration, the gentile, who was standing in the middle of the synagogue, exclaimed before the whole congregation, "Praised be the God of the Jews, who has such a holy people! Had one of my own kind bought this wood from me, I'm sure I wouldn't have gotten anything extra for my trouble in carrying it in!"

Later, the Besht's disciples—who were astonished by this whole episode, asked him why he had interrupted in the middle of the prayers to buy wood! He told them that, while praying, he saw that there was a heavenly accusation against the Jews who live in the villages, for some of them cheated the illiterate peasants on the bills for their purchases. "I had to find a way to counter this charge," he said, "and by this peasant praising the Jews—because most Jews are good and honest people, who treat the peasants decently and with respect—the Accuser's arguments were silenced."[20]

Every Action for the Sake of God

ONCE, WHEN THE BAAL SHEM TOV SAT WRAPPED IN HIS TALLIS AND *TEFILLIN*, teaching Torah to his disciples in his *beit midrash* before the morning prayers, he said, "When a person develops a new insight in his Torah study or does a *mitzvah*, such as putting on a tallis and *tzitzit* for prayer, he might think that he's doing something small and of little significance. Yet, the Holy One, blessed be He, creates from every new Torah interpretation and every *mitzvah* done with pure motives a new heaven and a new earth."[21]

His Pipe-Smoking

AFTER TEACHING FOR A SHORT WHILE, THE BAAL SHEM TOV LIT HIS PIPE and smoked meditatively to prepare for prayers. Every action and movement of the holy Baal Shem Tov was intentional and for the service of God, blessed be He. Even his pipe-smoking was accompanied by kabbalistic meditations, and the smoke that rose from his pipe was like the smoke of the incense that was burned on the altar in the Temple. Indeed, throughout the day, whenever he wanted to ascend to the higher worlds, he smoked his pipe; and each time he puffed, he went from one world to another. After the prayers that morning, Rabbi Gershon of Kitov said to a fellow disciple, "I wish I would have the paradise that our master acquires from smoking one pipeful of tobacco!"[22]

His Daily Schedule of Divine Service

WHEN THE BAAL SHEM TOV LIVED IN MEDZIBUZ, HIS DAILY SCHEDULE of divine service was regular: He went to the *mikvah* between 6 and 7 in the morning, whether summer or winter. By ten in the morning he had already finished *davvening*. He studied Torah until noon, wearing Rabbeinu Tam *tefillin**. He studied the *Zohar* every week, according to the *parashah*¶. If by chance he finished the whole *parashah* before *Shabbat*, he began it again; he did not proceed further, out of order. He never slept during the day, except for a nap on *erev Shabbat* to prepare for the Sabbath, and in the afternoon on *Shabbat* and *Yom Tov*§. The Besht ate only one meal a day, in the afternoon; he never ate at night. He occasionally ate meals with some of his disciples on weekdays. Every day, he had an hour of *hitbodedut* (seclusion with God) before *Minha* in his private room in the *beit midrash*. Between *Minha* and *Maariv*, he sat with his disciples and taught them Torah. Every evening after *Maariv*, he went to his room and received visitors who came to him for blessings, prayers, or advice; this went on for an hour or more. Then the Besht slept for two or three hours, waking up around

---

* Special *tefillin* worn by very pious men for the concluding part of the prayer service.
¶ Weekly Torah portion.
§ Holiday.

midnight for *Tikkun Hatzot*. Occasionally, when there were many visitors, he stayed up until the time for *Tikkun Hatzot*, performed the service, then slept for a few hours. Usually, after *Tikkun Hatzot*, the Besht studied Torah with Ahiyah ha-Shiloni until the morning.[23]

The Baal Shem Tov's Shoes

THE BAAL SHEM TOV HAD A BED IN HIS SMALL UPSTAIRS ROOM IN THE *beit midrash*, which he used Friday afternoon for a nap before the holy Sabbath. Once, a servant who had finished sweeping the *beit midrash* entered the room and quietly began sweeping there too. When he came near where the Baal Shem Tov was sleeping, he saw that the Besht's shoes were on the floor next to the bed, and did not know whether to move them or sweep around them. If he did not clean there, the synagogue officers might scold him; but if he moved them, the rabbi might be annoyed. He decided that since the holy Baal Shem Tov had put them in that place, he should leave them where they were, and clean around them.

Later, when the Baal Shem Tov awoke and saw that the room had been swept and cleaned, he asked the servant, "Did you move my shoes?" When the servant told him how he had decided the issue, the Baal Shem Tov approved, and blessed him with a long, healthy life.

One of the Besht's disciples who happened to be upstairs overheard this exchange between his master and the servant and later asked the Besht the meaning of what had happened. The Baal Shem Tov replied, "Everything in the world is determined down to its smallest details by divine providence—for example, where a pebble is on the road or how far a fallen leaf rolls when driven by the wind. A tzaddik's actions are also purposeful to the last detail. All of my movements," said the Besht, "are only for the sake of heaven. But how can someone else know the mystical intentions behind my actions? Every smallest human action has cosmic repercussions. You should believe with complete faith that if you even wave your little finger here on earth below, you're having an effect in the spiritual worlds above. A tzaddik knows what he's doing and his actions are intentional; it's not for someone else to change what he has set in place and arranged."[24]

Don't Focus on Stringencies

THE BAAL SHEM TOV ONCE ARRIVED IN THE TOWN OF KONSTANTYN IN Volhynia with his disciple, Rabbi David Forkes, and they stayed at a certain person's home. The Besht asked the *shochet* to come and show him his knife, to inspect it before they ate what he slaughtered. The *shochet* did not come promptly, however, and in the meantime the Baal Shem Tov began to pray *Minha* with the other men present. While this was happening, the *shochet* arrived but did not want to wait for the Baal Shem to finish his prayers. He angrily demanded that the householder's wife give him the chickens to slaughter immediately. She gave them to him, he slaughtered them, and left. When the Baal Shem Tov finished praying, he said, "Hasn't the *shochet* come yet?" "He came, slaughtered the chickens, and left," they said. The chickens were still lying there in the pan being salted. The Besht looked at them and said he would eat them, but Rabbi David Forkes said he would not. The Baal Shem Tov was not strict about this. He later said to Rabbi David, "Don't be too strict and punctilious about the *mitzvot* or your pious customs, because it's only a trick of the evil inclination to make you anxious and depressed." Unlike some of his contemporaries, the Baal Shem Tov did not lay great stress on stringencies in doing the *mitzvot*. He remarked to Rabbi Pinhas of Koretz, another of his close disciples, who was also present then, "I try not to be overly stringent in doing the *mitzvot*. In fact, this thought saved me when I was younger."[25]

The Hungry Preacher

THE BAAL SHEM TOV WAS ONCE STAYING IN BRODY AT THE HOME OF A certain wealthy man. His host made a large feast in his honor, and there were a number of prominent people sitting at the head of the table. Meanwhile, a certain itinerant preacher was sitting at the far end of the table and eating an enormous quantity of food. When some of the others saw this, they kept offering him more and more food, as a joke. The preacher, for his part, continued to eat whatever they put in front of him: If there was fish, where two people would eat one piece, he ate two pieces. So too with the soup and all the other dishes. When they saw that he kept on eating, they kept on giving him more, to make fun of him.

Finally, these people urged him to say words of Torah, and again, they were only interested in mocking him, for presuming to teach Torah at a table at which the Baal Shem Tov was present! Nevertheless, the preacher, in his simplicity, began to teach Torah to the gathering, while the instigators hid their laughter behind their hands. When he realized that they were laughing at him, he interrupted himself and said, "If someone can't say Torah well, does that mean he's not allowed to eat a piece of fish?"

Meanwhile, the Baal Shem Tov had looked over to see what was happening, and he was displeased and angered by their mockery of the preacher. The Besht then turned his ear to listen to what the preacher was saying, and found that it pleased him. After the preacher paused and made his remark, when he sensed that they were laughing at him, the Besht said to all those sitting at the table, "Friends, pay attention to what the preacher is saying, because these words of Torah are from Elijah the Prophet, may he be remembered for good."

After the meal, the Besht spoke to his disciples criticizing the behavior of those at the table who had mocked the preacher. He said, "Never mock anyone. Even the gentiles say that it's wrong to make fun of another person. They have a saying, 'If you pay attention to your own deeds, you won't mock others.' And there's something else to learn from this incident: People often judge and dismiss a Torah teacher because of his personal deficiencies. But if you're critical of the teacher, you won't be able to absorb the teaching. The Torah you hear is divinely intended for your ears, regardless of any faults in the person who delivers it." Listening to this precious lesson, the Besht's disciples also appreciated the humility of their own holy master, who was not offended that someone else had taught at a table over which he was presiding, and had even defended the man from mockery and condemnation.[26]

Eating His Fill

A CERTAIN JEW WAS ON THE ROAD TRAVELING IN THE VICINITY OF MEDZIBUZ and was very hungry, but there was no place to stop and have something to eat. So someone advised him, "Go to Medzibuz, where the Baal Shem Tov lives. He has an 'open house.' Everyone who shows up there is generously fed." Although it was somewhat out of the way, he went to Medzibuz.

When he arrived, it was *erev Shabbat*, so he went to the Baal Shem Tov's synagogue to *davven*. The prayers there took a very long time, because that was the way the Baal Shem Tov *davvened*. Meanwhile, he was experiencing terrible hunger pains. Afterward, they began arranging the table for the Sabbath meal, but by the time the Baal Shem Tov came in (because everyone was seated first and the Besht was preparing himself for the meal and so on), and they sang "*Shalom Aleichem*"* and until *kiddush*, he felt he was about to faint. So as soon as they made the *Motzi* (the blessing over the bread), he immediately devoured every bit of bread they gave him. And when he saw that the people around him were not very hungry, he ate their bread too, he was so ravenous. He even ate all of the special big challah that they put in front of the Baal Shem Tov! When the Baal Shem saw this, he realized that the man was extremely hungry and he ordered the *shammos* to serve him double portions of every dish. But when the meal was finished, the Baal Shem Tov saw that the guest still was not satisfied, so he told his wife to give him some of the *cholent* that was being prepared for the next day. Not only was it substantial food but it was still somewhat hard and would certainly fill him, which it did.

Now, the Baal Shem Tov had a custom that once a week he wanted to have someone rebuke him, to correct his ways for anything he might have done wrong, and—since who would presume to teach the Baal Shem Tov?—he appointed his holy wife, Chana, to perform that task. The time for this was after the Friday night *Shabbat* meal. And the Besht's wife said to him, "How could you give such honor and attention to this man the first time he came here, to the extent of having us serve him from tomorrow's

---

* The hymn "Greeting of Peace (to the Angels)," chanted at the table Sabbath evening.

cholent? Everyone will think you're running after followers!" The Besht told her why he gave the man the extra food: "I saw that he was very truthful, because when he was so hungry, he ate as much as he needed, without worrying about what other people thought of him. *When he's hungry for spirituality, he'll also eat his fill, despite what anybody else thinks.*" And that man did become an exceptional hasid.[27]

Honor and Pride

Escaping Pride

 THE BAAL SHEM TOV WAS ONCE TRAVELING TO BRODY, AND ON THE WAY HE spent the night at a village inn not far from the town. During the night he woke up so frightened that his knees were knocking against each other and he was shaking all over. The sound of his violent shaking woke up his scribe, Rabbi Tzvi, who asked him, "What happened? Why are you so frightened?" The Baal Shem Tov told him, "My master, Ahiyah ha-Shiloni, came to me in a dream, from the upper world, and asked me, 'Who is better, you or our Father Abraham, peace be upon him?' I was disturbed to hear such a strange question and said, 'Why are you asking me this?' He said, 'When you arrive in Brody, they'll honor you so much that if you don't prepare yourself to resist the temptation of pride—that there's no one greater than you—you'll lose all the spiritual levels you've attained until now.' Hearing this," said the Besht, "I became so frightened that I began to shake."

When the Besht arrived in Brody the next day, the most prominent townspeople, dressed in their best clothes, came out to welcome him to their city with the greatest honor. But he began to play with his horses, stroking them and patting them affectionately. All this was only a device to keep himself from pride, to disgrace and lower himself in people's eyes, that a great man should behave so frivolously at such a time, like a common wagon-driver. How profound was his fear of sin, that he trembled and shook, and went to such lengths to avoid falling through pride![28]

No Mirrors

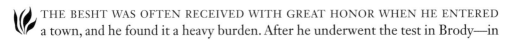 THE BAAL SHEM TOV AVOIDED PRIDE AND VANITY AT ALL COSTS. HE NEVER looked in a mirror.[29]

He Prays to Be Disparaged

THE BESHT WAS OFTEN RECEIVED WITH GREAT HONOR WHEN HE ENTERED a town, and he found it a heavy burden. After he underwent the test in Brody—in order to escape pride—he began to pray beforehand that some people in a town he visited would disparage and disgrace him.[30]

When Honored, Examine Yourself

THE BAAL SHEM TOV WAS ONCE INVITED TO A CERTAIN TOWN AND THEY gave him tremendous honor. He said to them, "When a person is honored on earth, his actions are immediately examined in heaven, to see if he's worthy of the honor. It would seem then that those who are honoring someone are actually harming him and doing him a disservice. But when a person who is wise and fears God is honored, he immediately repents and begins to carefully examine his deeds. Therefore, those who honor him are helping him by bringing him to repentance. And he should also always pray to attain the trait of equanimity, so that praise or blame are the same to him."

The Besht saw everything that happened to him as a divine message, as a hint from heaven. When he was honored, he knew that his deeds were at that moment subject to heavenly investigation and that he was being "told" that he should investigate himself. So he used the honor as a stimulus to repent and to reach an even higher level in his service of God.[31]

Equanimity

THE BAAL SHEM TOV SOUGHT AND ACHIEVED EQUANIMITY. WITH HIS mind always on God, he was unaffected by people's opinions about him. Whether they praised or criticized him, he said to himself, "Isn't this sent from God? And if it's good in His eyes, shouldn't it also be good in mine?"[32]

The Parable of the King in the Coach

THE BAAL SHEM TOV ONCE SPENT THE SABBATH IN A CERTAIN TOWN where there was an argumentative person who told everyone who would listen that in his view the coach the Besht rode in was too expensive and luxurious for a religious leader, and that it showed he was proud.

On hearing about this complaint against him, the Besht said to his disciples, "What is important is not the outer show of humility, but what is inside the heart." And he told them a parable: "There was a king who asked his doctors to find a medicine that would allow him to live forever. All the doctors worked diligently to accomplish this, but failed. One of them found a medicine that would allow the king to live ten years longer than normal, but they were not able to find a medicine that bestowed eternal life. Then, a certain beggar appeared and said, "I can prescribe something for the king so that he'll be able to live forever.' He advised the king that if he would be humble, he would live eternally. So the king decided to be humble. When he went for an excursion, he ordered that the royal coach go before him, while he walked behind on foot. But the wise beggar said to the king, 'That's not the correct way, my lord. True humility is when you ride in the coach but are still humble, for true humility is in the heart.' I tell you," said the Baal Shem Tov to his disciples, "humility gains one entry into God's presence and is a gateway to eternal life. But true humility is not a matter of outward behavior; it's within."[33]

An Envy for Insults

WHEN THE BAAL SHEM TOV VISITED PREMISHLAN IN REISSEN, HE DISCOVERED that a certain tailor reviled and humiliated his great disciple in that town, Rabbi Mendel, every day, and Rabbi Mendel received the abuse with love. "I envy you," said the Besht to his disciple. "If I only had the good fortune to hear insults every day!" And he explained that a person must struggle his whole life to avoid pride, and by listening to insults and abuse with love, Rabbi Mendel had a daily antidote to the deadly poison called pride.[34]

You Can't Tell Who Is Righteous or Wicked

THREE MEN ONCE VISITED THE BAAL SHEM TOV, AND SPOKE TO HIM ONE after the other. The first was a wealthy man, richly dressed; the second was a poorly dressed laborer; the third man was a rabbi, who wore traditional rabbinic garb.

After they left, the Besht said to his disciples, "Don't be deceived by appearances and think that you know what's inside a person. When you see someone in tattered clothing, sitting behind the stove in the *beit midrash*, studying Torah day and night, and going around the whole day in tallis and *tefillin*, eating bread with salt or fasting—you might think that he's pious, humble, and kind. And it might actually be so. But it might also be the very opposite! There are wicked people who act as if they're pious and do good deeds from bad motives. He may be completely wicked and full of pride; or everything he's doing may be just to deceive people.

"When you see someone living in luxury, wearing clothes fit for a king and eating rich food, you might assume that he's worldly and impious, without a single virtue: that he's proud, selfish, and unkind. And it might actually be so. But it might also be the very opposite! There are tzaddikim who behave in ways usually associated with the wicked, but they do so for a good reason and with a holy intention. For example, a tzaddik may wear fine clothes and eat the best food—but his real purpose is to expand his mind, so he can serve God joyfully. Or he may seem proud, but his real purpose is to fulfill the verse: 'His heart was lifted up in the service of the Lord.' He resists his evil inclination by saying to himself, 'How can I commit that sin? I'm a son of the King, the Holy One, blessed be He!'

"Understand then, that you can't tell who or what a person is. Only the One who searches hearts knows, not you, for the real difference between people depends on what's hidden from the eye. Only the Creator knows who is righteous and will inherit the World-to-Come. There's a person who dresses and eats well, and seems to be proud and arrogant, who'll inherit the Garden of Eden. And there's someone else who sits studying Torah, wearing tallis and *tefillin* the whole day, who'll inherit *Gehinnom*. God knows all these things, not you."

The Baal Shem Tov said that only God truly knows the inside of a person. But he also knew and saw much. Where others might see an ignorant, begrimed laborer, he could see a shining aura of holiness. Where others might see a pious ascetic or a great Torah scholar, he saw someone corrupted by arrogance. But not every ignorant person is holy, nor every pious Torah scholar proud (God-forbid)! These are matters of the heart, of the inside, not the outside; it is not for us to judge, but for God.[35]

The Parable of the Two Princes

THE BAAL SHEM TOV THEN TOLD HIS DISCIPLES A PARABLE ABOUT THE value of humility and lowliness. "A king had two sons. He sent one son to another kingdom to learn military strategy and tactics. Being a prince, he was treated in that foreign country with great honor. The king sent his other son to a different kingdom, but as a simple person who had to struggle to earn a living. Being a poor stranger, they treated him with contempt. As a result, he became humble and broken-hearted. Later, when both sons returned to their father the king, and he conducted wars, the son who had experienced many humiliations and learned lowliness, conquered many more lands than the other brother conquered with his military strategy and tactics. I tell you," said the Baal Shem Tov to his disciples, "a poor, uneducated person who has learned humility from life's hardships and suffering achieves more spiritually than a Torah scholar achieves with all his knowledge."[36]

The Besht Lodges with a Sinner

THE BAAL SHEM TOV ONCE VISITED A CERTAIN CITY AND STAYED AT THE home of a wealthy man, a notorious adulterer, whom people spoke of with contempt. They could hardly believe that, of all people, the Baal Shem Tov had chosen to stay with this sinner, and they asked the Besht, "Why don't you stay with the rabbi?" "Although this man is an adulterer," replied the Besht, "he knows who he is and is lowly in his own eyes. And it's written that God 'dwells with them in the midst of their uncleanness.' Although the rabbi is a Torah scholar, he's arrogant and thinks he's a great man. And it's written that God says: 'Whoever is of haughty glance and proud of heart, him I cannot bear.' The Sages explain that the Holy One, blessed be He, says, 'He and I cannot dwell together in the same world.' If the Holy One, blessed be He, can't dwell with him," said the Besht, "how can I? But I don't want to criticize the rabbi himself, God-forbid! I'm only criticizing his bad traits—of pride and arrogance."

It was the Baal Shem Tov's way to befriend sinners, when they were not proud, and to push away Torah scholars who were righteous but proud, for he used to say, "When a sinner knows who he is and is lowly in his own eyes, God is with him. When someone is righteous but proud, God is not with him."[37]

Testing a Teacher about Advice for Pride

SOME OF THE BAAL SHEM TOV'S DISCIPLES ASKED HIM IF THEY COULD visit a certain famous teacher to see who he was. When the Besht gave his permission, they asked him, "How can we know if he's a true teacher?" "Ask for his advice on how to remove pride and arrogance," the Besht replied. "If he gives you such advice, there's nothing to him. But if he answers, 'God help us, there's no advice for this!'— he's a true tzaddik, because you must struggle with pride your whole life." The Baal Shem Tov constantly prayed to be saved from pride.[38]

An Achievement

A CERTAIN TZADDIK SAID TO THE BAAL SHEM TOV, "I'VE LABORED FOR MANY years in the service of God, but in the end I've achieved nothing, because I'm an ordinary and lowly person." "You've achieved that you're lowly and small in your own eyes," replied the Besht.[39]

Glory and Humility

THE BAAL SHEM TOV'S DISCIPLES SAW WITH THEIR OWN EYES THAT THE glory and majesty of the greatest king was insignificant next to the glory and splendor of their holy master. And the self-effacement of the lowliest beggar, who is contemptible in his own eyes, was insignificant next to the self-effacement and humility of the holy and pure Baal Shem Tov. His light was like the light of the Holy One, blessed be He, which is infinitely high and exalted above everything, yet is infinitely low, descending to the lowest depths.[40]

Pray with Humility Also

THE BAAL SHEM TOV ONCE PRAYED WITH HIS *MINYAN* AND THEY ALL PRAYED with fervor, as usual. But when they concluded the prayers, the disciples saw that the Besht was angry. Later, he explained to them that the Accuser had incited every one of them to proud and arrogant thoughts—that they were praying with such extraordinary fervor and *d'vekut*. "Because of that, a severe accusation was aroused against you in heaven, and I had to exert myself to sweeten it."

The Baal Shem Tov told them about this to make clear to them that they had to constantly work on themselves to be free from pride, which is an abomination to God. Although one prays with great *d'vekut*, one must still have humility and a broken heart.[41]

No Better than a Worm: The Parable of the Humble Prince

THE BAAL SHEM TOV THEN EXPLAINED TO HIS DISCIPLES THAT THE SECRET of coming close to God in prayer and in other divine service depends on humility. "You mustn't think that you're better than someone else because you serve God with more *d'vekut*, for you should understand that you are like all the other creatures in the world that have been created to serve Him, blessed be He. God gave the other person his intelligence just as He gave you yours. How then are you greater than a worm? A worm also serves its Creator according to its intelligence and ability. And a human being is like a worm, as it is written: 'I am a worm, and not a man.' If you're not more important than a worm, how can you think that you are more important than a fellow human being? So you should realize that you and a worm and all the other insignificant creatures are comrades in this world, for all are created, and none of them has any abilities beyond what the Creator, blessed be He, gave it."

The Baal Shem Tov then told them a parable. "There was once a king who kept all his subjects away from him because he hated their pride. No one was allowed to approach him. The king's son, however, was very humble, and lowered himself to the dust, making himself like nothing. Everything he did was for God alone, and he joined himself with all creatures, for all of them were created only to do the will of his Father. Therefore, he had no arrogance at all about anything. His single desire was to do his Father's will, like the lowly worm that crawls along the ground. And because of his great humility, which was absolutely sincere and from the heart, his Father the King allowed his son into his presence. When you are praying," said the Besht, "remember to be humble in the presence of your Father in Heaven, the King of the Universe.[42]

Father! Father!

ONE YEAR, DURING THE DAYS OF AWE, THE BAAL SHEM TOV TAUGHT THAT the inner meaning of the *shofar* blast is like crying out: "Father! Father!" He said that one should not cry out and weep over past suffering—about the trials and tribulations one had experienced in the past—but plead and beg for the future, "Father, save me! Father, have mercy on me!"

The Baal Shem Tov was usually involved in the *shofar* service with his special *minyan* of disciples. But, once, he had Rabbi Yaakov Yosef of Polnoye take care of that, while he arranged a separate *minyan* for the simple people and young people. He had them cry out, at appropriate times during the *shofar* service: "Heavenly Father, have mercy!" He said that this had the greatest effect in heaven and helped more than anything else.[43]

Preparing the Prayer-Leader for Yom Kippur

ONE YOM KIPPUR DAY, THE BAAL SHEM TOV DID NOT COME TO THE synagogue to pray very early in the morning as was his custom. He was extremely late, and they were all waiting for him, to begin the service. When he finally arrived and sat in his place, he put his head down on his hand on the prayer-desk, then he lifted it up and put it down again, several more times. After this, he signaled to them that someone should go before the Ark and begin the morning service. Rabbi David Forkes went forward to be the prayer-leader, since he always led the prayers on the Days of Awe.

But when Rabbi David approached the Ark to begin praying, the Baal Shem Tov started to vilify and humiliate him in front of the whole congregation, saying things like, "You wicked old man, where are you going?" He heaped scorn and abuse on him for a few long minutes. While this stream of invective was pouring over him, Rabbi David, bent and humbled, returned to his seat, for he said to himself, "He must see something despicable in me."

As soon as he sat down, however, the Baal Shem Tov immediately scolded him again, saying, "Stand up!" Then he ordered him to begin the prayers, which he did, amidst much crying and sobbing. He did not even know what he was praying, he was weeping and crying out so much, for his heart was utterly broken.

After the conclusion of Yom Kippur, the pure and upright Rabbi David went to the Baal Shem Tov and said to him, "Master, what disgusting things did you see in me?" "God-forbid," the Besht replied, "I saw nothing wrong in you at all. But before I left for the synagogue in the morning, I saw that the Satan was waiting on the path by which the prayers ascend to heaven, to block the way and take all the prayers into his possession, God-forbid. I said to myself, 'Why should I go to pray and deliver the prayers to him, God-forbid? So I delayed going to the synagogue. I prayed and meditated for hours, pouring my heart out in pleas and supplications, with self-sacrifice, and, praise God, I was finally able to clear a single narrow path for the prayers to ascend, without his being able to grab them. But afterward, I was still afraid that something improper might enter your heart and spoil all my efforts. That's why I broke your heart, so that you wouldn't have any foreign thoughts whatsoever, and not give him the slightest entry into your heart. Then I ordered you to pray."[44]

Not Keys, but an Axe

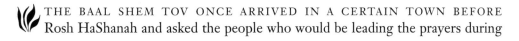 RABBI ZEV WOLF KITZES WAS THE *SHOFAR*-BLOWER IN THE BESHT'S synagogue during the Days of Awe. The Besht called out the order of the blasts, and Rabbi Wolf blew the *shofar*. Rabbi Wolf had long been familiar with various kabbalistic *kavvanot* for *shofar*-blowing, but one year he devoted a great deal of time and effort to prepare himself thoroughly for this holy task, with fear and awe, studying and reviewing all the *kavvanot* of the Ari. Worried that he might forget some of them, he wrote them all down on a piece of paper that he could look at during the *shofar*-blowing. He then put the paper between the pages of his *mahzor** and, before the services, placed the *mahzor* on the *bimah*, to be ready when he needed it.

The Baal Shem Tov became aware of this and was displeased. When he ascended the *bimah* during the services to call out the order of the *shofar* blasts to Rabbi Wolf, he quietly removed Rabbi Wolf's notes from the *mahzor*. When Rabbi Wolf opened the *mahzor* to say the blessing before blowing the *shofar*, he realized to his great dismay that the paper with his notes had disappeared. He was crushed. He had gone to such lengths to prepare himself, and now it was all for nothing! He was so upset that he became confused and even forgot the *kavvanot* that he had always been familiar with and knew. He had no other choice than to blow the *shofar* with the simple intention of fulfilling the commandment of his Creator.

After the service, the Baal Shem Tov said to him, "Today you blew the *shofar* better than ever." And he explained, "In the King's palace there are many halls and chambers, and there are different keys for each gate. The *kavvanot* serve as keys to open the various gates of heaven, but it's not always possible to find the right one for each lock and to make them fit what you are doing or saying at the moment. Furthermore, these keys tend to become rusty—when someone meditates on the formulas by rote. But there's one simple and direct way," said the Besht, "to open all the gates—and that's with an axe, which can smash open every lock so that one can gain entrance to all the chambers. A broken heart is like an axe that can break through all the barriers and reach right to the Throne of Glory."[45]

The Parable of the Sweeper

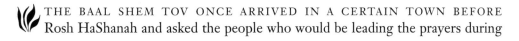 THE BAAL SHEM TOV ONCE ARRIVED IN A CERTAIN TOWN BEFORE Rosh HaShanah and asked the people who would be leading the prayers during

* High Holiday prayer book.

the Days of Awe? They replied that it was the rabbi of the town's religious court. "And how does he lead the prayers?" the Besht asked. "On Yom Kippur," they said, "he chants the whole confession of sins in a cheerful tune." The Besht sent for the rabbi and asked him about his strange custom. The rabbi replied, "The least and lowliest of the king's servants, who cleans out the sewers and sweeps the garbage and filth from the courtyard, is as happy as can be while he cleans, because he's cleaning the court-yard of the king, and he sings a cheerful tune as he sweeps, for his work pleases the king." "If that's the intention with which you pray," said the Baal Shem Tov, "may my lot be with yours!" Later, the Besht explained to his disciples that a happy melody while chanting the confession sweetens the heavenly judgments.[46]

The Prayers of Simple People

THE BAAL SHEM TOV'S DISCIPLES WERE ONCE AMUSED AT OVERHEARING a common laborer mangle the words of a prayer. The Besht later said to them, "The essence of prayer is that it be from the heart; that's why the prayers of simple people, who pray with great faith and a broken heart, are valued so much in heaven. Although they may not understand the Hebrew and mispronounce the words, God judges their prayers according to the faith of their heart. When a small child, whose father loves him very much, asks for something and babbles the words, his father still gets pleasure from what he says and gives him whatever he wants. So when a simple person prays sincerely, would his Heavenly Father, who loves him so very much, be strict with him or care if he mispronounces the words?"[47]

Strange Movements and Cries While Praying

WHEN OPPONENTS OF THE BAAL SHEM TOV CRITICIZED SOME OF HIS followers for making strange movements and shouting while praying, the Besht answered, "When someone is drowning, he makes wild motions to save himself and yells at the top of his lungs: 'Save me! Save me!' Would anyone watching his thrashing about make fun of him? When somebody is making wild gestures and shouting while praying, he's trying to save himself from being drowned in the 'arrogant waters'—the negative forces of his lower nature—that are distracting him and keeping him from focusing on God. Why should anyone laugh or criticize him?"[48]

Annulling Accusations by Prayer

THE BAAL SHEM TOV—TO WHOM THE PATHS OF HEAVEN WERE AS FAMILIAR as the paths of Medzibuz—knew when the Satan made accusations against the

Jewish people. He also knew that sometimes it was not his own or his disciples' prayers that were able to annul the accusation and the evil decree, but the prayers of pious, simple people.

Aren't You Our Father?

WHEN THE BESHT ONCE SAW THAT THERE WAS A SERIOUS ACCUSATION in heaven against the Jewish people, he and some of his close disciples fasted and prayed, but did not succeed in changing the situation for good. The Besht then used his influence with the rabbi of Medzibuz to declare a fast for all the townspeople, so that they would offer prayers on the fast day for the annulment of the heavenly decree. (The rabbi did not know the real reason; but by giving him various justifications as an excuse, the Besht was able to convince him to declare a fast.)

Both men and women came to the synagogue, where they wept, prayed, and recited psalms. But even the communal fast, the prayers, and the tears did not remove the evil decree. Suddenly, the Besht's face, which had been clouded over with worry, began to shine joyfully. He turned to his disciple, Rabbi Nachman Horodenker, who stood beside him in the synagogue, and said, "Thank God, the decree has been annulled in heaven."

Later, after the conclusion of the fast, when the Besht was sitting with his disciples, he told them in whose merit the decree was annulled. "There was a certain simple woman in the women's section of the synagogue who didn't even know how to recite psalms. But when she heard the congregation sobbing, she said to the Holy One, blessed be He, 'Master of the world, aren't You our Father and aren't we Your children? I have five children and when they all begin to cry at once, my *kishkes** turn over inside me. And You, our Heavenly Father, have so many children who are crying pitifully now. Do you have the heart of a Tartar that You don't hear their cries and pleas? Shouldn't You answer them? Master of the world, answer us!' At that moment," said the Baal Shem Tov, "a heavenly voice proclaimed, 'The decree is annulled!'"[49]

Squeeze the Heavens!

ANOTHER TIME, WHEN A TERRIBLE DROUGHT AFFLICTED THE COUNTRYSIDE in the vicinity of Medzibuz, a special prayer service and communal fast were called to beg for divine mercy. But although the congregation prayed for a long time, they were not answered.

Then the Baal Shem Tov saw a simple, unlearned man, who was weeping and praying with fervor, loudly call out the verse from the *Shema*, that if the Jews worship idols, God will be angry with them, "and He shall close the heavens so that there shall be no

---

* Innards.

rain." What could be more confused and inauspicious! But the Besht did not rebuke him, because he saw with his holy spirit—to his surprise—that this man's prayer was favorably received in heaven.

Later, when abundant rains had already fallen, he called the man to him and asked, "What were you thinking of when you were reciting that verse?" "The way I translated it to myself," the man replied, "was that God would squeeze the heavens with His hand like a sponge so that not a drop of rain remains above!"

With his poor grasp of Hebrew, he mistakenly thought that the word "close" in the verse (which means that God will shut up the heavens and allow no rain to fall) meant that God would close His fist and squeeze out the water above, so that it would all fall as rain below. Later, when the Besht was alone with his disciples, he said to them, "'God desires the heart.' He doesn't judge a person's prayers according to whether he knows Hebrew or pronounces the prayers correctly, but according to his faith and sincerity. So this simple man's prayers, said so sincerely, greatly pleased Him, and God, blessed be He, answered his prayer, with mercy and with plentiful rain."[50]

A Drunkard's Prayer on Yom Kippur

ONCE, DURING THE AFTERNOON PRAYER ON YOM KIPPUR, THERE WAS a grave accusation in heaven against the Jewish people, and the Baal Shem Tov and his holy disciples were praying loudly and exerting themselves to the fullest, to open the closed gates of heaven.

Now, the man who stoked the oven in the Besht's synagogue was a habitual drunkard. Since he would not be able to drink during the fast, he had "prepared" by imbibing so much liquor on the eve of Yom Kippur that he became miserably drunk. He lay down and slept in the synagogue the whole evening and the following morning too. He slept right through the services, evening and morning.

When he awoke the next afternoon in the middle of the *Minha* service, he saw that the Baal Shem Tov and his disciples were praying urgently, with raised voices. He was deeply moved by the dramatic scene around him and thought, "If these holy people, who are so devoted to God and His Torah the whole year, have to repent like this on Yom Kippur, crying out and pleading with the Master of the world to forgive them, what about someone like me?" He became so bitter and disgusted at his own lowliness—being drunk and unconscious in the synagogue on the holiest day of the year and sleeping through almost all the services!—that he started to sob uncontrollably. He also began to cry out loudly in prayer from the bottom of his heart, joining his raised voice with the voices of the holy congregation. His sincere repentance made such a powerful impression above, that the gates of heaven, which until then had been shut fast, flew open at the sound of his anguished cries.

After Yom Kippur, the Baal Shem Tov, who knew what had happened and wanted to reward the man, had a new set of clothes made for him. Clothes change a person, and the Besht hoped to take advantage of his Yom Kippur repentance to make a new man of him. But this drunkard did not change his ways, and after Yom Kippur he went right back to being exactly as he was before. But at that time, his prayer had been from the very depths of his heart. As the Rabbis say: "There is no man, who has not his hour," And in his hour, he had accomplished a great deed.[51]

The Boy with the Flute

A JEWISH VILLAGER, WHO EVERY YEAR PRAYED IN THE BESHT'S SYNAGOGUE on the Days of Awe, had a retarded son who was not even able to learn the letters of the Hebrew alphabet, and he certainly could not recite any of the prayers or blessings. When the boy was still a child, his father did not bring him to the city on the Days of Awe, since he could not participate in the service in any way. But when he became bar mitzvah and was obligated to fast on Yom Kippur, his father took him along, to make sure that the boy did not eat on the holy day, due to his lack of knowledge and understanding.

The boy had a simple flute that he always played when he sat in the fields looking after his father's sheep and calves. He could not actually play music; he simply blew on the flute to make a sound. Without his father's knowledge, he took this flute in his pocket to the synagogue. If his father had known about it he certainly would not have allowed his son to take the flute, since it is forbidden to play a musical instrument on Yom Kippur or even to carry or touch it on the holy day. But the boy knew nothing about such things.

He sat in the synagogue the whole evening and the next morning, and was not able to recite or participate in the service in any way. Meanwhile, the Baal Shem Tov and his disciples were praying with tremendous fervor, which aroused the boy greatly. A powerful urge to do something for God burned in his heart; yet he did not know what to do; he could not take part in any way. During the *Musaf** service, he said to his father, "Father, I brought my flute, and I want to blow on it!" His father was vexed to find out that he had brought the flute and was very upset at the thought that his retarded son might suddenly cause a disturbance in the middle of the prayers on this holiest day. He scolded him severely and said, "Don't you dare do any such thing!" So the boy had to restrain himself.

During *Minha*, he begged his father again, "Father, *please* let me blow on my flute!" His father became angry and sternly warned him against it. But he could not take the flute away from the boy because it was *muktzeh* and he could not touch it. After the *Minha* prayer, the boy again began pestering his father, and begged him, "Father, I don't care, *please* let me blow on my flute!" Seeing how desperately and urgently the boy wanted to play on his flute, the father realized he might not be able to control his

---

* Additional morning prayer service recited on Sabbath and holiday.

son much longer, so he said, "Where is the flute?" When the boy pointed to his pocket, the father clamped his hand forcefully over the pocket to make sure that his son could not take it out and blow on it. The father prayed the final *Ne'ilah** prayer that way, holding his hand on his son's coat pocket.

But in the middle of this decisive prayer that ends Yom Kippur, the boy suddenly pulled out of his father's grasp, took out the flute, and blew a long, powerful note. All the people in the congregation were startled by the sound and cringed when they heard it. When they realized where it came from, they stared disapprovingly and frowned at the boy and his father. But the Baal Shem Tov continued praying, seemingly undisturbed. After this, however, he shortened his praying from what was typical for him for the final prayer of Yom Kippur.

When the service was over, he told his disciples why he did not extend his pleas for divine compassion, as he usually did during the *Ne'ilah* prayer, saying, "The sound of that boy's flute raised all the prayers to heaven and made things much easier for me." He explained why. "This boy didn't know how to pray at all, and when he sat in the synagogue for the whole day and saw how everyone else was praying, he also wanted to pray. The holy spark in his soul was burning within him like a fire. Someone who knows how to pray can clothe that longing in words of prayer. This boy knew nothing; he had no way to express his yearning, except by blowing on his flute before God, blessed be He. But his father wouldn't let him and the flame of his longing burned more and more strongly within him, until he couldn't contain it! Then, with all the power of his longing, he blew on the flute from the depths of his heart, without any other motive, but for God alone. And 'God desires the heart,' so the pure and innocent breath of his child's mouth was received with favor before Him. That boy and his flute caused the prayers of the whole congregation to ascend into heaven."[52]

Helping Thieves

ONCE, A GANG OF JEWISH THIEVES IN MEDZIBUZ WAS CAUGHT AND turned over to the police. They were all tried in court, found guilty, and sentenced to years in prison. Their families, who were penniless and had nothing, were living in misery. But the Baal Shem Tov stepped in and supported the wives and children for all the time the men were in prison. He always gave all his money to the poor, even to those whom others thought were unworthy of support.

When their jail terms were up and the men were released, none of the Jews in Medzibuz wanted to hire any of them for a job. So the former thieves were forced to go from house to house asking for charity. But that still did not help. No one would even open the door of their homes to them to let them beg, because they were afraid of them.

---

* The concluding, "Closing the Gates" prayer of Yom Kippur.

After becoming aware of the situation, the Baal Shem Tov did everything he could to help the men and their families. He either got jobs for them or saw that they were taken care of.

Some of the Besht's family and his disciples were surprised at the trouble he was taking to assist and support these former thieves. Who even knew if they had changed their ways? Many people suspected that they were still working at their old trade "on the side." When the Besht's disciples asked him why he helped such people, he said, "There are times when *I* need help from thieves. When there are serious accusations in heaven against the Jewish people, on account of their sins and misdeeds, the prosecuting angels have the upper hand. Although I plead and pray for the Jews, the heavenly gates of mercy are closed before me. But then the merit of the *tzedaka* I give to people like these former thieves stands me in good stead! In heaven, they say, 'He helps those who are unworthy; it's only right that we should too.' When the heavenly gates are locked shut to my prayers," said the Baal Shem Tov, "these thieves come, break the locks, and throw the gates wide open in front of me!"

Later, the Besht spoke again to his disciples about this incident, saying, "If you forgive others their sins and do good to 'unworthy' people, God will forgive you your sins and shower blessings on you, although you too may be 'unworthy.'"[53]

A Tzaddik Saves Sinners from Gehinnom

THE BAAL SHEM TOV WAS ONCE SITTING IN HIS *BEIT MIDRASH* WITH SOME of his disciples and the question was asked whether the prohibition on *hadash**applied in this time. The great scholars present, such as Rabbi Yaakov Yosef of Polnoye and Rabbi Meir Margoliot, vigorously debated the issue to determine the *halacha*. It was pointed out that the Bach[¶] had ruled that the prohibition on *hadash* does not apply in the present day outside the Land of Israel, while his great son-in-law, the Taz[§], as well as many other famous halachic authorities disagreed with the Bach in this matter. The Baal Shem Tov had the highest regard and respect for the Bach, who had once been the rabbi of Medzibuz. When the Bach's name was mentioned, the Besht's eyes lit up with a holy fire and he said, "The Bach was the rabbi in Medzibuz and we should certainly follow his ruling here, especially since he was not only a great scholar but a great tzaddik." He then explained to them why he considered the Bach to be such a holy man.

"A great tzaddik," he continued, "can't bear to see Jews suffer, even those who are completely wicked. That's true even after his death, when he refuses to enter the

---

* The new crop of grain. Jewish law forbids consuming new grain crops until after the second day of the next Passover (*Code of Jewish Law*, chapter 172).
   ¶ Rabbi Yoel Sirkes—called the Bach, from the acronym of his famous commentary, the *Bayit Hadash*. He lived from 1561 to 1640.
   § Rabbi David ben Shmuel HaLevi—called the Taz, after his famous commentary, the *Turei Zahav*.

Garden of Eden straightaway and enjoy himself there, leaving the wicked Jews to suffer in *Gehinnom*. He insists on entering the Garden of Eden by way of *Gehinnom*. And once he's in *Gehinnom* and sees the torments of those trapped there, he refuses to leave unless they come with him to the Garden of Eden. It's told," the Besht concluded, "that in heaven, they knew that a holy man like the Bach would certainly demand to pass through *Gehinnom* on his way to the Garden of Eden, so a decree was issued by the heavenly court to cool down *Gehinnom* for forty days before the Bach's death, so as not to trouble that tzaddik by exposing him to the terrible fires of hell. We can certainly rely on a tzaddik like that and follow his ruling, even when there's no urgent need to find a leniency in the law." The Besht then sent someone to buy liquor made from *hadash* and had it served to his disciples.

The Besht's disciples later discussed their master's teaching and the story he told, and what they showed about *his* attitude to the suffering of Jews, even those completely wicked—that he too was willing to pass through *Gehinnom* to save them. He was willing to make sacrifices and undergo torments in this world or the next for their sake. That was what he wanted to teach his disciples.[54]

Love Him More

ONCE, THE SON OF A CERTAIN MAN STRAYED FROM THE PATH AND BECAME an atheist. The distraught father ran to the Baal Shem Tov, desperately seeking advice for what to do. The Besht told the father, "Love him more." The man did so and his son abandoned his atheism and returned to Judaism.

In the Besht's time, it was typical for religious parents of a child who left Judaism to shun him, to "sit *shiva*" and mourn for him as if he had died. The Baal Shem Tov did not shun those who had strayed. He tried every way he could to bring them close to him and to God. He could see a spark of life where others saw only a corpse. And he knew that love could raise even the dead to life.[55]

He Should Save, Not Destroy

AFTER RABBI YAAKOV YOSEF OF POLNOYE BECAME A DISCIPLE OF THE BAAL Shem Tov, the people of his town, Sharogrod, became extremely hostile to him, because he adhered to the new hasidic path and also insisted on strict righteousness, refusing to compromise or bend. The dispute intensified until they expelled him from the town on *erev Shabbat* and he had to spend the Sabbath in a nearby village. The Baal Shem Tov happened to be traveling not far away and, when he saw this with his holy spirit, he said to the disciples who were with him, "Let's go to that village, because I know that he's very upset. Let's spend the Sabbath with the rabbi of the holy community of Sharogrod, to comfort him and help him deal with this adversity." So they traveled to that village.

Rabbi Aryeh Leib, the Preacher of Polnoye, one of the Besht's great disciples, was in the group. On *Shabbat*, after the *Musaf* prayer, he saw that Rabbi Yaakov Yosef was still deeply disturbed at having been expelled from the town. He said to him, "Don't be troubled, for I heard a heavenly proclamation that this one of your enemies will be murdered and that one will die on the road, and the whole city will be burned down in a fire!"—for expelling their righteous rabbi. Hearing this, the Baal Shem Tov yelled at the preacher, "You fool! Are you too hearing heavenly proclamations?" The preacher immediately became silent.

Later, the Baal Shem Tov explained to Rabbi Yaakov Yosef, "Do you think the preacher was lying, God-forbid, when he said that he heard a heavenly proclamation? He heard it. The reason I was angry at him was that he uttered it with his mouth. If he hadn't spoken it aloud, I would have been able to completely nullify the decree against the city. As it is, I was only able to delay it, so that one fire will destroy one part of the city and a later fire will destroy another part; and those who are doomed will have their punishment delayed." The Baal Shem Tov then told Rabbi Yaakov Yosef that, despite his anger at the people of Sharogrod, who had persecuted and expelled him, he should continually pray for the city, to save it from harm. "A leader in Israel should not arouse judgments on the Jewish people," said the Besht, "but annul them; he should save, not destroy."[56]

The Parable of the King's Treasury

IN A CONVERSATION ONE DAY WITH RABBI YAAKOV YOSEF OF POLNOYE, the Baal Shem Tov claimed that he (the Besht) was being punished by being made to see so much suffering of the Jewish people. He continued, "I'll explain why, with a parable. A king appointed four ministers to supervise his treasury. The four of them stole the money and fled. One repented of what he had done and returned on his own. A second was advised by a sage who spoke to him about his wrongdoing and persuaded him to return. The third reached a place where tribunals appointed by the king were judging and punishing people for crimes such as absconding with stolen money, and he returned out of fear. The fourth minister did not return at all. Now, the king appointed the first one who had returned on his own to a higher post than the second one who had consulted with the sage—because he had returned as a result of his own repentance, whereas if the other one had not been advised by a sage, he would not have returned. The king appointed the third one, who had returned because he saw people being judged and punished, to oversee that place of tribunals, to constantly view the suffering. That's me," said the Baal Shem Tov.

The Baal Shem Tov taught that God sends a person thoughts of repentance every day; but most people ignore these messages and do not "hear." The one who does hear his soul teaching him is appointed to the highest level spiritually. Another, who needs to be taught by a sage, is the next level. But someone who does not listen to his conscience, his inner teacher, or to an outer teacher, needs to see others who are suffering and being punished, in order to wake up and repent. The Baal Shem Tov believed that whatever a person experiences or encounters in life is a heavenly lesson. Why, then, the Besht asked himself, did his own religious mission involve seeing so much suffering of other people? Judging himself harshly, he concluded that it must be a heavenly punishment for his own previous sins and because he needed to see this to keep himself from falling into sin. He was fated to witness all these afflictions suffered by the Jewish people, as a heavenly judgment against him, so to speak, despite the fact that it was his task and mission to relieve their suffering by deeds and by praying for them before the heavenly court. He applied this parable to himself in a spirit of humility and in a moment of weakness.[57]

Repairing the Damage

A RESIDENT OF MEDZIBUZ CAME TO THE BAAL SHEM TOV AND COMPLAINED about his difficulties in life and his disappointment at unfulfilled wishes. The Besht told him to travel to the distant city of Kuzmir (near Cracow) and investigate the doings of a certain man there. The Besht gave him the man's name and said that when he accomplished his purpose, he should return to him. It was unclear what this all had to do with his problem, but the man implicitly followed the Baal Shem Tov's instructions.

When he arrived in Kuzmir, he went to a synagogue and asked about the person whom he had come to investigate. But no one there had heard of him. He went from one synagogue to another, asking, until he had gone through the whole city, but no one knew of anyone by that name. This man greatly revered the Baal Shem Tov and would not simply give up his search. So he next went to the town's old men and asked them if they remembered someone by that name. Finally, a very old man said that his grandfather had told him about a person of that name who had lived in the city. He was wicked to the core and had not left a single sin undone. That is why the townspeople had totally forgotten about him. Having accomplished his task, the man still could not see how this would help him in his troubles.

When he returned to Medzibuz, he reported to the Besht what he had uncovered about that former resident of Kuzmir, and added some details of what the old man had told him about that person's many evil deeds. After listening to his story, the Besht stood up and said to him sternly, "You are that man! In a previous life you were completely wicked and you only reincarnated now, to repair the damage you did to your soul then. Why, then, are you complaining about the Holy One, blessed be He?"

When the Besht revealed to a person who complained about his bitter lot in life the root of his soul and the source of his problems, he was soothed, and justified the judgment against him, because now he knew the task facing him and how to fix what needed fixing.[58]

The Death of a Baby

ONE DAY A POOR AND BROKEN WOMAN CAME TO THE BAAL SHEM TOV TO weep in front of him about her baby son who had died immediately after being circumcised. The Besht asked her to sit down and began to tell her a story.

"A certain great king had an only son who was learned in all the wisdoms of the world; but his soul yearned for the Torah of Israel. Finally, he fled the palace and traveled to a distant city, where he converted and devoted himself to study and prayer. His fame spread far and wide as an amazing prodigy. One of the town's wealthiest men, who appreciated his talents and perseverance in Torah study took him as a groom for his daughter and promised to support him as long as he remained committed to a life of piety and study. The young prodigy continued to diligently pursue his studies, in holiness and purity, in a special room that his wealthy father-in-law had built for him, and where his meals were brought. Over a number of years he became a *gaon*, as he sat in solitude within his room studying. But as he ascended in Torah and piety, his body became thinner and weaker from day to day. Seeing this, his father-in-law was deeply worried about his health but did not know what to do.

Once, late at night, this wealthy man returned home from a business trip and found his whole house dark, except for his son-in-law's room, which was lit up. When he passed by the window and looked in, he was astonished to see him stretched out on the floor, weeping bitterly. The next day, he asked his son-in-law what was troubling him so terribly, but the young scholar evaded answering. When the family continued to pressure him to explain, he revealed to them that he was a convert. He told them that in addition to his studies in the revealed Torah, he delved into the wisdom of the Kabbalah. And he made soul-ascents to the upper worlds, to the chambers of the heavenly palace. But he was not permitted to enter one chamber, because only those born as Jews and circumcised on the eighth day are allowed to enter that chamber. He then explained to them why he was so emaciated. He lifted up a floor board and showed them where he had been disposing, daily, of the food brought to him. He said, 'I'm so grief-stricken about being denied entry to that exalted chamber, that I've been fasting and praying about it before God.' When he finished telling his story, the young *gaon* broke down weeping and said, 'My only prayer is that I be reincarnated as a Jewish child, for after I'm circumcised, I'll be able to enter that awesome chamber that's withheld from me now.'"

The patience of the poor, troubled woman listening to this story was about to burst, when the Baal Shem Tov said to her, "That pure and holy soul was reincarnated in your son. Immediately after it was brought into the covenant of Abraham [circumcision], it was allowed to enter that heavenly chamber for which it had yearned for so many years. And the angels greeted it with songs and shouts of joy. You can be happy that you merited to be its mother and give your milk—even if only for eight days—to that holy soul."[59]

What to Fix

IN THE TOWN OF MIKOLAIYEV IN PODOLIA LIVED TWO HASIDIM OF THE Baal Shem Tov, both named Rabbi David. One was elderly; the other was young. They were once riding with the Besht in his coach and they asked him, "Rebbe, tell us what we need to fix in ourselves." He asked each of them to read aloud from *Ein Yaakov*. After they both read from the book, he said, "Now I know." He told one of them about the sin he needed to fix, in front of his friend, but he got down from the coach with the other hasid to tell him his sin, because it was an embarrassing matter.

The younger Rabbi David died while still a young man, and the elderly Rabbi David mourned him for a long time, because they were close friends. This Rabbi David once visited the Baal Shem Tov, who, wanting to comfort him, said, "Don't worry about your friend, because I was in the heavenly chamber of King David, and I saw him there, and asked him if he had fixed what he needed to fix. He told me he had already done so while alive. And I saw Rabbi Akiba standing there on guard," said the Besht, "wearing red and with a spear in his hand."

The Baal Shem Tov could tell from a person's voice when he read aloud from a holy book what *tikkun* (soul-repair), he needed to accomplish in his lifetime. This was an invaluable insight he could offer to a sincere disciple.[60]

A Night Visit

ONE *MOTZA'EI SHABBAT**, THE BAAL SHEM TOV ASKED RABBI YOSEF ASHKENAZI to read to him from *Ein Yaakov*, as Rabbi Yosef often did, while the Besht listened as he lay on his bed. At a certain point, the Besht expounded on a particular saying in the *Ein Yaakov*. Then, Rabbi Yosef continued reciting from the book. While he was reading, Rabbi Yosef suddenly saw the *maggid* of Medzibuz—whose name was also Rabbi Yosef, and who had died about nine months earlier—enter the room dressed in Sabbath garments, wearing the same hat that he used to wear when alive and with the same walking stick that he was accustomed to carrying; and he said loudly, "*Gut vorch!*" (Have a good week!)[¶]. Rabbi Yosef Ashkenazi was so terrified that the *Ein Yaakov* fell from his hands. The Baal Shem Tov immediately passed his hand over Rabbi Yosef's face and Rabbi Yosef no longer saw the deceased. Then the Besht said to him, "Take one of the candles from the table and stand over there on the other the side of the room." He did so, while the Besht continued to talk with Rabbi Yosef the Maggid for another half an hour. Rabbi Yosef saw the Besht talking with the *maggid*, but did not hear what the *maggid* was answering.

---

* The period after the Sabbath ends, i.e. Saturday night.
¶ The traditional greeting after *Shabbat* ends and the new week begins.

Afterward, the Baal Shem Tov called to Rabbi Yosef and said, "*Deutsch*, come here!" (The Baal Shem Tov sometimes called Rabbi Yosef "Deutsch" [German] which is the meaning of his name Ashkenazi.) Rabbi Yosef went over to the Besht and read again from *Ein Yaakov*. As they continued studying, the Besht began to be annoyed at Rabbi Yosef, saying, "Why were you afraid? Did Rabbi Yosef the Maggid slaughter a *deutsch* like you while he was alive, that you're so afraid of him after his death? Don't you know that he was a great tzaddik while alive, how much more so after his death!* Isn't it an insult to be afraid of him?" The Besht was also angry because he knew of what Rabbi Yosef had deprived himself by his weakness and unworthy fear. Rabbi Yosef said humbly, "Master, why did I merit to see him?" "Because you were reciting the *Ein Yaakov* before me," said the Besht. "And when I taught Torah before you, I purified you with my words, so that we formed a bond and became united. That's why you saw him. But if you had disciplined your mind, you would have heard what he said to me, and you would have been able to ask him whatever you wanted, and he would have answered you. And once you became known to him, you would have been able to see him regularly, and he could teach you many secrets." Hearing this, Rabbi Yosef became despondent, because he knew that seeing the soul of a deceased tzaddik is a form of prophecy. He then asked the Besht, "Why did he come to you?" "For something he needed," said the Besht.

It is considered a great attainment to see a deceased tzaddik, who can help a person spiritually and teach him mystic secrets. But the souls of the dead, even tzaddikim, came to the Baal Shem Tov for various kinds of *tikkun*, for spiritual repair and help.[61]

Healing by Repentance

THE BAAL SHEM TOV HAPPENED TO BE PASSING THROUGH A CERTAIN town and was called to the bedside of a sick man whose condition was considered hopeless after having been examined by an important Jewish doctor. As soon as the Besht arrived, he ordered that beef soup be prepared for the sick man and as they fed him the soup, the Besht talked to him about repenting. The man listened and repented. Soon, his condition began to improve, until finally he completely recovered.

The doctor, who was present, asked the Baal Shem Tov, "How were you able to heal him, since I know that his blood vessels were so damaged they couldn't be repaired?" "You diagnosed him physically," replied the Baal Shem Tov, "I diagnosed him spiritually. According to our tradition, a person has 248 limbs and organs and 365 blood vessels, which correspond to the 248 positive *mitzvot* and the 365 negative *mitzvot*. When someone transgresses a *mitzvah*, God-forbid, the limb or blood vessel corresponding to that sin is damaged. Since this man sinned a great deal, many of his blood vessels

---

* Tzaddikim are considered greater in death than when alive.

were damaged, his blood didn't flow properly, and his condition became critical. I urged him to repent and he agreed and resolved to correct all his sins and repair whatever he had damaged spiritually. And, with that, his blood vessels were healed. That's how I was able to cure him."[62]

Taking a Pulse

A FAMOUS DOCTOR ONCE VISITED THE DUCHESS OF THE TOWN OF Medzibuz, and she expressed her pride that the Baal Shem Tov lived in her town, saying he was a great man and, among other things, an expert in medicines. The doctor was skeptical, and had no doubt that the man spoken of was an uneducated charlatan. Intending to expose him before the duchess, he said, "Send for him to come here, I'd like to meet him." "He's a great man," said the duchess, "I can't just summon him. I have to invite him and send a special coach to bring him here, as I would do for an important government minister." So she sent a special coach for the Besht, which brought him to the citadel.

With contempt and mockery in his voice, the doctor asked the Baal Shem Tov, "I'm told that you're knowledgeable about medicines. Is that so?" "Yes," replied the Besht. "At which medical school did you study?" the doctor asked drily, "Who taught you medicine?" "God, blessed be He, taught me," answered the Besht. The Besht believed that everything he knew—all his knowledge and expertise—came from God alone. To the doctor, such an answer was ludicrous, and he laughed at him. (The Besht was also unwilling to explain, because he did not want to reveal himself to a hostile non-believer.)

"Do you know how to diagnose a pulse?" asked the doctor. "I have a certain irregularity in my pulse," the Besht replied. "Why don't you diagnose my pulse and then I'll diagnose yours." The doctor took the Besht's pulse and immediately realized that there was indeed something highly unusual, but he did not know what it was—because the holy Baal Shem Tov's love-sickness for God often made his heart pound, his pulse irregular, blood rush to or from his face, and so on. But all this was beyond the understanding and expertise of the doctor! How would he know of such things? Then, the Besht took hold of the doctor's wrist and checked his pulse. While still holding him, he turned to the duchess and asked, "Have you had any valuables stolen from your house recently? Perhaps a golden hand mirror and a pearl necklace?" "Yes," the duchess answered in surprise. "Just yesterday, I found those very items missing and haven't the slightest idea where they could have disappeared to." "Send some servants to the doctor's room at the inn," said the Besht, "and have them open his trunk. They'll find both the necklace and the mirror, for I can detect those thefts from his pulse." She immediately sent people to search the doctor's room, and the stolen objects were found there exactly as the Baal Shem Tov had said. Needless to say, after this the doctor left town in utter disgrace.[63]

Don't Waste Heaven's Blessings

THE BESHT WAS ONCE WALKING WITH SOME OF HIS DISCIPLES, WHEN a young gentile prince rode by mounted on a magnificent horse. The prince was wearing exquisite garments and his horse was wonderfully equipped. Everything about the horse and its rider bespoke glory, contentment, and delight.

The Baal Shem Tov commented to his disciples, "This prince's star* is so high in heaven that he would be fated to become king. But because of his immense pleasure and pride at being outfitted so beautifully on such a splendid horse, he's received his portion here and now, and has lost what heaven wanted to give him. It's the same with worldly pleasures. When a Jew is satisfied with lowly, mundane pleasures and accepts them as his reward, he wastes what heaven wanted to give him."

Later, when they arrived at their destination, the Besht explained further, "The pleasures a person merits are fixed in measure. But if he doesn't accept a lower pleasure that comes to him, it's as if he hasn't received anything yet, so they offer him something more elevated. If he refuses that too, they offer him something still higher. And so on. A person should 'manage' his pleasures wisely, and accept only the highest pleasure there is: intimacy with the *Shechinah*."[64]

Market Day

THE BAAL SHEM TOV TRAVELED TO HUNGARY AND HIS FIRST VISIT WAS TO the town of Serentch. He arrived on the big market day when many Jews went there to trade. The Besht walked through the market in the late afternoon accompanied by his disciples and attracted everyone's attention with his radiant appearance and the holy aura that surrounded him. When a crowd had gathered to him, he addressed them, "My brothers! Today is the big market day and everyone has come to buy and sell. Those who are clever hurried to buy or sell merchandise as soon as they arrived and when they finished they were able to enjoy in leisure all the different kinds of amusements and entertainments available here. But those who were foolish and lazy, first strolled about admiring all the sights and diversions in the marketplace. When they finally got around to taking care of their business, night came, it grew dark, and they accomplished nothing. It's the same with us," continued the Besht. "Life is like a market day. Every Jew has a lot of buying and selling to do to prepare for the long journey on which we're all going. Those who are clever will hurry to prepare everything while there's still time. But a lazy person whiles away his time with empty amusements and distractions. When he finally wakes up and wants to prepare some-

---

* *Mazal*, destiny.

thing for the journey, he suddenly realizes: It's too late, he waited too long—the day is gone, night has come, and with it darkness and death."

Later, the Besht confided to his disciples, "I don't usually speak like this, because arousing the fear of death is not the best way to bring people to religion; it's much better to arouse their yearning to approach the source of eternal life. But when I saw how all these merchants were oblivious to their real situation and were immersed head to toe in vanities, I felt I had to speak to them sternly."[65]

A Matter of Blindness

A *MOCHSIN* WHOSE FORTUNES HAD TAKEN A DOWNTURN, CAME AND ASKED the Baal Shem Tov to pray for him. The Besht did not respond to his request, because he saw the Angel of Death standing behind him. Instead, he admonished the man and urged him to repent. Why should he bother running after the vanities of this world and worry needlessly about his trouble making a living? He'd do better to repent and mend his ways! These words made no impression at all on the *mochsin*, who was a worldly man and suspected that the Baal Shem Tov was not answering his request, and talking about repentance, because he wanted money from him. He offered him money, but the Besht refused to accept it.

When he left, the Besht said to those present, "The fool! Today or tomorrow he'll die, and he's worried about making a living!" His brother-in-law, Rabbi Gershon, scolded him, "Why do you let a bad word out of your mouth, saying that some evil will befall a Jew?" The Besht answered back, "What can I do if you're all blind and don't see that the Angel of Death is walking behind him?" The Besht's other brother-in-law, Rabbi Yaakov, was there and also heard all this.

The *mochsin*, who was accompanied by his wife, was preparing to return home. Rabbi Yaakov, who had been widowed of his first wife, was traveling to a certain town to remarry. Since he had to go the same way as the *mochsin*, they arranged to travel together. When they stopped at an inn on the way, the *mochsin* ordered a hearty meal for himself. Rabbi Yaakov, who for reasons of piety did not eat meat, asked for some dairy food, which he ate sitting at the other end of the table (to avoid eating meat and milk in proximity at the same table). The *mochsin*—a worldly man, with no understanding of piety—ridiculed him for not wanting to eat meat.

Later, they all went to sleep. During the night, the *mochsin* woke up screaming, with a terrible headache and, feeling his end was near, asked for someone to say the rite of confession with him. Since there was no one to do it except Rabbi Yaakov, he recited the confession and the sick man repeated it after him.

Rabbi Yaakov was amazed that the Besht's prediction was coming true. After an hour, the *mochsin*'s wife left his side, saying that perhaps he would feel better after a little sleep. But a short while later she looked in on him and found him dead.

When Rabbi Yaakov returned home after his trip, he told everyone the story and about the Baal Shem Tov's comments, and said, "Indeed, we are blind!"[66]

A Mature Teacher Full
of Wisdom and Love

Judging Favorably

Judge Not

ONE *SHABBAT*, DURING THE THIRD MEAL, THE BAAL SHEM TOV TAUGHT HIS disciples, saying: "Don't judge someone else, because you have the same fault in yourself. Learn to judge other people favorably, since loving your neighbor as yourself is a great principle of the Torah and the basis for all spiritual perfection. How can you love another person when you are judging him? So when you see someone sinning or acting wrongly, or hear people talking about another person's sin or wickedness, consider it as certain that there is at least a trace of that same sin in you, and God has brought this seeing or hearing before you to remind you of *your* fault and so that *you* will repent, for your responsibility is to fix what needs fixing in *you*.

"For example, if you see someone desecrating the Sabbath, examine your own deeds and you'll certainly find something similar. I was once pained to see someone desecrating the Sabbath, and became depressed about it. I asked myself what had I done that heaven made me see this desecration of the holy Sabbath? I searched my deeds and remembered that years earlier I had remained silent when people were denigrating a great Torah scholar. By not speaking up, I had become a party to desecrating that scholar's holiness and, according to the Rabbis, a Torah scholar is on the spiritual level of '*Shabbat*.' For someone like me, this was equivalent to that other person's Sabbath desecration, and God had made me see it, so that I would reflect on my own ways, remember, and repent for the desecration that I had committed.

"Everything a person experiences is intended by divine providence to lead him to repentance and spiritual elevation. If God makes you see or hear another person's sin it's only to remind you to repent for your own, similar sin. So if you hear some profanity, reflect on your own impudence, and remember when you didn't act modestly. If you hear some skeptical or atheistic talk from someone, it's a sign for you to concentrate on strengthening your faith and trust in God.

"Certainly, anyone who acts in this way won't judge someone else unfavorably, for he realizes that he's no better than the other person and that he has the same fault and blemish in himself. And he'll be grateful to God for reminding him of sins he'd forgotten about long ago, so that he may repent and purify himself. The truth is that nothing happens in this world without a purpose, and everything that takes place before your eyes was sent from heaven for you to see, and everything that enters your ears was sent for you to hear. I tell you, someone who is completely pure, who had never sinned at all, would not even be able to see evil in another person or to hear about it. If the face looking in a mirror is clean, the reflection won't be unclean. If you see an unclean face in the mirror, it's only because your own face is unclean.

"When you see someone acting in a lowly way or committing a serious sin, try to find an excuse for him. Tell yourself that he did what he did because of the coarseness of what he's made of; or because his evil inclination, burning within him, overpowered him; or because he didn't know the seriousness of the sin. Accustom yourself to judge people who transgress for their personal benefit or to satisfy their lusts and desires, favorably, as innocent. You also have something similar to that sin in you, only that, for yourself, you find excuses to justify your actions. In the same way, learn to find excuses and justifications for every Jew, because they are all righteous and pure, and deserving of every blessing. Just as you make excuses for yourself and your behavior, find excuses for your neighbor. That's the meaning of loving your neighbor as yourself. Everyone loves himself and won't allow anyone else to criticize him, even though he himself knows that he's as full of sins as a pomegranate is of seeds. And when you judge the other person favorably and charitably, heaven will also judge you that way." Later, when the Besht spoke again to his disciples about this teaching, he added, "If you want to be perfect, instead of justifying yourself, learn to admit your own sins and only justify the sins of others."[1]

Are You Better than Him?

WHEN THE BAAL SHEM TOV ONCE LEFT MEDZIBUZ TO VISIT THE NEARBY town of Chemelnik, the rabbi of Chemelnik saw that a certain notorious adulterer went to the Besht, who befriended him and conversed with him. The rabbi was scandalized and complained to the Besht, saying, "Why do you associate with someone who is a well-known adulterer?" "Are you better than him?" retorted the Besht. Taken aback by this sharp answer, the rabbi reflected for a moment to consider his deeds, but he found nothing to warrant such a remark from the Baal Shem Tov. "I swear that you're speaking lies," he said. The Baal Shem Tov responded, "I can see an impression of adultery on your forehead. I'll tell you about it in detail tomorrow."

That night, the Baal Shem Tov made a soul-ascent to the heavenly palace of the Rambam (Maimonides) and learned why the rabbi bore an impression of adultery. The next day he said to him, "You made a commitment to refrain from marital relations with your wife for a certain period of time and violated it. Last night, I heard the Rambam give a ruling in the heavenly academy that such an act is equivalent to a person vowing to refrain from conjugal relations with his wife by saying, 'You are to me as my mother.' That's why I saw a trace of adultery on you. Look in the Rambam's books.

Perhaps you'll find this ruling there." The rabbi admitted that what the Besht said was true. And when he looked in the Rambam, he found that that is how the Rambam had ruled.[2]

Your Own Sins

THE BAAL SHEM TOV WAS ONCE IN A CERTAIN TOWN WHERE HE MET A preacher who was constantly inveighing against the evil inclination that leads people to the gates of hell. "Tell me," the Besht asked him, "how do you know so much about the ways of the evil inclination, when you've never committed any sins of your own?" The preacher was puzzled. "How do you know that I haven't sinned?" "My friend," said the Besht, "if you have sinned, then first rebuke yourself. Don't go on making a long list of other people's sins."[3]

The Stolen Harness

THE BAAL SHEM TOV WAS ONCE ABOUT TO BEGIN A JOURNEY, BUT SINCE IT was the evening for blessing the new moon, he delayed his departure from Medzibuz until nighttime. He told his attendant to have the horses harnessed to the coach and ready to travel, so that he could leave as soon as he returned from the synagogue. The attendant did as he was told, getting the horses' equipment, harnessing the horses to the coach, and bringing the coach out to the front of the house.

Then, the Baal Shem Tov, accompanied by one of his disciples, left his house to go recite the new moon blessing with the congregation. As they began walking down the street, the disciple wanted to turn around to look back, but the Besht told him not to, saying, "Don't look. Someone is stealing the harness from the horses." The disciple was surprised at the Besht's words and even more surprised at his explanation, which followed. "He's stealing because he needs money for Sabbath expenses." So they went on to the synagogue and out in front of the synagogue, on the street, they blessed the new moon with the congregation.

When they were walking back and nearing the house, the Besht's attendant had just discovered that the harness was missing and began to shout, "Who stole the harness?" But the Besht hushed him, saying, "Don't shout! The thief pawned it with a certain person. Take this money"—he handed him a specific sum—"and go to him and redeem it. And don't publicize the matter."

The holy Baal Shem Tov judged the thief favorably, for good—that he was stealing for his Sabbath expenses. Later that night, the Besht reached the town to which he was traveling. And after *Shaharit* the next day he taught his disciples there about judging others favorably. He said, "I once made a soul-ascent and saw the angel Michael, the great heavenly intercessor for Israel, defending the Jewish people by arguing that all their vices in money matters, such as cheating in business, were really virtues, because all their lowly acts were done in order to be able to serve God—to have money to make a *shidduch* [marriage-connection] with a Torah scholar or to give *tzedaka* and so on. From Michael," said the Besht, "I learned how to defend the Jewish people before the heavenly court.

"Last night in Medzibuz, I saw a thief stealing something from me. I didn't try to stop him and told myself that he was stealing for his Sabbath expenses. It might seem farfetched to say that the thief was stealing, so to speak, for the honor of the Sabbath. But why did God—who created everything for a purpose—give us the ability to be illogical? The answer is: So we could justify the faults of others. Most of us twist logic to justify our own behavior, but we should actually use our irrationality only to justify others.

"Never speak ill of any Jew, or when the Satan accuses him, he'll call you to be his witness. When the Satan accuses a Jew before the Throne of Glory, his single accusation is not accepted as true, because the Torah says: 'According to two witnesses shall the matter be established.' Therefore, the Satan waits until he can find a partner to defame the person. If you have to mention a particular person when condemning some bad trait, say explicitly that you're not talking about the person himself, but just about his bad trait."[4]

Speak Well of Fellow Jews

THE BAAL SHEM TOV INSTRUCTED EVEN SIMPLE JEWS TO SPEAK WELL of one another—praising other people, complimenting them, excusing other people's faults, and so on—because doing so sweetened the heavenly judgments.[5]

Like Fish in the Sea

THE BAAL SHEM TOV WAS ONCE WALKING WITH SOME DISCIPLES IN Medzibuz, along the bank of the Bug River, when he stood for a few moments and silently peered into the water, looking at some fish that were swimming close to the surface. He then turned to his disciples and explained to them how he defended the Jewish people in heaven when they are accused of engaging in cut-throat business practices and harming each other's livelihood. "Normally, animals don't eat their own kind. Lions don't eat lions, wolves don't devour wolves. But with fish, the big ones eat the little ones. In the Talmud, our Sages, of blessed memory, interpreted the verse from the prophet Habakkuk, 'You [God] make men [*adam*] like the fish of the sea': Just like fish in the sea, where the big one swallows the small one, so too with human beings, the big swallows the little." At first, it seems strange, for our Sages say elsewhere in the Talmud that the term *adam* refers only to Jews. Why then are Jews particularly compared to fish, where the big one swallows its neighbor? The answer is clear: All the other peoples are free to enter whatever occupations they want and to make a living however they can. So it's easier for them to earn a living. But Jews, who are in exile, are oppressed and persecuted in foreign lands. The gentiles restrict where they can live and enact repressive decrees against them. Jews can't enter many occupations and trades and many government positions are forbidden to them. How can they survive under such conditions? They have to scramble for crumbs! They're forced to scrape and fight and desperately compete against each other, like fish in the sea, where the big ones eat the little ones!" The Besht concluded his teaching to his disciples by saying, "When Samael*, the angel of Esau, accuses the Jewish people, saying that each one eats the flesh of his neighbor, and each Jew undermines his fellow Jew's livelihood, I take him over to the river here and show him the fish that are forced to struggle to survive by eating each other, and immediately his accusations are silenced."

The Besht did everything possible to prevent Jews from competing harmfully in business and encroaching on each other's livelihood. But he understood the economic distress that drove them to it and in his great love for the Jewish people defended them in heaven from the Satan's accusations.[6]

Before and after the *Mitzvah*

ONCE, AFTER THE YOM KIPPUR PRAYERS, THE BAAL SHEM TOV TOLD HIS disciples that there had been a serious judgment in heaven against the Jewish people. "The Satan didn't accuse wicked people; he accused religious Jews who go to synagogue every day to pray with a *minyan*, but on their way there, when they see a wagon on the street with firewood for sale, they stop to buy the wood and stand there haggling until they get the lowest price. For the sake of a few pennies, they're willing to be late to synagogue and miss reciting the *Borechu* and *Kedushah*¶. None of the defending angels in the heavenly court could find anything to say to refute this accusation and excuse this kind of behavior. But I came up with a good argument. 'It's true,' I said, 'they're willing to lose the *mitzvah* of saying these prayers to save a few coins. But after they do the *mitzvah*, if you'd offer any religious Jew a treasure to sell it, he wouldn't do it!' And by this argument I sweetened the judgment."

The Besht himself was certainly pained by the impious behavior of some religious Jews. But he never judged or criticized others. Instead, he perceived any accusation against fellow Jews as satanic and searched until he found an excuse and a defense.[7]

Compassion for a Thief

THE BAAL SHEM TOV WAS ONCE AT A VILLAGE INN IN PODOLIA WITH A number of his disciples, when they became aware that the Jewish innkeeper was

---

* A name of Satan, here said to be the angel of Esau, the symbol for gentiles who persecute and defame the Jewish people.
¶ Two important prayers that can only be said with a congregation.

exploiting a pair of orphans by using them as servants without paying them properly. The Besht's disciples began to angrily rebuke the innkeeper for his wrongdoing, but the Besht said to them, "I received a tradition from my father, of blessed memory, that the thief needs more compassion than the person he's stolen from! The person whose possessions were stolen will get over his loss, but how will the thief get over his wickedness? There are many accusers in the heavenly court against someone who's guilty of sin. There's no need for us on earth to add fuel to the fire." After this, the Besht took care of the orphans' needs and also brought the innkeeper and his wife to repentance.[8]

Arousing an Accusation Above

DURING THE PRAYERS ONE ROSH HASHANAH, THE SNUFF BOX OF ONE OF the Baal Shem Tov's disciples fell to the ground, whereupon he picked it up and sniffed the tobacco. This disciple, like some others at that time, used snuff to keep alert and increase his concentration while praying. But another disciple was annoyed at seeing this and thought, "How can he interrupt in the middle of the prayers and sniff tobacco?" This tzaddik's annoyance aroused an accusation in heaven and caused a heavenly decree that the man he criticized die that year.

The Besht saw all this with his holy spirit and made a soul-ascent to defend the accused before the heavenly court, "How can a punishment of death be decreed for such a minor transgression?" But none of his arguments succeeded and he could not cause the decree to be annulled. As a result, the Besht was upset and troubled.

On *Hoshanna Rabba**, he made another soul-ascent, and he argued and complained and cried out, until he achieved by his prayer that if the accuser himself found a justification for his comrade, the decree would be ripped up and the other disciple pardoned. The Besht then entered his *beit midrash*, and found the accusing disciple sitting reciting the *Hoshanna Rabba Tikkun*¶. By mystical means, the Baal Shem Tov removed the disciple's power of concentration so that he could no longer recite the *tikkun* with *d'vekut*! He then got up and began to walk around thinking about various matters, such as, "Why did divine providence arrange for snuff and smoking tobacco to be introduced into Europe in recent generations?" It occurred to him that certain souls were only able to meditate and concentrate with the help of tobacco. When he thought this, he regretted having been critical of his fellow disciple, who had been sniffing tobacco while praying.

Now, on *Hoshanna Rabba*, the Baal Shem Tov's custom was to answer questions of all sorts. And this day he was in a very good mood and was answering questions put to him by his disciples. This disciple asked him, "Why was tobacco introduced in recent generations?" "What do you think?" replied the Besht. The disciple told him what he

---

* This holiday is the seventh day of *Sukkot* and occurs about three weeks after Rosh HaShanah. According to tradition, the decree of the High Holidays—for life or death—is finalized on this day.

¶ A compilation of scriptural recitations composed by the kabbalists for the holiday.

had thought. Then the Besht asked him why he had been thinking about this. The disciple remembered, and told him how he had been critical of his comrade and had only now found a justification for what he had done. The Besht knew that because the accuser had repaired the damage by finding an excuse, the decree was nullified. He then revealed to the disciple what had happened and told him the danger his fellow disciple had been in because of his judgmental attitude and his critical thoughts. The Besht went on to rebuke him severely about this and warned him not to judge another person, saying, "When you see someone acting badly, don't judge him, because it arouses an accusation against him in heaven. Judge others favorably, and then you too will be judged favorably."[9]

Riveleh the *Tzaddeket*

THE BESHT ONCE TRAVELED TO SATINOV IN PODOLIA AND, AS HE approached the city, saw with his holy vision that a divine light was shining above one of the townspeople. Stopping briefly and standing in place to look more closely, he saw that the light was resting on a woman. When he entered the town and was greeted by its prominent men, he told them what he had seen and asked if they knew which woman might be the one over whom he had seen the light. They replied that undoubtedly it was the Pious Riveleh. Anxious to meet this holy woman, the Besht asked them to send for her, but they told him it was unnecessary, since she was always collecting money for *tzedaka* and performing deeds of kindness and would certainly come on her own to ask him for a donation.

The next day, after the morning prayers, the Baal Shem Tov saw with his holy spirit that she was on her way, and he said to the people with him, "I see her coming here. And she's made up her mind not to accept anything less than a certain large sum of money from me. Pay attention to how I act with her and how she responds, and you'll see her holiness."

When Riveleh came, she said to the Baal Shem Tov, "Holy Rabbi, there are several sick poor people in town. Will you please make a generous donation for them?" When the Besht offered her a small amount of money, she said nothing, but made a slight gesture with her hand to indicate that she would not accept it. He then offered her twice that amount, which was still a small sum, but she would not accept that either. Feigning anger, he rebuked her, saying, "Who made you the charity collector, so that you could steal from the fund whenever you pleased?" She did not answer a word or show the least anger or annoyance at this insult; the words made no impression on her whatsoever, because she was as humble and lowly as the dust. But she refused to leave until the Besht had given her the entire amount she had decided she would take from him. For although she was as soft and pliant as a reed in the face of abuse to her own person, she was as hard and unyielding as a cedar when it came to doing good and helping the needy. The Besht, who had seen her great light, had tested her resolve and patience by offering her small donations and trying to provoke her, so that the townspeople would see her pious humility as he saw it.

That evening, Riveleh came to the Baal Shem Tov a second time and said, "A certain doctor in the city is very ill. Please pray for him to live, because he's in critical condition." "Let there be one less adulterer in the world," said the Besht. "Who told you that he's an adulterer?" she protested. The Besht turned to the men standing there and said, "Is what I say true?" "Yes, it's true!" they answered. She responded firmly, "First, they haven't the least evidence for this. And second, he's a complete innocent, sexually; he's the sort of person who's never even seen a paintbrush in a tube. Even if he did what they say, it's only because he's ignorant of the Torah, and didn't know the severity of the sin. If he had known how serious it was, he would never have transgressed!" Kind and compassionate as she was, she readily found reasons to judge others favorably and excuse their faults, just as the Besht taught his disciples and followers to do.

The Baal Shem Tov, who had heard an accusation about the doctor's adultery made against him in heaven, repeated it to her intentionally so that she would defend him and speak in his favor. When she did so, her arguments on his behalf were accepted above, and the doctor immediately recovered from his illness.[10]

Persecuting the Satan

THE BAAL SHEM TOV WAS SO STRICT ABOUT REFUSING TO JUDGE OTHERS and so unyielding in opposing any attempt of the Satan to accuse the Jewish people, that in his time the heavenly court actually persecuted the Satan, who constantly blamed Jews, and often denied him the chance to accuse.[11]

The Informer

A CERTAIN JEW WHO COMMITTED EVERY SIN AND TRANSGRESSION POSSIBLE, was close to the feudal landowner and regularly informed on his fellow Jews. One day, the lord called this informer to him and said, "Look, basically, you're already a gentile like me. I want you to convert to our religion." The Jew said, "I need a few days to think it over." The lord gave him three days. Finally, the informer said, "I've committed every sin there is, but I won't change my religion." The lord had him shot. When the Baal Shem Tov heard of this, he said, "God, blessed be He, got a good bargain when He chose the Jews as His people. Even a lowly soul like this informer nevertheless martyred himself and sanctified God's name publicly!"[12]

According to One's Thoughts

A CERTAIN POOR MAN IN MEDZIBUZ, WHO HAD NO WOOD TO HEAT HIS home, once saw, while praying in the Baal Shem Tov's synagogue, right before

Kedushah, that a wagon was standing on the street with wood for sale. He was thinking about what to do, whether to exit to buy the wood and miss the *Kedushah* or to forget about the wood, although he was worried that someone else would buy it before him. He decided not to leave the synagogue. Another poor man there had similar thoughts. But he decided to miss the *Kedushah*. So he went outside and bought the wood.

Later, the two of them were talking and found out what had happened and they went to ask the Baal Shem Tov which of them had acted correctly. The Besht turned to the one who had bought the wood and said, "You were right. Because all the time you were buying the wood you were thinking about having missed the *Kedushah*. But you," he said to the second man, "were thinking about the wood while reciting the *Kedushah*. It would have been better for you both to have stayed for the *Kedushah* and kept your mind on the prayer. But since neither of you was capable of that, everything follows your intention. Because where your thoughts are, there you are, all of you."[13]

Comforting an Isolated Jew

A SIMPLE JEW ONCE CAME TO THE BAAL SHEM TOV AND COMPLAINED THAT he lived in an isolated village far from other Jews, and had no *minyan* to pray with. He never had a chance to hear and respond to *Borechu* and *Kedushah*. But he could not leave the village to live with other Jews, because he had to support his family and he was already established where he was! The Baal Shem Tov told him, "Try to perform the *mitzvah* of hospitality as much as possible. Whenever any Jew passes through your village, always try to serve him a meal. And when you serve *borsht*, have it in your mind to fulfill your obligation of *Borechu*; and when you serve *kasha* have it in your mind to fulfill your obligation of *Kedushah*." [*Borsht* (beet soup) sounds vaguely like *Borechu* and *kasha* (buckwheat groats) sounds like *Kedushah*.] The Baal Shem Tov comforted the man with this novel solution to his problem. By means of this substitute practice, this isolated villager would not only enjoy regular Jewish companionship, but also gain the spiritual benefits of participating in congregational prayer.[14]

The Seer

THE BAAL SHEM TOV WAS A SEER WHO SAW EVENTS HAPPENING FROM AFAR. He was not limited by space or time. His physical sight extended to an area of four hundred miles by four hundred miles. His spiritual sight was unlimited—from one end of the world to the other. He saw the future and heard heavenly proclamations.

The Besht once said to Rabbi Yaakov Yosef of Polnoye, "I achieved my spiritual levels because of my frequent immersions." Particularly when he was younger he was continually immersing in rivers and *mikvahs*. The Besht often prayed for others when he was in the *mikvah*, to strengthen the force of his prayer. The pure waters of the *mikvah* also allowed him to see farther. On one occasion, he asked Rabbi Yaakov Yosef why he stayed so long in the *mikvah*, saying, "When I go into the *mikvah* and under the water, as soon as I open my eyes, I see all the worlds." Later that same day, he taught his disciples, saying, "The eye, being an eye, should be able to see from one end of the world to the other; and the ear, being an ear, should be able to hear heavenly proclamations. But one's sins create a barrier, because a person's soul is, as it were, in exile within his evil inclination, and the three evil Shells surround the soul and block his ability to see and hear. But you must break through those Shells; then, you will be able to see and to hear."[15]

The Delayed Homecoming

THERE WAS A VERY SUCCESSFUL MERCHANT IN MEDZIBUZ WHO WAS among those who were still opponents of the Baal Shem Tov. This merchant had an only son who was a brilliant scholar and had many other virtues. The son used to travel to the German city of Breslau on business and would usually stay away for four weeks on one of his trips. Once, however, he was gone for ten weeks, without sending any message home, and both of his parents were very worried. The merchant's wife said to her husband, "Why are you so stubbornly against the Baal Shem Tov? Everybody is running to him from all over the world, and he's doing miracles for them, while you live next door to him and refuse to walk over to his house and ask him about our son! This is a serious matter. I tell you, something has happened to him!" But her husband ignored her pleas and refused to go. After a few more days passed with no news from their son, she became even more insistent, until finally he had to give in to her.

On Friday afternoon, he went to the Baal Shem Tov and said, "Rabbi, it's more than ten weeks now since my son went to Breslau and we haven't heard a thing from him. We're very worried. We don't know what's happened to him." The Besht had someone bring him a copy of the *Zohar*; he opened it and looked inside. Then he said, "With God's help, your son is alive and well. He's on his way home this very moment and will spend *Shabbat* in a village one mile from the city." The man could not believe this. If his son was so close, why would he not make every effort to be home for the Sabbath? He must know that his parents are worried to death about him! Regardless, just to be certain, he sent a gentile servant (who could travel on the Sabbath) to the village, and told him to stay there until evening.

That night, the servant returned and said there was no sign of their son. "It's just what I told you," said the merchant to his wife. "Our 'seer's' words are pure fantasy." That Sabbath could not have been more gloomy in their household. They were like mourners.

But after *havdala*, they heard the sound of a coach outside. The father looked out of the window and, to his astonishment, saw his son climbing down from the coach. He ran out and embraced and kissed him. But before they even went inside, the father asked his son what had happened to him and why he had not even sent a message. In a single breath, the young man explained why he had been delayed and all the mishaps that had occurred on the way back—that his coach had broken down several times and he was not able to reach the village before nightfall; he had to walk there on foot and arrived in the middle of the night. But immediately after the Sabbath, he hired another coach and came home.

The merchant then realized that everything the Besht had said was absolutely true. So the next morning he went to him and begged his forgiveness for having doubted and maligned him. "You fool!" said the Besht. "Didn't Adam use the light that the Holy One, blessed be He, created on the first day of creation, to see from one end of the world to the other? The Sages tell us that God hid that light away for the use of the tzaddikim in each generation. Where did He hide it? In the Torah! When I open the holy *Zohar* and look inside, I see the whole world within the book. And, with God's help, I make no error in what I see." That man became a follower of the Baal Shem Tov and a completely pious person.[16]

Torah Enlightens the Eyes

RABBI MEIR MARGOLIOT, WHO WAS IN MEDZIBUZ THEN, HEARD ABOUT what the Baal Shem Tov had said to the merchant and asked his master to explain further. How could he see all these things in the *Zohar*? The Besht said, "Meir, when a person studies Torah for its own sake, without any ulterior motive, and focuses his mind and speech to cleave to the letters in holiness and purity with all his might, then he'll see from one end of the world to the other. He'll see future events from the letters themselves. That's why the Torah is said to enlighten a person's eyes, because it enlightens the eyes of someone who cleaves to its letters, just like the letters of the *Urim* and *Tumim* on the high priest's breastplate. And, Meir, the *Zohar* is especially potent for this."[17]

Kefitzat Ha-Derech

WHEN THE BAAL SHEM TOV TRAVELED TO A DISTANT PLACE ON A HOLY mission, in his horse-drawn coach, he often used a divine Name for shortening the journey. Ahiyah had once given him this Name to use on a single occasion. But the Besht had since received heavenly permission to use this miraculous power of *kefitzat ha-derech** whenever needed. Soon afterward, he hired a gentile named Alexei, who

---

* "Road-leaping."

drove his coach and served him in other ways. After Alexei would drive the coach outside Medzibuz and away from the eyes of men, the Besht would ask him to put down the reins and turn around in his seat, facing backward; sometimes Alexei would even take a nap. The horses then raced off on their own, under divine guidance, the ground contracting under their flying hooves. When they stopped, it was a sign from heaven that the Besht had arrived at his destination.

A Trip to Lubar

THERE WAS A WEALTHY MAN IN THE CITY OF LUBAR WHO HAD A DEAR friend who lived in Ostropol (both in Volhynia). When his friend's wife gave birth to a baby boy, he of course received an invitation to the *bris*, which would be performed on a Friday. There was a problem, however, because he had a pressing reason why he had to be at home that Sabbath after the *bris*, and the return trip would take more than half a day. He was at a loss at what to do. How could he attend his friend's celebration? But he certainly had to be there; how could he miss it? He decided to ask his friend if he would please make the *bris* as early as possible in the morning, so he would be able to return home for the Sabbath. His friend promised him that he would surely do as he asked.

The man arrived in Ostropol on Thursday evening, and early Friday morning his friend made every effort to hurry things up and to speed up everyone connected with the *bris*, so that it would take place at the earliest possible hour. Just as they were about to begin they saw through the window that a coach had pulled up and stopped near the house. Curious to know who had arrived, they all went outside and were delighted to see that none other than the holy Baal Shem Tov, accompanied by some disciples, was sitting in the coach! Overjoyed at this unexpected, eminent guest, they invited him inside for the *bris*.

He agreed, but because of his arrival, the *bris* was delayed. They first had to wait until the Baal Shem Tov immersed in the *mikvah* and then prayed the morning prayers; that itself took a long time. They then performed the *bris* without rushing, with great holiness, and had a festive meal afterward. And, of course, the Besht taught Torah at the table, and everything else that was done was done with great holiness and devotion, and nothing at all was rushed; just the opposite. Moreover, this was during the winter, when the days are short. So, when they finally finished the feast, it was almost evening, no more than ten minutes before the time for lighting the Sabbath candles.

Understandably, the friend from Lubar was forlorn, since he had no hope anymore of getting home for the Sabbath. His plans had come to nought. When the Besht saw him standing there, pensive and dejected, he went over to him and said, "If I take you home, can I stay with you for the Sabbath?" "Yes!" the man answered. Without further ado, they immediately set out on the long journey. But to his utter astonishment, the man saw that after just five minutes, they were in Lubar! He took the Baal Shem Tov into his home as his Sabbath guest, in a manner befitting a great tzaddik, and from then on he became the Besht's loyal follower and hasid.

The Baal Shem Tov did not live according to the clock; all his doings were beyond time and space. He might occasionally delay others, for example, by praying at length, without regard to the hour. Sometimes it seemed that others were inconvenienced by him. But just as he could be devotedly slow in his divine service, so too was he quick to fly with holy speed when necessary for the good of those who were with him—as on his trip to Lubar, when he traveled by *kefitzat ha-derech*.[18]

The Besht Shows His Disciples Elijah

THE BAAL SHEM TOV HAD ACHIEVED SO MANY AWESOME MYSTICAL LEVELS: He had revelations of Elijah and Ahiyah, and of deceased tzaddikim, like the Ari; he made soul-ascents to heaven; his eyes saw from one end of the world to the other and his ears heard heavenly proclamations; he knew the language of animals. Seeing what their master had attained, his disciples also yearned to have mystical experiences.

One day they asked him to let them see Elijah the Prophet just once. Since, as is well known, Elijah attends every *bris*, the Besht promised them that the next time there was a *bris*, he would let them see Elijah. But by the time one of the townspeople in Medzibuz made a *bris*, the disciples had already forgotten what they had asked of their master. The prophet Elijah, disguised, came to the synagogue where the *bris* was going to be, took a holy book from the shelf, and sat down to study. Some time later, the Baal Shem Tov arrived at the synagogue and asked his disciples to bring him that same book. They searched for it, but could not find it. They said, "A short while ago there was a stranger here studying from that book; he must have it." They looked around for him in the synagogue, but he was not there. Then they searched on the street for him. When they found him, they also found that the book was concealed beneath his coat. "This is terrible!" they said. "You came to the synagogue to study a holy book and then you steal it? You should be ashamed of yourself!" Despite his denials, they dragged him back to the synagogue and then wanted to give him a good beating, but the Besht would not let them, saying, "Can't you tell from his face that he's not a thief?"

A few weeks later, there was another *bris*, and again Elijah appeared in disguise. This time, they caught him after the festive meal as he was trying to sneak out with a silver spoon concealed in his hand. Some of the men recognized him and said, "This is the same one who stole the book the other time! And the last time too he denied it, although he had the book with him!" They were about to give him a good pummeling, when again the Besht intervened, saying, "You can see from his face that he's not a thief!"

Later, the Besht said to his disciples, "You've now seen Elijah twice. He was the one you thought was a thief. That's why I didn't let you beat him." The disciples were upset at having missed their chance twice and became dejected at not having recognized Elijah. Once more, they begged their master to show Elijah to them, but this time when they would be traveling. If they were on the road with fewer people and fewer distractions, they were sure they would be able to recognize him.

Some time later, when they had already forgotten what they had asked, they were traveling with their master in his coach. Suddenly, they saw a Russian cavalry soldier riding toward them. He pulled his horse up beside their coach and asked them if they had a flint to light his pipe. The Besht told them to give it to him, and they did. The cavalryman then looked into the coach and saw the Baal Shem Tov. He smiled broadly and said to him in Russian, "My dear Mister Jew! How are you?" and he reached into the coach and embraced the Besht and kissed him. The Besht also kissed him, and then the soldier rode off. The Baal Shem Tov said to his disciples, "That was him. You've now seen Elijah a third time." They raced after him, but could not find him. Again they were disappointed. They asked the Besht, "Master, why were we not able to recognize him?" The Baal Shem Tov answered, "Sometimes Elijah appears as a thief, a stranger, or a gentile. As long as you judge by the outside, you'll never be able to see what is inside, and you won't recognize what is concealed."[19]

The Besht's Humor

THE BAAL SHEM TOV HAD A LIVELY SENSE OF HUMOR, AND OCCASIONALLY spoke holy words in a light-hearted vein. But even his humorous comments contained mystical meanings of awesome profundity. Once, before teaching his disciples, the Besht made an especially good joke and everyone was laughing. After they recovered, the Besht said, "We know that one of the talmudic sages always opened a study session with a joke or humorous remark. I'll tell you why. The divine vitality that gives a person life and awareness is always fluctuating between expanded and constricted consciousness. Humor takes you from a state of constricted consciousness into a more expanded state of mind, so that you can learn Torah deeply and cleave to God, blessed be He. The Talmud tells of two holy jesters who went around cheering up the downcast. They'd befriend a person by means of jokes and humor and elevate him spiritually. Indeed, Elijah the Prophet told Rabbi Beroka that these two jesters would inherit the World-to-Come. I tell you," said the Besht, "through humor and laughter for the sake of heaven, you can also elevate your own childishness and raise it to spiritual heights." The Besht elevated others through humor and he elevated his own childishness. He also knew how to laugh at the world. He once said, "Who is a holy jester—like the two mentioned in the Talmud—who will inherit the World-to-Come? It's someone who has reached the level that when everyone is laughing at his piety, he laughs at them, unconcerned at their mockery."[20]

Elijah Sent and Recalled

THE BESHT ONCE MADE A JOKE THAT BROUGHT SMILES TO THE FACES OF the angels in the highest heaven. Another time he told a story of how he was once infected with the angels' laughter.

One year, just as the Baal Shem Tov sat down to conduct his Passover *seder*, he began to laugh gently to himself. None of his disciples present at the table had the courage to ask what was so amusing, but after the holiday was over, one close disciple questioned his master about it. "Why did the Rebbe laugh at the beginning of the *seder*?" he asked.

The Besht explained that he had seen something that had transpired simultaneously on earth in Poland and in the heavenly realms. "In the forest north of Krasnopol," he said, "there lives a very simple farmer and his equally simple wife. The couple perfectly complement each other, which is fortunate, since they live alone, far from any town. The little of *halacha* that the farmer, Shraga Shmeryl, knows, he observes meticulously. For example, Shraga Shmeryl is always zealous to have a poor guest at his Passover *seder*. As a child, he had been told that it is an important *mitzvah* to have a poor man at the *seder* and so he made every effort to comply. This at first involved an annual, exhausting pre-Passover journey to Krasnopol. Wandering through the various synagogues, he sought out a beggar to invite to his *seder*. After a few years of this, however, word spread, and Shraga Shmeryl never had to search for a guest again. The beggars of the area learned that it was worth the long and tiring trip out to the farm, for they were treated like kings and the hospitality was not restricted to the first two nights of the holiday on which there are *seders*. With time, the local *shnorrers** devised a scheme to exploit their gullible host. They claimed that since it was such a difficult journey to the farm, they had to set out well in advance to make sure they would arrive in time for Passover; then they needed some time to rest before Passover so they would be prepared to celebrate the holiday as was fit. Thus, not long after Purim, about a month before Passover, the first few guests would arrive, soon joined by additional freeloaders. Invariably, they explained to the naive Shraga Shmeryl that a *seder* invitation included the entire eight-day Passover festival, and needless to say, a host should not evict his guests the moment a holiday is over! Thus, Reb Shraga Shmeryl and his wife had steady company for five straight weeks every spring.

"One year, however, guests failed to arrive after Purim and the simple couple began to worry. *Rosh Hodesh Nissan*[†] rolled around and, still, no beggars appeared at their door. The farmer was distraught. How would he fulfill the important *mitzvah* of hosting the poor at his *seder*? *Shabbat HaGadol*[§] came and went and so too the night of

---

* Beggars; freeloaders.
[†] The first day of the month during which Passover falls.
[§] The Sabbath preceding Passover.

bedikat hametz*. It would soon be time for the *seder* and the couple were still all by themselves. As Passover eve approached, a pall of sadness descended on them. Shraga Shmeryl scaled the tallest tree in the area as the sun was about to set, hoping to spot a Jewish vagabond lost on the way, but all of the paths were empty, bare of a living soul. Depressed, he sat down at his *seder* table, but the sight of the tears flowing down his wife's cheeks made him unable to begin the service.

"Now, this pitiful scene," the Baal Shem Tov explained, "caused quite a commotion in heaven. It was decided in the heavenly court that a guest would have to be sent at once, and who would be more appropriate for this mission than Elijah the Prophet, who is supposed to visit every *seder* table during the evening? Just as Elijah was preparing for the journey, however, the farmer had an idea. 'Don't worry,' Shraga Shmeryl comforted his wife, 'we'll still have a guest!' The woman straightened herself up expectantly as her husband dashed out of the house and into his barn. Carrying a nice afghan blanket, he approached his favorite horse and gave him a gentle pat on the head. With a jubilant expression on his face and the rapture of victory adding a bounce to his step, Shraga Shmeryl led the afghan-draped horse to his table. The farmer threw a triumphant arm around the horse's neck and happily informed his wife that a guest had arrived after all! The angels in heaven were incredulous at this scene. Immediately, they aborted Elijah's mission amidst laughter. When I saw the angels laughing," the Baal Shem Tov concluded, "I couldn't keep from laughing myself!"

The Baal Shem Tov's disciples were also amused by this story, but afterward they discussed it more seriously, because everything their master said—even his jokes and ordinary conversation—contained profound spiritual lessons. When they later asked the Besht about it, he added, "Although what happened was humorous, there's another side to the story too. This simple couple's childlike piety is precious. But in this instance Shraga Shmeryl was actually too clever in devising a scheme to solve his problem. He helped himself when he should have relied on God. As a result, he foolishly lost a rare visit by Elijah the Prophet."[21]

The Dancing Bear

ONE YOM KIPPUR, BEFORE THE BLOWING OF THE *SHOFAR*, THERE WAS a serious heavenly accusation against the Jewish people, which the Baal Shem Tov was unable to nullify by his prayers. So he stayed in his private room and did not enter the synagogue to begin the *shofar* blowing. Sensing the gravity of the situation, his disciples sat in the synagogue in great fear and dread.

A simple Jewish villager, seeing the glum looks on their faces, ran home and came back dressed in the bear costume he wore on Purim, to lighten the mood and cheer everyone up. He cavorted and danced until he succeeded in making everyone laugh.

* The final search for leavened bread on the night before Passover, when one destroys any leaven one might have overlooked.

Immediately, the Baal Shem Tov entered for the *shofar* blowing, and said, "This decree couldn't be nullified except by joy."

The anxiety of the Besht and his disciples prevented them from canceling the heavenly accusation and judgment. Only when the spirit of joy and laughter passed through them was the decree cancelled.

Later, the Besht explained to his disciples what had happened, commenting on the verse in Ecclesiastes: "What, after all, is joy?" He said, "Even joy that is not from a high and holy source, but merely foolishness of the category 'what, after all?' or 'so what?' makes an impression in heaven."[22]

Avoid Depression

THE BAAL SHEM TOV ONCE ENTERED HIS *BEIT MIDRASH*, AND NOTICING that a few of his disciples sitting and conversing there seemed to be in a depressed mood, sat down with them and asked one of them to light his pipe. Then, while puffing on his pipe, he said, "If a person truly believes that God is good and everything that He does is good, he can't be sad. Sadness is actually a sign of atheism. The Rabbis commented on the Torah verse, 'There is strength and gladness in His place,' saying that one isn't allowed to enter the gates to the king's palace wearing a mourner's sackcloth. Depression blocks the divine light and keeps a person from approaching God. I love joy and laughter and hate sadness and depression. I have a relative who is a complete tzaddik, but I find it difficult to speak to him because he's so gloomy and depressed. I tell you, a Jew who wants to cleave to God, blessed be He, can't allow himself to become sad. If a Jew has forgotten to be happy, it's a sign that he's forgotten God. You should avoid sadness at all costs!" The Besht then put down his pipe, closed his eyes and began to sing a soft, joyful *niggun*. His disciples joined in, they all raised their voices, and in a short while the mood had changed from sadness to great joy.[23]

How Could I Wait?

THE BAAL SHEM TOV WAS ONCE IN A CERTAIN CITY WHOSE RABBI WAS a great Torah scholar. This rabbi did not believe in the Baal Shem Tov, but, having heard the extraordinary things people were saying about him and the miracles he was performing, very much wanted to meet the Besht and talk with him. However, he was reluctant to lower his own dignity by going to the Besht. He felt that since he was the rabbi of the city it was proper that the Baal Shem Tov come to him, and visit him in his house. When they reported this to the Baal Shem, he said, "Not only doesn't he come to me to welcome me to his city, he wants me to go to him."

Finally, the rabbi went to the Baal Shem Tov, but when he entered the room where the Besht was staying, the Besht was not there, for he had gone to the outhouse. An *agunah** was also there waiting for the Baal Shem Tov. When he returned, he picked up the vessel with water to ritually wash his hands. But before he could pour the water, the woman immediately began to weep and plead hysterically that he tell her (by means of his holy spirit) about her husband—was he alive or dead (God-forbid)? If he was alive, where was he? She did not even allow the Besht to wash his hands. Finally, he told her that her husband was alive, and in such-and-such a city, and that if she went there, she would find him.

After she left, the rabbi, who had observed all this, said to the Baal Shem Tov, "If you were speaking words of prophecy, shouldn't you first have washed your hands, and then spoken to her in a state of cleanliness?"

The Baal Shem Tov replied, "If you came into your house after having relieved yourself, and saw that two chickens had gotten in from outside, and were jumping up on a table on which there were expensive glass objects, would you wash your hands first before you chased them out? Because, meanwhile, the glass would be broken. And I, praise God, see her husband walking around in that city, and he is actually before my eyes—just as you would see the glass objects on the table and the chickens. And you are standing there and able to do something. In the same way, I see her husband there, and she's here, weeping and crying out in front of me. Can I wait until I wash my hands first? Every minute, her heart is breaking into a thousand pieces and she's dying a thousand times. How could I wait?"

The Besht, with his holy spirit, could see the wayward husband at a distance, but his greater achievement was that he could see and share the suffering of the woman who was standing right in front of him. And he was ready to help her in any way that he could.

Later, when the Baal Shem Tov told his disciples about this incident, he said, "The moment you see anyone suffering, no matter who it is—whether someone important or ordinary, whether someone righteous or wicked, and whether a Jew or a non-Jew, even animals, birds or insects—you must act immediately to relieve their pain and suffering, doing everything you can, even beyond your ability, to help them, for that's the essence of Judaism."[24]

He Revives a Boy and Receives Fiery Lashes

ONCE, WHEN THE BAAL SHEM TOV WAS TRAVELING AND ARRIVED IN A certain town before the Sabbath, he heard a heavenly proclamation telling him to lodge with a particular family. But when he appeared at their home, they refused to offer him hospitality because their young son was seriously ill. When the Besht sent in his scribe, Rabbi Tzvi Hirsh, to try to persuade them to receive him, the mistress of the house yelled at him, "How can you stay here? Don't you see that our child is sick

---

* A woman whose husband is missing and, according to Jewish religious law, cannot remarry. See endnote.

and I'm falling to pieces?" She then cursed the Baal Shem Tov for troubling her. The husband did not dare say anything to his wife, who was terribly upset, but he went out to appease the Besht and begged him not to be angry. He explained the situation and told him that it was impossible for him to stay there. The Baal Shem Tov then *swore* to the man that if he stayed with them, the child would live. Hearing this, he received the Besht into his home.

Immediately after this, the Baal Shem Tov went to the *mikvah* to immerse for the Sabbath and to pray for the child. While in the water, he saw with his holy spirit that the child's condition was not good, and he realized that much prayer and effort would be needed to save him. When he returned to his hosts, he ordered everyone to leave the house, and they all did so and went elsewhere. He also ordered his scribe out and told him to return only when he called him to bring wine for the *kiddush*.

The Baal Shem Tov remained there alone and prayed *Minha*, *Kabbalat Shabbat*, and *Maariv* at the child's bedside. He stayed awake late into the night, until Rabbi Tzvi Hirsh became worried that the Besht might harm himself by his extreme exertions in praying for the child—for he was able to pray so strenuously that he could actually endanger his life. So, ignoring the Besht's order, he went to the house and opened the door of the room slightly, and he heard the Baal Shem Tov order the child's soul, "Reenter the body! You *must* reenter, for I won't swear falsely!" The scribe did not know if the boy was dead or was still clinging to life.

He went away but returned after a short while to take another look, and found the Baal Shem Tov fully prostrated on the floor. The Besht then got up and said (to the soul), "Didn't I order you to reenter the child's body!" Then he called out, "Hirsh, bring me the wine for the *kiddush*!" He recited *kiddush* and ate the Sabbath meal with the scribe. The Besht did not sleep that whole night. In the morning, he gave medications to the scribe and instructed him regarding what treatments to apply, while he went to the synagogue to pray *Shaharit*.

Seeing that the Baal Shem Tov was confident enough to go to the synagogue to pray, the child's mother realized that her son had begun to recover, and she began to sob. The scribe heard her and asked, "Why are you weeping?" "How can I not weep," she said, "when I cursed such a tzaddik!" "Don't weep," he told her, "my master has a good heart; he'll certainly forgive you."

When the Baal Shem Tov returned from the synagogue, he also heard her weeping and asked the scribe the reason. Rabbi Tzvi told him, and the Besht sent the scribe to her, saying, "Tell her not to weep. Let her prepare a fine third Sabbath meal, and I promise her that her little boy will sit with us at the table." And so it was.

Later, the Besht said to Rabbi Tzvi, "The reason I fell down prostrate on the floor was to receive fiery lashes from heaven as a punishment for the oath I swore. But the boy's soul was forced to reenter his body."

When the Baal Shem Tov realized that the child's time to die had arrived and the heavenly decree had been sealed, he nullified the decree by his oath, forcing heaven to return the soul to the boy's body. Because of his brazenness in troubling his Creator, the Besht received a punishment from heaven, but he accepted it willingly, with love, to save a child.[25]

Anger

The Unclean Spirit of Anger

THE BAAL SHEM TOV ONCE WENT TO VISIT HIS CLOSE DISCIPLE, RABBI Baruch of Kaminka. When the Besht arrived at his home, Rabbi Baruch was inside angrily rebuking his servants. When they told him that the Besht was at the door, he dropped everything and went to greet him. The Besht looked at him carefully, and said to him, "If I didn't know you well and know that you live here, I wouldn't have recognized you, for an unclean spirit of bloodshed has clothed you from head to toe because of your anger." Then the Besht said, "From now on, I resolve never again to become angry, even with my gentile servant, Alexei."

Rabbi Baruch was disfigured spiritually by his anger, but when the Besht saw someone else's poor behavior and its consequences, he learned a lesson *for himself.*[26]

Pregnant Potential

A CERTAIN JEW IN MEDZIBUZ, WHO WAS INVOLVED IN A FIERCE DISPUTE with his neighbor, rushed into the Baal Shem Tov's *beit midrash* looking for the man, and he was so enraged that he was gnashing his teeth. When he looked around with wild eyes and did not see his enemy, he shouted out, his voice choking with anger, "Where is that miserable wretch? If I get my hands on him, I'll rip him apart like a fish!" He then ran out.

The Besht and his disciples, who were sitting in the *beit midrash*, witnessed this revolting scene. After the man had left, the Besht told his disciples to stand and hold hands forming a circle, with their eyes closed. He then held the hands of those nearest to him. Suddenly, they all groaned in horror—because they actually saw in a vision this Jew cruelly and viciously beating the other. After they sat down again, the Besht explained to them what they had seen. "It's a spiritual principle that everything potential has an immediate effect. It's only because our eyes are weak that we don't see it."

Anger is evil and ugly. And it contains the seed of murder. A person loses his temper and commits an act that may ruin someone else's life and his own life. If we only saw with the Besht's clear vision the way we appear when we are angry and the potential results of our anger, we would surely despise our anger and repent.[27]

The Besht Tells a Tale about Uncontrolled Anger

THE BAAL SHEM TOV ONCE TRAVELED TO A CERTAIN TOWN TO SPEND *Shabbat* there with his hasidim and followers. The whole town was excited by the visit of the famous teacher. But the town rabbi, a sharp scholar and a confirmed opponent of the Besht's new path, refused to greet him despite pressure from some of the town's prominent men, who were greatly impressed by everything that they had heard about the Besht. At the first meal on the night of *Shabbat*, the Besht sat in the *beit midrash* and taught Torah teachings that greatly inspired everyone who heard him. Some of what he said was passed on to the rabbi and he too was impressed; but he still refused to welcome the Besht or to go see him. At the second *Shabbat* meal the next day, the Besht again taught Torah about exalted spiritual matters and revealed awesome Torah secrets. Again, what he said was passed on to the rabbi, who this time was moved to the depths of his soul. Before evening, as darkness descended, the Besht was sitting in the *beit midrash*, fulfilling the *mitzvah* of the third Sabbath meal, as his hasidim and the townspeople sat crowded around him eager to listen to his teaching. Meanwhile, the rabbi, desiring to hear the Besht firsthand, quietly slipped into the dark room without being noticed and stood in a corner so no one would realize he was there. Only the Baal Shem Tov himself, with his holy spirit, sensed the rabbi's presence and knew that he had joined them.

Then the Besht began to tell a story. "There was a certain rabbi who was a sharp and accomplished Torah scholar, who every year, from the beginning of the month of *Nissan* and on, immersed himself in one of the most difficult sections of the talmudic tractate *Pesahim*, to prepare a penetrating sermon for the upcoming *Shabbat HaGadol*. But because the rabbi this year was so busy with his many obligations before Passover, with people constantly coming to him to ask him questions about *kashrut*, he was not able to finish preparing his speech. So a few days before *Shabbat HaGadol* he decided to leave his home and spend the whole day in the town's *beit midrash*, to work there preparing his talk. He sat and studied with great intensity and then walked the length and the breadth of the *beit midrash* rehearsing his sermon, until he became so overheated in the hot weather that his tongue almost cleaved to his palate he was so thirsty. Just then, he happened to look out of the window and saw a Jewish boy carrying a pail of water on his shoulder. He called the boy to come over, but the boy ignored him and went on his way. The rabbi became very annoyed at the boy. Meanwhile, his thirst became even stronger. A little while later, he again saw the boy passing by with the water bucket on his shoulder. This time too the rabbi called out to him, but again the boy paid no heed to his cry and hurried along on his way. The rabbi became enraged at the boy's chutzpah and in a fit of anger and fury, he ran out of the *beit midrash*, ran after the boy and, catching up with him, gave him a stinging slap on the cheek. Afterward, he discovered that this boy had been orphaned of his father, that his mother was very ill with a high fever, and that the doctors had told him to put a cold water compress on her head and brow every half hour to lower her temperature. So this orphan was running back and forth from the well, bringing water for his sick mother, and paid no attention to the rabbi! Realizing his own lowliness," said the Baal Shem Tov finishing his story, "this rabbi was full of regret that he had hit the boy in his rage and he tried to repent for his sin by means of fasts and self-afflictions . . . but his methods to cleanse himself and atone didn't work. Why? Because this angry rabbi needs a spiritual master; there's no other way to cure his disease."

When the rabbi in the audience heard this, his heart began to pound within his chest and the blood rushed to his face, because he realized, "That's me! That happened to me! And that's the story of my life—losing my temper, flying into a rage, regretting it, but not being able to do anything about it. I can't control my anger or fix myself either!" But aside from himself and the boy he had struck, no one else knew of this incident. How did the Baal Shem Tov know his secret? He must have the holy spirit! After the third meal had concluded, the rabbi went over to the Besht and, with tears in his eyes, greeted him and begged him to accept him as his disciple and teach him how to overcome his sickness of anger.[28]

Ripples

WHEN THE BAAL SHEM TOV WAS ONCE SITTING IN HIS *BEIT MIDRASH* IN the company of a few disciples, he said, "I saw someone commit a serious sin today, and I feel partly responsible. A tzaddik has a share in all the sins of the people. If he commits even a very minor sin, someone else is sure to commit a major sin of that same sort. If you are angry, someone else with less control than you will hit another person, God-forbid, or do even worse, God-forbid. That is one aspect of the teaching of the Sages, 'All Israel are responsible for one another.' So avoid anger or you'll be held accountable for the even worse things that others will do!"[29]

The Anger of a Tzaddik

ONE OF THE BAAL SHEM TOV'S DISCIPLES ONCE ASKED HIM, "MASTER, YOU teach us not to become angry, yet we occasionally see you in an angry mood, when you yell at someone for doing something wrong." "A tzaddik sometimes uses traits characteristic of wicked people," replied the Besht, "but he uses them for the sake of heaven. For example, he may seem angry at bad behavior. But although he shows anger outwardly, inwardly he's still joyful and laughing. He may appear angry when he's rebuking someone, but inside he's not only not angry, he's not even annoyed or upset."

"But there's something else involved here that you should understand," continued the Besht. "There's a doctor who has expert knowledge of the physical makeup of different people. He can accurately diagnose a sick person's condition and prescribe strong drugs that are so dangerous that someone could actually die from taking them, God-forbid. But this doctor has the expertise to know that this person with this condition needs this particular drug in this or that exact dosage. Another doctor who's not as knowledgeable, however, is not permitted to use these powerful drugs, because he could easily make an error in the dosage and kill someone, God-forbid. I can use anger and rebuke and even humiliate someone when necessary because, thank God, I know what I'm doing. It's not for everyone to act like me."[30]

The Proofreader and His Wife

🔥 THE BAAL SHEM TOV WAS VISITING THE TOWN OF CHEMELNICK, WHERE there lived a proofreader whose wife was sick. The Besht was staying at the home of the head judge of the rabbinic court. When the proofreader came to ask the Besht to heal his wife, not only did the Besht decline, but he got angry at the man and spoke to him harshly. This was difficult for the rabbi and, in the evening, when they were walking together, he asked the Besht, "Why didn't you want to heal the proofreader's wife?" "I didn't want to heal her because she's a *tzaddeket*," replied the Besht, "and her illness is protecting the whole town from robbers hiding in the nearby forest, waiting to rob from and murder everyone here. Soldiers have already been sent to deal with them and they'll arrive in three days. As soon as the robbers are captured or removed, she'll recover and return to health." The rabbi continued to ask, "And why were you angry at the proofreader?" "I saw judgments hovering over him," said the Besht, "and my anger dissipated them."

The Baal Shem Tov lived on a plane different from normal human beings and his actions could not always be easily understood. The mystic tradition tells us that sometimes a person is under a "cloud" of heavenly judgments (accusations) that may cause bad things to happen to him. A great tzaddik like the Besht can see this and can disperse the "cloud" by acting harshly, by yelling at the person, and so on. The Torah says that there is no one who is wholly righteous and never sins. But one should not quickly judge a great tzaddik like the Baal Shem Tov.[31]

Divine Providence with a Leaf

🔥 ONE SUMMER DAY THE BESHT ORDERED THE HORSES HARNESSED TO HIS coach and took a few of his disciples for a ride in the countryside. After traveling for a while, they stopped at a pleasant spot and climbed down for a short stroll. They then sat under a tree, next to a newly ploughed field with row after row of ridges and furrows.

The Besht spoke to them about divine providence, how everything that happens is from God's hand alone, and how He provides for every living thing. He said, "Divine providence controls every detail of existence. If the wind carries a fallen leaf from one place to another, it is by divine providence, and the number of times the leaf rolls and the exact spot where it comes to rest are also determined by divine providence. God provides the sustenance for every living thing and for our livelihood too, as it says in the Talmud: 'He provides sustenance for every creature, from the long-horned wild ox to the tiniest insect eggs.' If He provides for the needs of even the smallest of creatures, the worms and insects, why should we trouble ourselves worrying about our livelihood? We should believe and trust with complete faith that our Heavenly Father will provide for our needs too."

Then the Baal Shem Tov pointed out to them a leaf that was being blown by the wind from one place to another. It soon came to rest on a ridge near them and rolled no more. The Besht kept his glance fixed on the leaf, and his disciples did so too. Then, as they looked on with rapt attention, a worm slowly crawled out of the earth and began to chew on the leaf. After having listened to the profound words of their holy master, and watching the scene before them, they felt that they were seeing with their own eyes how divine providence controls every movement in Nature and had brought the worm the food it needed to live. They felt certain, too, that providence had arranged for this very scene to unfold before their eyes to illustrate their holy teacher's lesson.[32]

A Thirsty Disciple

THE BAAL SHEM TOV AND HIS DISCIPLE, RABBI MENDEL OF BAR, WERE once traveling in the Besht's coach through a dry and desolate region without having brought any water with them. Rabbi Mendel became very thirsty and said, "Rebbe, I'm parched. I need something to drink." The Besht did not answer and they continued on their way. After some time, the disciple's thirst became even more urgent, and he said anxiously, "Rebbe, I'm very, very thirsty. I'm worried that if I don't get something to drink soon, I'll be in danger."

The Baal Shem Tov said to him, "Don't you believe that the Creator, blessed be He, foresaw at the creation of the world, every future event? Even your thirst at this moment was foreseen and is known to Him. Certainly, He prepared water for you to drink. If you have unwavering trust in Him, He'll bring it to you." Rabbi Mendel, who was agitated, did not speak for a while, until he regained his composure and absorbed what his master had said. Then he exclaimed, "Rebbe, I believe!" "Then wait just a little while longer!" said the Besht.

After traveling some distance farther, they saw a man riding in a wagon and coming toward them. When they met, the man asked them if they had seen his lost horses, which he had been searching for for three days. They told him no, and asked him if he had any water with him. He said he did, and gave them some water to drink.

After he had gone, Rabbi Mendel asked the Besht, "Master, if it was the divine will that this man be here to give me water, why did he have to travel for three days?" The Besht replied, "God, blessed be He, made him set out earlier, so that if you had had absolute trust, your need would have been fulfilled immediately."[33]

Feeding the World

THE BAAL SHEM TOV ONCE SAID THAT, WITH HIS COMPLETE AND TOTAL trust in God, he could feed and sustain the whole world, but he had no cook to prepare such a large quantity.

The Besht had enough faith and trust to save the world, but he had no disciple with the total faith and trust in him to "cook" what he could provide, who had the vessels to draw his light down to all those who needed it.[34]

A Debate with a Misnagid

ALTHOUGH THE BAAL SHEM TOV'S FAME WAS SPREADING RAPIDLY, AND his hasidim were proclaiming his greatness, there were many who opposed him. One of his most vociferous opponents, a rabbi of great Torah knowledge, wisdom, and piety, even made it his custom, when saying in the morning prayers, "Blessed is our God, who has created us for His glory, and separated us from those who go astray"— to always thank God for granting him his part in opposing the Besht. Nevertheless, he began to crave a face-to-face meeting with the Baal Shem Tov, so that he could debate the Besht, to bring him back from the false path he had chosen and was misleading others to follow. The rabbi traveled to Medzibuz and, throughout the journey prayed, "O God, save me from the clutches of this sect, that I not fall into heresy through them!"

The Baal Shem Tov, who had heard of this rabbi's bitter opposition, received him warmly when he arrived—for the Besht always treated his opponents graciously, without taking offense—greeting him and inquiring about his welfare and the welfare of his town. Afterward, the Besht invited him to speak freely and criticize him or his religious path. "Please don't spare me," he said, "because if I don't know what you object to, I won't be able to defend myself. Since we're both seeking the truth, it shouldn't make any difference to us who wins our debate, for what do false honor or the pride of victory count, compared with the obligation we both have to honor God?"

After pausing to consider how to best present his arguments, the rabbi said, "Let me say at the outset that if I speak too harshly during our debate, please forgive me. The Torah tells us to avoid flattery and not respect persons, especially when discussing basic matters of faith. The most serious questions I have to ask you are these: First, we've been told that you claim to possess some sort of exclusive, exalted secret about divine service that was not revealed to the sages of previous generations, and which can only be grasped by someone with a uniquely elevated soul. Whether this 'secret' is something new or added to our faith, either way you'll be judged by the heavenly court, for anyone who innovates or adds to Judaism's essential tenets is either a heretic or he violates the commandment not to add to the Torah. Second, we've been told that you say that Torah mysteries are revealed to you from heaven, and that anyone who interprets the Torah using his own intellect, without heavenly inspiration, is engaged in a worthless activity. To us, this seems like impudent nonsense, as if you are a prophet with the holy spirit and all the other Torah scholars are inferior to you. Third, almost all the sermons and teachings that we've heard in your name seem to have as their main object to lessen people's reverence for the revealed Torah and to insult the rabbis and scholars who study the Torah day and night." After opening the debate this way, the rabbi waited for the Besht's reply.

The calm expression on the Besht's face made it clear that he felt he would have no trouble answering the rabbi's questions. "First of all, my friend, you should know that my basic belief is that the glory of the Holy One, blessed be He, fills the earth, and that He is actually with me, and with anyone who seeks His presence. What I teach is how to attain this awareness in actual experience—by constantly remembering that God is with you and never letting this thought out of your mind even for a moment. And 'in the way a person wants to go, heaven leads him.' As I pursued this goal in my earlier years, I saw that I was being given divine help in everything I strived to achieve, and by God's will, I merited to see and hear awesome and wondrous things. With each step I took, I saw Godliness revealed, and I found that Godliness can be seen by the eyes of the mind. In everything that happened, I clearly perceived that the world is directed by divine providence, in even its smallest details. And because of the intensity and constancy of my spiritual quest at that time, even my worldly activities became equal to Torah study, prayer, and *mitzvot*, because I engaged in them with total dedication and devotion.

"Anyone who calls what I teach a 'new' way or an 'addition' to Judaism is completely mistaken. There's nothing new or added in what I teach. It's simply what we've received from our holy ancestors and rabbis. I've only tried to reinforce what's been forgotten over the years by many of the Torah scholars and by the rest of our people.

"Let me explain: We all know that faith in God's existence is the basis of the whole Torah. Anyone who says that there's no order or wisdom or purpose, and that random events produced this world, is lacking in intelligence. The Torah never even addresses those who deny God's existence. Leaving atheists aside then, there are four ascending levels of faith: First, there are those who say that they believe in God, but deny divine providence. But what does it matter if they believe in a Creator who's not involved with the world, which goes its own way without His help? What do we need a God like that for, since His existence is of no consequence? Practically, there's little difference between those who hold this view and atheists.

"A person who truly believes, realizes that this world points to a perfect God for whom nothing is impossible. He understands that God each day renews the work of creation. A faith like this is enough to guarantee adherence to the Torah and the fulfillment of its commandments. However, those who hold such a belief often mistakenly imagine God as sitting high above in heaven and descending only on rare occasions, but, generally, leaving people to do as they please without any interference on His part. Nevertheless, they have a strong faith in divine providence since they believe that God watches the world from on high, and they know that He has the power to reward and punish. So their belief leads them to be religious and keeps them from sinning.

"Above this class of believers are those who realize that the Holy One, blessed be He, has caused His *Shechinah* to dwell below on earth, that the Torah's letters are supernal lights, that the ancient Temples were filled with God's radiant glory, just like the houses of Torah study and synagogues today; that the dreams of the tzaddikim are sometimes visions, that a true tzaddik or hasid sometimes hears a heavenly voice, and that a holy spirit rests on him. Most of the more pious religious people are believers of this kind.

"But there's an even higher level, when a person realizes that the Torah's sole purpose is to lead him to faith in the perfect unity, the belief that there's no ultimate reality to anything in existence other than God's essence. Even what appears at first sight to be a separately existing thing is actually completely Godliness, and everything that happens—although it has natural causes or is due to the free choice of human beings—yet its inner cause is divine providence. After becoming aware of God's infinite ability and power, it's not hard to believe that He can hide Himself so as to be revealed and concealed, visible and invisible, at the same time. When looking at a created object, nonbelievers see only its superficial exterior, but intelligent believers see its interior divine reality. They find within every thing the divine power that keeps it in existence and gives it all its qualities.

"I'm sure you know the famous story of Rabbi Akiba, who was traveling with his donkey, a rooster to wake him for divine service, and a torch for protection and nighttime Torah study. When he arrived at a certain town and tried to find a place to lodge, there was no room in the local inn and the innkeeper made no attempt to accommodate him. 'Everything that God does is for good,' said Rabbi Akiba, and he went to sleep in an open field outside the town. That night, a lion devoured his donkey, a wildcat ate his rooster, and a wind blew out his torch. 'Everything God does is for good,' he repeated each time with the same trust in God. Later that night, foreign troops raided the town and took captive all the people in the inn. If his donkey had brayed, or his rooster crowed, or his torch had been lit, the troops would have discovered him. If he'd been in the inn, they would have taken him captive too. He said, 'This is what is meant by the pious saying: "Everything that God does is for good."'

"Certainly," said the Besht to the rabbi, "these were all separate, independent events that happened to Rabbi Akiba: The lion and wildcat were predators that killed because of their hunger; the wind was an act of Nature; and the innkeeper acted by free will. If these things had happened to someone who wasn't pious, he would have considered them as due to natural causes and attributed everything to chance; but Rabbi Akiba saw nothing except the hand of God. When the innkeeper didn't offer him a place to sleep, he said, 'Everything that God does is for good,' not supposing that the innkeeper's free choice in any way denied the deeper divine causality. So too with the other 'natural' causes that might afflict anyone who sleeps out in the open where there are wild animals. All Rabbi Akiba saw was Godliness face-to-face.

"Let me give you another example of a series of incidents that occurred to someone I know, who was suddenly awakened by a mosquito bite, jumped out of bed, and ran behind the porch of his house to relieve himself. Half asleep, he crashed so hard into a barrel of water that it overturned and spilled onto the ground. He immediately realized that at that moment some smouldering coals that had begun to set the house on fire were put out by the water. When he got back inside, he found that the roof beam above where he'd been sleeping, had fallen on his bed!

"If this man weren't religious, he would have considered this only an amazing but random series of coincidences, separate events, each of which had no relation to the other, and certainly not with all the others. But a religious person who believes with simple faith, sees in a sequence of incidents like this, Godliness face-to-face. When during his lifetime he's seen things like this two or three times, his faith becomes stronger, and he attributes to divine providence even matters that are less obvious. Finally, he fully adopts a pious perspective and testifies without any doubt or hesitancy that God exists and there is none other, blessed be He, and that the verse, 'There is none but Him,' is literally true, according to its plain and simple meaning.

"Our thoughts also are Godliness. The countless thoughts that flit through a person's mind every moment have no reality; there's no need to ask why they come or what their purpose is. But thoughts that linger somewhat . . . the pious view is that each is a message and a heavenly reminder of something important; it's come into a person's mind with a purpose. A man of faith should believe that heaven is showing him by subtle hints things necessary for his soul.

"The Rabbis say that everything happens by divine guidance, that an angel hits each blade of grass and commands it, 'Grow, grow!' People of pure and holy vision see, as if with their eyes, each angel—that is, the divine vitality and power—when it strikes the blade of grass; and they hear, as if with their ears, the voice of each angel when it calls out, 'Grow, grow!' These awakened ones hear all the heavenly proclamations that go forth and echo throughout the world.

"Many religious people think that only certain special places are sanctified, but those with a deeper understanding realize that all places are holy. They know that not only prophecies and visions come from heaven, but every spoken word is a message from God, and that by reflection a person can find in it a divine purpose and intention. Someone on this spiritual level can see mountains of meanings even in events that appear trivial to others. To holy people who've grasped this secret, that everything is holy, it's not important whether they pray in a synagogue or in a forest. When they are meditating in *d'vekut* with the Creator of the world, blessed be He, they see no difference between words of Torah and the offhand remarks and idle conversation of anyone on the street. Although the speaker may be unaware of the significance of his own words, that doesn't contradict the fact that the One who gave man a mouth and the ability to speak has put in his mouth the words he utters, and they can have many meanings. Holy people in a state of *d'vekut* hear only the divine inner voice; and they become so attuned that, even when they fall from their *d'vekut*, they still hear in others' speech only the inner voice arousing them to return to their divine service. A person on the highest level of faith sees no difference between studying holy books and reflecting on the words of a child or a gentile, or on a thought that entered his mind and was slow to leave—to him they're all words of Torah. If he sees that a thought about worldly matters, or one that comes from his evil inclination or lust, keeps returning to his mind—he takes it as a heavenly sign. When he feels an urge to expand some seed of an idea that can't yet be clothed in speech or even in a clear concept, it's a sign that this thought belongs to him in a special way, that it's linked to his soul's root and contains a heavenly message.

"What is my view about rabbis and teachers of Torah? A teacher should only speak when he's completely convinced of the truth of what he wants to communicate, for 'What comes from the heart, enters the heart.' And he should only teach what he knows from his own spiritual experience. He himself must be on the spiritual level that he's speaking about; any virtues that he praises must be reflected in his own life. That's my own practice and that's what I encourage among my followers.

"Most rabbis and Torah scholars have abandoned what's essential and instead waste their time finding farfetched solutions to remote talmudic and halachic 'problems'; instead of studying and teaching in order to spiritually elevate the generation, they create convoluted arguments about trivial matters. I revere the rabbis and scholars, and respect their Torah knowledge, but they're making a terrible mistake by doing this, because the simplest Torah discussion about piety and ethics is better than all their complicated talmudic analyses. 'Happy is the generation whose great men listen to reproof,' because even the greatest of the great have some fault that needs correction or a virtue that needs improvement."

Just then a gentile cooper with a bunch of hoops around his neck knocked on the window and asked if there were any split buckets or barrels that needed repair. "No thanks," said the Baal Shem Tov, "everything's in fine condition." "Look carefully," insisted the cooper, "and I'm sure that you'll find things that need fixing." The Baal Shem Tov then turned to the rabbi and said, "Isn't this man a heavenly messenger? He's repeating what I was just saying: that even someone who thinks he's without faults will find, after looking carefully, flaws in his character and behavior that need improvement." After asking the cooper to return later when there would be more time to check for items that needed repair, the Besht said to the rabbi, "I believe with perfect faith that there's no such thing as coincidence. So I'm certain that this gentile interrupted me at this exact moment, to remind me of what I'm constantly meditating on.

"I remember seeing an interpretation in a holy book about God's words to Moses: 'Get you up from the midst of this congregation'—that every Jew should consider himself elevated above the congregation of all other Jews. A true tzaddik must nullify himself completely and act only according to what he thinks is right, even if great Torah scholars disagree with him. Everyone should worry about himself and his own soul, without concerning himself about whether his views agree with those of others. I know that my teachings have brought me many critics, but 'Where there is a desecration of God's name and honor, we do not worry about the honor of the rabbis.' So, my friend, I've tried to explain to you my essential views; I hope that I've answered your questions. If you accept what I've said, I'd like to invite you to stay as a guest in my home for a while, and I'll spend as much time with you as I can, until you're able to absorb these teachings fully."

The rabbi, who had bowed his head in concentration and stood unmoving all the time the Besht was speaking, now paced back and forth, while considering how to respond; then he began. "I find most of what you say reasonable. But your belief that even chance conversations are words of Torah, that gentiles can be heavenly messengers and their words prophecy, I consider contemptible; for according to your view, holiness can rest on heresy or evil, and the *Shechinah* can be revealed even in sinful thoughts. No rational person can tolerate such a view and the Torah totally rejects it. Anyone who accepts this perverted perspective is destined to be punished for it. I certainly can't accept it!"

"It's not a matter of what you *can* accept," replied the Baal Shem Tov forcefully, "but what you *want* to accept. You *can*, but you don't *want* to accept this viewpoint. It all depends on your will and desire. Instead of saying, 'I can't,' say, 'I don't want to'; then you'll be speaking the truth." "No," said the rabbi, "because when you claim that the conversation of a gentile in the marketplace can be the Word of God, as if it were a prophecy or a revelation of the *Shechinah*, that's something I simply can't accept or agree with. "You can, you can," insisted the Besht. "You simply don't want to." With these words, the debate and discussion ended.

The rabbi left the Baal Shem Tov's house and was ready to return home to his own city. As he walked back to his inn, he came across a gentile peasant whose cart, loaded with rocks, had turned over on its side. "Jew!" he called out, "Please come over here and help me lift this cart. It's too heavy for me!" "I don't have the strength; I'm weak," the rabbi replied. "I can't help you." "You can," said the peasant angrily, "you just don't want to!" These words so astonished the rabbi that he did not know whether to try to help the man, or run immediately back to the Baal Shem Tov to tell him what had happened. He helped the man first and also called over a few passersby, for them to lend their assistance. When they succeeded in righting the cart, and the peasant went on his way, the rabbi returned to the Besht's house, his heart pounding in his chest; but he was still uncertain whether or not to believe.

When he entered, the Besht listened to the story the rabbi breathlessly recounted and said, "Maybe now you understand what I meant when I said that you can but don't want to, because this subject has become clear to others of my followers too from incidents like the one that happened to you."

The rabbi decided to stay in Medzibuz for a few more days, in order to continue discussing this profound topic of divine providence with other disciples of the Baal Shem Tov. And he resolved to look with open eyes at everything that happened to him, as the Besht had told him. In a short while, he became a devoted hasid of the Baal Shem Tov.[35]

A *Defective* Mezuzah

 THE BAAL SHEM TOV ONCE VISITED THE CITY OF NEMIROV. ONE DAY, when he was going from one room to another in the house where he was staying, he mistakenly opened the door to the cellar and began to enter. After realizing his error, he told them to check the *mezuzah*. Someone asked him, "If a person goes the wrong way, should he immediately attribute it to some cause? Maybe it's just an accident." "I don't believe in accidents," replied the Besht. "One should have faith that everything that happens occurs by divine providence, and not attribute anything to chance or accident."[36]

His Grandchildren from Edel

TEN YEARS AFTER HER MARRIAGE, THE BESHT'S DAUGHTER EDEL HAD HER first child, a son, Moshe Hayim Ephraim. Then she gave birth to a girl, Feiga, and years later to another boy, Baruch. So Moshe Hayim Ephraim, Feiga, and Baruch were the Besht's three grandchildren from his holy daughter, Edel.[37]

The Day of Judgment

AT THE END OF ONE ROSH HASHANAH, THE BAAL SHEM TOV WAS WITH his young grandson, Ephraim, and described to him what happens in heaven on that day. "The Patriarchs—Abraham, Isaac, and Jacob—and all the Seven Shepherds*, stand before the King of Judgment, showing him all the merits of the Jewish people, all the *mitzvot* and good deeds they did the whole year. Our teacher Moses, peace be upon him, is there too, acting like a middleman, rushing back and forth, bringing in all the merits, and watching carefully to make sure that no accusing angels or sins can come in." After vividly describing the scene to the wide-eyed boy, the Besht said to him, "Isn't that nice?"[38]

Lifting up the Prayers

ONCE, IN THE SYNAGOGUE AFTER THE MORNING SERVICE, THE BAAL SHEM Tov taught his disciples about prayer. He said, "If a person prays without vitality, his prayers can't ascend to heaven and are cast into the treasury of defective holy things. But if at a later time, he becomes aroused and even once prays as he should, all the earlier prayers that had remained below for years latch onto that prayer, and they all ascend and are received with favor by the Holy One, blessed be He. The great advantage of praying with a tzaddik is that he's able to lift up the prayers of other people that wouldn't otherwise have the power to rise, and to take prayers that have already been cast aside into the treasury of defective holy things and raise them up."[39]

---

* The three Patriarchs, and David, Aaron, Moses, and Joseph.

Word for Word

🔥 ANOTHER TIME, WHEN THE BAAL SHEM TOV SERVED AS PRAYER-LEADER, he told the congregation, "Whoever wants his prayers to ascend to heaven should pray with me word for word." So when he recited the hymn *Adon Olam* (Lord of the world) and said *Adon* (Lord), they said *Adon*; when he said *olam* (of the world), they said *olam*.[40]

Waiting for a Powerful Prayer

🔥 ONE YOM KIPPUR, THE BAAL SHEM TOV DELAYED RECITING THE FINAL *Ne'ilah* prayer. He later explained that a certain sinful man in the western lands had repented from the depths of his soul, and his repentance was greatly valued in heaven. This man had said, "God, there's no one in the world who needs to repent more than me!" The Besht said that he delayed *Ne'ilah* so he could join this powerful prayer to the prayers of the rest of the Community of Israel, and elevate them all together.[41]

The Prayers of Eighty Years

🔥 AT THE END OF ONE YOM KIPPUR, THE BESHT SAID THAT HIS PRAYERS THAT day had raised up all the rejected prayers that had been cast aside for eighty years—and now he had elevated them to their proper place.[42]

He Hears Torah from God Himself but Fears the Pit

🔥 ONE SABBATH EVENING, THE BAAL SHEM TOV WAS WITH HIS GRANDSON Ephraim and after hugging and kissing the boy was explaining to him the verse: "Who shall go up for us to heaven and bring it [the Torah] to us, that we may hear it and do it?" He said, "Ephremele, I swear to you that there's someone in this world who can go up to heaven and hear Torah, not from an angel and not from a seraph*, but from the mouth of the Holy One, blessed be He, and His *Shechinah*—yet he still doesn't trust himself that he won't be pushed away. Because the least bit of pride can cause a person to be cast into the fathomless pit, may God save us."[43]

---

* An exalted and fiery angel.

Having This World and the World-to-Come

🔥 THE BAAL SHEM TOV ONCE SAID TO SOMEONE, "IF YOU RECEIVE EVERYTHING that happens to you with love for God, you'll have both this world and the World-to-Come." The man answered, "May God, blessed be He, help me to receive everything with love." "Well spoken," said the Besht.

When a person accepts everything that happens to him, even what seems bad, with love, he has "this world"—he enjoys his life now. Because of his piety, he also inherits the World-to-Come. The Besht taught his followers to have faith and rely on God in all things. If so, this man was right—as the Besht acknowledged—to ask God's help to attain faith and trust. One must certainly train oneself by saying, when bad things happen, "Everything God does is for good." But one must also pray to be able to take this to heart and actually receive everything with love. One can only learn to rely on God by relying on God's help in attaining this precious, pious quality.[44]

Trusting in God's Goodness

🔥 TWO GREAT DISCIPLES OF THE BAAL SHEM TOV, RABBI YAAKOV YOSEF OF Polnoye and Rabbi Nachman of Horodenka, were once traveling from Nemirov to Medzibuz, to spend the Sabbath with their master. On the way, they came up behind a carriage that was having problems with its wheels and moving very slowly. When the two rabbis saw that a high government official was inside, they were afraid to pass it on the side of the road, so they also had to travel slowly behind it. "*Oy, oy,*" said Rabbi Yaakov Yosef, "This is causing me grief. If this keeps up, we won't reach the Baal Shem Tov for the Sabbath." Then, remembering his piety, he muttered, "Everything God does is for good." Rabbi Nachman said, "I trust that this is good and for good. It's not only 'for good' later, it's 'good' now too, you'll see!" "God-willing," said his friend.

As they traveled on, they came to a narrow section of the road where there was no place to go off to the side on the right or left. One wagon had broken down and many others—all loaded with barrels of milk—had backed up behind it unable to pass. But when the official's carriage reached the spot, he yelled at them to clear the way for him, and the gentiles had to unload the milk barrels from the disabled wagon and push it to the side. Then, immediately, all the other wagons were able to travel, including the official's carriage and the rabbis' carriage. A short distance farther on, the official turned off onto another road and the two rabbis were able to speed ahead on their way to Medzibuz. At that moment, Rabbi Yaakov Yosef also realized that the earlier delay of getting caught behind the official's slow-moving carriage was "for good," because the men had only moved the broken wagon out of the way because of him; who knows how long they would have been delayed otherwise?

When they recounted the incident to the Baal Shem Tov, he told them that they were on different levels in their belief in divine providence. "You," he said to Rabbi Yaakov Yosef, who had been upset, "felt that the delay caused by the official's carriage was bad now, bad in itself, though you reminded yourself of your trust that it would be for good later. But you," he said to Rabbi Nachman, "trusted that it was good at that very moment. Although the good would only be revealed later, your trust was so strong, you felt certain that what happened was good now. There are different levels in faith and trust," said the Besht. "In the story of Rabbi Akiba with his donkey, the rooster, and the torch, he said after each seemingly bad event, 'Everything God does is for good.' He trusted that what seemed bad would eventually be for good. Yet, though he trusted that good would come of it, he felt upset as it occurred. When a person has this kind of belief, God fulfills his faith and trust by turning the bad to good. But there's an even higher level of faith and trust, as in the story of Rabbi Akiba's master, Nachum Ish Gam-Zu*, who always said, 'This *also* is for good'—that is, what happened is *itself* good; there's nothing bad about it. He didn't just console himself that in the future good would come of it. He felt at the very moment the seemingly bad event occurred that *this* also *is good now* and that what seems bad is really *better* than it would be if there were revealed good. When a person has this great faith and trust, God does more than in the other case: He changes what seems bad to be even better than if it had been revealed good. It's like what happened to both of you with the official's carriage. Not only wasn't it bad, it was very good, because if the official hadn't been there, the broken-down wagon wouldn't have been cleared from the road. If something that seems bad happens to a Jew, God-forbid, he should consider it right then and there to be actually and certainly good. Then, God, in the merit of his strong faith and trust, will help him by turning what seems bad to the best good possible. But what is the very highest level of faith and trust? The truth is, the thought that something is bad should never even occur to us at all. It's not enough to say: 'This *also* is for good.' Why should we even have to say 'also'?—since *there isn't anything bad at all. What is bad is good.*" After pausing, he looked at both of his disciples one after the other and said, "*There is no bad or evil.*" They then realized that this was the exalted level in faith of their holy master.[45]

This Is Not for Good

RABBI NACHMAN OF HORODENKA'S PIOUS CUSTOM WAS TO SAY ABOUT everything that happened to him, that it was "good and for good." His faith was as strong as an iron pillar. Once, when the Polish army barracked soldiers in Jewish homes in Medzibuz, which caused great inconvenience and suffering, the Besht told Rabbi Nachman to pray for this to stop. Rabbi Nachman answered piously, "This too

---

* Nachum "This-also."

is from heaven. It's good and for good." The Besht became angry at him and said, "I'm glad you didn't live in the time of Haman, who tried to destroy all the Jews, because you would have said that that decree too was for good. And Mordechai wouldn't have shaken the worlds in prayer to annul the decree. The only good thing that happened then was that Haman was hung. Say: 'It's good' for your own affairs, but for others and when a Jewish community is involved, you should pray for their relief. A tzaddik realizes that suffering comes from a heavenly decree, but he also knows that his task is to pray to nullify the decree." The Baal Shem Tov himself constantly prayed for the annulment of decrees against the Jewish people.[46]

Trust and Simplicity

A HASID ONCE ASKED THE BAAL SHEM TOV TO PRAY FOR HIM TO ATTAIN trust in God. The Besht took a small piece of parchment, wrote some words on it, sealed the parchment in an amulet and gave it to the hasid to carry on his person. Years later they opened the amulet and found written in it Rashi's comment on the verse, "Be simple with the Lord your God"—"Walk with Him in simple piety and look only to Him. Do not worry about what will happen in the future, but receive everything that happens with pious innocence. Then you will be with Him and will be His portion."[47]

A Prayer for When Bad Happens

THE BAAL SHEM TOV COMPOSED A PRAYER FOR HIS DISCIPLES TO SAY when bad befell them: "I know that the bad too is for good. But You are God and not a human being, and can turn bad to good. May everything, then, be not the kind of good that is concealed from our understanding, but revealed good, so that what needs fixing will be accomplished through good itself." The Besht himself was on a higher level than this prayer, but this was the level in faith and trust that he encouraged most of his disciples to have and which they could achieve.[48]

The Icicle

ONE COLD, WINTER NIGHT, WHEN THERE WAS SNOW COVERING THE ground and icicles hanging from the roofs, the Baal Shem Tov recited *Tikkun Hatzot* and afterward said, as usual, "Master of the world, I'm healthy, so I can serve You!" Then the Besht's aide and disciple knew it was time to take an axe and accompany his master to the *mikvah*, walking in front of the Besht and lighting the way with a lantern. They entered the *mikvah* building and the disciple broke a hole in the ice with the axe. Then the Besht went down into the frigid water and remained there for almost an hour—immersing himself many times, engaging in many meditations and offering many prayers. Finally, the candle in the lantern began to sputter. "Rebbe," the disciple said, "What should I do? The candle is going out!" "You fool," the Besht answered, "break an icicle off the roof and light it! He who decreed that the wax burn can also make the icicle burn and give light." The disciple did as he was told and held the flaming icicle in his hand for a long while in the *mikvah* and for the walk back. When he reached the Besht's house, he looked down, and all that remained was a little water in the palm of his hand.[49]

Why the Besht's Prayers Were Answered: The Parable of the Shepherd

SOME VERY RELIGIOUS PEOPLE ONCE ASKED THE BAAL SHEM TOV, "RABBI, we also study Torah and pray, and do the *mitzvot* and good deeds, yet, when we make requests in our prayers, they seem to have little effect. But your supplications are heard in heaven and when you ask for something, we see with our own eyes that your prayer bears fruit."

"Let me explain with a parable," replied the Besht. "A prince once lost his way in the woods and, after wandering for hours, finally came to a field where a shepherd was grazing his flock. The prince was famished and exhausted, and when the shepherd saw him he took him into his cottage. But what did a poor shepherd have with which to receive or honor a prince? What could he offer him? So he took out a clean white cloth from his shepherd's pouch and, with great care, spread it over his crude table. He placed a single piece of dry black bread on the cloth and poured water into a clay cup. Then he humbly and reverentially invited the prince to sit down and partake. The prince revived himself with the simple food and drink. Seeing that the prince was exhausted, the shepherd would have wanted to offer him a comfortable place to rest; but he slept on the ground and had no bed. So he gathered some soft grass, carefully placed it on the ground, covered it with his sheepskin coat, and humbly with great reverence asked the prince to please lie down and rest. The prince lay down gratefully and slept a sweet sleep. That was all that the shepherd could offer; he had nothing else with which to honor the prince—no good food and no pillows or sheets for a bed, because a pauper has nothing. But what he was able to do, he did with great reverence. Later," continued the Besht, "when the prince returned home, he ordered his servants to summon the shepherd to his palace, and elevated him above all his ministers. 'Why do you raise up a simple shepherd like this?' they asked. 'Don't we always do everything that you command us?' 'All the honor and greatness that I'm bestowing on him,' said the prince, 'is because of the way he honored me by putting a clean white cloth on his table, by serving me black bread and plain water, and by spreading his sheepskin coat over some grass for a bed.'"[50]

Preparation for Receiving Musar

A MAN ONCE CAME TO THE BAAL SHEM TOV TO LEARN WISDOM AND TO improve his character. The Besht kept the man with him for a year and a half before he even began to instruct him. The Besht explained to him that a person's sins dull his heart, covering it over with layer after layer of thick crust, so that it rejects reproof. Therefore, before he could instruct him by teaching him *musar*, he first had to remove the covering over his heart.[51]

Uncovering One's Heart

THE BAAL SHEM TOV ONCE SAID TO HIS DISCIPLES, "A JEWISH HEART IS alive, but a person has to dig within himself to uncover it. It's like digging a well: Sometimes water is discovered immediately; other times they have to dig for a long while and remove a lot of earth before they find the water."[52]

Rejoicing in Your Portion

A HASID OF THE BAAL SHEM TOV WANTED TO LIVE COMFORTABLY, LIKE A normal person, but also to be properly religious. So he went in to the Besht and said, "Rebbe, I'm not capable of doing anything extraordinary in serving God. Please give me some divine service to concentrate on so that I'll have this world and also the World-to-Come." The Besht answered him, "I'll give you the service of being happy with your portion in this world." "Rebbe," said the man, "that's still very difficult." "That's what I intended," replied the Besht.

The Baal Shem Tov prescribed for the man the easier path in divine service—focusing not on increasing his efforts to do God's will but rather on accepting God's will in the events of his life. Yet, although an ordinary person may not be able to perform the extraordinary divine service of a tzaddik, there is nothing gained spiritually without difficulty, for, as the Rabbis say: "According to the painstaking is the reward."[53]

The Katinka

A WOMAN WENT TO THE BAAL SHEM TOV, WHO WAS VISITING HER TOWN, and begged him to "give" her a baby boy. She had faith that if he gave his blessing it would certainly be fulfilled. "What will you give me?" he said, since people usually

offered a tzaddik a gift for his blessing. She told him that she was poor and had nothing to give—except a *katinka*, an inexpensive fur cape. The Besht told her to give it to
him and then she would have the boy.

The woman went home to get the *katinka* but, as soon as she left, the Baal Shem
Tov got into his coach and began to travel back to Medzibuz. She took the cape and
followed him, walking on foot from city to city, suffering great hardship, until she
finally arrived in Medzibuz. When she entered to see the Baal Shem Tov, he took the
katinka from her, hung it on a peg on the wall, and blessed her that now she would
have a son who would be a great rabbi and tzaddik.

Why did the Baal Shem Tov ask for the poor woman's only possession, and leave
without waiting for her? Because he knew that if she gave him her gift and followed
him with self-sacrifice, her reward would match her effort.[54]

The Besht's Book

AMONG THOSE LISTENING TO THE BAAL SHEM TOV'S TEACHINGS IN
his *beit midrash* in Medzibuz, was someone who, afterward, wrote down everything he heard. One day, the Besht saw a demon walking along holding a book in his
hand. "What is that book you're carrying?" asked the Besht. "It's the one you wrote,"
answered the demon. The Baal Shem Tov then realized that someone was recording
his Torah teaching without his knowledge. He called all of his followers together and
asked them, "Which of you is writing down my Torah?" The one who was doing it
admitted that it was he. When the Besht asked him to show him his notebook, the man
brought it to him. After looking through it, the Besht said, "There's not a single word
here that's mine."

Later, the Baal Shem Tov explained to his disciples, "Since he wasn't listening for
the sake of heaven, an evil spirit entered his heart and twisted everything he heard to
something different from what I said."

After this incident, Rabbi Yaakov Yosef of Polnoye asked and received the Besht's
permission to write down what he heard from his holy master, and he listened and
wrote purely for the sake of heaven.[55]

The Besht Cannot Enter a Synagogue

THE BAAL SHEM TOV ONCE WENT TO A SYNAGOGUE WITH SOME OF HIS
disciples, but as he tried to enter, he moved back, as if rebuffed. He tried to enter
again, but again abruptly moved back as if rebuffed. This happened a few times, to the
surprise of his disciples, who questioned him about it. He said, "This synagogue is full
of prayers, I can't get in!" "Isn't that the best recommendation for a synagogue?" they
said. "The holy *Zohar*," he explained, "says that love and fear of God are 'the two wings
of the bird' that enable prayers to ascend into heaven. Without sincerity, they remain

below on earth. This synagogue is full of prayers. There's no room for me; I can't get in!" The Besht could not bear the stultifying atmosphere of rote religion. When he stood on the threshold of a synagogue, he could tangibly sense the sanctity within, or the lack of it. If he felt an impenetrable emptiness, if he did not feel the radiance of the *Shechinah* inside, how could he enter? Why would he enter? Such places were not for him.[56]

I Know I've Not Even Begun: The Parable of the Treasure

ONE DAY, AFTER *SHAHARIT*, THE BAAL SHEM TOV TOOK SOME OF HIS DISCIPLES to the fields outside Medzibuz and sat down with them under a tree. Then he began to teach them Torah and the words were rejoicing as when they were given at Mount Sinai. In the midst of his teaching, his disciples saw that the Besht's face was shining and the air surrounding him seemed to glow with divine light. Just at that moment, he paused and then said, "When I reach an elevated spiritual state, I know that there's not even a single letter of the Torah within me and that I haven't progressed even a single step in the service of God."

Then he told them a parable. "A man once found an enormous treasure, way beyond his ability to carry. Even if he returned countless times to the site, he'd never be able to carry more than the tiniest fraction of it home. He was overjoyed at the wealth he was able to take back, but he also realized that he had to leave behind thousands of times more.

"When a tzaddik studies Torah for the sake of heaven, he's filled with joy, but he also realizes that he hasn't learned anything compared to what remains, and the more he learns, the more he realizes how little he knows. And when a tzaddik serves God sincerely, and enjoys even the least glimpse of His awesome glory, he realizes that he hasn't even begun to serve Him according to His greatness."

The Besht continued, "The psalm verse says: 'God's Torah is perfect, restoring the soul.' I tell you, the Torah is still perfect; no one has yet touched even the tip of its smallest letter. As of this hour, it's still quite perfect." He went on, "This verse can also be translated and understood another way: 'When God's Torah is studied with perfect simplicity'—that is, when a person studies the Torah with pious innocence, believing that he's not even begun to comprehend its depths, that he hasn't yet plumbed the meaning of even one letter, then 'it restores the soul.'"[57]

Remember God When Studying

THE BAAL SHEM TOV ONCE ENTERED A *BEIT MIDRASH* AND COMMENTED TO a disciple about a scholar sitting there immersed in Torah study, "He's so absorbed in the text that he's forgotten there's a God in the world!"[58]

Scrubbing Off the Logic

THE BAAL SHEM TOV ONCE MET RABBI AVRAHAM OF POLOTZK (LITHUANIA), an elderly scholar who was one of the great *gaonim* of the generation and whose mouth never ceased from study. He had a sharp mind that worked with a powerful logic. He could clearly explain any section of the Talmud. Yet, even when he was eighty years old and studied by himself, he translated the text word by word into Yiddish, like a child, explaining to himself out loud the meaning of each sentence.

The Besht greatly appreciated this childlike quality of the venerable *gaon's* Torah study. But after meeting with Rabbi Avraham, he remarked to his disciples, "A whole troop of angels has a lot of work to do to scrub away the thick crust of logic that covers the pure, childlike words the *gaon* utters when he translates the Talmud for himself. What heaven really delights in is Rabbi Avraham's innocent and childlike love for Talmud study."[59]

Correcting Their Path

THERE WERE FAMOUS RABBIS WHO HAD MANY DISCIPLES AND STUDENTS, and who thought that their heart was burning up with divine service—but when they visited the Baal Shem Tov they realized that they were not on the path of truth. And he instructed them how to correct themselves. They took off their honored rabbinic garments and sat like ordinary people in his *beit midrash*, repenting over all their deeds. Some of these people later became great disciples of the Besht's inner circle.[60]

Lighting a Candle

THE BAAL SHEM TOV ONCE SAID ABOUT A NUMBER OF HIS DISCIPLES, "They're candles but they need to be lit." It was not simply that they did not shine out to others; their divine souls were not shining even within themselves. It is possible for everything to be ready—there is a vessel, a candle, a wick—but there is no light. When these rabbis came to the Baal Shem Tov, they were already great scholars, they were men of deeds, they had purified their character—they had prepared the vessel, but there was no light. The Besht lit up their souls so that they shined.[61]

The Parush *and the White Horse*

A CERTAIN *PARUSH*—WHO SOUGHT A REVELATION OF ELIJAH—DRESSED only in white, was silent except for words of Torah and prayer, drank nothing but water, rolled naked in the snow, and put nails inside his shoes. Yet he did not succeed in attaining a vision of Elijah. He had heard that the Baal Shem Tov did experience such revelations of Elijah, so, on a winter day, with snow covering the ground, he traveled to Medzibuz to ask the Besht why he had not succeeded.

When he came to the Baal Shem Tov, he asked his question. The Besht responded by taking the visitor out into the courtyard. He then told his coach driver Alexei to take his white horse from the stable and bring it to the courtyard, along with a bucketful of water, and let it run free. When the horse was taken out of the stable and smelled the brisk, fresh air, it snorted with delight. When it was led into the snow-covered courtyard and let loose, it first took a drink from the bucket of water and then began to roll in the snow.

"Do you see this horse?" said the Besht. "It also wears white, drinks only water, rolls in the snow, and has nails in its shoes; and it hasn't spoken a single word for ten years—yet it's never had a revelation of Elijah! Why? Because, when all is said and done, it's still just a horse! All these things that you're doing—wearing white, drinking only water and so on—are just external. Don't worry about Elijah; let him reveal himself or not as he wants. What you should worry about is yourself and revealing your own soul."

Later, the Besht explained to his disciples, "Being pious is more about cleaving to God than about neglecting the body and worldly affairs. Instead of fasting from food, eat in the presence of God. Instead of fasting from speech, infuse all of your words—whether of Torah, prayer, or conversation—with holiness. I tell you, having heavenly visions, even of Elijah, is a lesser spiritual level than having a revelation of your own soul, meaning that you are totally authentic and live from your deepest self, your divine soul."[62]

The World of Exchanges

WHEN THE BAAL SHEM TOV ONCE SAW A CERTAIN "HOLY MAN" WHO mortified his body, he said to the disciples who were with him, "In the World of Exchanges, they're mocking him." Asked to explain, he said, "There are intensely pious people whose motives slowly become false. Without their realizing it, they begin to deceive themselves and others. They pridefully seek miraculous powers and visions. Sometimes they're given what they desire. This *parush* is excessively devoted to ritual purity and is detached from worldly affairs; he's had many extraordinary spiritual experiences and visions. But a drop of impure desire for honor has contaminated his motivation—he sought the holy spirit and other spiritual attainments out of pride. Therefore, the spiritual energy created by his deeds flows to the World of Exchanges, and they are mocking him there by bestowing on him higher and higher rungs of these 'mystical' experiences that he wants, to fool and mislead him. Even the slightest deviation from truth can cause a person to lose everything that he's gained in holiness." If not for the Baal Shem Tov, this *parush* would have been lost both in this world and the next. But the Besht had compassion on him and saved him.[63]

His Prayer Answers a Torah Problem

THE *GAON*, RABBI YISRAEL HARIF OF SATINOV, HAD MET THE BAAL SHEM TOV, but did not believe in him. The Besht, for his part, very much wanted to make him a disciple.

Once, Rabbi Yisrael was confounded by an extremely difficult talmudic problem. The Baal Shem Tov, who was visiting Satinov, told him the correct interpretation, according to its plain meaning. Rabbi Yisrael was pleased and appreciated the Besht's help, but remarked, "The interpretation you've given is so good I might've considered becoming your disciple—if only you weren't a *baal shem*"—because he did not think it fitting for a serious Torah scholar to be a faith healer.

After this, Rabbi Yisrael's son became gravely ill and was in bed from before Passover almost until the end of the summer. His wife kept pressing him to visit the Besht, saying, "Doesn't everybody go to the Baal Shem Tov for help, and doesn't he perform miracles for them? Why can't you go to him? Perhaps he'll cure our son!" "Even if there is something to the Baal Shem Tov," he replied, "and he can help, if I travel to him it disrupts my regular schedule of Torah study, and I don't believe that any good can come to our son from my neglecting my Torah study." Like most Torah scholars at the time, Rabbi Yisrael considered any neglect of Torah study a serious sin. He felt that no benefit could come to his son if he committed this "sin" in order to visit the Besht.

Later, when more time had passed and their son remained seriously ill, his wife bothered him without letup, saying she would not stop until he agreed to go to the Baal Shem Tov. "The days of *Selichot* will soon be here," he said, "and the holy books say that it's proper to somewhat reduce one's Torah study then and to increase one's involvement in matters of piety. I'll travel to the Baal Shem Tov then." That was what he did, for although he thought it unworthy that the Besht was a faith healer, when his own son was sick he was forced to go to him.

He traveled to the Baal Shem Tov and arrived at his synagogue on the first night of *Selichot*. When he realized that he had forgotten to take a book of penitential prayers with him, he stood next to the prayer-leader's stand and recited the prayers along with the cantor from one book. The Baal Shem Tov's custom was that he himself would lead the congregation in reciting two prayers: *El Rahum* (Compassionate God Is Your Name) and *Aneinu* (Answer Us). (The Besht once said that if someone else could say those two prayers like him, they would bring the Messiah.) When the congregation reached "Compassionate God Is Your Name," the cantor left the prayer-leader's stand and they waited for the Besht to come up. Rabbi Yisrael was still there next to the stand and, *gaon* that he was, was taking advantage of those few moments to ponder, from memory, a difficult talmudic comment in the *Tosafot** that he had long been

---

* A medieval talmudic commentary that usually takes its start from Rashi's commentary.

unable to understand. He became so absorbed in his thoughts that he did not notice when the Baal Shem Tov came to the stand and began praying. But the moment the Besht began to pray "Answer Us!" the correct interpretation of the *Tosafot* fell into Rabbi Yisrael's mind, for the Besht's prayer had opened for him channels from the fountains of wisdom and his mind was expanded. When the Besht concluded praying "Answer Us!" he said to Rabbi Yisrael with a smile, "My 'Answer Us!' gives a good interpretation of a *Tosafot*, doesn't it?" "I see now," said Rabbi Yisrael, "that you have a part in the Torah of each and every Jew, so I'm ready to become your disciple whole-heartedly, without reservation." Later, the Baal Shem Tov prayed for Rabbi Yisrael's son, who was completely cured. From then on, Rabbi Yisrael Harif was a sworn disciple of the Baal Shem Tov.

The Baal Shem Tov not only opened the knots people encountered in their Torah study, he put them in touch with their soul's Torah. Each Jew has a special and unique connection to the Torah, as the Rabbis say: "Every Jew is connected to one letter in the Torah." By connecting every Jew more closely with his letter, the Baal Shem Tov had a part in everyone's Torah.

At first, the Besht had given *his own* answer to the rabbi's knotty Torah question, but Rabbi Yisrael Harif was not won over. Finally, the Besht showed that he had a part in *the rabbi's* Torah by inspiring *him* with the prayer of "Answer Us!" to receive an answer from heaven. Later, when the Baal Shem Tov cured the rabbi's son, Rabbi Yisrael also appreciated that the Besht was a *baal shem*.

The Baal Shem Tov showed great love for his new disciple, Rabbi Yisrael Harif. When the Besht occasionally visited Satinov, he stayed at Rabbi Yisrael's home. And when he sat at Rabbi Yisrael's *Shabbat* table, he did everything possible to please him, like a father with his only son. He sometimes even kissed Rabbi Yisrael on the forehead out of his great love for him.[64]

Three Times

WHEN THE BAAL SHEM TOV WAS VISITING A CERTAIN TOWN, HE ENTERED the local *beit midrash* on three separate occasions and each time the Torah problems of all the scholars studying there were immediately resolved. When asked about this, he said, "When I arrive, the *Shechinah* arrives with me. And when the *Shechinah* is present, there are no longer any problems."[65]

Speaking to Each One

EVERY NIGHT AFTER THE EVENING PRAYERS, THE BAAL SHEM TOV WENT TO his room and sat behind a table on which were placed two candles (for he said that one candle or three are not good for the eyes, but two are good). He always had on the

table the same books, among them *Mishnayot Kodashim* and *Taharot*, the talmudic trac-
tates *Zevahim* and *Menachot*, the *Zohar*, and the kabbalistic *Sefer Yetzirah*. For an hour
or more, people who needed to speak with him about personal matters were permitted
to enter.

Once, a group of hasidim went in together and stayed there for the whole time. The
Baal Shem spoke to them intimately, giving them spiritual instruction and advice on
how to advance in the ways of God. When they exited, one of them turned to his
friend and told him what the Baal Shem Tov had said to him. The other replied,
"What are you talking about? We went in and left together, and the whole time we
were standing there the Baal Shem Tov spoke only to me and to no one else!" But the
first one insisted that the Besht had spoken just to him the whole time. He was certain
of it. A third overheard their argument and claimed that the Besht had addressed
everything he said to him. Then a fourth said the same, and a fifth, and they discovered
that every one of them had thought that the Besht was speaking to him alone. This
awesome occurrence astonished them all and made them realize that when the Baal
Shem Tov spoke, everyone who heard him felt that he alone was being spoken to, and
that he personally was being addressed.[66]

Seeing Providence

A CERTAIN MAN WHO HAD DIFFICULTY IN UNDERSTANDING THE EXTENT
of divine providence traveled to Medzibuz to ask the Baal Shem Tov about it.
Early one morning, he and the Besht were walking to the synagogue to pray, and they
were discussing the matter.

On the way, they came across a peasant taking a wagon full of hay, to sell in the market. Just then, they saw another man walking in the opposite direction, holding his
hand to his jaw and groaning from what was obviously a painful toothache. As this
man and the peasant with the wagon crossed paths, the man with the toothache
reached out and took a single stalk of grass from the wagon. He put it in his mouth,
stuck it into his gum, and it was evident from his face that his pain was immediately
relieved.

The Baal Shem Tov and his visitor had both been watching this unusual incident,
and the Besht said to him, "Did you see what happened here? There's a kind of grass—
called *ruta*—that cures toothaches, and this man found a stalk of it when he put his
hand to the hay. [Being a *baal shem*, the Besht knew about medicinal herbs.] Someone
might think that the peasant's leading the wagon full of hay is a natural event, and
what's providential is that, today, God arranged for the grass to be there to ease the
man's suffering—but it's much deeper than that. When the Holy One, blessed be He,
created the world, He foresaw and arranged the details of every event: that this man
would have a toothache today, that the peasant would take the hay to market, that
there would be a stalk of *ruta* grass in the hay, that the man would reach into the hay,

that the grass would come to his hand, that he would recognize it for what it was, and that he would use it and be healed."

The visitor was stunned at seeing this incident. And once the Baal Shem Tov explained it, everything seemed so clear. Hearing this teaching about divine providence from a man of perfect faith, the words entered his heart and found a home.[67]

Repenting for One Miracle with Another

WHEN THE BAAL SHEM TOV WAS STILL A YOUNG MAN, HIS KABBALISTIC knowledge and his intense piety and spiritual practice won for him miraculous powers. In his youthful exuberance, he had once tested his powers and wrongly used a divine Name to do a miracle unnecessarily—by crossing the Dniester River standing on a belt. The Besht repented his sin for many years, performing numerous fasts. Finally, he succeeded in fully repairing the spiritual damage, and this is how: He once urgently needed to cross the Dniester River to flee from some Turkish Muslims who were a threat to his life (the river was the border between Poland and Turkey). So he again placed his belt on the water and crossed over on it, this time without using any divine Name, but only by his great faith in the God of Israel.[68]

Simple Faith

AT A *MELAVE MALKA* FEAST, THE BESHT ENCOURAGED HIS DISCIPLES TO strengthen their faith. He said, "Abandon idle doubts, for when you have doubts, God is not with you. It says in the Talmud, 'Are there doubts before God?' The Rosh HaShanah prayers say, 'Certainty is His name; that is His praise.' When you doubt, you're not before God and in His presence. God's glory fills the earth, for the whole world is pervaded by His *Shechinah*. Remember that your doubts are divorcing you from the living God and separating you from the Life of all life. Strive for perfect faith, because doubts cause the flow of divine blessing to cease. And when you achieve *d'vekut* with the Source of all, you transcend all doubting and questioning; when you are in God's very presence, all doubts disappear."

Although the Baal Shem Tov attained extraordinary wisdom and awesome spiritual levels, involving countless visions and revelations, while still in his youth he came to believe that the essence of religion is simple faith. That is why he envied pious common people, whose simple faith became his standard for what he desired to achieve, first for himself and later for his disciples. He once said to his disciples, "After all that I've achieved—all the wisdom, all the spiritual levels—I forget everything and cling to simple faith. I'm a simple fool and believe, for although it's written: 'A simple person believes everything,' isn't it also written: 'God protects the simple'?" When a person of great Torah knowledge and divine wisdom achieves truly simple faith, he becomes very great indeed—like the holy Baal Shem Tov.[69]

Praying for Faith

RABBI PINHAS OF KORETZ, THE BESHT'S YOUNG DISCIPLE, WAS DEEPLY involved in studying the Rambam's books on religious philosophy and became confused in his faith. He realized that he needed to visit the Baal Shem Tov to have his doubts resolved, but did not have enough money for the trip. Just then, he heard that the Besht had arrived in town, and he joyfully ran to the house where his master was staying. When he arrived, he found that all of the Besht's followers had gathered to welcome him, and he was teaching them about faith. He said, "When a person begins to have doubts, he should pray to God to strengthen his faith. This prayer itself will increase his faith, because he's demonstrating his belief that everything, including faith, is in God's hands, and there is not the slightest basis for doubt."

The Besht then explained further by interpreting the story where Moses prayed on the mountain with his arms stretched out to heaven, while Joshua led the people in battle against the Amalekites down below. "Everyone knows that the wicked tribe of Amalek cooled off the Jewish people's fiery faith. When they were at the Red Sea, it's written: 'They believed in God.' Then, as Amalek approached to attack, they became mired in doubts, and questioned: 'Is God with us or not?' At that time, our teacher Moses taught them how to repair the damage they'd done to their faith—by standing on the mountaintop, where everyone could see him, and stretching out his hands in prayer." As he said this, the Baal Shem Tov showed what Moses had done by standing with his own arms raised and turning his gaze to heaven. Seeing his master, the holy Baal Shem Tov, in this pose of total faith, tears began to stream from Rabbi Pinhas's eyes like faucets. He became another man and his faith in God was completely restored.[70]

The Innovation

THE LARGE CITY OF SLUTZK IN LITHUANIA WAS RENOWNED FOR ITS outstanding Torah scholars and great rabbis. Once, when the Baal Shem Tov visited there, he was invited to the dedication of a *beit midrash* and the laying of a foundation stone. The gathering was in the courtyard of the future *beit midrash*, and they greatly honored the Besht and asked him to say words of Torah. In the courtyard was a large foundation stone, which the Jews had brought there by their own efforts, without relying on the workers, to show their devotion to the house of Torah study that they were building. The Baal Shem Tov sat on the stone, which had not yet been placed in the ground, and taught Torah. Among other things, he said, "A stone that a Jew brings for building a *beit midrash* is very precious. The *Midrash* tells how the pious Galilean, Rabbi Hanina ben Dosa, saw the men of his city setting out with their dedicated gifts for the Temple in Jerusalem. Despondent, because he was too poor to afford the kind of offerings they were making, he said to himself, 'Everyone is bringing something to Jerusalem for their vows and freewill offerings, except me!' He then went to the open country outside the town, where he found a large stone, which he cut, chiseled, and polished with his own hands—hopefully, to be used in the structure of the Temple. When it was finished, he went to hire workers to transport the huge stone to Jerusalem, but he soon discovered that the cost was also beyond his means.

"Then, the Holy One, blessed be He, sent him five angels disguised as men, who said that they would transport the stone for him for a small sum, on the condition that he also put his hand to the work. But the moment he touched his finger to the stone, he and it were suddenly, miraculously, in Jerusalem, and the men had disappeared. Being scrupulously honest, and not knowing what to do with the wages he had promised the workers, Rabbi Hanina ben Dosa went to the Sanhedrin* in the Temple, to ask the rabbis. When they heard what had happened, they told him, 'It seems that angels have taken your stone up to Jerusalem.' So," said the Besht, applying the story, "the foundation stone you've brought here with your own sweat and effort is very precious to God."

The Besht's teaching greatly pleased his audience, most of whom were simple laborers. However, when he ended his talk, the town's scholars turned the discussion in a different direction and asked him what was new in his approach to the Torah. They said, "We also studied Torah before you came. Doesn't it say: 'For I have given to you good doctrine'? The Torah has always been good, even before you arrived on the scene. Why is anything new necessary?"

The Besht answered them, "I have not come to innovate or teach anything new, only to explain the simple meaning of the scriptures. In fact, let me explain the meaning of the verse you've just mentioned: 'For I have given to you good doctrine; forsake not My Torah.' The 'good doctrine' is the revealed Torah. But by studying that part of the Torah a person may come to think that the Torah, which is 'given to you,' is *yours*, and he forgets the Giver of the Torah. Through his Torah insights and interpretations, he becomes proud. Instead of you becoming the Torah's, the Torah becomes yours, and a person feels he even has the right to look for loopholes and leniencies to evade the demands of *halacha*. Arrogantly wielding his intellect, he sees problems and difficulties in the text that are simply not there. Then, because he has forgotten the Giver of the Torah, his faith is weakened and he begins to have questions and doubts about divine providence; for example, he asks, 'Why do the wicked prosper?'

"But the second half of the verse provides the cure for this disease. It says: 'forsake not *My* Torah.' When you study the Torah according to its inner meaning, realizing that it is *God's* wisdom, then you study with humility. You are the Torah's; you remem-

---

* The supreme Jewish political, religious, and judicial body during the time of the Second Temple.

ber God every minute and believe in divine providence. Then you come to the level of 'forsake not': You never lose yourself in the subject matter of your Torah study, forgetting God's presence. You don't forsake the Giver of the Torah, and He doesn't forsake you. When you study this way, you no longer seek leniencies or create artificial problems by idle speculation." Then, looking at them all intently, the Baal Shem Tov concluded, "The greatest 'innovation' I teach is one thing only—simple faith."[71]

Without Questions or Doubts

THE BAAL SHEM TOV HAD CHOSEN HIS GENTILE SERVANT AND COACH driver, Alexei, because he was a very simple person who would not question or pry into what his master was doing. That way the Besht could maintain secrecy about his piety and his mystical doings. Alexei just followed his master's orders, even if they were peculiar. He did not question the Baal Shem Tov. He was a simple peasant who would occasionally drink to drunkenness. Even if the Baal Shem Tov told him to put down the reins and sit with his back to the horses (when the Besht traveled by *kefitzat ha-derech*), Alexei did not ask, "How is it possible for the coachman to drive the horses when he's facing the passengers?" His lack of inquisitiveness was not because he understood that the holy Baal Shem Tov should not be questioned, but because he was too simple to question.

One of the Baal Shem Tov's disciples once unburdened himself to the Besht, telling him that he was troubled by questions and doubts about the way God ran the world. The Baal Shem answered him, "You can learn a good trait from my coach driver, who doesn't even doubt or question what I, a creature of flesh and blood, do. He has no doubts; in fact, he's incapable of questioning or doubting, because he hasn't attained the level of desire or will. This is the mystic secret of the saying of the Rabbis: 'Nullify your will before His will,' that you shouldn't even have any will or desire to question or to doubt God."

Later, when the Besht was teaching his disciples and discussing the mystic concept of "the two extremes meeting," he said, "The very same qualities that make my servant Alexei so simple and lowly—that his will and awareness of existing as a separate, individual being are nullified—can lead a person to the highest spiritual level."[72]

A Scholar and a Simple Man Compared

ONE OF THE BAAL SHEM TOV'S MANY FOLLOWERS WAS A MAN FROM THE large city of Brody, a linen merchant named Reb Noson. He was an outstanding Torah scholar and, any time during the day when he was free from his work, particularly during the evenings, he sat and studied Torah with great diligence. But when it came to his character and his conduct with his fellow men, Reb Noson was a very ordinary person. His main concern was studying the Torah and fulfilling the commandments in the most exacting way. He also fulfilled the commandments concerning conduct with other people, but he did them without any concessions to piety. His enthusiasm was exclusively for the in-depth and analytical study of the Torah. As for divine service—actually *serving* God by laboring with effort, he was minimally involved. The Baal Shem Tov encouraged him to engage more in actual *service* and to work on himself and his conduct with others, but Reb Noson continued in his own way. Years passed, and he raised his children according to the path he had established for himself, and they also became outstanding Torah scholars.

Another follower of the Baal Shem Tov was a simple Jew named Reb Avraham, who lived in the small village of Belishtzenitz. He was very ordinary when it came to Torah study. He only studied books written in Yiddish, and even those he could barely comprehend. Nor did he understand the meaning of the Hebrew of the prayers, the psalms, or the *Chumash*. But he was a devoted servant of God and labored in his divine service. Everything that involved the fulfilling of the commandments he did with zest and joy. His divine service also included matters of personal character and conduct with others, for he worked on himself in those areas.

Now, the Baal Shem Tov's custom was that the disciples and followers who came to him for a Sabbath ate their meals with him. One Sabbath, when Reb Noson and Reb Avraham were both visiting the Baal Shem Tov, he taught Torah at his table on the verse in Ezekiel: "When you spread forth your hands, I will hide My eyes from you. Even though you make many prayers, I will not listen. Your hands are full of blood." The Besht explained, "Despite the fact that the main forms of divine service are the service of the mind and the service of the heart—namely, Torah study and prayer— and, by concentrating on them, the service involving activity in the world, that is, matters of personal character and conduct with others, usually develops by itself and in the correct way . . . nevertheless, it's possible that this will *not* happen. Instead, it will be that 'your hands are full of blood'—meaning that even though you give generously to a poor man, you lack any feeling for his suffering; and that is actually like spilling blood! 'When you spread forth your hands'—although you stretch out your hands and give charity generously, 'I will hide My eyes from you'—I will not see it, because it is not true service. For true *service* must involve your heart, when you *feel* another person's pain and suffering. 'Even though you make many prayers'—for the poor man— you do it only as a service of the mind. That also is not true service, because when you pray for him, you don't really feel his sorrow and distress. All these things are like spilling blood: 'your hands are full of blood'—the 'hands' of your deeds in the world, your conduct with others, and even the good deeds you do, are 'full of blood.'"

Reb Noson and Reb Avraham both heard this Torah teaching. Reb Noson understood the teaching in the way to which he was accustomed. He delved into it and analyzed the concepts involved. He thought deeply about the different kinds of divine service, of the mind, the heart, and the service of character and behavior with others. But the truth is he made almost no effort to practically fulfill these teachings. Reb

Avraham, on the other hand, who understood just those few parts of the Besht's teaching that dealt with matters of concrete and practical significance, according to his level of understanding, came to the conclusion that he had to occupy himself with purifying and refining his character and conduct much more than he had until then. And he firmly resolved to do that. The words "your hands are full of blood"—that not truly feeling the other person's misery is like spilling blood, even when you give generous help, did not allow Reb Avraham to have any peace of soul. When he returned home, he began to work harder on himself, and from time to time he made real progress and grew in this divine service of feeling for other people's suffering.

The following Passover, at the first *seder*, the Baal Shem Tov sat at the table with his closest disciples. He was in an exalted spiritual mood and talked about how there was greater pleasure in heaven from the divine service of simple people than from the service of those who knew how to study Torah and pray (understanding the Hebrew and so on). He continued, "The verse in Proverbs says: 'Better a dry crust of bread eaten with peace and quiet, than a house full of feasting with strife.' That's true not only in a person's worldly life, but in his spiritual life as well. A little divine service with an effort that leads to actual realization—which always brings peace and tranquillity—is better than a lot of divine service without the resolve that brings matters to their true completion, for that kind of religiosity always results in strife and bitterness." Then, after telling his disciples to place their hand each one on the shoulder of his comrade, and to close their eyes, the Baal Shem Tov put his own hands on the shoulders of the two disciples sitting at his right and left, and began to sing a soft *niggun*.

The disciples were then drawn into the Baal Shem Tov's vision and saw things far away. They saw Reb Avraham, in his small village of Belishtzenitz, sitting at the *seder* table with his wife and children. They were in a tiny room, dimly lit by one small candle burning on the table, on which there were a few clay dishes and bowls. The food was of the poorest kind and there was not enough for the whole family. But although their home was humble and poorly lit and lacking sufficient food, Reb Avraham and his family were sitting in a festive mood of mutual peace and love, performing the Passover *seder* with great joy.

Then the vision changed and the disciples saw Reb Noson, sitting with his family in his house in the large city of Brody. They were in a well-lit, spacious room, sitting around a festive table that had on it expensive dishes and silverware, and a large quantity of delicious food. But all those reclining there were self-centered and irritated at each other, making the mood gloomy and depressed.

When the Baal Shem Tov removed his hands from the shoulders of the two disciples at his sides and ceased singing, he instructed them all to open their eyes, and said, "That is the difference between someone who *serves* God and works on himself, and someone who does not. Despite Reb Avraham's being a simple person, he *works* on himself and notices his own defects and faults. He also sees other people's virtues and the many ways in which they are superior to him. Therefore, he's always happy and satisfied with his lot, because of his humility. He doesn't assume he deserves everything as his right. Even when he's unable to feed his children, not even on a holiday, he's still happy with holiday joy. That's the meaning of: 'Better a dry crust of bread eaten with peace and quiet.' On the other hand, someone who serves God through Torah study and prayer—despite these being important kinds of divine service—yet who lacks the true completion of actually having purified his character and his conduct—that is 'a house full of feasting with strife.' But when a gathering is with the joy of a *mitzvah*, as at Reb Avraham's house, that is where the *Shechinah* comes to rest."[73]

Liquor on the Table

WHEN THE BAAL SHEM TOV TAUGHT TORAH, HIS FACE WOULD REDDEN from his intense *d'vekut*. He was drunk but not from wine. Yet he always had a half-full glass of liquor put on the table in front of him so that if strangers were present and saw that his face was red, some of them might think it was because he had imbibed liquor.

His disciples asked him why was he encouraging people to suspect him? He answered, "It's written: 'He that hears, let him hear; and he that refuses to hear, let him refuse.' Just as it's a *mitzvah* to see that the one who hears, hears, so is it a *mitzvah* to see that the one who refuses, refuses. If someone comes here who should attach himself to me, he'll think that my face is red from speaking Torah; but if someone comes who doesn't belong here, he'll think that it's from drinking liquor."[74]

Hiding before Scholars

THE BAAL SHEM TOV'S DISCIPLES USED TO LAUGH WHEN THEY HEARD that someone was saying that the Besht was not a Torah scholar. They knew that not only was his expertise in the revealed Torah and *halacha* extraordinary, but that heaven had not granted such knowledge to anyone else in his generation. Some of the Besht's disciples were renowned Torah scholars themselves, yet they brought their Torah problems to him, and he answered all their questions, not withholding anything from them. But when great scholars visited him to test him to see if he was knowledgeable in Torah, he pretended that he was ignorant and did not know how to study. He had revealed himself in order to be a leader in Israel, but his instincts of holy modesty remained intact. He would not put his scholarship on display. And he felt that a spiritual leader should not be judged by an external standard of Torah knowledge.

Once, a great scholar, who had investigated and knew that the Besht could perform awesome miracles, came to see if he was a learned man and knew how to study. If yes, good; if not, he would oppose him. The Baal Shem Tov, knowing this, concealed himself from him. But this scholar was clever and realized that the Besht was a person of immense intellect. As he saw it, it was simply that the Besht was not an expert in *halacha.* He said to him, "What will you do if, God-forbid, a fire breaks out in the town on the Sabbath and, not having studied beforehand, you're not expert in the relevant halachic rulings? While you are researching the subject in the *Shulchan Aruch* to know which things it's permitted to save and which are forbidden, everything will go up in flames!"* The Besht, who knew what this sage thought about him, but still did not want to reveal himself, replied, "You consider me to be a miracle worker, though, don't you?" "Yes," he replied. "In that case," said the Besht with a smile, "I'll decree that the fire not burn, while I have a chance to study the matter thoroughly."

The Baal Shem Tov deflected this scholar's test with a joke, without revealing his Torah knowledge, because he did not want to support the false evaluation of a spiritual teacher based primarily on Torah expertise. To the Besht, direct knowledge of God was more important than book knowledge. But how could he explain that to someone whose heart was closed?[75]

Worthy Opponents

SOME OF THE TORAH SCHOLARS OF THE BRODY *KLOIZ* WERE TRULY GREAT tzaddikim but they were firmly opposed to the Baal Shem Tov. When the Besht was revealed, the holy *gaon*, Rabbi Hayim Tzanzer, the greatest among the great sages of the Brody *Kloiz*, said, "Is the midwife's son also among the miracle workers?" because the Besht's mother had been a midwife and he had been called in his younger days, "Israel, the son of the midwife." Rabbi Hayim sent one of his outstanding disciples to test the Besht, to form an opinion about him from firsthand knowledge, not hearsay. This scholar, who remained with the Besht for a few weeks, became attached to him heart and soul and accepted his authority. When he was about to leave and asked for a parting blessing, the Besht said, "I order you to report to your rabbi everything you saw here that seemed improper or peculiar. Rabbi Hayim is one of the great sages and tzaddikim of the generation, and he's a spark of the soul of Rabbi Yohanan, who never laughed, as in the saying of Rabbi Yohanan in the Talmud: 'It is forbidden to fill your mouth with laughter until the final redemption.' Whoever gives Rabbi Hayim such pleasure that he laughs, will win for himself the World-to-Come. Since he's my sworn opponent, perhaps when you fulfill his desire that you speak against me, telling him something about me that seems strange or peculiar, you'll make him laugh."

Another of the great scholars of the Brody *Kloiz*, the *gaon* Rabbi Yehezkel Landau, the famous author of the *Noda BeYehuda*, also opposed the Baal Shem Tov, although he was actually his relative. The Besht visited him a number of times, and the Noda Be-Yehuda's *rebbetzin* believed in the Besht's miracles; but the Noda BeYehuda did not

---

* Work is forbidden on the Sabbath, and there are restrictions even in this situation. The rulings are in the code book of Jewish law.

believe in him. Nevertheless, when the Besht visited Brody, he stayed in his home. The Noda BeYehuda would himself perform the *mitzvah* of hospitality and personally served the Baal Shem Tov tea. When the Besht saw that the Noda BeYehuda was being distracted from his Torah study because of him, he ceased staying in his house and lodged in the *beit midrash*. From time to time, the Noda BeYehuda's *rebbetzin* would go to the *beit midrash* with her children to make sure that he was being taken care of and to see if he needed anything, and the Besht would ask her about her husband's welfare.

Once, when the Baal Shem Tov was visiting Brody, some valuable object in the Noda BeYehuda's house was lost. The *rebbetzin* went with her son, Rabbi Yekovke, to the Besht, and told him about it. The Besht told them where to look for it and they found it. Thrilled about this, the *rebbetzin* said to her husband, "So, *misnagid*, what do you say now?" But the Noda BeYehuda was not impressed and dismissed the incident with various arguments.

Another time, when the Baal Shem Tov was together with the Noda BeYehuda, a chicken bone was brought to Rabbi Yehezkel, for him to rule whether the chicken could be eaten. He permitted it. "I also see that it's kosher," said the Besht, "because there's a spirit of purity resting on it." Rabbi Yehezkel gently mocked the Besht's claim of spiritual vision and, with a smile on his face, answered, "That's the difference between you and me. I can rule if a chicken is kosher without having to see it, just by being told of its condition. You actually have to see it. From that, we can understand the saying of our Sages: 'In the future, the Torah will be forgotten in Israel, and a woman will take a loaf of bread in her hand and go from one synagogue and *beit midrash* to another, to ask if it is pure or impure.' At first it seems hard to understand: Why does she need to carry the loaf of bread around with her? But because the Torah will have been forgotten, they will have to decide if it's kosher by means of the holy spirit, and look to see if a spirit of purity rests on it." Rabbi Yehezkel considered the Besht to have only a limited knowledge of *halacha*. And like other scholarly opponents of the Besht's hasidic way, Rabbi Yehezkel denigrated what he perceived as a reliance on spiritual gifts to the detriment of Torah expertise.

The *gaon* Rabbi Yitzhak HaLevi, another member of the Brody *Kloiz*, was also an opponent of the Baal Shem Tov. Yet once, when the Besht was visiting Brody, he appeared one night at the home of Rabbi Yitzhak HaLevi to ask him a question in Kabbalah, which the rabbi was not, however, able to answer. But from that time on, Rabbi Yitzhak ceased to persecute the Baal Shem Tov. How could he persecute someone humble enough to ask a Torah question to his opponent? It was clear that the Besht only sought the truth.

On another occasion, the Besht spent the Sabbath in Brody, and after the two great rabbis, his opponents, Hayim Tzanzer and Yehezkel Landau, had made *havdala* over the wine at the conclusion of the Sabbath, and lit their pipes, they said to each other, "Let's go to Rabbi Israel, the rabbi of the hasidim, to see what he's doing on *motza'ei Shabbat* after *havdala*." When they arrived there, they found that the Baal Shem Tov and his disciples, in the hasidic way, had not yet concluded the Sabbath and were still sitting in the dark at the third meal, singing mellow Sabbath table hymns with great devotion. The two rabbis stood to the side, unrecognized in the darkness, and secretly smiled at the peculiar proceedings. Suddenly, the Besht, who had been sitting in a profound trance of *d'vekut*, opened his eyes and said, "I sense that some here are mocking us." One of the rabbis spoke up and said, "How do you know that, sir? Do you have the holy spirit?" "I'm neither a prophet nor the son of a prophet," replied the Besht, "but when someone truly loves another individual, with a pure heart, they become one, and he knows the other person's thoughts as if they were his own."

The Besht's disciples were often astonished by their master's mild reaction to his opponents' provocations and insults. When they asked him about this, he said, "The Torah teaches, 'You shall not hate your brother in your heart,' and so on, 'and you shall love your neighbor as yourself; I am the Lord.' If someone has harmed you, how can you hate him, since he's merely an agent of God? If it's against God's will, no human being can harm you; so, by hating him, you're denying God and divine providence. That's why it says: 'You shall not hate your brother in your heart . . . I am the Lord': *I* have sent him to you to cause you this harm.'"

On another occasion, when the Noda BeYehuda persecuted the Baal Shem Tov—sending out letters warning various communities about him—the Besht said, "Why should I hate him and bear him a grudge, if God has commanded him to do it?"

The Baal Shem Tov was always deeply respectful of his great adversaries and appreciated their holiness. He once said about another famous opponent, Rabbi Hayim Rapaport, the rabbi of Lvov, "He's a big liar. How can he say in the Yom Kippur confession, 'I've sinned, I've transgressed,' and so on, when I know that he's never sinned in his whole life!"[76]

Dust and Ashes

 THE FAMOUS RABBI OF A LARGE CITY WAS A VEHEMENT ADVERSARY OF THE Baal Shem Tov and his new way, although he had never met him. Once, when the rabbi was sitting studying Torah, a visitor, who appeared to be a beggar, with a knapsack over his shoulder, entered the room. The rabbi greeted him in a friendly manner and asked him his name. "I'm dust and ashes," he replied, "that's my name. Who are you?" The rabbi, who was now paying close attention, answered, "I too am dust and ashes." "If that's the case," said the mysterious visitor, "and we're both dust and ashes, why should there be a dispute between us?" Immediately the rabbi knew that his visitor was the Baal Shem Tov. At that moment, he became attached to him with cords of love.[77]

Sincere Piety

SINCE GREAT RABBIS OPPOSED THE BAAL SHEM TOV, SOME COMMON people followed the lead of their teachers. A woman once saw the Besht walking down her street and tried to lift a large stone to throw at him. But it was too heavy for her. She looked up to heaven and called out, "Master of the world, let it be accepted before You as if I had thrown it at him!" Hearing this, the Besht said to a disciple walking with him, "There's great joy in heaven at her sincere piety."[78]

He Supports the Brody *Kloiz*

THE BAAL SHEM TOV HAD GREAT REVERENCE FOR THE SCHOLARS OF the Brody *Kloiz*, because the sound of Torah study never ceased there for even one minute; when one scholar slept, another stayed awake to study. The Besht was not disturbed by the fact that many of these scholars opposed him. Once, the hasidim of the Baal Shem Tov in Brody came to him, and complained bitterly that they were being persecuted by his opponents among the sages of the Brody *Kloiz*. "They're constantly harassing us and making up false stories about us, that we don't observe Jewish customs." They asked the Besht to retaliate against his opponents. But he did not allow them to respond at all, saying, "Their intention is for the sake of heaven."

One year, some brazen and insolent people in Brody had the stipend for the *Kloiz* eliminated, and as a result the great scholars who studied in the *Kloiz* dispersed. Hearing about this, the Baal Shem Tov was greatly upset, and said, "The *Shechinah* is lamenting that She has no place to rest there!"[79]

The Man Who Murdered the Prophet Zechariah

LATE ONE NIGHT, THE BAAL SHEM TOV SAT IN HIS *BEIT MIDRASH* AND told his disciples stories of tzaddikim. One story was of a tzaddik in a German-speaking land who predicted that he would die a violent death at the hands of murderers. He said that he had already been in this world one hundred times, and each time he had died violently or in a strange manner. It was all measure for measure, for when the first Temple was standing he had been the head of the Sanhedrin and was very sharp-witted and sharp-tongued. Although he was a great Torah scholar, his desire was not to seek the truth but to defeat and humiliate his opponents. The Rabbis say that if one studies the Torah with pure intentions it is an elixir of life, but if one studies with evil intentions, it becomes a deadly poison. He studied the Torah with perverted motives, until it acted as a corrosive poison in his soul; so that he became increasingly caustic and argumentative. In a previous life, he said, he had been the first one to strike the prophet Zechariah on the cheek, screaming, "You ignorant fool! Are you prophesying?" Because of him, other completely wicked people fell on the prophet and murdered him. And this tzaddik, who told the story, ordered that when he died they should write on his tombstone: "Here lies the man who murdered the prophet Zechariah."

The Baal Shem Tov said that this tzaddik's soul had now finally been repaired and brought to its eternal rest. The Besht also said to his disciples that he told them this story to show them that a person must be careful not to study the holy Torah with impure motives—turning it to poison, to bitter waters—in order to provoke and humiliate others. Because the essence of Torah study is to study in order to fulfill the commandments of the Creator, blessed be He.[80]

He Takes Torah Away from a Scholar

ONCE, THE BESHT ACCOMPANIED A DISCIPLE OF HIS, RABBI YEHIEL MICHAL, the head of the religious court of Kovel in Volhynia when he traveled to Horodni, Lithuania to assume the post of rabbi. On the Sabbath, Rabbi Yehiel Michal gave a talmudic discourse in the synagogue, but there was an unpleasant incident during the talk, because an argumentative scholar named Rabbi Michal the Dayan (religious judge) challenged everything the rabbi said, suggesting problems and difficulties concerning every point he made. Rabbi Yehiel Michal, who was disturbed by this harassment and unable to respond adequately on the spot, excused himself by saying that he would answer all the questions at the third Sabbath meal. Meanwhile, the Baal Shem Tov looked on with displeasure at this unbecoming spectacle.

The community owned a large house that they used only for special occasions. So to welcome their new rabbi, they made a third Sabbath meal there for the whole town. Everyone was seated according to his honor: Rabbi Michal the Dayan sat next to the rabbi, who himself was next to the Besht, who had the place of honor at the head of the table. Rabbi Zev Kitzes, the Besht's great disciple, who had also come with them, seated himself at the far end of the table; but the Besht scolded him, saying, "I can't stand your humility! Come sit here with us!"

Rabbi Yehiel Michal began to go over the talmudic discourse he had given earlier and Rabbi Michal the Dayan again harassed him with his questions. Rabbi Zev, who was now sitting near the head of the table, began to engage Rabbi Michal in debate (as the Besht had intended), defending the rabbi's position, and he defeated Rabbi Michal. Rabbi Michal was embarrassed by this and refused to admit the truth; he kept insisting on his position, even though he had to make forced and farfetched arguments. At this point, the Besht, who had watched this whole scene, said to him, "Stop disturbing my table!" Finally the quarrelsome *dayan* became silent.

After the Sabbath, the Baal Shem Tov and Rabbi Zev were setting out to travel to a nearby village to attend a *bris* the next morning. Rabbi Michal the Dayan pushed his way into the coach without being invited, and they took him along also. On the way, this Rabbi Michal began to discuss astronomy, thinking that Rabbi Zev would certainly not be able to compete with him in that subject, since the Besht's disciples and pious people generally did not study such topics. But Rabbi Zev made astute comments about everything he said, and Rabbi Michal the Dayan was at a loss to understand how a hasid came to know these things.

When they returned to Horodni, and the Besht began thinking about leaving for home the next day, he became worried that this Rabbi Michal, with his continual arguing and debating, would make Rabbi Yehiel Michal's life miserable and make his job as rabbi impossible. So by mystical means, he took away Rabbi Michal's Torah knowledge and he became an unlearned man. Rabbi Michal's daily custom was to wake at midnight to study *Gemara*, halachic codes, and the Rambam. That night, when he opened the book, he knew nothing. Assuming that his mind was unclear because he had drunk a lot of mead at the *bris*, he decided that he should sleep a little; so he closed the book, smoked his pipe for a while, and then lay down and slept until morning. In the morning, his custom was to study Torah after the daily prayers. He opened a book and again saw that he knew nothing; then he realized that the Besht had done this to him. He went to the Baal Shem Tov and pleaded, "Rabbi, give me back my Torah knowledge!" "Is the purpose of studying Torah to be able to defeat people in debates, to torture and harass them?" said the Besht. He rebuked him until Rabbi Michal was humbled and clearly saw his own lowliness. As a result, he changed his ways and became a completely righteous person.[81]

Torah into a Cossack's Pouch

THE BAAL SHEM TOV ONCE TRAVELED TO A DISTANT CITY TO ATTEND THE wedding of a disciple's son. The whole time he was there, the grandfather of the bride, who was a stern opponent of the Besht, rudely ignored him and would have nothing to do with him. This elderly man was an exceptional Torah scholar, who almost never ceased studying. He had a study room in his house whose walls were covered from floor to ceiling with books, and he studied there day and night. But he was very caustic in his manner. Shortly before the Besht was to travel home to Medzibuz, he said that he wanted to say goodbye to the old man—which surprised everyone— because they had all seen how the grandfather had not even wanted to look at the Baal Shem Tov's face.

When the old scholar saw through the window that the Besht was coming to visit him, together with a few other people, he got up from where he was sitting and stood by the window, with his back to the door. When the Baal Shem Tov entered, he did not even turn around to greet him. The old man's study had just a single desk and a chair. The Besht sat down on the chair, while the old man stood silently staring out the window. The Besht began to speak and, as Torah scholars do when they meet, he opened a Torah discussion. He quoted a passage in the Rambam, and after posing a profound question, asked the old man to explain the matter. The aged scholar was so excited by the sharp question that he could not help himself. He turned to the Baal Shem Tov and began to explain the passage. When he concluded, the Besht said, "That's not what I had in mind." Realizing that he had to probe the matter more deeply, the old man reflected again and suggested a second, deeper explanation. When he concluded, the Besht said again, "That's not what I had in mind." He once more pondered the problem and gave a third explanation, even more profound.

The moment he finished speaking, an armed Cossack suddenly entered the room, but the Baal Shem Tov immediately ordered him not to harm anyone there. The Cossack had a big leather mail pouch slung over his shoulder. The Besht reached in and took from it three large envelopes. He then removed from the envelopes three pieces of paper, and showed the old man that his three interpretations were written on them. "Do you see into whose pouch your Torah study is going?" he said. "You can study Torah day and night, but if your heart is full of pride and anger, all your studying is worthless!" After saying this, he immediately left.

The old man, who understood that this was a vision—and that the Cossack was an evil spirit—was stunned and remained standing there in a state of shock. He realized that the Baal Shem Tov, whom he had treated with such disdain, was an awesome tzaddik, while he was nothing, and all the spiritual energy of his Torah study had been flowing to the Other Side (of Evil). When he thought how he had wasted his years, his heart sank and he felt faint. But the spark of holiness within him was not extinguished. He revived and went after the Baal Shem Tov and when he came before him, he began to weep and beg forgiveness. He repented completely and, old as he was, in his final years was a devout follower of the Besht.[82]

The Joy of Torah Study

THE BAAL SHEM TOV TAUGHT HIS DISCIPLES THAT THEY MUST NOT STUDY Torah or do the commandments for the joy and pleasure it brought them, but only to give joy and pleasure to their Father in Heaven. Some of his disciples came to him and anxiously asked, "Master, what should we do? We try to study Torah with purity of heart and to give pleasure to our Heavenly Father. But we still get great joy from studying." "You misunderstood me," replied the Besht. "It's the Torah's nature to give joy to whoever studies it, even if he does so only to give pleasure to God, blessed be He. Isn't it written: 'The precepts of the Lord are true, rejoicing the heart'? Since a true servant of God can't help delighting in his Torah study, and his pleasure comes without his seeking it, God is greatly pleased by his happiness."[83]

The Antisemitic Student

ON A VISIT TO VIENNA, AUSTRIA, THE BAAL SHEM TOV ONE DAY WENT out into the courtyard of the hotel where he was staying. Several gentile university students who were loitering there noticed him, for a traditional-looking Jew was a rare sight in that city; moreover, the Besht attracted people's attention, since he was a handsome man with reddish-blond hair and a beautiful beard. But when one of the students, who was a vicious antisemite, saw the holy Baal Shem Tov, he mocked him and said loudly to his friends, so the Besht could hear, "Look at that Jew with his ugly beard!" because his heart was burning with the impure fire of hatred for the Jewish people. The Baal Shem Tov did not respond with hate; he walked right over to the student, placed a hand on his shoulder in a friendly way and looking deeply into his eyes, whispered, "Be a Jew!" Then the Baal Shem returned to his room in the hotel.

A few minutes later, the student came running to the Baal Shem Tov's room, his heart burning like a torch with the pure fire of his desire to be a Jew; and he converted.[84]

Absolute Unity

THE BAAL SHEM TOV WAS ONCE TRAVELING IN THE COUNTRYSIDE WITH a wagon of his hasidim, and in the late afternoon he ordered them to stop and *davven* at a roadside Jewish inn. The hasidim climbed down from the wagon and followed the Besht inside. After receiving the innkeeper's permission to use his inn as a place for prayer, the Besht and his *minyan* began to *davven* loudly, with tremendous fervor, as always.

In the quiet countryside, their heartfelt cries and pleas could be heard at a great distance. When the gentile peasants who lived nearby heard the commotion and cries, they assumed it could mean only one thing: a fire had broken out! In those days, a fire could wipe out a whole village of wooden buildings in a matter of hours. The peasants jumped up, grabbed water buckets, and ran to help. When they reached the inn, however, they were surprised to find not a fire that people flee from, that destroys, but a fire that brings people together, that produces love and joy, a fire of prayer. And if a person is praying for real, with all his heart and soul, whoever hears it also has to pray.

When these peasants heard the Besht and his hasidim crying out with all their might to the Master of the world, they put down their water buckets, entered the inn, and started yelling and shouting to God as never before in their lives. Their voices joined with the voices of the hasidim; these were calling out in Hebrew and those in Russian, but the mixed sounds rose to heaven together and ascended before the Throne of Glory.

After finishing the afternoon prayers, the hasidim began to sing and dance. And the peasants joined them. There was absolute unity and so much love and joy in the air. The Besht stood marveling at the sight of his hasidim dancing arm in arm with the gentile peasants.

When night came on and it grew dark, the Besht and his *minyan davvened* the evening prayers accompanied by their gentile companions. Then the peasants paid the innkeeper to provide a good meal for themselves and their new Jewish friends, and they all ate and drank together.

Afterward, the Besht announced that it was time to leave. The peasants all hugged and kissed the Besht and his disciples, and escorted them to their wagon. When the hasidim climbed onto the wagon, everyone was weeping. As the Besht was leaving, he whispered, "*Ribono shel olam*, Master of the world, surely this is what it will be like when the Messiah comes! Make him come soon!"[85]

The Council of the Four Lands

◖ THE BAAL SHEM TOV'S RAPIDLY GROWING HASIDIC MOVEMENT AROUSED intense opposition not only from individual rabbis but also from the religious establishment. The Council of the Four Lands, the central institution of Eastern European Jewry, sent a delegation of three rabbis to the Baal Shem Tov, to investigate him. The Besht debated and defeated them and before they left, said to them, "What is the root of the difference between us? There are two kinds of knowledge: head-knowledge and heart-knowledge. The head understands, the heart feels. You know the Torah as it's understood by the head and the mind. I have come to reveal the Torah as it's understood by the heart."[86]

Visions and Visitations

Hallel

◖ THE BAAL SHEM TOV'S POWERFUL SPIRITUAL EXPERIENCES OFTEN PRODUCED changes in his physical appearance. Ordinary hasidim and outsiders, who were unfamiliar with such manifestations of extraordinary spiritual states, could easily mistake these bodily symptoms as coming from a physical rather than a spiritual cause. When the Besht was in a trance, they thought he was sleeping or had fainted; when his face suddenly flushed, or he became unsteady on his feet, they thought that he had drunk too much. His closest disciples, however, recognized these bodily signs and knew what and what not to do when they occurred.

The Baal Shem Tov made soul-ascents while praying, and sometimes while teaching Torah or during sleep. He usually made a soul-ascent during *Minha* of *erev Shabbat* and also during *Shabbat*, his soul ascending to the upper worlds and to all the heavenly palaces. When he chanted the Great *Hallel* during the Sabbath morning service, he did not say a verse until he had first seen and heard the angel that sings that verse of the psalm, and then said it together with him.

One *Rosh Hodesh*, the Baal Shem Tov's disciple, Rabbi Abba, was in front of the Ark leading the prayers in the Besht's synagogue and the Baal Shem Tov was praying in his usual place. It was the Besht's custom to lead the prayers beginning with the Half *Hallel*. When the *Shemoneh Esreh* (the prayer right before the *Hallel*) was being repeated aloud by Rabbi Abba, they saw that the Besht was trembling greatly, as usual when he prayed. When Rabbi Abba finished the repetition of the *Shemoneh Esreh*, the Besht stood in his place trembling, without going forward to lead the *Hallel* and the remainder of the prayers. Everyone was waiting for him without knowing what to do, but Rabbi Zev Kitzes went over to him, and looking in his face, saw that it was burning like a torch and that his eyes were bulging—they were open, but fixed and unmoving, as if he were dying. Rabbi Zev, a close disciple of the Baal Shem Tov and a hasid on a high spiritual level, was familiar with the Besht's spiritual moods and states, and realized that he was in a trance and his soul had ascended to the upper worlds. He motioned with his hand for Rabbi Abba to come over, and, each of them holding the Besht under an arm, they gently led him to the prayer-leader's stand before the Ark. He went with them slowly and stood shaking before the Ark for some time. Then, he recited the *Hallel*, shaking and quivering all the while. After he concluded the *Kaddish*, he stood there trembling for a long while so that they had to delay the Torah reading until his trembling subsided. Such events were typical when the Baal Shem Tov prayed. Sometimes, he would later tell his disciples what he had seen and done in the upper worlds during a soul-ascent. Other times no one knew.[87]

Visions While Eating

THE BAAL SHEM TOV HAD MANY VISIONS INVOLVING VISITATIONS BY THE Seven Shepherds. Moses often came to the Besht while he was eating, because Moses is the master of spiritual eating. The Besht once taught at the table during a Sabbath meal, "The Torah nowhere describes Moses as eating. It only says the opposite, that when he was on Mount Sinai 'he ate no bread.' Why? Because Moses' eating was so spiritual that it can't really be called 'eating' in a worldly sense."

Once, during a *pidyon ha-ben* feast celebrating the redemption of a firstborn son, the Besht began to eat a slice of bread. Suddenly, his face reddened and his expression changed. Some of those at the table thought he was choking on the food and wanted to run to his aid and save him. But Rabbi Zev Kitzes looked at his face and said, "Leave him alone." He could tell that the Besht's flushed face was from a spiritual not a physical cause. After being in a trance for a long time, the Besht finally returned to the normal plane of consciousness and regained his usual appearance. Later, Rabbi Zev asked him what had happened. The Besht said, "While eating the bread, I was meditating the same way that Moses did when he was serving at the feast for his father-in-law, when Jethro visited the Children of Israel in the desert. At that moment, Moses came to me—that's why my appearance suddenly changed."[88]

Serving God in All Your Ways

THE BAAL SHEM TOV'S GRANDSON, RABBI MOSHE HAYIM EPHRAIM OF Sudilkov, was a great *matmid**, studying Torah constantly. He sat in the study hall

---

* Someone who studies the Torah every possible minute.

day and night and immersed himself in the Torah without cease. Most of his study was concentrated on the *Gemara*. He had deviated somewhat from the hasidic way of his holy grandfather, which did not emphasize continual Torah study and did not focus on *Gemara* and other legal studies.

The Baal Shem Tov, for his part, was constantly traveling here and there in his coach—to meet, teach, heal, and save. Now and then he liked to take his grandson, Ephraim, with him on these excursions. This caused the young man, in a typically *misnagid* way, anguish at having to interrupt, if only briefly, his Torah study.

Once, the Besht asked a visitor from another town about a certain householder from that place. The visitor answered with praise, saying that the man was a great *matmid*. "I'm jealous of his ceaseless studying," replied the Besht, "but what can I do? I don't have time to study, for I have to serve God, blessed be His name." When the Besht's grandson heard these words, uttered in holiness and purity, they entered his heart, and he began to conduct himself in the hasidic way from that moment on.

The religious path emphasized by Torah scholars in the Besht's time was continual Torah study, almost to the exclusion of all else. Their ideal was a one-sided, bookish person who sits indoors studying Torah day and night. This is holy, but there is something higher: The Besht himself was hardly a person to neglect the Torah! Yet he was not merely a book person, but a God and a people person. As a teacher who led people back to God, he traveled constantly, meeting merchants and robbers, Jews and gentiles, men, women, and children. He was always racing about, seeing and experiencing the richness of God's creation. The Besht's way was to be with others and to be in this world. How could he bring the light of Hasidism to people if he confined himself to the study hall? His ideal was not the scholar, the intellectual, but something broader and more many-sided. Two of his favorite Torah verses were: "Know Him in all your ways"—to serve God in all one's varied activities, and "I have placed God before me always"—to have *d'vekut* at all times. Whereas Torah scholars sought to avoid the sin of "Torah-neglect"—not leaving an idle moment without Torah study—the Besht's concern was to avoid, so to speak, "*d'vekut*-neglect." His focus was to have God-consciousness at all times, in whatever activity one is engaged. His goal was not simply book knowledge, not even of Torah, but direct knowledge of God, *d'vekut* with the Holy One, blessed be He and blessed be His name.[89]

To Labor in Prayer

A NEW DISCIPLE OF THE BAAL SHEM TOV, NAMED RABBI MORDECHAI, who came to the Besht at middle age when he was already an accomplished scholar and kabbalist, had, after seeing the Besht's awesome *davvening* for a few days, completely changed his ideas about prayer and his own preparation for praying.

Yet, even after lengthy meditation to prepare for *davvening*, his praying was not always what he felt it should be. More than once he complained about this to his master, and asked the Besht to bless him to be able to pray with real devotion. "You have to plough more deeply," replied the Besht. "Then the seeds that you plant will sprout and produce better fruits." He needed to go deeper and labor more in the divine service of prayer.

During that first long stay with the Baal Shem Tov in Medzibuz, Rabbi Mordechai had often wondered why he had such great pleasure in studying Torah, whereas he found prayer so difficult and alien to his nature. There was even a period, at the beginning of his first stay with the Besht, when he did not want to bother about prayer; he prayed the ordained services in the minimal time necessary, and that was it. Yet, while he almost discounted prayer and had no time for it, he was very careful not to waste any opportunity, even a minute, to study Torah, and he studied continuously.

Just then, the Besht gave a talk comparing Torah study and prayer. The essence was his comment: "By studying the Torah, we learn how to act in the world and do God's will. But by praying, we learn how to turn to God at every minute during the day."

When Rabbi Mordechai heard this teaching from the Besht, its profound truth caused a spiritual revolution in his attitude and behavior. Now, he not only prepared well for praying, he also began to actually *labor* with great effort in the divine service of praying; and on a day that he prayed fluently with real *d'vekut*, he considered it an occasion for celebration.[90]

The Secret to Elevating Spiritually

ONE OF THE BAAL SHEM TOV'S DISCIPLES ASKED HIM, "MASTER, WHAT IS the secret to elevating spiritually?" The Besht replied, "One can elevate by the power of yearning. You have to be on fire to get close to God. When I was younger, there was a period when I would run around and cry out, 'Why should I continue to live if I can't see You?' Isaiah says: 'I saw the Lord [*Adonai*] sitting upon a high and exalted throne. . . . *Serafim* [fiery angels] stood above Him. . . . And one cried to another, "Holy, holy, holy is the Lord of hosts; the whole earth is full of His glory!"' Everyone asks: How can the *serafim* stand above *Adonai* who creates them? But because their deepest yearning when they cry 'Holy!' is to be nullified in the transcendent light of the *Ein Sof* [Infinite] that surrounds all worlds, they are elevated above the name *Adonai* that creates them and fills the worlds with glory*. Then, it's as if they were actually standing in that place of God's infinite light. Why are they called *serafim* [fiery]? Because their very essence is a burning desire to elevate to what is transcendent. And wherever someone's will is, there he is, all of him. Therefore, when your greatest desire is to reach an exalted place, so that you are ready even to nullify yourself to get there, you transcend your own spiritual level and begin to elevate."[91]

---

* According to Kabbalah, there are different levels and aspects within divinity. The transcendent light of the *Ein Sof* [Infinite] is above the Name *Adonai* (Lord).

The Sabbath

The Day of the Soul

ONE *EREV SHABBAT*, AFTER THE MORNING PRAYERS, THE BAAL SHEM TOV sat down in the synagogue and taught his disciples. "The essence of *Shabbat* is to cleave to God, blessed be He, through Torah study, prayer, and meditation in purity. That's why the holy *Zohar* says about *Shabbat*: 'This day is the day of the soul, not the day of the body'—meaning that the Root of all souls shines into the souls that are in bodies, and they yearn for Him. That is the extra soul power on *Shabbat*, which the pure of heart actually feel."[92]

Anticipation

ON *EREV SHABBAT*, WHEN NOON ARRIVED, THE BAAL SHEM TOV'S HEART began to pound so loudly and his insides started to churn and make such noises, that everyone near him heard the sound. His fear and awe of God were so great that all his limbs trembled and shook in anticipation of the Sabbath holiness that was coming into the world.[93]

How to Prepare

ONE MORNING ON *EREV SHABBAT*, THE BAAL SHEM TOV SPOKE TO HIS disciples about how to prepare for *Shabbat* by immersing in the *mikvah*. "A person should prepare himself to receive the Sabbath with holiness and purity. Before entering the *mikvah*, he should first break his heart within him and accept on himself the yoke of the kingdom of heaven. Then, abandoning his sins and dedicating himself in total self-sacrifice to God's holy Name, let him immerse."[94]

Like a Coat

THE BAAL SHEM TOV AND HIS HASIDIM TOO ALWAYS WENT TO THE *MIKVAH* before *Shabbat*. They removed their weekday clothes, immersed in the *mikvah*, then donned their Sabbath clothes. The Besht himself not only changed his clothes; he also altered his consciousness. Every week on Friday before going to the *mikvah*, he secluded himself in his room to prepare for the holy Sabbath. One of his disciples who had eyes to see once looked in and saw that the Besht separated himself from materiality and hung his body on a peg on the wall above his bed, like someone hangs up a coat. And it stayed there until after the conclusion of the Sabbath.[95]

A Head Taller

WHEN THE BAAL SHEM TOV WALKED BACK FROM THE *MIKVAH* ON *EREV Shabbat*, people could see that he was a head taller than when he went. The tailor who made his clothes said that he had to make the Besht's Sabbath clothes longer than his weekday clothes, and yet, on *Shabbat*, one could see that they fit him perfectly.[96]

Beyond Conversation

AFTER THE BESHT LEFT THE *MIKVAH* ON *EREV SHABBAT*, HE WAS SO FOCUSED on *Shabbat* that it was no longer possible to talk with him.[97]

From One World to Another

THE RABBIS SAY THAT IF SOMEONE DIES ON *EREV SHABBAT* IT IS A GOOD SIGN for him. The Besht interpreted this to mean that one should die to all the desires and concerns of this world on *erev Shabbat*, to prepare oneself for *Shabbat*. His disciples saw that when he welcomed the Sabbath his face was like that of a dying man. Passing from weekdays to the Sabbath is similar to the passage from this world to the next at the time of death—in each case the transition requires dying to one world in order to enter a higher one.[98]

Answering Questions

WHEN THE SABBATH ARRIVED AND ALL THE WORLDS ELEVATED TO THE highest levels, the Besht's soul would be elevated to a rung so exalted that he was no longer able to descend in order to answer a question about mundane matters. In his later years, he prayed and fasted to reach an even higher level, and then, since the one who is higher can descend lower, he was able to converse about such things even on *erev Shabbat*.[99]

The Parable of the King's Letter

AT ONE FRIDAY NIGHT SABBATH MEAL, THE BESHT TOLD A PARABLE TO explain the reason for Sabbath feasts. "A prince was sent by his father the king on a mission to a small village in a distant country, where he lived among coarse and common people. After a long time had passed, a letter from his father reached him, and he was so elated that he wanted to celebrate. He was worried, though, that the villagers would ridicule him, saying, 'Why is today special? He's making a fool of himself.' So he made a party for all the villagers and gave them plenty of wine and liquor. Then, while they were rejoicing in their drunkenness, he could rejoice in his father's love, without being noticed. That's the reason," said the Besht, "that we entertain and divert the body by eating three meals on the Sabbath. For the soul, which is like a prince, is ashamed to rejoice in front of the body, which is like a villager. So while the body rejoices in its things, the soul can rejoice in its *d'vekut* with its Father the King, the Holy One, blessed be He."[100]

Eating with the Rebbe

SOME WEEKDAYS AND ALWAYS ON SABBATHS AND HOLIDAYS THE BAAL Shem Tov ate together with his followers. On *Shabbat*, he brought them into his Sabbath joy. Tables were set up and large numbers of people gathered for the meals. From near and far people came to bask in the Besht's holy light and to inhale the fragrance of his teaching. On Friday night and Saturday late afternoon, at the first and third Sabbath meals, he ate in his house with all the visitors. Most of his public teaching was delivered during the third Sabbath meal. But the second Sabbath meal, after the Saturday morning prayers, was reserved exclusively for disciples. Before the Sabbath, the Besht prepared a list of guests who were invited to his table for the second meal. Although the door of his house was always open during that meal, no one ever dared enter without having been invited, because of their awe of the holy Baal Shem Tov.[101]

At the Table before God

THE BAAL SHEM TOV ATE WITH HIS FOLLOWERS ON THE SABBATH SO THAT through his holy influence they would realize that they were sitting at the table before God and would receive the flow of divine abundance from the side of holiness. Eating with a tzaddik is like eating in the presence of the *Shechinah*, and, when someone is elevated to the level of divine awareness and wisdom, all his bodily lusts disappear, because of his *d'vekut* with the *Shechinah*. The Besht once said at his Sabbath table, "A person who's wise can eat good food and enjoy all the other pleasures but be fasting and denying his lower self at the same time. He can look wherever he wants and not see anything beyond his personal space. All this is according to the secret of: 'I have placed the Lord before me always,' for he relates only to the spiritual aspect of everything he eats or sees or encounters. He knows the mystic meaning of what the Rabbis say: 'Look not at the jar, but at its contents,' for the essence of everything in the world is Godliness."[102]

The Tzaddik's Medicine

THE BAAL SHEM TOV CLOSED HIS EYES, THEN OPENED THEM AND continued, "I infuse into anyone who eats at my Sabbath table a life-giving drug that acts like a medicine to cure him from all bodily lusts and desires. This medicine continues working in him even when he leaves here, so that he'll conduct himself with holiness and purity in his home. Ordinary medicines only cure the sickness a person already has, but they can't protect him for the future, and the illness can return, God-forbid. But the 'medicine' a tzaddik gives a person who eats at his pure table is so potent that it protects him even for the future, to be saved from all evil."[103]

Where a Person's Mind Is

ONCE, WHEN THE BAAL SHEM TOV WAS VISITING A CERTAIN TOWN AND sitting at the Sabbath table with his hasidim, he said to them, "Where a person's mind is, there he is, all of him. If he's thinking of spiritual things, that's where he is. If he's thinking of material things, that's where he is, all of him. If he's thinking of God, at that moment he's in heaven and before God. If he's thinking evil thoughts, God-forbid, he's actually standing with both feet in hell. He can't be half above and half below. He's either here or there. So be careful of what you're thinking about and where your mind is, because there you are, all of you."

He then whispered to Rabbi Zev Kitzes and the other disciples sitting near him, "The rabbi sitting at the end of the table thinks that he's eating meat in honor of the Sabbath, but look." The Besht mystically caused them to see in a vision the way that rabbi appeared in the spiritual realms. As the rabbi was eating, he had taken on the form of an ox wearing a *shtreimel**, because his mind was on the meat and not, to make a distinction, on God, blessed be He.[104]

Rejoicing in the Sabbath Itself

ONCE, WHEN THE BESHT'S DISCIPLES WERE IN A JOYFUL MOOD, THEY ASKED him to show them something wondrous. He agreed, but made a condition with them that no matter what they saw, they would not laugh. They promised him.

That Sabbath morning in the synagogue, the Besht pointed out to them a certain man who was praying with great joy and fervor. After the prayers, this man said "Good *Shabbos!*" to every one of the worshipers in a voice brimming with happiness. From his face, it could be seen that he was in an exalted mood; he was floating in a sea of Sabbath joy. When the man left the synagogue to go home, the Besht and his disciples followed him quietly at a distance. When he entered his humble home—no more than a hut—they stood near the half-open door and looked in. Inside, on the table, were two tiny Sabbath candles, so small that the house was almost dark; and, being windowless and without a chimney for ventilation, it was full of smoke. The lady of the house was

---

* A festive fur hat worn by male hasidim on Sabbaths and holidays.

wearing a worn-out dress and shuffling about without shoes on her feet, making last-minute preparations for the Sabbath meal. When her husband walked in, he said, "Good *Shabbos* to you, my dear," and she answered, "A peaceful *Shabbos* to you, my precious husband."

After singing the hymn "*Shalom Aleichem*" in a tone that made evident his peace with the world, the man of the house said, in a voice suffused with the joy of the holy day, "Please bring me the wine, dear wife, so we can fulfill: 'Remember the Sabbath day to sanctify it.'" The woman put two little rolls of the poorest, dark bread on the table, and said, "My dearest dear, won't you say the *kiddush* on the bread tonight?" (Being too poor to afford wine, he had to recite the *kiddush* over bread.) He answered happily, "Certainly, my dear wife, we'll make *kiddush* on the bread, which will taste as sweet as the wine concealed in the grapes since the Six Days of Creation." After washing his hands, he recited the *kiddush* over the bread, and his face now wreathed in smiles, said to his devoted wife, "My dear, please bring to the table the fish you've prepared, which is always so delicious and tastes like the Garden of Eden, and we'll fulfill: 'And you shall call the Sabbath a delight.'" Since they could not afford fish, the lady of the house brought a plate of beans to the table, ladled some out for her husband, then for herself, and said, "Eat and enjoy, dear husband, and may it be God's will that these beans taste on your tongue like the most delicious and tastiest fish."

The man ate the beans with blissful contentment, his face beaming radiantly, as if he were enjoying royal delicacies from a king's table. Then he said, as if to himself, "Praise God, for we are not lacking any good thing for the honor of our guest the Sabbath Queen, to fulfill what is said: 'The Sabbath is like a taste of the World-to-Come; it is a day that is wholly good.'"

After joyously singing some Sabbath table hymns, he said, "And now, my woman of valor, please bring to the table your supremely delicious soup." Again, she dished out a ladleful of beans, first on his plate, then on her own, and said, "Eat the soup, my dear husband, and may it taste as delicious as can be. And let us not say, God-forbid, that we lacked any good food on the holy Sabbath." The man ate the beans with obvious relish and exclaimed aloud, "How tasty this soup is! It couldn't be better!" Then, overwhelmed with Sabbath bliss, he said, "Oh, oh, what delicious food! Oh, oh, Sabbath day, day of delight!"

After this, his wife gave him a third ladleful of beans instead of a meat course and a fourth ladleful instead of dessert. But he was so happy, he was as if drunk with Sabbath joy and, almost reeling from his great delight, raised his voice, sweetly singing the Sabbath table hymn, "*The Rock, from whose bounty we have eaten, bless Him my faithful friends! We have eaten our fill and left over, according to His word.*" He ended his meal with a few more Sabbath table hymns and said to his wife, "And now, my sweetest dear, come, let's dance in joy for the honor of Queen Sabbath, to fulfill: '*Whoever hallows the seventh day as fitting . . . his reward is exceedingly great, in accordance with his deed.*'" Then they got up, held hands, and began to dance in a rapture of joy around and around in a circle, singing the song, "Happy are we, how goodly is our portion and how pleasant is our lot!"

The Besht's disciples who were watching this whole scene, finally could not contain themselves and began to laugh quietly. "Didn't you agree not to laugh if I showed you something wondrous?" said the Besht. "But since you didn't keep your promise, you won't be able to receive the gift I intended to give you after you'd seen the Sabbath joy of this poor couple." "Master," they said in disappointment, "what was the gift?" "I wanted to bless you," said the Besht, "that you too would attain the exalted rung of these poor people, to rejoice not in the physical pleasures of the Sabbath, but in the day itself. But you weren't worthy, and lost that precious gift I'd hoped to give you."

If we laugh at the pious innocence of those who put God at the center of their lives and actually experience the sweetness of His presence, we make ourselves unworthy of attaining that same blissful state. May we have the devotion and simplicity to rejoice in God under all circumstances and at all times.[105]

Sabbath Soul-Ascents

EVERY SABBATH, THE BAAL SHEM TOV MADE A SOUL-ASCENT, EITHER during prayer (usually during the *Shemoneh Esreh* of the *Musaf* service), or during his Sabbath afternoon nap, or during a meal—often the third Sabbath meal. Then, at the conclusion of the Sabbath, he went to his room, lit his pipe and, while smoking, revealed to his disciples what he had seen in the upper worlds.[106]

Elijah

AT THE CONCLUSION OF EVERY SABBATH, WHEN THE BAAL SHEM TOV sang the hymn "*Eliyahu HaNavi*," the prophet Elijah, may he be remembered for good, appeared to the Besht to bless him for the coming week. Once, when Elijah came to wish him: "A good week!" the Besht was sitting deeply immersed in his holy thoughts, in a state of supernal awe. Elijah was so overwhelmed with holy fear that he fled.[107]

A Meditative Excursion

AFTER *HAVDALA*, IT WAS THE BAAL SHEM TOV'S CUSTOM TO GO OUT FOR an excursion in his horse-drawn coach. He would travel half a mile and then return to the town. He usually invited a few disciples to accompany him, and it was considered a great honor to be in such intimate contact with the rebbe. Why did the Besht make a short trip after the Sabbath ended? *Shabbat* is a sedentary God-meditation when it is forbidden to work or to travel. A person immerses himself in Godliness through peacefulness and quietude. But once the work week started Saturday night, and it was permitted to travel, the Besht would continue his meditative God-awareness, this time when moving.[108]

Toward Redemption
with the Sting of Persecution and Heresy

The Besht Appoints Rabbis and Others

WHEN THE BAAL SHEM TOV REACHED THE HEIGHT OF HIS INFLUENCE, his movement numbered tens of thousands of followers and scores of disciples, many of them great rabbis and scholars. His authority had grown and become established to such an extent that he appointed and removed rabbis, *maggidim* (preachers), *shochtim*, and cantors in many towns and villages.

He encouraged his rabbi-disciples to follow his compassionate path of caring for their flocks, rather than being strict, legalistic, and aloof; he encouraged *maggidim* to inspire people by speaking of God's love, rather than by threatening them with punishment for their sins; he encouraged *shochtim* to be God-fearing and scrupulous in their work; and he encouraged cantors to lead their congregations in serving God with joy, rather than giving in to vanity and showing off their voice. He also encouraged some of his followers to be religious school teachers. A hasid once asked him if he should become a *melamed*. "It's good to be a *melamed*," replied the Besht. "The happiest time of my life was when I was a teacher of little children."[1]

Servants of the Redemption

WHEN THE MONTH OF *KISLEV* ARRIVED, THE BAAL SHEM TOV EVERY evening gathered together the children from the *cheder* after their studies were finished, including his own grandchildren, and told them the story of the miracle of Hanukkah. He would sit among the children and with their help construct a new *menorah** each year. They made a base, eight branches with cups to serve as vessels for the oil, two decorative lions with their red tongues extended, and a kind of finger on the right side for the *shammos*, the "servant" candle used to light the other candles.

The Besht spent every evening with the children making the *menorah*, while they used little saws, knives, glue, and pieces of wood. The hasidim said that the form of the *menorah* that the Besht and the children constructed was like the form of the *menorah*

* Hanukkah candelabra.

288

in the Temple, which never fell into Roman hands when they destroyed the Temple, but ascended into heaven; when the Redeemer comes, that *menorah* will descend and light the path for the redeemed.

On the first night of Hanukkah when the first candle would be lit, the *menorah* that the Baal Shem Tov and the children built was prepared and ready. Hasidim were arriving from near and far and the fervor was great. The Besht always taught Torah before lighting the candle. One year he said, "The verse says: 'When you light—literally, 'elevate'—the candles.' Why does it say: 'When you elevate'? because someone who lights the Hanukkah candles must also light himself; someone who elevates the candles must also elevate himself, to the level of self-sacrifice." Then the Besht began to burn with fervor and asked, "Is everyone ready for self-sacrifice, like that of the Maccabees—Matisyahu and his sons?" All the hasidim, together with the children who had constructed the *menorah*, answered in one voice, "We're ready!" Then they started to sing a *niggun* and began to dance—and as they sang, it seemed to them that they were lifted up in flames above the ground on which they danced. They danced for hours, pouring out their very souls, the Besht dancing with them, hand holding hand, shoulder against shoulder. Every once in a while, a certain hasid jumped up on the shoulders of his comrades and called out loudly, *Shema Yisrael*, "Hear O Israel!"

Before the Baal Shem Tov lit the candle, he gazed fixedly at the congregation and at the hasid who had been calling out *Shema Yisrael!* Then, after meditating with closed eyes for a long while, he opened his eyes and said, "Why do we draw out the final syllable of the word *ehad*, 'one,' when we chant the *Shema Yisrael*—'Hear O Israel, the Lord our God, the Lord is *o—n—e*'? Because the essence of everything is the One—One above and One below; without 'One' there's no *Shema Yisrael*." The hasidim, who were listening to this teaching with their eyes closed, absorbed it fully, and their feeling of brotherhood, their feeling of oneness, immediately increased and was strengthened, because they understood that the essence of Hasidism is: "One." The chorus of singers began a new *niggun* for *Shema Yisrael*—for that year. The hasidim used to say that whoever had not heard the yearly melody for *Shema Yisrael* had never truly heard a *niggun* in his whole life.

When the time came to light the first candle, the Baal Shem Tov began to teach about the *menorah* that they had built for that year, mentioning its different parts, beginning with the base on which rested the eight branches with their eight cups to hold the pure oil, in which the oil-saturated wicks floated, waiting to be lit. He said, "The power of the branches is in their all having one foundation and base, which unites them and brings them to the level of holiness. Although each wick burns in its own cup—yet, because they all have a common base, it's as if they're all a single branch, and that's why we make only one blessing over the candle lighting, saying, 'Blessed are You, O Lord our God . . . who has commanded us to light the *candle* of Hanukkah'—because all eight candles are like one candle that's completely holy." A great silence descended on the room, as the Besht stood in front of the eight-branched *menorah* surrounded by the hasidim and the children who had climbed up on the benches to be able to see him when he would light the candle.

Suddenly, a voice broke the silence, the voice of a grandson of the elderly villager Pinhas, one of the foremost hasidim. This little boy called out, 'What about the *shammos*, Rebbe?' The boy's voice rose up, as if from the hearts of all the children there, for they were all wondering why the Besht had not yet taught about the "servant candle." Even the hasidim and those in the Besht's inner circle, who were startled by the cry that disturbed the silence, opened their eyes wide, expectantly wondering what the Besht would say. He stood there quietly for a little while, then looked tenderly at the child—who was himself surprised by his own voice and question—and said, "The holiness of the *shammos* is not less than that of the other candles. In fact, it even has an extra degree of holiness, because one is permitted to use its light, different from the other candles, whose light one is not permitted to use for any purpose, but only to view. And that is the special merit of the 'hewers of wood and the drawers of water' among the Jewish people, that thanks to their help and supplies, the *kohanim* can offer up the sacrifices on the altar in the Temple. Then, turning to the little boy who had called out the question, the Baal Shem Tov added, "And you, *boychik'l*, may God grant that you have the merit to be one of the holy servants, one of the *shammosim*, who bring the redemption!"*[2]

He's Coming Today!

THE SON OF RABBI YITZHAK DOV MARGOLIOT, ONE OF THE BESHT'S FIRST disciples, became seriously ill and his father took him to the doctors, who told him that the boy's condition was dangerous and they could not help. Rabbi Yitzhak Dov then ran to the Baal Shem Tov to ask him to pray for his son, whose name was Shmuel. Before the Besht had even answered him, Rabbi Yitzhak Dov saw from the Besht's face that he too considered the boy's condition serious and the rabbi became frightened. But the Besht quickly told him, "Don't worry. I have a cure for him. Send him to me. He'll stay with me for a year, he'll eat at my table, and I hope that with God's help, he'll recover. I know it'll be difficult for you to leave him with me for a year, but I promise you that I'll treat him like my own son and take him with me wherever I travel." That is what they did and in time Shmuel recovered. It was the Besht's custom that whenever he traveled, he had someone in the coach read aloud from the psalms or from *Ein Yaakov*. During the year that Shmuel was with him, the Besht always asked him to read.

Now, the Holy Society of the Baal Shem Tov's intimate disciples had a special house on the outskirts of Medzibuz where they gathered after their master taught them Torah, to review and discuss his teaching. Shmuel who was only sixteen years old, knew where their meeting-place was, but did not dare to join them, being so young and not a member of their circle.

---

* A *shammos* is a "servant candle" but also a human servant; plural *shammosim*.

On the first day of Rosh HaShanah, after the Grace said following the festive meal, the Besht taught Torah at his table, on the words in the prayer: "Sound the great *shofar* for our freedom!" Immediately afterward, he retired to his room and locked the door behind him, while the Holy Society went away to their special house. Young Shmuel remained alone in the Baal Shem Tov's home, and he began to think that the Messiah would come that day. As every minute passed, the thought became stronger and stronger in his mind—that the Messiah was on his way and would soon enter the town. His heart began pounding within his breast, as the imminence of this awesome event became more and more real to him. There was no one in the house, none of the leading disciples, who would have been able to calm his spirit and dissipate the enormous tension building up within him. Finally, he felt that his very soul was in pain and anguish, because it had become fixed as a certainty in his brain that in a very short while the Messiah would arrive in the town. In a fever of anticipation, and not knowing what else to do, he decided to run to the Holy Society and tell them; perhaps they could calm him. So he ran out of the Baal Shem Tov's house and down the main street of the town in such wild haste that the people who saw him were startled. Why was he running like that? What was happening? for everyone in town knew him. They called out to ask him, but he did not answer; he just kept running until he reached the house where the disciples were.

He rushed into the house and saw the Holy Society sitting around the table, all of them having lost the power of speech, because it was absolutely clear to every one of them that the Messiah would arrive at any moment. Shmuel calmed down by sitting among them. He sat silently with them there for hours. Only when the stars came out and the second night of Rosh HaShanah began, did this thought break off from all of them and they returned to the town.

The Baal Shem Tov's teaching about the redemption was so powerful that his words became a reality in the souls of those who heard him.[3]

Rabbi Tzvi the Scribe

RABBI TZVI WORKED AS A SCRIBE FOR THE BAAL SHEM TOV, WRITING amulets. But the Besht wanted him to also write for him, when needed, *tefillin* and Torah scrolls. When he began to teach Rabbi Tzvi the holy meditations to have in mind while writing *tefillin*, the Besht told him that in order to instruct him, they must seclude themselves in a certain place in the forest, where he would show him the *tefillin* of the Master of the world. (Jewish men wear *tefillin* that say: "Hear O Israel, the Lord our God, the Lord is one!" The Rabbis teach that the Holy One, blessed be He, also wears *tefillin*, which say: "Who is like My people Israel, a unique nation on earth!") When the Baal Shem Tov and Rabbi Tzvi reached the spot, which was deep in the forest and surrounded by tall trees, the Besht drew a circle on the ground and called out, "The *mikvah* of Israel is the Lord, their savior in time of trouble!" At that moment, a spring was miraculously created in the earth, and the Besht and Rabbi Tzvi immersed in it. Then, the Besht taught Rabbi Tzvi the secrets of holy writing. Rabbi Tzvi, like other pious scribes, always immersed in a *mikvah* each time before writing the four-letter divine Name. Now, the Besht taught him how to meditate and immerse himself in God while in the water. From this time on, while writing *tefillin*, Rabbi Tzvi saw from one end of the world to the other. And the *tefillin* he wrote were prized beyond all others by the Baal Shem Tov's disciples and by the most devout people of the generation.[4]

The Cantor

RABBI MORDECHAI OF ZASLOV WAS A HIDDEN TZADDIK AND A DISCIPLE OF the Baal Shem Tov. Years after the Besht had revealed himself, Rabbi Mordechai decided to change his way of life. When he asked his master what he should do to earn a living, the Besht told him to be a cantor. Rabbi Mordechai was astonished and said, "But Rebbe, I can't even sing!" "Then I'll bind you to the world of song," said the Besht. That is what he did, and Rabbi Mordechai of Zaslov became one of the most famous cantors of his generation, and the sweetness of his *davvening* melted the heart of everyone who heard him.

The Baal Shem Tov could not bear cantors who were proud of their fine voices and sang to please their audience, rather than standing before the Master of the world and seeking to please Him. As with all other talents, someone who has a beautiful voice should devote it to God's service; but the Besht taught that a good voice is not the essence of prayer, for God desires the heart. If a prayer-leader binds himself to God through singing, his voice is certain to sound sweet to the ears of pious people, and he will elevate everyone who hears him, so that they yearn to repent and return to the Source of their soul.[5]

The Teaching of the Palm Tree and the Cedar

THE BAAL SHEM TOV INSTRUCTED ALL OF HIS CLOSE DISCIPLES TO TRAVEL from place to place to "fix the world" by bringing people to repentance. Before sending each of them out, he told them a teaching on the psalm verse: "The righteous shall be fruitful like a palm tree and grow like a cedar in Lebanon." He said, "There are two kinds of tzaddikim. One is like a date palm, the other is like a cedar. A cedar has many good qualities: It's tall, strong, and beautiful; but it produces no fruits. The palm tree lacks the other qualities, but has the most important one of all: It produces sweet fruits—dates—that nourish and heal those who eat them. So too with tzaddikim. There are two ways to serve God, blessed be He. There is a tzaddik," explained the

Besht, "who is like a cedar. He studies Torah and fulfills the *mitzvot*, but it's all for himself, for his own benefit; he doesn't influence others. Yet he's still a tzaddik and he receives a reward from the Holy One, blessed be He. He's like a cedar—tall, strong, and beautiful. But that's not the purpose for which the Holy One, blessed be He, created a person. What God wants is for a person to be like a palm tree that produces sweet fruits. God wants everyone to devote some of the time, energy, and effort that he might have used for his own needs, to influence and affect another Jew for good, so that this other Jew may also become someone about whom the Holy One, blessed be He, can say, 'He's a good and sweet fruit!' When someone influences others, he's called 'a fruitful palm tree.' That's why I'm sending you out to influence other Jews to return to their Source—so that you too will be called 'a fruitful palm tree.'"[6]

The Parable of the Broom

ONCE, WHEN RABBI MENDEL OF BAR RETURNED FROM A PREACHING TRIP to bring others to repentance, the Besht said to him, "Just like a broom cleans the courtyard, but itself becomes dirty, so someone can clean the whole world, but a bit of its evil clings to him. You have to be willing to descend to *Gehinnom* for the sake of God, blessed be He. That's what the Talmud hints at in saying: 'A sin for the sake of heaven is greater than a *mitzvah* not for the sake of heaven.' You might think that when you act for the sake of heaven you don't have to go that far, to descend to *Gehinnom*, but it's not true! You must sweep the house, even though the broom—you yourself—becomes dirty. Then you must clean the broom too. Therefore, when you've cleaned the world and brought others to God, don't be proud, because who knows what evil has clung to you?"[7]

The Preacher's Pride

ANOTHER OF THE BAAL SHEM TOV'S DISCIPLES, RABBI ARYE LEIB OF Polnoye, also traveled around as a preacher according to his master's instruction. He even preached in the prestigious Great Synagogue in the large city of Lvov and was honored everywhere he went.

When he returned to Medzibuz after one preaching trip, he stayed at the Baal Shem Tov's house for the Sabbath. After the Sabbath evening services, when they came back from the synagogue, the Besht stood by the table and chanted "*Shalom Aleichem*," as customary. Rabbi Arye Leib saw that the Baal Shem Tov turned toward the door and motioned with his hand as if telling someone to go away. It occurred to him that the Besht was pretending to be having a vision, but actually was just acting crazily and saw nothing. Because of the honor he had received for his preaching, he had become so infected by pride that he was able to have such low and impure thoughts about his holy master, the Baal Shem Tov. Then, the Besht turned around a second time and again waved his hand as if he was motioning to someone to go away. But during the Sabbath, Rabbi Arye Leib did not dare ask him about his peculiar behavior.

After *havdala*, the Baal Shem Tov lay down to rest and while smoking his pipe related the visions he had seen during the Sabbath. Rabbi Arye Leib asked, "Master, why did you turn around to the door twice while chanting *Shalom Aleichem*?" The Besht answered, "The Satan came and wanted to snatch you from me and take your soul. While reciting *Shalom Aleichem*, I rebuked him and prayed for you—so he went away. When he came a second time, I had to concede, 'He'll be punished, but you won't take him from me!'"

And so it was, for when Rabbi Arye Leib left the Besht's house and went home, he became ill and the Baal Shem Tov had to exert himself mightily to pray for him, until he was cured. The preacher also forgot all his memorized sermons and he had to undergo severe trials and labor with much effort before he was once again fit to preach.[8]

The Importance of Parables and Stories

ONE DAY, BETWEEN *MINHA* AND *MAARIV*, THE BAAL SHEM TOV SAT WITH his disciples and taught them exalted teachings, including a generous assortment of stories and parables, as usual. He then told them this parable: "There was once a king," he said, "whose sons ate with him at his table. Even though a king's table is laden with all the finest delicacies, they became so accustomed to this rich food that they derived no special pleasure from it. One day, their father the king said to them, 'My advice is that you fill large sacks with the leftovers, and store them away in a safe place. A time will come when you'll enjoy the leftovers even more than you did the full meals.' That's what actually happened. Once, during a wartime siege of the city, they brought out the stored leftovers and enjoyed them tremendously. The meaning of this," said the Besht, "is that you should carefully store away in your memory what may seem like the 'leftovers'—the stories and parables—that you hear from me, because there will come times when they'll be of great use to you. And in truth, stories and parables are not 'leftovers' at all. In fact, only an expert preacher can find the right story to illustrate his teaching, or create a parable that can be understood even by simple people."

Hearing the rich philosophical and mystical lessons of their master, the Baal Shem Tov—eating at the king's table—every day, his scholarly disciples tended to overlook the simpler and more homely stories and parables he used to explain his teachings. The Besht told them by means of this parable to carefully memorize these useful illustrations, because there would be occasions when they would derive more benefit from them than from the most exalted teachings. Sometimes when they were in low spirits a story or parable would revive them, and when they preached and taught, stories and parables would be indispensable, for a story brings a teaching to life and a parable makes a teaching understandable.[9]

The Tree of Life

RABBI ALEXANDER WAS THE BAAL SHEM TOV'S FIRST SCRIBE; WHEN THE work became too much for one man, he had been joined by Rabbi Tzvi. After many years working as a scribe for the Besht, Rabbi Alexander felt he needed to earn more money to support his family. He asked the Besht to get him work as a *shochet*, and the Besht arranged for him to be appointed as a *shochet* in Whitefield. Once, when he was visiting his master in Medzibuz, the Besht (who called him by his nickname) said to him, "Sendril, I once made a soul-ascent to the Garden of Eden and I saw many Jews accompanying me. But the closer I came to the Garden, the fewer there were, until, at last, when I reached the Tree of Life, there remained only a very few—I also saw you among them, Sendril, but you were standing off at a distance."

How could Rabbi Alexander leave eternal life to pursue what is temporary? How could he abandon the chance to be close to his master, the holy Baal Shem Tov—who was a tree of life—and keep himself at a distance merely to earn extra money for his family?[10]

Witness to a Debate

THE BAAL SHEM TOV FREQUENTLY CONVERSED WITH THE SOULS OF deceased tzaddikim, especially with the great kabbalist, the holy Ari.

The Besht once asked the Ari why he had revealed the secrets of the Kabbalah in a way that they could not be easily applied in divine service. Indeed, a person can study the Ari's teachings and wonder how knowing about such heavenly matters can improve him spiritually. The Ari answered that if he had lived two more years he would have done that—because the Ari died when he was only 38.

Once, the Besht sat around a table with his disciples and gave a discourse about the *kavvanot* for *mikvah* immersion. His disciples, who were all great kabbalists, said to him, "Master, isn't what you're teaching different from what's found in the writings of the Ari?" When the Besht heard this question, he leaned his head back on the chair, directing his face and eyes heavenward. His face began to burn like a torch and his eyes bulged out, as always when he made a soul-ascent to the upper worlds. And, as always, his disciples were overcome with feelings of intense awe as they sat in deep silence, watching their holy master in this state of trance.

The Baal Shem Tov was sitting at the head of the table, while Rabbi Nachman Horodenker, one of his youngest disciples, sat at the end. Suddenly, a powerful drowsiness began to descend on Rabbi Nachman and, to his dismay, he found himself falling asleep. He became upset with himself, thinking, "How can this be happening? Everyone is sitting in fear and trembling while our master is making a soul-ascent, and I'm falling asleep?" He did everything he could to stay awake. He even tried to hold his eyelids open. But, against his will, he fell into a deep sleep.

He dreamt he was walking on the street and saw many people running. He ran after them and asked them why they were running. They said that their holy rabbi was about to give a discourse. He asked them who their rabbi was, but they were too much in a hurry to answer him. He followed them until he came to a magnificent mansion. He went in and saw that it was completely filled from wall to wall with great tzaddikim, as was evident from their appearance. Then the Baal Shem Tov entered and, his face glowing with divine light, began to deliver his talk about the kabbalistic meditations for the *mikvah*. There was a young man of striking spiritual beauty present, who stood opposite the Besht and contradicted what he said. Rabbi Nachman, who avidly followed the debate, asked who the young man was and was told that it was the Ari, of blessed memory. The debate and discussion between the Ari and the Baal Shem Tov continued for a long time, until the Ari finally conceded that the Besht was correct.

At that moment, Rabbi Nachman woke up, and the Baal Shem Tov, who had just returned to normal consciousness, called to him, "Nachman! I took you along with me as a witness. Tell them who is correct!" With that, the Besht got up from his chair and left, while Rabbi Nachman reported to the other disciples what he had seen and heard.[11]

The Ark of the Covenant

RABBI NACHMAN HORODENKER HAD ALREADY VISITED THE LAND OF Israel and now wanted to return there, but the Baal Shem Tov would not agree. (A disciple under his rebbe's discipline will not act without the rebbe's permission.) So he did not go. Yet every time he felt a yearning and desire to travel to Israel, he went to ask the Besht, who still would not agree. Once, a very strong yearning arose within him to travel to Israel and he went to ask for the Baal Shem Tov's consent. The Besht responded, "If you want to travel, go. But first go to the *mikvah*." He went immediately to the *mikvah* and immersed many times. When he returned afterward to the Baal Shem Tov, the Besht asked him, "What did you see during the first immersion?" Rabbi Nachman said, "I saw the Land of Israel." "What did you see during the second immersion?" "I saw Jerusalem," he replied. "What did you see during the third immersion?" "I saw the Temple." "What did you see during the fourth immersion?" "I saw the holy of holies, but I didn't see the Ark." "The Ark is in Medzibuz," said the Baal Shem Tov. Rabbi Nachman then understood that the Besht did not want him to travel, so he did not persist and stayed with his master, the Baal Shem Tov.

Why did Rabbi Nachman want to travel to the Land of Israel? to be elevated by the

land's holiness. It became clear to him that his master, the Baal Shem Tov, would elevate him and that the greatest holiness was in the Besht's presence, for he was the Ark
of the Torah.[12]

Knowing His Own Level

THE BAAL SHEM TOV WAS AS HUMBLE AND LOWLY AS THE DUST, YET HE
knew his own spiritual level. Once, after teaching Torah to his disciples, he said,
"Before I came to the world, the Torah was wearing sackcloth; and if I had not come,
she would by now be totally covered in sackcloth. But I rescued her from her mourning." He paused and was silent for a while. Then he said, "A tzaddik should act with
such holy force that every sinner is at least somewhat affected for good. I tell you, it's
impossible that there's a Jewish sinner in any corner of the world who's not been
touched by my divine service." On another occasion, he said to Rabbi Yaakov Yosef of
Polnoye, "Sometimes the world is in a low state; at other times, it's in a high state.
Because of me, the world is now in a high state." Indeed, because of the merit of his
great soul having descended to this world, all the souls of his generation were great.[13]

The Tale of the Wife's Test

ONCE, IN DISCUSSING THE FIRST VERSES IN THE BOOK OF LAMENTATIONS
and the destruction of the ancient Temple in Jerusalem, the Baal Shem Tov told
Rabbi Yaakov Yosef of Polnoye the following story:

"A Jewish merchant was once on a ship at sea when a great storm arose and threatened the lives of everyone on board. The merchant stood and prayed to be saved in the
merit of his chaste wife. A gentile merchant, overhearing him, said that he was astonished that the Jew prayed to be saved because of his wife. When the Jew answered that
she was worthy of such praise, the gentile replied, 'You may think that she's chaste, but
I'm willing to bet that I can seduce her. What proof do you want that I've succeeded?'
The Jew said, 'She wears an expensive ring on her hand. If you bring it to me, I'll know
that you seduced her.' They agreed that whoever lost the bet would forfeit all his merchandise to the other.

"After the ship arrived safely in port, the husband stayed away from home. The gentile went to seduce her, but he could not even approach her. He visited her several
times, claiming to have a secret message from her husband, but she wouldn't have anything to do with him. Finally, he bribed her maid to steal the ring and succeeded in
obtaining it. He brought it to her husband, who had to forfeit all his merchandise. The
husband then returned home empty-handed. He not only had lost all his merchandise
from the trip, but believed that his wife was unfaithful.

"When the woman heard that her husband had returned, she put on her best clothes and went out of the house to greet him lovingly. But he totally ignored her. She was confused, not knowing why his love for her seemed to have disappeared. He went inside with her, but was cold, showing no feeling for her at all.

"Finally, he decided to test her a second time. He sent her away from his house and put her on a boat that had no captain, just a single sailor, who was actually the husband himself, who had disguised his dress and speech. The 'sailor' made advances to her, but she harshly rejected him and pushed him away. He then refused to give her anything to eat or drink. After sailing on the boat for several days without food or even water, she was forced to plead with the sailor to give her something to eat and drink to stay alive. 'If you kiss me,' he replied, 'I'll give it to you.' She was forced to kiss him. Later, he demanded that she lie with him and she could not refuse.

"Afterward, when they sailed near a coast, she jumped from the boat and swam ashore. While looking for food, she saw two fruit trees. When a person ate the fruit from one of them, he became leprous; when a leprous person ate fruit from the other, he was cured. She took fruit from the second tree in her bag. When she arrived at the king's palace, disguised as a man, and the king needed that cure, she gave it to him and was rewarded with great wealth.

"She then returned home to her husband and angrily complained about what he had done to her, sending her from his house in a boat with a single, vile sailor, whom she was forced to kiss and lie with, because she was starving! Her husband inwardly rejoiced at her extreme anger, which proved her chastity. After that, when he investigated, he discovered that the gentile had lied about her and had stolen her ring. Once this was revealed, he severely punished the man."

After finishing the tale, the Besht said to Rabbi Yaakov Yosef, "This story applies to everything that's happened and will happen in the world, from the destruction of the Temple until the coming of the Messiah, soon and in our time. I once made a soul-ascent to heaven and saw that the archangel Michael argued on Israel's behalf that all their sins and lowly acts in their business dealings were really virtues, since they were all done to obtain money to arrange a marriage for their daughter with a Torah scholar, or to give charity and so on. The 'chaste wife' is the *Shechinah*, according to the secret of 'a woman of valor is the crown of her husband.' Samael [the Satan] became jealous and said to God, 'Now they have the Temple and sacrifices and obey You, but if You want to test them, destroy the Temple and I'll seduce them, so to speak.' *By means of the maid, he stole the ring*—these are the lots for the two goats, one for God, the other for Azazel [another name for the Satan] and because of sin, the left side won and the Temple was destroyed. *He sent her away in a boat.* God, blessed be He, so to speak, disguised Himself within the name Sa"l. This is the secret of *the wife's confession about being forced to give in to the sailor's sexual demands*, which represents the complaint of the *Shechinah* against God, blessed be He, that She—the Congregation of Israel—was forced by the suffering of the exile to sin. *Later, it was revealed that she had been falsely accused.* Then, there will be 'a slaughter by God in Bozrah.' Even when it seems as if the Jewish people have been abandoned by God," said the Besht, "like when the husband sends his wife away in the boat with the sailor, He is still with them all the time."

The Baal Shem Tov heard in heaven the intercessor for Israel, the archangel Michael, justifying the Jewish people's venal sins by claiming that their motives were pure. The Besht's telling of the story of "The Wife's Test" to his disciple similarly justified the Jewish people by showing that they were forced to sin by the suffering of the exile. This effective "argument" restores Israel into God's good graces and speeds the redemption. The Rabbis teach that the Satan (the "Adversary") is an angel of God who performs God's will to test people. The Besht's bold mystic teaching in this story is that God has disguised Himself, so to speak, as Satan, and when the suffering of the exile causes the Jewish people to submit to their evil inclinations and they are seduced to sin, they are really only seduced by their disguised "Husband." In their hearts, they remain pure. Who compelled the wife in the story to sin by starving her? her own husband. When she "sinned" it was really with him. The two fruit trees that she encountered after jumping from the boat represent the two trees in the Garden of Eden—the Tree of the Knowledge of Good and Evil, which makes a person sinful and "leprous," and the Tree of Life, which cures leprosy. The wife is the tzaddik—like the Baal Shem Tov—who eats fruit from the Tree of Life, is cured and possesses the power to cure others, spiritually and physically. When the wife returns "home," she complains to her husband, meaning that the tzaddik, representing the *Shechinah*, complains to the Holy One, blessed be He, Her Husband. By means of this tale, the Baal Shem Tov complained to God about the suffering of the Jewish people and begged that they be redeemed.

After interpreting this story to Rabbi Yaakov Yosef, the Baal Shem Tov explained further that sometimes, as here, he had mystic purposes in his storytelling. "When I see that there are obstacles to prayer—that the supernal channels are defective and the flow of divine goodness is blocked and can't be fixed by prayer, I have to unite them by storytelling." By telling this story to Rabbi Yaakov Yosef, the Besht was pleading in heaven on behalf of the Jewish people.[14]

Ascending by Prayer

RABBI YOSEF ASHKENAZI, WHO FOR A TIME WAS THE PRAYER-LEADER IN the Baal Shem Tov's synagogue, once saw in his dream a certain deceased hasid of the Besht, who had passed away leaving behind a very special and intelligent young son. The widowed mother was about to make an inappropriate match for the boy, and the hasid asked Rabbi Yosef to go tell his wife, in his name, not to make the match, because it was against his wish and was disturbing his heavenly rest. Let her instead make a match with the daughter of the first man that came to her house that day.

After this, Rabbi Yosef saw an altar in his dream, and the deceased man ascended the altar, sat with his head between his knees, and began to cry out the *Selichot* prayer, "Answer us, O Lord, answer us! Answer us, our Father, answer us!"—saying the whole prayer, until the end. Then he said, "Answer us, God of our fathers, answer us! Answer us, God of Abraham, answer us! Answer us, Dread of Isaac, answer us! Answer us,

Mighty One of Jacob, answer us! Answer us, Shield of David, answer us! Answer us, God of the Chariot, answer us!" Then he flew upward into heaven.

In the morning, Rabbi Yosef went to the Baal Shem Tov and told him the dream. "That wasn't a dream you saw," said the Besht, "but a vision. I also saw it. The altar is the one on which the angel Michael sacrifices the souls of the righteous who offer themselves up before God." Rabbi Yosef asked him why the deceased hasid said the "Answer Us" prayer. The Besht replied, "Angels and souls are only able to ascend from one world to another by means of the prayer 'Answer Us.'" Rabbi Yosef asked further, "Why did he say the prayer in a version different from the one we use?" "Because that's the version used in heaven," replied the Besht.

Then the Baal Shem Tov sent for the deceased's wife, and told her her husband's message about the match for her son.[15]

The Palace of the Bird's Nest

🕯 THE BAAL SHEM TOV USUALLY STOOD PRAYING THE *SHEMONEH ESREH* FOR a very long time. Whereas an average person might take five minutes and a pious person ten or even twenty minutes, the Besht often prayed for several hours. Since the rest of the congregation found it difficult to wait until he completed this prayer, they would go home and have something to eat, to fortify themselves. When they returned for the conclusion of the service, they would usually find the Baal Shem Tov still standing finishing the prayer. However, the Holy Society, the disciples of his inner circle, would not go home to eat. They would wait for hours until the Besht finished praying the *Shemoneh Esreh*.

It happened once that all the disciples of the Holy Society felt weak, so that they also went home to have something to eat. Knowing how long the Besht usually remained in the *Shemoneh Esreh*, they expected when they returned to find him still praying it. But when they came back to the synagogue they were surprised to find that he had completed the *Shemoneh Esreh* and was waiting for them in order to conclude the service.

Whenever they noticed something unusual in the Besht's behavior, the leading disciples always asked him about it. Later, they asked him why he had shortened his prayer. He answered, "When you all went away and left me alone, you caused a serious breach in our unity. Let me explain with a parable: Everyone knows that birds migrate south for the winter, seeking warmer climates. Once, the people of a southern land saw among their avian visitors the most beautiful bird they had ever seen, whose brilliant plumage contained all the colors of the rainbow. This gorgeous bird had built its nest in the uppermost branches of a tall tree so high that no one could catch it. When the king of that land heard about it, he ordered some of his servants to stand on each other's shoulders in a pyramid, so that the one on top would be able to capture the bird and bring it to him. But when they all stood on each other's shoulders, the ones on the bottom, who couldn't see what was happening above them, became impatient and suddenly walked away, each to his own affairs. Of course, the pyramid immediately collapsed! Without the support of those below, the ones on top came tumbling down and were injured. And they all became a laughingstock throughout the land, because they had disobeyed their king's order to form a pyramid, one on top of the other, and they had failed to accomplish anything.

"Before we pray, we follow the instruction of the holy Ari, to resolve to love our neighbor as our self, so that while praying we'll be bound together in love and not be separate from each other. When you were praying together with me, I was accomplishing things, but when you all left me alone, everything fell apart, and what I'd hoped to achieve escaped my grasp.

"All Jews should join together—one to the other and one above the other—so that they all can receive the heavenly flow of blessing by way of those above them who are closer to the source of supernal goodness. When you all left me for your own private affairs, it showed that your love for each other and for me during prayer isn't what it should be. So everything was ruined. The only way to repair the damage is for you to love each other with unwavering devotion and strongly attach yourselves to me, so that I'll be able to reach and grasp the supernal goodness.

"This applies every day, but today there was even more at stake, for what are we ultimately praying for? When I make a soul-ascent during the *Shemoneh Esreh*, all the worlds are revealed to me, and my single desire is to ascend to the highest heights, to what the *Zohar* calls 'the Palace of the Bird's Nest,' that is, the Palace of the Messiah. But it's very high and the ascent dangerous. I can't reach it without your supporting me. When you're praying with me, everything I'm able to accomplish is with your help, even if you have no idea of what I'm trying to do. When you left me alone today, I fell from the place to which I'd ascended and wasn't able to accomplish anything more in the *Shemoneh Esreh*, so I concluded my prayer."[16]

It's Time to Put the Angel Michael to the Side

IT WAS THE BAAL SHEM TOV'S CUSTOM ON THE FINAL DAY OF PASSOVER to make a feast with matzah and four cups of wine for the last meal of the holiday and invite everybody. During the feast, he would distribute his matzahs (that he baked or that were baked for him) to everyone present, even the simple people, to eat. He called this "The Feast of the King Messiah." Whereas the *seders* at the beginning of Passover look back to the first redemption from Egypt, this special feast at the end of the holiday looks forward to the final redemption and the coming of the Messiah.

Once, during this feast, the Besht said, "It's time to put the angel Michael to the side." He went on to explain, "Michael is the angel-prince of Israel and also the angel-prince of the world. But there's a difference in the way he acts toward the two. When it comes to the Jewish people, if he finds something positive to say about them, well and good; but if he doesn't find anything, he manufactures it! When it comes to the nations of the world, however, he begins to stammer—he has nothing good to say about them. My master and teacher, the Baal Hai*, said to me, 'It's necessary to work with the nations of the world,' to transform them. So it's time to put the angel Michael to the side."

One of his close disciples asked, "Master, explain your meaning further." The Besht continued, "The angel Michael is the angel-prince of Israel. One of his main tasks is to justify and praise the Jewish people, to defend them against their detractors in heaven. Tzaddikim take on themselves this angelic task; they too always defend the Jewish people from their enemies and detractors on earth by justifying their faults and praising them before God and arguing their merits before the heavenly court. But for the Messiah to come, the nations too must be transformed. On the final day of Passover, when the Messiah's light is revealed, when the whole creation strives for fulfillment and all limitations become apparent, it becomes clear that even the angel Michael and his heavenly defense of the Jewish people are limited. Michael is supposed to be the angel of the whole world, not just of the Jewish people. But he hasn't fulfilled his task. And neither has the Jewish people, who are supposed to be a kingdom of priests for the whole world and a light to the nations. Jews must now find justifications and good things to say about the gentiles too, not only about Israel. Michael's exclusive focus on the Jewish people, the chosen people, must be put aside, for the final redemption and the work of the Messiah must also involve transforming the nations of the world. At the least, that means that the Jewish people must teach the gentiles the seven *mitzvot* of the Children of Noah. May the redemption come soon in our day!"[17]

Love for the Creation

THE BAAL SHEM TOV LOVED ALL OF THE CREATION AND EVERY ONE OF God's creatures. He once said to his disciples, "I love my fellow Jews like my own self, but I love gentiles too. I feel love for every animal and for every tree and plant in the forest."[18]

The Besht's Soul and the End

THE BAAL SHEM TOV ONCE RAISED A STORM OF PRAYER PLEADING FOR THE coming of the Messiah. He heard a heavenly voice answer, "There was once a great clamor in heaven urging the advent of the Redeemer. But many tzaddikim argued that the time for the End had not yet arrived, since many souls still needed fixing. Better that the judgment be delayed, to spare these souls from being lost. Other

---

* Ahiyah.

tzaddikim countered, saying, 'Must all of Israel suffer because of those unrepentant souls?' The two sides agreed to ask the view of the great unborn soul of the Baal Shem Tov. The Besht said then, 'It is written that God "devises means so that none should be outcast before Him," for He does not desire that any remain outside the fold and unsaved.' They said to him, 'And what will happen to the Jewish people, which suffers because of the outcasts who are slow to repent?' So after discussion and debate, it was decided that if that was the position of the Baal Shem Tov, it was only fitting that he himself descend to this world and bring all the outcast souls to repentance. "If so," the heavenly voice concluded, "what are you demanding now? You yourself rejected the early coming of the End!"

The Besht did not accept this answer. He continued to work to bring lost souls back to their Source, but he also prayed with all his might for the coming of the Messiah.[19]

His Soul-Ascent to the Messiah

AT THAT TIME, THERE WERE MANY MEETINGS OF THE HIDDEN TZADDIKIM, who were continually occupied in efforts to improve the material and spiritual standing of the Jewish people. They also worked to counteract the effects of the terrible flareups of antisemitism that afflicted the Jews. The Baal Shem Tov himself was troubled to his soul by these recurring persecutions and pogroms. In his love for the Jewish people, he felt their suffering as his own. With loving eyes he saw all the goodness of the Jewish people and the repentance that he and those who followed him had inspired. Yet these same pious Jews who fulfilled the Torah and *mitzvot* with self-sacrifice were persecuted by wicked gentiles! Since the Rabbis say that if Israel repents they will be redeemed, the Besht could not understand why the Messiah had not come. He decided that he and his comrades among the hidden tzaddikim—some of whom were men on awesome spiritual levels—would do everything they could to bring the revelation of the Messiah. After one such meeting with some of his comrades among the hidden mystics, at which he had spoken to them about acting to bring the Messiah, the Besht resolved to make a soul-ascent to ask the Messiah himself why he had not come.

The following Rosh HaShanah, in the year 1747, he made a soul-ascent, by means of an invocation, to the upper Garden of Eden and witnessed wondrous visions such as he had never before seen. When he returned to the lower Garden of Eden, he saw innumerable souls of the living and the dead, people both known and unknown to him, who were ascending in the manner of forward and back from world to world by means of the column that connects the worlds. They were all in a state of ecstatic bliss and joy. He also saw many sinful people who had repented and whose sins were forgiven, as it was a time of great divine favor, and the Besht was amazed that so many were received in repentance. They too were consumed in joy and ascended through the worlds with the others. All of them together pleaded with him insistently, saying, "Because of your supremely profound Torah knowledge, God has graced you with

extraordinary understanding. Therefore, ascend with us, to help and support us."
Because of the awesome joy he witnessed among them, he agreed to ascend with them.

He also saw in his vision that the Satan too, joyful as never before, ascended to make accusations and instigated a decree of religious persecution and forced apostasy, so that a number of Jews would be put to death by terrible means. The Besht was seized with terror and resolved to do everything to save them, even offering his life if necessary.

He begged his master and teacher, Ahiyah ha-Shiloni, to accompany him on his ascent, since it is extremely dangerous to travel to the upper worlds and he had never ascended so high. He ascended by stages until he entered the Palace of the Messiah, where the Messiah studies Torah with the Seven Shepherds and with all the *Tannaim** and tzaddikim. There, the Baal Shem Tov witnessed extraordinary joy without knowing its cause. He thought that, perhaps, the rejoicing was because he had died and left this world behind. But they told him that he had not yet died, because they derived great pleasure and delight in heaven when he performed unifications joining cosmic spiritual forces by means of the holy Torah.

He asked the Messiah, "Master, when are you coming?" The Messiah answered, "This shall be the sign for you: When your teachings have spread throughout the world and your fountains have overflowed in all directions—east, west, north, and south—and what I will teach you, and you have grasped, becomes accessible to others and they too are able to perform unifications and soul-ascents like you, then all the Shells shall be destroyed and the hour for salvation will have arrived."

The Besht was surprised and disturbed by this and his heart fell, grieving at how long this would take. Who knew when it might happen? But while there he learned three mystically potent secrets and three divine Names, which are easy to teach and explain, so his mind was put at ease, thinking that perhaps it was possible that, through these, some of his close disciples would also succeed in attaining the spiritual rung he had reached and they too would be able to ascend and learn and comprehend. But he was not given permission to reveal these things as long as he lived. Nor did he ever learn what had caused the great joy in heaven.

While in the upper worlds, the Besht also prayed regarding the vision he had seen about the terrible persecution of Jews that would soon occur, "Why did God do this? Why was His anger so great, to deliver these Jews into the Satan's hands to be put to death by horrible tortures, and some of them will apostatize to save their lives and yet still be killed?" He was given permission to ask the Satan himself. So he asked, "Why are you doing this and why will they be put to death even after they convert?" The Satan answered, "My intention was for the sake of heaven, for when other Jews see that converting will not save them, they will face martyrdom bravely and withstand the test. They will refuse to convert and will sanctify God's name." After hearing this, the Besht prayed to God that the merit of the sacrifice of these martyrs speed the coming of the Messiah. Then he descended to the earthly plane.

---

* Sages of the *Mishna*.

Having been told that the redemption depended on the spread of his teaching, the Besht's outlook changed and all his efforts took on a new urgency. He now was a disciple of the Messiah. And he now conceived the essence of his spiritual path to be to teach Jews how to perform the divine service that will be in the days of the Messiah, a divine service that overcomes all fear and is filled with joy. The Messiah had not yet come, and the Jewish people would still experience persecution; the Baal Shem Tov would still struggle with grief and sadness at their suffering. But the task of attaining a joyous service of God was now clear. That is how the Baal Shem Tov tried to serve God and that is the way he revealed the spark of the Messiah in his soul. After this soul-ascent, he later taught his disciples on that Rosh HaShanah, "Each Jew must fix and prepare the spark of the Messiah in his own soul, and when all these sparks come to fulfillment and are joined, the Messiah will be revealed and the redemption will come."[20]

Bringing the Messiah

AT NIGHT, AFTER THE CONCLUSION OF ROSH HASHANAH, THE BAAL Shem Tov taught further:

"Adam's soul extended from one end of the world to the other—and the souls of all Israel were included within it—but because of his sin, his soul was reduced. The Messiah's soul also includes the souls of all Israel, like Adam before his sin. ADaM stands for the first letters of Adam, David, Messiah. When each Jew fixes the Messiah portion of his own soul, the complete form of the Messiah's soul will be prepared, and there will be an enduring and perfect unity among all of the Jewish people, soon in our days."

The Besht continued, "The words in the psalm: 'Draw near to my soul; redeem it!' are a prayer for the redemption of the soul from the exile of the evil inclination. When each soul will have accomplished its own individual redemption, the Messiah will come and the world will be redeemed, soon and in our days, Amen. And they all shall know, from the least to the greatest, to do everything for God's sake alone, blessed is He and blessed is His name."

The advent of the Messiah began from the time of the revelation of the holy Baal Shem Tov.[21]

His Soul Taken without Speech

ONE EVENING WHEN HE WAS ALONE WITH HIS GRANDSON, RABBI EPHRAIM, the Besht told him that his (the Besht's) father had taken his soul from the treasury of souls without speech or prayer—as happened to Moses, who because of that stuttered. "If my father had brought down my soul by speech," said the Besht, "my Torah teaching would have been so powerful and persuasive that I would have convinced everyone who heard me to repent. My teaching would have filled the whole world and would immediately have consumed all the Shells and brought the Messiah!"[22]

Persecution

SINCE THE MIDDLE AGES, RIVERS OF JEWISH BLOOD WERE SPILLED because of the false accusations of Christian antisemites. Sometimes these were libels that Jews had slaughtered Christians to use their blood in making Passover matzahs; other times that Jews had desecrated the communion wafer. These false accusations led to persecutions and pogroms in which many thousands of Jews were murdered. In Poland, these vicious libels were almost commonplace and they took many innocent sacrificial victims among the Jewish people. The Baal Shem Tov was born and revealed in Podolia, a land that was drenched in the blood of Jewish martyrs. During his lifetime there were constant blood libels.[23]

The First Zaslov Blood Libel (1747)

ON ROSH HASHANAH IN 1747 THE BAAL SHEM TOV HAD MADE HIS GREAT soul-ascent to the Palace of the Messiah and had learned about a terrible decree of persecution and forced apostasy. Later that year there occurred a grievous tragedy in the city of Zaslov (in Volhynia about fifty miles from Medzibuz), which the Besht had foreseen in his vision in the upper worlds. At the end of the winter, when the ice was breaking up in the rivers and the heavy snow melting, the body of a dead gentile was found near one of the villages, on the road from Zaslov to Bilogorodka. The decomposed body had undoubtedly been under the snow for some time. Probably, the man had lost his way during a storm because of the bad condition of the roads.

But a peasant came and testified that one evening he had seen a horse-drawn sleigh with Jews in it stop at the Jewish inn in that village, where they had some sort of celebration. They slept there overnight and the next day prayed with their prayer-shawls on and then made a feast and celebrated some more; afterward, they returned to Zaslov.

This happened before Passover, when blood libels were typically made. It was easy then for the officials of the lord of the area—Prince Sengosciu—and the priests to solve the puzzle: The Jews had gathered to ritually slaughter the Christian to use his blood for their Passover matzahs. And in honor of the commandment that they had been fortunate enough to fulfill, they celebrated at the inn. The innkeeper was imprisoned and, during his interrogation, told them that indeed there was a celebration in his inn for a circumcision. The rabbi, the cantor, the *mohel**, the *shammos*, and one of

* Ritual circumciser.

his relatives were all present at the circumcision feast. The authorities took them all into custody, except for the rabbi, who managed to escape to Medzibuz, and they tortured the Jews to extract confessions from them. All five captives were sentenced to horrible deaths. One was cut up into four parts, three others were nailed hanging to posts, a sharp metal peg at their head and a heavy load at their feet, so that the body was pulled down until the intestines came out; another one was beheaded with a sword. Before their deaths, the last two of them had been persuaded to convert by the priests, who told the Jews that they would save them from torture and death. But the unfortunate victims did not know that the compassionate priests were only anxious about their souls in the World-to-Come; they would still be put to death. When these Jews saw that they had been deceived and were being led out to execution, they regretted their conversion and called out loudly, *Shema Yisrael, HaShem Elokeinu, HaShem ehad*—"Hear O Israel, the Lord our God, the Lord is one!"

After this incident there were blood libels in the towns of Sivtovka and Dinovitz and—as was revealed to the Besht in his vision—the Jews did not apostatize, having heard what had happened in Zaslov. All of them withstood the test of martyrdom and gave up their lives to sanctify God's name.

These tragic events caused the Baal Shem Tov terrible anguish, and he prayed that, in the merit of the sacrifice of these holy martyrs, atonement be made for the Jewish people, that the Messiah would come to avenge their suffering and lead them up to their land.[24]

The Second Zaslov Blood Libel (1750)

THREE YEARS LATER, IN 1750, THERE WAS A SECOND BLOOD LIBEL IN Zaslov. The Baal Shem Tov visited Zaslov for several Sabbaths that year, on one occasion staying with Rabbi David, formerly the head of the religious court of Ostrog. Rabbi David's son, Rabbi Yitzhak, also lived in Zaslov. During one of the Besht's visits, on a Sabbath before Passover, a gentile was found dead in a field. After bringing him into the city, they went to the duchess and accused the Jews of having murdered him. The duchess was afraid to go along with them because her husband the duke had himself died a contemptible death on the road as a heavenly punishment for having martyred the Jews in the earlier false accusation. So she said to them, "It's impossible to condemn people to death unless the matter has been thoroughly investigated and it's clear that the Jews murdered him."

When the Jews of the city learned about these events, they were terrified and sent Rabbi Yitzhak to the inn where the Baal Shem Tov was staying, to tell him about it. When he arrived, he found the Besht standing with one foot on a stool and the other foot on the floor, listening to his scribe, Rabbi Tzvi, read to him from the *Zohar*. Rabbi Tzvi read, and the Besht repeated the words after him, with intense fervor, his face burning in such rapture that it glowed. Rabbi Yitzhak was standing in the doorway, and the Besht motioned to him with his hand to leave; so he left.

Meanwhile, the terror among the Jews was growing, and they sent Rabbi Yitzhak to the Besht a second time, but again he motioned to him to leave. Finally, they urged Rabbi Yitzhak's father, Rabbi David, to go to the Besht, because he was a venerable, elderly rabbi and the Besht would certainly not dismiss him. So Rabbi David himself went to the Baal Shem Tov to tell him of the danger from the blood libel that was hovering over their heads. "I don't hear them discussing this in the citadel of the duchess at all," said the Besht. "Don't worry about it." (The Besht did not hear with his holy spirit any discussion, because the duchess had delayed judgment on the accusation.)

Later during the week, the Besht was lying down in the middle of the day after a meal, with his head propped up on his hand, and his disciples were standing around him in the room. Suddenly, he inclined his head like someone who is listening to something, and then he said that they were discussing the blood libel in the citadel. He told them to heat the *mikvah* quickly, so he could immerse and pray about it. After returning from the *mikvah*, he said, "Don't worry; there's nothing to be concerned about."

Nevertheless, the frightened community leaders sent a representative to the citadel to speak on their behalf. He heard the gentiles complaining to the duchess about the dead man, and she ordered her doctor to examine the cadaver to determine whether or not the man had died from natural causes. The doctor was bribed by the Jewish community leaders, who were afraid to rely on the Besht alone. The doctor reported that the man had died a natural death. So nothing came of the accusation.

The head of the religious court of Zaslov, Rabbi Mordechai, who was the brother-in-law of Rabbi David, was skeptical about the Baal Shem Tov and asked him why he had not used his holy spirit to tell them beforehand that the body would be found in the field, so that they could prepare themselves and would not be so frightened when it occurred. "I prayed about this when I was in the *mikvah*," the Besht replied, "and asked why heaven concealed this from me at first. They answered that it was to punish me for being lax in eulogizing a Torah scholar and opponent of mine, Rabbi Hayim Tzanzer of Brody, who recently passed away." Rabbi Mordechai was listening to this explanation skeptically, thinking that it was probably just a lie, and the Besht had no holy spirit at all. Then the Besht said to him, "Do you think I don't know that you were so frightened of being accused and martyred that you hid yourself several times—once under the benches in the bathhouse and other times elsewhere?" He told him every place he had hidden himself, and the rabbi confessed that he was correct about each one.[25]

The Conceit of Martyrdom

SOME TIME AFTER THIS, WHEN THE BESHT WAS WALKING IN THE countryside with his disciples and heard an ox in the field bellow, he emitted a loud groan. Asked by his disciples why he had groaned, he said, "A Jew was just burned as a martyr and, at the moment of his death, he felt satisfied at having withstood the test. The shame! Because this ox will go to its death without the least pride or self-satisfaction, simply to fulfill the purpose for which it was created. Should a man not know how to fulfill his duty and mission to sanctify the name of God, without it being tainted by pride and self-satisfaction?"[26]

The Martyrs of Pavlitch

THREE YEARS LATER, IN 1753, THERE WAS ANOTHER BLOOD LIBEL BEFORE Passover in the city of Pavlitch in the Polish Kiev region—that Jews had murdered a Christian child who was found dead. Eight righteous and innocent men—Rabbi Akiba, the rabbi of Pavlitch, and seven others—were seized. The rabbi of the nearby town of Korotchishov, Rabbi David, fled, and wanted to continue to Walachia, which was under Turkish rule, because all the prominent people in the area were afraid that they too would be falsely accused. When Rabbi David arrived in Medzibuz, the Baal Shem Tov kept him with him and told him not to be afraid and not to flee to Walachia. He also told him a number of times that those seized in the blood libel would escape harm.

But they were killed. Afterward, a letter from Pavlitch reached Rabbi David in Medzibuz, describing the gruesome details of how each of the martyrs had met his death by being subjected to severe and bitter tortures. Rabbi David went with the letter to the Baal Shem Tov, who grieved so after reading it that he fell into a deep depression. This happened on a Friday, and when the Besht went to the *mikvah* to prepare for the oncoming Sabbath, he wept while in the *mikvah*. He prayed *Minha* with such grief that his disciples were not able to lift up their heads. They said, "Perhaps when he receives the Sabbath, he'll do so joyfully." But he was also grieving when he prayed *Kabbalat Shabbat* and *Maariv*, and made *kiddush* over the wine while weeping. He washed his hands for the Sabbath meal, sat down at the table for a few minutes, and ate a bite of the bread over which he had made the blessing, although the guests had not yet eaten. But he then left the table and went to his private upstairs room in the *beit midrash*. He prostrated on the floor and lay there for a long while. His family and the guests waited for him until the Sabbath candles began to go out. Then his wife went in and said to him, "The candles will soon go out, and the guests are waiting for you." "Let them eat, say the Grace After Meals, and go home," replied the Besht. After the others had left, Rebbetzin Chana also went to the room where the Besht was and lay down on her bed.

The Besht was still lying on the floor, with arms and legs outstretched. Rabbi David of Korotchishov, who had fled the blood libel and taken refuge with the Besht, stood near the door of the Besht's room to see what the outcome of this would be. Eventually, he became tired from standing and sat down on a stool outside the door. About midnight, Rabbi David heard the Baal Shem Tov say to his wife, "Cover your face." Suddenly, the room was filled with brilliant light, which shone through the cracks around the door. He heard the Besht say, "Welcome, Rabbi Akiba of Pavlitch!" and he heard him greeting by name the other holy martyrs who had come to him from the next world. When Rabbi Akiba of Pavlitch spoke, Rabbi David recognized his voice because he knew him.

The Besht said to the martyrs, "I order you to go and take revenge on your persecutors!" "Holy Rabbi," they responded, "Don't let such words out of your mouth, and annul what you've already said. Because you don't know your own power. When you disturbed your Sabbath, there was a tremendous commotion in the Garden of Eden, and souls were fleeing from all the heavenly palaces, as people flee from a battlefield during a war. We also fled and, when we arrived at a higher palace, they were fleeing from there too, although no one knew why. Finally, we came to an even higher palace where they did know. They shouted to us, 'Go quickly and console the Baal Shem Tov!' That's why we're here. And we can tell you," they continued, "that all the suffering a person experiences in his whole life is as insignificant as the skin of a garlic compared to the suffering we endured in being martyred to sanctify God's name, may He be blessed and exalted. And the evil inclination didn't slacken its efforts even then and it succeeded in confusing our thoughts ever so slightly, although we pushed it away with both hands. As a result, we were forced to undergo a half hour's punishment in *Gehinnom*. Afterward, we were immediately escorted to the Garden of Eden and we began to argue that we wanted to take vengeance against our persecutors. 'The Accuser still has the upper hand,' they said to us. 'If you wish to take vengeance, you must agree to be reincarnated and return to that lower world.' We said, 'Praise God, we overcame our weakness and martyred ourselves to sanctify God's name, but we still had to endure the suffering of *Gehinnon* for having succumbed ever so slightly to the evil inclination. And all the tortures of martyrdom are like the skin of a garlic compared to the awful torment of that half hour in hell. Who knows what will happen if we are reborn? What if this time we are tested somehow and succumb to our evil inclination in a more serious way, God-forbid, so that there's no way to repair our sin? Therefore, it's better for us to forgo vengeance, to avoid being reborn.' So we beg you, Holy Rabbi, to nullify what you just said."

"Why did heaven mislead me," asked the Besht, "so that I thought you would escape harm? Why wasn't it revealed to me that you would be martyred?" "If you had known about this," they answered, "you would have prayed until heaven was forced to cancel the decree, and later there would have been an even greater catastrophe. Our martyrdom atoned for many sins of the Jewish people and a worse disaster was averted. That's why heaven concealed it from you."[27]

Comforting a Martyr's Mother

ONCE, WHEN THE BAAL SHEM TOV WAS IN POLNOYE, HE VISITED THE HOME of the mother of a Jewish youth who had been martyred as the result of a blood libel and had greatly sanctified God's name by his conduct. The Besht comforted her, saying, "Know that at the hour of his death all the heavenly worlds opened up before him, as they did for Isaac when he was bound on the altar."[28]

If I Don't Succeed

❧ THE BAAL SHEM TOV USED TO VISIT A CERTAIN TOWN EVERY YEAR, AND stayed at the home of one of its wealthy men. Once, he arrived there suddenly on a Friday afternoon, not at the usual time of year, and arranged to stay in the synagogue. His regular host came to him and asked him to be his guest, as always, but the Besht said that this time he wanted to spend the Sabbath in the synagogue. Soon, everyone in the city had gathered in the synagogue and after the Sabbath welcoming service, the Besht, who looked grave, told them to recite psalms. They were all wondering what this meant and became anxious, because they realized that they were in dire need of heavenly mercy. Close to midnight, he asked them to bring him his Sabbath meal, and he told the people to go home to eat their meal and to return to the synagogue afterwards.

When they returned later, they continued reciting psalms for the whole night, until dawn. They prayed the morning service, and then the Baal Shem Tov told the wealthy man that now he would go to his house for a Sabbath meal. When everyone saw that the Besht's mood had changed and he was now smiling and full of Sabbath joy, their mood also changed and they too relaxed. After *kiddush*, when they were all sitting at the table, a gentile suddenly entered the synagogue and asked for a glass of liquor in reward for some news. The Besht told them to give it to him, and then asked the man to tell them what he knew. He told this story:

"Yesterday evening," he said, "the lord of this area gathered all the peasants from the local villages and armed them with staves, knives, pitchforks, and swords, so that they would go and wipe out all the Jews in the town. The whole night they stood around impatiently waiting for his command. Before dawn, a high government official arrived in a carriage, went in to the lord, and stayed with him for some time. Afterward, the lord came out and ordered the peasants to disperse and return to their homes."

The Besht told the gentile he could leave and then revealed the rest of the story to those at the table. "The lord is a very wealthy man. Since he wasn't in need of money, he was in no hurry to sell his crops, and the Jewish merchants found it impossible to come to terms with him on a price. As a result, the produce from many years piled up in his storehouses until it began to rot. Antisemitic friends of his blamed the Jews and convinced him that they were plotting to keep buyers away from him. Believing what they told him, he grew increasingly angry about it, until he decided to make a pogrom and murder all the Jews living on his estate. I knew the situation was desperate and prayed with all my energy, while you were reciting psalms. Thankfully, my prayers were answered and God prevented the disaster. God, blessed be He, caused an old school friend of the lord to visit him, someone whom he'd not seen in forty years.

When they were young, this government official and the lord were schoolmates in the capital city. But as they lived very far from each other, they hadn't seen each other even once since they had graduated. By divine providence, the friend was traveling nearby and God put it into his head to remember his old schoolmate and to visit him. When he arrived, he asked the lord why all the peasants were milling about with weapons in their hands. The lord replied that they were getting ready to take revenge on his enemies, the Jews, who had caused his crops to rot in their storehouses. "What are you talking about?" his friend said to him. 'I deal with Jews all the time and they're decent and honest people. Tomorrow, after their Sabbath, see if what I'm saying is true. Call the Jews here and tell them your problem. I'm sure they'll offer to help you sell all your produce.' Convinced by these words of his old friend, the lord ordered the peasants to disperse."

After hearing this story from the Besht, some of his disciples could not understand why he had troubled himself to make a special visit to the town to deal with this problem. Couldn't he have stayed in Medzibuz and prayed there; and his prayers could have been answered here? When they asked him about it, the Baal Shem Tov said, "When I realized that these Jews' lives were in danger, I said to myself, 'If I succeed and my prayers are answered, good; but if not—I want to be here with them.'"[29]

The Killings Will End

ONE DAY, THE BAAL SHEM TOV WAS DEPRESSED BECAUSE OF A NEW report of pogroms and persecution of Jews. Rabbi Pinhas of Koretz, who was outside the Besht's room later that night, heard the Besht praying as he wept: "To whom shall we turn? We're fleeing to You! Don't deliver us to the wicked oppressor! We cry out while disaster after disaster befalls us. Was it not enough that we suffered the destruction of the Temple? Today none of us lives happily, as we once did in our Holy Land, each man under his fig tree. When will the Temple be rebuilt? When will we hear the sound of the Messiah's *shofar*?" After concluding his anguished prayer, the Besht left his room and discussed the situation with Rabbi Pinhas, saying to him, "When the Messiah comes, there won't be any more killing of Jews."[30]

Rabbi Dov Ber of Torchin (the Maggid of Mezritch)

He Refuses to Visit the Besht

RABBI DOV BER OF TORCHIN IN VOLHYNIA WAS A GREAT TORAH SCHOLAR who was expert not only in the Talmud and halachic codes, but in the Kabbalah as well. There was not a book of the revealed or concealed Torah that he had not reviewed one hundred and one times. Following the ascetic kabbalistic teachings, he engaged in much fasting and self-mortification. While this life of self-denial and self-sanctification led him to towering spiritual heights, it also took its toll on his health. Never too strong or healthy, and afflicted with a painful lameness in his left foot that made him use crutches—his neglect of his body aggravated his already poor health.

Once, he fasted successively seven times from Sabbath to Sabbath and became ill. Rabbi Mendel of Bar happened to visit Torchin then, and met Rabbi Dov Ber. Rabbi Mendel was very upset to see him so emaciated and sick, because he realized that Rabbi Dov Ber was a rare individual, who could accomplish great things if he was taught the true path in the service of God by the Besht. "Haven't you heard," he said to him, "that there's a Baal Shem Tov in the world, who can heal sick people? Travel to him and he'll cure you." "It's better to take refuge with God than to trust in a man," Rabbi Dov Ber replied, and he did not want to go.

Rabbi Mendel left the town and, when he visited the Besht, told him about Rabbi Dov Ber, saying, "I was in Torchin and saw there a beautiful vessel ready to receive every good thing." "I've been aware of him for a number of years," said the Besht, "and I long for him to come to me." When a great teacher sees someone who is able to receive what he has to bestow, his longing knows no bounds until he makes that person his disciple. That is the kind of powerful longing that the Baal Shem Tov felt for Rabbi Dov Ber.[31]

The First Visit

RABBI DOV BER'S FAMILY ALSO PRESSURED HIM TO VISIT THE BAAL SHEM Tov for a cure, but he absolutely refused, saying that it is forbidden to seek a cure from a *baal shem* who uses practical Kabbalah. He said, "I have one hundred questions about the Baal Shem Tov's behavior. When I receive explanations for all those questions, I'll consider visiting him."

Yet, Rabbi Dov Ber's health kept deteriorating. He tried household remedies, went to doctors, but nothing helped. Finally, his wife yelled at him, "How long will you ruin yourself? The Baal Shem Tov is doing miracles for everyone and will help you too. Why be stubborn? Go to him just once. Maybe you'll also learn something from him!" By this time, Rabbi Dov Ber had heard so many stories about the Besht's piety that his curiosity had been aroused. It had occurred to him more than once that perhaps he should make a visit to test the Besht and see if what they said about him was true. His wife's scolding finally impelled him to go. So he traveled to Medzibuz to the Baal Shem Tov.

Being a great *matmid*, it took Rabbi Dov Ber only one day of traveling before he regretted going, when he saw that he could not study as at home. At last, he arrived and went to see the Baal Shem Tov. When he entered, the Besht was receiving *pitka'ot* (prayer-request notes) and the rabbi saw that many women were standing there and the Besht was conversing with them about what Rabbi Dov Ber considered petty matters—this one wanted a son, that one could not pay her rent, and so on. It seemed to him that the Besht was not a serious spiritual person, to be discussing such trifles with women. (The Besht obviously did not share his view about talking with women). Taken aback by this sight, he thought, "Is this person going to teach me?"

Later, when he had his own audience with the Besht, and thought that he would be treated as a scholar deserved and would hear Torah teaching from him, all he heard were peculiar stories and parables, the kind of things one might tell simpletons or children! All these stories and parables were full of profound wisdom, but Rabbi Ber was not used to this sort of communication, and failed to understand it. He went back to his room at the inn thoroughly disappointed, feeling that he was wasting his valuable time. He told his servant, "I want to begin the trip home tonight. But since it's already late, let's sleep until the moon comes out. Then we'll travel."[32]

The First Midnight Session

AT MIDNIGHT, JUST AS RABBI DOV BER WAS PREPARING TO LEAVE, THE Baal Shem Tov sent his servant to summon him. When Rabbi Dov Ber entered the Besht's room, he found the Besht sitting with a small cushion on his head and wearing a wolf-skin coat turned inside out. The Besht asked him, "Have you studied Kabbalah?" When he said yes, the Besht told him to read aloud from the kabbalistic book, *Eitz Hayim* (Tree of Life), that was on the table. After he had read half a page, the Besht stopped him, saying, "That's not the way to read. Let me have the book!" Then the Besht began to read, and as he did so he began to tremble. Suddenly, he jumped up and said, "We're engaged in studying the Account of the Divine Chariot and I'm sitting?" He then continued to read while standing, with great awe.

But he made the rabbi lie down on his bed in a fetal position. From that moment, Rabbi Dov Ber no longer saw the Besht. He just heard thunder and saw lightning and awesome flames. This went on for two hours. Just as the Jewish people received the Torah at Mount Sinai, that is the way the Baal Shem Tov transmitted to Rabbi Dov Ber his soul's Torah. When Rabbi Dov Ber finally opened his eyes, he looked at the Baal Shem Tov and wondered if this person he saw before him was a man or an angel. It was difficult for him to conceive of the vision he had seen coming from the influence of a mere human being. He innocently stretched out his hand to touch the Besht's arm, to see if he actually had a physical body.

After returning to his room later, he remembered what he used to say about having one hundred questions about the Baal Shem Tov's behavior. Now he realized that he had no more questions, because one had questions about a human being, not about an angel. He then told his servant to go home with the horses and wagon; he would remain in Medzibuz.

Why had the Besht, at his first meeting with Rabbi Dov Ber, worn a cushion on his head and a wolf-skin coat inside out? The Besht sometimes spoke in riddles and sometimes acted symbolically. The cushion on his head meant that the Besht was a throne or resting place for the *Shechinah*. The reversed wolf-skin coat meant that he was ready to reveal the inner teachings to Rabbi Dov Ber.[33]

Love the Stranger

THE NEXT DAY, RABBI DOV BER CAME TO THE BAAL SHEM TOV AND found him sitting on his bed and studying. Rabbi Dov Ber greeted the Besht and asked him to cure his bad health and fatigue. The Besht scolded him, saying, "My horses don't eat matzah!" Surprised and confused by the Besht's vehemence and his peculiar manner of expression, Rabbi Dov Ber began to perspire and feel weak. He exited and sat down to rest on the stone bench outside the house, to reflect on what the Besht had said to him. At first perplexed by these enigmatic words, he finally realized that the master was criticizing the excessive fasting that was leading to his ill health. Horses are animals of flesh and blood and need proper food if they are to perform their task of pulling a coach. If the body, with its animal powers, is to perform its task of being the vehicle for the soul, it cannot subsist on matzah—the "bread of affliction"; it needs real bread.

Rabbi Dov Ber received this lesson humbly, but he still was crushed by the stern way it was delivered. He sat there physically and emotionally drained and devastated. When a young disciple of the Besht passed by, the rabbi called him over and said, "Please go in to the Baal Shem Tov and ask him why he doesn't fulfill the commandment to love the stranger." Seeing Rabbi Dov Ber's distraught state, this young man's sympathy was aroused and he went in to the Besht. But afraid to speak words suggesting reproach to the master directly, he cleverly went into the house the back way and, as he quickly walked out again, called out, "Someone very depressed is sitting in front of your house, and he asked me to say to you, 'Why don't you fulfill the verse: "Love the stranger"?'" The Besht immediately gathered ten men and went to apologize to Rabbi Dov Ber for the harsh way he had spoken to him. As a spiritual master, the Besht usually knew when a strong rebuke was required, but he realized that this time he had been too forceful.[34]

A Cure

AS RABBI DOV BER'S HEALTH DETERIORATED STILL MORE AND HE became extremely weak, he had to remain in bed. But he now began to eat properly, according to the Besht's order. For the next two weeks, the Besht visited him in his room at the inn every day and sat opposite him reciting psalms. The Besht also went to the *mikvah* to pray for Rabbi Dov Ber's recovery. But his condition did not improve quickly. When he asked the Besht to heal him with medicine, the Besht replied, "I wanted to heal you with words—with psalms and prayers—because that healing lasts longer; but now I'll give you medicine." The Besht then began to treat him with herbs and medicines. He also provided Rabbi Ber with a place to live, for himself and his family, and a weekly stipend for them to live on. Rabbi Dov Ber was helped by the Besht's treatment, but his healing was not long-lasting and he was never fully cured.[35]

Learning How to Eat

AT FIRST, RABBI DOV BER COULD NOT GO TO THE BESHT BECAUSE OF his infirmity, but after a short time his condition began to improve and he was able to be at the Besht's table on the Sabbath. There, Rabbi Dov Ber watched closely and saw how the Baal Shem Tov ate like an angel, not a man, and how he spiritually elevated all the food that he put into his mouth. It was then that Rabbi Dov Ber, who used to starve himself to achieve holiness, began to learn how to eat. He abandoned the ascetic path and followed the new hasidic path of his master, the Baal Shem Tov.[36]

Yom Kippur

The Feast before the Fast

RABBI DOV BER STAYED WITH THE BESHT THROUGH YOM KIPPUR. On *erev* Yom Kippur, when he sat at the Besht's table for the final meal before the fast, he saw that the Baal Shem Tov was all flaming fire. His hands were hands of fire and each piece of food he ate was fire. Later, when Rabbi Dov Ber spoke to him, the Besht told him that when Rabbi Ber had seen him, "I was meditating using the *kavvanot* that Moses meditated on while ascending Mount Sinai, where he remained for forty days and forty nights without eating; and at that moment Moses came to me." The Besht then taught Rabbi Dov Ber how to eat without eating and how to partake of all enjoyments by deriving not just physical but spiritual pleasure from them and by enjoying the radiance of the Divine Presence.[37]

His Tallis

LATER THAT SAME *EREV* YOM KIPPUR, WHEN THE BAAL SHEM TOV WAS leading the prayers in the synagogue, he was praying with intense fervor, and his tallis slipped off his shoulder. Seeing that the Besht was not in this world, Rabbi Dov Ber went over and lifted it back up. But as soon as he touched the Besht's tallis, he was struck with such awe of God that he began to tremble and shiver violently. He grabbed the table and it too began to shake. When others present saw that the rabbi was actually in danger, they woke the Besht from his trance of *d'vekut* and he was able to calm the rabbi down from his intense fear and awe.[38]

Studying with Spirit

RABBI DOV BER WENT TO THE BAAL SHEM TOV EACH NIGHT AT MIDNIGHT and the Besht taught him the deepest secrets of the Kabbalah. During one session, he showed Rabbi Dov Ber a saying in the *Eitz Hayim* and asked him to interpret it. Rabbi Ber said, "I have to review it first." After studying the saying, he told the Besht his interpretation. The Besht listened closely and said, "Let me interpret it for you." He then began to interpret the saying, which was about various angels, and as he did so he was burning with holy fervor. Whenever he mentioned the name of an angel, Rabbi Ber saw the angel with his own eyes. When the Besht finished, he said to Rabbi Dov Ber, "Your interpretation was correct, but it was without life!"[39]

You Too Cry Out!

RABBI DOV BER ONCE ASKED THE BAAL SHEM TOV WHY IN KABBALISTIC *siddurs* they printed next to each verse of the Great *Hallel* the name of the angel who recites it. Why is it that during an angel's whole life it recites only one verse? The Besht replied, "Why do you care if the angel cries out one verse all the time? Don't bother yourself about such questions. You too cry out!"

The Baal Shem Tov himself never recited the Great *Hallel* without first hearing an angel say each verse and reciting it with him. But he taught Rabbi Dov Ber that the purpose in knowing the divine service of the angels is not intellectual but spiritual. One must imitate the angels by one's own fervor and devotion until one becomes an angel and even greater than an angel.[40]

A Fountain of Torah

ONCE, WHEN RABBI DOV BER VISITED THE BAAL SHEM TOV, THE BESHT kept Rabbi Ber with him for a long time and did not allow him to return home. When Rabbi Dov Ber asked the Besht why he was keeping him, he replied, "When you're with me, my Torah teaching flows freely, for the more water one draws from a fountain, the more water flows out."[41]

Teaching Kabbalah in Public

THE BAAL SHEM TOV ONCE ENTERED A *BEIT MIDRASH* AND FOUND A scholar teaching Kabbalah to a small group. After listening for a while from a distance, the Besht sat down elsewhere and began to study Torah. When the scholar finished the class, the Besht went over to him and told him that he should not teach Kabbalah publicly. "But you too teach Kabbalah publicly," the man protested. "My style of teaching is very different from yours," said the Besht. "You teach about divine reality according to how it's described in the *Eitz Hayim*, whereas I teach that all these aspects of divinity are found in this world in human beings. I make what is material into something spiritual, while you—by using physical metaphors and parables to explain divine realities—make what is spiritual material!"

The Ari charted the paths of heaven, while the Besht revealed the interpenetration of heaven and earth in every movement in the world, in a person's every action, speech, and thought. He revealed divinity in every detail of this lower world, especially in human beings, because there is no action or limb that has not a spark of divinity concealed within it, for there is no place where God is not present.[42]

Hearing with an Open Ear

THE BAAL SHEM TOV DREW SIMPLE PEOPLE CLOSE AND SHOWED THEM the greatest affection. His attitude was well known, and it was the main reason that the numbers of his followers among the masses of people grew so rapidly in a short time. But some of his foremost disciples—tzaddikim and *gaonim*—were not at ease with their master's practice, even though he sometimes sent them to learn lessons in piety from the common folk. They found it difficult to accept this approach of his, and certainly could not conduct themselves that way.

One Sabbath during the summer, something happened that made a powerful impression on all the Holy Society of the Besht's disciples. On that Sabbath, a large number of guests arrived in Medzibuz, among them many simple people: farmers, innkeepers, craftsmen, shoemakers, tailors, merchants, and so on. During the Sabbath evening meal, the Baal Shem Tov showed great affection for the simple people among the guests. He poured a little of the wine remaining from his *kiddush* into the cup of one of them; he gave his own special cup to a second, to use to make *kiddush*; he gave bread from the loaves over which he had made the *Motzi* to some; and fish or meat from his own plate to others. These and other notable signs of affection surprised the disciples and left them wondering.

When the time came for the second meal, after the Sabbath morning prayers, the guests were not permitted to be present. The custom in the Besht's house was that the guests ate only two of the three Sabbath meals at his table. The second meal was reserved for the disciples, the Holy Society; the guests were not permitted to come, not even to stand at a distance and look on. The visitors knew this, so they ate that meal elsewhere and then gathered in the Baal Shem Tov's synagogue, where they began, each individually, to recite the *Chumash* or psalms. Being very simple people, they only knew how to recite the Hebrew, without understanding the meaning of the words.

When the Baal Shem Tov sat down for the second Sabbath meal, he arranged the seating of his disciples in proper order, as was his custom, because he did everything in an orderly way. When they had been sitting for a short time, the Baal Shem Tov began to teach Torah, and the disciples were basking in divine pleasure. As usual, they sang various *niggunim*, and when they saw that their holy master and teacher, the Baal Shem Tov, was in good spirits, their own joy and delight knew no bounds. They were all lifted to heights of ecstasy and felt a tangible holiness and gripping inspiration; it was an experience of pure spirituality. Within themselves, they silently gave thanks for all the kindness that God had shown them, in allowing them to be disciples of His favorite, the Baal Shem Tov.

Some of them thought to themselves, "Now, it's so good. This is the way a Sabbath meal should be, not like when all the simple people—who don't even understand what our holy master, the Baal Shem Tov, is saying when he teaches—gather at the Sabbath table." They even began to question why the Besht drew these simple people close—showing them such extraordinary signs of affection—pouring wine from his cup into their cups, even letting one of them use his own *kiddush* cup!

As they were mulling over these thoughts, they saw that the Besht's face became serious and he entered into a state of profound *d'vekut*. While in this deep mood, with eyes closed, he began to teach them from a verse in Isaiah, saying, "'Peace, peace to him who is far off and to him who is near, says the Lord.' Our Sages, of blessed memory, say, 'In the place where the repentant stand, even the perfectly righteous cannot stand.' Why did they use the expression 'perfectly righteous'? because there are also those who are repentantly righteous, for there are two ways in the service of God: that of the righteous and that of the person who is repenting. The service of the simple people is on the level of the repentant, for they are humble and lowly in their own eyes and their attitude is like that of someone who repents and regrets his past and resolves to do better in the future."

When the Baal Shem Tov concluded his teaching, they began to sing various songs and melodies. The disciples who had entertained critical thoughts about the great affection that the Baal Shem Tov had shown for the visiting simple people understood that he knew their thoughts and doubts, and that was why he had given them this teaching, explaining how special and precious the divine service of the simple people is, that it is on the exalted level of penitents, whose service is higher than that of the perfectly righteous.

The Baal Shem Tov was still in a state of intense *d'vekut*, and when they finished singing, he opened his holy eyes and looked around the table, gazing for a long time into the faces of his disciples. Then he told them to each put his right hand on the shoulder of his comrade sitting next to him, so that all the disciples sitting around his holy and pure table would be joined together in a closed circle.

The Besht, who was at the head of the table, told them which melodies to sing while they had their hands on each other's shoulders. When they finished singing, he told them to close their eyes and not to open them again until he asked them to do so. Then he put his two holy hands on the shoulders of the disciples sitting at his right and left. Suddenly, all the disciples heard the sweetest and most beautiful singing and chanting of the psalms, interspersed with soul-stirring pleas and prayerful endearments to God. One chanting voice cried out, "*Oh, Master of the world!* 'The sayings of the Lord are pure, silver refined in the furnace seven times.'" Another said, *"Master of the world!* 'Test me, O Lord, and try me; examine my reins and my heart.'" In heart-rending tones, one sang, *"Dear Heavenly Father!* 'Be gracious to me, O God, be gracious; for in You has my soul taken refuge and in the shadow of Your wings will I seek shelter, until the storm has passed.'" Another sang, *"Oh, Beloved Father!* 'Let God arise, let His enemies be scattered and let those who hate Him flee before Him.'" A plaintive voice called out, *"Father!* 'Even the sparrow finds a home and the swallow a nest where she can put her young . . . Your altars, Lord of hosts, my King and my God. . . .'" Another pleaded, *"Compassionate Father!* 'Return us to You, O God of our salvation, and remove Your anger from us!'"

The disciples, who heard these soulful voices singing and chanting the psalms, were shaking and trembling; shivers ran through their bodies from the overwhelming holiness. Although their eyes were closed, tears streamed down their cheeks, and their hearts were broken and crushed, hearing the pleading voices of those singing and chanting. Each of them silently prayed from the depths of his heart for God to help him to be worthy of serving Him like this.

The Baal Shem Tov removed his hands from the shoulders of the disciples at his right and left, and all of them ceased to hear the voices singing and chanting the psalms. Then he told them to open their eyes and he sang with them the melodies they had heard. When the Besht stopped singing, all of the disciples became silent, and the Besht remained immersed in intense *d'vekut* for a period of time. Afterward, he opened his eyes and said, "The singing and chanting you heard was that of the simple people who are in the synagogue now, reciting psalms from the depths of their hearts with utter simplicity, with piety and simple faith. Consider then, my disciples: What are we, who are just the 'lip of truth'? For only the soul is true, not the body. And even the soul is just a part of the divine essence, and so is called the 'lip of truth,' for we only perceive the merest bit of reality. Yet we too recognize the truth and sense it and are powerfully affected by it. How much more so then does God, blessed be He, who is completely and absolutely true, recognize the truth and sincerity in the recitation of psalms by the simple people!"

The Baal Shem Tov gave his disciples the ability to hear a little bit of how the humble divine service of simple pious Jews is heard by God, even when they can only recite psalms without understanding the words; for their prayerful cries of "Master of the world!" and "Compassionate Father!" are not uttered by their mouth alone but from their heart. That was how the Besht himself always perceived these simple folk. Only this time he lifted up his disciples, so that they too could hear and see and understand.[43]

Redeeming a Melody

 THE BAAL SHEM TOV WAS ONCE WALKING WITH HIS DISCIPLES IN THE countryside outside Medzibuz, when he saw a gentile shepherd playing his flute.

The Besht approached and stood quietly as he listened in rapt attention to the beautiful melody. When the shepherd finished, the Besht gave him a coin and asked him to play the melody again. The shepherd enthusiastically played it again, while the Besht listened intently, in a state of great *d'vekut*, with his eyes closed. When the shepherd finished, the Besht put another coin into his hand, and asked him to play the melody for a third time—but the shepherd suddenly realized that he had forgotten it.

The Besht left the coin with the shepherd, thanked him, and he and his disciples continued on their way. As they walked, the Besht led them in singing the *niggun* for an hour. They were all transported in ecstasy. When he stopped singing, he said to them, "Praise God, for having let me fulfill the commandment of ransoming captives. The Levites used to sing this awesome melody in the holy Temple, but after Jerusalem was destroyed, the melody went into exile among the gentiles, until it reached this shepherd who guarded it. Today, we've redeemed this precious melody from the realm of the profane and elevated it back to its holy source."[44]

Good Influence

RABBI YOSEF OF KAMINKA, A DISCIPLE OF THE BESHT, MARRIED THE eldest of two sisters, who also had six brothers, all of whom were the Besht's disciples. When shortly after the wedding, Rabbi Yosef's wife passed away, the Baal Shem Tov ordered him not to marry someone else, but to wait until her younger sister came of age, although she was still a girl then. The Besht wanted him to remain part of this family of his followers, who were all pious and holy, brothers and sisters alike. But Rabbi Yosef said to the Besht that if he had to wait until the girl grew up and was of marriageable age, he was worried about having lustful thoughts during that time. The Besht told Rabbi Yosef to stay with him and to sleep in his room for a year. After that, he would have no more lustful thoughts. That is what Rabbi Yosef did. He stayed with his master, the Besht, a whole year, sleeping with him in his room, and then he returned to Kaminka. After a few years—during which time he never had a lustful thought—he married the younger sister and was again a member of that holy family.[45]

The Besht Gives Medical Advice to a Duke

THE BESHT WAS ONCE TRAVELING WITH HIS GRANDSON, BARUCH, WHO was still a boy. When their coach passed by a certain feudal lord's mansion in an area of the estate where travel was forbidden, the servants ran at them to give them a beating. But the Baal Shem Tov told them that he was a famous doctor, and they took him to the duke, who was sick. The Besht said to him, "You'll recover, but you should know that you've developed this illness because you engage in excessive sexual activity. In the future you should reduce your lust for sex." "Is that possible?" asked the duke incredulously. "Are *you* able to control yourself?" "I'm already an old man," the Besht answered, "and all my desires have long since disappeared."

When they were traveling home, Baruch asked his grandfather, "*Zeyde*, why didn't you tell him that you're a Jew and that this lust is prohibited?" "Then," said the Baal Shem Tov, "I would have had to explain to him what a Jew is and I didn't want to do that." Later, when they were at home in Medzibuz, the Besht spoke to his grandson again, saying, "It's impossible to explain to a gentile what a Jew is. It's even impossible to explain to a Jew what a Jew is, because a person can't really understand a spiritual level more elevated than his own. That's why a Jew so easily forgets the great dignity of being a Jew and the special responsibility for pure behavior required of someone who's been drawn close to God. That lustful gentile lord would never have understood that a pious Jew controls his instincts and impulses for the sake of God."[46]

The Impure Bed

THE BAAL SHEM TOV ONCE TRAVELED TO LUDMIR IN VOLHYNIA AND received hospitality from a certain wealthy man there. When the Besht sat down on the bed in his room, he immediately jumped up and said, "Someone has committed adultery on this bed!" His host told him, "It's not my bed." When a Jewish informer who had harmed many of his fellow Jews had died, everyone in the town pillaged his belongings. The Besht's host had taken his bed.

Very holy people, like the Baal Shem Tov, are extremely sensitive to spiritual impressions and vibrations. Even his body reacted strongly to any contact with impurity. Sitting on a bed in which adultery had taken place was, for the Besht, like sitting on burning coals.[47]

Rabbi Zev's Prayer Saves the Besht

ONE YOM KIPPUR, AFTER THE MORNING PRAYERS, THE BAAL SHEM TOV walked over to Rabbi Zev Kitzes and whispered something in his ear. That whole day it was bright and sunny, but toward evening, at the time of the final *Neïlah* prayer, the skies darkened with clouds. The congregation prayed and finished *Neïlah* and the evening prayer, but did not recite the blessing over the new moon, which could not be seen because of the clouds. The Baal Shem Tov made *havdala* over the wine cup and ate a little something to break the fast, as did his disciples.

Then, to celebrate the successful conclusion of the holiday, the disciples danced, as was their holy custom, until the Baal Shem Tov also danced with them. Just then, one of the disciples realized that Rabbi Zev Kitzes was not there and asked, "Where is Rabbi Zev?" The Besht signaled to him to act as if he had not noticed Rabbi Zev's absence. Afterward, they all went home and lay down to sleep.

A short time later, Rabbi Zev came to the Baal Shem Tov's house, tapped on the window to wake him, and said, "Master, get up and we'll make the blessing over the moon, because the clouds have dispersed." The Baal Shem Tov and all his disciples got up and blessed the moon with great rejoicing. Then the Besht and Rabbi Zev were very happy and began to dance together. All the disciples danced with them, although they did not know the reason for their jubilation. They realized, however, that something extraordinary had happened.

It was the Besht's custom at the conclusion of every Yom Kippur to tell his disciples what had transpired that day in the upper worlds. So he told them that when he had prayed the morning prayer, it had been revealed to him from heaven that there was a serious accusation against him and he would soon have to depart from this world. They gave him a sign, moreover, that at the time of the *Neïlah* prayer the skies would darken with clouds, so that it would be impossible to make the blessing over the moon. Therefore, he whispered this to Rabbi Zev, who exerted himself in prayer until he succeeded, for good, on behalf of his master.

Not being able to perform the *mitzvah* of blessing the new moon at the proper time may be a bad omen for a person. The Baal Shem Tov himself was like the moon reflecting God's sunlight. The hidden moon hinted that the Besht's light would be taken away. But his great disciple saved him and extended his life.[48]

The Besht Visits Rabbi Nachman Kossover in the Other World

RABBI NACHMAN OF KOSSOV, THE BESHT'S FRIEND, HAD PASSED AWAY IN 1746. In 1757, on *Shabbat Shuvah*, the Sabbath between Rosh HaShanah and Yom Kippur, the Baal Shem Tov lay down on his bed in his room in the *beit midrash* to take his usual Sabbath afternoon nap after the meal. His wife, Chana, also lay down on her bed to rest. After an hour, she was wakened from her sleep when she heard the Besht emit a loud cry. She jumped up, went to him quickly, and called to him loudly, "Israel!" He woke up and said, "Yes. I'm here." "Why did you just cry out in your sleep?" she asked. "It's good that you woke me," he answered. "If not, I'd have died in my sleep." Then he washed his hands and face, and asked that his close disciples be called to his side, because he wanted them also to hear what had happened.

After they had gathered to him, he told Chana and his disciples what he had seen in the upper worlds. "Every Sabbath, during the *Shemoneh Esreh* of the *Musaf* service, when I make a soul-ascent, I'm shown heavenly worlds and meet holy souls in the heavenly academy who are studying the Torah's secrets. I have permission to listen, to learn, and to teach in this world some of what I hear. Some of it I reveal to you during the third Sabbath meal. But for several years now, I've longed to visit my dear, departed friend, the holy tzaddik Rabbi Nachman of Kossov and see what has become of him in the upper world. Yet, no matter how I searched, I couldn't find him. I prayed, using certain unifications and divine Names that I know, trying to make a soul-ascent to his resting place, but I never succeeded. I was not given permission to visit him. So I pleaded with God, blessed be He, saying, 'Master of the world, You've allowed me to know so many secrets and so many divine Names. Why aren't I considered worthy to see the resting place of this tzaddik in the upper worlds?' I received the answer, 'If you will perform these certain unifications, then you will be able to see him.'

"Today, on my bed, I meditated on those unifications and saw an awesome vision. I came to a place in the upper worlds where there were many buildings of a splendor that I'd never before seen, made of fine gold and precious stones—diamonds, rubies, and sapphires. These buildings were large and spacious houses of Torah study, each one of huge dimensions in length, breadth, and height. And all the houses of study are filled with Torah scholars, whose faces are like angels of God, all of them studying Torah according to their heart's desire—*Tanach, Mishna, Gemara, Aggada*. Some are outstanding scholars, who are studying the Torah's secrets, others are reciting psalms and singing songs and praises to God. And there are thousands in each house of study. I was astonished at this amazing sight and at the mighty sound of their voices, like the roar of waves rising in the sea of holiness, for it could be heard from afar.

"I asked, 'To whom does all this glory belong?' They answered, 'To the pious hasid, the favorite of God, Rabbi Nachman of Kossov.' When I inquired about his resting place, one of the venerable elders arose and said to me, 'Take my hand, and let us go to the house of study where our holy master, Rabbi Nachman, sits and studies.' When I arrived at his abode, it was surrounded by glowing flames, so brilliant that my eyes were almost blinded by the light. Then I saw him face-to-face, and his appearance was that of an awesome angel of God, clothed in a white robe that shone with divine splendor and, over his head, a tallis whose light radiated from one end of heaven to the other. 'Who are the souls in all these chambers?' I asked. 'My dear brother,' he said to me, 'these are the souls whom I fixed during my lifetime by teaching them the good and upright way. Some of them were great scholars who had lost their faith and turned away from God's Torah, and I brought them back to goodness. They are the ones studying the Torah's secrets. Others were confirmed sinners, addicted to their lusts, but by my repeated admonitions, spoken respectfully and without contempt, I brought them back to goodness. They are the ones reciting psalms and praising and glorifying the King, the living God.'

"When he saw how my heart melted at the holy beauty and charm of this scene, he went on to say, 'If you desire to be with me in this eternal world, deliver your soul to the angel known to you, and your body will remain dead in the lowly world below. Perhaps your passing will atone for the sins of your generation and bring the final redemption and the miracles of the end-time. Your death will be good for your generation and good for you also—since you won't have to meet the Angel of Death or experience the bitter taste of death. Simply stay here with me, and I and the souls of the other tzaddikim will lead you to the place prepared for you, and we'll be friends and comrades in this eternal world also.'

"I said to him, 'What can I do, since my heart yearns to be buried in the Land of Israel, for the soul attains a greater elevation from there.' 'Know for sure,' he answered, 'that you will die outside the Land, for so have I heard several times in the heavenly academy. I'm not permitted to reveal the reason to you as long as your soul is bound to your body. It was decreed that I also would die outside the Land because of this hidden reason. But if you give your soul to the angel, as I said, then I'll reveal everything to you.'

"When I heard these words from his holy mouth, I longed to deliver my soul to the angel, but I also longed to see my son and daughter, Tzvi and Edel, again. I didn't want to die without directing them on their path in life, to prepare them for the future. I was at war within my own mind. And how my heart ached for all my disciples and followers! How could I leave them without a shepherd to guide them? When I told that tzaddik about my inner struggle, he urged me saying, 'Why worry now about the lower world, if you won't have to return there again?' and I made my decision to remain with him. Then I burst out weeping at the thought of being separated from my wife and children and grandchildren—and especially from my disciples. Yet, though at that moment my soul was still attached to my body, if you, Chana, had not wakened me, I would have remained above and died in my sleep, for I had already decided to follow that tzaddik's advice and do as he said. But because of your crying out, my soul returned to my body."[49]

Fixing Souls

WHEN RABBI GERSHON RETURNED FROM ISRAEL IN 1757 TO ARRANGE A marriage for his son, he traveled to visit his brother-in-law, the Baal Shem Tov. On *erev Shabbat*, the Besht prayed *Minha* and stood praying the *Shemoneh Esreh* for a long time, until the stars came out. While the Besht was still praying, Rabbi Gershon finished his prayers and reviewed the weekly Torah portion, twice in Hebrew and once in the Aramaic translation, as customary. Then he asked for them to bring him some pillows, to take a nap before *Shabbat*.

Later, during the Sabbath evening meal, Rabbi Gershon asked the Baal Shem Tov, "Why did you pray the *Shemoneh Esreh* for so long? I also prayed using the *kavvanot* from the Ari's *siddur*, yet I finished and even had time to go over the weekly Torah portion and take a nap, while you remained standing and praying, trembling as you do." The Besht had also made strange movements during prayer. Rabbi Gershon was being purposely provocative in order to try to get the Besht to reveal what he had been doing. The Baal Shem Tov just laughed off his question and did not answer.

But Rabbi Gershon persisted and asked a second time. Then the Besht said to him, "When I reach the words in the *Shemoneh Esreh* that God 'revives the dead,' I meditate on certain unifications, and thousands of dead souls come to me; and I have to speak to each one and find out why it hasn't been permitted to reach it's heavenly resting place. Then I make a *tikkun* to fix it and pray for its elevation. I deal with them in order of importance because they are so many that if I wanted to elevate all of them I would have to stand praying the *Shemoneh Esreh* for three years. But when I hear the heavenly proclamation, 'Sanctified, sanctified!' it's impossible to continue, so I conclude my prayer and step back." Rabbi Gershon responded with some skeptical teasing, "Oh, so that's it! Then why don't these souls come to me?" The Besht said, "Stay with me for another *Shabbat* and I'll write down for you the *kavvanot*, so they'll come to you too." And he wrote the *kavvanot* down for Rabbi Gershon on a piece of paper.

When they were praying on the next *erev Shabbat*, and the Baal Shem Tov had finished the *Kaddish* that precedes the *Shemoneh Esreh*, Rabbi Gershon stood up to pray too, but the Besht did not begin because he knew that Rabbi Gershon would not be able to bear what would happen and would become frightened. So while Rabbi Gershon started praying, the Besht began adjusting his watch and sniffing tobacco until Rabbi Gershon would reach the part of the prayer about reviving the dead, for which he had given him the special *kavvanot*. When Rabbi Gershon meditated according to the *kavvanot* the Besht had written down, he saw a great many souls, like a large flock of sheep, come to him, and feeling faint, he collapsed. The Baal Shem Tov helped him up and sent him home to recover.

Later that evening, at the Sabbath table during the meal, the Baal Shem Tov asked him, "Why did you feel faint?" Rabbi Gershon replied, "When I meditated the way you said, many dead souls came to me, like a great flock of sheep." The Besht then said jokingly to his disciples sitting around, "Give him a *potch* [playfully hit him], so he won't make fun of the Baal Shem Tov!"[50]

He Rebukes Rabbi Gershon

THE BAAL SHEM TOV GAVE GREAT HONOR TO HIS BROTHER-IN-LAW, Rabbi Gershon Kitover, and even passed on some of Rabbi Gershon's teachings to his disciples. But the Besht also did not hesitate to rebuke him. Once, during the *Shema* of the evening prayers on the night of *Shabbat*, the Besht went over to Rabbi Gershon and knocked off his *shtreimel*, crying out, "Ah!" Rabbi Gershon became so upset that he trembled. He then went to the private room of his friend, Rabbi Dov Ber of Mezritch (who was also in Medzibuz then), broke down and began to weep. The Besht's disciples went and told him, "Rabbi Gershon is weeping." The Besht replied, "When I saw during the recitation of the *Shema* that he had succeeded in reaching the exalted level of stripping off all materiality, I feared that he would become proud." The Baal Shem Tov was more concerned to protect Rabbi Gershon from spiritual harm than worried about his wounded feelings. The Besht was an expert doctor in treating the fatal disease of pride.[51]

The Time and Circumstances Are Not Right

RABBI GERSHON LATER RETURNED TO ISRAEL AND REGULARLY EXCHANGED letters with his beloved brother-in-law, the Baal Shem Tov. In one letter, he pleaded with the Besht to join him in Israel, saying, however, that he was doubtful if the Besht would come, knowing how attached the Besht was to his *minyan*. The Besht wrote back, "God knows that I've not despaired of traveling to Israel. If God wills, I'll be with you in Israel, but now the time and circumstances are not right."[52]

The Parable of the Frightening Mask

WHEN ONE OF HIS DISCIPLES WAS SUFFERING GREATLY FROM PERSONAL troubles, the Baal Shem Tov said to him, "When you experience afflictions, you should recognize God behind the mask. It's like a father, who's playing with his little son by putting on a frightening mask to see if he'll recognize him. The boy is scared, but when he realizes that it's his father, he calls out, 'Father, Father!' Then, the father, seeing that his son is frightened, takes off the mask and embraces him, to remove his distress and comfort him.

"When you are suffering, understand that there's nothing but God, blessed be He, and it's your own Father in Heaven who has put on this frightening mask to see if you'll recognize Him. If you call out, 'Father, Father!' your suffering and distress will be removed. But if a person doesn't realize that everything that happens is from God, blessed be He, and, when afflictions come, seeks only worldly means and remedies to escape them, then his troubles and distress will remain. I tell you, when you realize that God is everywhere and there's nothing separating you from Him, blessed be He, all your fears and troubles will disappear."[53]

Yenta the Prophetess

YENTA, THE DAUGHTER OF THE BESHT'S GREAT DISCIPLE RABBI YEHIEL Michal of Zlotchov was extremely pious. She immersed in the *mikvah* several times a day and prayed with great devotion while wearing a tallis. As she listened in the fields or forests to the birds singing, she would "jump *Kedushah*," rising on her toes three times while saying the "Holy, holy, holy" response, as in the *Kedushah* prayer recited in the synagogue, in which Israel below imitates the adoration of the angels above.

Once, her husband, Reb Yosef, saw Yenta, as she was sweeping the house, suddenly throw her broom away and "jump *Kedushah*." Reb Yosef thought that she had lost her mind due to the severe poverty that reigned in their home. When he asked her what she was doing, Yenta told him that, while sweeping, she had heard the angels singing hymns before God's throne and saying "*Kadosh, kadosh, kadosh, HaShem Tzeva'ot*" (Holy, holy, holy is the Lord of hosts, the whole earth is full of His glory)! So she said *Kedushah* with them.

Hearing this, Reb Yosef ran to the Baal Shem Tov and anxiously told him about his wife Yenta's delusions. The Baal Shem Tov comforted him, "Your Yenta has seeing eyes and hearing ears. She hears the angels singing and understands the language of the birds and animals. Don't trouble Yenta the Prophetess or interfere with her. She has the holy spirit."[54]

At His Wife's Death

WHEN HIS WIFE CHANA DIED, THE BAAL SHEM TOV WAS DEJECTED AND forlorn. His disciples knew that their holy master was beyond being sad about anything that could happen in this world—even his beloved wife's death—and they asked him about it. He told them, "I'm depressed that the great God-awareness residing in this body of mine will one day have to rest in the earth. I expected to ascend into heaven alive in a whirlwind, like the prophet Elijah, may he be remembered for good. But now that my holy wife is gone, and I'm only half a body, that's impossible. That's what saddens me."

According to the Rabbis, a man or woman is only half a person before marriage. Then, husband and wife "become one flesh" and are one body; as soul-mates they share a single soul. The Baal Shem Tov knew that his wife had given him a wholeness that he now lacked. But his sadness was not personal; it was a spiritual sadness over the dimming of God's light in the world.[55]

Why Remarry?

WHEN THE YEAR OF MOURNING WAS COMPLETED AFTER HIS WIFE'S DEATH, those close to the Baal Shem Tov suggested that he remarry. But he replied in wonder, "Why do I need to remarry? For the last fourteen years I didn't lie with my wife, and my son, Tzvi, was born because I was compelled by the divine Word." Like Moses, the Baal Shem Tov had ceased having marital relations with his wife after producing two children, so that he would always be in a state of holiness and ready at any moment to commune with the *Shechinah*.[56]

Shabtai Tzvi and Yaakov Frank: The False Messiahs

Shabtai Tzvi

THE FALSE MESSIAH, SHABTAI TZVI, DIED ABOUT TWENTY-FIVE YEARS before the Baal Shem Tov's birth, but his movement and evil influence survived him. All his life the Besht had to fight against the followers of Shabtai Tzvi.

Fixing His Soul

SHABTAI TZVI, LONG DECEASED, CAME TO THE BAAL SHEM TOV SEEKING redemption for his soul. The work of redemption, the fixing, is done by binding *nefesh* to *nefesh*, *ruach* to *ruach*, and *neshamah* to *neshamah* (life to life, spirit to spirit, and soul to soul). But because he had been such a terribly wicked man, the Besht was afraid to engage him so intimately and therefore began slowly and cautiously to bind himself to him.

Once, when the Besht was sleeping, Shabtai Tzvi came to him in his dream and tried to entice him to apostasy and evil (God-forbid). The Besht hurled him away so strongly that he plunged to the lowest pit in hell. The Besht later told his disciples that Shabtai Tzvi had a spark of holiness in him, but that the Satan had trapped him in his snare. And his fall was due to pride and anger, for the sin of pride goes very deep. It rots to the core and is extremely dangerous.[57]

Shabtean Books

THE BESHT OPPOSED THE DISSEMINATION OF BOOKS CONTAMINATED with Shabtean influences. Once, when he visited Rabbi Yaakov Yosef of Polnoye and walked in the door, he saw a book lying on the table and said, "A forbidden book is on your table." The rabbi asked, "Which one?" and the Besht pointed at it with his finger. The rabbi picked up the book with a rag, wrapped the book in it, and then disposed of it.

Yaakov Frank

IN THE LAST YEARS OF HIS LIFE, THE BAAL SHEM TOV FOUGHT WITH ALL his might against the heresy of Yaakov Frank and his followers, who continued in the contemptible ways of the earlier false messiah, Shabtai Tzvi. Frank, the prince of impurity, was born in Karolovke, a small town not far from Okup, the hometown of the Baal Shem Tov, the prince of holiness! That the two were born close to each other in the same province of Podolia fulfilled the verse in Ecclesiastes: "This, equal and opposed to that, has God created." After spending many years in areas under Turkish control, where he learned the depraved customs of the followers of Shabtai Tzvi, Frank returned in 1756 to the land of his birth, to revive that heresy among its secret adherents and to recruit new members. Frank, who rejected and attacked the Talmud, led his followers into immorality and licentiousness, covering up their perversion with a veneer of kabbalistic justification. The Besht said that Frank and those with him went astray because they studied the Kabbalah without the fear of heaven. Ultimately, this wicked man, like Shabtai Tzvi, also claimed to be the Messiah. But he was utterly false.[58]

The Shabtean *Shochet*

SHABTAI TZVI AND YAAKOV FRANK AFTER HIM TAUGHT THEIR FOLLOWERS a perverted and evil philosophy: that the redemption would come from immersion in sin (God-forbid)! The Frankists sinned and seduced others to sin. The Baal Shem Tov once sent a letter to the rabbi of Butchatch telling him that the *shochet* of his community was secretly a member of the sect of Shabtai Tzvi and causing them to eat *treifot* (non-kosher meat). The *shochet* would show the rabbi his knife, but afterward strike it with a hammer to cause nicks that made the slaughtering unkosher. The rabbi investigated, found that the Besht's claims were true, and removed the *shochet*.[59]

The Threefold Cord Unravels

IT WAS REVEALED TO THE BAAL SHEM TOV FROM HEAVEN THAT YAAKOV Frank was greater in impurity than he was in holiness. They also revealed to the Besht that he, Rabbi Meir of Premishlan, and Reb Moshe the Shepherd would together be able to overcome and defeat Frank. Rabbi Meir had been one of the earliest disciple-friends of the Besht, even before he was revealed to the world. He was a great kabbalist, who had the holy spirit. Reb Moshe was a holy shepherd, whom the Besht had met many years earlier. So the Baal Shem Tov traveled first to Rabbi Meir in Premishlan. When he arrived, he was told that Rabbi Meir was not at home and had gone into the woods for solitude in his divine service. The Besht followed him there and told him why he had come and what he wanted from him. Then the two of them went to seek out their third partner, Moshe the Shepherd, so that the three of them together could nullify the schemes and plots of the wicked Frank.

The two tzaddikim went to the town where Moshe the Shepherd lived, they asked about him and were told that he was grazing his flock in the nearby hills. So they looked for him and found him tending his flock. The sheep were scattered over the hillside and he was loudly singing shepherd songs and dancing with great devotion in God's honor. Seeing his incredible fervor, the Baal Shem Tov remembered their first meeting, and his realization then that the shepherd's service of God was greater than his own. The two tzaddikim went over to him and the Besht said, "I must speak with you." "I'm paid by the day," the shepherd answered, "and I'm not permitted by God to take time from my work to talk to you; that would be stealing!" (for he was scrupulously honest). "Aren't you taking time from your work to sing and dance?" replied the Besht. "That's permitted," he said, "because it's for God's glory! But other than that, I can't!" "It's about God's glory and His service that I want to talk to you," said the Besht. Hearing this, Moshe the Shepherd immediately became aroused and full of fervor. The Besht could see that everything this simple man did for the service of God was with such fiery enthusiasm that his deeds split the firmaments and shattered the Shells of impurity. "With only the least bit of Torah knowledge, this Moshe the Shepherd has risen to great heights," thought the Besht. "If I can only teach him how a Jew should really serve God, who knows what he could attain? Nothing would be beyond his grasp! With his help, we could not only overcome the threat from the wicked Frankists, we could bring the Messiah!" "There's a man who wants to destroy our religion!" said the Besht to him. "Who?" the shepherd asked, his fervor and zeal increasing by the minute. When the Besht saw that his words were having an effect, he decided that, right then and there, he would teach him the basics of Judaism. And to gain the extra spiritual power provided by the *mikvah*, he asked him, "Is there a stream or spring nearby? Let's go there to immerse, and I'll teach you God's Torah!" "There's a stream near the foot of the hill," said the shepherd and, burning with fervor, in one minute, he rushed down from the hilltop to the stream below. They immersed themselves and, while they were standing in the water, the Besht began to teach him the *aleph-bet* and continued his teaching and explanations, until he told him that the holy Temple had been destroyed and was in ruins. He also told him about the terrible persecutions the Jewish people had suffered and were still suffering, and said, "Now we must pray that the *Shechinah's* exile be ended!" The Besht realized that the hour had arrived, for there were three times of divine visitation: Once, at the time of the Spanish Inquisition, when the Satan prevailed and the Jewish people suffered terrible persecutions; a second time in 1648, when there were dreadful pogroms and massacres against the Jewish people and many thousands were martyred for God's name; and the third time was now. The Besht saw that the three of them—Reb Moshe and Rabbi Meir, the simple devout Jew and the scholar, united by the Baal Shem Tov—standing together in prayer could bring the redemption.

The three of them then prayed with such holy fervor that there was a great uproar in heaven. But the Satan exerted all his might until he was conceded fifteen minutes. If in that time he was able to disperse the three tzaddikim, he would prevail. If not, the Messiah would surely come. Just then a great fire broke out in the town, and the church bells pealed an alarm that echoed through the hills, summoning all the townspeople to gather and fight the raging fire. At the sound of the bells, Moshe the Shepherd began to shake in fear and started to run back to his flock. "Where are you going?" the Besht called to him. He answered anxiously that the flock's owner would certainly come now to see about their safety and, if the owner saw that he had abandoned them, he would have him beaten and deny him his wages! His family would not have anything to eat! The Besht pleaded with him to stay and continue praying, but the shepherd was too confused and distracted to listen. The Baal Shem Tov understood that this was the work of the Satan, who had gained the victory by dispersing these three great tzaddikim, so that the threefold cord of their praying would be broken and come to nought. All the Besht's pleas were in vain; Moshe the Shepherd fled back to his flock, and the whole plan was undone.

But the Satan's plan succeeded and, exploiting his advantage, he tried to harm the Baal Shem Tov and Rabbi Meir. Disguising himself in human form, he went to the nobleman of that town and said, "Two Jewish sorcerers are now immersing themselves in the stream on your land, casting a spell to destroy everything you own." The nobleman shouted for all the peasants to gather, and they marched out with pitchforks and clubs and wanted to kill the Besht and Rabbi Meir. But God saved them from the grasp of their enemies. They fled and escaped. Then they returned to their homes, their plan having failed.[60]

The Decree against the Talmud

IN 1757, DURING THE TEN DAYS OF REPENTANCE, THE BAAL SHEM TOV said that he had been shown in heaven that there would be good news that year— but he did not know what.

On *erev* Yom Kippur, the Besht, who was aware that Yaakov Frank and his followers were inciting the Catholics against the Talmud, saw a serious accusation in heaven against the Jewish people that would cause the Talmud to be taken from them. He was utterly despondent the whole day of *erev* Yom Kippur. As evening arrived and everyone in the city came to his house, as customary, to receive his blessing before the holiday, he blessed one or two and said, "I can't continue"—because of his great sorrow—and he did not bless them. Then he went to the synagogue for services and harshly admonished the congregation. He opened the holy Ark, put his head in, and cried out, "Woe! They want to take the Torah from us! How will we be able to survive among the nations for even half a day?" He was very angry with the rabbis and scholars of his generation, saying that the accusation was because of them, since they made twisted and false Torah interpretations. He said that all the *Tannaim* and *Amoraim** were brought before the heavenly court and made to stand for judgment.

He continued, "Let me tell you a parable: After a king's wife died, he married a maidservant and dressed her in royal garments. At first, the queen was always with her husband the king, but later she began to spend more and more time with her former friends, the other maidservants, joining them for strolls as she used to do before her marriage. The king commanded that during the night, while she slept, they should remove her royal garments from her room and in their place put the servant's clothes

---

* Sages whose teachings are found in the *Mishna* and *Gemara* respectively.

she used to wear. When she woke up in the morning and saw that her royal garments were gone, she had no choice but to put on the maidservant's clothes. Wearing those clothes, she went in to the king to ask him why he had done this. The king answered her, 'I had royal garments made for you because I wanted you to be with me. But if you want to spend your time with the maidservants—then these clothes are good enough for you.' "The Torah scholars," said the Besht explaining his parable, "used to study for the sake of heaven. But now they're all studying to advance themselves and increase their own honor. That's why the 'royal garments' are being taken away from us and there will be a decree against the Talmud."

Then he went to the adjacent *beit midrash*, to pray with his disciples, separate from the congregation. Once there, he again preached in harsh words to arouse them to repentance, and they prayed the opening *Kol Nidre* service. After *Kol Nidre*, he said that the heavenly accusation was gaining strength.

In the morning, he prayed with the whole congregation and made the prayer-leaders pray speedily, so that he could recite the closing *Ne'ilah* prayer while it was still broad daylight and there would be enough time for him to annul the decree before the heavenly gates closed at sunset—because he himself always led the prayers for *Ne'ilah*. Before *Ne'ilah*, he again severely admonished the congregation and wept. Putting his head down on the prayer-leader's stand, he also groaned and cried out. Then he began to pray. He prayed the whispered *Shemoneh Esreh* and then the vocal repetition. On the Days of Awe, his custom was not to look in the *mahzor*. Rabbi Yehiel of Medzibuz prompted him by reciting the prayer or hymn, and the Baal Shem Tov repeated it after him.

When Rabbi Yehiel reached the words: "Open for us the gates of heaven!" and saw that the Besht did not repeat them, even after he said them twice, he fell silent. Then the Besht began to make strange movements and gestures, bending and contorting himself grotesquely. Everyone was worried that he would fall down and they wanted to grab and support him, but they were afraid to interfere with him when he was in such a state. They called to Rabbi Zev Kitzes, who came forward and looked in the Besht's face. Realizing that the Besht was in the midst of a soul-ascent and should not be disturbed, he motioned to them not to touch him. The Besht's eyes were bulging out and he was groaning like a slaughtered ox. This went on for about two hours. Suddenly, he returned to normal consciousness, straightened up, and prayed very quickly to finish the service.

After the conclusion of Yom Kippur, everyone in the city came to see him, as customary, and they asked him what had happened with the accusation. "As I was praying *Ne'ilah*," he said, "I saw that I was able to ascend from world to world without any hindrance during the whispered *Shemoneh Esreh*. During the repetition, I also kept ascending until I reached a certain heavenly palace and there was one more gate to pass through before I would enter God's presence. In that palace I found the prayers of 50 years that had not ascended and, now, since we had prayed with *kavvanah* this Yom Kippur, all those prayers had ascended and were shining as brightly as the dawn.

"I said to the prayers, 'Why haven't you made the final ascent?' 'We were commanded to wait for you to lead us in!' they said. I called out, 'Come with me!' The open gate was as big as the whole world. But when I was about to enter, an angel suddenly came and shut it, placing a huge lock on it that was the size of the whole city of Medzibuz. [This was when Rabbi Yehiel had recited "Open for us the gates" and the Besht had not repeated it.] I began to turn the lock, searching for some way to open it, but I wasn't able to do so. Then I ran to my master, the prophet Ahiyah ha-Shiloni, and pleaded with him to help, saying, 'The Jewish people are in great danger, and heaven is not allowing me to enter! At another time I wouldn't try to force my way in, but now . . . !' 'I'll go with you,' said my master, 'and if I can open the gate, I will.'

"When Ahiyah came to the lock and turned it around, he also couldn't open it. 'What can I do?' he said. I began to complain bitterly to him, 'How can you abandon me at such a critical time?' 'I don't know what I can do for you!' he answered. 'But let's both go to the Palace of the Messiah. Perhaps he can help us.' With much clamor, I ascended to the Messiah's Palace, shouting and pleading as I went. [This was when the Besht was groaning and bellowing like a slaughtered ox.] When the Messiah saw me from a distance, he called out, 'Stop shouting. All will be well!' Then he gave me two letters of the *aleph-bet*—as a key. I went to the gate and, praise God, unlocked it and led in all the prayers. Because of the great rejoicing as the prayers ascended, the mouth of the Accuser was silenced, and I didn't even need to plead or argue. The decree was annulled and only a mere impression of it remains in heaven." The Baal Shem Tov said that this was the good news he had seen earlier, during the Ten Days of Repentance, but he had not been told then what it was. And he said that that year there would be a miracle as in the days of Mordechai and Esther, when the Jews were saved and their enemy Haman destroyed. But although the main part of the decree was annulled, the impression that remained still caused a tremendous tumult.[61]

The Debates with the Frankists

WHEN YAAKOV FRANK HAD MOVED BACK TO POLAND, THE STRIFE between him, his followers, and the Jewish community intensified and became increasingly fierce. Frank made an alliance with the Catholic bishop of Kamenitz in Podolia, and began to incite the Catholics against the Talmud, claiming that it defamed the Christian religion. To gain the Church's sympathy, the Frankists also twisted their own doctrine toward Christianity, pretending that they were an intermediary between the two religions. When the bishop of Kamenitz, a sworn antisemite named Dembowski, saw an opportunity to harm the Jewish community, he intervened, and in 1757 forced the rabbis to engage in a public debate with the Frankists. He then declared the rabbis losers in the debate and, as a punishment, forbade the study of the Talmud, on penalty of death, and ordered all copies confiscated and burned. The Frankists went with soldiers and police to all the cities in the region. They went from house to house and from *beit midrash* to *beit midrash*, grabbing volumes of the Talmud from the hands of the Jews. They brought all the books to the city of Kamenitz, where approximately one thousand volumes of the Talmud were made into a large pile and burned. As word of this terrible desecration spread to the Jewish communities in all the cities and towns, there was great mourning and lamentation among the Jews, with repentance, prayer and charity, to annul the evil decree.[62]

Fighting Fire with Fire

ON THAT DAY APPOINTED FOR THE BURNING OF THE TALMUD, THE BAAL Shem Tov was visiting at the home of his disciple, Rabbi David Leikes, in the town of Bar in Podolia. The hour of noon had been fixed for the commencement of the decree. Anyone found studying the Talmud after that would be burned together with the book. That morning, Rabbi David hid himself under a large vat used for cooking liquor and was studying the Talmud there. He was ready to sacrifice his life for Torah study. This would be his "study house" from now on, or his grave if it came to that.

When noon arrived and Rabbi David heard the church bells ringing to announce that the decree was in effect, he could not contain himself. Moaning and weeping, he ran home, where he found the Besht pacing back and forth, deeply absorbed in his holy thoughts. Rabbi David rushed in, burning up with his fervor and zeal for the Torah, and shouting out his anguish. "Master," he cried, "why has this terrible decree come upon us!" "It's because of the rabbis and scholars who study Torah for their own honor," said the Besht. "It's because of them that the antisemites can throw the Talmud into the fire." "Rebbe," Rabbi David shouted, "*I* don't study for my own honor! How can you be silent at a time like this?" The Besht replied, "Know that with your fire, you've extinguished their fire!" At that moment, God, blessed be He, who answers the prayers of His people in times of trouble, heard their cries now also. The heavenly decree was changed; but the earthly decree was still in force.

The Baal Shem Tov immediately sent one of his most trusted comrades among the hidden tzaddikim, Rabbi Hayim Yisrael the Potter, to Bishop Dembowski in Kamenitz to warn him that if he did not retract the decree to burn the Talmud, he would die a sudden death. Dembowski responded, "Tell your master that I have only contempt for him and his threats." Dembowski then ordered one of his leading priests to continue to seize copies of the Talmud, pile them high in the town square, and invite the whole populace to come view the burning of the despised Jewish books and see how their enemies were dealt with.

The order of Bishop Dembowski was immediately fulfilled. Then the Baal Shem Tov quickly traveled to Kamenitz. A few days later, while Bishop Dembowski himself threw volumes of the Talmud into the fire, the Besht stood and watched from a distance, leaning on his walking stick, as tears streamed from his holy eyes in torrents. Then, Dembowski suddenly collapsed and started screaming in agony, yelling that the burned pages of the Talmud were beating him cruelly. The priests thought he had gone insane, but were terrified nonetheless. They did everything possible to save him, but he died on the spot. The bishop's sudden, bizarre death, while he was engaged in burning the Talmud, stunned both Jews and gentiles alike. It shocked the priests and made an even greater impression on the peasants. It was clearly a punishment from heaven. This was the miraculous destruction of a "Haman" that the Besht had foreseen.

For a time, the decree against the Talmud was annulled. The Jews rejoiced at this great *kiddush ha-Shem*, while the Frankists mourned the death of their ally. But the Frankists appealed to the Catholic hierarchy again and urged that another debate be held with the rabbis. So once again, in 1759, the rabbis were forced into a debate, this time in Lvov, by Bishop Mikolski. Forty prominent rabbis were made to attend and three of them who spoke Polish represented the Jewish side: the Baal Shem Tov; Rabbi Hayim Rapaport, the rabbi of Lvov; and the Besht's disciple, Rabbi Yitzhak Dov Margoliot of Yazlovitz. Although Rabbi Hayim Rapaport and many of the other rabbis were hostile to the Baal Shem Tov, they made a temporary alliance with him to fight Frank, for they realized that the Besht's special talents and abilities could help in the critical struggle with their greater enemy. The debate lasted four days. During this debate, different from the first, the fear of the Torah fell on the bishop, for he knew what had happened to Dembowski. Not daring to harm the Jews, he declared the rabbis the victors, and the decree against the Talmud was finally and completely annulled. Then Bishop Mikolski disgraced the Frankists by having one half of their beard and one side curl shaved off, to show that they were neither Jews nor gentiles. Because of their great shame, they all converted to Christianity—more than one thousand people.[63]

The Wailing of the *Shechinah*

MANY OF THE RABBIS REJOICED AT THIS MASS CONVERSION, BECAUSE the Frankists, who were inciting the Catholic priests against the Jews, had become a serious threat to the whole community. The Baal Shem Tov, however, was deeply depressed by this event, for although he fought the Frankists with every ounce of his energy, he had always hoped and prayed, until the last moment, for their repentance. He could not conceal his compassion for even wicked Jews like the Frankists, who caused such terrible suffering for the Jewish community. When he heard about their conversion, he began weeping and said, "The *Shechinah* is weeping and wailing over them. As long as a diseased limb is attached to the body, there's hope that it may recover. But once it's cut off, all hope is gone—for the Community of Israel is the body of the *Shechinah* on earth, and each Jew is a limb of the *Shechinah*."

Only because his heart flowed with such a strong current of love for every Jew could the Besht speak this way about dangerous heretics! But the Torah teaches that "love covers all transgressions." When a certain rabbi criticized the Baal Shem Tov's attitude, one of the Besht's disciples answered sharply, "Our master says, 'A little tzaddik loves little sinners, and a great tzaddik loves great sinners. The Messiah will find excuses and justifications for everyone of Israel!'"[64]

Renewed Hostility

WHEN THE BAAL SHEM TOV'S RABBINIC OPPONENTS HEARD ABOUT HIS expressions of sympathy for the converted Frankists, their suspicion and antagonism to him were renewed. Some of them had never approved of the temporary alliance with the Besht for the sake of the debate with Frank. With that episode in the past, and now that Frank had been dealt with, they all decided it was time to deal with the Baal Shem Tov and his followers. But Rabbi Hayim Rapaport had been so influenced by his association with the Baal Shem Tov during the course of the debate that his attitude toward the Besht totally changed. As the rabbi of Lvov, Rabbi Hayim had also been influenced by the Besht's two great disciples, Rabbi Meir Margoliot, chief rabbi of the district of Lvov and Ostrog, and his brother, Rabbi Yitzhak Dov Margoliot of Yazlovitz, who had also participated in the debate. But now Rabbi Hayim was finally won over by the Besht and became his disciple.[65]

The Ban

AT THIS TIME, SEVERAL EXTREME OPPONENTS OF THE BAAL SHEM TOV, AMONG them some great and learned men, gathered in the city of Shklov in Lithuania to denounce and issue a ban against the "cult of the Hasidim and their leader, Israel of Medzibuz." This was but the first of a series of hostile acts they directed against the Baal Shem Tov.

Although the Besht realized that these steps taken against him and his followers were contrary to *halacha* and legally invalid, the viciousness of the opposition pained him greatly. But he made an effort to calm his disciples' feelings and not inflame them. Despite the fact that they were being persecuted, he sternly warned them not to retaliate in any way. At a gathering of his close disciples in Medzibuz, shortly after the ban was issued, he told them, "Don't answer the malice of our opponents and persecutors in kind. Forgive them completely, because God's promise is that sins will be removed from the earth, not sinners. It was revealed to me in a soul-ascent that they'll fall before us like stubble in any case. The more silent we are, the more we'll succeed. In my earlier days before I became well known, I also was persecuted by some rabbis, including some who are righteous and upright. Even my dear and pious brother-in-law, Rabbi Gershon, harassed me! Remember that 'God favors the persecuted,' and that 'When a man's ways please God, He makes even his enemies to be at peace with him.'" Yet, to appease his disciples and followers, he formed a religious court of some of his greatest disciples to nullify the ban. They signed a statement that read:

> We, as one, together with all those who confess to truth, and together with all of our brethren of Israel who believe in the Holy One, blessed be He, and in His

servants, the pious tzaddikim who are upright and pure, declare absolutely void the ban issued by those irresponsible and reckless individuals in the city of Shklov against our master and teacher, the Rabbi of all the Jews in the Exile, the Baal Shem Tov (long may he live!), and against us, the undersigned, and those of our brethren of Israel who are associated with us.

Even though according to the holy Torah a ban may only be annulled by those who declared it, our saintly master has given us the power of authority to annul it by ourselves, in order to ease our minds. Therefore, we declare, with all force and vigor, that the evil ban is null and void, because it is based in falsehood from beginning to end. Thus, there is no ban and no execration (God-forbid). But there is in it vanity and emptiness; there is nothing to it. It is completely abrogated, like the dust of the earth. Upon this, we herewith sign, in the community of Medzibuz.

Israel son of Eliezer, Baal Shem of Medzibuz
Yaakov Yosef of Polnoye
Yeshayahu of Yanov
Yitzhak of Drohobitch
Leib Pistriner
David Forkes
David of Mikolaiyev
David Leikes
Menahem Mendel of Bar
Dov Ber, son of Rabbi Avraham, of Mezritch
Zev Wolf Kitzes
Shimon, son of Rabbi S. of Hanipol
The least of the company, Rabbi Tzvi Hirsh, scribe in the home of our holy master.
Written and signed before me here in Medzibuz. And I have added my signature. Meir Margoliot, chief rabbi of the district of Lvov and Ostrog.[66]

The Cause of Death

NOT LONG AFTER THIS, THE BAAL SHEM TOV TOLD HIS DISCIPLES THAT he would come to his death because of the Frankists and because of the rabbis who had issued the ban in Shklov. He said that among Frank's followers were several great Torah scholars, who had been led astray. By separating from the Jewish community and speaking against the Talmud, they slandered the community as a whole. Since the leader of the generation represents the community, their slanders fell on the Baal Shem Tov. The baseless accusations made by the great rabbis in the Shklov ban added to the Besht's grief and suffering. He said that two holes were made in his heart because of Frank and because of his rabbinic opponents in Shklov. And these events finally led to his death.[67]

His Spiritual Power Ebbs

DEFENDING THE JEWISH PEOPLE AGAINST PERSECUTION AND POGROMS, against Christian antisemites, and Frankists; and defending his movement against *misnagdim* all began to weaken the Baal Shem Tov physically and spiritually. He no longer had access to all the spiritual levels that he had so long taken for granted. He felt his powers beginning to ebb and he was distressed. This was why his soul had refused to descend to this world—he had feared that the grief caused by the enmity of vicious opponents would weaken him and separate him from his spiritual root. His enduring consolation in these troubles was his Holy Society of disciples.

To Death and Beyond

The Besht's Death

The Koretzer Neglects the *Mikvah*

ON PASSOVER IN 1760, RABBI PINHAS OF KORETZ WAS VISITING THE Baal Shem Tov. Rabbi Pinhas usually went to the *mikvah* to purify himself before a holiday, and he did so on the eve of the first day of Passover. But he did not feel well during Passover; because of that he hesitated going to the *mikvah* on the eve of the final days of the holiday, worried that it might affect his health. He debated with himself whether or not to go and finally decided against it.

As he was praying the morning prayers on the seventh day of Passover, he perceived with his holy spirit that it had been decreed in heaven that the Baal Shem Tov would soon pass away, because of the strains he suffered in his confrontations with the Frankists and with the rabbis in Shklov. The previous year, the Besht had said that he would come to his death because of these matters, but his disciples did not take his words literally. Rabbi Pinhas began to pray with great intensity to nullify the decree—but to no avail. He then became very depressed and regretted not having gone to the *mikvah*. He felt that if he had seen this while in the *mikvah*, the extra potency the *mikvah* added to his prayer would have helped him annul the decree.

After the morning prayers, the Baal Shem Tov asked him if he had gone to the *mikvah* the previous day. Rabbi Pinhas said, "No!" "What's done is done," said the Besht. "It can no longer be changed."[1]

He Sends Disciples Away

AFTER PASSOVER, THE BAAL SHEM TOV BEGAN TO SUFFER FROM DIARRHEA, but he still led the prayers before the Ark. Those disciples whom he knew would sacrifice themselves to the utmost in praying to annul the decree against him—if they knew about it—he told nothing. He either sent them home or elsewhere on missions to promote the hasidic movement, so that they would not be present at his passing. The Besht had ordered Rabbi Pinhas of Koretz, who knew about the decree, not to reveal anything; Rabbi Pinhas did not go home after the holiday, but stayed with his master.[2]

340

A Sick-Bell for the Servant

THE BAAL SHEM TOV WAS VERY SICK BEFORE HIS DEATH, BUT HE WAS not bed-ridden, although he became thin and his voice was affected. He sat in his small house of seclusion, and his voice was so weak that he could not call his servant when he needed him. So they hung a bell in the main house and ran a rope from it to where he was in his small house. When the Besht pulled on the rope, the bell rang and the servant came to him.[3]

Healing with Stories

ONE DAY, HIS DISCIPLE, RABBI DAVID FORKES, WHO WAS THE *MAGGID* IN Medzibuz, came in to the Baal Shem Tov and asked him how to pray for a sick person by telling stories. (When there were obstacles to prayer, the Besht occasionally healed a person by telling a story. Since direct prayer can arouse contrary forces, an indirect prayer that is clothed in a story can sometimes more readily succeed.) The Baal Shem Tov began to explain the matter to him and, as he talked, he became inspired and his face was aflame with his fervor. Such a great fear and awe fell on Rabbi David, that he wanted to flee from the Besht's holy presence. But because the Besht was speaking to him face-to-face he could not leave.

Just then, the Besht's daughter, Edel, entered and interrupted him, saying, "Father, it's time to eat. It's very late already." Immediately, all the blood left the Besht's face, which had been flushed to a fiery red, turning it to a deathly pallor. And he lay down to rest on his bed; in a moment, he had become drained and fatigued. "My daughter, what have you done to me!" he said. Rabbi David defended her, saying, "She's right, it's time to eat." "Don't you know who was here?" the Besht said to him. "Elijah the Prophet, may he be remembered for good, was standing on one side of me, and my master, Ahiyah ha-Shiloni, was standing on the other side. They were speaking to me and I was repeating to you what they said. But when she came in and disturbed me, they left!" Rabbi David, who had sought this knowledge of praying through stories in order to pray for the Besht himself, never learned its secret.[4]

My Life for Yours!

A FEW WEEKS BEFORE THE BAAL SHEM TOV'S DEATH, HIS DISCIPLE, Rabbi Leib Kessler, came in to him. When the Besht said that he would surely die, Rabbi Leib said, "Rebbe, my head for yours, and my eyes for your eyes!"—because he was ready to offer his life in exchange for the Besht's, so that his rebbe could live. But the Baal Shem Tov would not hear of it, since he had lost his interest in remaining in this world. He said, "Let them [heaven] return to me what they've taken from me this past year, and I'll want to live." He had no desire to live without his spiritual levels, saying, "Who needs this kind of life?"

Later that day, the Baal Shem Tov complained to Rabbi Pinhas of Koretz, "When I was young, and I lifted up my arms in prayer, I felt all the worlds moving. Now I feel nothing."[5]

The Spirit Returns

W AT THE FEAST ON *LAG B'OMER*, WHEN THERE WAS GREAT REJOICING, the Baal Shem Tov taught his disciples a teaching based on *gematria**, saying, "'And you shall love the Lord your God'—the [Hebrew] letters of the [single] word for 'And you shall love' [*v'ahavta*] add up to two times the numerical value of the word 'light' [*or*]. 'Light' numerically equals 'secret' [*raz*], which equals and is the mirror image of 'stranger' [*zar*]. What do these equivalences mean? The Kabbalah speaks of two kinds of light: a direct light and a reflected light that emerges from what is at first dark. A tzaddik is a direct light, and his divine service of love is to reveal the *secret*—the reflected light hidden in the *stranger*, someone far from God and spirituality. That has been my mission and task in life."

The Besht paused, then continued, "'And you shall love' is two times 'light'—direct light and reflected light. 'Light,' according to the small number[¶] equals 9, and two times 9 equals 18. In another eighteen days, I'll merit to the reflected, returning light, as it is written: 'And the spirit returns to God who gave it.' Spirit brings spirit and draws spirit, with a new light that will shine until the coming of the Messiah."

Thus, on the joyous holiday of *Lag B'Omer*, the Baal Shem Tov predicted that in eighteen days (18 signifying *hai*, "life"), on the first day of *Shavuot*, his soul, which was a direct light of love for God, would return to its source and merit a more powerful reflected light. After the darkness of his death, his light and influence would become even greater than during his lifetime. But his disciples who heard these words did not understand their full meaning.[6]

Fulfilling "To Dust Shalt Thou Return"

W ON *LAG B'OMER*, THE BAAL SHEM TOV HAD QUOTED ECCLESIASTES 12:7, which speaking of human mortality, says: "The dust returns to the earth, as it was; and the spirit returns to God who gave it." Some days later, he alluded to the same verse, saying, "When my wife died, I realized that I would no longer be able to ascend to heaven in a whirlwind, like Elijah [who never died]. Now I want to fulfill: 'Dust thou art and to dust shalt thou return.'"

---

* Jewish numerology; each Hebrew letter has a numerical value (*aleph* is one, *bet* is two, etc.), so each word has a cumulative value, which according to *gematria* can be related to other words with similar values.

¶ The "small number" in *gematria* means that each value is without zeros; thus, the three Hebrew letters for "light" are *aleph* = 1, *vav* = 6, and *resh* = 200 (where only the two is counted). 1 + 6 + 2 = 9.

The Baal Shem Tov's holy mission was to refine everything connected to the body and materiality, to elevate the whole world and raise up the *Shechinah* from the dust. Only a tzaddik willing to descend to the lowest levels, to *Gehinnom* if necessary, can accomplish this, and lift up the Jewish people and the gentiles too. By descending to the dust in utter humility the Besht could ascend to the highest heights in life and beyond death. After his dust returned to the earth, his spirit would return to God, receive new light, and radiate great light.[7]

The Doctor

A FAMOUS DOCTOR HAPPENED TO BE IN MEDZIBUZ THEN. THE BAAL Shem Tov's disciples wanted to call him, but they were afraid to mention it to the Besht. Rabbi David of Ostrog spoke to him about it. The Besht replied, "David, are you too so mistaken? What do I have to do with a doctor?"[8]

The Day of Death

AS *SHAVUOT* APPROACHED, THE BAAL SHEM TOV'S CONDITION DETERIORATED and he was bed-ridden, although he was occasionally able to briefly sit in his room or to walk to the outhouse.

On the night of *Shavuot*, his close disciples gathered to his side, to stay awake the whole night in the traditional vigil, reciting the *Tikkun Leil Shavuot* of the Ari. The Besht taught them about the Giving of the Torah and about the subjects of the *Tikkun*. Before dawn, he told them to return to where they were staying, for a brief nap.

Early in the morning, the Baal Shem Tov sent for his close disciples and told them that he would die that day. Then he delegated Rabbi Leib Kessler and another disciple to care for the purification of his body after his death. He explained to them how the soul gradually leaves the body, indicating the signs to know when it is departing first from this limb, then from that one. He taught them this so they would understand what was happening with sick people who were expiring, because they were members of the *hevra kadisha* (burial society).

Then the Besht told them to bring a *minyan* to his room for the morning prayers. He also asked them to give him a *siddur*, saying, "Let me speak a little more with God, blessed be He."

After the prayers, Rabbi Nachman of Horodenka went to the synagogue to pray for the Baal Shem Tov. The Besht said, "He's shouting for nothing. If he could enter the door that I used to enter, he could accomplish something. I used to be able to pray and shake the worlds, but now's not the time for that. I'll soon be standing for judgment, not before the heavenly court and not before an angel, but before the Holy One, blessed be He, Himself."

At that moment, the soul of a dead man entered his room, asking for fixing and redemption. The Besht scolded him, saying, "For eighty years you've been wandering and you didn't hear until today that I was in the world? Leave, you wicked one!" The Besht realized that the appearance of this dead soul was a satanic attempt to distract him during his final hours; but it failed.

After this, all the townspeople came to visit the Baal Shem Tov to offer their holiday greetings, and he taught them Torah. When they left, he asked that the traditional dairy meal be served, but without delay. During the meal, he told the servant to bring him a large glass of mead. When the servant brought a small glass instead, the Besht joked, "'There is no lordship on the day of death'—even my servant doesn't obey me!" Then, the Besht told each of his disciples present how to conduct himself and how to earn a living after his passing. He also told a few of them what would happen to them in the course of time. The Baal Shem Tov called his disciple and personal attendant, Rabbi Yaakov, to him and said, "Yaakov, travel to all the places where they know of me and tell stories about what you saw when you were with me, and that will be your livelihood." Then he said to his disciples, "Until today, I've shown kindness to you. Now show kindness to me by properly caring for my burial." He then told them to leave him for a while and remain together until he called them back to him.[9]

The Final Hours

THE BAAL SHEM TOV KNEW HE HAD ONLY THREE HOURS TO LIVE. WHEN he saw that he could accomplish his final preparations in one hour, he said to God, with total self-sacrifice, "I give You these two hours as a gift." No one knows what he accomplished by willingly leaving this world two hours before his time.

Shortly after this, the Angel of Death appeared to him. When the Besht's servant entered the room, he overheard the Besht say under his breath, "I've renounced two hours. Don't trouble me in the brief time I have left!" The servant asked, "Sir, who are you speaking to?" "Don't you see the Angel of Death?" the Besht replied. "He always used to flee from me—as the saying goes, 'Banish him to where the black peppers grow'—but now that he's been given power over me, his shoulders have broadened and he can't contain his joy."

Then the Besht went to the outhouse to purify himself for his end, and the servant began to walk after him, to watch over him because of his weakness. The Besht said to him, "Why are you following me around today? Why is today special?" So the servant did not follow him. After the Besht returned from the outhouse, he got back into bed and asked his servant to call his daughter Edel. When she came to him, he directed her, after his passing, to guide those people to whom he had given specific instructions or orders and to help others to whom he had made specific promises. And if there was something too difficult for her to understand and she did not know what to tell them, she was to go to his grave and ask him and he would answer her. He then transmitted to her a *yihud** and divine Name to use to contact him after his death to ask his advice. The Baal Shem Tov also gave Edel his secret kabbalistic manuscripts and his book of remedies.

The Besht then told his servant to call back his disciples. He had earlier given them a sign, saying that at the hour of his death the two clocks in his room would stop. When he had returned from the bathroom and washed his hands, the big clock had stopped. His disciples stood around the bed blocking his view so he would not notice that it had stopped running. When he saw the grief on their faces, he said to them, "I know that the clock has stopped. But I'm not worried for myself. I know clearly that I'll exit through this door and immediately enter through another door."

He told them that he had given Edel charge over certain matters after his death. They said that they knew that Edel could guide them in some ways, but who would be their rabbi and teacher? Only a man could fulfill that role. "Master," they said, "to whom are you leaving us?" He answered, "To my son, Tzvi. But know that the bear is in the woods and there is the sage Pinhas." They understood that he was speaking of Rabbi Ber, the Maggid of Mezritch, and Rabbi Pinhas of Koretz. Until this moment, the Besht's son, Rabbi Tzvi, had remained in the shadows and had hidden his great holiness. But now, the Baal Shem Tov revealed his true nature.

Then the Besht told his disciples a parable. "A certain land had a great warrior and hero. Because of their trust in him, his countrymen neglected to learn the ways of war, for they relied on the hero who lived among them. Later, during wartime, when the hero wanted to ready his weapons, the clever enemy stole them from him one by one until he had nothing with which to fight. His countrymen, who depended on him, were captured with him. I tell you, everyone should learn to use weapons and fight. No one should rely on the tzaddik of the generation to act for him. Only then will they see the light of the King's face."

Although the Baal Shem Tov told them that he would pass away that day, his son, Rabbi Tzvi, was sleeping. They said to the Besht, "Why don't you give your son final instructions?" "What can I do?" replied the Besht, "he's sleeping." Rabbi Tzvi had stayed up the whole night for *Tikkun Leil Shavuot* and was now sleeping because he did not believe that his father would die that day. They woke him and said to him, "Your father said he'll certainly die today." Rabbi Tzvi went to his father's bedside and began to weep. The Besht said, "I gave you a holy soul. Your soul will teach you how to act; you don't need instructions from me. If I wanted, I could infuse into you the soul of Adam, by the secret of impregnation, and you would know everything you need to know. But you have a holy soul and don't need all that." Rabbi Tzvi begged him, "Father, in any case, tell me something!" So the Baal Shem Tov began to speak to him. But Rabbi Tzvi, who was dismayed and confused, said, "I don't understand anything you're saying." "I'm close to death," replied the Besht, "and can't speak with you any more." So the Besht taught him a *yihud* to use to meditate on a certain divine Name, and said, " I know that you're afraid to be appointed in my place after my passing. But

---

* A kabbalistic unification meditation.

I promise you that whenever you need me and call me by meditating on this Name, I'll come to you in a vision and teach you."

The Besht then told Tzvi and Edel and his other disciples to stand around his bed—because it is good for the soul to exit in a *minyan*, where there is a greater revelation of the *Shechinah*. The Besht had earlier said he had no desire to live without his spiritual levels. Now he told his disciples that he willingly gave up all the spiritual levels he had attained. His single purpose was simply to declare before the whole world the inheritance he had received from his ancestors, "I believe with perfect faith." He also said, "I now understand why I was created."

He then urged his disciples to constantly strive to free themselves from pride. He interpreted the verse: "You will offer to sell yourselves to your enemies [as servants] and no one will buy [or "rule"]. "How can you free yourself from the contamination of evil? By being lowly in your own eyes and believing that you've never truly served God as He deserves, that you've not even begun to do the will of your Creator. If you judge yourself, you'll escape heavenly judgment. If you continually suspect yourself with a broken heart of having 'sold yourself to your enemy,' your evil inclination, 'as a servant,' that all your life you've never done anything purely for God, but have only 'sold yourself,' with the intention of gaining a reward, like a servant for pay, then, 'no one will buy,' no one will be able to possess you or rule over you. No judgments or accusations will ever have any dominion over you and you'll cleave to the Life of all living, blessed is He and blessed is His name."

The Baal Shem Tov then asked his disciple, Rabbi Yehiel Michal of Zlotchov, to sing a *niggun* that Rabbi Michal had composed. The Besht loved this *niggun*, which he called "The Melody for Arousing Great Compassion Above." When Rabbi Michal had finished singing it, the Besht sat up in bed and said to them, "I promise you for all your generations that whoever sincerely repents and sings this *niggun* for awakening heavenly mercy—no matter where he is and when he sings it—I'll hear it in whatever heavenly palace I am, because there are angels who bring announcements and tidings to souls in heaven. And I'll join in the song and arouse great compassion for the singer who is repenting."[10]

The Passing

HE THEN TAUGHT THEM TORAH ON THE VERSE: "THUS CAME EVERY maiden unto the king"—teaching about the column by which the soul ascends from the lower to the upper Garden of Eden. He described to them the transformations that take place in the kabbalistic categories of World, Time, and Soul, during the transitions from world to world as one ascends. He also explained to them how one ascends from world to world during prayer. The Besht had often made such soul-ascents, during prayer and at other times. He would soon make his final soul-ascent, willingly and according to the will of God.

He told them to recite *Vayehe No'am* ("May the favor of the Lord our God be upon us") and he lay down on the bed. He then sat up and lay down several times. Finally, he lay down and repeated aloud various *kavvanot*, until he began to speak unclearly and they could not make out what he was saying. Then he told them to cover him to his shoulders with a blanket, and he began to shake and tremble as he did when he made a soul-ascent while praying the *Shemoneh Esreh*. He entered a state of such awe of God that the bed too was shaking.

As his soul was departing, his disciples saw his lips moving, and they bent down to listen. They heard him whispering in prayer the psalm verse: "Let not the foot of pride come upon me." He had often taught them that a person must guard against egoism until the last clod of dirt is thrown on his grave. He should not stretch out his feet pridefully even as he breathes his last breath. Now that the Baal Shem Tov had reached his final moments, his own last temptation was pride—at having accomplished the purpose of his creation. When the Besht saw legions of angels coming from the Garden of Eden to escort his soul home, he prayed that he not be affected by arrogance. Then, slowly, the trembling ceased, and the disciples saw that the small clock had stopped running. After waiting for a long time, they put a feather under his nose and saw that he had ceased breathing and was dead. It was midday when his soul departed in holiness and purity.

The soul of the holy and pure Rabbi Israel Baal Shem Tov left this world on the first day of *Shavuot* in the year 1760. May the memory of a tzaddik and holy man be for a blessing for the life of the World-to-Come.

Rabbi Leib Kessler (who had earlier been taught by the Baal Shem Tov the signs of the soul's departure) said that he saw the Besht's soul exit in the form of a blue flame. Those of the Baal Shem Tov's disciples who saw his face at his passing said, "When he received the holy Sabbath, the Baal Shem Tov's face looked like the face of someone expiring from intense longing. And when the Besht died, his face looked like it did when he received the Sabbath. In reality, it is all one, because in receiving the Sabbath or in dying, the soul ascends from one world to another."[11]

The Funeral

RABBI ZEV WOLF KITZES WAS THE OLDEST AMONG THE HOLY SOCIETY of the Besht's disciples. When they had gathered for the funeral procession, he addressed them and said, "How shall we praise our holy rebbe? If the holy Ari was no greater than what is written about him, we saw more from our holy rebbe. And if the Torah had not written that no prophet has arisen like Moses . . . ." The fiery Rabbi Leib Saras, the youngest of the disciples, said, "If the Baal Shem Tov had been in the generation of the *Gaonim*, he would have been a *gaon*; if he had been in the generation of the *Amoraim*, he would have been an *amora*; in the generation of the *Tannaim*, he would have been a *tanna*; in the generation of the Prophets, he would have been a prophet. And if he had been in the generation of the Patriarchs, he would have been unique; just as we say 'the God of Abraham, Isaac, and Jacob,' we would say 'the God of Israel.'"

Then, Rabbi Zev Kitzes ordered them to begin the funeral procession and he walked at their head as they followed the Baal Shem Tov's coffin. When they arrived at the cemetery, Rabbi Zev announced, "While he was alive, angels longed to gaze at his holy face, but could not, because of the radiance of his countenance. At the hour of his death, however, they all gathered to welcome him—like a large crowd gathered to hear the joyous music at a wedding—for only now were they able to at least briefly glance at his holy face."

At the time of the Baal Shem Tov's funeral procession and at the cemetery, Rabbi Nachman of Horodenka was puzzled, because he saw nothing special and he did not understand why. But when they left the cemetery, he saw amazing and awesome visions. And Rabbi Nachman said to Rabbi Zev Kitzes that that is undoubtedly the way it had to be.

The Baal Shem Tov's final resting place is in Medzibuz in Ukraine, to this day. At the time of his death the hasidic movement numbered about forty thousand souls.[12]

After the Baal Shem Tov's Death

Yankele the Thief

THERE WAS A JEW WHO DWELT IN A TOWN NEAR MEDZIBUZ WHO MADE his living as a thief. This Yankele the Thief was also a devoted follower of the Baal Shem Tov, and although he was a very simple man (and too busy with his "work" and evading the police to study Torah), he had great faith in the Besht. So whenever he was in danger of being caught, he immediately ran to his rebbe for a blessing and somehow or other the authorities would forget about him or lose a document and the matter would quiet down. This happened a number of times.

One might wonder how a thief can be a hasid of the Baal Shem Tov. But not everyone can change overnight and, since he began to associate with the Besht, Yankele did develop some principles and reform somewhat: He only stole from the rich.

Once, he stole a large sum from a certain nobleman and was in imminent danger of being caught. The nobleman made an intensive investigation of the theft and finally found someone who informed on the culprit. The police were closing in and Yankele realized that he might soon find himself in prison. So he ran to the Baal Shem Tov to seek his help. On his way to Medzibuz, however, he met some Jews who told him that the Baal Shem had departed this world a few days earlier. Understandably, he took this news very hard. He sat down in the middle of the road and wept like a child. Not only was he crushed by his rebbe's death, but he was left like an orphan at a critical moment. If he was captured and thrown in prison, his life was over. What was he to do? Then he remembered that he had been told that the Baal Shem Tov had a great disciple named Rabbi Yaakov Yosef of Polnoye, who was also a holy man whose blessings were fulfilled.

Not knowing what else to do, he asked as to the whereabouts of Rabbi Yaakov Yosef and discovered that he had just arrived in town after hearing of the Besht's passing. Yankele quickly went to the house where the rabbi was staying, and excitedly began to tell the rabbi about his predicament, how he was a thief, and how the Baal Shem Tov would bless him and save him from his troubles. But as soon as Rabbi Yaakov Yosef heard that his visitor was a thief, he refused to listen further. He jumped up and kicked him out, yelling, "Chutzpah! You're a thief and you come to see me? Do you want me to be your accomplice perhaps? Get out! Get out!" Shattered and confused, Yankele did not know where to go or what to do. His lone support had been removed and his world was crumbling around him.

Finally, in desperation, he went to the cemetery where the Baal Shem Tov was buried and threw himself down on his master's grave and wept. He pleaded, "Rebbe, you saved me while you were alive; please, save me now in my time of need! Speak to God on my behalf, to save me!" So he pleaded and wept for a long time. Then, physically and emotionally exhausted, he fell asleep lying on the grave.

The Baal Shem Tov appeared in his dream and asked him, "Yankele, why are you here? How can I help you?" He wept before the Besht and told him of the danger he was in. "You've always saved me," he cried. "But now that you're gone, what am I to do?" The Besht asked him who he had gone to before this. "I went to Rabbi Yaakov Yosef, your disciple," he said. "But he didn't want to have anything to do with me. He kicked me out of his house. I don't know what to do or where to turn. What will happen to me?" "Don't be afraid," said the Besht. "Go to my son, Rabbi Tzvi, and tell him in my name that he should have compassion on you and give you his blessing." "How will he know that I'm speaking the truth?" Yankele cried. "I'll give you a sign, so he'll believe that I sent you," said the Besht. "Tell him that this past week, in *parashat* Naso, I taught him the Torah he should say before the guests at his Sabbath table," for after his passing, the Besht had appeared to his son to teach him. "Only he and I know about this," said the Besht. "Give him this as a sign, and with God's help, you'll be saved from your trouble." Yankele woke up from his sleep and remembered all of the dream.

He immediately traveled to Rabbi Tzvi. When he came before the rabbi, he asked to speak to him privately. Rabbi Tzvi took him to another room, away from his father's hasidim, and Yankele told the rabbi everything on his heart, and how when the Besht was alive he always helped him whenever he was in trouble, and how he had gone to Rabbi Yaakov Yosef, who had thrown him out. And now, when he had visited his master's grave and wept there, Rabbi Tzvi's father, the Besht, had appeared in his dream and sent him here, giving him the sign. Rabbi Tzvi listened closely to the whole story and, when he heard the sign, he realized it was all true. He then blessed Yankele and promised him that nothing bad would happen to him.

After Yankele left, Rabbi Tzvi went and told the whole story to the hasidim and said, "See how great faith is—even the faith of a thief, because this thief won my holy father's blessing by the power of his simple faith! And I had to obey my father's command to bless and promise him, which I did." And the rabbi's blessing was fulfilled.

Precious Jews, open your hearts to this profound story. There is a kind of tzaddik who loves good people, and there is another, higher tzaddik who loves even sinners. The Besht's love extended to the lowest of the low, even to the wicked and sinful, even to thieves. And who knows how broken Yankele was at being a thief? Do we know if he may have tried to change himself, and failed? One may ask how the Baal Shem Tov could bless a thief. The Rabbis say that there are thieves who pray for God's help even while breaking into a house. They say elsewhere that faith in God is so great that even sinful people who trust in Him are surrounded and protected by His kindness. If God, blessed be He, sometimes shields such a "pious" thief from punishment, if He answers his prayers, it can only be to raise him up from his lowliness. If the Baal Shem Tov protected this thief with his blessings, it was only to lift him up, slowly but surely, through love. Yet Rabbi Yaakov Yosef of Polnoye could not tolerate the thief and the Besht's son, Rabbi Tzvi, needed a sign from his father before helping him. After the Besht's death, even his great followers sometimes fell below his elevated ideals, for who could reach the level of the Baal Shem Tov?[13]

The Besht Tells His Disciples What to Focus On

AFTER THE BAAL SHEM TOV'S DEATH, HIS CLOSE DISCIPLES GATHERED TO collect all of his Torah teachings, each one relating what he had heard. Rabbi Tzvi, the Baal Shem Tov's son, sat at the head of the table. Suddenly, he fell into a deep sleep and the Besht appeared to him and said, "Why are you all concentrating so much on my teachings, and not on stories about my love and fear of God?"[14]

His Successor

RABBI TZVI BECAME THE BAAL SHEM TOV'S SUCCESSOR AS THE HEAD OF the hasidic movement. But he was not a strong leader and after a year, on his father's *yahrzeit*, he abdicated in favor of Rabbi Dov Ber, the Maggid of Mezritch.[15]

Burning the Polnoyer's Book

RABBI YEHIEL MICHAL OF ZLOTCHOV WAS ONE OF THE GREATEST DISCIPLES of the Baal Shem Tov. Many years after the Besht's passing, Rabbi Yehiel Michal's young son, Yosef, became critically ill and his condition steadily deteriorated until he was on the verge of death. Just then, news reached Rabbi Michal that opponents of the Baal Shem Tov were planning to burn the first hasidic book—*Toldot Yaakov Yosef* (The Generations of Yaakov Yosef) in a certain city. This book, written by Rabbi Yaakov Yosef of Polnoye, was the first and at that time the only book that contained the teachings of the Baal Shem Tov.

Rabbi Yehiel Michal realized that this was an attempt to suppress the new hasidic movement and that the situation was urgent. He decided to travel to that city and try to prevent this terrible desecration. He instructed his family that if (God-forbid) his son died when he was gone, they should delay the burial until he returned home. Shortly after he left, Yosef entered a deep coma. He seemed to have stopped breathing and they thought he was dead, but they delayed his burial as they were told. After three days, however, Yosef began to perspire. He opened his eyes and told this story:

"When I went into the coma, I felt my soul leave my body. Immediately, an angel came to take me to a certain heavenly palace. Since the angel was not permitted to enter that palace, I entered alone and stood by the door. Inside, the heavenly court was in session and I saw two angels arrive with a book that contained a record of all my sins. It was so large and heavy that it was difficult for them to carry. As I looked on, another angel came with a thin book of my good deeds, but they were not equal to the sins, which outweighed them. Then a third book was brought in, of my sufferings, and they caused many of my sins to be erased. Nevertheless, because of the sins that remained, the court decided to condemn me to die from my illness and they were about to pronounce the sentence and write the decree.

"At that moment, my father—who had made a soul-ascent to appear before the heavenly court—came to that palace, entering with a commotion and loudly complaining about the *misnagdim* who wanted to burn the book with the Baal Shem Tov's teachings. He vigorously protested, saying, 'It will be a terrible *hillul ha-Shem** if it's burned. It can't be allowed!'"

Just then, Rabbi Yehiel Michal noticed his son standing near the door, and said, "Yosef, why are you here?" "Father, I don't know," he said. "But please speak to the court on my behalf." "I certainly will," his father answered. Then, Rabbi Yehiel Michal continued to protest about the book burning as before, and pleaded passionately that it not be permitted. But the court answered, "This matter belongs to a higher jurisdiction," because in heaven there are higher and higher courts, one above the other—an appellate court, a supreme court, and so on. Rabbi Yehiel Michal then left to make an appeal to a higher court and completely forgot about his son Yosef.

Yosef stood near the door, worried and troubled. Not long after this, Rabbi Yaakov Yosef of Polnoye also made a soul-ascent and came to that heavenly palace where the court was sitting. He entered and also shouted and pleaded while weeping, complaining about those who wanted to burn his book. Then, he noticed his friend's son standing by the door, and said, "Yosef, why are you here?" "Rabbi, I don't know," said the boy. "But please speak to the court in my behalf." "I'll certainly say something in your behalf," said Rabbi Yaakov Yosef. The court then told him too that the issue of the book was a matter for a higher court. Rabbi Yaakov Yosef immediately left to appeal to the higher court and totally forgot about Yosef. Yosef, meanwhile, continued to stand there worried and troubled, because he had no one to help him or to be his advocate.

Suddenly, there was such a great commotion that all the worlds trembled, and a

---

* Desecration of God's name.

proclamation echoed throughout the heavens, "Make way, make way; the holy Baal Shem Tov is entering the palace!" (The Besht had passed away and was in the other world.) As soon as the Besht came in, he saw his disciple's son standing alone by the door, and said, "Yosef, why are you here?" "Holy Rabbi, I don't know," said Yosef. "Could you please speak to the court on my behalf?" "I certainly will," said the Besht, and he immediately went and spoke to the court about the boy, asking them to dismiss his case and let him go in peace. He then returned to Yosef and said, "You can leave now and go home."

By this time, Yosef was curious about what would happen in heaven and wanted to stay a little longer to see what the Baal Shem Tov would do there. But two burly angels immediately came, took him under the arms and escorted him out. They then took him down, down, down, to the lower world, "Until," he said, "I saw a repulsive corpse lying on the floor," for his family, thinking he was dead, had taken him off the bed and put him on the floor with his feet pointed toward the door, according to custom. And the angels said, "Enter that corpse!" They wanted him to return to his body. But he was disgusted by the body and the suffering in this world and absolutely refused. He cried and pleaded with them, but they forced him to enter against his will. "Then," he said, "I began to perspire, opened my eyes, and am telling you this story."

Rabbi Yehiel Michal of Zlotchov, the father, forgot about his own son in his zeal to defend the book that contained the Baal Shem Tov's teachings. Rabbi Yaakov Yosef of Polnoye, the author of the book, forgot about his friend's son in defending his book that contained the Besht's teachings. But the holy Baal Shem Tov, whose teachings were in the book, did not forget a Jewish child. A child was more important to him than a book. The Baal Shem Tov put people before books, before studying. Some of the holiest people do not write books. The Besht focused on living the teachings, not recording them. He never wrote a book, but he never forgot a child. The Baal Shem Tov's legacy was not of books, but of people. What he left behind were disciples and followers in whose hearts burned love of God, love of Israel, and love of the Torah, with an eternal fire. Yet few of the Besht's disciples approached his spiritual level. Shortly after his passing, the emphasis began shifting once again, even among some of his closest disciples, away from people back to books and studying.[16]

The Mezritcher Envies the Besht

THE MAGGID OF MEZRITCH ONCE SAID, "I WISH THAT I COULD KISS A Torah scroll like my holy master, the Baal Shem Tov, kissed a child." I, Yitzhak Buxbaum, son of Meyer and Charna, am dust under the feet of an awesome tzaddik like the Mezritcher, who had scores of great disciples, all tzaddikim with the holy spirit. But I ask: Why did the Maggid not pray to be able to kiss a child like the Baal Shem Tov kissed a child? Then, he might have reached that level too. But although the Maggid was a holy man of awesome greatness, he retained some of the limitations of a scholar, a book-person, and did not attain to what the Besht attained.[17]

Rabbi Tzvi's Dream

THE BAAL SHEM TOV OFTEN APPEARED IN THE DREAMS OF HIS SON, Rabbi Tzvi. Once, in a vision, Rabbi Tzvi saw a lofty mountain under the open sky, and next to it was a very deep valley. The Baal Shem Tov was standing on the top of the mountain and threw himself off, falling into the valley, where all his limbs were shattered to pieces. Rabbi Tzvi asked, "Father, why are you appearing to me in this manner?" The Besht answered, "Because this is the way I served God, blessed be He."[18]

A Form of Fire

THE MAGGID OF MEZRITCH ONCE PRAYED TO BE SHOWN HIS MASTER in the World of Truth. They showed him the bodily form of the Besht, made completely of fire.[19]

The Vision of a Great Fire

REBBE ELIMELECH OF LIZENSK, THE MAGGID'S GREAT DISCIPLE, WAS extremely grieved that he had never seen the Baal Shem Tov during the Besht's lifetime and he longed to have a vision of him. One day, he was told from heaven, "Look to the skies at midnight." As midnight arrived, Rebbe Elimelech went outside and lifted his eyes to the heavens. At that moment, the door of the heavens opened above him and an awesome fire emerged. In the fire was the likeness of a man and from it 600,000 sparks burst forth and scattered, filling the sky. In each spark, there was the likeness of the Baal Shem Tov. Suddenly, the heavens closed, the fire disappeared, and he heard a heavenly voice saying, "Now you know what the Baal Shem Tov was. This great fire was the soul of the holy Baal Shem Tov." "Why was there a likeness of the Besht in each spark?" Rebbe Elimelech asked. "The Baal Shem Tov was on the level of the Messiah," the voice answered, "and his soul has a connection with each and every Jew in the world."[20]

The Messianic Spark in Our Souls

THE HOLY BAAL SHEM TOV REVEALED THE GREAT MESSIANIC SPARK IN his own soul and lived in the manner of after the coming of the Messiah, "when our mouths shall be filled with laughter." If we read the stories about him and study his teachings with devotion, we can learn how to reveal the messianic spark in our soul. Then we too will laugh at the final day. And when the Baal Shem Tov's wellsprings have spread abroad, and we have done what we must do, the Messiah will come, soon in our days. Amen.

On the Walls

THE PROPHET ISAIAH SAID IN THE NAME OF THE HOLY ONE, BLESSED be He, "I have set watchmen upon your walls, O Jerusalem, who shall never be silent day or night. You that make mention of God, take no rest and give Him no rest until He establishes and until He makes Jerusalem a praise in the earth."

Many years after the Besht's passing, Rebbe Shalom of Belz said, "I once had a dream in which I was taken to the upper Garden of Eden and was shown the walls of the heavenly Jerusalem that are in ruins. On them, there walked a man from wall to wall. When I asked who it was, they answered, 'That is our master, Rabbi Israel Baal Shem Tov, who swore that he would not descend from there until the holy Temple is rebuilt,' speedily in our days."[21]

Cleaving to the Baal Shem Tov

ONE CAN CLEAVE TO THE HOLY BAAL SHEM TOV BY PRAYING AT HIS grave site in Medzibuz. One can cleave to the Besht by singing the *niggun* to arouse great compassion, for he promised to aid those who sincerely repented while singing that *niggun*. One can also cleave to him, spirit to spirit, by devotedly studying his life and teachings, absorbing his love of God, the Torah, the Jewish people, and all people. The Messiah told the Baal Shem Tov that he would come when the Besht's teachings were spread abroad. When a book about the Baal Shem Tov is revealed, the redemption is brought closer. The stories and teachings in this book are the true praises of the Baal Shem Tov. May his light and fire lead us on the path of holiness until the coming of the Messiah, speedily in our days. Amen.

From the depths of my heart, I thank my God and the God of my parents for allowing me to finish this book in praise of His chosen and beloved servant, Rabbi Israel, son of Eliezer and Sarah, the holy Baal Shem Tov. I raise my arms to God above, in gratitude for His inspiration. May the offering of my heart be acceptable before You, my Rock and my Redeemer. Amen and amen.[22]

The Baal Shem Tov's *beit midrash* (Torah study hall and synagogue).

The Baal Shem Tov's *siddur* (prayer book) with his hand-written reminders in blank spaces on the page to pray for particular disciples, for example, on the page shown: "A reminder to pray for children for Moshe ben Pini and Sarah bat Yitta."

גּוֹ רָאֵל בְּ"הֹ"רר אֱלִיעֶזֶר בֶּ"שׁ מִמֶדְזְבוּז

The Baal Shem Tov's signature: Yisrael B"H"RR [ben HaRav Rabbi] Eliezer Besh [= Israel son of the rabbi, Rabbi Eliezer, Baal Shem] (of) Medzibuz

The musical notation for a favorite *niggun* of the Besht—"The Melody for Arousing Great Compassion Above"—composed by Rabbi Yehiel Michal of Zlotchov.

The Besht's grave in Medzibuz.

Appendix

Baal Shem *and Faith Healer*

A *BAAL SHEM*, A "MASTER OF THE DIVINE NAMES," WAS A FOLK HEALER and a faith healer. Typically, a *baal shem* was a combination of a practical kabbalist who cured by means of prayers, amulets, and incantations using holy Names; and a popular healer familiar with such common techniques as bleeding by lancet or leeches, *segulot* (mystically potent items or techniques), and remedies concocted from animal, vegetable, and mineral matter. *Baal shems* were considered especially effective in expelling *dybbuks*, evil spirits, and other demons. The poor people, particularly those in small towns and villages, did not have access to doctors; in essence, these *baal shems* were a kind of folk doctor. While some of them were great Torah scholars and kabbalists, others simply knew the techniques of healing and writing amulets using divine Names. Although the educated elite and the uneducated common people generally believed in the *baal shems*, some people, both secular and religious, did not. Some rabbis respected *baal shems*, but others considered them of little worth; still others disapproved of their use of the divine Names. Sometimes, a doctor might work together with a *baal shem*, one caring for the natural, the other for the supernatural aspect in dealing with a patient. Simple folk doctors were likely to be more respectful of a *baal shem*. But some medically trained doctors considered them frauds, especially when they felt themselves in competition with the *baal shems*.[1]

About Towns and Places

THROUGHOUT HIS LIFE THE BAAL SHEM TOV TRAVELED WIDELY AND lived in a number of different areas. To help the reader grasp the nature of his movements I've made great efforts to locate the places mentioned. The task has been difficult because there is conflicting information in different sources about the names of provinces and regions within Poland during the Besht's lifetime. Different maps found in various books show town locations but fail to show the borders of provinces and regions, or they show borders and leave out many towns. As a result, it is sometimes difficult to determine to which province a town belonged.

359

Some relevant facts, all of whose veracity I can't absolutely attest: Poland was composed of many lands, including Lithuania. Poland was joined with Lithuania to form Poland-Lithuania under the Polish crown. I will refer to it throughout this book as "Poland." Much of Ukraine was part of Poland (the rest was in Russia), although I am unclear about the borders of the Ukrainian area. Reissen, which means "Russia," was the name for an area in Poland; it was also called "Ruthenia." Galicia was part of Poland and known as Little Poland (*Encyclopedia Judaica*, vol. 7, 266). The name Galicia is referred to in some sources about the Besht's time, but other sources claim that the name was created after the Besht's death when Austria took over Little Poland and Ruthenia. The areas called Reissen or "Russia" or Ruthenia or Galicia or Little Poland seem to overlap but the reality is unclear. One source refers to two provinces of "Little Poland, [and] Red Russia (Podolia and Galicia)." The main areas of the Besht's activity were Podolia, Volhynia, Reissen, and Galicia. I have provided an amateur map on p. 10 that gives the approximate location of the various places visited by the Besht and mentioned in the book.

How This Book Was Constructed

THIS BOOK IS COMPOSED ALMOST EXCLUSIVELY OF HASIDIC TALES about the Baal Shem Tov, and some of his teachings, that I have translated from the Hebrew; I have not "novelized" the material, but I did reconcile and merge different elements. Most of the stories came into being independently and stand on their own. We usually do not know their origin or authenticity and most have no reference to an overall chronology. The exceptions are that there is a general chronological sequence of tales for the beginning of the Besht's life, until his revelation as a great teacher, and for the very end of his life, from his final sickness to his death. I have put these two segments, the beginning and end of his life, chronologically, and collected some of the other stories according to category, for instance, the Besht's humility, or his love of fellow Jews. However, although I occasionally group stories by category in order to make them more understandable, the overall arrangement of this book is narrative, with a pretense of chronology. This is because when grouped by category, the conceptual mind is activated and I want the reader to be in a narrative consciousness. I don't want this to be a book about the Besht, I want it to be a book in which the Besht is alive. So I have tried to make it approximately and plausibly chronological. When stories about the Besht relate to historical events whose dates are known, I try to respect that reality. The broad sweep of the chronology of the main events of his life is generally known. Otherwise, stories that would likely have taken place when the Besht was younger are usually put earlier; stories that seem to show a more mature leader are usually put later. Stories that would only be understood if preceded by other stories are put in that order, and so on. However, I could not be accurate about every date or know when each event took place, whether earlier or later in the Besht's life. Most stories provide no clue to their dating. And it is almost impossible to establish a correct time line for the Besht's age. Thus, a story may say that the Besht was fourteen, but because of the context and other stories that would contradict that figure, I may have had to change the age. This editing has not been done casually. And, as stated, some later events have been put earlier or vice versa, for explanatory reasons. As the Rabbis say about the *Chumash*, there is no before and after in the Torah—meaning that the placement of events in the Torah is not always chronological. Why? Because the main point is to express spiritual truth, not to write a chronologically correct history. One can sometimes approximately date certain stories, because, for example, certain disciples appear in them, and we know more or less if those disciples attached themselves to the Besht earlier or later in his career. But the creators of these tales did not always have accurate information. A tale may place the Besht in Medzibuz because that town became his base and more than any other town is associated with him; yet the story may be about matters early in his career, before he had moved to Medzibuz. Hasidim who told these tales often did not really know details of the Besht's whereabouts. If all the stories about the different places he lived in were true, the Besht would have had to have moved twenty times. I've done the best I can do to properly place him and to be chronological but have not always made either aspect paramount. The main goal is spiritual understanding and I've put tales where they will be understood best. For example, a story about the Besht teaching his disciple, Rabbi Pinhas of Koretz, to pray for faith occurred shortly before the Besht's death, but I've put it earlier, to be in a section about faith. Most of the original tellers of these different tales were not historians or experts in the Besht's life. The stories they told may therefore contradict one another and contradict known historical facts. I have had to sort these matters out from a great number of sources, and connect, reconcile, edit, remove, reorganize, etc. The difficulty of this task is certainly one reason why there has been no previous comprehensive attempt to accomplish it. I may use a tale that is clearly invented or an unhistorical legend that communicates something more important than the history. As to the veracity of the tales: There is no sure way to tell in every case which stories are historically true and which legendary, yet certain stories present a character so original and unique that one is almost certain that they couldn't have been fabricated. Some of the tales in this book do not have strong religious or spiritual messages, but have been included because they provide valuable information about aspects of the Besht's life or even about the legends surrounding him. Recording or combining legendary stories is not a science. But I've done the work with reverence for the holy Baal Shem Tov. Sometimes, stories or versions of the same story contradict each other and I had to choose one or the other, whichever seemed best and most likely. All the tales are drawn from hasidic sources. I have used material from Chabad sources, some of which seem to be of later vintage. But almost all the stories are legendary and I need not be purer in my attitude to sources than the hasidim themselves. However, I do give earlier legends more credence in certain circumstances. There are still stories about the Besht floating around in oral form, which have not yet been recorded. I included a few stories told by my rebbe, Rabbi Shlomo Carlebach, and from other oral hasidic sources. If a story was mainly about a disciple or someone other than the Besht, I used it only if it showed something important about the Besht. So some readers may "miss" what they always felt was a great "Baal Shem Tov story." I left it out because the Besht was basically a secondary figure or the story showed little about him. I have used primary and secondary hasidic sources as well as academic scholarly sources about the Besht. If a story that the reader is familiar with is different from what he remembers, let him not assume that I've made an error or am editing willfully. There are different versions of many stories. And there are reasons for my editing. A reader may note that something is left out of a Besht legend that he knows. He may not realize that I left out a part of that legend because it contradicts something else important and I had to choose which to include. When there are different versions of the same tale, there are two possibilities: to choose one or the other or to reconcile the different versions. Sometimes I followed one path, sometimes the other. I may have left a piece of a story out for another reason. For example, the story about the young Besht and Rabbi Adam Baal Shem's son calling down from heaven the angelic Prince of the Torah has that they err in their kabbalistic rite and cause the whole town to be almost burned down. Not only does the Besht show no remorse about this, but he accedes to his friend's request to try a second time and risk disaster again. This is simply not credible to me even as a legend and I've removed that motif. Rabbi Shlomo Carlebach once told me that when telling hasidic tales, he would "change stories without changing them," because his "nose told him that it could not have happened that way." As a person totally immersed in hasidic literature and as a hasid of Reb Shlomo and of the Baal Shem Tov, I trust my nose too. But only occasionally, because, again, I have not edited casually but with reverence. When I've changed stories without changing them, I've tried to describe what I've done in an endnote and explain why. I have also in a few instances made a teaching of the Besht into a simple story by creating a setting, for example, saying that the Besht was in the synagogue and sat down with his disciples after the morning prayers and taught them. Such created settings are standard in legendary works. The only difference in my work is that I've admitted what I've done and tried to record what I've invented in the endnotes. There is little radical about such created settings since they are probably not far from the historical reality. In a few instances, I've added a sentence or two of teaching from a later hasidic rebbe to fill in a gap in the text so as to help the reader better appreciate a Baal Shem Tov story or teaching. Again, this has been indicated in endnotes. In three instances I've created sermons for the Baal Shem Tov, joining together related teachings of the Besht to produce "The Sermon in Kolomaya about Love of Israel," "The Sermon to the Pious of Kitov," and "The Sermon in the Field about Love of Israel." This device allowed me to present the Besht's major ideas, which I felt was required for the book's message. In one case I used an existing story as the setting for a sermon, and in the other two cases I created a simple fictional setting.

I criticized *Shivhei HaBaal Shem Tov* (in the Preface) because it includes too many miracles. I believe in miracles, but they are not the essence. Miracle-mongering lowers the teaching and spoils it. I've included a fair share of miracle tales because the stories have other qualities, but also because miracles show that a tzaddik is beyond material constraints and limitations. There is another aspect to my writing and editing to be noted: I don't like to record stories that will be incomprehensible to most people. So I have sometimes added an explanation within or at the end of tales that would otherwise be opaque.

Everything in this book has been thoroughly researched. It is an accurate portrayal of hasidic tradition about the Baal Shem Tov. But in the development of that legendary tradition about the Besht, many hasidim have creatively added their own handiwork and interpretive thoughts. I've occasionally, very rarely, done the same; but I've been open and honest about it. May God protect me from falsehood and misrepresenting the Baal Shem Tov! Books about hasidic rebbes often lack endnotes. That option appealed to me because the book should be taken on trust once a reader senses its authenticity. Yet I also wanted readers to see the traditional sources for the material, so I decided to include endnotes. Scrupulous readers can use my notes to check the references and investigate the sources. I trust that they'll find I've been a faithful transmitter of our holy tradition, especially if they recognize the difficulty and complexity of the task involved.

I was not able to give all the references I used in every instance. I may have seen some stories in ten or more versions, including later, secondary sources. I could not include all the citations. I sometimes use a secondary reference in an endnote where I later checked the primary one but did not have the time during the work of writing to record it. I sometimes referred to a secondary source for convenience; I may have seen the quotation in many early sources but when I decided to use it did not remember where the sources were and cited the later reference. I drew from so many sources and intermixed their details that the references could not always be kept separate. For example, I might use a story from one source and later insert scattered related details known from three other sources that have nothing to do with the first story. In writing the book it was simply impossible to keep track fully of all such occasions. Because of the interweaving of so many sources and the number of sources involved, I'm certain I have not avoided mistakes in the references; but I tried my best. To conclude, I want to assure readers that although I cannot promise to have met everyone's scruples, and although no one is exempt from errors, I believe that this tribute to the Baal Shem Tov is highly authentic.

Note: Would anyone who is interested in translating this book into Hebrew, please contact the author at yitzhak@att.net.

Notes

About Source References and Endnotes

I CONSOLIDATED ENDNOTES AT THE END OF EACH SECTION, SO THE reader wouldn't be distracted by countless superscript numbers. But as a result, many notes are no longer attached to their exact piece of text, which makes it more difficult to trace the references. A reader who wants to check sources will have to pay attention. If a section is basically composed of a central story, with details from elsewhere inserted, I cite the main sources first and then add sources for the details. If, however, a number of stories or teachings were strung together within a section, the references are ordered sequentially, as they occur in the section. Multiple references for the same item are separated by semicolons. A period means that the reference is for a different and separate part of the section. Not infrequently I appended a comment of my own interpretation to the text, and it looks as if my comments are part of the referenced source; there was no help for this. I regret the inconvenience and invite scholars who want assistance with references to contact me at yitzhak@att.net or through my web site www.jewishspirit.com.

Abbreviations

Agnon	*Sippurei HaBesht*
B	Buber, *Tales of the Hasidim: Early Masters*
Circle	*The Circle of the Baal Shem Tov*
DA	*Devarim Areivim*
DD	*Dor Daiya*
DME	*Degel Machane Ephraim*
Dubnow	Simon Dubnow, "The Beginnings: The Baal Shem Tov (Besht) and the Center in Podolia," in *Essential Papers in Hasidism*
E	Edelbaum, *HaBaal Shem Tov: Ha'Ish V'Torato*
Etkes	*Baal HaShem*
G	Glitzenshtein, *Sefer HaToldot: Rabbi Yisrael Baal Shem Tov*
Gutman	*Rabbi Yisrael Baal Shem Tov: Hayav, Pe'ulotav V'Torato*
H	*HaBesht U'Vnai Heichalo* [Note: Unfortunately, this excellent and reliable book usually does not give its sources.]

Hilsenrad	*The Baal Shem Tov: His Birth and Early Manhood*
Horodetzky	*Rabbi Yisrael Baal Shem Tov: Hayav V'Torato*
IE	*Ikkarei Emunah*
Ishti	*Ishti Ahuvati, Bo'i V'Nirkod*
K	*Kol Sippurei Baal Shem Tov* [Note: Since this source often truncates stories quoted from earlier books, I have not said, when giving its sources, "quoting" but "from."]
Kahana	*Rabbi Yisrael Baal Shem Tov: Hayav, Shitato, U'Pe'ulato*
KE	*Kovetz Eliyahu*
Komarna	*Ma'aseh HaShem HaShalem: Komarna*
KRY	*Kitvei Rabbi Yoshe Shochet U'Vodek*
KST	*Keter Shem Tov* (Kehot)
MEY	*Me'ir Einei Yisrael*
MRT	*Midrash Rivash Tov*
N	*Nezer HaBaal Shem Tov*
P	*In Praise of the Baal Shem Tov*
R	*Reshimot Devarim*
Raz	*Ma'aseh B'Rabbi Yisrael Baal Shem Tov*
S	*Shivhei HaBaal Shem Tov HaShalem*
Sadeh	*Sippurei HaBesht*
Schochet	*Rabbi Israel Baal Shem Tov*
SM	*Sarei HaMaiya*
Steinman	*Be'er HeHasidut: Sefer HaBesht*
SBST	*Sefer Baal Shem Tov*
SSKB	*Siach Sarfei Kodesh* (Breslov)
TYY	*Toldot Yaakov Yosef*
TZR	*Tzava'at HaRivash*
TZR-E	*Tzava'at HaRivash*: The Testament of Rabbi Israel Baal Shem Tov (English)
TZR-K	*Tzava'at HaRivash* (Kehot Hebrew edition)
Y	*HaYahid B'Dorot*
Z	Zevin, *Sippurei Hasidim*

Preface

1. In his preface, the compiler/editor of *Shivhei HaBaal Shem Tov* says that because there are fewer miracles in his day, there is less faith, and his motive in writing the book is to record miracles! The author was related to R. Alexander, the Besht's scribe, who wrote his amulets and was most interested in that aspect of the Besht's work, involving practical Kabbalah and miracles. The author derived much of his information about the Besht from this scribe.

Light and Fire

1. *Likkutei Dibburim* (English), vol. 3, pp. 65–66; vol. 5, pp. 101–2.

Introduction: Praise, Promise, and Prayer

1. Amos 8:11; Isaiah 55:1.

2. Divine service primarily means praying or worship, but also other forms of serving God.

3. *Rabbi Nachman's Wisdom*, p. 268, *Sichos HaRan*, #138. *No'am Elimelech*, Parashat Shmot, p. 28b. Psalms 113:1; Malachi 3:16.

4. *Likkutei Moharan*, I, #248. K, vol. 3, p. 44, from *Knesset Yisrael*. Unlike the Besht, neither the Maggid of Mezritch nor any of the later hasidic rebbes was a *baal shem* (a master of divine Names) and an adept at Practical Kabbalah. *HaNiggun V'HaRikud B'Hasidut*, p. 28. *Yeshu'ot Yisrael*, p. 135. Ahiyah the Shilonite (from Shiloh), a biblical prophet who was Elijah's teacher, came to the Besht from heaven and instructed him. The text states that whoever tells stories of the Besht "after the Sabbath at the beginning of the week—will have salvation and success that week; if at the beginning of the month, he will have success all that month; if he speaks of him at the beginning of the year, he will have a good and blessed year." Many rebbes taught that this is inaccurate and the promise and blessing apply to all times that one tells stories of the Besht; so I adapted the text accordingly.

5. SBST, vol. 1, Preface, p. 22, #43, quoting *Zichron L'Rishonim*; #45, quoting a letter by the author of *Da'at Torah*. Agnon, p. 53. DD, vol. 1, p. 57. The text says that "none" of the miracles happened, but I don't believe the Ropshitzer said this, and changed it to "most." The Ropshitzer's son said after his father's death that the many miracles his father is claimed to have done never happened, but his father actually performed a few miracles, only not those in the stories.

6. *Ateret Menahem*, p. 73, #130. K, vol. 2, p. 138, #12, from *Degel Machane Yehuda*.

7. MEY, I, p. 76; H, p. 295; *Shalshelet HaKodesh: Komarna*, p. 374. *Otzar Yisrael* (Rosenzweig), vol. 1, p. 24, #6.

8. *HaMered HaKadosh*, p. 18. *Yehi Or*, p. 17, #20.

The Setting

1. All sections of this Setting are based on: E, pp. 17–21; Y, pp. 17–31, 56–58; *Bain Pshis'cha L'Lublin*, pp. 3–8; Hilsenrad, p. 10; see also the whole of *The Founder of Hasidism*, and H, pp. 11–17.

2. See n. 1 and the Appendix: *Baal Shem* and Faith Healer. G, vol. 1, p. 205; B, vol. 1, pp. 92, 154.

Beginnings to Revelation

1. N, p. 27; G, vol. 1, p. 55; E, p. 293; R, vol. 3, p. 6, #6.

2. MEY, I, p. 39, quoting *Beit Aharon*. The subject of souls not tasting from the Tree of Knowledge is found in *Sha'ar HaGilgulim*.

3. KE, p. 115, #370; *Kitvei Maran HaRamach*, p. 21, #1. The text says the Besht's soul could not descend for five hundred years. But I wanted to use a story that the Besht's soul had previ-

ously incarnated in a hidden tzaddik who lived in Tzfat around 1573 and passed away, let's guess, around 1640. I reconciled these by a vague "many years." See p. 107 and n. 93 for the story "Ahiyah Tells Him of the Previous Incarnation of His Soul" for more about this. The reference to tzaddikim praying for the soul to descend probably means tzaddikim on earth and in heaven. Compare the story "The Besht's Soul and the End," p. 302.

4. SBST, vol. 1, Preface, p. 11, #1, quoting *Rachmei HaAv*, ot 50; a somewhat different version of this tale is found in *Sefer HaToldot: Rabbi Shneur Zalman, Rabbeinu HaZaken*, vol. 1, p. 189. E, p. 224, quoting *Imrei No'am*. Some doubtful late sources claim that the Besht was descended from King David (R, vol. 3, p. 5, #1; MEY, I, p. 36, quoting R. Nachman of Bratzlav in *Likkutei Moharan*, II, #100). A more credible tale tells that the Besht wanted to marry one of his family into the family of a disciple, but the disciple's wife objected because whereas they had high lineage, the Besht didn't (MEY, II, p. 91). If the Besht was descended from King David, the fact would not have escaped earlier sources and been unknown to his close disciples. Dubnow, p. 26, mentions that just at the time the Besht was born, Podolia was ceded to Poland by Turkey after their war that ended in 1699. The location of Okup was long unclear. Recently, R. Shlomo Abish discovered Okup on an old Ukrainian map; it was a small habitation three miles from Kamenitz-Podolsk (*Heichal Habesht*, p. 44, n. 5; Issue 3, 2003). Today, Podolia is in the territory of Rumania. In the original versions, it is not stated why Elijah replaces the Satan. The reason I've given reflects my own understanding, following an identical motif with this reason in another hasidic story (*Sippurei L'Shabbat*, p. 94). Another reason is that Elijah is often disguised as a wandering beggar and appears in stories where the test involves hospitality.

5. SBST, vol. 1, Preface, p. 11, #4, quoting *N'tiv Mitzvotecha*; MEY, I, p. 37; *Otzar Yirat Shemayim (Breslov)*, vol. 7, p. 76. R. Yaakov Yosef of Polnoye explained, based on the teaching of the Ari in *Sefer HaGilgulim*, that a great soul that descends to elevate others is reluctant to do so for fear it may be led to sin; it only descends when promised that it will not sin (SBST, vol. 1, p. 198, #8). R. Yaakov Yosef also taught in the Besht's name that the Satan complains when a great soul is born, and as a result, a scholarly opponent, a "Jewish demon" (a traditional phrase), is born with him (MEY, II, p. 185, quoting TYY, parashat Shoftim). See "Protecting the Besht from Opponents," on p. 180 and n. 5 there.

6. "*Sippurim Na'im Shel Rabbi Yisrael Baal Shem Tov*," S.Y. Agnon, *Molad*, vol. 18, 1960, pp. 357–64.

7. "*Sippurim Na'im Shel Rabbi Yisrael Baal Shem Tov*," Agnon, *Molad*, vol. 18, 1960, p. 357. Adapted from Hilsenrad, p. 23 and expanded; see G, vol. 1, p. 41 and E, p. 77. Song of Songs 4:1. *Ishei HaTanach*, "Sarah," p. 428, quoting *Bereishit Rabba*, 53–90, states that Sarah imparted fear of heaven to Isaac with her milk. See *Nedarim* 32 about Abraham recognizing his Creator at three, and *Michlol HaMa'amarim V'HaPitgamim*, vol. 1, on *ben shalosh l'otiyot*. IE, p. 11 and G, vol. 1, pp. 31, 34. N, p. 32.

8. IE, p. 11; S, p. 11; K, p. 13; Hilsenrad, p. 25; B, p. 36; G, vol. 1, p. 31. See *Pe'ulat HaTzaddik*, vol. 1, p. 44 and *The Divine Conversation*, p. 65, for a different, Breslov, version. Psalms 16:8.

9. K, vol. 1, p. 14. The *Kaddish* does not mention the deceased. It is a prayer for the coming of God's kingdom. Traditionally, a pious parent might call a son his "Kaddish," because the son would say the *Kaddish* to elevate the parent's soul after death.

10. G, vol. 1, pp. 31, 34.

11. E, pp. 77–78; SBST, vol. 1, p. 266, n. 7. One source has that this occurred when the Besht was three years old; like Abraham, mentioned in the previous section, he first knew his

Creator when he was three years old (MEY, I, p. 38, quoting a Lubavitch source in manuscript). Psalms 139:12; 92:10. Daniel 2:22.

12. Raz, p. 15 (no source cited). Psalms 2:7.

13. E, pp. 56–57; K, vol. 1, p. 19; Hilsenrad, pp. 25–26; G, vol. 1, p. 41; N, p. 33, #3. SM, vol. 3, p. 51. *Zohar*, vol. 3, p. 225a. Psalms 92:10. *Pe'ulat HaTzaddik*, vol. 1, p. 44. Although legend, particularly from Chabad sources, says that the Besht's mother died when he was young, she seems to have lived for quite some time. E, p. 78 gives all the sources—that *Shivhei HaBaal Shem Tov* indicates she was alive and the date of death on her tombstone is 1740 (when the Besht was forty). I've chosen to follow the legend, since we have no additional information about the mother during the Besht's mature years.

14. R. Moshe Weinberger of Long Island, New York, on tape 3 of his Baal Shem Tov series. He told me personally that he heard this story from an elderly Tzanz-Shinova hasid, about 1990. The sentence about the Besht's being troubled about how to fulfill his father's instruction is mine.

15. P, pp. 11–12; S, p. 13, #2. There is no information about how the young Besht was supported or where he lived at this time or about his activities; my comments are speculative.

16. Hilsenrad, p. 26 f.; K, vol. 1, pp. 19–22; G, vol. 1, pp. 31–34; R, vol. 3, p. 9; H, p. 30. The Besht's parents were members of a pre-hasidic movement, "hidden tzaddikim," who should not be confused with the legendary thirty-six hidden tzaddikim in whose merit the world exists (although the young Besht here does "confuse" them and make the connection). It seems that Rabbi Eliezer and Rebbetzin Sarah kept their association with the movement from the boy. In the original version of our tale, the hidden tzaddik is unnamed. Legend sometimes leaves people unnamed because they are unimportant for the story or as here because it fosters an atmosphere of mystery (or, because to the intensely spiritual, names are not important). But in our culture, the effect is disturbing, since one wonders: What is his name? Schochet, p. 39, identifies him as R. Hayim, who is mentioned later as the one who taught the Besht kabbalistic praying. This identification is unlikely. But to avoid the awkwardness of such an important character, whom the young Besht spends years with, being unnamed, I've given him the name Shlomo Zalman. Tractate *Pesahim* is about Passover.

17. Hilsenrad, p. 26 f.; K, vol. 1, pp. 19–22; G, vol. 1, pp. 31–34; R, vol. 3, p. 9; H, p. 30. See G, vol. 1, p. 178. One wonders what Reb Shlomo Zalman was doing most of the day, that the boy didn't realize he was a hidden tzaddik.

18. R, vol. 3, p. 10, #8; Hilsenrad, p. 26 f.; K, vol. 1, pp. 19–22; G, vol. 1, pp. 31–34; H, p. 30.

19. An academic scholar, Hana Shmeruk, recently discovered a Yiddish pamphlet that contains miracle stories about R. Adam Baal Shem. Shmeruk dates the pamphlet to the seventeenth century; see Etkes, p. 79, and H, pp. 338–42. H, p. 25 ("Camp of Israel"). According to Lubavitch traditions, R. Adam Baal Shem was from the town of Ropshitz in Galicia, Poland (*Likkutei Dibburim* [English], vol. 3, p. 67; G, vol. 1, p. 298, and elsewhere). But other traditions that seem more likely place him farther away with less possibility of contact with the young Besht. I've combined the traditions by saying that he was originally from Ropshitz.

20. G, vol. 1, p. 32. H, p. 31. *Baruch hu u'mevorach l'olam va'ed. Yevorach yihiyeh sh'mo hakodesh.* Each year on one's birthday and each day throughout the year it is a hasidic custom to recite the psalm whose number matches the number of years of one's life (*Sichos in English*, vol. 45, p. 108). The Besht, on his sixteenth birthday, would have begun reciting Psalm 16 (whose v. 8 contains: "I have placed God before me always"). The text of the story says "psalms" in the plural, though perhaps it means one psalm from the Book of Psalms. The Besht was meditat-

ing, literally, on "the unifications of the holy Names that are in the first and last letters of the words of the psalms arranged by David, King of Israel."

21. SBST, vol. 1, p. 107, #179 f.; *Hedvat Simhah*, p. 57. Enoch is the biblical figure from the time before Noah. "Blessed is God's glorious kingdom" is the phrase that follows the *Shema Yisrael* in the prayers. While chanting his mantra, Enoch was meditating on heaven and earth being one, what Kabbalah calls the "lower unity"—that all the world is permeated with divinity, is "God's kingdom"; KST, ## 356, 42, 91. Genesis 5:23 says that Enoch "walked with God; then he was no more, for God took him." The Rabbis comment: "He ascended to heaven on God's command and [became an angel who] was given the name Metatron" (*Targum Yerushalmi* to Genesis 5:4; *Midrash Aggada* on Genesis 5:18); see TZR-E, ## 356, 42, 91. The Rabbis in *Derech Eretz Zuta* 1 listed nine biblical figures who they said entered heaven alive. Psalms 16:8. The mantras are: *baruch hu u'mevorach l'olam va'ed; yevorach yihiyeh sh'mo ha-kadosh; baruch shem kavod malchuto l'olam va'ed; shivitti HaShem l'negdi tamid; ko'ach ha-po'el b'ni-fal, baruch HaShem*. The Besht taught common people to use the latter mantra (see p. 29), which can also be translated "Blessed is God." He taught his disciples to use the next to last one (see p. 125). One can deduce that the Besht may have used Psalms 16:8, the most traditionally popular Jewish mantra, and the one used by Enoch, because he taught about Enoch and his mantra, and an important disciple of his, R. Yaakov Koppel used Psalms 16:8 as a mantra. G, vol. 1, p. 71. *Kavvanot*. SBST, vol. 1, p. 173, #134, also n. 126. The Besht spoke approvingly of Nechunya ben HaKaneh who prayed like a child. And one can see from the preceding story in my book that this is the lesson of Elijah. So I consider this a proper characterization of the Besht too.

22. G, vol. 1, p. 35.

23. G, vol. 1, p. 35; pp. 178–79.

24. G, vol. 1, pp. 420–21; Hilsenrad, p. 32. "I thank You [God]"—the first prayer said in the morning, upon awakening, thanking God for restoring one's soul. "Firing": Heard from R. Shlomo Carlebach, in the name of Rebbe Y. Y. Schneersohn of Lubavitch. SM, vol. 3, p. 52. Deuteronomy 4:9. "*Shavuot*": Adapted from *Ma'aseh HaShem HaShalem: Dinov*, vol. 1, p. 30, #5, quoting *Shomer Emunim*, p. 92; KE, p. 15, #52. N, p. 74, #2. "Precious": Adapted from a comment of the Lubavitcher Rebbe (based on *Shabbat* 119), discussing the Besht's teaching of children.

25. B, p. 37; E, p. 57; S, p. 13; P, p. 12; K, vol. 1, p. 23. N, pp. 72–73, #1. During one of the wars in modern-day Israel, parents wanted to keep their children at home, but the tzaddik, R. Reuven Yosef Gershonowitz, promised them that in the merit of the children's Torah study, they would come to no harm (*Netzotzei Aish*, pp. 208, 243). Hardly anyone today, I imagine, believes in werewolves. Perhaps the Besht saved the children from a wolf, as he saved a gentile peasant boy from wolves ("The Besht Protects a Shepherd Boy," p. 45). The Lubavitcher Rebbe referred to the Besht saving the children from vicious dogs (N, p. 72, #2).

26. K, vol. 1, p. 22, #10; cf. p. 25, #13.

27. S, p. 14; P, p. 13; E, p. 58; B, p. 37; Hilsenrad, p. 34; IE, p. 12; TZR-E, p. 130, #33. Micah 6:8.

28. Based on Horodetzky, p. 12.

29. S, pp. 14–20, 31; P, pp. 15–18, 31; K, p. 130, from *Sippurei Nifla'ot*; Hilsenrad, p. 38. "In Galicia, there were books containing prescriptions for medicines, such as *Toldot Adam* and *Mifla'ot Elohim*, both printed in Zolkiew, 1720 and 1724. These were based on the books of the Kabbalah and on the writings of famous *baalei shem* (Rabbi Yoel, Rabbi Eliyahu, and others).

But most often, these books were not printed, and circulated in manuscript as secret writings, known only to a few initiates" (Dubnow, p. 31). The source text says that this manuscript had only been revealed to four individuals before the Besht, including Abraham and Joshua bin Nun. Abraham is traditionally held to have been at the origin of the Jewish mystic tradition and the author of *Sefer Yetzirah*. For Joshua's connection with the mystic lineage, see Etkes, pp. 80–81. One other of the four is not mentioned, with the fourth being R. Adam Baal Shem, who passed it on to the Baal Shem Tov (S, p. 31, #9; P, p. 31). *Baal HaShem* has a different Hebrew version of this than does S. That the Besht is called "Rabbi" by a heavenly voice indicates that he has *s'micha* (ordination) from heaven. Another tradition (see p. 86) says that Elijah and angels ordained the Besht. I've removed from the text a statement that R. Adam realized that this message about his successor meant that he would soon leave this world; since there were reasons that made me have the Besht assuming leadership ten years hence, my chronology would not support this comment. In the sources, R. Adam's son is not named, perhaps because his main importance is as an agent for his father and because his name was not known. But also, perhaps, because leaving a character nameless lends an atmosphere of mystery. There is a tradition in the Tchernobil hasidic dynasty that his name was Nachum (*Beit Tzaddikim Ya'amod*, vol. 3, p. 76). The source text leaves the Besht's first wife nameless. I've created a name for her, Chava. In Temple times, ashes of a pure red heifer were required to purify ritual uncleanness caused by contact with a corpse. "The Ari admonished his disciples to avoid the practical arts of Kabbalah, as he deemed such practice unsafe so long as the state of ritual purity necessary for service in the Holy Temple remains unattainable" (*Zohar: Selections*, Moshe Miller, p. 20; the source for this is R. Hayim Vital in *Sha'arei Kedushah*, part 3, gate 6). The Besht taught: "It is very dangerous to perform *yehudim*, and there were many who, because of a slight error, were cast out of both worlds" (SBST, vol. 2, p. 135, notes, quoting *N'tiv Mitzvotecha*). "Overnight annulment" is a rule of Jewish law.

30. S, pp. 20–23; P, pp. 18–22; B, p. 39; K, vol. 1, p. 135; Hilsenrad, p. 41. Circle, p. 45 (about R. Gershon Kitover's family). E, p. 62. H, p. 320. His full name was Avraham Gershon, but he is often referred by the second name alone. Kitover means "from the town of Kitov." H, p. 35. Chabad tradition has her name as Leah Rachel (Schochet, p. 46; Hilsenrad, p. 42). SBST, vol. 1, p. 87, #10 and n. 8; see also *The Lubavitcher Rebbe's Memoirs*, vol. 1, p. 309 about the clothes of the hidden tzaddikim and their goal of blending in with the working class. *HeHasidut*, p. 13.

31. G, vol. 1, p. 73. S, p. 23, #5; P, p. 22, #8. What if there was no sun? Kahana, p. 33. TZR-E, #s 35, 42, 57; G, vol. 2, p. 682; SBST, vol. 1, p. 128. TZR, p. 7, #s 7–8; see "The Parable of the Magic Palace," p. 114 in my book. Psalms 42:3 (see *Jewish Spiritual Practices*, p. 24, n. 12 about the translation). About the Besht reciting psalms in a *mikvah*: *Mazkeret Shem HaGedolim*, p. 139. TZR-E, #41; MEY, II, p. 126. *Sefer HaSichot* (Hebrew), vol. 2, 1943, p. 196; G, vol. 2, p. 679. *Israel Baalshem: His Life and Times*, pp. 13, 15. Proverbs 3:6. Intense longing: adapted from the Besht's remarks about King David (G, vol. 2, p. 607). Proverbs 5:19. S, p. 26; P, p. 24; K, vol. 1, p. 149. K, vol. 1, p. 25 and B, p. 46, both quoting *Gedolei Yisrael B'Yaldutam*. The Maggid of Mezritch said that the Besht taught him the language of the birds and animals. Details of the immersion scene were filled in from descriptions of Rebbe Hayim of Ribnitz immersing in the same Dniester River in which the Besht immersed. (*Halichot Hayim*, pp. 60–64). *Yeshu'ot Yisrael*, p. 138; K, vol. 1, pp. 146, 148; B, p. 44; *Sippurei Yaakov*, I, #14; *Imrei Pinhas*, Gate 9, #84. N, p. 70, 19:8, quoting the Lubavitcher Rebbe.

32. K, vol. 4, p. 281. Raz, p. 32; SM, vol. 3, p. 52. See "Redeeming a Melody," p. 320.

33. K, vol. 1, p. 145; *Mazkeret Shem HaGedolim*, p. 147; *Shemu'ot V'Sippurim* (no volume or page); *Imrei Pinhas*, p. 245, Gate 9, #84; *Yeshu'ot Yisrael*, pp. 141–42. That the Besht wore this wolfskin a long time is known from a much later tale about his initial meetings with the Maggid of Mezritch. In the source text, the Besht kills the wolves by uttering a divine Name that removes their life-force. This is problematical because of issues about whether and when the Besht used practical Kabbalah; so I've changed the text here. I've based this alteration on the previous tale in which the Besht protects the schoolchildren by killing a wolf with his stick. The reason I like and included this tale is because it shows that the Besht was not only helped by gentiles but that he helped a gentile shepherd boy.

34. S, pp. 23–25; P, p. 22; K, vol. 1, pp. 108–9; B, p. 41. Children (descendants) of Noah is a term that includes both Jews and gentiles but usually, as here, refers to gentiles. According to Jewish law, they are obligated to perform seven *mitzvot*, one being not to steal or rob.

35. S, p. 24; P, p. 22. Psalms 91:11–12. Angels protected the Besht.

36. MRT, II, p. 56, #2. The Komarner Rebbe said that many secrets of Torah are revealed in the merit of voluntary wandering in "exile." "Exile subdues a person's heart in a way that all other sufferings cannot. Then he becomes bound to the Torah and the *Shechinah* rests on him" (H, p. 232). MRT, I, p. 71, #19; G, vol. 2, pp. 635, 637. "Not assimilate, etc." is from a Chabad source whose reference I've misplaced.

37. *Otzar Sippurei Chabad*, vol. 1, p. 72. N, p. 99, #3 states that the Besht instigated this new program to help first materially and only later spiritually. G, vol. 1, pp. 48–50; E, p. 83, quoting G.

38. G, vol. 1, p. 42; see also p. 421; G, vol. 2, p. 645; a few details have been added from the similar practice of R. Chaim Gelb (*A Life of Chessed*, p. 113).

39. *Ner Yisrael*, vol. 4, p. 41; *Tiferet Sh'B'Malchut*, p. 149. This was R. Levi Yitzhak of Berditchev. DD, vol. 1, p. 32. MRT, I, p. 71, #19; SBST, vol. 1, p. 29, #66, quoting *Toldot Aharon*.

40. *Emunat Tzaddikim*, story 2; quoted in E, p. 132; quoted in K, vol. 4, p. 154, but not fully. The boy in the story became one of the Besht's great disciples, R. Meir Margoliot. He became a disciple later as an adolescent (see "Attraction," p. 75). I left out his name here because the preceding related story has no name for the boy and the two tales together would otherwise seem awkward. I also left out the name of the town, which was Yazlovitz. When a child begins to study *Chumash*, usually at the age of five, there is a feast to celebrate the *mitzvah*. He is put on a table, his father at the head, and he gives a little talk of the following nature: He is asked, "What do you learn?" He answers, "*Chumash*." "What is that?" He answers with the verse, "Moses commanded us this Torah, etc." "Who gave the Torah?" etc. (The custom is described in *Through Fire and Water*, p. 644, n. 6.)

41. G, vol. 1, pp. 65, 350–51; vol. 2, p. 637; p. 641, n. 204.

42. N, p. 315, quoting *Sefer HaSichot* (1944), p. 140. Note that although the Besht was at this time a hidden tzaddik, he preached publicly. Psalms 65:5. In the source text, the Besht said that the letters of the word *ashrei* (Happy) of the verse are an acrostic that stands for *amen, y'hai shmai rabba* (not in order, though: *alef-yud-shin-resh*). *Shabbat* 119b.

43. This sermon was constructed from the Besht's teachings and set in Kolomaya, where the Besht lived for a period and also visited, because of my own father's origins there. G, vol. 2, pp. 638–42, 677; vol. 1, pp. 72–73, 75, 78. MEY, II, p. 15, quoting *Likkutei Dibburim*; N, pp. 208, 55–5. E, p. 145, quoting *Ktav Shem Tov*, 150–51. The text specifically mentions R. Yishmael, a righteous high priest. Traditional Torah study is usually verbal not silent, and involves either reading from a book or recitation from memory. *Avodah Zarah* 3a. Genesis 1:26. Psalms 8:5.

44. *Shemu'ot V'Sippurim*, vol. 2, p. 10; G, vol. 1, pp. 9–10.

45. G, vol. 1, pp. 396–400. The Besht left Brody under pressure from his brother-in-law, R. Gershon, and one might wonder at his presence there. But Brody was a big city and it would be possible for him to avoid R. Gershon. *Gehinnom*: To be purged and cleansed; then one is admitted to paradise.

46. G, vol. 1, p. 411. The name Yonah has been created for the nameless tinsmith. Study in a *cheder* was private and expensive; study in a *Talmud Torah* was funded by the community and inferior. In many ways this tale parallels the Besht's own recruitment, as a boy, in the woods etc., studying, and going off with the mystic for three years, which seems to have been the period required for a novice before joining the movement of hidden tzaddikim. MRT, II, p. 56, #3, quoting *Notzair Hesed* about the Besht's practice of "exile."

47. *Shemu'ot V'Sippurim*, vol. 2, p. 10. I changed the source text, which has this event taking place a full fifteen years after the new program was instituted. G, vol. 1, p. 72; B, p. 9; H, p. 32.

48. G, vol. 1, p. 83; vol. 2, pp. 605–6; N, p. 170, #5; E, p. 130; *Sippurei Tzaddikim HeHadash*, p. 16, #4. *Yoshaiv*—literally: sit or dwell; idiomatically: make a living from. "Israel provides a livelihood " (*Zohar Hadash*).

49. Raz, p. 249 (no source cited). *Sotah 2*.

50. *Biyeshishim Hochmah*, pp. 16, 265. Malachi 3:16. Some details were taken from the similar story told about the Seer of Lublin, in *Sippurei Tzaddikim*, Preface, p. 5. See SBST, vol. 1, p. 227, #9, and my book *Storytelling and Spirituality in Judaism*, p. 12 and n. 18 and p. 45 about the teaching. I seem to remember having seen a version of this tale with the Besht being with another hidden tzaddik; or I may have changed the version in *Biyeshishim Hochmah*, which on one page has the Besht with "another person" and in another place with a disciple, because I felt this tale belonged earlier, when the Besht was a hidden tzaddik and before he had disciples. The main branch of Jewish mysticism is *Maaseh Merkavah*: the "Account of the Divine Chariot." S, p. 233, #160; P, p. 199, #194; G, vol. 1, p. 111.

51. E, pp. 31, 42. K, vol. 4, pp. 74, 81; G, vol. 1, p. 328.

52. R, vol. 1, p. 7, #12; *Sneh Bo'ar B'Kotzk*, p. 183; *Hasidim M'Saprim*, vol. 2, p. 17, #58; Raz, p. 161.

53. G, vol. 1, pp. 371, 328; E, pp. 162–63, 158; DD, vol. 1, p. 35. Psalms of Ascent are Psalms 120–134. E, p. 158; G, vol. 1, p. 328. IE, p. 25; KE, p. 94, #7. Reciting the whole book of 150 psalms is a tremendous undertaking that requires hours and is a practice of piety and repentance. *Avot* 5:10–11. I couldn't find the source for the *midrash* about Moses "chastising" God. Perhaps it relates to Exodus 5:22 where Moses, so to speak, rebukes God, saying, "Why have you dealt ill with this people?" Presumably, since the *Shechinah* spoke through Moses' throat, God "told" Moses to say these words and to "rebuke" Him. It's an awesome concept.

54. K, vol. 1, p. 152, from *Sippurei Yaakov*, I. On *Sukkot*, four plant species—*esrog* (citron), *lulav* (date palm), myrtle, and willows—are ceremonially waved during the prayer services. The Torah calls the *esrog* a "splendid fruit" and pious people make great efforts to find a splendid and perfect *esrog*, and they spend as much money as they can to acquire one for the *mitzvah*. *Esrogs* are not grown in Eastern Europe and imports from other countries were sometimes not available.

55. KRY, p. 7, #18; Agnon, p. 17; DD, vol. 1, p. 26. R, vol. 3, p. 13, #13. The source text does not have the words about "How can I slaughter, etc." Marcus, in *HeHasidut*, p. 13, says that the Besht innovated the Ukrainian method of sharpening slaughtering knives because the sharper knife made the animal's death less painful. A hasidic tale tells of a pious *shochet* who before slaughtering an animal, wept, thinking, "How can I slaughter a living creature? Am I

better than it?" (*Ner Yisrael*, vol. 4, p. 14, #29). The Besht taught that a person should consider himself at one with all living creatures and no better than a worm. This seems to be why the Besht was weeping, so I added that motive; see also E, pp. 343 f.; P, pp. 133–34. The Torah teaches that meat eating is wrong but God compromised with human weakness to allow the consumption of strictly regulated kosher meat, until the end of days, when the vegetarianism of the Garden of Eden will be restored.

56. KRY, p. 7, #19; Komarna, p. 49, #30. Rabbinic authors are sometimes known by the name of their most famous book, as here.

57. *Emunat Tzaddikim*, p. 10, #7; DD, vol. 1, p. 26; H, p. 43; R, vol. 3, pp. 12–14, #12, 13; E, pp. 112, 131; B, p. 42. H, p. 371 (no source cited; I've seen the source, which I don't remember, numbers of times). E, p. 131. See "Arousal by a Glance," p. 49 and n. 40 on p. 372. Undoubtedly, the Besht revealed to the two young men some of his spiritual levels, taught them secrets of the Torah, and how to pray and study with true devotion

58. *Sippurim Nechmadim*, p. 2b, in *Sippurei Nifla'im*; *Emunat Tzaddikim*, p. 13 (7a), #20; K, vol. 1, p. 151; H, p. 45. About those who test others and are not able to stand a test, see a story about the Belzer Rebbe in *Dover Shalom*, p. 141.

59. S, p. 41, #12; P, p. 36, #22; E, pp. 107, 109–10. H, pp. 44, 150.

60. K, vol. 2, p. 121, #21; E, p. 212; *Ta'amei HaMinhagim*, p. 325; MRT, II, p. 32, #4—all quoting *Divrei Yehezkel*; *Hasidic Anthology*, p. 513, quoting MRT, II, 32; B, p. 45; N, p. 91, #10.

61. H, p. 207; KE, p. 114, #366. The source text has that the Besht was told "during a soul-ascent to the Garden of Eden" to learn from this man; for editorial reasons, I changed it to his being told by Elijah. There are a number of stories of Moses coming to teach the Besht *kavvanot* while he was eating (see, for example, p. 279). I've created the scene with Elijah and the initiation of these encounters.

62. Raz, p. 84; H, p. 169. My text is a composite of these two versions. The source text has that the Besht was told "from heaven" about the man; for editorial reasons I changed it to his being told by Elijah. Leviticus 19:16, 18.

63. S, p. 27, #7; P, p. 26, #13; K, vol. 1, p. 140.

64. S, pp. 4, 28, 39; P, p. 27, #14, and p. 34, #19; K, vol. 1, p. 140, #2; B, p. 46; R, vol. 3, #16, 17. *Israel Baalshem: His Life and Times*, p. 7; Dubnow, p. 30. There is confusion in the sources about whether the Besht resided in Kitov or Brody and regarding his relations with the Pious of Kitov or the Pious of Brody, the members of the renowned Brody *Kloiz*. It seems that the Besht and his wife ran an inn near Kitov, not near Brody. The Besht and Chana had earlier in his career lived in that area and dug clay. R. Gershon, from Kitov, had moved to Brody, but his presence in later stories with the Besht in Kitov may be explained by his visiting that familiar area where his relatives lived. Etkes, pp. 169–85, compares the Brody *Kloiz* and the Pious of Kitov. R. Gershon of Kitov was a link between the two groups, being a member of both (at the same or different times of his life?). R. Gershon and R. Moshe, the rabbi of Kitov and a leading member of the pietists there, were brothers-in-law (Circle, p. 45; see pp. 45–55 for R. Gershon's movement between the groups; see also P, p. 31, note). One washes in the bathhouse before the ritual of *mikvah* immersion. Horodetzky, p. 14. *Jewish Spiritual Practices*, p. 205 (cf. p. 203), quoting *Derech Tzaddikim*, p. 55. Kahana, p. 54, estimates that Edel was born about 1720. Her son, Moshe Hayim Ephraim, was born approximately in 1744 (*Tehillot Baruch*, p. 12) and it seems that she didn't give birth for ten years after her wedding (which must have been around 1734). Kahana assumes she was about sixteen at her wedding, putting her birth as 1720. My time line doesn't allow this exact dating.

65. K, vol. 1, p. 150, #10; R, vol. 3, p. 15, #16; cf. *Gevurat Ari*, p. 7, in *Kahal Hasidim HeHadash*, what the Besht says about R. Leib Saras. MEY, p. 56*; *Even Yisrael: Beit HaBaal Shem Tov*, p. 38, n. 21, quoting *Da'at Moshe*. The source text has that the tale involves the Besht's son, Tzvi. But this is impossible if, as likely, the event took place when the Besht was still a hidden tzaddik and he and Chana lived in the inn. Kahana, p. 54, states that Edel was born about 1720 and Tzvi about 1740. The Besht was revealed in 1736, when he was thirty-six. One could either change the time and location, making the story not in the inn, but later. Or, one could change the story to be about Edel not Tzvi. I've chosen the latter. Kahana could be wrong about the dates for Tzvi and Edel. But Tzvi is mentioned in the 1747 letter of R. Gershon to his brother-in-law and it is likely he was still a boy then. As for the story, it being a *mitzvah* for a man to grow a beard, the beard is considered holy, especially if the individual is holy. The Besht taught that one can bring God's attention down to the lower world by prayer, using a metaphor of a child grabbing its father's beard (SBST, vol. 2, p. 77, n. 13). The final comment about children is based on a similar tale told by the Lubavitcher Rebbe, who taught that although a person is engaged in mystic meditation he still must be alert to the needs of a child, who is a part of God (*An Open Heart: The Mystic Path of Loving People*, p. 54, quoting *Kovetz Sippurim*).

66. MEY, p. 60, note. See *Kohen Gadol M'Sharait*, p. 90, and *Yafa Sichatan Shel Avdai Avot*, p. 155 about the *shterntichel*.

67. S, p. 48, #17; P, p. 42, #29; K, vol. 1, p. 144, #5. Unattended, unguarded flour is considered *hametz* and ritually unusable in making matzahs. Psalms 127:1. "With God's help": *Jewish Spiritual Practices*, p. 511, #26:10, 11, quoting *Kaf HeHayim*, p. 281, #2, and *Otzar HaSippurim*. The Besht taught that when a person realizes that he cannot help himself, then God helps him (see MEY, p. 141, quoting *Likkutim Yekarim*). One can only properly understand the meaning of the Besht tale from what is basically a version of this story, in which a disciple of the Besht exerts himself to guard wine from losing its kosher status, and fails. The Besht teaches him that in addition to his own efforts, he must also rely on God (SBST, vol. 1, Preface, p. 21, #40; K, vol. 2, p. 142, #16; R, vol. 3, p. 276, #2).

68. S, p. 50, #17; P, p. 43, #29, p. 27, #14.

69. S, p. 50, #18; P, p. 44, #30. "They" is often used in Jewish religious writings to refer to the inhabitants of heaven—the angels or God. The source has that the horse was returned a year later. Since it seems unlikely that the Besht would remain without a horse if it was needed for tasks, I've changed this to two months. The final quotation is from the Talmud, *Mo'ed Katan* 16.

70. *Ma'amar Mordechai*, vol. 1, p. 2, #3. The source says "they seated the Besht on a fallen tree," which is a motif paralleling the scene when the Besht is revealed to the world and accepted as a leader (see p. 113 in this book). Because of the similarity, I have changed this to a laying on of hands traditional in giving *s'micha*. There was a previous indication that the Besht had received heavenly *s'micha*—a heavenly voice had told R. Adam Baal Shem about him and called him "Rabbi Israel." But now, before the Besht began to be instructed by Ahiyah, Elijah gave him his *s'micha*.

71. G, vol. 2, p. 625. According to the mystic teachings, everything that happens to a person is divinely directed, and meaningful. Job 32:8: "the soul of a man makes him to understand" is often understood to mean that a person's soul teaches him. The Besht said his "soul taught him" that he attained his spiritual levels not by Torah study, but because of his fervent prayer. One can learn the way of God from a book, but the Torah is also written in the divine soul. The

Besht's disciple, R. Pinhas of Koretz, said that your soul is always teaching you, but it never says the same thing twice. The Lubavitcher Rebbe said that the Besht taught, "Everything a person sees or hears is, in a sense, a heavenly message about divine service. But one has to understand what one sees and hears. This comes from 'a man's soul teaches him,' which means that his mind becomes illumined so that thoughts fall into his head explaining what he heard or saw. That is how he can understand the heavenly instructions about divine service." (G, vol. 2, p. 635). Comparison of Chabad sources indicates that the level of "a person's soul teaches him" is the same as what is elsewhere spoken of as "revelation of the soul" (G, vol. 1, p. 73; vol. 2, p. 635). See also n. 102 on p. 380. TZR-E, #41; MEY, II, p. 126. TZR-E, p. 46, #56. G, vol. 2, p. 448; KRY, p. 13, #33. SBST, vol. 2, pp. 64–65, n. 12. G, vol. 2, pp. 448, 447, 593. See p. 144, "When to Visit the Teacher?" G, vol. 2, p. 679. The source refers only to children; the other elements have been added from G, vol. 1, p. 73; vol. 2, p. 640. DD, vol. 1, pp. 40–41.

72. R, vol. 2, p. 30, #13; cf. SBST, vol. 1, Preface, p. 20, #35. *Kitzur Shulhan Aruch* 2:6. See "A Form of Fire" and "The Vision of a Great Fire," p. 353; KRY, p. 33, #88.

73. SBST, vol. 2, p. 169, #17, quoting *Sichot HaRan*, #48. See also *Rabbi Nachman's Wisdom*, p. 152 and B, p. 52.

74. MRT, II, p. 150; *Ma'amar Mordechai*, vol. 2, Sippurim, p. 13, #29.

75. G, vol. 1, pp. 35f., 42. One Chabad tradition has that Ahiyah revealed himself to the Besht on *Hai Elul*, which was his twenty-sixth birthday; but another has that this occurred on *parashat* Vayeshev in winter (R, vol. 3, p. 15). I have adapted the text to fit the former view. Only "a book" is mentioned, but from other indications I deduce that it was the *Zohar*. It is a traditional spiritual practice to nap before *Shabbat*, to gather all one's energies and to be fully awake and alert on the holy day. The Besht interacted with members of the Pious of Kitov and of the Brody *Kloiz*, two similar groups of hasidim. See n. 64 on p. 374. "Elijah the Prophet" is sung at the end of the Sabbath. Elijah appears to mystic adepts in visions to teach them Torah secrets. R. Shimon bar Yohai was the greatest of the ancient mystics. Ahiyah, then, is the teacher of the teachers of mystics.

76. G, vol. 2, p. 679; K, Preface, p. 12. The mystic tradition is usually described as beginning with Abraham. Here, as with the transmission of the revealed Torah, it starts with Moses, and goes to David. *Netivot Emunah*, p. 4, says that Adam saw the newly created world, told about it to etc. Amram to Ahiyah to Elijah, etc., and he cites a *Baba Batra* commentary. That Ahiyah was a disciple of Moses is from *Ma'aseh Avot*, p. 15, #2, in the words of the Spinker Rebbe. It seems that, like Elijah and Enoch, Ahiyah became an angel.

77. R. Shimon bar Yohai, the great mystic and author of the *Zohar*, said, "Let Abraham bring people back to God, from his time to mine. I will bring people back from my time to the end of generations. If my merit is not sufficient, let Ahiyah ha-Shiloni be joined with me, and I can bring the whole Jewish people back to God" (*Y. Berachot* 9:27). According to the Ari, R. Shimon bar Yohai was the reincarnation of Ahiyah (N, pp. 277–78). Why was Ahiyah the Besht's teacher? One reason might be that whereas many mystics merited to have Elijah teach them, the Besht was on a higher level, being a teacher of mystics, and he merited having Elijah's teacher teach him. The authors of N (pp. 277–78) and of *Sefer HaToldot: Rabbi Shneur Zalman, Rabbeinu HaZaken* (vol. 1, p. 141, n. 159 and p. 143, n. 172) discuss this issue. *Sefer HaSichot* (1940), p. 163; *Likkutei Dibburim* (English), vol. 2, p. 110; *Sefer HaToldot: Rabbi Shneur Zalman, Rabbeinu HaZaken*, vol. 1, p. 141, n. 159; G, vol. 2, p. 655. According to Kabbalah, everyone receives a *nefesh* at birth. *Ruach* and *neshamah* are acquired, the former when one rises above the lower animal self and becomes spiritual, the latter for special people. The higher lev-

els *haya* and *yehida* are for the even more special few (*Kabbalah*, G. Scholem, pp. 155, 157). *Sefer HaToldot: HaMaggid MiMezritch*, p. 7. Ordinary people may attain a level where the higher two soul levels, *haya* and *yehida* are in constant *d'vekut*, but souls of *Atzilut* may attain a level where all their soul levels are in constant *d'vekut* (*Sefer HaToldot: HaMaggid MiMezritch*, p. 7). *Sefer HaToldot: Rabbi Yosef Yitzchok, Admor Moharayatz*, II, p. 6. *Sefer HaToldot, Rabbi Shneur Zalman, Rabbeinu HaZaken*, vol. 1, p. 143, n. 172. *Atzilut* is the essence of the *pardes* of the Torah; the Messiah is *haya-yehida*. Previously, on p. 89, it is said that Ahiyah taught the Besht the Torah's secrets and that the Torah's hidden light evoked the hidden light of his soul. Here, it is said that the higher soul levels enable one to comprehend the mystic Torah. The relation between soul revelation and comprehension of the mystic Torah is dialectic. "There is a very tiny spark in which God, blessed be He, so to speak, concentrates Himself; this is the last level of the Creator of the world. This spark clothes itself in the spark that is the choicest and finest level of the soul, the level of *yehida*. This spark called *yehida* is the source that includes the four other soul levels—*nefesh-ruach-neshamah-haya*. And by this level the created being-Israelite unites with the Creator of the world and attains prophecy and the holy spirit, and God, blessed be He, actually speaks with him" (SBST, vol. 2, p. 130, n. 2, quoting *Zohar Hai*). See "He Hears Torah From God Himself but Fears the Pit," p. 250.

78. G, vol. 1, pp. 37, 41; vol. 2, p. 587. MEY, II, p. 193, quoting *Zohar Hai*, and referring also to DME. See n. 2 on p. 380.

79. SBST, Preface, p. 20, #36; DD, vol. 1, p. 43. The Besht said: "By the power of faith a Jew can lay a scarf on a river and cross over on it" (N, p. 203). The miracle story about the Besht may have evolved from such a saying. Some versions have a scarf or handkerchief, which suggests that one needs only the flimsiest support if one trusts in God. The belt comes from familiar sayings about faith and trust as a belt around one's loins. *Ner Yisrael*, vol. 1, p. 44 says the belt in this tale symbolizes faith. The tradition says that the Besht was under a vow not to use divine Names until the age of thirty-six, although this matter is nowhere explained. Yet it must be explained. I've created here a likely reason, according to the lines of other stories and teachings.

80. *Funim Rebben's Hauf*, p. 90, #23; Connections/Hakrev Ushma, 1985, 1 (3), 2.

81. *Sippurei Kedoshim*, pp. 21–23, 67–68; *Adat Tzaddikim*, p. 14; K, vol. 2, p. 122.

82. This tale is a composite from a number of sources (there were reasons that required this). K, vol. 1, p. 225, #6, from *Likkutei Sippurim*; *Ta'amei HaMinhagim*, p. 13 and B, p. 77, quoting *Sha'arei Yisrael*; E, pp. 77–78 and *Rabboteinu M'orai HaGola, Beracha M'shuleshet*, p. 372, quoting a Lubavitch source; Horodetzky, p. 113. Some versions have that the Besht wanted the one divine Name he didn't know, which was in Satan's hand—how to bring the redemption. See E and *Rabboteinu M'orai HaGola*. See also KRY, p. 12, #30. The motif in one version of this tale, of the Satan being pacified when seeing the divine image on the Besht's disciples' faces, didn't fit with the motif I used from another version, that the Besht wanted the key to piety (if his disciples were on such a high level, how could he lack the "key to piety"?). So I made the Satan pacified by the divine *light* on the Besht's face, earlier in his career, when he still sought the key to perfect piety.

83. K, vol. 1, p. 250, #5, from *Sippurei Besht*. The original tale is about a woodcutter, but since I used another story shortly before this about another woodcutter I thought it would be confusing, so I changed it to a tailor; it is not an essential aspect of the tale.

84. SBST, vol. 1, p. 253. *Jewish Spiritual Practices*, p. 474, quoting TZR, and p. 467, quoting *Likkutim Yekarim*, p. 5a. TZR, p. 12. G, vol. 2, pp. 655–66. S, p. 157; P, p. 129. *Admorei Belz*,

vol. 1, p. 8; Nigal, *Moro V'Rabo Shel Rabbi Yisrael Baal Shem Tov*, p. 157. G, vol. 2, p. 668, n. 18; K, vol. 2, p. 220, quoting *Torat Hayim*.

85. G, vol. 2, p. 631. Horodetzky, p. 14, quoting *Keter Shem Tov*. MRT, p. 52, quoting *Likkutei Yekarim*; *Jewish Spiritual Practices*, p. 17. The number 18 in Hebrew numerology stands for "life."

86. MEY, I, p. 39. *Zohar*, Mishpatim, p. 94b.

87. Based on SM, vol. 3, pp. 51–56. *Perek Shira* tells which Torah verses different species of animals and birds sing in praise to their Creator. "Who has all this in His world" is part of the ordained blessing made upon seeing goodly trees or beautiful animals (*Kitzur Shulchan Aruch* 60:15). The Besht said (p. 151) that his disciples "hear and see the song that emanates from each and every thing that God, blessed be He, has created." Genesis 2:5. *Bereishit Rabba* 13.

88. SBST, vol. 2, p. 50, ##29–31, quoting various sources; G, vol. 2, p. 668 and n. 18; B, p. 75; *Ner Yisrael*, vol. 2, p. 140; *Or HaShabbat*, pp. 66–67; *Ma'asiyot U'Maamarim Yekarim*, p. 6a (11) in *Sippurim Nifla'im*. R. Yaakov Yosef of Polnoye taught that when the Messiah comes even animals will recognize their Creator (SBST, vol. 1, p. 262). One can guess that this legend about the Besht elevating the flock of sheep comes from the Besht's teaching on Leviticus 1:2. See SBST on that verse, where the key line of the Besht is: "From the flock"—the secret of a flock of sheep or goats is the aspect of *aliyot ha'olamot*, "the ascension of the worlds." The point there is mystical, having nothing to do with actual sheep. H, p. 147, notes that at *Minha* and *Kabbalat Shabbat* all the worlds are elevated and that the Besht then raised all the prayers and *mitzvot* of the week.

89. G, vol. 1, pp. 35, 42; R, vol. 3, p. 11, #9. Various authors make different guesses at what age the Besht became leader of the Society of Hidden Tzaddikim. Schochet, p. 45, guesses age thirty-four. B, p. 9 says at nineteen he was chosen as one of committee of three and soon afterward chosen as the leader. G, vol. 1, p. 42 has at twenty-six, which is based on the Chabad tradition about the age at which Ahiyah was revealed to him. H, p. 32, quoting *The Lubavitcher Rabbi's Memoirs* of Rebbe Y. Y. Schneersohn. Horodetzky, p. 20.

90. R, vol. 3, p. 16, ## 17, 18. Cf. R, vol. 3, p. 15, #16; G, vol. 1, p. 41; vol. 2, p. 682. The sentence about *s'micha* is inserted, based on *Shalshelet HaZahav MiGalitzia V'ad Yerushalayim*, p. 14.

91. R, vol. 3, p. 16, #18. A person who is given greatness or honor should ponder whether heaven has bestowed this on him to mock him, and as a punishment (*Toldot HaYismah Yisrael*, vol. 1, p. 141). See *Souls on Fire*, Wiesel, pp. 23–24, for a story about why the Besht was punished while a spiritual twin was not. G, vol. 2, p. 704. N, p. 32, #1. K, vol. 1, Preface, p. 12. R, vol. 2, p. 37. *Likkutei Dibburim* (English), vol. 1, pp. 299–307; G, vol. 1, pp. 42–44. R, vol. 1, p. 38. R, vol. 2, pp. 665–66, 682. The tradition indicates that during the Besht's lifetime others were the tzaddik of the generation, the sage of the generation, etc. It seems that the Besht was the leader of the generation.

92. K, vol. 1, p. 196, #22, from *Sippurim Yekarim*, and K, vol. 1, Preface, p. 12; B, p. 45. In *Emet V'Yatziv*, vol. 3, p. 178, the editor adds a bracketed comment to the tale to indicate that the Besht and his wife were trying to nullify the decree that the Besht be revealed. This might be a normal understanding of the tale, but I made it vaguer, to "asking God's help," because it is unworthy to imagine the Besht would have to be forced to save his people. But I struggled with this issue, for what about Moses? Didn't he refuse to lead at first? Here is what my alternate text would be: Finally, the Baal Shem Tov confided in his wife and told her what was being demanded of him. "What shall we do?" she asked. He said, "We must afflict ourselves and beg God to spare me this burden."

93. *Beit Tzaddikim Ya'amod*, p. 164; G, vol. 1, p. 30, quoting *HaTamim*. The latter source (not the former) has this matter communicated by R. Adam Baal Shem. But I consider the sources that have the Besht never meeting R. Adam as more authentic. So I have put this story in the mouth of Ahiyah. See n. 3 on p. 381 about the need to reconcile this tale with the story about the Besht's soul not being able to descend for a long period of time.

94. K, vol. 1, p. 197, from *Sippurei Hasidim* and *Eretz HeHayim*; *Eretz HeHayim*, p. 19 (10), #9; DD, vol. 1, pp. 27–28. The Talmud says that personally serving sages is more spiritually beneficial than learning their teachings. Serving a tzaddik like R. Yitzhak in his home was like serving God in His House, the Temple.

95. S, p. 29, #9; P, p. 28, #15; K, vol. 1, p. 200, #25; E, pp. 68, 72, 77; B, p. 46. "By mystical means": Or, it was the Besht's expressed wish, the wish of a tzaddik, that was fulfilled by heaven.

96. S, p. 28, #8; p. 32, #2; P, p. 27, #14. Certain Jewish holidays extend over a week and the beginning and end days are more sanctified, no work being allowed. The "intermediate days" are still holidays but less holy. The custom of Ashkenazi Jews is to wear *tefillin* on the intermediate days of a holiday and to remove them before reciting *Hallel*. Comments about "deserving death" should not be taken literally! They mean that such an offense severely damages a person spiritually. Etkes, pp. 170–71. "Defective": Some of the Jewish legal requirements for the scroll inside a *mezuzah* to be kosher (fit) were not present.

97. S, p. 48, #16; P, p. 42, #28.

98. S, p. 39, #11; P, p. 34, #20; K, vol. 1, p. 142, #4; E, p. 73. The text says: "For I know that you've been warned not to make use of the divine Names until you are thirty-six years old." (The Besht wasn't yet thirty-six at this time.) The Besht threatens her that he'll convene a religious court to release him, presumably from a vow not to use divine Names. This matter is nowhere explained. The specific age can also not be reconciled with other traditions, including the tradition that Ahiyah teaches the Besht for ten years, from ages twenty-six to thirty-six, and then demands that he be revealed. *Imrei D'vash*, p. 39, has a story about R. Levi Yitzhak of Berditchev with a similar motif, that the Berditchever would not be revealed before he was thirty-six years old. There, it is said to be a condition demanded by the Satan, so that his task will not be impossible, and the condition is granted to placate him. See n. 79 on p. 377. *Dybbuk*: The man's soul became a *dybbuk* after its death, as a punishment for its sins; it then entered the woman. In the merit of their Torah study for its sake, it would be released from its punishment.

99. S, p. 31, #9; P, p. 31, #15; K, vol. 1, p. 202; R, vol. 3, p. 16, ##19, 20. Etkes, pp. 181–86, particularly p. 186 and n. 85 establishes that this was the Society of the Pious of Kitov and not the Pious of the Brody *Kloiz*. E, p. 75 agrees. See also H, p. 255.

100. Psalms 97:11. G, vol. 2, p. 639; S, p. 79, #29; H, pp. 131–32; SBST, vol. 1, Preface, p. 29, #69. G, vol. 2, pp. 447–48, 593; P, p. 63. SBST, vol. 2, pp. 64–65, n. 12. Careful study of this note indicates that the teaching in the name of the Besht's disciple, R. Nachman of Horodenka, was also shared by the Besht, which is the reason that it was included in SBST. Cf. also in my book the Besht's teaching that eating at his Sabbath table acts like an elixir of life (p. 284). SBST, vol. 2, pp. 64–65, n. 12. G, vol. 1, pp. 72, 75; G, vol. 2, p. 640. KST, p. 28b (56), #219; MRT, I, p. 38, ##6, 7, quoting *Sippurei Tzaddikim* and *Imrei Tzaddikim*. Kabbalists already used the *mikvah* daily. The Besht was encouraging its use in place of fasting. S, p. 79; H, p. 132. Psalms 139:7, 8. R, vol. 2, p. 33, #17. The two verses quoted are Isaiah 58:7 and Job 19:26. G, vol. 2, pp. 561, 562, #15 and on; E, p. 216, quoting *Pri HeAretz*, Ki Tissa, from R. Menahem Mendel of Vitebsk quoting the Besht. SBST, vol. 1, p. 156, #2, quoting *Likkutei Moharan*, #133; B, p. 74; H, p. 5. MRT, II, p. 62 (31b), quoting *Likkutei Yekarim*. TZR-E, p. 133, #137. Deuteronomy 4:35. Isaiah 6:3. Jeremiah 19:13. IE, p. 24; KE, p. 93, #1; the sentence about the

"speck" is from Raz, p. 27 (no source cited). "The Parable of the Magic Palace" is a composite of the 8 versions in SBST, vol. 2, p. 235 f.; see also: E, p. 191; Kahana, pp. 42–43; *Eretz HeHayim*, pp. 69 (35), 72 (36), #217. Composite from *Eretz HeHayim*, p. 36b (72), #217; SBST, vol. 1, p. 263, n. 5. SBST, vol. 2, p. 90 quoting TZR (with minor alterations). Proverbs 3:6. The "mask" comment is derived from "The Parable of the Magic Palace," as well as from two other Besht parables, one in which a king sent fearsome or gentle messengers to someone, with the parable's lesson being to react not to the external aspect of the "messenger," but to the One who sent them. See also "The Parable of the Frightening Mask" on p. 327. The Torah says that God created light on the first day of creation but the sun only on the fourth day. The Rabbis explained that the first was the spiritual light, by which Adam could see from one end of the world to the other. But God hid that light so it would not be misused by wicked people. It is "reserved" for the use of the tzaddikim, the righteous. MRT, II, p. 44, #1; p. 45, #2; Raz, p. 278; *Armon Knesset Yisrael*, vol. 2, p. 486, quoting *Otzar HeHayim* (Komarna); *Bas Ayin*, Issue 9, January 1995, quoting *Otzar Mishlei Hasidim*. SBST, vol. 1, p. 116, #7, quoting *Turei Zahav* and other sources. SBST, vol. 1, p. 92. S, p. 31; P, p. 31; R, vol. 3, p. 16, #20; K, vol. 1, p. 202. R, vol. 3, p. 16, #20. In a letter to the Besht, R. Gershon of Kitov calls him by the title "Rabbi of all the Jews in the Exile." (Etkes, p. 184).

101. Based on G, vol. 1, p. 71. G, vol. 1, pp. 30, 42; SBST, vol. 1, Preface, p. 15, #17.

102. G, vol. 2, pp. 617, 667, quoting a teaching of the Besht as transmitted by the Lubavitcher Rebbe in *Sefer HaSichot*. The wording of the teaching alludes to a verse "the soul of a man makes him to understand" (Job 32:8) that is often understood to mean that a person's soul teaches him. See n. 71 on p. 375 for an explanation. Another tradition says that on Sabbaths the Besht was 2/3 above and 1/3 below, while on weekdays he was 1/3 above and 2/3 below. I have inserted here about the "house" and "garment" from related material in *Even Yisrael*, p. 69, n. 25; ibid, p. 68, n. 21, end.

A Mission as a Teacher and Baal Shem

1. S, p. 40, #11; P, p. 35, #20.

2. See the Appendix: *Baal Shem* and Faith Healer. *Encyclopedia Judaica*, "Ba'al Shem," vol. 4, p. 6; Etkes, pp. 15–53 (see p. 48 for the views of a contemporary of the Baal Shem Tov, R. Yoel Baal Shem, on when use of divine Names is permitted). Many later hasidic rebbes were troubled by the fact that the Besht seems to have engaged in practical Kabbalah and used divine Names to perform miracles, a practice frowned upon by many great rabbis. So they sought to explain why he was called the Baal Shem Tov, that is, master of divine Names, if he did not use divine Names, and they produced various, often strained, interpretations. A story tells that R. Yitzhak of Drohobitch opposed the Besht's use of Names in amulets and the Besht showed him that his amulets contained not divine Names but only his own name, which was effective to ward off evil. This story may be true or it may be an attempt to explain away the issue. It seems clear to me that the Besht at least sometimes used divine Names. Yet we know that there is a strong stream in the tradition which teaches that great tzaddikim can work miracles by prayer or even decree alone. Some rebbes discussed this issue and tried to explain limitations the Besht would have put on the use of Names. The Tzemach Tzedek of Lubavitch, for example, said that the Besht did not use divine Names to help individuals and that he could produce miracles

without using them. When it came to helping a Jewish community in distress, communal prayer was needed; but in such cases the Besht occasionally used divine Names, although the Tzemach Tzedek qualifies this by limiting the use to thought alone and not in speech (G, vol 2, p. 673). R. Yitzhak Eisik of Komarna said to R. Shalom of Belz that there was a tradition that the Besht said that it was permitted to used divine Names to heal; the Belzer disagreed, and said it was not permitted (*Shalshelet HaKodesh Komarna*, p. 408). S, p. 41, #12; P, p. 36, #22. See Kahana, pp. 59, 63 about the healing techniques of two other *baal shems* that legend connects with the Besht: Rabbis Eliyahu and Yoel Baal Shem. *Toldot Adam* contains some of the healing techniques of R. Eliyahu Baal Shem. See the insightful discussion about the Besht's overcoming fear in DD, vol. 1, pp. 25–26.

3. S, p. 37, #10; P, p. 32, #17. The source says that R. Tzvi was added as a second scribe after a few years of R. Alexander carrying the workload alone. I changed the time frame for editorial reasons. S, p. 41, #13 ; P, p. 37, #23.

4. H, p. 199 (no source given). The text only refers to medicinal herbs; the rest has been added. Etkes, p. 267.

5. At some time, both R. Meir Margoliot, one of the Besht's first disciples, and R. Gershon Kitover, who later became his disciple, were both members of the Brody *Kloiz* (H, p. 320). *Otzar Yirat Shamayim (Breslov)*, vol. 1, p. 37 says that the Besht's disciples—Rabbis Nachman of Horodenka, Nachman of Kossov, and Menahem Mendel of Bar—were also members of the *Kloiz*. R. Nachman of Kossov was previously mentioned as a member of the Pious of Kitov, so I left him out here. H, p. 54.

6. S, p. 44, #13; P, p. 39, #25. The *Kedushah* ("Sanctification") is an important communal prayer that pious people desire to hear and respond to even if they did not pray with that congregation. Most traditional synagogues have a picture or plaque of a candelabra motif with a psalm verse highlighted about keeping God always before you; its purpose is to remind the prayer-leader to concentrate and to provide a focus for him while praying. A (literally) "foreign thought" is a profane or unholy thought during a religious activity. The final sentence comes from a similar tale (S, p. 43, #15; P, p. 38, #25).

7. R, vol. 3, p. 25, #34.

8. *Ko'ach ha-po'el b'nifal.* MEY, II, p. 33, quoting *Shomer Emunim.* The Lubavitcher Rebbe said that when a person, like the Besht, separates himself from materiality (*hitpashtut ha-gash-miyut*), he "sees the power of the Maker in what is made and sees Godliness revealed" (N, p. 49). See "Attraction," p. 75. MEY, I, p. 73, quoting *Emunat Tzaddikim*, #132. *Jewish Spiritual Practices* , pp. 132–33 and elsewhere, for information about the traditional use of such a card. H, p. 62 (no source given). Setting created. *Emunat Tzaddikim*, #132.

9. *Even Shtiya*, p. 17, #1. I have added that it was the Besht who taught him the practice of using the *shivitti* mantra.

10. Horodetzky, p. 53, quoting a letter from R. Gershon to the Besht; Circle, pp. 47–49; cf. R, vol. 3, p. 16, #19; G, vol. 2, pp. 705, 709, 710, 719.

11. Based on Komarna, p. 39, which cites *Zohar Hai*, section 3, p. 27a. This is how the Besht taught others to pray; see TZR-E, p. 27, #35 and p. 30, #42. R. Aharon of Zhitomir said that Ahiyah ha-Shiloni taught the Baal Shem Tov the true way in prayer—to strip oneself of any awareness of one's body or surroundings, until one is as if not in this world; and to cleave to the holy letters with fiery *d'vekut* (*Tiferet Beit Levi*, p. 8; H, p. 80). K, vol. 4, pp. 68, 71; I applied this description about a disciple of the Besht to the Besht himself. *HaNiggun V'HaRikud*, p. 28 (see p. 4 in my book). *Yeshu'ot Yisrael*, p. 102, #6. KST, p. 44 (22b), #177; p. 116 (58b), #396; *Israel*

Baalshem: His Life and Times, Simon, p. 17. Based on SBST, vol. 1, p. 143, #89, quoting KST. The beginning verse of the *Shemoneh Esreh*, the main prayer of every service, is interpreted to suggest that the *Shechinah* prays the prayer. *Likkutei Yekarim*, p. 21, 1:18. MEY, I, p. 56, quoting *Shivhei HaBaal Shem Tov*, #21. G, vol. 2, p. 469. This is said of a disciple of the Besht and it was certainly true of the Besht himself. S, p. 56, #22. SBST, vol. 2, p. 198, #23, quoting *Rishpei Aish HaShalem*, parashat Aikev, #85; B, p. 58. R, vol. 3, p. 28, #38. S, pp. 58, 60; P, p. 52, #37 and p. 53, #39. *Ratzo v'shov*. In the vision of the prophet Ezekiel (1:14), the angels ("living creatures") move in the way of "running and returning," running toward the transcendent God and then returning to the immanent divine reality. G, vol. 2, p. 467. S, p. 237, #165; P, p. 203, #200. DD, vol. 1, p. 29. K, vol. 1, p. 207, from *Zohar Hai*, parashat Vaiyechi. *Imrei Pinhas HaShalem*, p. 245, #86. The woman in the tale is identified only as "the mother of R. Shimon Ashkenazi." I've not been able to identify this rabbi and didn't find his name in lists of the Besht's disciples. Too often women are not named in traditional tales. I've honored this unnamed woman with my own mother's Jewish name: Charna.

12. S, p. 164, #86; P, p. 137, #114; the verse quoted is Deuteronomy 33:2. The Rabbis said that because the Jews are a fiery people, God had to tame them by giving them a fiery Torah.

13. H, p. 282 (no source given). When the congregation heard the *shofar* under his supervision, he knew that the blasts would be properly sounded and everyone would fulfill the *mitzvah*. The story is also in *Even Yisrael*, p. 71, n. 28, without the ending about the Besht immediately going off to the *shofar* blowing. The editor interprets Edel's comment to mean that her trust in God was so great that she was not afraid to sleep in the face of the judgment on Rosh HaShanah. And the Besht appreciated her remark.

14. MEY, II, p. 141. This recitation includes these gates: "the gates of light, the gates of long life (days and years), the gates of patience, the gates of blessing, the gates of understanding, the gates of joy, the gates of greatness, the gates of redemption, etc. (*Or HaShabbat*, p. 110) *Biyeshishim Hochmah*, p. 266, #5.

15. DD, vol. 1, p. 47; Kahana, p. 103. *Kahal Hasidim HeHadash*, p. 14, #23; SBST, vol. 2, p. 153, n. 4; *Seder HaDorot HeHadash*, p. 2; K, vol. 4, p. 181, #1; p. 184, #2; *Sippurei Nifla'im*, Likkutei Ma'asiyot, p. 2.

16. DD, vol. 1, p. 47; K, vol. 4, p. 181, #1 and p. 186; *Kahal Hasidim HeHadash*, p. 14, #23; SBST, vol. 2, p. 153, n. 4. This section is legend but based on historical reality, as can be seen from a letter of R. Gershon in Israel to the Besht (see E, pp. 249 and 350; Etkes, p. 183). Some scholars think the Or HaHayim died before R. Gershon arrived in 1747. DD, vol. 1, p. 48 records the legend and gives the text of the letter, pointing out the claimed contradiction. But other scholars like Kahana, pp. 96–97, think R. Gershon made an earlier trip to Israel, returned to Poland and went back to Israel in 1747. Kahana says that R. Gershon therefore could have met the Or HaHayim. Kahana suggests 1740 for the first trip, but I've chosen 1742 because the Besht would have sent R. Gershon after he had encountered the Or HaHayim's newly published interpretation of the *Chumash* in that year.

The Or HaHayim certainly died before the Besht set out for Israel. Moreover, the letter from R. Gershon in Israel to the Besht refers to a vision the Besht said he had of a great sage residing in Israel who was a spark of the Messiah. The Besht later said that he no longer saw him in vision. This parallels the legend of the exchange of letters between the Besht and the Or HaHayyim, and that the Besht saw him in vision but didn't see his heels, etc. and that the Besht considered him to be a spark of the Messiah. In the same letter of R. Gershon, he tells the Besht that he has made his greatness known to the Sephardic sages in Israel and that they yearn for him to come; this is different from the legend that R. Hayim ben Attar said it would be fruitless to come. See Etkes, p. 70 for a partial text of the letter. The detail about the cave is from SSKB, vol. 5, p. 196, #478. The yeshivah's name is from Etkes, p. 181; H, p. 324.

17. SBST, vol. 2, p. 151, #1 and p. 152, #2, quoting DME and TYY; H, pp. 222, 207; G, vol. 2, p. 595. Although heaven told the Besht not to go, Ahiyah still helped him.

18. *Adat Tzaddikim*, p. 11; R, vol. 2, p. 18, #2 and p. 21, #3; K, vol. 4, pp. 201–3; Horodetzky, p. 64. *Kerem Beit Yisrael*, p. 16, #2. Versions of the story say that the captain was Elijah, but since this conflicts with the place of Ahiyah in the larger story, I've left it out.

19. *Adat Tzaddikim*, p. 10; K, vol. 4, pp. 191 and 199, #6; Z, vol. 2, pp. 255 and 261, #291; H, p. 178; B, p. 78; R, vol. 2, p. 18, #2; *Yeshu'ot Yisrael*, p. 124, #6; *Sippurei Yaakov*, II, #34. "Although it is forbidden to drink wine, that is only for a fourth of a cup, because: 'A little satisfies, but a lot whets the appetite'" (R, vol. 2, p. 18, #2, version of this tale). The *Hallel* is psalms of praise in the latter part of the *Haggadah*.

20. H, p. 230 (no source cited); R, vol. 1, p. 23, #22. I saw this exact reaction when I was in Jerusalem and told my own rebbe, R. Shlomo Carlebach, about a new incident of Arab terrorism; his head shot back as if he had been struck in the face. The latter clause about the Messiah is added, in line with a story of the Besht telling R. David Forkes who had returned from Israel, that if, when he had been asked about the condition of the Jews in exile, he had spoken of their intense suffering, he could have brought the Messiah. That is the inner meaning of the story of the groan, as when the Children of Israel groaned from their slavery in Egypt and God heard.

21. *Kahal Hasidim HeHadash*, p. 14 (7b), #23; H, p. 222; SBST, vol. 2, p. 153n.; B, 79; DD, vol. 1, p. 49; *Yeshu'ot Yisrael*, #6; *Kitvei Kodesh Rabbi Moshe Minder*, #19. *HeHasidut*, p. 300. *Kerem Beit Yisrael*, p. 16, #2. That the Besht was specifically tempted by the Satan to apostasy comes from Breslov sources, such as SSKB, vol. 6, p. 235, #536. The *Shema* (Hear O Israel) is called out at the time of death. At the end of TYY, p. 729, #10, it says that Ahiyah showed him what worlds he was in then, and the Names were *Ehyeh* and the permutations of *Ehyeh*, etc. Then the Besht strengthened himself and sweetened them in their source. *Gevurat Ari*, p. 6 (3b); K, vol. 4, p. 187.

22. *Founder of Hasidism*, pp. 51, 52, 64, 165, 168–69; Dubnow, p. 35, says the Besht moved to Medzibuz about 1740–1745. Gershom Scholem, *Demuto HaHistorit Shel Rabbi Yisrael Baal Shem Tov*, p. 342, says he moved about 1740. *Even Yisrael*, p. 74, n. 37; *Kedushat Baruch*, p. 177. SBST, vol. 2, p. 51, #33, quoting *Zichron Tov*; Sadeh, p. 204. Eating fish on *Shabbat* has mystical significance. R, vol. 3, p. 21, #25. E, p. 119.

23. *The Story of the Baal Shem Tov*, p. 143 (no source cited). The Hebrew word *yud-chet-yud-heh* may be read as *yichyeh* or *yichayeh*. I've been unable to find a source for this Besht teaching (it is not in *Even Yisrael*, about R. Tzvi). But it's found in the name of Rebbe Shlomo of Karlin in *Beit Tzaddikim Ya'amod*, vol. 3, p. 128; and see my p. 128 for the tradition that the Besht related his daughter Edel's name to a Torah verse. Kahana, p. 54, and DD, vol. 1, p. 35 say that Tzvi was born about 1740. Habakkuk 2:4.

24. S, p. 205, #120; P, p. 173, #152; p. 136, #114. Y, p. 383. Kahana, p. 106.

25. S, Preface, pp. 31, 38; P, pp. 5–6. The text continues: "because he is R. Shimon bar Yohai and his companions"—meaning that the Besht and his disciples are the reincarnations or the equals of R. Shimon, etc. H, p. 364 leaves off this end, as I did; I don't know if he had a different source. Cf. KE, p. 113, #364.

26. K, vol. 4, p. 141, from *Ma'asiyot U'Maamarim Yekarim*; SM, vol. 3, p. 30; B, p. 56; E, p. 127; *Sippurei HaTzaddikim HeHadash*, p. 18, #7. The parable may also relate to the rabbi's

being too strict with the different individuals of his community—"dark brown, chestnut, and white." He must loosen the reins of his authority. Etkes, p. 192, says that the Polnoyer came to the Besht between 1747–1752. H, p. 360, and E, p. 130, say it was shortly before the Besht tried to go to Israel (1743). In *Shivhei HaBaal Shem Tov* the author says he heard from the Polnoyer himself that sometime after he met the Besht in Mohilev, the Besht went to Israel. The Besht moved to Medzibuz in about 1740; so the Polnoyer became his disciple not long after that.

27. S, p. 73, #28; P, p. 61, #47.

28. *Sefer HaSichot* (1940; Hebrew), p. 134, #8 and (1942) p. 96, #8. "Meritorious" means that you derive a spiritual benefit to influence yourself for good. The text has that the rabbi walked from Polnoye to Medzibuz, but I put the story about him leaving his position as rabbi of Sharogrod later, so I've changed the location to Sharogrod, like the preceding tale. The inclination of a storyteller would be to identify R. Yaakov Yosef with Polnoye regardless of the accuracy anyway. Polnoye is forty miles from Medzibuz while Sharogrod is sixty miles (Etkes, p. 14, map), so instead of the original two-day walk, I have made it three. Steinman, pp. 43, 89.

29. P, p. 62, #47.

30. S, p. 78, #29; P, p. 63, #49; B, p. 57. The loss of a possession or domestic animal may serve as an atonement so that a human not be punished. "Sweetened" means "ameliorated" or annulled. *Sippurei Tzaddikim HeHadash*, #16; E, p. 224. In the source, this was spoken to the Zlotchover, but there's no reason to think the Besht did not make this remark to the Polnoyer too.

31. MEY, I, p. 72; H, p. 363.

32. Steinman, pp. 43, 89.

33. KRY, p. 13, #33; KE, p. 118, #388. The sentence about R. Yosef attaining the holy spirit and the final sentence comparing the disciples and master are mine.

34. KE, p. 115, #37. MEY, p. 239, quoting TZR, ot 56. I've speculated as to why the Besht had a pet bear cub, which is not explained and nowhere mentioned later. Genesis 9:2 expresses the spiritual level of Adam outside the Garden of Eden.

35. Schochet, p. 53. G, vol. 2, p. 452. H, p. 34.

36. *Sefer HaSichot* (1941), p. 130 #7; *ra'ah elokut bimuchash*.

37. *Sichot Moharan*, p. 85, #109; *Tzaddik* (English), p. 430, #552. That he recited a blessing over his pipe-smoking and over the snuff tobacco he used during *davvening* (to keep alert) is from H, p. 287, quoting *Shulhan HaTahor* by R. Yitzhak Eizik of Komarna.

38. *Gevurat Ari*, p. 7 (4a), #3; SM, vol. 3, pp. 117 and 118; H, p. 367. For help in understanding this tale, compare the tale about R. Aharon of Karlin in Ishti, p. 101. It is known from many stories that R. Leib Saras was a liason between the "above ground" world and the "underground" of hidden tzaddikim. He was appointed to this task by the Besht (*Zechut Avot*, p. 243, quoting *Siach Zekanim* 2; *Gevurat Ari*, p. 4 [2b] #1 end).

39. Heard from R. Shlomo Carlebach, Sept. 3, 1994. Shlomo referred to both Edel and Hersh, but since they seem to have been twenty years apart in age they could not have both been children at the same time. According to Kahana, p. 54, Edel was born around 1720 and Tzvi before 1740. DD, vol. 1, p. 35 also mentions the latter date.

40. *Sifran Shel Tzaddikim*, p. 12, #10. SBST, vol. 2, p. 263, #2. SBST, vol. 1, p. 77, #106, quoting *Likkutim Yekarim*; also, vol. 2, p. 205, n. 40. SBST, vol. 2, p. 175, #41 (see also n. 39), quoting TYY; the setting is created. K, vol. 1, p. 217, from *Sippurei Besht*. S, p. 133, #58; P, p. 107, #83; H, p. 102.

41. S, p. 52, #20; P, p. 46, #32; K, vol. 4, p. 52, #22. One changes a dream by saying: "Good it is and good may it be! May the All Merciful turn it to good!" (*Berachot* 55b).

42. K, vol. 4, p. 229, from *Sippurei Hasidim*. Isaiah 38:19.

43. *Sippurei Ya'akov*, p. 22, #30; K, vol. 2, pp. 118–19; Y, p. 377. The source says that they were so poor they didn't have a penny even on weekdays, but this contradicts the preceding tale that Rabbi David enjoyed treating them with mead; so I've reconciled the two tales.

44. E, pp. 338–39; Kahana, pp. 80, 81n.

45. K, vol. 1, p. 233, #9, from *Sippurei Nifla'ot*. I was able to appreciate the tale properly and adapted it with the help of two clearer versions of an almost identical tale about R. Moshe Leib of Sassov (*MiDor Dor*, vol. 2, p. 220, #1584; *Shoshelet Spinka*, p. 159). A similar story is told about the Alexanderer Rebbe (*Toldot HaYismach Yisrael*, vol. 1, p. 166) and, amazingly, about a Hindu guru of the nineteenth century, Sarada Devi (*In the Company of the Holy Mother*, 218)!

46. *Kovetz Sippurim* (1960/5720), p. 31, #31. The Besht could not easily succeed against the kind of religious opposition he faced in Lithuania. But, as in this story, the better rabbis recognized his greatness, although they refrained from joining his movement. The younger scholars, again as here, were divided, some joining his movement, perhaps most not.

47. G, vol. 2, p. 483. In many stories, the Besht asks his disciples to make a circle by putting their hands on each other's shoulders, and to sing. See, for example, "Hearing with an Open Ear," p. 318 (note that this tale relates to love of Israel). R. Shlomo Carlebach explained the significance of this custom (*Reb Shlomele*, p. 108). G, vol. 2, p. 678; KST, Hosafot, p. 274, #266—about the revival of circle dancing by the Besht; the equality of first and last in the circle also comes from a Lubavitch source that I can't find. But G, p. 678, does say that the circle dance is kabbalistically a *makif*, a surrounding supernal light, meaning that all in a circle dance are equal. *Ish HaPele*, p. 69. KST, #34; the Besht quoted the *Zohar* on 2 Kings 3:15. The "*shofar*" teaching is based on the Besht about praying, not singing (SBST, vol. 1, p. 143, quoting KST). *Jewish Spiritual Practices*, p. 487, quoting *Encyclopedia Judaica*; Raz, p. 223. KST, p. 45 (23a), #179. *Ta'anit* 31; the quote is from Isaiah 25:9. R, vol. 3, p. 281, #12; Etkes, p. 138 and B, p. 53, both quoting DME, parashat Yitro, p. 101. Some of this teaching seems to contradict certain stories where the Besht is portrayed as being depressed. Perhaps he was not always able to fulfill his teaching, or perhaps he was saddened only by spiritual matters or by Jewish communal suffering (see "At His Wife's Death," p. 328). G, vol. 2, p. 647; K, vol. 4, pp. 229–230; Z, vol. 2, p. 214, #250. K, vol. 4, pp. 229–30. *Kovetz Sippurim* (1955/5715), p. 31. "Always joyful" is a teaching of the Lubavitcher Rebbe that I've put in the Besht's mouth.

48. *Divrei David*, p. 66 (33a); H, p. 139 (no source quoted). See the Besht teaching that clouds symbolize mental confusion (SBST, vol. 1, p. 193, #171).

49. K, vol. 1, p. 207, #6, from *Sippurei Besht*; B, p. 53. *Kovetz Sippurim* 5714–5715, p. 31, #48. I've put a teaching of the Lubavitcher Rebbe in the Besht's mouth. According to a hasidic author, one of the Besht's principles is: "Each person, if he follows the way of God, is a complete spiritual Torah, which clothes itself in him according to his spiritual level" (IE, p. 25, #8).

50. S, p. 99, #40; P, p. 80, #61; K, vol. 4, p. 171; B, p. 53; E, p. 168.

51. SSKB, vol. 3, p. 192, #516; vol. 6, p. 239, #547; vol. 4, p. 24, #67.

52. Steinman, p. 318; H, p. 283; Raz, p. 248. The first two books have that the Besht sent R. Yaakov Yosef of Polnoye and the latter, R. Arye Leib of Polnoye; none of them gives sources. According to DD, vol. 1, p. 35, Edel married Yehiel Ashkenazi in 1735. If that is true, R. Yaakov Yosef can't be in the story, because he only became a disciple of the Besht later. The matter and the dates remain unclear but that is why I used the source about R. Arye Leib. The text in Steinman has the Besht say, *zehu ben zug tov*, literally, "That's a good marriage-partner." Another understanding of these words might be that such humility makes one a good spouse.

53. *Otzar Yirat Shemayim (Breslov)*, vol. 1, p. 63; SSKB, vol. 2, p. 18, #72. DME, Toldot, p. 2

and n. 8. The original source is the Cherson *geniza* material which is of questionable authenticity.

54. N, p. 211, #57 (see the good discussion of the story there); G, vol. 2, pp. 630–31. According to the Rabbis, the angel Sandalfon weaves crowns for God (see *Otzar HaMachshavah*, p. 158, quoting the *Tosafot* on *Hagiga*, chapter 2). Perhaps this angel with a name related to sandal has something to do with the Besht's teaching about weaving shoes (sandals) into crowns for God.

55. Raz, p. 225 (no source cited). Pious Jews mourn the "exile" of God from the world, which is drowned in injustice and evil; some mourn excessively.

56. *HaNiggun V'HaRikkud B'Hasidut*, p. 17, quoting KST and giving no source for the second anecdote. SBST, vol. 2, p. 82, n. 1, quoting multiple sources. That the Besht did not dwell on the sin is from the version in *Shalshelet HaKodesh Komarna*, p. 301, #8, quoting *Ma'aseh HaShem*. Job 11:11.

57. H, p. 181; DA, pp. 5b–6a, #14. The custom is to bring a gift of "soul-redemption" money (*pidyon nefesh*) to a holy man when asking for help.

58. H, p. 180; G, vol. 2, p. 607. The Rabbis said a person should not *bazbez*, "squander," his money. Playing on the Hebrew root, the Besht said it was from *baz*, "take spoil"—a person should not give more than a fifth if he had to fight with himself to take spoil.

59. Heard from R. Shlomo Carlebach, in the name of Rebbe Y. Y. Schneersohn of Lubavitch.

60. S, p. 224, #143; P, p. 190, #176.

61. S, p. 211, #128; P, p. 179, #160; E, p. 153; H, p. 181; K, vol. 1, Preface, p. 21. The text says just the Rabbi of Kitov, whom I assume is the Rabbi Moshe mentioned elsewhere.

62. SSKB, vol. 2, p. 109, #329.

63. SM, vol. 3, p. 48. See the story "Eating His Fill," p. 195.

64. S, p. 211, #128; P, p. 179, #161; E, p. 153; K, vol. 2, p. 148; K, vol. 1, Preface, p. 21. *Sefer HaBesht* (Maimon), pp. 18–19. The Besht traveling to earn money most probably means money for his work as a *baal shem* to pay his personal debts.

65. *Kahal Hasidim HeHadash*, p. 7, #7; K, vol. 3, p. 44, #11; SBST, vol. 1, p. 215 note; *Emunat Tzaddikim*, p. 7 (4a), #7.

66. *Imrei Pinhas HaShalem*, p. 248, #102; H, p. 180. The accusing angels are literally, the *kelipot*, or "shells," that is, evil forces.

67. R, vol. 3, p. 30, #45; DD, vol. 1, p. 34. Verses quoted: Proverbs 19:14 and 14:1. The Besht's comment is based on a teaching in the *Zohar* on Genesis 12:13 that he applied to himself. *Shivhei HaBaal Shem Tov* mentions that the Besht had a large and a small house; no explanation is given. Traditional sources don't mention that the Besht was given a house by the Jewish community of Medzibuz. This information was discovered by a modern academic scholar using the town's archives (*Founder of Hasidism*, pp. 165, 168–69). I've tried to reconcile the different pieces of information.

68. S, p. 137, #62; P, p. 110, #87; B, p. 68 (oral source); E, p. 152 (source: S); K, vol. 1, p. 263, #16. Rabbinic quote: *Berachot* 6.

69. *Kahal Hasidim HeHadash*, p. 6 (3b), #4; K, vol. 1, p. 261, #13; *Emunat Tzaddikim*, p. 6 (3b), #4. Verses quoted: Proverbs 20:29 and 16:31.

70. Steinman, p. 186, #5; K, vol. 2, p. 93; SSKB, vol. 3, p. 215, #604; *Beit Tzaddikim Ya'amod*, vol. 2, p. 166. The text has: "Our Sages taught: 'Though a person is judged on Rosh HaShanah for the whole year, he's also judged each day.' Since his livelihood is fixed from one Rosh

HaShanah to the next, Heikel must be a water-carrier every day of the year. But he's judged anew each day—by himself!—whether he'll labor joyfully or, God-forbid, drudge away in bitterness and misery." I like the story better without the scholarly reference.

71. G, vol. 1, p. 72, 75. N, p. 70, #8, in the name of Rebbe M.M. Schneersohn of Lubavitch. See n. 69 on p. 375 about *pidyon nefesh*. "Love the person you are with" and "Shivered" heard from R. Shlomo Carlebach, the latter at a talk in The Carlebach Shul in New York City on May 15, 1992, quoting Reb Shmuel, "an old Lubavitcher hasid." Genesis 15:5. SBST, vol. 1, p. 212, #27. G, vol. 2, pp. 637, 640, 594, 638. N, pp. 102–3, #1 (the Lubavitcher Rebbe explaining the teaching of the Besht). R. Abraham Joshua Heschel in *Passion for Truth*, p. 66, points out that although the *Zohar* puts the order: God, Torah, Israel, the Besht would say: God, Israel, Torah (on p. 52 the order is reversed because of the point being made). The significance is that the Jewish people precede the Torah in importance. R. Tzaddok HaCohen in *Otzar HaMachshava*, p. 162, refers to *Tanna D'Vei Eliyahu Rabba*, chapter 14, which seems to be the source of this reversal of order, that God loves Israel more than the Torah. G, vol. 2, pp. 639, 677. The teaching of R. Nachman of Bratzlav (source unknown) to justify a fellow Jew well explains the teaching of the Besht, his great-grandfather. One can see from the story further on, p. 185, "Curing a Spiritual Sickness," that this was the Besht's own view, for there he parallels doubts about faith in God, doubts about the Torah, and doubts about a fellow Jew. G, vol. 2, p. 639, E, p. 144, quoting *Ktav Shem Tov*.

72. MEY, II, p. 4. *Kitvei Rabbi Moshe Minder*, #16.

73. KST, p. 120, #407. KE, p. 3, #9; Horodetzky, p. 69; N, p. 236, #74. A *tzitzit* is a ritual thread of fringe on the corner of a tallis. *Likkutei Dibburim* (English), vol. 3, p. 71. *Sefer HaToldot: Rabbi Shmuel, Admor Moharash*, p. 173.

74. G, vol. 1, pp. 65, 70, 328. MEY, II, p. 160, quoting *Sefer HaMa'amarim*, p. 202.

75. G, vol. 1, p. 75. See *Avot* 4:2, 6:4. Hershel the Ditch-digger earned his living by the labor of his hands and ate the minimum necessary to have strength for his spiritual purposes. For the Besht, he epitomized the pious laborer.

76. G, vol. 2, pp. 611–12; *Chassidic Discourses*, vol. 2, pp. 405–11. Lamentations 5:1. The Besht read *herpah*, shame, as *heref*, risk ("endangering their lives"; *The Great Mission*, p. 65).

77. Z, vol. 1, p. 30, #21; K, vol. 3, p. 62, #14.

78. G, vol. 1, pp. 75 and 129; vol. 2, p. 643. The point may also be that God's holiness, as reflected in the holiness of Israel *as Israel*, is manifested more in people who have no special virtues other than that they are Jews. *Sefer HaSichot* (1940), pp. 84–85.

79. SBST, vol. 1, p. 61, n. 12, quoting *Leket Imrei P'ninim*; K, vol. 1, Preface, p. 20; E, p. 211; B, p. 72. G, vol. 1, p. 70, 69; vol. 2, pp. 611, 650. Verses quoted: Malachi 2:10; Deuteronomy 14:1; Malachi 1:2.

80. *Otzar Sippurei Chabad*, vol. 1, p. 403; *Sefer HaSichot* (1940), p. 134, #10.

81. MRT, I, p. 71, #15, quoting *Mayim Rabim*.

82. G, vol. 2, p. 644. I've lost the source for the sentence about hidden treasures of virtues; it is most likely G (cf. G, vol. 2, pp. 605, 617). Rabbis' quotations: *Avot* 4:1; *Yevamot* 69.

83. G, vol. 1, p. 78, and vol. 2, pp. 475, 493; E, p. 145; K, vol. 4, pp. 74, 81.

84. K, vol. 1, p. 253, from *Sichot Yekarim*; see also: DA, p. 7a, #19; E, p. 259; *Ma'alat HaTzaddikim*, p. 123; *Seder HaDorot HeHadash*, section on R. Meir of Premishlan; K, vol. 3, p. 213; B, vol. 1, p. 80; *Aspaklaria HaMe'ira*, vol. 1, pp. 41–43; R, vol. 1, p. 6, #10.

85. SM, vol. 3, p. 44; Raz, p. 287.

86. G, vol. 1, p. 78, and vol. 2, pp. 475, 493; E, p. 145; K, vol. 4, pp. 74, 81.

A Movement Forms and Opposition Grows

1. Based on Horodetzky, p. 58 and elsewhere. See P, p. 90, #71; p. 166, #141; p. 254, #246, where the Besht discharges *shochtim*.

2. The list of reasons for opposition to the Besht is from a hasidic book (I think a Lubavitch source, G or N), but in moving this paragraph around the reference was lost. The final sentences are from G, vol. 2, p. 512.

3. MEY, I, p. 87, quoting *Shailot V'Tshuvot Divrei Hayim* and *Divrei Shalom*. The rabbis could tolerate that a rare *minyan* of kabbalists prayed with the Ari's *siddur*, but they opposed this custom spreading beyond those limited bounds. Horodetzky, p. 190 (no source given), based on the comments of R. Yaakov Yosef of Polnoye.

4. S, p. 244, #173; P, p. 211; Etkes, pp. 233–38. I added the last sentence to temper the idea of opposition to the Besht, because there is a story I include later about another visit. The hasidic source for the Besht's use of the phrase "Jewish demons," which I inserted in this tale, is found on p. 368, n. 5.

5. Combination of TYY, vol. 2, p. 666, #8, and SBST, vol. 2, p. 133, n. 4. The setting has been created based on information in Horodetzky, pp. 35, 57 and elsewhere. See "Sixty Heroes" on p. 18 and n. 5 there. There are different traditions with the motif that heaven arranged the Besht to have an opponent or opponents. Some versions make the opponents demonic, others make them worthy. The Besht had opponents of both types. His most notable worthy opponent was the Noda BeYehuda (see "Worthy Opponents, end, p. 270); his most notable "demonic" opponent was the heretic Yaakov Frank (see "Yaakov Frank," p. 329).

6. SBST, vol. 2, p. 149, n. 10 (four versions); H, p. 103.

7. S, p. 220, #139; P, p. 187, #172. I translated *b'katnuto* to refer to a minor sin committed "in his boyhood"; it could also mean when he was "in small-consciousness" and committed a minor sin that was otherwise foreign to him. The Latin *matronita* means "matron," or "lady," and was used for women of status. S has in parentheses: "Queen." I've replaced the source's "winnowing shovel" with a scythe.

8. G, vol. 1, pp. 49–50; Horodetzky, pp. 188–89.

9. *Israel Baalshem: His Life and Times*, p. 10. Simon gives no hasidic source for this comment but I suspect he had one. See "His First Visit" about the Maggid of Mezritch on p. 313. R. Aryeh Kaplan in *Meditation and Kabbalah*, p. 266, says that the Society of Hidden Tzaddikim, which was eventually led by the Baal Shem Tov, had a program to elevate the status of women; he too gives no source, but perhaps he had one. *Kedushat Baruch*, p. 173.

10. Heard from R. Shlomo Carlebach (date, place unknown). In I. B. Singer's largely fictional book about the Besht, *Reaches of Heaven*, there's a version of this tale, in which Edel actually dances with the hasidim, provoking opponents of the Besht to anger. I don't know where R. Carlebach saw or heard the story, which seems intended to counter a rumor of the nature of the Singer story.

11. K, vol. 4, p. 37, #13, from A. M. Haberman; S, p. 255, #182; P, p. 222, #221. Rabbinic quote: *Avot* 2:6. Dubnow, p. 41, claims that the question asked the Besht was not simple: "This was a classic test question on which volumes had been written. The one being tested was expected to demonstrate virtuosity in the scholastic literature." The point of the parable about the horses is unclear in the text. The parable is found in K and in *MiDor Dor*, vol. 2, p. 191, #1477, but not in the *Shivhei HaBesht* version of this tale. However, the same parable is found

in *Once Upon a Chassid*, p. 242, in a story about an early Lubavitcher Rebbe. That tale helps explain the meaning here. I've adapted the material to clarify the point.

12. S, p. 214, #132; P, p. 182, #65; E, p. 164; SBST, vol. 2, p. 111 n. 12 (multiple versions). G, vol. 1, p. 371; *Likkutei Dibburim* (English), vol. 2, p. 123. Torah verse: Ecclesiastes 3:14.

13. Raz, p. 137 (no source cited). Verse quoted: Numbers 20:10.

14. G, vol. 2, p. 522; K, vol. 4, p. 93. The end of this story is missing in the source. From "The touch" on I've created an ending. Although the story might have concluded differently, my ending is not entirely imaginary: In what seems to be another version of this tale (K, vol. 3, p. 57, #9; vol. 4, p. 93; S, p. 262, #186; P, p. 229, #225), the sick man is healed. I've also truncated the tale, which in its source is about three brothers and their uncle; the changes affect only details. Verse quoted: Leviticus 19:17. The chanted words of the Besht in the original text would be almost impossible to understand by the average reader, so I've "translated" them into a simpler, more comprehensible form. I've also used teachings of R. Nachman of Bratzlav, clearly derived from the Besht, to clarify the Besht's point, particularly that doubts about a fellow Jew produce doubts about the Torah. This connection is not obvious in the Besht's words, but is certainly what he meant. R. Nachman taught that just as one should not doubt any part of the Torah, so one should not harshly judge or have doubts about any Jew. See *Rabbi Nachman's Wisdom*, p. 212, #91 and *Tzaddik*, p. 157, #160.

15. *Imrei Pinhas HaShalem*, p. 205, #81, and p. 204, #77. It's clear from internal and external evidence that R. Pinhas of Koretz's teaching reflects the teaching of his master, the Besht. "Aaron" rabbinic quote: *Avot* 1:12. Verse quoted: Proverbs 27:19. The "Congregation of Israel" (*Knesset Yisrael*) is the Jewish people's ideal, spiritual aspect, equivalent to the *Shechinah*, which manifests God's presence on earth.

16. Composite of: Etkes, pp. 170–71; Circle, p. 134, quoting TYY, p. 44b; *Mishnat Hasidim*, p. 304, #36; KRY, p. 21, #57; *Kitvei Rabbi Moshe Minder*, I, #42; SBST, vol. 1, p. 228, #10 and n. 8; *Otzar Sippurei Habad*, vol. 1, p. 37 (about arousing indirectly). This was said to another disciple of the Besht who was a preacher, and I've generalized the thought; the actual words were: "You should arouse a conceited Torah scholar to repent by your love of Israel, by drawing him so close that, even without your saying anything directly, he becomes aware of his arrogance and corrects himself"; Etkes, p. 118, quoting TYY, parashat Kedoshim, p. 94a; *Great Jewish Personalities*, "The Baal Shem Tov," p. 300; Raz, p. 75. See p. 305 about the Besht's recognition of his lesser speaking ability.

17. *To'afot HaRim*, pp. 138, 140; Horodetzky, p. 125; B, p. 142, quoting *Mifalot HaTzaddikim*; N, p. 80. I've removed a motif from the source text—that at first a black dog (= demon) ate the candles and the Besht realized that there was a heavenly obstruction, namely, R. Yehiel Michal's desire. So the Besht told the man to offer candles again, and he resolved to teach R. Yehiel Michal a lesson. Y, p. 426. K, vol. 4, p. 124 from *Sippurei Hasidim B'Yiddish*; *Pe'ulat HaTzaddik*, vol. 1, pp. 224, 225.

18. SSKB, vol. 6, p. 233, #530. The Besht's explanation of his remark is my interpretation of the editorial comment in the source text (which contains the phrase "measure for measure" after "accordingly"). Also, the final piece about his telling the man to be a warm Jew is taken and adapted from another Besht anecdote (see p. 49), because it seemed to fit here too.

19. SBST, vol. 2, p. 111, n. 12, quoting *N'tiv Mitzvotecha*; E, p. 226, quoting *Arvei Nachal*.

20. S, p. 274, #197; P, p. 242, #236; E, p. 173. The prayer-leader's stand is near or faces the Ark, the cabinet containing the Torah scrolls, which is the central focal point of the synagogue.

21. SBST, vol. 1, p. 192, note, quoting KST.

22. SBST, vol. 2, p. 60, n. 3. S. Dresner, *The Tzaddik*, p. 52, quoting *Butzina D'Nehora HaShalem*. S, p. 132, #56; P, p. 105, #80; cf. E, p. 289, quoting *Zohar Hai*.

23. The clause about the nap is inserted from the story "The Baal Shem Tov's Shoes," p. 193. There is no mention of what the Besht did between noon and *Minha*. R, vol. 2, p. 31, #14. H, p. 150. MRT, I, p. 105, #8. *Emunat Tzaddikim*, p. 8, #11; K, vol. 1, p. 215, and E, p. 283 (source of both: *Emunat Tzaddikim*). B, p. 55; *Kahal Hasidim HeHadash*, p. 8, #11. The sentence about Ahiyah is from KE, p. 112, #355. The Besht's times of sleeping are unclear. My conjectures try to reconcile various sources. See KRY, p. 26, #34; p. 14; K, vol. 1, p. 216. After a number of years, the Besht changed his practice and ceased reciting *Tikkun Hatzot*. He stayed awake during the earlier part of the night, performing divine service, and went to sleep shortly before midnight (Steinman, p. 92 [no source cited]; but compare SSKB, vol. 3, p. 214, #602).

24. R, vol. 1, p. 2, #4; Ishti, p. 181. "Wave finger" saying is from MRT, II, p. 24, #3; Horodetzky, p. 67.

25. S, p. 226, #145; P, p. 192, #178; Horodetzky, p. 40. Salting is necessary to make meat kosher for eating. Although I consider my interpretation of this incident to be correct, the story is not totally clear. It could mean that the Besht saw with the holy spirit that the meat was kosher, although he had not seen the knife. Another tale, "Worthy Opponents," p. 270, tells that the Besht looked at a chicken bone and ruled, using his holy spirit, that the chicken was kosher. But if that was the case here, why doesn't the tale say so? Rather, the point seems to be that he was not strict. Yet, *lo hikpid al zeh* could mean that the Besht was not strict about inspecting the knife when circumstances dictated otherwise. Or it could conceivably mean that the Besht was not angry at R. David for refusing to eat meat that his spiritual master was willing to eat. Also relevant to the issue is the story in S, p. 230, #155, in which the Besht was willing to use *tzitzit* for his tallis that a disciple was afraid of using, because the Besht "recognized" that they were woven with pious intentions. This suggests that, contrary to my interpretation, our tale too is about seeing with the holy spirit. The teaching at the end has been added and the application to this scene created. TZR, #44, 46, 56. E, p. 214, quoting *Midrash Pinhas*. The story, "The Two Thrones," p. 92, shows the Besht overcoming a tendency to be excessively sin-fearing and excessively stringent.

26. Agnon, p. 17, quoting *Ma'asiyot Pliyot*, 17; *Ma'alat HaTzaddikim*, p. 7; Ishti, p. 14. The Torah someone speaks or writes can be mystically inspired by the prophet Elijah. When a person speaks from inspiration it may be a "revelation of Elijah" (*Nifla'ot HaTiferet Shlomo*, beginning essay, p. 5, #2). In R. Nachman of Bratzlav's version of this tale the preacher is a hidden tzaddik whose final words had a mystic meaning (*Otzar Yirat Shemayim* [Breslov], vol. 4, p. 48). Aside from MEY, II, p. 100, quoting *Likkutim Yekarim*, most of the lessons appended to the tale are mine.

27. *No'am Siach*, p. 1 (R. Eliezer Fish). *Cholent* cooks overnight for the next day's meal; by then it is soft. In S, p. 66, #25, the Besht's wife rebukes him for being harsh with guests.

28. S, p. 138, #63; P, p. 112, #88; K, vol. 2, p. 139; E, p. 155; *Imrot Tzaddikim*, p. 188, #3; *Rachmei HeAv*, #32.

29. *Legends of the Hasidim*, pp. 91, 229.

30. S, p. 185, #101; P, p. 155, #132; K, vol. 2, p. 137, #11.

31. K, vol. 2, p. 137, #11; H, p. 205; SBST, vol. 2, p. 127, #7; TZR, p. 1, #2. Based on H, p. 205.

32. TZR, p. 1, #2; KST, p. 56, #220.

33. SBST, vol. 2, p. 96, note; R, vol. 3, p. 276, #1; E, p. 225 and MEY p. 162 both quoting *Siftei Tzaddikim* and MEY, p. 162, quoting *Tzafnat Pane'ach*; Steinman, p. 205.

34. Komarna, p. 56, #42.

35. SBST, vol. 1, p. 221, n. 55 (two versions). Verse quoted: 2 Chronicles 17:6.

36. Gutman, p. 206; MEY, II, p. 167, quoting TYY; TYY, vol. 2, p. 731, #23.

37. KE, p. 114, #369; KRY, p. 21, #55; K, vol. 2, p. 138; SBST, vol. 2, p. 104, #5. Verses quoted: Leviticus 16:16; Psalms 101:5. Sages quoted: *Sotah* 5a. The text story ends with the sentence about not being able to dwell with an arrogant person. One might ask if this is not *loshon hara*, slanderous speech, about the rabbi. I am unsure. If it were, the Besht would certainly not have spoken it and the story would be unauthentic. In a similar story about the Apter Rebbe, the rebbe's words are slightly more indirect. My guess is that in certain circumstances a rebbe is permitted to make such a comment. At the end of the story "The Stolen Harness," p. 221, the Besht says: "So never speak ill of any Jew. If you must mention a particular person when condemning some bad trait, explicitly say that you are not talking about the person himself, but just about his bad trait." To deal with the question of possible slander, I've added a sentence at the end of this tale along these lines. SBST, vol. 2, p. 104, #6; K, vol. 2, p. 138, #11.

38. MRT, I, p. 76, #9, and MEY, II, p. 111, both quoting *Divrei Yehezkel*; K, vol. 4, p. 253; vol. 2, p. 138; vol. 2, p. 144, #7. Many versions have this story take place shortly before the Besht's death. I don't think the Besht would send his disciples to an unknown teacher and not to his own senior disciples. For these reasons, I preferred this version, which has no connection to his later years and passing. *Ma'alat HaTzaddikim*, p. 79.

39. MRT, I, p. 106, #12, quoting *Ginzei Nistarot*, p. 30b, #80; MEY, II, p. 162, quoting *Imrei Pinhas*. Horodetzky, p. 111 (no source cited), seems to have another version.

40. G, vol. 2, p. 670.

41. *Kochavei Or*, Anshei Moharan, p. 72, #10; Sadeh; K, vol. 2, p. 137, #11, from *Darkei Tzedek*; Komarna, p. 63. "Sweetening" an accusation means to ameliorate it.

42. SBST, vol. 2, p. 97, #9, quoting *Tzava'at HaRivash*, p. 2b, and *Hanhagot Yesharot*, p. 14b; SBST, vol. 1, p. 152, note 83, which begins on p. 150. Verse quoted: Psalms 22:7.

43. G, vol. 2, pp. 628, 680.

44. S, p. 58, #23; P, p. 52, #38; H, p. 82. Another story has that R. Zev Kitzes would pray *Kol Nidre*, R. David Forkes *Musaf*, and the Besht *Ne'ilah*.

45. Z, vol. 2, p. 21, #15; K, vol. 2, p. 103, #10; H, p. 81; B, p. 64, from *Or Yesharim*.

46. *Or Yesharim*, p. 139 (70a), #187; Agnon, p. 32, quoting *Or Yesharim*; B, p. 70; Horodetzky, pp. 91, 135. "Heavenly judgments" are divine decrees for bad things to happen, but they may not yet have taken effect on earth, so they can be countered and ameliorated.

47. SBST, vol. 2, p. 286, #7; vol. 1, p. 125, #30.

48. N, p. 234, #73; E, p. 220, quoting *Or Tzaddikim*; MEY, II, p. 251, quoting *Likkutei Yekarim*, #167. Horodetzky, p. 49, quoting *Imrei Tzaddikim*, #9. The Besht too sometimes made strange movements while praying, though I don't know if his intention was to ward off negative forces and distracting thoughts.

49. G, vol. 1, p. 75; K, vol. 1, p. 251, #6, from *Likkutei Dibburim*. R. Nachman Horodenker lived in Israel after 1740–1741, so this tale would have taken place before then. (Circle, pp. 92–93).

50. Agnon, p. 32, quoting KST; KST, p. 110, 385; K, vol. 1, p. 250; SBST, vol. 2, p. 207, #61, quoting KST, II, p. 176 and *Be'er Moshe*. The text has "like olives and grapes are squeezed out/pressed." Since that image would be less clear to the reader, I changed it to a sponge, although I do not know if sponges were used then.

51. Ishti, p. 9 (no source given); KRY, p. 27, #72.

52. *Eser Tzachtzachot*, p. 12 (6b), #18; *Kahal Hasidim HeHadash*, p. 11 (6a), #17; B, p. 69, from *Kvutzat Ya'akov*; *Ma'aseh HaShem HaShalem: Dinov*, vol. 1, p. 61, #23.

53. SM, vol. 3, p. 47. I've slightly expanded the text here to develop the thought more fully. My rebbe, R. Shlomo Carlebach, said that the Besht used to pray with a *minyan* of thieves because when the heavenly gates were closed, they would know how to break open the locks. See *Lamed Vav: A Collection of the Favorite Stories of Rabbi Shlomo Carlebach*, p. 104.

54. SM, vol. 3, p. 8; MRT, I, p. 71, #18, quoting *Derech Emunah U'Ma'aseh Rav* (in which the Besht is told about the Bach and *Gehinnom* in response to a dream-question; he then serves liquor made from *hadash*); DD, vol. 1, p. 27, note, quoting *Zichron Tov*, p. 24. I have replaced the text that the prohibition does not apply "to the produce of non-Jews," with "outside the Land of Israel." This correction concerning the *halacha* is based on an explanation of R. Meir Fund of Brooklyn.

55. *Imrei Pinhas HaShalem*, p. 205, #81, and p. 204, #77. See "Loving Those Who Seek to Harm You," p. 187 and n. 15 on p. 389, about loving someone who withdraws from you, *more*. Horodetzky, p. 124 (no source cited) seems to have another version.

56. S, p. 74 (where an addition from the Yiddish version of *Shivhei HaBesht* at the end gave me a clue to understand the events), and the continuation of the story on p. 80; P, pp. 62 and 66; K, vol. 3, p. 223; Y, p. 437, which ends with the preacher silenced. Unwilling to endure rote praying, the rabbi formed a separate *minyan*. He was also strict about ritual slaughter and refused to eat the meat slaughtered by the community's *shochet*. Both of these acts were taken as insults by the community (Etkes, p. 192). I made some slight changes in this story. The Besht's words to Yaakov Yosef were later in time than I suggest, and I added about not arousing judgments, which is the true meaning but not explicit here. The story literally ends: "The Baal Shem Tov's prophetic words at that time came true, for over a period of years the city experienced a number of fires. And those for whom death was decreed were murdered about twenty years later, in 1768, when the Haidamaks killed many Jews and Poles near Uman in the Ukraine. Sharogrod is about one hundred miles west of Uman." This story with the Besht occurred, then, in 1748.

57. TYY, parashat Tzav, edition Jerusalem, 1973, vol. 1, p. 281; Scholem, *Demuto*, p. 348, quoting TYY; KRY, p. 21, #54. The setting is created.

58. H, p. 136; Raz, p. 87 (no source cited in either book). H also tells how R. Yaakov Halperin of Zevanitch asked the Besht about the rabbi's previous incarnations. The Besht used a dream-question to find out.

59. H, p. 237; Z, vol. 1, p. 138; Sadeh, p. 80.

60. S, p. 232, #157; P, p. 197, #190. R. Akiba, wearing red and holding a spear, represents judgment, fitting for the honor guard of King David's heavenly chamber. R. Akiba had militantly declared Bar Kochba the Messiah. In "Hearing the Inner Song," p. 157, the Besht knows a singer's sins from his voice.

61. S, p. 152, #74; P, p. 124, #100. R. Yosef is here called the Besht's "nephew." His relation to the Besht is unclear. The Hebrew is *hatan horgo* and the Yiddish version understands this to mean that the Besht's wife was his aunt, that is, he was the Besht's nephew. See S, p. 124 and the footnote, where the Hebrew is understood to mean that he was the Besht's stepfather's son-in-law, indicating that the Besht's mother had remarried. There is a possibility that the Besht's wife Chana, who was a divorcee, had a daughter by her first marriage and R. Yosef was her son-in-law and the Besht's "son-in-law"-in-law (see Y, pp. 409, 566–67).

62. MEY, II, p. 264, quoting *Nifla'ot HaBaal Shem Tov*; K, vol. 3, p. 47. This story seems like a "partial version" of the story "Curing a Spiritual Sickness," p. 185. I've removed the most dis-

tinctive parallel piece (about the sick man not being able to speak), but retained the rest, which is unique to this tale, and adapted it by adding what was left out—about what the Besht said to the sick man. The positive and negative *mitzvot* are what to do and what not to do. The 248 and 365 add up to 613, the traditional number of *mitzvot*.

63. S, p. 288, #206; P, p. 253, #245; DA, p. 12a; E, p. 171; there is an interesting variant of this story in *Heichal Bobov*, p. 153. For a kabbalistic explanation from the teaching of the Ari, of spiritual diagnosis by taking a pulse, see *Physician of the Soul, Healer of the Cosmos*, p. 164. The main idea is that the divine life-force that resides in the blood can be blocked by sinful activity, producing sickness.

64. MEY, II, p. 173. *Tzaddik Yesod Olam*, vol. 2, p. 307.

65. K, vol. 2, p. 115, #18, from *Gedolei HeHasidut*. IE, p. 25. Cf. the fuller, more exact and literally rendered quote in "The Besht Opposes Preachers of Rebuke," on p. 68.

66. S, p. 42, #14; P, p. 37, #24. Traditionally, it is called "opening your mouth to the Satan," that is, giving the Satan an opening to argue for evil before the heavenly court; it is almost like a curse and is considered bad luck. R. Yaakov was a second brother of the Besht's wife, Chana.

A Mature Teacher Full of Wisdom and Love

1. *Zichron L'Rishonim*, p. 70; K, vol. 2, p. 130, #5, from *Heichal HaBeracha*; K, vol. 2, p. 131, #5, from *Sippurei Besht*; N, p. 84, #3. That a Torah scholar is equivalent to the Sabbath, is found in the *Zohar*, Raiya Mehemna 96, 29a. R, vol. 2, p. 35, #22; K, vol. 2, p. 130, #5; *Jewish Spiritual Practices*, p. 32. G, vol. 2, p. 642. SBST, vol. 2, p. 106, ##2, 3. E, p. 222, quoting *Tefillah L'Moshe* and *Shivhei HaBaal Shem Tov*; *Seder HaDorot HeHadash*, p. 59 f.; R, vol. 2, p. 35, #22; K, vol. 2, p. 130, #5, from *Arvei Nachal*; SBST, vol. 2, p. 106, ##2 and 3; SM, vol. 3, p. 27; DD, vol. 1, p. 35. The tradition judges people who transgress for their personal benefit or to satisfy their lusts more leniently than those who transgress to express their antagonism to religion and to defy God.

2. S, p. 88, #34; p. 167, #90; p. 264, #88. His act was equivalent to fornication with a woman other than one's wife, that is, adultery. The Baal Shem Tov had learned this by hearing it directly from the Rambam in heaven and had not seen if it was written in the Rambam's books.

3. *Hazulat Hu HaRe'i*, p. 3 (no source cited); *Once Upon a Chassid*, p. 181, quoting *Hazulat Hu HaRe'i*. There is a truncated version of this in Steinman, p. 152, quoting *Emtachat Binyamin*. *Even Yisrael*, p. 70, n. 32, has a version of this, quoting *Emtachat Binyamin*.

4. S, p. 114, #46; P, p. 90, #70. SBST, vol. 2, p. 158, #9. *Ish U'Ra'ayhu*, p. 87. Verse quoted: Deuteronomy 19:15. SBST, vol. 2, p. 59, #6.

5. N, p. 114.

6. SM, vol. 3, p. 174, Talmud quotes: *Avodah Zarah* 4a; *Yevamot* 61a. Habakkuk 1:14; cf. 1:13, one person swallowing up the other. Aside from *adam*, other Hebrew terms for humans are either more general or have different specific references.

7. *Degel Machane Reuven*, #59; SBST, vol. 1, p. 126, #34; Gutman, p. 42; Steinman, p. 318.

8. SM, vol. 3, pp. 174, 20.

9. MRT, I, p. 43, #21, quoting *Otzar HeHayim*; MEY, II, p. 98, quoting *Notzair Hesed*. It should be understood that the person using the tobacco was not a simple Jew but an elite disciple who might be expected to know better than to interrupt his prayers.

10. S, p. 145, #70, 71; P, p. 120, #95, 96; *Likkutim Yekarim*, p. 1, #1.

11. G, vol. 2, p. 681; N, p. 59, #1.

12. *Biyeshishim Hochmah*, p. 266, #6. The feudal lords often used Jewish informers to spy on the Jewish community. They were despised by the people.

13. *Ma'aseh HaShem HaShalem: Dinov*, vol. 1, p. 76, #36, quoting *Even Shlaima*, IV, p. 113. The *Kedushah* is a congregational prayer that it is important to participate in.

14. SSKB, vol. 5, p. 197, #481.

15. K, vol. 1, Preface, p. 13; MEY, I, p. 46. SBST, vol. 2, p. 37, #14 and n. 18, quoting *Likkutim Yekarim*. S, p. 240, #168; P, p. 206, #206. I changed the original "as soon as I close my eyes" to "open," because of the story on p. 89. SBST, vol. 1, p. 47, #29; K, vol. 2, p. 151. According to the Kabbalah, the three lowest kinds of *kelipot*, Shells, are altogether unclean and evil; they cannot be transformed and no good can come from them (*Tanya*, chapter 6).

16. S, p. 54, #21; P, p. 48, #33 (see also p. 164, #139); K, vol. 2, p. 195, #19 (source: S). The Rabbis asked how the light of the first day of Creation ("Let there be light") could have existed before the creation of the sun on the fourth day. They explained that the original light was a divine light for the exclusive use of the tzaddikim, not the ordinary sunlight, which came into being days later.

17. *Sod Yachin U'Vo'az*, p. 6a. See the comments about this practice from the Lubavitcher Rebbe (N, p. 127, #7). The Slonimer Rebbe says in *Netivot Shalom*, p. 22, that at Sinai the heavens opened because that is the essence of Torah. The letters of the Urim and Tumim on the high priest's breastplate glowed and lightened his eyes with prophecy.

18. K, vol. 3, p. 44, #12; *Sippurim Nechmadim*, p. 12 (6b) in *Sippurei Nifla'im*. The bris is performed on the eighth day after birth.

19. *Sippurim Kedoshim*, p. 42; second version on p. 81; Steinman, p. 204.

20. MRT, II, p. 91 (46a), #2, quoting *Ben Porat Yosef*; KST, p. 6, #37. Steinman, p. 320. Talmud quotation: Ta'anit 22.

21. *Tzaddik*, p. 406, #495; *Otzar Yirat Shemayim (Breslov)*, vol. 4, p. 65. *The Bostoner* by Hanoch Teller, pp. 39–42, from a story told by Shea Friedlander, a Bostoner hasid.

22. *Netivot Shalom*, p. 288. The Rabbis say there is a mystical connection between Yom Kippur, the most solemn holiday, and Purim, the most frivolous holiday, that the Hebrew *Yom Kippurim* means *Yom Ki-Purim*, a day like Purim. This story "illustrates" the connection. The final comment plays on the Hebrew in Ecclesiastes 2:2: *simha **mah** zo osah* and the phrase ***mah** b'kach*, meaning "nothing."

23. *Kovetz Tshuvot B'Inyanei Simha U'Vitahon BeHashem*, p. 18. MEY, p. 213, quoting *Kitvei Kodesh Rabbi Moshe Minder*, ot 92. TZR-E, p. 37, #44. The remark about his relative is the Besht's, as is the instruction to avoid depression, but the rest is based on stories and teachings of the Rizhiner Rebbe and the Seer of Lublin, which I've used to explain the Besht's remarks (*Ohel HaRebbe*, p. 8, #12; B, vol. 1, p. 315; *BeHetzer Pnima*, vol. 1, p. 109). The setting is created.

24. *Sippurim Nechmadim*, p. 3a (5), in ed. H. Y. Malik, *Sippurei Nifla'im* (Jerusalem, 1976); *Emet V'Yatziv*, vol. 1 (Shivhei Emet), p. 276, #5. According to Jewish law, a woman whose husband is missing or believed dead—but without witnesses—cannot remarry. Sometimes an irresponsible and cruel man would desert his wife, and start a new life in a distant area, unconcerned with his wife's fate. This *agunah* status could produce terrible consequences, particularly for young women, and the rabbis were sensitive to their plight. They usually did everything within the boundaries of the law to find some justification to free them from this status and permit them to remarry; but, ultimately, there were limits to what they could do, for

the law about the *agunah* was God-given. Sometimes an *agunah* who could not be helped by the rabbis would go to a hasidic rebbe who had the holy spirit and was known as a seer, to ask him to tell her where her husband was, if alive, so she could seek him out and force him to give her a divorce that would free her. But if the husband was not alive, and there were no witnesses to his death, even the rebbe could not help. Or perhaps he could—in some other way. Hand-washing is required by Jewish law after going to the bathroom. The final words of teaching are from the Maggid of Tcheidinov, a disciple of the Maggid of Mezritch. They are found in a very similar story about not making a needy person wait (*Beit Pinhas*, p. 80, n. 19). I think they express the views of the Baal Shem Tov too.

25. S, p. 157, #79; P, p. 129, #105; K, vol. 3, p. 240, #3, quoting *Hitgalut HaTzaddikim* (this reference seems to be wrong; I didn't find this tale there).

26. *Imrei Pinhas HaShalem*, Sha'ar 4, #133; MRT, I, p. 105, #10, quoting *Ginzei Nistarot*; Sadeh, p. 78. In MRT, the Besht says that R. Baruch is clothed with *shin"dalet*, an abbreviation for *shvichat damim*, bloodshed or murder. The same letters, unabbreviated, spell *shed*, a demon. *Imrei Pinhas* has *kelipa*, synonymous with demon. If bloodshed is original, an editor along the way failed to notice that *shin dalet* was an abbreviation. In any case, the meaning is largely the same. Yet, the thought of bloodshed casts light on the following tale, "Pregnant Potential," p. 238.

27. Steinman, p. 166; *HaYom Yom* ("From Day to Day"), p. 100. The phraseology about the worlds of speech and action are from the language used by Lubavitcher R. Aaron Raskin, when telling this story on *Shabbat* in Cong. Bnai Avraham, Brooklyn Heights, New York, in June 2004.

28. Adapted from SM, vol. 1, p. 76, citing an oral rendition by D. B. Weiss and referring to DD, vol. 1, p. 77. Another version is found in Ishti, p. 84. This is one of the many different stories about how R. Yaakov Yosef of Polnoye became a disciple of the Besht. Because I used another tale for that purpose, this one could not be used if it is about R. Yaakov Yosef; so I removed the identity of the rabbi. *Shabbat HaGadol*, the "Great *Shabbat*," before Passover was one of the two times a year that European rabbis traditionally gave a sermon.

29. MEY, II, p. 183, quoting *Rav Yaiva*, Tehillim, #22. The source text has that if a leader makes servile use of a *talmid hacham*, who is considered spiritually equivalent to *Shabbat*, someone else will actually desecrate *Shabbat*. But since these terms are too similar to another, different teaching (see p. 219) and would be confusing, I've changed this teaching to be about anger and violence. I've also added the final line about the saying of the Sages, to give the story an appropriate ending.

30. MEY, II, p. 97, quoting *Turei Zahav*; Horodetzky, p. 51, quoting *Porat Yosef*, Bereshit. MEY, II, p. 92, quoting DME, Aharai. Setting created.

31. S, p. 166, #89, P, p. 139, #117; *Ma'aseh HaShem HaShalem: Dinov*, vol. 1, p. 86, #47 and n. 46.

32. R, vol. 2, p. 34, #19.

33. *Mishnat Hasidim*, p. 320, #42; K, vol. 2, p. 117; R, vol. 3, p. 32, #47.

34. K, vol. 2, p. 122, #21, from *Divrei Yisrael*; *Likkutei Aytzot HaMeshulash*, vol. 1, p. 143b, quoting the *Zohar*, says the "cooking" is trust.

35. IE, pp. 9–23; K, vol. 4, p. 10, #4, from *Shalom Al Yisrael*. "Akiba" story: *Berachot* 60b. Numbers 17:10.

36. S, p. 230, #153; P, p. 196, #186; SBST, vol. 1, p. 211.

37. H, p. 285 has about Feiga. Kahana, p. 4, n. 2, says that Edel was born in 1720 and did not

give birth until ten years after marriage. Her first son, Moshe Hayim Ephraim, was born in 1742 according to Kahana (see Y, p. 238). Her second son, Baruch, was born much later but still during the lifetime of his grandfather. *Ma'alat HaTzaddikim*, pp. 84–85, says that Moshe Hayim Ephraim was born in 1748 and Baruch in 1753. *Tehillot Baruch*, pp. 12–13, written by a descendant of R. Baruch of Medzibuz, gives the dates 1744, 1748, and 1750 for the three children.

38. SBST, vol. 2, p. 258, #46, quoting DME; G, vol. 2, pp. 627–28.

39. SBST, vol. 2, p. 256, ##38–40 and nn. 20, 21.

40. Z, p. 448, #451.

41. *Imrei Dvash*, p. 15 and n. 5.

42. SBST, vol. 2, p. 256, n. 21. The rejected prayers were of the community or of the whole Jewish people.

43. SBST, vol. 2, p. 233, #12, quoting DME, end; SBST, vol. 2, p. 134. Deuteronomy 30:12.

44. SBST, vol. 2, p. 144, #16, and MRT, I, p. 76, #8, both quoting *Ben Porat Yosef*. See "The Gates of Divine Help" on p. 129.

45. Agnon, p. 173, translating *Nifla'ot HaTzaddikim* (Yiddish), and K, vol. 2, p. 95, #5; see also: S, p. 198, #111; P, p. 167, #142; Steinman, p. 312; SBST, vol. 1, p. 258; *Emet V'Yatziv*, vol. 1, p. 148, #2. K, vol. 4, p. 229. See p. 245 of this book for the Akiba story from *Berachot* 60b. In the source text, the Besht refers to the story about Nachum Ish Gam-Zu (*Ta'anit* 21a), who took a chest full of precious stones as a gift to the emperor on behalf of the Jews. The gems were stolen and the chest filled with mere dirt. When he found this out, Nachum said, "This also is for good" and gave the dirt to the emperor! As a result of his faith, a great miracle occurred by means of that dirt, which resulted in good that even the gift of the gems could not have effected. The Besht always sought the highest spiritual level, where one's divine service is focused on the present, not on what will happen later. Thus, he taught how to eat meditatively so that eating is divine service in the present not just strengthening oneself to be able to study Torah or pray later. The same principle applies here: One believes in God's goodness now, in the moment and does not need to wait for good to be revealed later.

46. S, p. 198, #111; P, p. 167, #142; MEY, p. 40, quoting *Likkutei Divrei Torah*.

47. *Ma'aseh B'Rabbi Yisrael Baal Shem Tov*, p. 285 (no source cited). Deuteronomy 18:13.

48. MEY, p. 70, quoting *Mishmeret Itamar*.

49. K, vol. 3, pp. 38, 39 (2 versions); Z, vol. 2, #358; R, vol. 1, p. 10, #16; B, p. 74 and E, p. 290 (the source for both: *Notzair Hesed*, p. 56); SBST, vol. 1, Preface, p. 20, #34; *Zechut Avot*, p. 260.

50. SBST, vol. 1, Preface, p. 23, #51, and MEY, II, p. 256, both quoting *Shoshanim L'David*; H, p. 130; Steinman, p. 312. See also K, vol. 1, p. 256; vol. 2, p. 131; *Tzaddik*, pp. 488–89; and *Ma'aseh B'Rabbi Yisrael Baal Shem Tov*, p. 288.

51. H, p. 154; SBST, vol. 2, p. 200, #29, n. 27.

52. G, vol. 2, p. 637.

53. *Kitvei Kodesh Rabbi Moshe Minder*, #27.

54. *Sippurei HaBesht* (Agnon), p. 48 and B, p. 286, both quoting *Likkutim Hadashim*, 104. One brings the tzaddik a *pidyon nefesh*, a "soul-redemption" gift. A *katinka* is a catskin cape.

55. S, p. 210, #127; P, p. 179, #159; SBST, vol. 2, p. 181, note; *Midrash Pinhas HeHadash*, #52; Scholem, *Demuto*, p. 346, quoting Gustman, *MiTorat Rabbi Pinhas MiKoretz*, p. 14. In Judaism, demons are not as uniformly malevolent as in Christianity. R. Yaakov Yosef of Polnoye wrote down many of the Besht's teachings and is the main source for them, but I connected that fact with the preceding tale. In a similar story about R. Nachman of Bratzlav, a

disobedient hasid was replaced as scribe by a better hasid (his greatest disciple, R. Noson). They both took notes at the same talk; R. Nachman read their notes and stated that one had recorded what he said and the other hadn't. (*Otzar Yirat Shemayim [Breslov]*, vol. 7, pp. 232–235).

56. SBST, vol. 2, p. 179, #58; R, vol. 3, p. 281, #13; *Kahal Hasidim HeHadash*, p. 13 (7a), #22; K, vol. 2, p. 214, #39; B, p. 73.

57. SBST, vol. 2, p. 28, n. 13; B, p. 52. If the word *temimah* refers to the Torah itself, the verse is understood one way; if it refers to the person studying Torah, it is understood the other way. G, vol. 2, p. 605; SBST, vol. 1, p. 48, n. 27 and #34; SBST, vol. 2, p. 47 and p. 171, #29; H, p. 143; B, p. 48; *Ma'or Einayim* on *Avot*, p. 37 (19a), last teaching in the book; see also *Rabbi Nachman's Wisdom*, p. 212.

58. Kahana, p. 95; *A Passion for Truth*, p. 58; SSKB, vol. 3, p. 216, #608.

59. *Sefer HaSichot* (1943), #12, p. 160.

60. *Imrot Tzaddikim*, p. 189.

61. N, p. 238, #76, quoting *Sichot HaKodesh* of the Lubavitcher Rebbe.

62. R, vol. 2, p. 26, #5; *Midor Dor*, vol. 1, p. 250; *Hasidic Anthology*, p. 17, 7:2, quoting *Midor Dor*. I constructed the final paragraph based on the Besht's teaching in *Jewish Spiritual Practices*, p. 466, quoting the Besht in *Sefer HaBaal Shem Tov al HaTorah*, vol. 1, p. 253; G, vol. 1 p. 79, quoting *Sefer HaSichot*; E, p. 145, quoting *Ktav Shem Tov*.

63. SBST, vol. 1, p. 106 n. (2 versions); *Or HaMe'ir*, parashat Sh'mot, p. 43b; B, p. 74, quoting SBST. *Olam ha-temurot*. The man thought he was cultivating purity and holiness, but the spiritual energy he created, being contaminated by pride, actually gave strength to the Other Side, of evil, and that side "encouraged" him. R. Prof. Miles Krassen: "*Temurot* are related to the *herev ha-mit'hapechet* [the ever-turning sword guarding the Garden of Eden] and the angel Metatron. Usually, the implication is a power that changes *hesed* into *din* [compassion into severity]."

64. *Ma'asiyot U'Ma'amarim Yekarim*, p. 11 (6a) in *Sippurei Nifla'im*; K, vol. 4, p. 152, #19. H, pp. 366–67.

65. MEY, I, p. 49.

66. *Emunat Tzaddikim*, p. 8, #11; K, vol. 1, p. 215 and E, p. 283 (source of both: *Emunat Tzaddikim*). B, p. 55; *Kahal Hasidim HeHadash*, p. 8, #11. The presence of the *Zohar* on the Besht's table has been added, as this fact is known from other stories. The original "a number of hours, until 11 p.m" has been changed to reconcile with other traditions.

67. R, vol. 1, p. 14, #19; K, vol. 4, p. 174, #18.

68. SBST, vol. 1, Preface, p. 20, #36, quoting *Notzair Hesed*; vol. 1, p. 215, note, quoting *Heichal HaBeracha* and others; MRT, II, p. 24, #5; *Ma'aseh HaShem HaShalem: Dinov*, vol. 1, p. 84, #43, quoting *Shomer Emunim*, p. 133, and Komarna, I, #18. The circumstances here were similar to the earlier instance, but also different, because here the Besht's life was threatened. Therefore, in this case, he would have been justified in performing a miracle using a divine Name. Yet he did not use a Name and relied instead on his faith alone. This is according to Jewish teaching that discourages the use of divine Names to perform miracles, as it seems to approach magic in attempting to coerce divine forces, so to speak.

69. SBST, vol. 1, p. 194, #175 and n. 165; MEY, II, p. 29, quoting *P'ri Hayim*. The Talmud (*Berachot* 3b) quotation meaning that God has no doubts, is interpreted to mean that when one has doubts, one cannot be before God. MEY, II, p. 34, quoting *Be'er Ya'akov Hayim*. SBST, vol. 1, p. 7, #10; B, p. 67; K, vol. 2, p. 116; *Or HaNer*, p. 7, (4a), #28. Verses quoted: Proverbs 14:15; Psalms 116:6, meaning a simpleton.

70. SBST, vol. 1, p. 30, #20; H, p. 376. The Koretzer was in his thirties when he met the Besht, shortly before the Besht's death (Circle, p. 11). I've placed this tale earlier to connect it with other stories about faith. I added the Besht's dramatic pose; see a similar act by R. Nachman of Bratzlav in *Pe'ulat HaTzaddik*, vol. 1, p. 80. Verses quoted: Exodus 14:31, 17:7.

71. E, p. 166; *Sefer HaSichot* (1942), pp. 127–28; *Sefer HaMa'amarim* (1942), pp. 108–9; G, vol. 2, p. 611 and n. 95. Midrash: *Kohelet Rabba*, beginning; *Shir HaShirim Rabba*, beginning. The Sanhedrin was the supreme Jewish religious, political, and judicial body during the time of the Second Temple. Proverbs 4:2.

72. *Sarei HaMaiya*, vol. 3, p. 170. Rabbinic saying quoted: *Avot* 2:4.

73. G, vol. 1, p. 81; *Chassidic Discourses*, pp. 413–18. Verses quoted: Isaiah 1:15; Proverbs 17:1.

74. R, vol. 3, p. 36, #50; *Likkutei Sippurim* (R. Hayim Mordechai Perlov), pp. 14–15; N, pp. 136–37, #11 (the Besht put wine or liquor on the table but was drunk from the "wine," the mystical teachings, of the Torah).Verse quoted: Ezekiel 3:27.

75. *Kahal Hasidim HeHadash*, p. 11 (6a), #17. My understanding of the Besht's motives is based partially on similar behavior by a great hasidic scholar (*Yehi Or*, p. 299, #643 and p. 302, #649).

76. *Kerem Yisrael*, p. 2b (4), #12. Z, vol. 2, p. 138, #160. The Talmud quote is from *Berachot* 31a. K, vol. 4, p. 9; compare SBST, vol. 1, Preface, p. 23, #53, quoting *Beit Rebbe*. *Shabbat* 138. "Asked Kabbalah question": Literally, asked him the *pshat* of the permutation of three letters. Considering the awesome spiritual level the Baal Shem Tov was on, it's difficult to imagine him not knowing the whole Torah, and asking a question of a "mere" scholar. Perhaps he only asked the question to make peace and to give joy to the *gaon*. *Sippurei HaBesht* (Agnon), p. 106; Circle, p. 166. K, vol. 4, p. 7, from *Sichot Yekarim*. Leviticus 19:17–18. KE, p. 14, #50. "No hate or grudge": from a hasidic source whose reference I lost. K, vol. 4, p. 8, from *Sippurei Hasidim*; *Devarim Areivim*, p. 5b, #16; E, p. 271.

77. K, vol. 4, p. 51, #21, from *Sippurei Besht*; R, vol. 3, p. 278, #7. Genesis 18:27.

78. *Through Fire and Water*, p. 374; SSKB, vol. 3, p. 227, #641. Cf. the story in Gutman, *Rabbi Yisrael Baal Shem Tov*, p. 37, and H, p. 271 (both, no source cited).

79. H, p. 271 (no source cited). H, p. 145, quoting the Komarner Rebbe (no source cited).

80. *Kerem Yisrael*, p. 4b (8), quoting *Notzair Hesed*.

81. S, p. 222, #140; P, p. 188, #173.

82. *Sippurei Tzaddikim*, p. 30, #12; K, vol. 4, p. 42, #1. The Other Side = the *Sitra Achra*.

83. *HaRebbe Rav Tzvi Elimelech MiDinov*, vol. 1, p. 213; E, p. 227, quoting *Siftei Tzaddikim*.

84. R, vol. 1, p. 1, #3. One of the Lubavitcher rebbes said that the Besht had blond hair (R, vol. 1, p. 2, #4). The Rebbe of Karlin-Stolin said that the hairs from the Besht's beard that are in the Besht's copy of his volumes of the *Zohar*, which are in the possession of the Karlin-Stolin rebbes, are reddish-blond (*Shalshelet HaKodesh Komarna*, p. 412).

85. *Lamed Vav: A Collection of the Favorite Stories of Rabbi Shlomo Carlebach*, p. 129. The material has been adapted; see there. I've seen this story in Hebrew hasidic books.

86. G, vol. 1, p. 50; H, p. 350; E, pp. 140–44, 289; K, vol. 4, p. 251 and p. 37, #13; S, p. 258, #182; P, p. 222, #221. H, p. 261. The central institution of Jewish self-government in Poland, functioning from approximately the middle of the sixteenth century until 1764, and representing the Jewish communities associated in their respective provinces ("Lands"), principally four in number—Greater Poland, Little Poland, Red Russia (Podolia and Galicia) and Volhynia. (*Encyclopedia Judaica*, vol. 5, 993, 995; P, p. 222 n.).

87. S, p. 56, #22; P, p. 50, #34; SBST, vol. 1, Preface, pp. 17–18. S, p. 265, #188; P, p. 231, #227 (soul-ascent on *Minha erev Shabbat*; on *Shabbat*, see p. 287 and n. 105 on p. 400). The Great *Hallel* is Psalm 136, which is chanted during *Pesukei D'Zimra* in the morning prayer service on Sabbaths and festivals. The Half *Hallel* is recited on the new moon and the last six days of Passover.

88. SBST, vol. 2, p. 31, #1, quoting *Zera Kodesh*. "When a kabbalist meditates by means of a *yihud* (unification), the soul of a deceased tzaddik may become attached to him and reveal itself to him, through the mystery of *ibbur* [conception]" (*Meditation and Kabbalah*, p. 233, by Aryeh Kaplan). I've combined the similar tales in S, p. 238, #166; P, p. 204, #203; *Siftei Kodesh*, p. 84 (42b); *Caphtor U'Ferach* (Luchot Erez) p. 93. The Torah does not mention Moses' name at this feast given to honor Jethro, and the Rabbis interpreted this to mean that he was humbly serving others at the feast. The idea here is that Moses was eating spiritually without eating physically.

89. *Siftei Kodesh*, p. 85; *Jewish Spiritual Practices*, p. 64. Proverbs 3:6. Psalms 16:8. "Torah-neglect" = *bitul Torah*.

90. G, vol. 2, p. 460. The Besht's teaching depends on Hebrew wordplay and can't be well translated. He referred to the Talmud (*Shabbat* 10a) teaching that the Torah is considered *hayei olam* (usually translated "eternal life"), whereas prayer is *hayei sha'ah* (usually translated "transient life"). The Baal Shem Tov interpreted and translated this way: By studying the Torah, we learn how to act in the world (*olam*). But by praying, we learn how to turn (*sha'ah*) to God at every minute during the day.

91. G, vol. 2, pp. 602–3 and n. 65 there; MEY, p. 199. Setting and question created. Isaiah 6:2–3.

92. SBST, vol. 1, p. 71, #83. Another source says that the Besht taught that one should decrease Torah study on *Shabbat* and concentrate on kabbalistic meditation (*yihudim*), so I added meditation here.

93. K, vol. 2, p. 139, #12, from *Sippurei Hasidim*.

94. H, p. 148.

95. KE, p. 3, #7.

96. R, vol. 1, p. 3, #6.

97. S, p. 173, #95.

98. SBST, vol. 1, p. 68, #79; *Netivot Shalom*, p. 67. KRY, p. 18, #47.

99. K, vol. 2, p. 220, #1, from *Torat Hayim*; G, vol. 2, p. 668, and n. 18 there. *Torat Hayim* interprets the story about the Besht not being able to talk or answer questions on *erev Shabbat* as referring to the time when the sun sets and the worlds elevate. This could be true, but a person like the Besht may begin to elevate even earlier and the phenomenon may not apply only to that late hour.

100. SBST, vol. 1, p. 71, #85, 86; KE, p. 115, #373; *Mazkeret Shem HaGedolim*, helek 1.

101. H, p. 150. Kahana, p. 100. *Emunat Tzaddikim*, p. 6 (3b), #5. It is hard to see how the Besht could serve meals for all the guests in his house (one would have supposed that the meals would be in the *beit midrash*, as with later rebbes) but the most pertinent reference, in *Emunat Tzaddikim*, seems to suggest that.

102. SBST, vol. 2, pp. 211, #58; 130, #8. Vol. 1, p. 55, #47, quoting *Likkutim Yekarim*. Psalms 16:8. Rabbis' saying: Look not at the physicality of the food, for example, but its spiritual essence, which is Godliness (*Avot* 4:27).

103. SBST, vol. 2, p. 51, quoting *Tiferet Shlomo*.

104. SBST, vol. 1, pp. 131, 91, 203 n.; G, vol. 2, pp. 603, 676, 678; H, p. 149; Sadeh, p. 67; SBST, vol. 1, p. 131; N, p. 86, #6; *Kovetz Sichot: Musar V'Hasidut*, p. 126.

105. *Sippurei Kedoshim*, p. 43; K, vol. 2, p. 106, #12; p. 177, #9; R, vol. 3, p. 17, #21; G, vol. 1, p. 403; KRY, p. 27, #70. In the tale, the poor couple have the traditional order of the Sabbath meal after the bread—fish, soup, meat, and dessert—but eat beans in place of each. The Rabbis interpreted the first mentioned verse as being fulfilled by remembering the Sabbath when making a blessing over the wine in the *kiddush*. And they said that when the Messiah arrives, the *kiddush* will be recited over the legendary "wine stored in the grapes," etc. The Rabbis interpreted the next mentioned verse as referring to delighting on the Sabbath in delicious foods.

106. K, vol. 2, p. 177, #9 (about his telling what happened when smoking). For his soul-ascents on Shabbat during *Musaf*, see the references for "The Besht Visits Rabbi Nachman Kossover in the Other World," p. 323. Many other stories refer to the Besht making soul-ascents; see in this book pp. 93, 99, etc.

107. *Sifran Shel Tzaddikim*, p. 12, #9.

108. Sadeh, p. 35. I've given my own speculation about the custom. Rabbi Dovber Pinson of Brooklyn suggested to me that the purpose is to release the spiritual tension of *Shabbat*.

Toward Redemption
with the Sting of Persecution and Heresy

1. Kahana, p. 107; H, p. 92. The question about whether to be a *melamed* and the answer, "Yes," comes from a hasidic source I can't recall. The Besht's remark about his happiness as a teacher is from N, p. 75, #4, and many other places.

2. Raz, p. 243 (no source cited). Numbers 8:2. Only when the Temple is supplied with wood, water, etc. can the priests perform the sacrifices. So too, only when ordinary Jews provide material support and other help can the leaders properly accomplish the spiritual mission.

3. *Emunat Tzaddikim*, p. 7 (4a), #6, p. 6, (3b), #3; E, pp. 120, 132; K, vol. 1, p. 217; KE, p. 6, #6; B, p. 79. This event occurred in 1749 as can be determined by the information in E, p. 132.

4. K, vol. 4, p. 180, #19; *Pe'er L'Yesharim*, p. 13a, #134; B, p. 77; SBST, vol. 2, p. 40n.; *Midrash Pinhas HeHadash*, ot 26; MRT, I, p. 37, #4; H, p. 57 (from a different source but it is not cited). The word *mikvah*, which literally means "hope" in the verse (Jeremiah 14:8), can also refer to the ritual bath (*mikvah*; constructed or natural—like a river or spring). The verse indicates that God is the true hope and "bath" in which Israel must immerse.

5. SBST, vol. 1, Preface, p. 17, #27; B, p. 61 (sources: SBST, *Megillat Starim, Sichot Yekarim*); H, p. 373 (no source cited).

6. G, vol. 1, p. 12. *Tikkun olam*. Psalms 92:13.

7. *Mishnat Hasidim*, p. 321, #43.

8. S, p. 187, #104; P, p. 156, #135. The Sabbath hymn *Shalom Aleichem* welcomes the angels. Here the Satan came and was made unwelcome.

9. MEY, II, p. 129, quoting *Ma'amarei Admor HaZaken*. Cf. Gutman, p. 23, n. 3, quoting DME. MRT, I, p. 70 (35b).

10. S, p. 37, #10; P, p. 33, #18; K, vol. 2, p. 239; SBST, vol. 1, p. 73, #89; B, p. 66; cf. Horodetzky, p. 35, quoting *Ben Porat Yosef*, Bereishit; H, p. 154 (no source cited). The source

text says R. Alexander left after eight years, but since that interfered with my time line I changed it to a vague "many years."

11. K, vol. 1, pp. 212–13, #9. I added the middle sentence of this paragraph for explanatory purposes. The Baal Shem Tov sometimes hosted meals at which only those who knew the writings of the Ari were permitted to sit at the table. The others stood around behind the chairs (E, p. 283, quoting KST, Hosafot, comment 198). K, vol. 4 (3 versions), p. 165 from *Kahal Hasidim*; p. 116, #3, from DA, p. 117 from *Shivhei HaBaal Shem Tov*; E, p. 304, quoting DA; H, p. 348 quoting *Shivhei HaBaal Shem Tov*.

12. *Pe'ulat HaTzaddik*, vol. 1, p. 37, #10; P, p. 152, #129 and p. 330; SSKB, vol. 5, p. 195, #474.

13. MEY, I, p. 69, quoting *Shomer Emunim*. MEY, I, p. 71. Scholem, *Demuto*, quoting DME, parashat Balak, p. 80a; Steinman, p. 89, quoting DME. Horodetzky, p. 9, quoting *Divrei Shalom*.

14. SBST, vol. 2, p. 158, parashat V'Et'chanan; MRT, II, p. 55. *Samech-mem-alef-lamed*; *Sam* = poison, *el* = (of) God; Samael = the angel who is "God's poison." Azazel: see Leviticus 16:5f. Isaiah 34:6 refers to Basra in present-day Iraq. Sa"l lacks the letter *mem* in Samael. The *mem* may stand for *mavet* = death. *Ma'aseh HaShem HaShalem: Dinov*, vol. 3, p. 785, #100 says that the name Sa"l is an acronym for *sof adam lamut* ("The end of a human is to die"). In *Toldot Yaakov Yosef*, VaYakhel, p. 252, R. Yaakov Yosef of Polnoye wrote that people on the highest spiritual level recognize that God's name is clothed within the Satan, and that Sa"l "sweetens" Samael. Once one realizes that the Adversary is acting in God's commission, one's relation to it changes. According to R. Dovber Pinson of Brooklyn, some kabbalists say that the name Sa"l comes from three letters in three words in Exodus 14:19–21 "*vayisa . . . Yisrael . . . ha-layla.* And Israel . . . traveled . . . [at] night." A real Jew can move spiritually, even when confronted by darkness and death. *Sippurei Ma'asiyot*, p. 7; *Rabbi Nachman's Stories*, p. 8.

15. S, p. 60, #24; P, p. 53, #40; K, vol. 2, p. 194, #17, from *Shivhei HaBaal Shem Tov*. Abraham, Isaac, Jacob, and David are the four legs of the Throne that rests on the Divine Chariot. After invoking these four divine forces, the mystic ascends in the chariot. See "His Prayer Answers a Torah Problem," p. 260 about the Besht saying that if someone else could pray the "Answer Us!" prayer like him, they could bring the Messiah. In the mystic tradition, the angel Michael, who is Israel's intercessor, "sacrifices" the souls of the righteous on a heavenly altar. The self-sacrifice of the righteous before God and their readiness to die in His service is their means of transformation by which they ascend from world to world. Michael "offers" their self-sacrifice to God to win them His favor. Our version does not have "Answer us, Shield of David," nor "Answer us, God of the Chariot"; it does have eight 'Answer us's including two not in the one the hasid said: 'Answer us, Help of the Tribes' and 'Answer us, Judge who protects widows.' There is also a manuscript version of *Shivhei HaBaal Shem Tov* in which the deceased hasid says the prayer 'Answer *me*'" in the singular. Perhaps that also is intended in R. Yosef's question about the form of the prayer" (S, p. 61, note).

16. K, vol. 2, p. 220, #2, and B, p. 54 (source for both: *Or HaHochmah*); Z, vol. 1, p. 337, #327.

17. *Kovetz Sippurim* (5720–5721), p. 29, #29. This tale was told by Rebbe M. M. Schneersohn of Lubavitch. *Yafeh Sichatan*, p. 54, quoting *Rav Yaiva* (parashat Vayeshev), who reports the Besht's comment about the Jewish obligation to teach gentiles the *mitzvot* of *b'nai Noah*; see all of #73 here for a discussion of this topic and the teaching of the Lubavitcher Rebbe about it.

18. N, p. 70, #8, in the name of Rebbe M. M. Schneersohn of Lubavitch. I have slightly

altered the original text, which reads: "He loved gentiles too. The Besht once said to a disciple, 'I feel love for every tree and plant, and for every animal in the forest.'"

19. *Kitvei Maran HaRamach*, p. 21. 2 Samuel 14:14.

20. KST, p. 3 (2a), #1; K, vol. 2, p. 225, #4; S, p. 302; Kahana, pp. 100–3. The Messiah's words that he'd come when the Besht's "fountains overflow" allude to Proverbs 5:16. G, vol. 1, p. 98. *Ratzo v'shov. Segulot.* The Rabbis say the Satan is God's agent to test people, and all his deeds are for the sake of heaven. The Besht's new "urgency" might seem to contradict the preceding tale, "The Besht's Soul and the End," p. 302, that he already knew this. But I surmise that he didn't remember this exchange and what had happened to his soul before birth until this moment. E, p. 78, quoting a Lubavitch version of *Shivhei HaBaal Shem Tov* quoted in G (no page number). SBST, vol. 1, Preface, p. 7; p. 16, #22; p. 103, #166; vol. 2, p. 231, #8.

21. SBST, vol. 2, p. 231, #8; p. 103, #166; vol. 1, Preface, pp. 7, 8, 16, 23. Psalms 69.

22. Scholem, *Demuto*, p. 348, quoting DME, end of book, p. 113a; *Sippurei Nifla'im*, Ma'asiyot U'Ma'amarim Yekarim, p. 8 (5a); Agnon, p. 10. According to Jewish mysticism, a soul is drawn down to this world from the heavenly treasury by the deeds of the parents. Many stories also tell of tzaddikim drawing down special children for themselves or for others by prayer.

23. E, p. 173. G, vol. 1, p. 28. Circle, p. 3.

24. S, p. 304. Literally, "make expiation for the land of His people" (Deuteronomy 32:43). Kahana, p. 99; S, p. 99.

25. S, p. 97, #39; P, p. 78, #60; E, p. 175. S says that R. Hayim of Brody died in *Shevat* 1750, which would mean a couple of months before Passover. However, P says (p. 80, note) that he died in 1783, which would mean that possibly another rabbi was the deceased opponent.

26. DD, vol. 1, p. 41.

27. S, p. 192, #106; P, p. 161, #137; E, p. 173. The text can be interpreted to mean the famous ancient martyr, Rabbi Akiba, and some scholars have taken the reference to be to him (for example, Dubnow, p. 40). The sources contain an added paragraph that the Besht later told a disciple that he had prayed and been promised from heaven that the decree would be nullified. But a certain preacher exploited the prisoners' situation in a sermon he gave in Brody, to make some money for himself, and this aroused heavenly accusations that caused the prisoners to be killed. I omitted this because it conflicts with a main motif of the story—that the Besht was not told, for his cancelling the decree by his prayer would have led to more suffering.

28. S, p. 232, #158; P, p. 198, #192; H, p. 173.

29. Z, vol. 1, p. 231, #232; K, vol. 1, p. 231, #8, from Z.

30. H, pp. 179 and 221 (quoting KST) combined with a created setting.

31. *Sefer HaToldot: Rabbi Dovber, HaMaggid MiMezritch*, pp. 21–22; Schochet, pp. 22–27, 41–49; S, pp. 100–107, #4; P, p. 81, #62; E, pp. 122–27; K, vol. 4, pp. 104–8.

32. K, vol. 4, pp. 111–114; SBST, vol. 1, Preface, p. 12, #8, quoting KST, p. 62b, #424.

33. S, p. 100, #41; K, vol. 4, p. 109, from *Kahal Hasidim*. MEY, I, p. 51; *HaMaggid*, p. 36; K, vol. 4, pp. 111, 115. Some versions (*Kahal Hasidim*) have the Besht with a cushion on his head and others (S) have a candle. These are spelled *caf resh* or *nun resh* (*kar* or *ner*); either *caf* became *nun* or vice versa. The meaning is basically the same: The cushion means that the Besht is a throne or resting place for the *Shechinah*, the candle, that he's illumined. The editor of S on p. 104 argues that cushion is correct. The reversed coat could also mean that some misguided scholars confused inside and outside in spirituality. A Tibetan Buddhist tale similarly has an enlightened lama (priest) who confronts some scholars wearing a wolfskin coat turned inside out, to symbolize that ignorance misconstrues what is perfect and imperfect (Surya Das, *A*

Snow Lion's Turquoise Mane, p. 183). *Eitz Hayim* contains the teachings of the Ari as transmitted by R. Hayim Vital. *Maaseh Merkavah* is the main branch of Jewish mysticism, about the prophet Ezekiel's vision of the heavenly Chariot composed of different kinds of angels.

34. S, p. 101, #41; K, vol. 4, p. 108. An apology offered in the presence of a *minyan* of witnesses shows the great regard the Besht had for R. Dov Ber as a very special individual.

35. S, p. 101; K, vol. 4, p. 107–9. H, p. 307 (no reference cited) has that the Besht asked him to choose whether to be healed with divine Names, in which case he would be completely cured, or to be healed in a natural way, with medicines. "I don't consider myself worthy to be healed with divine Names," said the *maggid*. So he chose medicines. The Besht later said that if the *maggid* had listened to his advice, he would have been healthy and strong enough to chop a wagonful of wood. After a few years of suffering from his condition, which occasionally caused him to cease from Torah study, the *maggid* regretted that he had not accepted the Besht's advice.

36. SBST, vol. 1, Preface, p. 12, #10; *Kahal Hasidim HeHadash*, p. 7, #9. The Besht elevated the experience, and the energy in the food, by meditating as he ate.

37. *HaMaggid MiMezritch*, p. 32, #1.

38. *Ma'amar Mordechai*, vol. 1, Ma'amarei Tzaddikim, p. 65, #70; S, p. 57, #22; P, p. 51, #36; KE, p. 112, #357; *HaMaggid MiMezritch*, p. 31; Zevin, p. 448, #451, KRY, p. 32, #86; *Ner Yisrael*, vol. 3, p. 150.

39. K, vol. 4, p. 114; *HaMaggid MiMezritch*, pp. 21, 24. "R. Ovadiah Bartenura . . . explains that *Maaseh Merkavah* is the practical use of divine Names to enable the kabbalist to view the angels in their various levels" (*Zohar*: Selections translated and annotated by R. Moshe Miller, p. 14).

40. *Ma'amar Mordechai*, vol. 2, p. 13, #31. According to the tradition, choruses of angels constantly praise God; also, each angel performs only one task. See "The *Hallel*," p. 278.

41. SBST, vol. 1, p. 13, #11, quoting *Lev Samayach*; H, p. 102; *The Great Maggid*, p. 54; see the Besht's teaching about this effect in MEY, II, p. 82, quoting DME.

42. MEY, I, p. 107, quoting *Likkutim Hadashim*; cf. G, vol. 2, pp. 673–74. H, pp. 60–61, quoting teachings of Rabbis Shlomo of Lutzk and Shneur Zalman of Liadi.

43. *Kovetz Michtavim* (in *Tehillim Ohel Yosef Yitzhak*), pp. 194–97; *The Great Maggid*, p. 61, quoting *Kovetz Michtavim*; Zevin, vol. 1, p. 517, #531; K, vol. 1, p. 246, #1, from *HaTamim*; *Sippurim Nifla'im*, p. 56, #37; *HaMaggid MiMezritch*, p. 37ff. Sharing food from the plate of a holy person conveys a blessing. Isaiah 57:19. Psalms 12:7, 26:2, 57:2, 68:2, 84:4, 85:5. Proverbs 12:19.

44. K, vol. 2, p. 281, #12, from *Sippurei Hasidim*. This legend reflects the fact that the Besht and the hasidic movement appropriated gentile melodies, but elevated them spiritually.

45. *Beit Pinhas*, p. 30, n. 18.

46. Ishti, p. 154. Lust is prohibited, not normal and sanctified sexual desire. An additional inserted explanation from "Later" to all but the final sentence is based on the comments of Baruch and on a teaching of the Slonimer Rebbe (*Netivot Shalom*, Avot, p. 146).

47. S, p. 218, #137; P, p. 185, #170; a different version is found in E, p. 141, quoting *Shivhei HaBaal Shem Tov*; perhaps it's a variant. I replaced "a serious (sexual) sin" with adultery.

48. *Ma'asiyot U'Ma'amarim Yekarim*, p. 10a (19), in *Sippurei Nifla'im*. R. Dovber Pinson of Brooklyn informed me that there is a kabbalistic source for this.

49. K, vol. 2, p. 222, #3, from *Siftei Baal Shem Tov*; KRY, p. 22, #57, 58; H, p. 336; Circle, pp. 143–45, citing *Ateret Ya'akov V'Yisrael*; *Hitgalut HaTzaddikim*, p. 7. *Shabbat Shuvah* is the Sabbath of Turning (Repentance).

50. S, p. 68, #27; P, p. 60, #46; Y, p. 516. Etkes, p. 185. The meditations, including *yehudim*

(unifications), involved in praying from a kabbalistic *siddur* are time-consuming. A soul whose deeds make it fit for neither heaven nor hell wanders after death in the world of *tohu*, which the Besht also called the "world of imagination" (according to R. Dovber Pinson). That soul remains in a state of confusion until a Jew or a tzaddik performs a redemptive act to release it. According to the Kabbalah, souls of the dead that are denied an eternal resting place can be "fixed" by prayer, particularly by the prayers of the great mystics. Just as many of the living flock to the rebbe in this world in order to be elevated spiritually, so do souls of the dead flock to him to receive their fixing and elevation in the next world. This is a traditional phrase ("Sanctified") "called out" after a holy man. It is unclear why it is used here, but the contextual meaning is "Enough, enough!" R. Meir Fund suggested to me that it means that the Sabbath is approaching and its sanctity requires that the Besht cease from this activity of helping dead souls that is designated specifically for *erev Shabbat*. The *Shemoneh Esreh* prayer begins by stepping forward and ends by stepping back.

51. Circle, p. 88, n. 187 (This story was told by R. Saul Bick of Medzibuz [no source cited]); H, p. 322 (no source cited). Stripping off materiality = *hitpashtut ha-gashmiyut*.

52. Y, p. 516.

53. SBST, vol. 1, p. 179, n. 148; p. 263.

54. *Froyen-Rebeim Un Barimte Perzenlekhkeytn In Poyln* (Women Rebbes and Famous Personalities in Poland) by Moyshe Fainkind, Warsaw, 1937. "Yente di Neviete" (Yente the Prophetess), pp. 22–23; another version in KE, p. 98, #305. Yiddish translated by Justin Lewis and edited by Yitzhak Buxbaum.

55. S, p. 200, #115; P, p. 169, #146; B, p. 82; *Aveneha Barzel*, p. 39, #58; *Tzaddik*, p. 71 n. 30; cf. R, vol. 1, p. 6, #11 and G, vol. 2, p. 541. Kahana, p. 104, claims Chana died about 1750, but he produces no supporting evidence. There is no sure knowledge when the Besht's wife passed away. A story about a soul-ascent the Besht made to visit his deceased friend, R. Nachman Kossover, takes place in 1757, and the Besht's wife appears in that tale (see p. 323); though that is less than proof. *Ner Yisrael*, vol. 2, p. 134, and *Kerem Beit Yisrael*, p. 16 #2, have a version from the Rizhiner Rebbe where the Besht says, "I hoped to be buried in the Holy Land, but now that I've become half a body outside the Land, I see that this other half will remain here." Compare this to the visit to R. Nachman Kossover, where the Besht, after having ascended to the upper worlds in a soul-ascent, is given the possibility of not returning and not tasting death. He refuses, saying he doesn't want to remain in heaven, because he hopes to be buried in Israel from where the soul attains a higher elevation. His wife appears in that tale. That version might actually be more original than the seemingly legendary desire to ascend to heaven alive. See further on, n. 7 on p. 406. The Besht tale alludes to the Talmud story (*Berachot* 5b) in which one of the rabbis weeps that R. Yohanan's beauty would one day rot in the earth. Genesis 2:24.

56. P, p. 258, #249. According to the tradition, a man is supposed to be married, and if his wife dies, he should remarry. The piece about the Besht's celibacy is not in S. The Hebrew is, however, found in Gutman, p. 45. The phrase *al pi ha-dibbur* "compelled by the divine Word" (which has reverberations from the Passover *Haggadah*) seems to mean that although the Besht had separated from his wife, in this instance God told him to have conjugal relations to produce a son. *The Story of the Baal Shem Tov*, p. 200, suggested to me to include the reference to the year of mourning.

57. S, p. 109, #42; P, p. 86, #66; H, p. 253 and B, p. 78 (source of both: *Shivhei HaBaal Shem Tov*); Kahana, p. 111; E, p. 44, suggests that Shabtai Tzvi was tempted by his charisma and success and fell into pride and then anger.

58. SBST, vol. 2, p. 184, note; Kahana, p. 108 f.; H, p. 244; *Aspaklaria HaMe'ira*, vol. 1, pp. 39–43. Maurice Simon, *Israel Baalshem: His Life and Times*, p. 26, says that in 1757 Frank claimed to be the reincarnation of Shabtai Tzvi. Ecclesiastes 7:14.

59. S, p. 226, #144; P, p. 192.

60. DA, p. 7a, #19; E, p. 259; H, p. 250; *Seder HaDorot HeHadash*, section on R. Meir of Premishlan (grandfather of the famous hasidic rebbe of the same name and town); K, vol. 3, p. 213; B, p. 80; *Aspaklaria HaMe'ira*, vol. 1, pp. 41–43. Y, p. 475; *Zechut Avot*, p. 328.

61. S, p. 61, #25; pp. 66–67, quoting *Imrei Pinhas*, p. 246, #88; P, p. 54, #41, p. 58, #42; *Kitvei Maran HaRamach*, p. 27, #24. Perhaps the Besht's criticism was against the methods of *pilpul* and *hilukim* (Etkes, p. 102). Since false *hakdamot* (introductions) are referred to, E, p. 261–62, speculates that he was taking issue with rabbinic authors who pridefully promoted their false principles and premises in the introductions to their books of talmudic novellae.

62. DD, vol. 1, p. 54.

63. DD, vol. 1, pp. 54–55; *Sippurei Nifla'im*, Sippurim U'Ma'amarim Yekarim, p. 5 [3a]); B, vol. 1, p. 174; *Kitvei Maran HaRamach*, p. 27, #24. H, p. 249; E, pp. 261–62; S, p. 64, P, pp. 57–58, #41; Kahana, p. 113; *HeHasidut*, p. 49; H, p. 244. G, vol. 2, p. 427. There is a question as to whether the Besht actually participated in the debate; see H, pp. 244, 248, 250.

64. S, p. 66, #25; P, p. 59, #44; E, p. 262; H, p. 248. The Besht's comment is based on R. Meir's famous teaching about the *Shechinah* lamenting the suffering of even a wicked Jew, "My head and arm are hurting!" Gutman, p. 27. Steinman, p. 139 (no source cited).

65. N, pp. 93–96, #12; G, vol. 2, pp. 425–43; *Likkutei Dibburim*, vol. 4, Likkut 32, p. 1192.

66. MRT, I, p. 39b (78), #23; p. 31b (62), #16; Schochet, p. 88; *Zechut Avot*, p. 262, quoting *Ma'or V'Shemesh*, Ruth. Dates have been removed to reconcile this section with the dates of the debates with the Frankists. The dates given for the ban are the 19th of *Tammuz*, 1757, and for the annulment the 8th of [the following month of *Av*], 1757. The sentence about forgiveness comes from *Zechut Avot*, where the date for the response is given as Yom Kippur, 1758. Ecclesiastes 3:15, as interpreted by the Rabbis, see *Kohelet Rabba* 3:19. The Rabbis say that God favors the persecuted, even if the persecuted is wicked and the persecutor is righteous. Proverbs 16:7.

67. *Likkutei Moharan*, #207 (that source also found in H, p. 253). Adapted to include the Shklov ban.

To Death and Beyond

1. S, p. 291, #208; P, p. 255, #247; E, p. 278; K, vol. 4, p. 209, #2; H, p. 273. The first two and the final two days of the eight days of Passover are special holidays when work is prohibited.

2. S, p. 293, #208; P, p. 255, #247; K, vol. 4, p. 209, #2; E, p. 279; H, p. 273.

3. S, p. 163, #86; P, p. 136, #114; H, p. 272; E, p. 277.

4. S, p. 163, #86; P, p. 136, #114; E, p. 277; K, vol. 4, p. 208; H, p. 272.

5. S, p. 296, #208; P, p. 257, #248; E, p. 278. H, p. 377 (no source cited).

6. G, vol. 2, p. 541 (see also p. 648); *Likkutei Dibburim* (English) vol. 4, p. 48; Schochet, p. 110. Between Passover and *Shavuot*, forty-nine days are ritually counted. Tradition mandates various mourning customs for this period. But on the thirty-third day, *Lag B'Omer*,

mourning is suspended and celebrations, such as weddings, may be held. Significantly, the passing of R. Shimon bar Yohai is celebrated on *Lag B'Omer*. Deuteronomy 6:5. Elsewhere (*Sefer HaSichot* [1940; Hebrew], p. 176, and G, vol. 2, p. 648), it says, discussing the Besht, that light in *gematria* equals *raz*, secret (*Tikkunei Zohar* 19 and *Zohar Hadash* 28:2), because whoever knows the inner secret of everything will shine (or: is able to illuminate). R. Dovber Pinson told me that the direct light is the tzaddik and the reflected light is the penitent Jew, the stranger who returns to God. R. Aaron Raskin thought that the Besht needed the higher, more powerful reflected light to love the stranger, to bring back all the alienated people to a renewed connection with Judaism. Genesis 3:19. The final paragraph is my own understanding of the preceding prediction.

7. R, vol. 1, p. 6, #11; G, vol. 2, p. 541. G, vol. 2, pp. 542–45, 551. There is a Breslover tradition: "The Baal Shem Tov once said [about his passing from this world], 'If I had my first wife, I would ascend to heaven in the middle of the day in the marketplace of Medzibuz in front of everybody, not like Elijah who ascended in the desert'" (*Avaneha Barzel*, p. 39, #58; *Tzaddik*, p. 70, n. 30). Note that this tradition refers to the Besht's first wife, who passed away early in his life. According to the Jewish tradition, a man has a special spiritual connection to his first wife. The Elijah episode is in 2 Kings 2:11. The final "dust" verse quoted is Genesis 3:19. The Besht's thought here may be hinted at by his exchange with the Kossover during a soul-ascent, where the latter says: Stay and don't experience death. The Besht answers that if one is buried in Israel his soul receives a greater *aliyah* (ascent), that is, by being buried, the soul goes higher (p. 323). I have tried to reconcile different traditions, one in which the Besht says that he wanted to go up to heaven like Elijah, but once his wife died he cannot, and the other in which he says that he can go up, but wants instead to fulfill: to dust, etc. Compare N, pp. 283–85, ##1–5. See MEY, I, p. 64 for a kabbalistic comment on the version that the Besht wanted to fulfill "returning to the dust."

8. Sadeh, p. 156 (no source cited).

9. S, pp. 291–96, #208; P, pp. 255–57; E, p. 278; *Adat Tzaddikim*, p. 20. Sadeh, p. 156 (no source cited). It is a widely practiced kabbalistic custom to stay up the first night of *Shavuot* to study *Tikkun Leil Shavuot*, which is a set order of Torah selections from the *Tanach*, rabbinic literature and mystic literature, such as the *Zohar*. "Dead soul": see "Fixing Souls," p. 325. Ecclesiastes 8:8. The verse literally means that no one has control over the day of their death.

10. For the whole section: S, pp. 291–96, #208; P, pp. 255–57, #247; E, p. 278; *Midrash Pinhas*, p. 36 (18b), #18; H, pp. 273–74; K, vol. 4, p. 210, #2; E, p. 280; KE, p. 112, #354; *Tzror HeHayim*, p. 75 (38a); DD, vol. 1, p. 56; *Adat Tzaddikim*, p. 20. That no one knows what he accomplished by giving up two hours is based on a comment by R. Moshe Weinberger of Long Island, New York, on his tapes about the Besht. The Besht went to the outhouse to remove waste from his body, so as not to soil himself in his final moments. *Tehillot Baruch*, p. 22. SSKB, vol. 2, p. 110, #334. See "Edel and the Book of Remedies," p. 154. K, vol. 1, p. 195, #22. *Even Yisrael*, p. 45. KST, I, p. 33 (17a), #133. He brought down by mystic means a soul that he had chosen. Some versions have the soul of Rabbi EBR"SH, seemingly an abbreviation for Rabbi Eleazar ben Rabbi Shimon (bar Yohai), that is, the kabbalist, son of the great kabbalist of ancient times. See S, p. 296, #208, and *Even Yisrael*, p. 33 and p. 61, n. 5. The Besht once compared himself and his companions to R. Shimon bar Yohai and his companions (ibid, p. 71, n. 29); by extension, his son would be like R. Shimon's son. The soul of a deceased prophet or tzaddik, etc. can mystically infuse a living person's soul and spiritually nurture him. The Besht said that he could mystically make this happen. S, p. 296, #208; P, p. 258, #249; K, vol. 4, p. 211, #3; H, p. 281; E, pp. 280–81; Gutman, p. 47. According to some traditions, the Besht

became, after his death, a divine Name, the Name of forty-two letters that is formed from the initial letters of the words of the kabbalistic hymn *Ana B'Koach*. When R. Tzvi used that Name, the Besht would come to him (*Even Yisrael*, p. 70, n. 26, and elsewhere in that book). According to the Rabbis, there is a greater revelation of God's presence in a *minyan*, a gathering of ten men. H, p. 274; SBST, vol. 2, p. 229, n. 12. Deuteronomy 28:68. SBST, vol. 2, p. 229, #11, and Komarna, p. 68, #57, both quoting *Heichal HaBeracha*. The Besht's thoughts on Deuteronomy 28:68 seem to have been inspired by *Zohar Hadash* on that verse (in parashat Ki Tavo), which mentions that no one will be able to rule over you. This is similar to the Besht's preceding reflection and joke—when the servant didn't bring him the full glass of mead he asked for—based on Ecclesiastes 8:8, that there is no rule on the day of one's death (translated in my text as "lordship"). For the final story about the melody: G, vol. 2, p. 541; K, vol. 4, p. 208; H, p. 274. About the melody, see Schochet, p. 116, and Horodetzky, pp. 136–37.

11. Esther 2:13. Gutman, p. 47, n. 1. The end of Psalm 90 is called "The Song to Overcome Harmful Forces" and is traditionally recited at the time of death to call down God's grace and ward off demons, accusers, etc. "May the favor of the Lord our God be upon us; and establish Thou the work of our hands upon us. The work of our hands, establish Thou it." Psalms 36:12. Komarna p. 68, n. 47; *Zichron Tzaddik*, p. 25, #58. Etkes, p. 266; E, p. 278; H, p. 275; G, vol. 2, pp. 541–42; *Even Yisrael*, p. 70, n. 27. KYR, p. 18, #47; H, p. 275.

12. MEY, I, p. 66. *Gaon, amora, tanna* are, respectively, terms for the Jewish religious leaders from a later to an earlier period in history. H, p. 275. S, p. 179, #98. H, p. 189 (no source cited, though I have seen this figure of 40,000 in earlier sources).

13. *Sippurei Nifla'im*, Ma'asiyot U'Ma'amarim Yekarim, p. 12b; K, vol. 4, p. 224. Cf. p. 220; *Sippurei Tzaddikim*, #14; *Shlomo's Stories*, p. 157. In a story in *Rabbeinu HaKodesh MiShinova*, vol. 2, p. 396, the Besht prayed for a thief to escape punishment after he promised never to steal again. In K, vol. 3, quoting *Sippurei Ya'akov*, the Besht tells a young thief, who is desperately poor and must support himself and his mother, that a Jew should not steal, but if circumstances are such that he falls into it, he should at least avoid stealing from the poor (p. 108) and from fellow Jews (pp. 109–10). See the story "The Mountain Moves," p. 46, where the Besht took a similar tack with gentile robbers. In *Michtav Mai'Eliyahu*, vol. 1, p. 291, R. Dessler explains, based on the Talmud, how precious it is to God when people on a low spiritual level, such as Jewish robbers or thieves, struggle with their evil inclination to have some principles in their wrongdoing. As for the presence of a descendant of the Besht in the tale: There seems to be confusion in the text. The Besht had a son Tzvi, and a daughter Edel who had three children (the Besht's grandchildren)—the eldest being Ephraim of Sudilkov. He appears in the original source text, but when the Besht died his grandson would not have been a rebbe with hasidim. This is probably therefore his son, Tzvi, and I have changed it accordingly. However, a different version of the tale has the action and timing proceed in a way that R. Ephraim is clearly intended (in the biography preceding DME [Jerusalem: Mir, 1995], p. 20, quoting "the book of Rebbe Yitzhak of Skver"). The source text refers to *parashat* Korach. Previously it had said that the Besht had died a few days earlier. Yet *parashat* Naso always follows *Shavuot*, so something is amiss. I changed the *parasha* to Naso. If it was *parashat* Korach it would be not a few days but weeks and one would wonder if the thief would not have heard that the Baal Shem Tov had passed away. As for the significance I give the tale, it might seem to intend only a contrast between the Besht's disciple, Yaakov Yosef of Polnoye, who is typically presented as an irritable character, and the Besht's son, Tzvi, who was softer. Yet, even the Besht's son is shown as willing to bless the thief only after the sign from his father.

14. *Even Yisrael*, p. 37, quoting *Beit Avraham*, 161; *Sippurei Nifla'im*, Sippurim Nechmadim, p. 6. *Toldot Yitzhak*, Preface; DD, vol. 1, p. 56; K, vol. 4, p. 226; KE, p. 112, #358.

15. *Even Yisrael*, p. 46; *The Great Maggid*, pp. 89–90.

16. S, p. 298, #210; P, p. 260, #251. TYY was published in 1780. A few of the sections in my book that follow this one took place earlier in time, but for the sake of the inner meaning, I've put this story out of place. The Rabbis say: "Afflictions cause a person's sins to be forgiven" (*Sifre*, V'Etchanan, 32). "The Rebbe of Alexander said, 'What was the difference between Rabbi Israel Baal Shem Tov and the *gaonim* of his generation? They left behind books; he left people'" (*Torat Hanoch*, p. 84).

17. G, vol. 2, p. 665. See also p. 639 about the Maggid of Mezritch saying that the Besht taught that love of Israel should be expressed in kissing, just as one kisses a Torah scroll. Yet this teaching does not affect my understanding of the Maggid's remarks.

18. DD, vol. 1, p. 56; KE, #363; *Kerem Yisrael*, p. 6 (3b), #6; B, p. 85.

19. K, vol. 4, p. 211, #5.

20. *Otzar HaSippurim*, IV, pp. 22–23; K, vol. 4, p. 213; B, p. 85; SBST, vol. 2, Haskamah.

21. H, p. 318; K, vol. 4, p. 227. Isaiah 62:6.

22. H, p. 277, quoting R. Nachum of Tchernobil, without citing a source. H, p. 287, quoting R. Yitzhak Eizik of Komarna.

Appendix

1. *Encyclopedia Judaica*, "Ba'al Shem," vol. 4, p. 6.

Glossary

Adam Kadmon. The Cosmic Man, the highest world discussed in Kabbalah. See **Five worlds**.

Adon Olam. "Lord of the World" hymn.

Aggada. Nonlegal sections of the Talmud containing homiletic expositions of the Torah, stories, legends, folklore, parables, anecdotes, and maxims. In contradistinction to *halacha*.

Agunah. A woman whose husband is missing and, according to Jewish religious law, cannot remarry.

Aleph-bet. Hebrew alphabet.

Aleph, bet, gimel, dalet. First four letters of the Hebrew alphabet.

Aliyah. The honor of being called up to the synagogue platform when the Torah is read publicly, to recite the blessings over one of the sections.

Aliyat neshamah. The mystic soul-ascent, in which the soul exits the body, ascending to heaven to receive Torah secrets or to plead before the heavenly court.

Amen, y'hai shmai rabba mevorach! Amen, blessed be His great name!; congregational prayer response.

Am-ha'aretz. A religiously ignorant person.

Amidah. The Standing Prayer, the main prayer of a Jewish service; also called the *Shemoneh Esreh*.

Amora. (pl. Amoraim). A sage whose teachings are found in the *Gemara*.

Ari. The great kabbalist, Rabbi Yitzhak Luria, also called the Ari, the "Lion."

Ark. The cabinet at the east wall of the synagogue that contains the Torah scrolls, the holiest ritual objects in Judaism.

Ashkenazi. An ethnic definition for German that includes most of European Jewry.

Asiyah. See **Five worlds**.

Atzilut. See **Five worlds**.

Baal Hai. Ahiyah ha-Shiloni, the Baal Shem Tov's angelic teacher, who is the "Master of Life" and of the higher soul levels.

Baal shem. Master of the divine Names; kabbalistic faith healer.

Baal Shem Tov. Rabbi Israel, the founder of the hasidic movement, was called by this title, which literally means "Master of the Good Name." The idiomatic Hebrew has two meanings: "a person who has a good reputation in the community" and "a righteous *baal shem*," a kabbalistic faith healer who uses divine Names to work miracles. Rabbi Israel was beloved as a great teacher and a faith healer. See **Besht**.

Baruch HaShem. "Praise God"; "Thank God"; traditional response to the question "How are you?"

Bedikat hametz. The final search for leavened bread the night before Passover, when a person searches his house to remove any leaven he might have overlooked.

Beit din. Religious court.

Beit midrash. Torah study hall, often adjacent to a synagogue or also used as a synagogue.

Beracha. A blessing uttered over food or other pleasure or benefit, or before doing a *mitzvah*.

Beriyah. See **Five worlds**.

Besht. Acronym for Baal Shem Tov.

Bimah. The raised synagogue platform where the prayer-leader stands and from which the Torah is read.

Borechu. The call to prayer: "Bless the blessed Lord!" which can only be said with a *minyan*.

Boychik'l. Little boy.

Bris. Circumcision.

Cheder. Religious primary school.

Cholent. Traditional Sabbath meat and bean stew.

Chumash (pl. Chumashim). Five Books of Moses.

Chutzpah. Brazen behavior.

Counting the Omer. The forty-nine days, from the second day of Passover to the holiday of *Shavuot*, are ritually counted.

Davven (davvening). Ordained form of Jewish prayer.

Days of Awe. The High Holidays—Rosh HaShanah, Yom Kippur—and the days between.

Deutsch. A German, which is the meaning of the surname Ashkenazi.

Din Torah. Torah judgment, ruling.

Divine service. Praying, worshiping, studying Torah, doing *mitzvot* and other forms of serving God.

D'vekut. Cleaving with intense love to God; God-consciousness.

Dybbuk. The spirit of a deceased individual that possesses a live person.

Ein Sof. The Infinite, a kabbalistic appellation for God.

Ein Yaakov. A book containing the *Aggada*, the legends and parables of the Talmud.

Eitz Hayim ("Tree of Life"). A kabbalistic book containing the teachings of the Ari, as transmitted by his disciple, Rabbi Hayim Vital.

Eliyahu ha-Navi ("Elijah the Prophet"). A hymn sung at the end of the Sabbath.

Elokim. God; the name of God that refers to His quality of judgment.

Erev. Eve. The day before a holiday; generally used for the daylight hours before the holiday that begins in the evening.

Erev Rosh HaShanah. The daylight hours before Rosh HaShanah, which begins at night.

Erev Shabbat. The eve of the Sabbath; Friday during the day.

Esrog. One of the four plant species ceremonially waved during the prayer services on *Sukkot*. The Torah calls the *esrog* a "splendid fruit," and pious people make great efforts and spend much money to acquire a splendid and perfect *esrog* for the *mitzvah*. See **Four Species**.

Farfel tzimis. A grain dish (like cous-cous) mixed with glazed carrots.

Four Species. On *Sukkot*, four plant species—*esrog* (citron), *lulav* (date palm), *hadasim* (myrtle branches), and *aravot* (willows)—are ritually waved during the prayer services.

Five worlds. Kabbalistic scheme of worlds. In ascending order of closeness to God: *Asiyah*, the world of Action (which includes our lower world); *Yetzirah*, the world of Formation; *Beriyah*, the world of Creation; *Atzilut*, the world of Emanation (or Nearness); and *Adam Kadmon*, the world of the Cosmic Man.

Gabbai. Manager.

Gaon (pl. gaonim). Great Torah scholar or genius. "The *Gaonim*" may refer to the era after that of the *Amoraim*.

Gehinnom. Hell.

Gemara. The completion of the *Mishna*, the two together constituting the Talmud; used as a synonym for the Talmud.

Gematria. Jewish numerology; each Hebrew letter has a numerical value (*aleph* is one, *bet* is two, etc.), so a Hebrew word has a numerical value, which in the method of *gematria* can be related to other words with similar numerical values.

Godliness (*elokut*). Divinity; used as a synonym for the *Shechinah* (not the human quality of being godly).

Gulden. A gold coin.

Gut vorch! "Have a good week!" The traditional greeting after *Shabbat* ends and the new week begins.

Hacham. A sage who excels in wisdom; Sephardic title for a rabbi.

Haggadah. The text of the story of the Jews' exodus from Egypt, recited on Passover.

Hai Elul. The 18th day of the Hebrew month of *Elul*; the number 18, in Hebrew *hai* (*het-yud*), means "life" and is auspicious.

Halacha. Jewish religious law.

Hallel. A group of psalms of praise recited in the prayer service on certain holidays. The Great *Hallel* is Psalm 136, chanted during the morning prayer service on Sabbaths and festivals. The Half *Hallel* is recited on the New Moon and the last six days of Passover.

Hametz. Leaven; leavened bread.

Hasid (pl. Hasidim) —A follower of the Baal Shem Tov; a member of the hasidic movement; literally, "a pious person."

Hasidism. A Jewish pietistic movement that was founded in eighteenth-century Poland by the Baal Shem Tov.

Havdala. End-of-Sabbath ceremony that separates sacred from profane time.

Haya. "Living" or "eternal life-force"; a high level of the soul discussed in Kabbalah. See **Neshamah l'neshamah** and **Soul levels**.

Hevra kadisha. Burial society.

Hillul ha-Shem. Desecration of God's name, that is, of God.

Hitbodedut. Seclusion with God, involving prayer, meditation, etc.

Hoshanna Rabba. This holiday is the seventh day of *Sukkot* and occurs about three weeks after Rosh HaShanah. According to tradition, on this day the decree of the Days of Awe is finalized. Legend says that if you see your shadow without a head on the eve of *Hoshanna Rabba* you will die during the coming year; if your shadow has a head, you will live.

Hoshanna Rabba Tikkun. A compilation of scriptural recitations for the holiday composed by the kabbalists.

Kabbalat Shabbat. The synagogue service for welcoming the Sabbath.

Kaddish. The memorial prayer for the dead.

Kaddish D'Rabbanan. The prayer said at the conclusion of a sermon.

Kadosh. Holy.

Kashrut. The matter of kosher status.

Katinka. A catskin fur cape.

Kavvanah (pl. kavvanot). Intention; brief formulaic kabbalistic meditation or incantation accompanying a prayer or religious action. There are numerous different *kavvanot* for particular prayers or actions, and a person might be familiar with a certain limited number of them, but not know many others.

Kavod. Honor.

Kedushah. The "Sanctification" prayer (Holy, holy, holy!).

Kefitzat ha-derech. "Road-leaping"; the miraculous means of speedy travel employed by the Baal Shem Tov and certain other holy individuals.

Kelipot (sing. kelipah). Literally, the "shells," meaning evil forces that oppose holiness; accusing angels.

Kiddush. Blessing recited by the man of the house over wine before Sabbath or holiday meals. If there is no wine, the blessing may be recited over bread.

Kiddush ha-Shem. Sanctification of God's name by a noble deed or by martyrdom.

Kittle. White robe worn by men on Rosh HaShanah and Yom Kippur, and by the Passover *seder* leader.

Kloiz. Yiddish for *beit midrash*; a Torah study hall or a house of prayer. The famous *beit midrash* in Brody was called a *kloiz*.

Kohen (pl. kohanim). A Jewish priest.

Kol Nidre. "All Vows" prayer that opens the Yom Kippur service and annuls all vows.

Lag B'Omer. "33rd day of the Counting of the Omer"; forty-nine days are ritually counted between Passover and *Shavuot*. Tradition mandates various mourning customs for this period. But on the thirty-third day mourning is suspended and celebrations, such as weddings, may be held.

Lulav. A date palm branch. See **Four Species**.

Machane Yisrael. The Camp of Israel, a name for the movement of hidden tzaddikim.

Maariv. Evening prayer service.

Maggid (pl. maggidim). Preacher.

Mah. "What"; the spiritual level of humility, self-sacrifice, or self-nullification.

Mahzor (pl. mahzorim). High Holiday prayer book.

Matmid. A diligent scholar who studies the Torah every possible minute.

Mazel tov, Kallah! "Congratulations, Bride!"

Mead. An alcoholic liquor made by fermenting honey and water.

Melamed. Children's religious school teacher.

Melave malka. A festive religious gathering and feast after the Sabbath ends to escort the departing Sabbath Queen.

Menorah. Hanukkah candelabra.

Mezuzah. A container, holding a parchment with Torah verses, which is attached to a door-post for divine protection and to remember God while entering and leaving.

Midrash. Ancient rabbinic commentary on Torah verses.

Mikvah. Ritual bath or a natural body of water used for immersion.

Minha. Afternoon prayer service.

Minyan. Prayer quorum of ten male Jews.

Mishna. A collection of mostly legal ancient rabbinic teachings; the core of the Talmud.

Misnagid (pl. misnagdim). An opponent (of the Besht or his movement).

Mitzvah (pl. mitzvot). Divine commandment of the Torah.

Mochsin. Agent who rented out properties for the feudal landlord and collected rents and taxes for him.

Modeh Ani. "I Thank You [God]"; the first prayer said upon awakening in the morning, thanking God for restoring one's soul.

Mohel. Ritual circumciser.

Motza'ei Shabbat. The period immediately after the Sabbath ends on Saturday night.

Motzi. The blessing over bread.

Muktzeh. The prohibition against touching an object used for work, such as a pen, that one is forbidden to use on a Sabbath or special holiday.

Musaf. Additional morning prayer service recited on Sabbath and holiday.

Musar. Teaching about character development and ethics; religious rebuke.

Nachas. Comfort; satisfaction; gratification.

Naran. *Nun"Resh"Nun*; acronym for the three soul levels—*nefesh, ruach,* and *neshamah.*

Nefesh. Life-force (or animating force); see **Soul levels**.

Ne'ilah prayer. The final "Closing of the Gates" prayer on Yom Kippur; last chance for prayers to be received.

Neshamah. Soul (or breath-soul). See **Soul levels**.

Neshamah l'neshamah. "Soul of the soul"; also called *haya* (living). See **Soul levels** and **Haya**.

Niggun (pl. niggunim). Melody, often wordless.

Omer. See **Counting the Omer**.

Or HaHayim. "The Light of Life," a book by Rabbi Hayim ben Attar.

Parashah. The weekly Torah portion publicly read in the synagogue.

Parush. An ascetic (literally, a separatist), who pursues piety by separating from sin and from worldly and bodily affairs.

Perek Shira. The mystic Book of Song that tells which Torah verse each species of animal or plant sings to praise its Creator.

Pesahim. Talmud tractate about Passover.

Pidyon ha-ben. The redemption of a firstborn son by making a ritual donation to a *kohen.*

Pidyon nefesh (pl. pidyonot). "Soul-redemption"; a money gift given to a holy man to bring divine grace.

Pirkei Avot. "Ethics of the Fathers," a book of ancient rabbinic religious maxims.

Pitka (pl. pitka'ot). A petition or prayer-request note given to a holy man or hasidic rebbe.

Purim. Holiday celebrating the Jews being saved from extermination in ancient Persia; it precedes Passover in the Jewish calendar.

Rashi. Acronym for Rabbi Shlomo ben Yitzhak of Troyes, France, the great medieval commentator on the Torah and Talmud.

Reb. Honorific equivalent to "Mr."; Reb Jacob simply means Mr. Jacob, Jacob being a first name.

Rebbe. Teacher or spiritual master; a hasidic sect leader.

Rebbetzin. Rabbi's wife.

Rheinish. Silver coin.

Rosh HaShanah. The Jewish New Year and Day of Judgment.

Rosh Hodesh. New Moon celebration on the first day of the month.

Ruach. Spirit. See **Soul levels**.

Sandek. Man honored to hold the baby boy on his lap during circumcision.

Sanhedrin. The supreme Jewish political, religious, and judicial body during the time of the Second Temple.

Seder. Festive meal celebrating Passover, during which the *Haggadah* is recited.

Seraph. Fiery angel.

Sefer Torah. Torah scroll.

Sefirot (sing. sefirah). Divine emanations as described in Kabbalah.

Selichot. Early morning penitential prayers in the days leading up to Rosh HaShanah.

Sephardic. An ethnic term for Jews of Middle Eastern origin, particularly descendants of those expelled from Spain.

Seudah shlishit. The third of the traditional three Sabbath meals.

Shabbat HaGadol. The "Great *Shabbat*" before Passover, is one of the two times a year that Eastern European rabbis traditionally gave a sermon.

Shabbat Shuvah. The Sabbath of Repentance between Rosh HaShanah and Yom Kippur, one of the two times a year that Eastern European rabbis traditionally gave a sermon.

Shabbos. Yiddish for Sabbath.

Shaharit. Morning prayer service.

Shalom aleichem. "Peace be upon you," which evokes the response "*Aleichem shalom*," "Upon you be peace"; the hymn "Shalom Aleichem," a greeting of peace to the angels, chanted at the table on Sabbath evening.

Shammos (pl. shammosim). Yiddish for caretaker, servant, synagogue attendant; the "servant" candle in the Hanukkah *menorah* that is used to light the other candles.

Shavuot. "Festival of Weeks" holiday commemorating the giving of the Torah to the Jewish people at Mount Sinai.

Shechinah. Indwelling Divine Presence; "female" immanent God.

Shechitah. Ritual kosher slaughter of meat animals.

Shells. Kabbalistic term for the negative forces of evil that surround and stifle what is holy. See **Kelipot**.

Shema. The "Hear O Israel" prayer; the central faith declaration of Judaism: "The Lord our God, the Lord is one."

Shemoneh Esreh. The most important prayer of Jewish prayer services; also called the *Amidah*.

Shidduch. Marriage-connection.

Shiva. The first seven days of most intensive mourning for a deceased.

Shivitti. A card, picture, or plaque of a candelabra motif, with a psalm verse about keeping God always before you highlighted ("I have placed God before me always" [Psalms 16:8]; the purpose of this kabbalistic picture is to remind the prayer-leader to concentrate and to provide a focus for his praying.

Shnorrer. Beggar.

Shochet (pl. shochtim). Ritual slaughterer for kosher meat.

Shofar. Ram's horn blown in the synagogue on Rosh HaShanah and Yom Kippur.

Shterntichel. A woman's decorated and bejewelled silk head-covering for *Shabbat* and holiday.

Shtreimel. A fur hat worn by male hasidim on Sabbath and holiday.

Shulchan Aruch. Code book of Jewish law.

Siddur. Prayer book.

Simhat Torah. "Joy of the Torah" holiday, when congregants dance with Torah scrolls.

S'micha. Ordination as a rabbi and teacher.

Soul levels. According to Kabbalah there are five soul levels, in ascending order: *nefesh, ruach, neshamah, neshamah l'neshamah* (= *haya*), and *yehida*. In English: animating force; spirit; soul; soul of the soul (= living or eternal life-force); single.

Sukkah. A temporary booth used for eating, living, sleeping on *Sukkot*. See **Sukkot**.

Sukkot. "Festival of Booths" commemorating that after the Exodus the Jewish people lived in temporary dwellings, booths, in the Sinai Desert.

Tallis. Prayer shawl, on whose corners are attached ritual fringes (*tzitzit*), that is worn by men while praying during daytime.

Talmud. The compendious series of volumes, which after the Torah is the most authoritative text in Judaism. It is comprised of the earlier *Mishna* and the later discussion and commentary, the *Gemara*. The terms Talmud and *Gemara* are often used interchangeably.

Talmud Torah school. Community funded religious school.

Tanach. Bible; acronym for the three sections of the Bible: *Torah, Nevi'im, K'tuvim*, that is, Torah (Five Books of Moses), Prophets, and Writings.

Tanna (pl. Tannaim). A sage whose teachings are in the *Mishna*.

Tefillin. Phylacteries; little leather boxes containing scriptural verses hand-written on parchment that men wear strapped to their head and arm while reciting the morning prayers. They symbolize a person's being bound to God and having his mind and heart directed to God continually.

Tikkun. Soul-repair; an ordained recitation of Torah selections to effect a soul-repair.

Tikkun Hatzot. Kabbalistic "Midnight Lamentation Prayer Service and Vigil" (or the "Midnight Fixing") lamenting the destruction of the ancient Temple, the Jewish people's exile from their land, all the injustices in the world, the exile of the *Shechinah*, and the "exile" of one's own soul from God.

Tikkun Leil Shavuot. A widely practiced kabbalistic custom to stay up the first night of *Shavuot* to recite and study a set order of Torah excerpts, including selections from the *Tanach*, rabbinic literature, and mystic literature, such as the *Zohar*.

Tohu v'vohu. The emptiness and void before Creation.

Torah. Jewish scripture; Five Books of Moses, whole Torah, or all of sacred literature. *Torah* means "teaching" or "instruction." The Torah has revealed and concealed aspects, namely: the Talmud, its commentaries, the halachic codes; and the Kabbalah.

Tosafot. A particular talmudic commentary.

Tzaddeket. A pious or holy woman.

Tzaddik (pl. tzaddikim). A pious or holy man; a hasidic rebbe.

Tzedaka. Charity.

Tzitzit. Ritual fringes on a square-shaped undergarment or *tallis*.

V'Ahavta. The prayer about love for God that follows the *Shema*.

Yaale V'Yavo. "Let our remembrance rise and come before You"; a special prayer inserted in the morning prayers on New Moon and other holidays.

Yahrzeit. The anniversary of a death; a candle is lit to commemorate the occasion.

Yehida. "Single"; the high soul level that is in constant contact with God, that is, singleness in union with the One. See **Soul levels**.

Yeshiva. Torah academy.

Yetzer ha-ra. Evil inclination.

Yetzirah. See **Five worlds**.

Y-H-V-H. The special four-letter name of God; the Tetragrammaton (in English, the letters are customarily separated by hyphens).

Yichus. Lineage.

Yihud. Kabbalistic unification meditation.

Yom Kippur. Yearly Day of Atonement, the holiest day of the Jewish religious calendar.

Yom Kippur Katan. A monthly Lesser Day of Atonement.

Yom Tov. Holiday.

Zeyde. Yiddish for grandfather.

Zohar. The "Book of Splendor," the main text of the Kabbalah.

Bibliography

Books about the Baal Shem Tov

Hebrew

Adat Tzaddikim. M. L. Rodkinson. Jerusalem, 1959.

Baal HaShem: HaBesht—Magia, Mistika, Hanhaga. Immanuel Etkes. Jerusalem: Merkaz Zalman Shazar L'Toldot Yisrael, 2000.

HaBaal Shem Tov: HaIsh V'Torato. Meir Edelbaum. Tel Aviv: Sifriat BE"M, 1986.

Be'er HeHasidut: Sefer HaBesht. Eliezer Steinman. Israel: Machon L'Hotza'at Sifrei Kabbalah, Machshavah, Hasidut, no date.

Even Yisrael: Beit HaBaal Shem Tov. Y. Y. F. Hager. Jerusalem: Ma'ayon HeHasidut, 2000.

Gedulat Rabbeinu Yisrael Baal Shem Tov HaKodesh. Edited by A. N. Bernotta. Brooklyn: Beis Hillel, 1996.

HaBesht U'Vnai Heichalo. Edited by B. Landau. Bnei Brak: Netzach, 1961.

Ikkarei Emunah. Lodz, 1933; reprinted, Brooklyn, 1961.

Ishti Ahuvati, Bo'i V'Nirkod. Edited by Pinhas Sadeh. Tel Aviv: Karta, 1988.

Keter Shem Tov. Edited by Aharon Tzvi Hirsh HaCohen. Brooklyn: Kehot, 1972.

Keter Shem Tov HaShalem. Edited by Aharon Tzvi Hirsh HaCohen. Jerusalem, 1968.

Kol Sippurei Baal Shem Tov. 4 volumes. Edited by Y. Klapholtz. Israel: Pe'er HaSefer, 1976.

Ma'aseh B'Rabbi Yisrael Baal Shem Tov. Edited by S. Raz. Israel: Kol Mivasair, 2001.

Me'ir Einei Yisrael. Edited by Y. Y. Kornblit. Jerusalem: Machon Da'at Yosef, 1991.

Midrash Rivash Tov. No date, etc.

Nezer HaBaal Shem Tov: Rabbeinu Rabbi Yisrael Baal Shem Tov B'Mishnato Shel HaRebbe MiLubavitch. Kfar Chabad: Iggud HaShluchim, 1998. No editor listed.

Rabbi Yisrael Baal Shem Tov: Hayav, Pe'ulotav V'Torato. Matityahu Yehezkel Gutman. Tel Aviv, 1949. No publisher listed.

Rabbi Yisrael Baal Shem Tov: Hayav, Shitato, U'Pe'ulato. Avraham Kahana. Zhitomir, 1900.

Rabbi Yisrael Baal Shem Tov: Hayav V'Torato. S. A. Horodetzky. Berlin, 1909.

Rabbi Yisrael Baal Shem Tov: Sippurei Hayav Shel Yotzair HeHasidut. Moshe Prager. Jerusalem: Yeshurun, 1960. Fictionalized and unauthentic.

Sefer HaToldot: Rabbi Yisrael Baal Shem Tov. 2 volumes. A. H. Glitzenshtein. Kfar Chabad: Kehot, 1986.

Sefer Baal Shem Tov. 2 volumes. Edited by S. M. Mendel. Jerusalem, no date.

Shivhei HaBaal Shem Tov HaShalem. Edited by Eli Hayim Carlebach. Jerusalem: Machon Zecher Naftoli, 1990.

Sippurei HaBesht. Edited by S. Y. Agnon. Tel Aviv: Schocken,1987.

Sippurei HaBesht. Edited by Pinhas Sadeh. Tel Aviv: Karta, 1987.

Tzava'at HaRivash. Brooklyn: Kehot, 1982.

Tzava'at HaRivash. Jerusalem: Machon Da'at Yosef, 1991.

HaYahid B'Dorot. Edited by Y. Alfasi. Tel Aviv: Machon Talpiot, 1997.

Yeshu'ot Yisrael. Edited by Eliezer Hayim of Yampoli. Brooklyn: Skolyer Congregation Toldot Yitzchok, 1986. Bound together with *Siach Hayyim* and *Imrei Aish*; pp. 31–159.

English

Buber, Martin. *The Legend of the Baal-Shem.* New York: Schocken, 1969.

Friedman, Eli, ed. *The Great Mission: The Life and Story of Rabbi Yisrael Baal Shem Tov.* Translated by Elchonon Lesches. Brooklyn: Kehot, 2004.

Hilsenrad, Z. A. *The Baal Shem Tov: His Birth and Early Manhood.* Brooklyn: Kehot, 1967.

Klapholtz, Y. *Tales of the Baal Shem Tov.* 5 volumes. Translated by Sheindel Weinback. Bnei Brak: Pe'er HaSefer, 1970.

Snitzer, J. L. *The Story of the Baal Shem Tov.* Translated by S. Rosenblatt. Edited by A. Burstein. New York: Pardes, 1946.

Rosman, Moshe. *Founder of Hasidism: A Quest for the Historical Baal Shem Tov.* Berkeley: University of California Press, 1996.

Schochet, Jacob Immanuel. *Rabbi Israel Baal Shem Tov.* Toronto: Lieberman's Publishing House, 1961.

Schochet J. I., trans. *Tzava'at HaRivash: The Testament of Rabbi Israel Baal Shem Tov.* Brooklyn: Kehot, 1998.

Simon, Maurice. *Israel Baalshem: His Life and Times.* Leading Figures in Jewish History. London: Jewish Religious Publications, 1953, reprinted 1961.

Singer, Isaac Bashevis. *Reaches of Heaven: A Story of the Baal Shem Tov.* New York: Farrar, Straus, Giroux, 1980. Mostly unauthentic fiction.

Selected Books in Which a Significant Number or a Section of Baal Shem Tov Stories Appear

Hebrew, Hasidic

Emet V'Yatziv, Shivhei Emet. Pp. 273–293. Monsey, N.Y.: Machon Or HaGanuz, 1990.

Dor Daiya. Y. A. Kamelhar. Vol. 1 (Tzaddikei HaDor), "Rabbeinu Yisrael Baal Shem Tov." Pp. 25–75. Israel, 1977.

Gedolei Yisrael B'Yaldutom. Y. Klapholtz. Pp. 7–122. Bnei Brak: no publisher listed, 1966.

Heichal Habesht (journal). Issue 3 (2003): 43–52. Monsey, N.Y.

Kahal Hasidim HeHadash. Rabbi Shmuel of Shinovi. Pp. 5–18.

Kitvei Maran HaRamah. Rabbi Mordechai Hayim of Slonim. Pp. 21–30.

Kitvei Rabbi Moshe Minder. Jerusalem, 1970.

Kitvei Rabbi Yoshe Sh"ub (Shochet U'Vodek). Pp. 1–35. Jerusalem, no date, etc.

Ma'aseh HaShem HaShalem: Komarna. Pp. 29–69. Monsey, N.Y.: Machon Or HaGanuz, 1990.
Ma'aseh HaShem HaShalem: Dinov. Pp. 27–96. Monsey, N.Y.: Machon Or HaGanuz,1995.
Reshimot Devarim. Y. Chitrik. Vol. 1, pp. 1–29. Vol. 2, pp. 5–39. Vol. 3, pp. 15–36. Brooklyn. Vol. 1, 1981; Vol. 2, 1989; Vol. 3, 1989.
Sarei HaMaiya. Y. L. Maimon. Vol. 3, pp. 28–71 and scattered throughout the book. Jerusalem: Mosad HaRav Kook, 1990.
Sefer HaBesht. Y. L. Maimon. Pp. 84–90. Jerusalem: Mosad HaRav Kook, 1960.
Sippurei Hasidim. Edited by S. Y. Zevin. 2 volumes. Jerusalem: Beit Hillel, 1955.
Sippurim Na'im Shel Rabbi Yisrael Baal Shem Tov. S. Y. Agnon. *Molad* 18 (1960): 357–64.

English

Buber, Martin. *Tales of the Hasidim: The Early Masters.* "Israel ben Eliezer, the Baal Shem Tov," pp. 35–86. New York: Schocken Books, 1947/1973.
Wiesel, Elie. *Souls on Fire.* Translated by Marion Wiesel. "Israel Baal Shem Tov," pp. 3–39. New York: Random House, 1972.

Academic Articles or Book Sections about the Baal Shem Tov

Dubnow, Simon. "The Beginnings: The Baal Shem Tov (Besht) and the Center in Podolia." In *Essential Papers in Hasidism,* edited by G. D. Hundert, 25–57. New York: New York University Press, 1991, reprinted from *Toldot HeHasidut,* 1944.
Etkes, Emmanuel. *"HaBaal Shem Tov V'HaHistoriah—Bain Reconstructzia L'Deconstructzia." Tarbiz,* 66 (1997): 425–42.
Etkes, Emmanuel. "Hasidism as a Movement—The First Stage." In *Hasidism: Continuity or Innovation,* edited by Bezalel Safran, 1–26. Cambridge: Harvard University Press, 1988.
Geshuri, M. S. *HaNiggun V'HaRikkud B'Hasidut,* 10–25. Tel Aviv: Hotza'at Netzach, 1954/55.
Ginzberg, Louis. "Baal Shem-Tob, Israel B. Eliezer." *Jewish Encyclopedia,* 2:383–86. New York: Ktav, 1964.
Heschel, Abraham J. *Circle of the Baal Shem Tov: Studies in Hasidism.* Edited by Samuel Dresner. Chicago: University of Chicago Press, 1985.
Heschel, Abraham J. *A Passion for Truth,* 3–69. Woodstock, Vt.: Jewish Lights, 1995.
Maimon, Y. L. *"MiTechum Rishonei HeHasidut."* In *Sefer HaBesht,* 13–20 (see above).
Marcus, Aharon. *HeHasidut,* 13–63. Tel Aviv: Netzach, 1980.
Newman, Louis. "The Baal Shem Tov." In *Great Jewish Personalities,* edited by Simon Noveck, 287–306. New York, 1959.
Nigal, Gedaliah. *"Demut HaBesht V'Haguto." Sinai* 120 (1997): 50–160.
———. *"Moro V'Rabo Shel Rabbi Yisrael Baal Shem Tov." Sinai* 71 (1972): 150–59.
Reiner, Elchanan. "The Figure of the Besht—History Versus Legend." *Studia Judaica* 3 (1994): 52–66.
Rubenstein, Avraham. "Israel ben Eliezer Ba'al Shem Tov." In *Encyclopedia Judaica,* 9:1049–58.

Schaeffer, Yitzhak. *"Rabbi Yisrael Baal Shem Tov U'Demuto B'Sifrut HeHasidut HaKeduma."* *HaDoar*, 39, 1 Sivan (1960): 525–32; (continuation) 15 Sivan: 551.

Scholem, Gershom. *"Demuto HaHistorit Shel Rabbi Yisrael Baal Shem Tov."* *Molad* (Av-Elul, 1960): 335–56.

Shmuel, Y.A. *"MiMishnato Shel Rabbi Yisrael Baal Shem Tov."* In *Sefer HaBesht*, 84–90 (see above).

Audio Tapes

Weinberger, Moshe. "The Baal Shem Tov." 8 tapes. Aish Kodesh Institute, Woodmere, New York.